# Language Issues in Literacy and Bilingual/Multicultural Education

Edited by
MASAHIKO MINAMI
BRUCE P. KENNEDY

Reprint Series No. 22
HARVARD EDUCATIONAL REVIEW

Library of Congress Catalog Card Number 91-75438

ISBN 0-916690-24-5

Harvard Educational Review
Gutman Library Suite 349
6 Appian Way
Cambridge, MA 02138

# Contents

MASAHIKO MINAMI and BRUCE P. KENNEDY
Introduction     viii

**Part I**
**Classic Theoretical Approaches to Language**
**Acquisition, Literacy, and Bilingual Education**     1

ROGER BROWN and URSULA BELLUGI
1    Three Processes in the Child's Acquisition of
Syntax     3

CHARLES READ
2    Pre-School Children's Knowledge of English
Phonology     20

CAROL CHOMSKY
3    Stages in Language Development and Reading
Exposure     48

KENJI HAKUTA and HERLINDA CANCINO
4    Trends in Second-Language-Acquisition
Research     74

*Essay Review*
JAMES PAUL GEE
Toward a Realistic Theory of Language
Acquisition     98

*Book Reviews*
ROBERT W. KOPFSTEIN
on *Stages of Reading Development* by
Jeanne S. Chall     117

Kenji Hakuta
on *Language and Learning: The Debate Between
Jean Piaget and Noam Chomsky* edited by Massimo
Piatelli-Palmarini                                          123

John B. Carroll
on *Thought and Language* by Lev Semenovich
Vygotsky                                                     127

**Part II
Literacy as a Social Product: A Sociocultural
Approach**                                                 **133**

Daniel P. Resnick and Lauren B. Resnick
5   The Nature of Literacy: An Historical
    Exploration                                             135

David R. Olson
6   From Utterance to Text: The Bias of Language
    in Speech and Writing                                   151

Kieran Egan
7   Literacy and the Oral Foundations of Education          177

Catherine E. Snow
8   Literacy and Language: Relationships during the
    Preschool Years                                         207

Sylvia Scribner and Michael Cole
9   Literacy without Schooling: Testing for
    Intellectual Effects                                    234

Paulo Freire
10  The Adult Literacy Process as Cultural Action
    for Freedom                                             248

*Essay Reviews*

James Paul Gee
The Legacies of Literacy: From Plato to Freire
through Harvey Graff                                        266

PETER L. MCLAREN
Culture or Canon? Critical Pedagogy and the
Politics of Literacy                                          286

HAROLD ROSEN
The Voices of Communities and Language in
Classrooms                                                   310

ERIC BREDO, MARY HENRY, and R. P. MCDERMOTT
The Cultural Organization of Teaching and
Learning                                                     320

*Book Reviews*

PATRICIA MARKS GREENFIELD
on *The Psychology of Literacy* by Sylvia Scribner
and Michael Cole                                             333

JOSEPH C. GRANNIS and ALEXANDRA WHARTON GRANNIS
on *Class, Codes and Control. Volume 1. Theoretical
Studies toward a Sociology of Language* by Basil
Bernstein                                                    339

## Part III
## Multicultural/Bilingual Issues in Literacy                 **345**

BERNARDO M. FERDMAN
11  Literacy and Cultural Identity                           347

JIM CUMMINS
12  Empowering Minority Students: A Framework
for Intervention                                             372

ELSA ROBERTS AUERBACH
13  Toward a Social-Contextual Approach to Family
Literacy                                                     391

RICARDO OTHEGUY
14  Thinking about Bilingual Education:
A Critical Appraisal                                         409

DAVID SPENER

15 Transitional Bilingual Education and the
Socialization of Immigrants                                         424


ALMA FLOR ADA

16 Creative Education for Bilingual Teachers              447


TAMARA LUCAS, ROSEMARY HENZE, and RUBEN DONATO

17 Promoting the Success of Latino Language-
Minority Students: An Exploratory Study of Six
High Schools                                                            456


LISA D. DELPIT

18 The Silenced Dialogue: Power and Pedagogy in
Educating Other People's Children                          483


*Essay Review*

CARLOS J. OVANDO
Politics and Pedagogy: The Case of Bilingual
Education                                                               503


*Book Reviews*

ROSEMARY C. SALOMONE
on *Bilingual Education: Theories and Issues* by
Christina Bratt Paulston                                      521


FRED GENESEE
on *Mirror of Language: The Debate on Bilingualism*
by Kenji Hakuta                                                    526


JOHN BAUGH
on *Twice as Less: Black English and the Performance
of Black Students in Mathematics and Science* by
Eleanor Wilson Orr                                               530


MASAHIKO MINAMI
Notes on Books                                                    542

About the Contributors                                     557

Author Index                                              565

Subject Index                                            573

# Introduction

Over the past two decades the *Harvard Educational Review* has published a number of impressive articles that address language acquisition, literacy, and bilingual and multicultural education. Thus, the Editors of the *Harvard Educational Review* are delighted to introduce a new collection of these articles, *Language Issues in Literacy and Bilingual/Multicultural Education.*

In the past the *Review* has published two reprint books, *Language and Learning: Investigations and Interpretations* (1972) and *Thought & Language/Language & Reading* (1980), both of which contained articles reflecting the current thinking in language studies of the times. Unlike these two predecessors, this new book addresses the distinct differences and transitions between the scholarship of the 1970s, which was generally theoretical, and that of the 1980s and 1990s, which focuses on literacy and bilingual and multicultural education within a sociocultural framework. This new look at how language shapes and is shaped by diverse cultural experience has emerged as the current "great debate" in education. Because language undergirds much of social activity, particularly participation in schooling and subsequent occupations that demand a high level of literacy, many language issues have now become issues of social equity and political empowerment. To date, educational discourse and learning environments have reflected only the discourse style of mainstream society, which often mitigates against achievement by those from different linguistic groups, thus limiting their access to and participation in higher educational and occupational opportunities. With the increased understanding of how variations in discourses contribute to success in school environments, it has become imperative to begin examining educational practice from this perspective (Gee, 1990; McCabe & Peterson, 1991). Therefore, we feel not only a strong need but also a responsibility to publish this new book, which comprehensively treats the issues that have emerged particularly in the 1980s and early 1990s.

This volume is organized into three parts. Part I provides an overview of the classic theoretical approaches to literacy with particular attention to psycholinguistic studies. In addition, a theoretical discussion of second-language acquisition is included. Part II considers literacy as a sociocultural product. More specifically, the articles in this section discuss issues related to literacy in different societies, such as the United States, Liberia, and Brazil. Part III further extends the issues discussed in Part II to bilingual and multicultural educational settings within a culturally diverse society such as the United States. The book concludes with the section Notes on Books, which contains brief reviews of recent books on language acquisition, literacy, and bilingual/multicultural education.

The first three articles in Part I are arranged in chronological order of child development: Roger Brown and Ursula Bellugi analyze toddlers' language acquisition; Charles Read considers preschoolers' invented spellings; and Carol Chomsky discusses elementary schoolchildren's continuing language development. These three articles, which represent classical developmental psycholinguistic studies, reflect the strong influence of the linguistic revolution originated by Noam Chomsky (1957). The studies, which are largely based on Chomsky's (1965) dichotomy of competence (i.e., a person's internalized grammar of language) and performance (i.e., the actual use of the language in concrete situations), try to reveal innate linguistic competencies by measuring aspects of language production performed by children in the process of their language development.

Roger Brown and Ursula Bellugi's syntactic-semantic approach provides beautiful accounts of young children's language development. In this seminal article, they discuss the spontaneous-speech samples of two children in part of Brown's (1973) now-famous longitudinal study of the linguistic development of three children, Adam, Eve, and Sarah. Brown and Bellugi's article, originally published in 1964, is also worthy of attention because here the incipient form of Brown's concept of the mean length of utterance (MLU)[1] was first introduced; since then, this measure has made an immense contribution to language studies. Perhaps more importantly, in this article Brown and Bellugi, while acknowledging the significant influences of environmental or parental interactions, pay particular attention to biological endowment to hypothesize the underlying rules of the target language. This notion closely corresponds to Noam Chomsky's (1965) conception of an innate language-acquisition device (LAD)[2] and reflects a major shift from behaviorist or Skinnerian approaches to language acquisition and learning to an organismic accounting of these phenomena. This concept served as a precursor to the Cognitive Revolution, which led to great advances in linguistics, psychology, and education.

Two other studies in Part I, also influenced by Chomsky, discuss the rule-governed nature of language acquisition. Focusing on invented spellings—a developmental feature of preschoolers' uncorrected spellings—Charles Read attempts to illustrate young children's unconscious knowledge of English phonology, which he believes to be mental representation of a biological endowment specific to human beings. Along the same lines, using the Chomskian concept of markedness, Carol Chomsky shows that the natural process of children's language development continues actively into their elementary school years. Researchers using the MLU are interested in investigating the rate of development of a child's linguistic ability at particular ages, and place much emphasis on similarities among children in the sequence of development. Likewise, Carol Chomsky applies the Minimal Distance Principle[3] (Chomsky, 1969) to her study and shows regularities across children in the language-acquisition process. By examining how children deal with grammatically marked or less marked sentences, she illustrates that, in spite of diverse individual differences in the rate of development, children proceed along similar developmental paths in constructing implicit grammatical rules.

Kenji Hakuta and Herlinda Cancino conclude the experimental psycholinguistic studies in Part I by exploring four theoretical approaches to second-language acquisition—contrastive, error, performance, and discourse analyses. The shifts among these methodologies reflect changes in the conceptions of the processes of language acquisition and the nature of learners. For example, within the framework of contrastive analysis, which was dominant up to the end of 1960s, errors that occur in the process of second-language acquisition are interpreted as a first-language habit interfering with a second-language habit. This notion mirrors the behaviorist approach represented by B. F. Skinner (1957), who argues that language development is largely determined by training based on trial-and-error and not by maturation.[4] On the other hand, error analysis in the 1970s (e.g., Corder, 1971, 1974; Richards, 1974) views the second-language-acquisition process as active hypothesis testing in which the language learner makes hypotheses and compares them with his or her innate grammar for syntactical and phonological similitude. This explanation clearly exemplifies how a generative grammar, outlined by Noam Chomsky, would function.

Concluding each section are essay and book reviews of publications that have greatly influenced the issues discussed in each section. These reviews also give the reader opportunities to appreciate distinguished researchers' interpretations of influential books. For example, James Gee's essay review in Part I, *Toward a Realistic Theory of Language Acquisition*, evaluates Noam Chomsky's and Steven Pinker's contributions to language acquisition studies. Next we present three book reviews. Since reading is one of the most significant communication skills taught at school, we include Robert Kopfstein's discussion of Jeanne Chall's *Stages of Reading Development* (1983), in which she analyzes the content of children's reading and characterizes a set of six stages in terms of underlying psychological processes, goals, modes of reading, and materials to be read. Kopfstein's review is of particular interest when read in relation to Carol Chomsky's notion of five stages in language development.

Kenji Hakuta discusses Massimo Piattelli-Palmarini's *Language and Learning: The Debate between Jean Piaget and Noam Chomsky*, which compares Chomsky's linguistic theory with Piaget's theory of cognitive development. Within the Piagetian framework, language plays a relatively secondary role; the sequence of general cognitive development determines the sequence of language development. This approach is very different from that taken by Noam Chomsky (1985), who believes in the LAD, a self-charged "bioprogram," whereby language acquisition is autonomous; that is, in the language-acquisition process, children automatically move from the initial state (an unspecified period of knowledge readiness) to the steady state (idealized adulthood, or speaker/listener), as if by flipping a switch.

It is also interesting to compare the contrast of these two theories with John Carroll's review of Lev Vygotsky's social-interactionist account, *Thought and Language*. Although language is a very special tool, Vygotsky (1978) argues, it is at first only a tool utilized for a young child's social interactions; as the child internalizes more complex linguistic forms, the role of language changes from a social tool to a private one, where thought can be used by the child independent of the immediate context. He therefore suggests that children's cognitive skills first develop through interactions with more mature members of society and are then internalized. As seen later, this social interaction approach plays an influential role in language studies of the 1980s and 1990s.

## Emerging Sociocultural Issues

In contrast to these psycholinguistic articles that appeared primarily in the early 1970s, the latter half of the 1970s and the 1980–90s in particular witnessed the emergence of more social and pragmatic linguistic concerns, which inevitably led language studies to further examine the nature of literacy within a sociocultural framework. To date, literacy issues have been an increasingly hot topic, and we deal with these issues in Parts II and III.

Daniel and Lauren Resnick's essay, which can serve as an overarching article for Part II, suggests one of the many prospective directions that may be taken with respect to literacy education. By situating literacy in a historical perspective, the Resnicks show that mass literacy education, which typifies the current practice, was brought about through the emergence and implementation of mass schooling. They argue that the literacy models introduced in the past fail to meet current educational needs, exemplified in the demand for high levels of literacy for the entire population. Marking historical shifts in literacy standards, the Resnicks not only argue the novelty of the current situation, but also propose the utilization of functional literacy as an alternative model for the 1990s.

David Olson and Kieran Egan, following the history from the Greek classical period—the foundation of Western literacy beginning with Plato—to the modern times, each discuss the meaning of literacy in relation to Western culture. Olson argues that, at the historical as well as at the individual level, the acquisition of literacy proceeds from context-dependent, oral language accounts of the "utterance" to context-free, written prose accounts of the "text." Based on this direction, he claims that the function of schooling is to make children's language increasingly explicit so that it can be utilized for higher-order intellectual skills such as reasoning and problem solving.

Brandt (1990) aptly characterizes Olson's view as the "strong-text" view of literacy, in which a child must acquire expository text-like, logical, literal, detached, and message-focused skills in order to be literate. In fact, the oral-literate continuum that Olson presents here has long been discussed in terms of an explicit, elaborated literate style versus an ambiguous, restricted oral style (Goody, 1987; Ong, 1982). This dichotomy originated in Basil Bernstein's (1971) theory of codes. The theory has been used to account for why some children do better than others in the schools (Torrance & Olson, 1985) and is discussed in more detail below. Brandt (1990) states that "in match-mismatch formulations, students are deemed to be at risk in school literacy performance to the extent to which their home language[5] is at odds with the so-called explicit, decontextualized language of the school" (p. 106). Thus, the oral-literate dichotomy has been closely associated with the match-mismatch conception in discourse patterns (Michaels, 1981; Wells, 1985).[6]

Egan takes a somewhat different view of the developmental path of literacy held by Olson or other "strong-text" proponents. Although orality tends to be undervalued in Western cultures, Egan acknowledges its historical contribution to intellectual resources and strategies. Extending this concept to child development, he argues that the developmental path of language should not be simply characterized as advancing from orality to literacy; instead he suggests that the evolution be understood as taking place from orality to a composite of orality and literacy. Egan then clarifies his educational ideal by stating that during the early school years children's orality should be used effectively, which would then lead to their later development of literacy.

Catherine Snow shows many similarities between learning to talk and learning to read and write. As a social interactionist, she emphasizes the role of environment and considers the functions of language in social communication to be important throughout the child's development. She explores the processes of a young child's language development in light of diverse theories, such as Bruner's (1977) "scaffolding," in which, for learning to take place, appropriate cooperative interactions must be provided to children.

Snow further argues that early oral language development is directly related to the later development of written language. Her approach, sharing some common elements with Olson's and Egan's, regards early oral language development as having direct bearing on later language skills development and emphasizes the importance of the interface between oral language and literacy (where oral literacy skills are seen as necessary precursors to later literacy skills). Applying this interface to an educational context, she assumes the existence of another interface (or, rather, a continuum) between home language use and school language use. She then points out the danger that the language and culture of the school may run counter to the language and culture of the home. This conflict has been a recurrent theme throughout the 1980s and 1990s. Thus, Snow considers young children's language acquisition, and their later acquisition of literacy, as products of social contexts as well as social interactions.

Sylvia Scribner and Michael Cole challenge the literacy-as-development view, in which literacy, in combination with schooling, is assumed to provide children with the skills necessary for the transition from context-dependent thought (such as buying and selling bolts of cloth in a market) to decontextualized abstract thinking (such as solving word problems in school or hypothetical dilemmas). Scribner and Cole closely study the literacy practices of the Vai of Liberia, who invented a syllabic writing system to represent their language. Using examples of contextualized communication among Vai literates, these researchers argue that the relationship between higher-level critical thinking skills and literacy activities is far more complex than the explanations provided in the literacy-as-development view suggest. Scribner and Cole's perspective challenges Olson's view by concluding that the relationship between literacy and schooling functions differently according to culture-specific norms and rules.

Scribner and Cole's discussion is interesting when compared with what Olson calls the essayist style of literacy, in which mainstream schooling is assumed to be the cultural norm and therefore functions as a gatekeeper in Western societies (Scollon & Scollon, 1981). This view is similar to that discussed by Paulo Freire in his article. Freire, a Brazilian educator and leading critical literacy proponent, sharply criticizes the use of social norms held by the dominant culture to legitimate only a few modes of communication. This restrictive approach leads to the devaluation and thus subtle oppression of minority language speakers and atypical language users. Instead he strongly advocates that the literacy process should play a role in empowering those who are oppressed within the system and thus function as a means of cultural action for freedom. Freire admits that literacy develops the capacity of expression, a view that may correspond to Olson's contention that literacy enhances higher-level critical thinking and problem-solving skills. More important, however, based on his experience with nonliterate farmers in Latin America, Freire emphasizes that learners should use their mental skills to analyze social reality and that, by so doing, they can participate fully in and thus alter social practices.

The essay reviews and book reviews that conclude Part II offer further opportunities to examine literacy in relation to the sociocultural matrix. Like some of the articles in Part II, James Gee discusses issues surrounding literacy using a genealogical perspective—from Plato, who strongly influenced Western thought and literacy, to Freire and Harvey Graff, who are both advocates of critical literacy. As he states elsewhere (Gee, 1990), Gee rejects the traditional view of literacy (the individual ability to read and write) and instead proposes a more sociocultural view of literacy.[7] Also, Peter McLaren compares functional literacy, cultural literacy, and critical literacy (with particular emphasis on the Freirean perspective). Reviewing Freire's *Literacy: Reading the Word and the World*, which is coauthored with Donald Macedo, McLaren explores the Freirean perspective on literacy in relation to U.S. society and its schooling practices.

The next two essays discuss ethnographic research with regard to community and classroom. Harold Rosen reviews Shirley Brice Heath's *Ways with Words*, and Eric Bredo, Mary Henry, and R. P. McDermott discuss Courtney Cazden's *Classroom Discourse*. Heath (1982, 1983, 1986) contends that children growing up in White middle-class, White working-class, and Black working-class families have different experiences and possibly develop different expectations concerning canonical forms of expressing behavior and attitudes. According to both Heath and her reviewer Rosen, each group's communicative style, and oral storytellings in particular, reflects a unique culture-specific perspective. Heath (1983) further states that "the traditional oral-literate dichotomy does not capture the ways other cultural patterns in each community affect the uses of oral and written language" (p. 344). Heath's argument corresponds to that presented in *Classroom Discourse*, in which Cazden (1988) argues that "narratives are a universal meaning-making strategy, but there is no one way of transforming experience into a story" (p. 24). These remarks are further reminiscent of Hymes's (1974) assertion that "it is impossible to generalize validly about 'oral' vs. 'literate' cultures as uniform types" (p. 54). These ethnographers therefore claim that describing language use as developing from context-bound orality to context-free literacy does not properly characterize literacy. This trend in thinking is also advanced by Bruner (1990), who argues that meaning creation is tightly yoked to a specific style of cultural representation.

These reviews pose an important question: If a child who has acquired a certain paradigm for communication in one culture is thrown into another culture, what happens? This question raises the potential problem of commensurability between different language users. A stronger restatement of this problem would suggest that the habitual way of communicating learned in one cultural setting may not necessarily work in a new setting. As Gee (1985) puts it, "Just as the common core of human language is expressed differently in different languages, so the common core of communicative style is expressed differently in different cultures" (p. 11). This problem becomes even more acute in the case of bilingual education (which we discuss further in Part III). To encourage and stimulate children from a different culture, one has to know something of the communicative style of that culture (Hymes, 1982). In the school setting, especially, teachers need to understand how children from different cultures communicate.

Two book reviews conclude Part II. Patricia Greenfield's review is helpful in reading Sylvia Scribner and Michael Cole's article. Joseph and Alexandra Grannis discuss British sociologist Basil Bernstein's controversial theory of codes—an "elaborated code" and a "restricted code." According to Bernstein (1971), in England middle-class speakers employ an extensive code that facilitates the verbal elaboration of subjective intent, while working-class speakers, in greater or lesser degree, employ a restricted code, a speech mode in which it is unnecessary for the speaker verbally to elaborate subjective intent. As seen later, both Delpit and Baugh in Part III refer to Bernstein's codes, but above all we believe it important to review Bernstein's perspective in this volume because it has often been confounded with social class and thus misused, especially in the United States (Brandt, 1990; Hemphill, 1989).

## Concerns about Plurality of Literacies in Society

Up to this point we have focused on the transition in concepts of language acquisition and development from the framework of generative grammar in Part I to the sociolinguistic perspective in Part II. While Hakuta and Cancino's discussion of second-language acquisition, which is presented in Part I, centers on methodologies, they predicted that studies of second-language acquisition in the 1980s would need to lay more stress on the learner's status as a member of society. The importance of this emphasis is now evident, especially when we consider that more than 4.5 million school-aged children speak their native languages, rather than English, at home (Hakuta, 1986). As implied in Part II, even if the same language is spoken, communication may be difficult if the manner of presentation and interactive style are different. If different languages are spoken, communication problems may become even more serious. Part III, which addresses bilingual and multicultural education, presents further discussions of the sociocultural embeddedness of literacy.

Bernardo Ferdman's essay serves as an overarching article for Part III. While acknowledging previous research that has examined the relationships between literacy, culture, and the human mind (e.g., Scribner & Cole in Part II), Ferdman advocates the need for studying these relationships within a culturally diverse society such as the United States. He argues that literacy is culturally framed and defined and that those who are from different ethnic groups in a multicultural society may differ from one another in what they view as literate behavior. According to Ferdman, the kind of literacy education the individual receives may also influence his or her cultural identity. He therefore proposes that literacy education in a multicultural society should be understood and addressed in consideration of the diverse cultures comprising that society.

Jim Cummins proposes a theoretical framework for analyzing minority students' academic success and failure. While highlighting the importance of home and classroom environments and family-school relationships, he argues that previous research (which has tended to discuss students' school success and failure by simply using the linguistic match-mismatch concept in discourse patterns) is inadequate. Instead, Cummins emphasizes ways in which educators can promote the empowerment of minority students so that they can become confident and capable in academic environments. Obviously, not only the empowerment of the students themselves but the empowerment of their parents and communities is crucial as well.

Elsa Auerbach emphasizes the need for designing and implementing family literacy programs that can support low-income, minority, and immigrant families in order to facilitate their children's literacy development. She proposes a social-contextual model of family literacy that reflects community concerns and culture-specific practices in curriculum development. In a more recent study, Snow, Barnes, Chandler, Goodman, and Hemphill (1991) report that in addition to the parents' communication with the school, diverse elements, such as children's outings with adults and even the presence of television rules, are critical home factors influencing literacy. Similarly, reflecting the family's social reality and thus broadening the definition of family literacy, Auerbach crystalizes the important factors that contribute to literacy development.

The next three articles by Ricardo Otheguy, David Spener, and Alma Flor Ada each discuss bilingual education from somewhat overlapping but different perspectives. From Otheguy's discussion, the reader will better understand the recent trend in bilingual education. The 1980s have witnessed a rapid influx of immigrants. According to a March 1987 report by the U.S. General Accounting Office (1987), the Department of Education estimates that between 1.2 and 1.7 million children 5 to 17 years old live in language-minority households, make substantial use of minority languages, and have limited proficiency in English (LEP). O'Malley (1982) estimates that the number of LEP children is much higher (1.5 to 2.4 million LEP children between the ages of 5 and 14). To master English, these LEP children are placed in English-as-a-second-language (ESL) programs.

Consequently, there have been heated discussions for and against bilingual education; but there generally seems to be a sentiment across the United States that people from countries of different languages should just learn English (Hakuta, 1986; Huddy & Sears, 1990). In his article, Otheguy examines the arguments that have been offered against using the home language of bilingual children in the schools. He claims that these arguments are simplistic and erroneous in their assumptions and that issues of bilingual education, combined with governmental policies, race, and ethnicity, are more complex than imagined.

Spener focuses his argument on the role of transitional bilingual education (TBE) programs with regard to U.S. governmental policies, the economy, and the employment situation. A variety of ESL programs, such as maintenance ("additive" or "late-exit") programs and TBE ("early-exit") programs, are representative of most bilingual education programs in the United States today. The purpose of these TBE programs is to help LEP children become familiar with subject matters without being handicapped by their native languages in the mainstream classroom. However, according to Spener, TBE programs provide only a limited period of native-language instruction and do not guarantee English mastery, thus these programs prevent LEP children from attaining fluency in either their native languages or in English; eventually, this deficit socially legitimizes their limited access to better jobs.

The quality of bilingual education programs obviously varies with the teachers. As previously discussed, educators need to promote the empowerment of minority students, their parents, and communities. Ada claims that bilingual teachers need to experience the elements necessary to empower language-minority students. By taking this approach, she argues, bilingual teachers will be able to clearly understand interpersonal, social, and political issues surrounding them; in other words, not only minority students, their parents, and communities, but bilingual teachers themselves should be empowered as well.

Tamara Lucas, Rosemary Henze, and Rubén Donato report on Latino language-minority students' success in secondary schools. In his book review of James Crawford's *Bilingual Education: History, Politics, Theory, and Practice,* Ovando (see below) mentions that people from Spanish-speaking countries are now the fastest-growing minority in the United States and are expected to become the country's largest minority group in the not-so-distant future. Unfortunately, most high schools have failed to meet the needs of Latino language-minority students; this is evident in their high dropout rates, low test scores, poor attendance records, and small numbers going on to college. Lucas, Henze, and Donato describe eight key features that promote the success of language-minority students. Parental involvement, one of these key features, is also mentioned in Snow et al.'s (1991) report, in which they argue that one factor in high school students' academic failure is that "parents were not as involved with teachers at the high school as they had been with teachers at the elementary school" (p. 191). The eight key features discussed by Lucas, Henze, and Donato are very helpful to those working with language-minority students.

Lisa Delpit addresses issues surrounding poor children and children of color; in this sense, the scope of her article is wider than those of the preceding articles. Delpit's anecdote about an Athabaskan Indian student in Alaska is reminiscent of an observation by Scollon and Scollon (1981), who noted that the speech of their two-year-old daughter, who could not read or write, reflected a discourse style similar to the literacy style necessary later in a Western school setting. Conversely, they found that, despite being grammatical, the discourse style of a ten-year-old Athabaskan girl was regarded as nonliterate and thus inappropriate according to the Western norm of literacy.

Citing similar examples used by Scollon and Scollon (1981), Delpit argues that children from middle-class communities are advantaged because they know the codes of power; on the other hand, children from lower-class communities or Black communities are disadvantaged because they lack the knowledge of the codes of power. Thus, according to Delpit, social injustice is embedded in the social norms of communicative interaction of the dominant group. Delpit argues that teachers must teach all students the explicit and implicit rules of power as a first step toward a more equitable education, and thus, society. This concept corresponds to the idea proposed by Robinson (1990), who advocates that opportunities should be equally provided to all students to practice and develop language competencies in response to concrete situations, especially in the classroom.

Part III includes one essay review and three book reviews. Reviewing James Crawford's *Bilingual Education: History, Politics, Theory, and Practice,* Carlos Ovando discusses pedagogical as well as sociopolitical issues surrounding bilingual education in the United States. Fred Genesee reviews Kenji Hakuta's *Mirror of Language: The Debate on Bilingualism,* and Rosemary Salomone discusses Christina Bratt Paulston's *Bilingual Education: Theories and Issues.* Each of these books about bilingual education has a general appeal. Hakuta (1986), for example, emphasizes that becoming fluent in a second language does not necessarily mean losing the first language, nor does maintenance of the first language retard the development of the second language. The belief that bilingualism confuses the mind and retards cognitive development, Hakuta argues, has its roots in some early attempts to explain why immigrants from southern and eastern Europe after the first World War were performing poorly on IQ tests. Genesee carefully summarizes such important issues discussed in Hakuta's *Mirror of Language.*

John Baugh concludes Part III by critically examining Eleanor Wilson Orr's *Twice as Less: Black English and the Performance of Black Students in Mathematics and Science.* In her book, Orr (1987) seems to believe in the concept proposed by Whorf (1956) that the language one speaks profoundly affects the manner in which one thinks about the world. Using this Whorfian concept, Orr argues that Black English vernacular serves as a barrier to Black students' success in mathematics and science. Judging this to be a misapplication of the Whorfian concept, Baugh sharply criticizes Wilson's unconscious inclination toward racist myths.

As we have shown, this book deals with diverse language-related issues, from psycholinguistic studies to different literacy practices in different cultures and, further, to literacy practices within a culturally diverse society. Multicultural/bilingual education plays a crucial role in helping minority children positively maintain their ethnic identities, and this adjustment, in turn, will eventually provide sociocultural stability not only to their own communities but to the larger society as well. In some sense, the issues dealt with in this book are no longer limited to language issues but, rather, extend far beyond to issues of social equity and political empowerment. Language is certainly a window onto the microcosm of the individual mind, but more than that it reflects the larger social world. As Brandt (1990) states, "It is not enough to say that everyone is welcome in the 'big tent' of literate culture without acknowledging that they will be bringing new materials with which to remake the tent" (p. 124). With the plurality of literacies in mind, we strongly believe that this book will serve as a valuable resource to those who are interested in language, literacy, and multicultural and bilingual education.

MASAHIKO MINAMI
BRUCE P. KENNEDY
*Editors*

## Notes

1. For instance, the word *kind* is a grammatical morpheme (the smallest meaningful unit in a language) because it cannot be divided without altering or destroying its meaning. On the other hand, *unkindness* consists of three morphemes: *un, kind,* and *ness.* The MLU is thus measured by counting the average length of a young child's utterances in terms of morphemes rather than words.
2. The LAD includes a universal grammar, a basic knowledge about the nature and structure of human language.
3. For example, "John told Jim to leave" can be more easily processed than "John promised Jim to leave" not only because the former is more usual and thus less marked than the latter, but also because the noun phrase to the immediate left of the infinitive serves as the subject of that infinitive (the distance is therefore minimal).
4. According to the behaviorist approach, infants acquire their native language as follows: At a certain stage, infants are rewarded because they make sounds that resemble the appropriate word for some person or object around them. With this repeated reinforcement, a habit is established, and children continue to imitate the same sounds. In this way, they learn to use words and sentences. Thus, the behaviorist approach views children as passive beneficiaries of the language training techniques employed by their caregivers.
5. Home language refers to the way language is spoken and used in the home and does not necessarily refer to a second language. Rather, this term may refer to dialectical differences and styles of communicative interaction.
6. Olson's argument that language influences higher level cognitive skills is further related to bilingual education, which is discussed in Part III. For example, Williams and Snipper (1990) criticize the "strong-text" view of literacy, which has been used to account for why certain groups of bilingual students tend to fail in school. They contend that Olson's idea implies that "children from backgrounds where written discourse may not be stressed will have cognitive deficiencies that will render them essentially incapable of academic achievement" (p. 71).

7. Gee (1990) proposes a notion of "Discourse," with a capital "D." According to his definition, Discourses, including more than sequential speech or writing, represent cultural models consisting of "words, acts, values, beliefs, attitudes, social identities, as well as gestures, glances, body positions and clothes" (p. 142).

## References

Bernstein, B. (1971). *Class, codes and control. Vol. 1: Theoretical studies towards a sociology of language*. London: Routledge & Kegan Paul.

Brandt, D. (1990). *Literacy as involvement: The acts of writer, reader, and texts*. Carbondale: Southern Illinois University Press.

Brown, R. (1973). *A first language: The early stages*. Cambridge, MA: Harvard University Press.

Bruner, J. S. (1977). Early social interaction and language development. In H. R. Schaffer (Ed.), *Studies in mother-child interaction* (pp. 271–289). London: Academic Press.

Bruner, J. S. (1990). *Acts of meaning*. Cambridge, MA: Harvard University Press.

Burton, D. (Ed.). (1972). *Language and learning: Investigations and interpretations*. Cambridge, MA: Harvard Educational Review.

Cazden, C. B. (1988). *Classroom discourse*. Portsmouth, NH: Heinemann.

Chall, J. S. (1983). *Stages of reading development*. New York: McGraw-Hill.

Chomsky, C. (1969). *The acquisition of syntax in children from 5 to 10*. Cambridge, MA: MIT Press.

Chomsky, N. (1957). *Syntactic structure*. The Hague: Mouton & Co.

Chomsky, N. (1965). *Aspects of the theory of syntax*. Cambridge, MA: MIT Press.

Chomsky, N. (1985). *Knowledge of language*. New York: Praeger.

Corder, S. (1971). Idiosyncratic dialects and error analysis. *International Review of Applied Linguistics, 9*, 149–159.

Corder, S. (1974). Error Analysis. In J. Allen & S. Corder (Eds.), *The Edinburgh Course in Applied Linguistics, 3*, Oxford: Oxford University Press.

Gee, J. P. (1985). The narrativization of experience in the oral style. *Journal of Education, 167*, 9–35.

Gee, J. P. (1990). *Social linguistics and literacies: Ideologies in discourses*. New York: The Falmer Press.

Goody, J. (1987). *The interface between the written and the oral*. Cambridge: Cambridge University Press.

Hakuta, K. (1986). *Mirror of language: The debate on bilingualism*. New York: Basic Books.

Heath, S. B. (1982). What no bedtime story means: Narrative skills at home and school. *Language in Society, 11*, 49–76.

Heath, S. B. (1983). *Ways with words: Language, life and work in communities and classrooms*. New York: Cambridge University Press.

Heath, S. B. (1986). Taking a cross-cultural look at narratives. *Topics in Language Disorders, 7*, (1), 84–94.

Hemphill, L. (1989). Topic development, syntax, and social class. *Discourse Processes, 12*, 267–286.

Huddy, L., & Sears, D. O. (1990). Qualified public support for bilingual education: Some policy implications. In C. B. Cazden & C. E. Snow (Eds.), *English plus: Issues in bilingual education* (The Annals, v. 508, pp. 119–134). Newbury Park, CA: Sage.

Hymes, D. (1974). Speech and language: On the origins and foundations of inequity among speakers. In E. Haugen & M. Bloomfield (Eds.), *Language as a human problem* (pp. 45–71). New York: Norton.

Hymes, D. (1982). Narrative as a "grammar" of experience: Native Americans and a glimpse of English. *Journal of Education, 2*, 121–142.

McCabe, A., & Peterson, C. (Eds.). (1991). *Developing narrative structure*. Hillsdale, NJ: Lawrence Erlbaum Associates.

Michaels, S. (1981). "Sharing time": Children's narrative styles and differential access to literacy. *Language in Society, 10*, 423–442.

O'Malley, J. M. (1982). *Children's English and services study: Educational needs assessment for language minority children with limited English proficiency*. Rosslyn, VA: National Clearinghouse for Bilingual Education.

Ong, W. J. (1982). *Orality and literacy: The technologizing of the word*. New York: Methuen.

Orr, E. W. (1987). *Twice as less: Black English and the performance of black students in mathematics and science*. New York: Norton.

Richards, J. (Ed.) (1974). *Error analysis*. London: Longman.

Robinson, J. L. (1990). *Conversations on the written word: Essays on language and literacy*. Portsmouth, NH: Heinemann.

Scollon, R., & Scollon, S. (1981). *Narrative, literacy and face in interethnic communications*. Norwood, NJ: Ablex.

Skinner, B. F. (1957). *Verbal behavior*. Englewood Cliffs, NJ: Prentice-Hall.

Snow, C. E., Barnes, W. S., Chandler, J., Goodman, I. F., & Hemphill, L. (1991). *Unfulfilled expectations: Home and school influences on literacy*. Cambridge, MA: Harvard University Press.

Torrance, N., & Olson, D. R. (1985). Oral and literate competencies in the early school years. In D. R. Olson, N. Torrance, & A. Hildyard (Eds.), *Literacy, language, and learning*. New York: Cambridge University Press.

U.S. General Accounting Office. (1987). *Bilingual education: A new look at the research evidence*. (GAO/PEMD-87-12BR). Washington, DC: U.S. Government Printing Office.

Vygotsky, L. S. (1978). *Mind in society: The development of higher psychological processes*. Cambridge, MA: Harvard University Press.

Wells, G. (1985). Preschool literacy-related activities and success in school. In D. R. Olson, N. Torrance, & A. Hildyard (Eds.), *Literacy, language, and learning*. New York: Cambridge University Press.

Whorf, B. L. (1956). *Language, thought, and reality: Selected writings* (J. B. Carroll, Ed.). Cambridge, MA: MIT Press.

Williams, J. D., & Snipper, G. C. (1990). *Literacy and bilingualism*. New York: Longman.

Wolf, M., McQuillan, M. K., & Radwin, E. (Eds.) (1980). *Thought & language/Language & reading*. Cambridge, MA: Harvard Educational Review.

# Part I
*Classic Theoretical Approaches to Language Acquisition, Literacy, and Bilingual Education*

# 1

# Three Processes in the Child's Acquisition of Syntax

ROGER BROWN, *Harvard University*

URSULA BELLUGI, *The Salk Institute for Biological Studies*

*In their insightful article, Roger Brown and Ursula Bellugi discuss data from his famous longitudinal study of the linguistic development of three children. Much of the thinking outlined in this article led to advances in language studies. Studying interactions between mothers and their young children, Brown and Bellugi discuss three processes to characterize the child's acquisition of English syntactic structures. Children who are in early phases of language development tend to imitate parental speech but reduce it into telegraphic utterances, only preserving (1) the word order of the model sentences provided by their parents and (2) content words, such as nouns and verbs. In response, mothers are likely to imitate and expand children's utterances, supplying words like articles that simply serve grammatical function. Mother–child interaction, which is a cycle of imitations, reductions, and expansions, further implies the third process, induction of the latent structure of the target language. Referring to this third process, which illustrates the inborn capacity to analyze the underlying rule-governed nature of the target language, the authors suggest that early social interaction is not enough to explain linguistic competence that young children develop and acquire.*

Some time in the second six months of life most children say a first intelligible word. A few months later most children are saying many words and some children go about the house all day long naming things (*table, doggie, ball,* etc.) and actions (*play, see, drop,* etc.) and an occasional quality (*blue, broke, bad,* etc.). At about eighteen months children are likely to begin constructing two-word utterances; such a one, for instance, as *Push car.*

A construction such as *Push car* is not just two single-word utterances spoken in a certain order. As single word utterances (they are sometimes called holophrases)

This investigation was supported in whole by Public Health Service Research Grant MH7088 from the National Institute of Mental Health.

*Harvard Educational Review* Vol. 34 No. 2 Spring 1964, 133–151 both *push* and *car* would have primary stresses and terminal intonation contours. When they are two words programmed as a single utterance the primary stress would fall on *car* and so would the highest level of pitch. *Push* would be subordinated to *car* by a lesser stress and a lower pitch; the unity of the whole would appear in the absence of a terminal contour between words and the presence of such a contour at the end of the full sequence.

By the age of thirty-six months some children are so advanced in the construction process as to produce all of the major varieties of English simple sentences up to a length of ten or eleven words. For several years we have been studying the development of English syntax, of the sentence-constructing process, in children between eighteen and thirty-six months of age. Most recently we have made a longitudinal study of a boy and girl whom we shall call Adam and Eve. We began work with Adam and Eve in October of 1962 when Adam was twenty-seven months old and Eve eighteen months old. The two children were selected from some thirty whom we considered. They were selected primarily because their speech was exceptionally intelligible and because they talked a lot. We wanted to make it as easy as possible to transcribe accurately large quantities of child speech. Adam and Eve are the children of highly-educated parents; the fathers were graduate students at Harvard and the mothers are both college graduates. Both Adam and Eve were single children when we began the study. These facts must be remembered in generalizing the outcomes of the research.

While Adam is nine months older than Eve, his speech was only a little more advanced in October of 1962. The best single index of the level of speech development is the average length of utterance and in October, 1962, Adam's average was 1.84 morphemes and Eve's was 1.40 morphemes. The two children stayed fairly close together in the year that followed; in the records for the thirty-eighth week Adam's average was 3.55 and Eve's, 3.27. The processes we shall describe appeared in both children.

Every second week we visited each child for at least two hours and made a tape recording of everything said by the child as well as of everything said to the child. The mother was always present and most of the speech to the child is hers. Both mother and child became very accustomed to our presence and learned to continue their usual routine with us as the observers.

One of us always made a written transcription, on the scene, of the speech of mother and child with notes about important actions and objects of attention. From this transcription and the tape a final transcription was made and these transcriptions constitute the primary data of the study. For many purposes we require a "distributional analysis" of the speech of the child. To this end the child's utterances in a given transcription were cross-classified and relisted under such headings as: "*A* + noun"; "Noun + verb"; "Verbs in the past"; "Utterances containing the pronoun *it*," etc. The categorized utterances expose the syntactic regularities of the child's speech.

Each week we met as a research seminar, with students of the psychology of language,[1] to discuss the state of the construction process in one of the two children as of that date. In these discussions small experiments were often suggested, experiments that had to be done within a few days if they were to be informative. At one time, for instance, we were uncertain whether Adam understood the semantic difference between putting a noun in subject position and putting it in object position. Consequently one of us paid an extra visit to Adam equipped with some toys. "Adam," we said, "show us the duck pushing the boat." And, when he had done so: "Now show us the boat pushing the duck."

Another week we noticed that Adam would sometimes pluralize nouns when they should have been pluralized and sometimes would not. We wondered if he could make grammatical judgments about the plural, if he could distinguish a correct form from an incorrect form. "Adam," we asked, "which is right, 'two shoes' or 'two shoe'?" His answer on that occasion, produced with explosive enthusiasm, was "Pop goes the weasel!" The two-year-old child does not make a perfectly docile experimental subject.

The dialogue between mother and child does not read like a transcribed dialogue between two adults. Table 1 offers a sample section from an early transcribed record. It has some interesting properties. The conversation is, in the first place, very much in the here and now. From the child there is no speech of the sort that Bloomfield called "displaced," speech about other times and other places. Adam's utterances in the early months were largely a coding of contemporaneous events and impulses. The mother's speech differs from the speech that adults use to one another in many ways. Her sentences are short and simple; for the most part they are the kinds of sentences that Adam will produce a year later.

Perhaps because they are short, the sentences of the mother are perfectly grammatical. The sentences adults use to one another, perhaps because they are longer

TABLE 1
*A Section from Adam's First Record*

| Adam | Mother |
|---|---|
| See truck, Mommy. | |
| See truck. | |
| | Did you see the truck? |
| No I see truck. | |
| | No, you didn't see it? |
| | There goes one. |
| There go one. | |
| | Yes, there goes one. |
| See a truck. | |
| See truck, Mommy. | |
| See truck. | |
| Truck. | |
| Put truck, Mommy. | |
| | Put the truck where? |
| Put truck window. | |
| | I think that one's too large to go in the window. |

5

and more complex, are very often not grammatical, not well formed. Here for instance is a rather representative example produced at a conference of psychologists and linguists: "As far as I know, no one yet has done the in a way obvious now and interesting problem of doing a in a sense a structural frequency study of the alternative syntactical in a given language, say, like English, the alternative possible structures, and how what their hierarchical probability of occurrence structure is."[2] It seems unlikely that a child could learn the patterns of English syntax from such speech. His introduction to English ordinarily comes in the form of a simplified, repetitive, and idealized dialect. It may be that such an introduction is necessary for the acquisition of syntax to be possible but we do not know that.

In the course of the brief interchange of Table 1 Adam imitates his mother in saying: "There go one" immediately after she says "There goes one." The imitation is not perfect; Adam omits the inflection on the verb. His imitation is a reduction in that it omits something from the original. This kind of imitation with reduction is extremely common in the records of Adam and Eve and it is the first process we shall discuss.

## Imitation and Reduction

Table 2 presents some model sentences spoken by the mothers and the imitations produced by Adam and Eve. These were selected from hundreds in the records in order to illustrate some general propositions. The first thing to notice is that the imitations preserve the word order of the model sentences. To be sure, words in the model are often missing from the imitation but the words preserved are in the order of the original. This is a fact that is so familiar and somehow reasonable that we did not at once recognize it as an empirical outcome rather than as a natural necessity. But of course it is not a necessity, the outcome could have been otherwise. For example, words could have been said back in the reverse of their original order, the most recent first. The preservation of order suggests that the model sentence is processed by the child as a total construction rather than as a list of words.

In English the order of words in a sentence is an important grammatical signal. Order is used to distinguish among subject, direct object, and indirect object and it is one of the marks of imperative and interrogative constructions. The fact that the

TABLE 2
*Some Imitations Produced by Adam and Eve*

| Model Utterance | Child's Imitation |
| --- | --- |
| Tank car | Tank car |
| Wait a minute | Wait a minute |
| Daddy's brief case | Daddy brief case |
| Fraser will be unhappy | Fraser unhappy |
| He's going out | He go out |
| That's an old time train | Old time train |
| It's not the same dog as Pepper | Dog Pepper |
| No, you can't write on Mr. Cromer's shoe | Write Cromer shoe |

child's first sentences preserve the word order of their models partially accounts for the ability of an adult to "understand" these sentences and so to feel that he is in communication with the child. It is conceivable that the child "intends" the meanings coded by his word orders and that, when he preserves the order of an adult sentence, he does so because he wants to say what the order says. It is also possible that he preserves word order just because his brain works that way and that he has no comprehension of the semantic contrasts involved. In some languages word order is not an important grammatical signal. In Latin, for instance, "Agricola amat puellam" has the same meaning as "Puellam amat agricola" and subject-object relations are signalled by case endings. We would be interested to know whether children who are exposed to languages that do not utilize word order as a major syntactic signal preserve order as reliably as do children exposed to English.

The second thing to notice in Table 2 is the fact that when the models increase in length there is not a corresponding increase in the imitation. The imitations stay in the range of two to four morphemes which was the range characteristic of the children at this time. The children were operating under some constraint of length or span. This is not a limitation of vocabulary; the children knew hundreds of words. Neither is it a constraint of immediate memory. We infer this from the fact that the average length of utterances produced spontaneously, where immediate memory is not involved, is about the same as the average length of utterances produced as immediate imitations. The constraint is a limitation on the length of utterance the children are able to program or plan.[3] This kind of narrow span limitation in children is characteristic of most or all of their intellectual operations. The limitation grows less restrictive with age as a consequence, probably, of both neurological growth and of practice, but of course it is never lifted altogether.

A constraint on length compels the imitating child to omit some words or morphemes from the mother's longer sentences. Which forms are retained and which omitted? The selection is not random but highly systematic. Forms retained in the examples of Table 2 include: *Daddy, Fraser, Pepper,* and *Cromer; tank car, minute, briefcase, train, dog,* and *shoe; wait, go,* and *write; unhappy* and *old time.* For the most part they are nouns, verbs, and adjectives, though there are exceptions, as witness the initial pronoun *He* and the preposition *out* and the indefinite article *a.* Forms omitted in the samples of Table 2 include: the possessive inflection -*s,* the modal auxiliary *will,* the contraction of the auxiliary verb *is,* the progressive inflection -*ing,* the preposition *on,* the articles *the* and *an,* and the modal auxiliary *can.* It is possible to make a general characterization of the forms likely to be retained that distinguishes them as a total class from the forms likely to be omitted.

Forms likely to be retained are nouns and verbs and, less often, adjectives, and these are the three large and "open" parts-of-speech in English. The number of forms in any one of these parts-of-speech is extremely large and always growing. Words belonging to these classes are sometimes called "contentives" because they have semantic content. Forms likely to be omitted are inflections, auxiliary verbs, articles, prepositions, and conjunctions. These forms belong to syntactic classes that are small and closed. Any one class has few members and new members are not readily added. The omitted forms are the ones that linguists sometimes call "functors," their grammatical *functions* being more obvious than their semantic content.

Why should young children omit functors and retain contentives? There is more than one plausible answer. Nouns, verbs, and adjectives are words that make reference. One can conceive of teaching the meanings of these words by speaking them, one at a time, and pointing at things or actions or qualities. And of course parents do exactly that. These are the kinds of words that children have been encouraged to practice speaking one at a time. The child arrives at the age of sentence construction with a stock of well-practiced nouns, verbs, and adjectives. Is it not likely then that this prior practice causes him to retain the contentives from model sentences too long to be reproduced in full, that the child imitates those forms in the speech he hears which are already well developed in him as individual habits? There is probably some truth in this explanation but it is not the only determinant since children will often select for retention contentives that are relatively unfamiliar to them.

We adults sometimes operate under a constraint on length and the curious fact is that the English we produce in these circumstances bears a formal resemblance to the English produced by two-year-old children. When words cost money there is a premium on brevity or to put it otherwise, a constraint on length. The result is "telegraphic" English and telegraphic English is an English of nouns, verbs, and adjectives. One does not send a cable reading: "My car has broken down and I have lost my wallet; send money to me at the American Express in Paris" but rather "Car broken down; wallet lost; send money American Express Paris." The telegram omits: *my, has, and, I, have, my, to, me, at, the, in*. All of these are functors. We make the same kind of telegraphic reduction when time or fatigue constrains us to be brief, as witness any set of notes taken at a fast-moving lecture.

A telegraphic transformation of English generally communicates very well. It does so because it retains the high-information words and drops the low-information words. We are here using "information" in the sense of the mathematical theory of communication. The information carried by a word is inversely related to the chances of guessing it from context. From a given string of content words, missing functors can often be guessed but the message "my has and I have my to me at the in" will not serve to get money to Paris. Perhaps children are able to make a communication analysis of adult speech and so adapt in an optimal way to their limitation of span. There is, however, another way in which the adaptive outcome might be achieved.

If you say aloud the model sentences of Table 2 you will find that you place the heavier stresses, the primary and secondary stresses in the sentences, on contentives rather than on functors. In fact the heavier stresses fall, for the most part, on the words the child retains. We first realized that this was the case when we found that in transcribing tapes, the words of the mother that we could hear most clearly were usually the words that the child reproduced. We had trouble hearing the weakly stressed functors and, of course, the child usually failed to reproduce them. Differential stress may then be the cause of the child's differential retention. The outcome is a maximally informative reduction but the cause of this outcome need not be the making of an information analysis. The outcome may be an incidental consequence of the fact that English is a well-designed language that places its heavier stresses where they are needed, on contentives that cannot easily be guessed from context.

We are fairly sure that differential stress is one of the determinants of the child's telegraphic productions. For one thing, stress will also account for the way in which children reproduce polysyllabic words when the total is too much for them. Adam, for instance, gave us *'pression* for *expression* and Even gave us *'raff for giraffe;* the more heavily-stressed syllables were the ones retained. In addition we have tried the effect of placing heavy stresses on functors which do not ordinarily receive such stresses. To Adam we said: "You say what I say" and then, speaking in a normal way at first: "The doggie will bite." Adam gave back: "Doggie bite." Then we stressed the auxiliary: "The doggie *will* bite" and, after a few trials, Adam made attempts at reproducing that auxiliary. A science fiction experiment comes to mind. If there were parents who stressed functors rather than contentives would they have children whose speech was a kind of "reciprocal telegraphic" made up of articles, prepositions, conjunctions, auxiliaries, and the like? Such children would be out of touch with the community as real children are not.

It may be that all the factors we have mentioned play some part in determining the child's selective imitations; the reference-making function of contentives, the fact that they are practiced as single words, the fact that they cannot be guessed from context, and the heavy stresses they receive. There are also other possible factors: for example, the left-to-right, earlier-to-later position of words in a sentence, but these make too long a story to tell here.[4] Whatever the causes, the first utterances produced as imitations of adult sentences are highly systematic reductions of their models. Furthermore, the telegraphic properties of these imitations appear also in the child's spontaneously produced utterances. When his speech is not modeled on an immediately prior adult sentence, it observes the same limitation on length and the same predilection for contentives as when it is modeled on an immediately prior sentence.

## Imitation with Expansion

In the course of the brief conversation set down in Table 1, Adam's mother at one point imitates Adam. The boy says: "There go one" and mother responds: "Yes, there goes one." She does not exactly reproduce the model sentence of the child but instead adds something to it or expands it. What she adds is a functor, the inflection for third-person on the verb, the very form that Adam had omitted when he imitated his mother.

One of the first things we noticed when we began to study child speech several years ago was the frequency with which adults imitated children. Indeed they seemed to imitate more often than did the children themselves. We later came to realize that adult imitations are seldom exact reproductions; they are usually expansions. The mothers of Adam and Eve responded to the speech of their children with expansions about thirty per cent of the time. We did it ourselves when we talked with the children. Indeed we found it very difficult to withhold expansions. A reduced or incomplete English sentence seems to constrain the English-speaking adult to expand it into the nearest properly formed complete sentence. Table 3 lists a few sample expansions from the hundreds in the records.

The first thing worthy of attention in the expansions of Table 3 is the fact that the words spoken by the mother preserve the order of the words in the child's sentences. To be sure, words and inflections are added but they are fitted in—before, and after and between the words the child used; they are not generally permitted to disturb the order of the child's words. It is as if these latter were taken as constants by the mother, constants to which some sentence had to be fitted. She acts as if she were assuming that the child means everything he says, all the words and also their order, but as if he might also mean more than he says. From the mother's point of view an expansion is a kind of communication check; it says in effect: "Is this what you mean?"

The second thing to notice about Table 3 is the character of the forms added to the child's utterances. They include the auxiliaries *is* and *will;* the prepositions *in, on, to,* and *up;* the verb forms *is, have, had,* and *having;* the articles *a* and *the;* the pronouns *her, he,* and *it.* For the most part, the words added are functors, and functors are of course the words that the child omits in his reductions.

The interaction between mother and child is, much of the time, a cycle of reductions and expansions. There are two transformations involved. The reduction transformation has an almost completely specifiable and so mechanical character. One could program a machine to do it with the following instructions: "Retain contentives (or stressed forms) in the order given up to some limit of length." The expansion accomplished by Adam's mother when she added the third-person inflection to the verb and said "There goes one" is also a completely specifiable transformation. The instructions would read: "Retain the forms given in the order given and supply obligatory grammatical forms." To be sure, this mother-machine would have to be supplied with the obligatory rules of English grammar but that could be done. However, the sentence "There goes one" is atypical in that it only adds a compulsory

TABLE 3
*Expansions of Child Speech Produced by Mothers*

| Child | Mother |
| --- | --- |
| Baby highchair | Baby is in the highchair |
| Mommy eggnog | Mommy had her eggnog |
| Eve lunch | Eve is having lunch |
| Mommy sandwich | Mommy'll have a sandwich |
| Sat wall | He sat on the wall |
| Throw Daddy | Throw it to Daddy |
| Pick glove | Pick the glove up |

and redundant inflection. The expansions of Table 3 all add forms that are not grammatically compulsory or redundant and these expansions cannot be mechanically generated by grammatical rules alone.

In Table 3 the topmost four utterances produced by the child are all of the same grammatical type; all four consist of a proper noun followed by a common noun. However, the four are expanded in quite different ways. In particular the form of the verb changes: it is in the first case in the simple present tense; in the second case the simple past; in the third case the present progressive; in the last case the simple future. All of these are perfectly grammatical but they are different. The second set of child utterances is formally uniform in that each one consists of a verb followed by a noun. The expansions are again all grammatical but quite unlike, especially with regard to the preposition supplied. In general, then, there are radical changes in the mother's expansions when there are no changes in the formal character of the utterances expanded. It follows that the expansions cannot be produced simply by making grammatically compulsory additions to the child's utterances.

How does a mother decide on the correct expansion of one of her child's utterances? Consider the utterance "Eve lunch." So far as grammar is concerned this utterance could be appropriately expanded in any of a number of ways: "Eve is having lunch"; "Eve had lunch"; "Eve will have lunch"; Eve's lunch," etc. On the occasion when Eve produced the utterance, however, one expansion seemed more appropriate than any other. It was then the noon hour, Eve was sitting at the table with a plate of food before her, and her spoon and fingers were busy. In these circumstances "Eve lunch" had to mean "Eve is having lunch." A little later when the plate had been stacked in the sink and Eve was getting down from her chair the utterance "Eve lunch" would have suggested the expansion "Eve has had her lunch." Most expansions are not only responsive to the child's words but also to the circumstances attending their utterance.

What kind of instructions will generate the mother's expansions? The following are approximately correct: "Retain the words given in the order given and add those functors that will result in a well-formed simple sentence that is appropriate to the circumstances." These are not instructions that any machine could follow. A machine could act on the instructions only if it were provided with detailed specifications for judging appropriateness and no such specifications can, at present, be written. They exist, however, in implicit form in the brains of mothers and in the brains of all English-speaking adults and so judgments of appropriateness can be made by such adults.

The expansion encodes aspects of reality that are not coded by the child's telegraphic utterance. Functors have meaning but it is meaning that accrues to them in context rather than in isolation. The meanings that are added by functors seem to be nothing less than the basic terms in which we construe reality: the time of an action, whether it is ongoing or completed, whether it is presently relevant or not; the concept of possession and such relational concepts as are coded by *in, on, up, down,* and the like; the difference between a particular instance of a class ("Has

anybody seen *the* paper?") and any instance of a class ("Has anybody seen *a* paper?");
the difference between extended substances given shape and size by an "accidental"
container (*sand, water, syrup,* etc.) and countable "things" having a characteristic fixed
shape and size (*a cup, a man, a tree,* etc.). It seems to us that a mother in expanding
speech may be teaching more than grammar; she may be teaching something like a
world-view.

As yet it has not been demonstrated that expansions are *necessary* for learning
either grammar or a construction of reality. It has not even been demonstrated that
expansions contribute to such learning. All we know is that some parents do expand
and their children do learn. It is perfectly possible, however, that children can and
do learn simply from hearing their parents or others make well-formed sentences
in connection with various nonverbal circumstances. It may not be necessary or even
helpful for these sentences to be expansions of utterances of the child. Only experiments contrasting expansion training with simple exposure to English will settle the
matter. We hope to do such experiments.

There are, of course, reasons for expecting the expansion transformation to be
an effective tutorial technique. By adding something to the words the child has just
produced one confirms his response insofar as it is appropriate. In addition one
takes him somewhat beyond that response but not greatly beyond it. One encodes
additional meanings at a moment when he is most likely to be attending to the cues
that can teach that meaning.

## Induction of the Latent Structure

Adam, in the course of the conversation with his mother set down in Table 1,
produced one utterance for which no adult is likely ever to have provided an exact
model: "No I see truck." His mother elects to expand it as "No, you didn't see it"
and this expansion suggests that the child might have created the utterance by
reducing an adult model containing the form *didn't*. However, the mother's expansion
in this case does some violence to Adam's original version. He did not say *no* as his
mother said it, with primary stress and final contour; Adam's *no* had secondary stress
and no final contour. It is not easy to imagine an adult model for this utterance. It
seems more likely that the utterance was created by Adam as part of a continuing
effort to discover the general rules for constructing English negatives.

In Table 4 we have listed some utterances produced by Adam or Eve for which
it is difficult to imagine any adult model. It is unlikely that any adult said any of

## TABLE 4
*Utterances Not Likely to be Imitations*

| | |
|---|---|
| My Cromer suitcase | You naughty are |
| Two foot | Why it can't turn off? |
| A bags | Put on it |
| A scissor | Cowboy did fighting me |
| A this truck | Put a gas in |

these to Adam or Eve since they are very simple utterances and yet definitely un-grammatical. In addition it is difficult, by adding functors alone, to build any of them up to simple grammatical sentences. Consequently it does not seem likely that these utterances are reductions of adult originals. It is more likely that they are mistakes which externalize the child's search for the regularities of English syntax.

We have long realized that the occurrence of certain kinds of errors on the level of morphology (or word construction) reveals the child's effort to induce regularities from speech. So long as a child speaks correctly, or at any rate so long as he speaks as correctly as the adults he hears, there is no way to tell whether he is simply repeating what he has heard or whether he is actually constructing. However, when he says something like "I digged a hole" we can often be sure that he is constructing. We can be sure because it is unlikely that he would have heard *digged* from anyone and because we can see how, in processing words he has heard, he might have come by *digged*. It looks like an overgeneralization of the regular past inflection. The inductive operations of the child's mind are externalized in such a creation. Overgeneralizations on the level of syntax (or sentence construction) are more difficult to identify because there are so many ways of adding functors so as to build up conceivable models. But this is difficult to do for the examples of Table 4 and for several hundred other utterances in our records.

The processes of imitation and expansion are not sufficient to account for the degree of linguistic competence that children regularly acquire. These processes alone cannot teach more than the sum total of sentences that speakers of English have either modeled for a child to imitate or built up from a child's reductions. However, a child's linguistic competence extends far beyond this sum total of sentences. All children are able to understand and construct sentences they have never heard but which are nevertheless well-formed, well-formed in terms of general rules that are implicit in the sentences the child has heard. Somehow, then, every child processes the speech to which he is exposed so as to induce from it a latent structure. This latent rule structure is so general that a child can spin out its implications all his life long. It is both semantic and syntactic. The discovery of latent structure is the greatest of the processes involved in language acquisition and the most difficult to understand. We will provide an example of how the analysis can proceed by discussing the evolution in child speech of noun phrases.

A noun phrase in adult English includes a noun but also more than a noun. One variety consists of a noun with assorted modifiers: *The girl; The pretty girl; That pretty girl; My girl*, etc. All of these are constructions which have the same syntactic privileges as do nouns alone. One can use a noun phrase in isolation to name or request something; one can use it in sentences, in subject position or in object position or in predicate nominative position. All of these are slots that nouns alone can also fill. A larger construction having the same syntactic privileges as its "head" word is called in linguistics an "endocentric" construction, and noun phrases are endocentric constructions.

For both Adam and Eve, in the early records, noun phrases usually occur as total independent utterances rather than as components of sentences. Table 5 presents an assortment of such utterances at Time 1. They consist in each case of some sort of modifier, just one, preceding a noun. The modifiers, or as they are sometimes called the "pivot" words, are a much smaller class than the noun class. Three students of child speech have independently discovered that this kind of construction is extremely common when children first begin to combine words.[5,6,7]

It is possible to generalize the cases of Table 5 into a simple implicit rule. The rule symbolized in Table 5 reads: "In order to form a noun phrase of this type, select first one word from the small class of modifiers and select, second, one word from the large class of nouns." This is a "generative" rule by which we mean it is a program that would actually serve to build constructions of the type in question. It is offered as a model of the mental mechanism by which Adam and Eve generated such utterances. Furthermore, judging from our work with other children and from the reports of Braine and of Miller and Ervin, the model describes a mechanism present in many children when their average utterance is approximately two morphemes long.

We have found that even in our earliest records the M + N construction is sometimes used as a component of larger constructions. For instance, Eve said: "Fix a Lassie" and "Turn the page" and "A horsie stuck" and Adam even said: "Adam wear a shirt." There are, at first, only a handful of these larger constructions but there are very many constructions in which single nouns occur in subject or in object position.

Let us look again at the utterances of Table 5 and the rule generalizing them. The class M does not correspond with any syntactic class of adult English. In the class M are articles, a possessive pronoun, a cardinal number, a demonstrative adjective or pronoun, a quantifier, and some descriptive adjectives—a mixed bag indeed. For adult English these words cannot belong to the same syntactic class because they have very different privileges of occurrence in sentences. For the children the words do

TABLE 5
*Noun Phrases in Isolation and Rule for*
*Generating Noun Phrases at Time I*

| | |
|---|---|
| A coat | More coffee |
| A celery* | More nut* |
| A Becky* | Two sock* |
| A hands* | Two shoes |
| The top | two tinker-toy* |
| My Mommy | Big boot |
| That Adam | Poor man |
| My stool | Little top |
| That knee | Dirty knee |

$$NP \rightarrow M + N$$

M → a, big, dirty, little, more, my, poor, that, the, two.
N → Adam, Becky, boot, coat, coffee, knee, man, Mommy, nut, sock, stool, tinker-toy, top, *and very many others.*

*Ungrammatical for an adult.

seem to function as one class having the common privilege of occurrence before nouns.

If the initial words of the utterances in Table 5 are treated as one class M then many utterances are generated which an adult speaker would judge to be ungrammatical. Consider the indefinite article *a*. Adults use it only to modify common count nouns in the singular such as *coat, dog, cup,* etc. We would not say *a celery,* or *a cereal,* or *a dirt; celery, cereal,* and *dirt* are mass nouns. We would not say *a Becky* or *a Jimmy; Becky* and *Jimmy* are proper nouns. We would not say *a hands* or *a shoes; hands* and *shoes* are plural nouns. Adam and Eve, at first, did form ungrammatical combinations such as these.

The numeral *two* we use only with count nouns in the plural. We would not say *two sock* since *sock* is singular, nor *two water* since *water* is a mass noun. The word *more* we use before count nouns in the plural *(more nuts)* or mass nouns in the singular *(more coffee)*. Adam and Eve made a number of combinations involving *two* or *more* that we would not make.

Given the initial very undiscriminating use of words in the class M it follows that one dimension of development must be a progressive differentiation of privileges, which means the division of M into smaller classes. There must also be subdivision of the noun class (N) for the reason that the privileges of occurrence of various kinds of modifiers must be described in terms of such sub-varieties of N as the common noun and proper noun, the count noun and mass noun. There must eventually emerge a distinction between nouns singular and nouns plural since this distinction figures in the privileges of occurrence of the several sorts of modifiers.

Sixteen weeks after our first records from Adam and Eve (Time 2), the differentiation process had begun. By this time there were distributional reasons for separating out articles *(a, the)* from demonstrative pronouns *(this, that)* and both of these from the residual class of modifiers. Some of the evidence for this conclusion appears in Table 6. In general one syntactic class is distinguished from another when the members of one class have combinational privileges not enjoyed by the members of

TABLE 6
*Subdivision of the Modifier Class*

A) PRIVILEGES PECULIAR TO ARTICLES

| *Obtained* | *Not Obtained* |
|---|---|
| A blue flower | Blue a flower |
| A nice nap | Nice a nap |
| A your car | Your a car |
| A my pencil | My a pencil |

B) PRIVILEGES PECULIAR TO DEMONSTRATIVE PRONOUNS

| *Obtained* | *Not Obtained* |
|---|---|
| That my cup | My that cup |
| That a horse | A that horse |
| That a blue flower | A that blue flower |
| | Blue a that flower |

the other. Consider, for example, the reasons for distinguishing articles (Art) from modifiers in general (M). Both articles and modifiers appeared in front of nouns in two-word utterances. However, in three-word utterances that were made up from the total pool of words and that had a noun in final position, the privileges of *a* and *the* were different from the privileges of all other modifiers. The articles occurred in initial position followed by a member of class M other than an article. No other modifier occurred in this first position; notice the "Not obtained" examples of Table 6A. If the children had produced utterances like those (for example, *blue a flower, your a car*) there would have been no difference in the privileges of occurrence of articles and modifiers and therefore no reason to separate out articles.

The record of Adam is especially instructive. He created such notably ungrammatical combinations as "a your car" and "a my pencil." It is very unlikely that adults provided models for these. They argue strongly that Adam regarded all the words in the residual M class as syntactic equivalents and so generated these very odd utterances in which possessive pronouns appear where descriptive adjectives would be more acceptable.

Table 6 also presents some of the evidence for distinguishing demonstrative pronouns (Dem) from articles and modifiers (Table 6B). The pronouns occurred first and ahead of articles in three-and-four-word utterances—a position that neither articles nor modifiers ever filled. The sentences with demonstrative pronouns are recognizable as reductions which omit the copular verb *is*. Such sentences are not noun phrases in adult English and ultimately they will not function as noun phrases in the speech of the children, but for the present they are not distinguishable distributionally from noun phrases.

Recall now the generative formula of Table 5 which constructs noun phrases by simply placing a modifier (M) before a noun (N). The differentiation of privileges illustrated in Table 6, and the syntactic classes this evidence motivates us to create, complicate the formula for generating noun phrases. In Table 7 we have written a single general formula for producing all noun phrases at Time 2 [NP → (Dem) + (Art) + (M) + N] and also the numerous more specific rules which are summarized by the general formula.

By the time of the thirteenth transcription, twenty-six weeks after we began our study, privileges of occurrence were much more finely differentiated and syntactic classes were consequently more numerous. From the distributional evidence we judged

**TABLE 7**
*Rules for Generating Noun Phrases at Time 2*

| | |
|---|---|
| $NP_1 \rightarrow Dem + Art + M + N$ | $NP \rightarrow (Dem) + (Art) + (M) + N$ |
| $NP_2 \rightarrow Art + M + N$ | |
| $NP_3 \rightarrow Dem + M + N$ | |
| $NP_4 \rightarrow Art + N$ | ( ) means class within |
| $NP_5 \rightarrow M + N$ | parentheses is optional |
| $NP_6 \rightarrow Dem + N$ | |
| $NP_7 \rightarrow Dem + Art + N$ | |

that Adam had made five classes of his original class M: articles, descriptive adjectives, possessive pronouns, demonstrative pronouns, and a residual class of modifiers. The generative rules of Table 7 had become inadequate; there were no longer, for instance, any combinations like "A your car." Eve had the same set except that she used two residual classes of modifiers. In addition nouns had begun to subdivide for both children. The usage of proper nouns had become clearly distinct from the usage of count nouns. For Eve the evidence justified separating count nouns from mass nouns, but for Adam it still did not. Both children by this time were frequently pluralizing nouns but as yet their syntactic control of the singular-plural distinction was imperfect.

In summary, one major aspect of the development of general structure in child speech is a progressive differentiation in the usage of words and therefore a progressive differentiation of syntactic classes. At the same time, however, there is an integrative process at work. From the first, an occasional noun phrase occurred as a component of some larger construction. At first these noun phrases were just two words long and the range of positions in which they could occur was small. With time the noun phrases grew longer, were more frequently used, and were used in a greater range of positions. The noun phrase structure as a whole, in all the permissible combinations of modifiers and nouns, was assuming the combinational privileges enjoyed by nouns in isolation.

In Table 8 we have set down some of the sentence positions in which both nouns and noun phrases occurred in the speech of Adam and Eve. It is the close match between the positions of nouns alone and of nouns with modifiers in the speech of Adam and Eve that justifies us in calling the longer constructions noun phrases. These longer constructions are, as they should be, endocentric; the head word alone has the same syntactic privileges as the head word with its modifiers. The continuing failure to find in noun phrase positions whole constructions of the type "That a blue flower" signals the fact that these constructions are telegraphic versions of predicate nominative sentences omitting the verb form *is*. Examples of the kind of construction not obtained are: "That (that a blue flower)"; "Where (that a blue flower)?".

For adults the noun phrase is a subwhole of the sentence, what linguists call an "immediate constituent." The noun phrase has a kind of psychological unity. There are signs that the noun phrase was also an immediate constituent for Adam and Eve. Consider the sentence using the separable verb *put on*. The noun phrase in "Put the

TABLE 8
*Some Privileges of the Noun Phrase*

| Noun Positions | Noun Phrase Positions |
|---|---|
| That (flower) | That (a blue flower) |
| Where (ball) go? | Where (the puzzle) go? |
| Adam write (penguin) | Doggie eat (the breakfast) |
| (Horsie) stop | (A horsie) crying |
| Put (hat) on | Put (the red hat) on |

red hat on" is, as a whole, fitted in between the verb and the particle even as is the noun alone in "Put hat on." What is more, however, the location of pauses in the longer sentence, on several occasions, suggested the psychological organization: "Put . . . the red hat . . . on" rather than "Put the red . . . hat on" or "Put the . . . red hat on." In addition to this evidence the use of pronouns suggests that the noun phrase is a psychological unit.

The unity of noun phrases in adult English is evidenced, in the first place, by the syntactic equivalence between such phrases and nouns alone. It is evidenced, in the second place, by the fact that pronouns are able to substitute for total noun phrases. In our immediately preceding sentence the pronoun "It" stands for the rather involved construction from the first sentence of this paragraph: "The unity of noun phrases in adult English." The words called "pronouns" in English would more aptly be called "pro-noun-phrases" since it is the phrase rather than the noun which they usually replace. One does not replace "unity" with "it" and say "The *it* of noun phrases in adult English." In the speech of Adam and Eve, too, the pronoun came to function as a replacement for the noun phrase. Some of the clearer cases appear in Table 9.

Adam characteristically externalizes more of his learning than does Eve and his record is especially instructive in connection with the learning of pronouns. In his first eight records, the first sixteen weeks of the study, Adam quite often produced sentences containing both the pronoun and the noun or noun phrase that the pronoun should have replaced. One can here see the equivalence in the process of establishment. First the substitute is produced and then, as if in explication, the form or forms that will eventually be replaced by the substitute. Adam spoke out his pronoun antecedents as chronological consequents. This is additional evidence of the unity of the noun phrase since the noun phrases *my ladder* and *cowboy boot* are linked with *it* in Adam's speech in just the same way as the nouns *ladder* and *ball*.

We have described three processes involved in the child's acquisition of syntax. It is clear that the last of these, the induction of latent structure, is by far the most

TABLE 9
*Pronouns Replacing Nouns or Noun Phrases and Pronouns Produced
Together with Nouns or Noun Phrases*

| Noun Phrases Replaced by Pronouns | Pronouns and Noun Phrases in Same Utterances |
|---|---|
| Hit ball | Mommy get it ladder |
| Get it | Mommy get it my ladder |
| Ball go? | |
| Go get it | Saw it ball |
| | Miss it garage |
| Made it | I miss it cowboy boot |
| Made a ship | I Adam drive that |
| | I Adam drive |
| Fix a tricycle | I Adam don't |
| Fix it | |

complex. It looks as if this last process will put a serious strain on any learning theory thus far conceived by psychology. The very intricate simultaneous differentiation and integration that constitutes the evolution of the noun phrase is more reminiscent of the biological development of an embryo than it is of the acquisition of a conditional reflex.

## Notes

1. We are grateful for intellectual stimulation and lighthearted companionship to Dr. Jean Berko Gleason, Mr. Samuel Anderson, Mr. Colin Fraser, Dr. David McNeill, and Dr. Daniel Slobin.
2. H. Maclay and C. E. Osgood, "Hesitation phenomena in spontaneous English speech," *Word*, XV (1959), 19–44.
3. Additional evidence of the constraint on sentence length may be found in R. Brown and C. Fraser, "The acquisition of syntax," C. N. Cofer and Barbara Musgrave, eds., *Verbal Behavior and Learning* (New York: McGraw Hill, 1963).
4. Brown and Fraser, *ibid.*
5. M. D. S. Braine, "The ontogeny of English phrase structure: the first phrase," *Language*, XXXIX (1963), 1–13.
6. W. Miller and Susan Ervin, "The development of grammar in child language," Ursula Bellugi and R. Brown, eds., *The Acquisition of Language, Child Developm. Monogr.* (1964).
7. Brown and Fraser, "The acquisition of syntax."

# 2
# *Pre-School Children's Knowledge of English Phonology*

CHARLES READ
*University of Wisconsin, Madison*

*In this now-classic study, Charles Read explores literacy issues at the most fundamental level—the relation between speech sounds and how they are represented graphically in spelling. He tries to disclose children's unconscious knowledge of English phonology by describing preschoolers' invented spellings, which are a developmental feature of uncorrected spellings. He argues that, irrespective of the arbitrariness of English spelling, preschoolers intuitively organize phoneme-grapheme correspondences, which are nothing but mental representations of a biological endowment to discover common principles and elements operating in their target language. The author advocates, with careful attention to each individual's stages of development, the construction of early reading instruction.*

The term *phonology* refers to the sound system of our language, a system of regular processes that determine the pronunciation of English. Part of what we acquire in learning a language is a mastery of these processes, so that when we encounter a new or unfamiliar word, we automatically (and for the most part, unconsciously) know some aspects of its pronunciation. In *telemorphic,* for instance, we know (without necessarily knowing what the word might mean) that stress falls on the third syllable and that the first and second vowels are not pronounced alike, despite the spelling. Linguists have shown that the processes determining these and many other details of English pronunciation are not simple "analogies" to familiar words (such as *telegraphic* in this case); they are a system of intricate but general rules of the language.[1] Exactly how and when we acquire our unconscious mastery of these rules remains largely a mystery; it is clear that we do not memorize individual pronunciations (since the rules extend to new words and sentences) and that we do not learn them directly from a study of English spelling.

*Harvard Educational Review*  Vol. 41  No. 1  February 1971, 1–34

In fact, a child must bring some knowledge of English phonology to his first encounter with reading and writing. Part of what he must have learned is that certain sounds are to be regarded as the same, despite differences in their pronunciation. For instance, the third segments ([n]) of *ten* and *tenth* are functionally the same in English, even though they are articulated differently; in another language, they might be as distinct as *tin* and *Tim* are to us. Variations in pronunciation take many forms; an example of a different sort is the contrast in timbre, pitch, and other qualities between the speech of a child and that of his father, even though they may be "saying the same thing." Such a contrast appears in all languages, of course, and perhaps need not be learned specifically for English; others must be learned as part of the particular language. For instance, in some languages the difference in aspiration between the [p] of *pit* and the [p] of *spit* would make them distinct sounds, while the difference in voicing between the first segments of *tin* and *din* might be entirely irrelevant; these would be two instances of the same word. As part of his knowledge of his language, a child must learn to attend to certain phonetic differences and to abstract from others in a specific and systematic way. Evidently, children possess some phonological knowledge of this sort in their pre-school years. Otherwise, they could not judge that two different speakers were saying the same thing; they could not understand a speaker of another dialect, however slightly different; ultimately, they could not understand English at all, for speech sounds can and do vary in a multitude of ways, many of which we must systematically disregard in understanding English.

Beyond the general observation that a pre-school child's conception of English phonology is sufficiently abstract to permit him to understand and be understood under normal circumstances, however, we know few details of when and how this conception develops. Evidence about the nature of the development must come from children's judgments of phonetic similarities and differences, and these have proven elusive indeed. This article will present some evidence of such judgments, specifically about how children in their pre-school and kindergarten years tacitly categorize the sounds of English. Which phonetic differences do they treat as important in relating one sound to another, which less important, and which ones do they regularly abstract away from? The evidence here suggests that the children's phonology is (necessarily) highly abstract, and that it differs in specific ways from that of adult speakers of English, including of course the children's parents and teachers.

In addition to its relation to the general question of how children learn a language, this evidence bears on a potentially more practical issue, namely, how a child's phonology compares to the abstract representation of speech that he learns in school—the standard English spelling system. It is obvious that any spelling system is highly abstract (again, necessarily so); in English, for example, all direct representation of pitch, stress, and intonation is entirely excluded. Further, as is well known, the standard alphabet does not provide enough characters to represent distinctly the forty-three or so autonomous "phonemes" that distinguish one word from another, and these phonemes are themselves classes of phonetically different sounds, as in the examples given for /p/ and /n/. A recent article in this journal[2] discussed and justified a class of still further abstractions, in which our spelling does not represent predictable phonetic variations in lexically related forms, as in the non-italicized vowels of *extreme/extremity*, even though we have the alphabetic means to do so. We can compare such an analysis of the abstractions inherent in our spelling system with what we learn about the abstractness of the child's conception of English phonology. Differences between the two systems may define a large and central part of what a child must learn in order to read and write. In making this comparison, I will be assuming that what the child learns in mastering the spelling system is a representation related in complex, but generally systematic, ways to the phonology of English. The contrary assumption—that the child memorizes a long list of generally unpredictable spellings—fails to account for the abilities of mature readers and writers.

The evidence of phonological knowledge comes from pre-school children who invented their own spelling system for English, influenced relatively little by the standard system. In each case, the child first learned the conventional names of the letters of the alphabet; then with blocks or some other movable-alphabet toy, began to spell words; and finally produced written messages of all kinds, including stories, letters, and poems. The writing began as early as age three and one half, usually before the child was able to read, and certain parts of the spelling system persisted well into the first grade, where they gradually gave way to standard spellings under the influence of formal instruction in reading and writing.

Such spontaneous spelling is relatively rare. Apparently, it depends on the coincidence of the child's interests and abilities with various other factors, such as the attitudes of the parents, particularly their tolerance for what appears to be bad spelling. In fact, the invented spellings sometimes look so little like English that parents and teachers may be unable to read them and may disregard or even suppress them. Hence, it is difficult to assess the actual (or potential) frequency of such early invented spelling. This report is based on twenty selected clear cases, together with some marginal ones.

What is significant, even from so few cases, is that each child arrived at roughly the same system, using certain spellings that seem implausible to his parents and teachers, but which can be explained in terms of hypotheses about the children's implicit organization of English sounds.

The structure of the argument, then, is this: to propose an explanation for the invented spellings by showing that they follow from certain assertions about English phonology, independently justified, together with certain hypotheses about how the children perceive and organize the spoken forms; that is, what they know about English phonology. "Knowledge" and "organization" in this context refer to unconscious beliefs about English sounds and their structure, in the sense in which a reader or listener has notions of sound-structure that enable him to judge two sequences as similar, as in the recognition of rhyme, without his necessarily being aware of either the beliefs or the rhyme itself. This sense of "knowledge" has been explicated more fully and defended elsewhere.[3]

Even for one who accepts, at least tentatively, this line of argument from observed language behavior (performance) to hypothesized judgments and knowledge that underlie it (competence), each step of the argument is open to various questions. Although the statements about English phonology have independent linguistic justification, they are hardly so well established as to be beyond question. For certain fine phonetic details, one can even ask whether the accepted description is based on a physical or perceptual reality that is stable and independent of the linguistic beliefs of the perceiver. There are also questions about the spellings, of course. Children's printing frequently includes marks that are difficult to interpret. Children, like adults, commit apparently non-systematic errors (even compared to the child's own spelling system), false starts, and inexplicable omissions. Sometimes conventional spellings occur; these may not reveal anything about the child's judgments, since one usually cannot know (certainly not from the written record alone) whether they are learned or created; they may have been copies or taken from dictation. Accordingly, I have usually left them out of this account.[4] It is also difficult to know about the children's language experience before they began to spell; none of the parents kept a systematic record of what their child heard or said, nor would such a record guarantee the accuracy of inferences from it about what the child knew. Some assumptions about the bases for the original spelling come from information provided by the parents, other investigations of children's language development, and the evidence of the early spellings themselves.

Consider the problem confronting the pre-school child who wants to spell English messages. He knows the pronunciation of the words; that is, he recognizes the words when someone else says them, and he may pronounce them more or less as an adult does.[5] Without being aware of it, he knows certain syntactic and semantic relations among words, such as that *-er* is an agentive ending in a pair like *ride/rider* or that *eat-* is a verb stem in *eating*. He may have mastered certain regular phonetic alternations, such as the [s]—[z] forms for plurals. He recognizes the letters of the alphabet and knows their conventional names, or most of them.

The letter-names provide only partial help to such a child. Assume for the moment that he wishes to represent English consonants at roughly an autonomous phonemic level of detail, and that he considers just those letters whose names contain consonantal segments, therefore leaving aside *a,e,i,o,u,* and *y,* whose names contain only vowels and glides. He has fairly direct clues to the representation of [p,t,k,b,d,f,v,s,z,ǰ,m,n,r, and l] in the corresponding letter-names, and [č] (as in *chin*) is the consonant in the name of *h.*[6] The names of *c,g,q,x,* and *w* provide no additional information, since they contain only consonants already accounted for. This leaves the child with no direct suggestion for representing [θ,ð,š,ž,g,ŋ and h].[7] The various English vowels are much less well provided for, but the children devise rather ingenious spellings for them, as we will see. Notice that to use even this information, the child must analyze the letter-names into their component segments and respect the consonantal or vocalic nature of each. There are indications in the invented spellings that the children can and do perform just such an analysis.

23

In addition, the children got information from their parents, but ordinarily only when they asked for specific help. Most of them apparently learned from adults the digraphic spellings of [θ], [ð], and [č], as in *thin*, *then*, and *church*. Certain common words, such as *the, day, Mommy, Daddy,* and the child's own name and those of his family were sometimes copied or dictated, but the evidence also includes invented spellings for each. In general, these pre-school writers are remarkably independent; they create most of their own spellings by trying to represent the sounds as they relate them to the letter-names they know. Occasionally these efforts lead to a standard spelling, but most of the results are non-standard, often extremely so, and they reveal aspects of the child's phonological system.

## Vowels

The children's representation of front[8] vowels presents a fairly clear system. The names of the letters *a, e,* and *i* correspond quite directly to the tense vowels in *bait, beet,* and *bite.* In the spontaneous spelling system these letters represent their own names in such words, usually without the standard devices, such as doubling or final "silent" *e,* to show the tenseness of the vowel. So we have:

| | | | | | |
|---|---|---|---|---|---|
| D*A* | (day) | L*A*D*E* | (lady) | T*I*GR | (tiger) |
| K*A*M | (came) | *E*GL*E* | (eagle) | L*I*K | (like) |
| T*A*BIL | (table) | F*E*L | (feel) | M*I* | (my) |

More interesting is the spelling of the lax vowels, as in *bit, bet, bat,* and *pot.* Altogether the children must extend the five vowel letters (or others, conceivably) to at least eight lax vowels, as well as some other tense ones. They choose a systematic phonological basis for making this extension.

Standard spelling accomplishes part of what is required by using the same letter to spell the distinct vowels italicized in the following pairs:

divine—divinity     extreme—extremity     phone—phonic

These pairs of vowels are related not only historically but lexically; that is, in the lexicon of an optimal grammar of English, the vowel segments of each pair will be represented in the same way. It is generally the case that standard spelling represents these lexical relationships; note that the relationships in meaning are thus embodied in spelling.[9]

Two general processes affect the actual pronunciation of the tense forms in contemporary English, however. The first combines them with a following [y]- or [w]-glide, converting them to diphthongs. The second, known as Vowel Shift, raises their place of articulation from that of the lax forms to the next highest position, lowering the highest to a low position. Other rules further modify their quality. Because all these rules affect only tense vowels, and because there was no corresponding change in spelling when Vowel Shift entered the language, the vocalic portion of a tense diphthong now differs phonetically in height and other qualities from the lax vowel that is usually spelled with the same letter. The phonetic correspondence is as follows:

|        | tense | lax | tense | lax | tense | lax |
|--------|-------|-----|-------|-----|-------|-----|
| Symbol | [īy]  | [i] | [ēy]  | [e] | [āy]  | [a] |
| Spelling | *ser*e*ne—div*i*nity* | | *c*a*me—extr*e*mity* | | *l*i*ne—ph*o*nic* | |

With these correspondences in mind, consider the following typical invented spellings:

| FES | (fish) | FALL | (fell) | SCICHTAP | (Scotch tape) |
|-----|--------|------|--------|----------|---------------|
| EGLIOW | (igloo) | LAFFT | (left) | GIT | (got) |
| FLEPR | (Flipper) | ALRVATA | (elevator) | CLIK | (clock) |

Such examples could be multiplied many times, for among the children under 5 years, these representations of the lax vowels are extremely regular. The [i] of *fish* and *igloo* is represented as *E*, the [e] of *fell* as *A*, the [a] of *Scotch* as *I*. In other words, the children pair lax vowels with tense vowels on the basis of phonetic relationships. The resulting spellings seem odd to most adults, just because adults have long since learned that spelling represents the lexical level at which the first vowel of *penalty* is related to that of *penal*. To adults this relation has become a perceptual fact, and not always an easy one for beginning students of phonetics to displace.

What is surprising is that the children are able to recognize the phonetic relationships they represent in spelling. The children do not pair lax with tense vowels as if these were unanalyzable segments, as they seem to most adults, but rather on the basis of similarity in place of articulation, abstracting from differences in tenseness, diphthongization, and possibly length. The children organize the vowels according to an analysis of their phonetic features.

Further evidence that the children are employing such a tacit analysis appears much later in their careers as original spellers. After they have learned the standard spellings for the lax vowels, many of the children make a rather systematic mistake. They occasionally spell a high or mid tense vowel with the letter they have recently learned to use for the phonetically corresponding lax form.

| SIKE | (seek) | CEME | (came) |
|------|--------|------|--------|
| AIRFILD | (airfield) | PLEY | (play) |
| FRONTIR | (frontier) | TEBL | (table) |

It is as if, having learned that the spelling of lax vowels is not based on what they can hear in the letter-names, the children attempt to save the phonetic correspondence between lax and tense forms, even at the expense of ignoring the obvious congruence between letter-names and tense vowels that they began with. This error, as they are on the verge of learning the standard system, actually carries them away from it momentarily, overthrowing the best-practiced vowel spellings of all. This seems a plausible error only if general notions of phonetic correspondence, not memorized sequences, underlie the spellings. It suggests that the children's knowledge of such relationships may be a more important basis for their spelling than the establishment of "habits" through practice.

Note that the children analyze the articulation of the three tense diphthongs considered so far in the same way, despite the considerable differences among them. For example, the vowel and glide of [īy] are sufficiently close that the segment is not considered diphthongal by many linguists (e.g., Jespersen, Jones); they consider the vowel of *beet* to be a tense, slightly higher and more fronted version of the vowel of *bit*. On the other hand, [āy] combines a low back vowel with a high front glide. Not surprisingly, the latter spelling is the first to disappear as a child's analysis develops. Children who at first have all three of the above tense-lax relationships later may have only [e]—[ēy] and [i]—[īy], employing a new spelling for [a]—not *I*, but *O* or *A*. Some preliminary counting suggests that a common reflection of this early system among the "errors" of first-graders who have, for the most part, learned the official spellings, is *A* for [e] as in KRAPT [crept].

Finally, in their analysis of front vowels all of the children seem to assume that the vowel of *bat* is to be spelled with an *A*—even at the same time that they are writing the "incorrect" forms just discussed. The vowel of *bat* is not a part of any letter-name, nor of any tense vowel in most northern U.S. dialects of English. Unless they learn the spelling of [æ] by asking their parents—and they clearly do not learn the spelling of any other lax vowel in that way—the children presumably choose the letter whose name is closest, in some sense, to it. In place of articulation, *A* [ēy] and *I* [āy] are the two possibilities. That the children always choose *A* may suggest that for them two vowels differing only in height of articulation ([æ—e]) are phonologically closer than two differing only in backness ([æ—a]); therefore they collapse the former pair in spelling. If the most fundamental phonological dimensions for the children are those along which contrasts are most likely to be preserved in spelling, this result contrasts with the suggestion of Jakobson, that height is the primary dimension for vowels.[10] On the same assumption, it is consistent with the hierarchy suggested by Chomsky and Halle, in which backness is the major dimension.[11] The entire discussion is highly tentative. At any rate, in the central and back vowels there is other evidence that backness is a more important determinant of the children's spelling than is height.

One result of the spelling of front vowels is that *bait*, *bet*, and *bat* all have the same spelling—BAT. Some homography is required by the lack of symbols, but the particular choices appear to reflect the children's own sense of phonological relations. The spellings are phonetic in the sense that they represent relations at a (broad) phonetic level of detail; they are abstract in that distinct segments are represented by a single symbol. The children evidently find this result acceptable enough that they do not introduce invented symbols, unlike those critics who reject standard English spelling for its lack of distinct representations for functionally distinct sounds.[12]

I will not discuss the invented spellings of back vowels in detail here. The phonetic relations are intricate, but the symbols available to the children from the standard alphabet are limited, so their spellings are highly abstract and reveal little internal structure. Also, there is a lack of clear evidence for some of the less frequent vowels. In general, the back rounded vowels of *boot*, *boat*, and *bought* are all spelled *O*. In this, the children disregard differences in height and tenseness, again choosing back-ness as the dimension to be represented. Typical examples at an early stage of development are:

| | | | | | |
|---|---|---|---|---|---|
| SOWN | (soon) | GOWT | (goat) | OL | (all) |
| EGLIOW | (igloo) | POWLEOW | (polio) | COLD | (called) |
| SOWTKAC | (suitcase) | WENDOWS | (windows) | SMOLR | (smaller) |

As these suggest, vowels with back glides, [w] as in *boot* [ūw] and *boat* [ōw], are often spelled *OW*. This remarkably accurate representation provides further evidence that the children can distinguish a vocalic segment from a glide, a distinction that is particularly notable for the vowel of *boat*, where *O* alone might have sufficed, had the children treated the letter-name as an unanalyzed whole.[13]

Further evidence that the children represent similarities in backness comes from their spelling of the lax, back, unrounded vowel [ʌ], the vowel of *hut*. The younger children (from three and a half to about four and a half years) spell this vowel *I*, indicating a relation to the other back, unrounded vowels [a] and [āy], not to [i].

| | | | |
|---|---|---|---|
| LIV | (love) | BRITHR | (brother) |
| DIZ | (does) | SINDAS | (Sundays) |
| WIS | (was) | WINTS | (once) |

Again the difference that the children abstract from is one of height and possibly tenseness. This fact, together with the treatment of back rounded vowels, is consistent with the system applied to front vowels.

The spelling of the "neutral" form to which unstressed lax vowels reduce is of some interest, because it illustrates both what the children know and what they do not yet know. Phonetically, this vowel is central, high or mid, and unrounded; the children pair it, accurately enough, with the vowel of *bit*, which they spell *E* at an early stage for the reasons mentioned above. This spelling appears in the italicized positions of:

| | | | |
|---|---|---|---|
| PLEM*E*TH | (Plymouth) | SEP*E*KOL | (Cepacol) |
| AN*E*MEL | (animal) | RAJ*E*LASNS | ([cong]ratulations) |
| B*E*NANE | (banana) | PANS*E*L | (pencil) |

Later, when the spelling of the vowel of *bit* develops to *I*, the reduced vowel also becomes *I*:

| | | | |
|---|---|---|---|
| SIG*I*RAT | (cigarette) | KRISM*I*S | (Christmas) |
| OV*I*N | (oven) | CER*I*T | (carrot) |
| ROC*I*T | (rocket) | SRK*I*S | (circus) |

In this detail again we see a system that abstracts from certain phonetic differences to relate one segment to another. Especially notable in this case is that the children give a consistent spelling to a segment that may be represented by various vowel letters in conventional spelling. Again, the reason is that standard spelling represents a lexical form which takes account of derivational relations like the one between *cigarette* and *cigar*, where the second vowel is not reduced. Pre-school children have little or no knowledge of these relations and the lexical forms that preserve them, of course; in fact, it is just such information that they must eventually learn.

## Vowel Alternations

As noted above, certain pairs of vowels alternate regularly in derivationally related forms in English. The following examples illustrate the major pairs:

| *Vowel Alternation* | *Spelling* |
| --- | --- |
| 1. [āy—i] | divine—divinity |
| | line—linear |
| 2. [īy—e] | please—pleasant |
| | serene—serenity |
| 3. [ēy—æ] | nation—national |
| | profane—profanity |
| 4. [ōw—a] | tone—tonic |
| | verbose—verbosity |
| 5. [āw—ʌ] | profound—profundity |
| | abound—abundant |
| 6. [ūw—ʌ] | reduce—reduction |
| | induce—induction |

Chomsky and Halle have shown that these phonetic alternations can be derived from lexical forms in which both members of a pair have essentially the same vowel. The phonological rules that predict the difference in pronunciation are each independently required in the grammar of English. As a result, the fact that English spelling uses the same letter for both members of each pair (except for dropping the *o* in case 5) becomes simply another instance of the general practice in the language, of representing lexical forms in spelling.[14]

The question of how to relate such forms in spelling surely does not arise for children in the age we are discussing. As the examples suggest, the derivational processes involved are typical of the learned vocabulary that includes many polysyllabic forms of Romance origin. One suspects that within young children's vocabularies there is little generality to such relationships as these. As a result, if a preschool child had occasion to write *pleasant,* he would probably not try to display its relation to *please.* Table 1 contrasts the standard spellings for such pairs with the results of the children's own phonological system.

TABLE 1

| Phonetic Pair | Examples | Adult Spelling[15] | Child Spelling |
|---|---|---|---|
| 1. [āy—i] | divine—divinity | I | Different: I—E |
| 2. [īy—e] | serene—serenity | E | Different: E—A |
| 3. [êy—æ] | nation—national | A | Same:    A |
| 4. [ōw—a] | tone—tonic | O | Different: O(W)—I |
| 5. [âw—ʌ] | abound—abundant | (O)U | Different: O(W)—I |
| | | | O—U later |
| 6. [ūw—ʌ] | reduce—reduction | U | Different: OW—I |
| | | | O—U later |

In general, the children spell differently the pairs that are the same in standard spelling. On this basis one can suggest some empirical hypotheses: for example, that children find it easier to learn the relationship and the first vowel spelling of *nation/ national* and similar forms than that of the derived forms in 1 and 2, and that the spelling of derived forms in 5 and 6 is easier to learn than that of their roots.

There are important questions yet to be answered, of course. We do not know what further development children's phonology may undergo before they begin to learn such words as these, nor do we know the exact role that the derivational relations play in the learning of spelling. Although these relations allow for a systematic account of English phonology and spelling, they may play little or no immediate role in learning. Furthermore, we do not know what individual differences there may be in pre-schoolers' conceptions of English phonology.

Nevertheless, one general insight seems clear: the children's created spellings, no less than the standard ones, are the results of a systematic categorization of English vowels according to certain articulatory properties. That children may tacitly recognize such phonological relationships spontaneously, even before their first formal encounter with reading and writing in the standard system, suggests that they need not approach the latter as a set of arbitrary sound-symbol correspondences—that is, as a long list of words to be memorized. Rather, the child's task is to master new principles that extend and deepen the already abstract conception of the sound system of English that he brings to school.

## Affrication

Turning now to consonants, we find other evidence of the pre-schoolers' phonological judgments embodied in their spelling. Consider the following:

| | | | |
|---|---|---|---|
| AS CHRAY | (ash tray) | CWNCHRE | (country) |
| CHRIBLS | (troubles) | JRADL | (dreidel) |
| CHRIE | (try) | JRAGIN | (dragon) |

The invented spelling of [t] and [d] before [r] is *CH* and *J*, respectively.

Again, these representations have a phonetic basis; the first segments of a pair like *truck* and *tuck* are not identical, in fact. Before [r] in English, [t] and [d] are affricated, i.e., released slowly with a resulting "shh" sound. They are articulated in the same place as the stops that we spell *t* and *d*, but in the manner of the palatal affricates [č] and [ǰ] that standard spelling represents as *ch* and *j* respectively. In that respect, they constitute a third possibility intermediate between the two phonological pairs that have distinct standard spellings. Because the affrication before [r] is predictable, standard spelling ignores it, using the lexical representations *tr* and *dr*. Evidently, the children perceive the affrication. Not knowing the lexical representations, they must choose between the known spellings *T/D* or *CH/J* for these intermediate cases. They consistently choose on the basis of affrication, abstracting from the difference in place-of-articulation. They always match affricate [t] and [d] with the affricates that correspond in voicing—[č] and [ǰ], respectively.

Sometimes this preference appears among first-graders, even those who have done no original pre-school spelling. A six-year-old, making average progress in reading and writing in first grade, wrote the following words for me when I asked what words begin with the same sound as *train*. (Note that *R* is usually omitted and *CH* is reversed):

| | | | |
|---|---|---|---|
| HCEAN | (train) | HCRAK | (track) |
| HCEK | (check) | HCICN | (chicken) |
| HCIKMANCK | (chipmunk) | HCITO | (cheetah) |
| HCRP | (trip) | HCAFE | (traffic) |

This boy's spelling is clearly different from that of the pre-schoolers—in the vowels, for instance—but he had no doubt that these words begin with the same sound. Similarly for [dr] sequences:

| | | |
|---|---|---|
| GIBOLL | (dribble) | (the word I asked about) |
| GIP | (Jeep) | |
| GIN | (Gene) | |
| GY | (draw) | (I attribute the *Y* to the [w] in the name of that letter.) |

Another first-grade boy independently produced very similar answers; *cheat, traps,* and *chap* were all words with the same first sound as *train*. He spelled that sound *H*—remember that the name of the letter includes [č]. He suggested *drink* and *Jim* as having the same first sound as *dribble*. For these boys, [t] and [d] before a vowel were clearly another matter; after they had given me the above answers, I asked each about *toy, table, Dick,* and *dog*. Those are *t* and *d*, they told me, and they wrote them out with those letters.

I have conducted an experimental investigation with 135 children who had done no original spelling, seeking to determine their judgments of these affricates. The details of the test and its results are beyond the scope of this article,[16] but the general outcome provides some support for the inferences drawn from the invented spelling.

For example, the children were asked to indicate which words in a set of examples like *train, turkey,* and *chicken* begin with the same sound as *truck*. The children supplied the words themselves, by naming pictures, so that I, as tester, rarely had to give my own pronunciation. There were at least 11 words in a set, so that the consistency of a child's judgment could be measured. Of the 80 kindergarten children, many could not make consistent judgments, but of those who could do so, fully half chose words like *train* and *chicken,* rejecting *turkey, tie,* and the like. The 28 nursery-school children had even more difficulty making the required judgment consistently, a fact which suggests, not surprisingly, that the children who spelled spontaneously were better than most at becoming conscious of their phonological judgments. But again, most of the consistent nursery-school children chose the affricates and rejected the stops.

In a class of 27 first-graders who had encountered *tr*-words in their early reading, most made the adult judgment. However, there were children even in this group who insisted on the similarity between [tr] and [č]. Furthermore, there were four who easily demonstrated their ability to read a set of words like *train, teddy bear,* and *chair,* and who asserted with equal confidence that it is the first and last that begin with the same sound, even while they looked at the printed forms. These children obviously distinguished standard spelling from their own phonetic judgments. Such results as these indicate at least that the spontaneous spellers are not unique in their phonological judgments, although they may be somewhat unusual in their ability to make them explicit, and that the affrication of stops before [r] in English may be an important phonetic fact for young children.

Just as there is no unaffricated [tr] cluster, there is no [čr] cluster within a syllable in English,[17] so, given the standard alphabet, either *tray* or *chray* would represent the word unambiguously. In a strictly taxonomic phonemic analysis, there is no relevant evidence for deciding whether the first segment of *tray* is to be classed with that of *toy* or that of *chin*. As usual, the standard spelling corresponds to the lexical representation from which the actual pronunciation is predictable by a general rule. That the children do not know this lexical representation is simply another instance of the general conclusion that it is such representations that they must learn in mastering standard spelling.

Perhaps the more remarkable fact is that knowing the usual uses of *T* and *CH,* the children are able to choose a consistent representation for this intermediate segment. They abstract from a difference in palatalization (so called because the tongue strikes the palate in the articulation of *chin*) in classifying the first segment of *tray* with that of *chin,* and they do so without parental guidance, obviously. Evidently affrication is for them a phonologically more influential feature than is palatalization, despite the otherwise general importance of place-of-articulation in their system. The children may represent palatalization if they have the alphabetic means to do so, as in SE (see) versus SHE, but they are capable of a more abstract spelling where it is needed, as in the [tr] and [dr] cases. In this, they are spontaneously employing one of the basic devices of spelling systems, namely consistent abstraction from phonetic variations.

The nature of this accomplishment is theoretically more important than the fact that they choose the wrong dimension, from the adult point of view. To learn standard (lexical) spelling, a child must acquire both the principle that spelling does not represent regular phonetic variation and a knowledge of just what is regular— affrication, in this case. The fact that children's spontaneous spelling is already systematically abstract suggests that it is chiefly the facts of English, rather than the principle of spelling, that they have yet to learn. We will examine other cases in which the original spelling is, or rapidly becomes, abstract in this sense. Teachers of primary reading and spelling should be aware of both the principle and the specific instances of it in English. In responding to children's first spelling, we should probably regard efforts that abstract in the wrong direction as misapplications of the right idea.

## Flaps

Another case that provides some information about the child's capacity for abstract representation is that of alveolar flaps, as in the following words:

| LADR | (letter) | PREDE | (pretty) |
| WOODR | (water) | BEDR | (better) |

Once again, the *D* in these words represents a phonetically correct perception. There is no contrast between [t] and [d] when they occur between vowels in English; both become a tap of the tongue against the alveolar ridge behind the upper teeth. Because this sound is voiced, it is closer to [d]. The same variation takes place across word boundaries, and the children do not fail to represent it:

AODOV   (out of)        GAD I CHANS   (get a chance)

In this case, the children represent a phonetic variation that the standard system does not. Presumably they have no basis for knowing that there is a lexical /t/ in such words. For the word-internal cases, they cannot receive any direct phonetic evidence, since [t] never occurs there.

Nevertheless, this is one of the earliest invented spellings to disappear. The child who wrote LADR and PREDE at age three and a half or four wrote LATR, SESTR (sister), and PRETE at age five. As these examples themselves show, other invented spellings, such as that of the lax vowels and the unigraphic representation of syllabic /r/ (see below), persisted longer, until age six in this case. Even children who at age six and later maintained some of the original spellings, such as CHR for [tr], stopped representing the flap even in internal positions, as in LETL (little).

How the children learn about the lexical /t/ in such words is not the issue. Most of these children were at least beginning to read at age five, and their parents say that they usually told their children the spelling of any word they asked about. Furthermore, at a boundary [t] alternates with the voiced flap, according to whether the following segment is a vowel, so that either may occur in the same word:

[gɨD ə čæns]     [gɨt səm]
get a chance     get some

More important than the source of evidence is the fact that the children learned to abstract away from this particular phonetic variation regularly. The relatively rapid development of this abstraction suggests that voicing contrasts may be less major determinants than others. Another section will present further evidence for this conclusion.

The extension of this abstract spelling to all appropriate instances despite deficient phonetic evidence supports the view that spelling is "rule-governed" behavior—that is, that spellings need not be learned one-by-one, but rather that what is learned is a principle. An important difference is that a principle extends to new instances. One cannot be sure what constitute "new instances" in children's writing, but the word-internal tongue flaps would seem to qualify, for phonetically they are always voiced, and the evidence that they are lexically (therefore graphically) /t/ is quite indirect. Yet once *T* appears in such a position, it appears consistently from then on, displacing *D* in words that the children have written previously. Accordingly, I suggest that the phonological relation between the voiced flap and the corresponding voiceless stop became a part of these children's knowledge of the language, and that they adopted the abstract form in their spelling as a result.

## Nasals

Another interesting feature of the children's spelling is the treatment of the nasals [m], [n], and [ŋ], as in *bumpy, end,* and *sing,* respectively. Initially within a syllable, only the first two occur in English, and in this position, the children spell them in the usual way:

> MARED   (married)     NIT   (night)

These two nasals in final position also receive standard spelling:

> POM   (palm)     WAN   (when)

But when any of the nasals occurs before a consonant, the children almost always omit it from spelling:

| | | | | | |
|---|---|---|---|---|---|
| BOPY | (bumpy) | AD | (and) | WOTET | (want it) |
| NUBRS | (numbers) | ED | (end) | DOT | (don't) |
| THOPY | (thumpy) | MOSTR | (monster) | PLAT | (plant) |

Velar nasals before phonetic consonants are slightly less common, but examples are:

| | |
|---|---|
| HACC | (Hanks) |
| THEKCE | (think(s?)) |
| AGRE | (angry) |

| | | |
|---|---|---|
| SIC | (sink) | written three times in my presence, along with a monologue on its nominal, transitive, and intransitive meanings. |
| FAC | (Frank) | the [r] is also omitted |
| NOOIGLID | (New England) | |

This treatment of preconsonantal nasals is quite general and consistent; it is the usual (almost without exception) spelling for all the children up to about age five. Then most of them begin to represent the nasal, but still frequently omit it. In fact, on an informal spelling dictation given to 49 first-graders, this spelling accounted for 15 of the 23 erroneous spellings of *went* and *sent*. Unfortunately, these examples are ill-chosen, since *wet* and *set* also happen to be English words, and on that account may be more likely errors. Some first-grade teachers have indicated, however, that the omission of preconsonantal nasals is extraordinarily common.

What appears at first to be another and extremely common instance of this spelling is the use of *EG* and *IG* for *-ing* endings, the former being used by those children who write *E* for [i].

| | | | |
|---|---|---|---|
| FEHEG | (fishing) | SKEEIG | (skiing) |
| SOWEMEG | (swimming) | CUMIG | (coming) |
| GOWEG | (going) | PLAYIG | (playing) |
| COLAKTGE | (collecting) | FILG | (feeling) |

One can not consider these as representing the *g* of conventional spelling and omitting the nasal, however, because the [g] is not realized phonetically in these forms in most dialects. The nasal is the final sound, and it seems plausible that the preschool spellings represent it, just as they do the other final nasals, but with *g*, since the alphabet provides no separate letter for [ŋ]. The stop [g] that the children otherwise spell *G* as in GEVS (gives) and EGLIOW (igloo) corresponds to [ŋ] in being velar. This suggests that place of articulation is a stronger determinant of the choice of symbol than is nasality, as indeed one would expect from the relative generality of these features in English. So when a nasal precedes a consonant (phonetically) it is not represented in the original spellings, but it is spelled (*M,N,* or *G*) when it does not precede a consonant. In the special case of the velar nasal, these rules give the same spelling for [ŋg] and [ŋ]: *G*. Words which include [ŋg] phonetically, such as *finger, longer,* or *linger,* the children spell FEGR, LOGR, etc., where the *G* evidently represents [g], and the nasal has been omitted.

When a nasal precedes a consonant in English, it must be articulated in the same place as the consonant; that is, within a syllable, only [m] precedes [p] and [b], only [n] precedes [d] and [t], and only [ŋ] precedes [g] and [k]. Thus, in the *-ing* of standard spelling, even when the *g* is not pronounced, we can regard it as corresponding to a lexical form, giving information as to where the nasal is articulated. In their original spellings the children are using *G* for a similar reason, apparently; when they learn standard spelling, they may find it natural in this respect.

The children do not often cooperate with direct requests to write particular words, but occasionally they provide some evidence that they distinguish the velar nasal and omit it before a consonant. One boy wrote FINGR for *finger* but then crossed it out, saying that that would spell [fingr]. He thought for a while, and then with a shrug, wrote FINGR anyway. He was older (6.2) and had begun to spell nasals before consonants in general. Another boy, who did not generally do so, wrote FIGR, sounding it out as [f-iŋ-g-r].

We would explain the children's treatment of nasals by assuming that they follow a strict segmentation principle under which a segment homorganic with and phonetically overlapping an adjacent one is not represented as a separate segment. There is no tongue-movement at all between a nasal and a following consonant, in fact. There is also support for the view that the children omit nasals on the basis of a systematic phonological abstraction.[18] Malécot has shown with spectographic and kymographic evidence that preconsonantal nasals have the effect of nasalizing preceding lax vowels. In fact, the nasals constitute distinct phonetic segments only before voiced consonants, as in *amble, candor,* and *anger.* Before voiceless consonants, as in *ample, cantor,* and *anchor,* the nasal is phonetically realized (and perceptually recognized) through vowel nasalization alone.[19] This result holds in most dialects of English for [ʌ], [i], and [æ], especially the last. Given these phonetic facts, any uniform representation of preconsonantal nasals is an abstraction. We could regard the children as generalizing in the direction of nasalized vowels, contrary to standard spelling, and then abstracting from that nasalization in their spelling.

Finally, the children's judgments may be abstract in a slightly different sense. Nasals are partially redundant in English in just the position in which the children omit them from spelling—preconsonantally. "Partially" in this case means that, given that a nasal occurs before a known consonant, one can predict all its other features, notably its place of articulation. For this reason, English spelling would carry the same information if a single symbol, say *n,* represented any nasal before a consonant. *Bump* would be spelled *bunp; bunt* and *bunk* would be spelled just as they are, and no ambiguity would be introduced. The children's spelling ignores just this one piece of information, albeit a crucial one. In this respect, it is an over-abstraction.

Treating a partially redundant segment as wholly so is not unprecedented. In Old English, and Germanic languages in general, alliteration depends on the second segment of a word if and only if the first is an [s] and the second is a true consonant. That is, [sp] must alliterate with [sp], not with [st] or [sk]. In such a cluster [s] was (and is) partially redundant in almost the same sense as preconsonantal nasals are: given that a consonant occurs initially before a true consonant, it must be [s]. Similarly, in folk-rhymes generally and Faroese Kuæði rhyme particularly, imperfect rhymes are tolerated where rhyming words differ by only one phonetic feature.[20] At the lexical level, *wet* and *went* differ by a segment specified by just one feature.

These three proposed explanations are alike in that they involve abstraction—from articulatory overlap, vowel nasalization, or partial redundancy. They all imply that nasality is a relatively minor, and place of articulation a relatively major, feature in the children's phonological system. The problem is to show how these proposals are empirically different and to obtain evidence that distinguishes among them. Confirmation for any of them would raise the problem of explaining how the children acquired the relevant principle. What is clear from the present evidence is that the original spellings are abstracted from a perceived phonetic contrast, even in a case in which the spellers have the appropriate letters available and indeed use them in other contexts.

## Syllabic Segments

When [r], [l], [m], or [n] occur in an English word between two consonants or at the end of a word after a consonant, they become syllabic—that is, the segment constitutes a sonority peak (in effect, a loudness maximum) and is perceived as a separate syllable. Because they know that the peak of most syllables is a vowel, and possibly influenced by the conventional spelling, adults perceive a vowel before the liquid or nasal. This perceived vowel is usually spelled *e* and may be represented either before or after the syllabic segment. The children virtually never represent such a vowel.

| | | | |
|---|---|---|---|
| TIGR | (tiger) | DIKTR | (doctor) |
| SOGR | (sugar) | OVR | (over) |
| AFTR | (after) | SMOLR | (smaller) |
| LITL | (little) | CANDL | (candle) |
| WAGN | (wagon) | OPN | (open) |

This spelling applies to medial syllabic consonants as well:

| | | | | | |
|---|---|---|---|---|---|
| GRL | (girl) | BRD | (bird) | HRD | (heard) |
| FRST | (first) | SRKIS | (circus) | SODNLY | (suddenly) |
| ALRVATA | (elevator, pronounced [elərvēytə], in a dialect common in the Boston area) | | | | |

This spelling is particularly persistent; it frequently appears even in words for which a child has otherwise learned aspects of the conventional spelling, such as the two T's in LITTL or the LY in SODNLY. On a spelling-dictation exercise, out of 47 first-graders, 21 (plus some who were inconsistent) produced:

BRATHR  (brother)     TABL  (table)     FETHR  (feather)

These same first-graders produced other spellings consistent with the invented ones (e.g., the nasals discussed above), but none so frequently as this one. Among the spontaneous spellers, this representation persists even in common kinship terms that the children might have occasion to learn the spellings of, to the extent that they learn any spellings.

FOT(H)R  (father)     MUTHR  (mother)     SESTR  (sister)

These spellings appear to be particularly independent of adult influence, and they occur quite consistently in every child's writing. Ultimately, we would like to explain both the occurrence of the spellings and their durability.

To adults these spellings seem to represent inadmissible consonant sequences—even whole words without a vowel—and on that account to violate an apparent principle of English, that each syllable contains a vowel. This principle is true, if at all, only of surface forms, however. A lexical representation that omits predictable detail need not specify the syllabicity—the apparent vocalic quality—of these liquid and nasal segments; it is an automatic effect of the rules of English phonology.[21]

The children's treatment of syllabic segments contrasts with that of syllables consisting of a reduced vowel and an obstruent (a non-nasal true consonant, restricted by definition from being syllabic). Where liquids and nasals are not involved, their general practice is to represent a vowel in each syllable, as in CERIT (carrot), the second syllable of SRKIS, and many other examples. It would be hard to argue that there is any consistent phonetic basis for this distinction, that is, a difference in vowel quality between the syllabic segments and [əC] syllables (where C represents any obstruent). Rather, the basis appears to be that the vowel is redundant in the former cases but not in the latter, generally. In other words, the children represent only lexical (unpredictable) vowels in their spelling.

The explanation must involve one of two assumptions—that the children's knowledge of English phonology is sufficiently abstract to eliminate predictable vowels, or that at some level of the tacit phonological analysis reflected in spelling, syllabics (liquids and nasals) are distinguished from other consonants.[22]

The latter appears to be more nearly correct, for after about age five, when the children begin to represent the (predictable) reduced vowel in past tense endings after [d] or [t], as in STARTID and WONTID, they still do not do so with syllabics.[23] As in other cases, there is phonetic justification for distinguishing liquids and nasals from other consonants. The fact that the former can become syllabic is related to their similarity to vowels, namely that in their articulation there is a less radical obstruction of the flow of breath than in true consonants. This explanation suggests once again that an abstract classification of English segments may be part of the knowledge of the language that a child brings to school. Again the conclusion may apply both to spontaneous spellers and to first-graders who have done no pre-school writing.

The children's spellings would be the conventional ones if the rules of English spelling were to change so that syllabicity was not represented. Although it would be an over-generalization, such a change would be appropriate to the lexical character of English spelling, since the syllabics are generally single segments at the lexical level. Perhaps it is just this property of these spellings that accounts for their slowness to change. In learning conventional spelling, the child is learning to represent his phonetic perceptions in a way that eliminates redundant variation. These representations of syllabic consonants are already of this sort, generally. In this case, as for preconsonantal nasals and certain others, all quite persistent, the child must learn to mark a phonetic detail.

An interesting footnote concerns the use of a letter to spell the syllable that is its name, as in

    STRT  (start)        GRDIN  (garden)

This phenomenon is not limited to liquids and nasals; occasionally the children use this rebus-device in other contexts. It is not typical of invented spelling, and in cases where I have been able to observe the writing first-hand, the child has been quite conscious of using it and somewhat amused at it. Frank, age five, wrote

    STṚT  (start)

When I asked him what the dot meant, he replied that it showed that the letter was spelling its own name. He applied this notation fairly regularly for a few months, but only where the syllable was exactly the letter-name, as in

    Ụ  (you)        ỌVR  (over)

    Ṛ  (are)        MẸ  (me)

This evidence suggests what I believe to be the general case: that the children distinguish the letter-names from the sounds that the letters represent. From the beginning of writing, they use a letter to spell only a certain segment of its name[24]; after some time, they may become conscious of this distinction and exploit it in rebus-fashion, but at no stage do they appear to be confused by the letter-names, as some have suggested in connection with proposals for teaching reading. This distinction is itself no trivial analytic accomplishment, especially for the vowels.

## Alternations

One effect of not representing predictable phonetic variation in English spelling is that the alternant forms of certain lexical items are spelled uniformly. The past tense ending is *ed,* whether it occurs in its voiceless variant as in *hopped* [hapt], voiced as in *hogged* [hɔgd], or with a vowel as in *wanted* [wantəd]. Exceptional spellings occur where some aspect of pronunciation is not predictable; for past tense, there are two main cases: (1) truly exceptional verb alternations, such as *go/went*, where presumably nothing in the past form is predictable, and (2) a tense-lax alternation in medial vowels, a subregularity of the language restricted to certain verbs and indicated by a final consonant cluster, as in *creep/crept.*

The same general principle carries over in part to the spellings of plurals, where the contrasts among the phonetic realizations [s], [z], and [əz] are completely predictable. [əz] occurs after coronal stridents as in *dishes*, [s] after voiceless consonants as in *cups,* and [z] everywhere else as in *bags*. English spelling marks the first as *-es,* noting its syllabicity, but uses *-s* for both of the others. For both inflections, the spelling system abstracts away from voiced/voiceless alternation. In general, only lexical contrasts are preserved in spelling.

With these facts in mind, we now consider how the children represent predictable contrasts. There are really two questions, although only rather indirect evidence could allow us to separate them: do the children recognize the various occurrences of past tense or plural as belonging to the same morphological item, and is there any evidence from their spelling that they perceive the predictability of the variation? Do they assign phonetic or morphophonemic spellings, and do they treat exceptional items in an exceptional manner?

The answer is that generally they assign phonetic spellings at age three or four, but that a dramatic change occurs around age five or six. For the younger children, the following are typical examples:

    MARED    (married)
    LAFFT    (left)
    HALPT    (helped)

all written at age four. The same child at age five, however, used *-d* fairly uniformly, as in

    WALKD     (walked)        ARIVD     (arrived)
    HAPPIND   (happened)      STARTID   (started)

But he treated irregular verbs differently, often with standard forms, as in *felt* and *slept,* but also:

    KUT    (cut)          CGOT    (caught)
    FOTE   (fought)

There are no exceptions to this general developmental sequence among the children for whom I have examples. For one child, Edith, there is a revealing month-by-month sequence from 5.10 to 6.3, during which time this change appears to have taken place. At 5.10 she began to mark past tense endings:

    HOP-T    (hopped)
    STOP-T   (stopped)

But she was unable to apply this diacritic orthography to past tense consistently:

    HOPPED-T   (hopped, apparently with adult coaching for HOPPED, since
               the double consonant and *-ed* do not otherwise occur)
    CAT-T      (cat)
    WAT        (went)
    WOCT       (walked)

The following month (5.11) showed more of the same; she had revised her notation slightly, and she treated an exceptional form as if it were regular.

    THA'T    (that)
    JUS'T    (just)
    WAN'T    (went)

At 6.0 (really almost two months later) we have the first uniform treatment of regular past forms. The diacritics disappeared, along with any apparent confusion between verbal inflections and the inherent segments of other words.

> PEKD    (peeked)
> FILLD   (filled)

The -D of PEKD was the only morphophonemic spelling in this month; it was also the only phonetic [-t] as an inflection. Otherwise, [t] was spelled phonetically.

Two months later (6.2) there was more evidence that Edith could spell past tense endings uniformly; she had also, however, begun to learn that exceptions may be spelled more phonetically, an insight that she applies correctly in one case, fails to apply in another, and over-generalizes in a third.

> LAFT     (left)
> WAND     (went)
> WISPRT   (whispered)
> RASTD    (rested)

Beginning the following month, and ever since, Edith treated regular and irregular forms correctly, except for the non-occurrence of the *e* in *-ed* endings.

> WALKD    (walked)
> SLAPT    (slept)

This girl's development in this detail is only a more fully illustrated and more explicit (with her diacritic innovation) version of what the other young spellers appear to have done.[25] Nevertheless, it would be hasty to base deep principles on so few cases. What does seem clear is that the invented spellings are phonetic in this detail until late in the pre-school period. Then rather suddenly the children begin to abstract from the phonetic contrast toward a uniform spelling of past tense inflections. At the same time, they rapidly develop a correct distinction of regular and irregular cases, even when the irregularity involves a rather limited class like *wept—slept—crept*.

It would be incorrect, I think, to attribute all of this development to adult teaching. The girl who wrote the last class of examples attended a Montessori school, even in her sixth year, where the practice was to accept all the children's writing with a minimum of correction. Her mother, who had gone to a Montessori school herself, followed much the same practice at home; she told her children spellings only when they asked, and she rarely corrected what they offered. In fact, almost all of these children got correction from their parents only when they asked; that seems to have been a necessary condition for the spontaneous spelling to occur at all. Of course the child has used information from adults—by age six, most children have acquired information from reading as well as oral instruction—but this information apparently has been "filtered" through the child's own notions, which exert a powerful influence on what he writes.

Notice, furthermore, that almost all the spellings deviate from the standard, if not in the ending, then in the vowel, and they do so in regular ways. A uniform *-D* may appear for both [d] and [t] in regular past forms long before the standard *-ed*. These spellings are certainly not copied from adults in any simple sense. The development from phonetic to morphophonemic is not a direct move from phonetic to adult spelling; rather, there is a dramatic change in the type of (non-adult) spelling the child creates.

The treatment of plurals appears to be a special case of the general conclusion; from the first writings on, the children spell plurals -*s*, marking no distinction between the voiced and unvoiced variants. They do (sometimes) mark the vowel of the syllabic ending [əz], as adult spelling does. The following examples are typical:

| WENDOWS | (windows) | RASIS | (races) |
|---|---|---|---|
| WANSAS | (Wednesdays) | CIDEJCHES | (sandwiches) |
| LADYS | (ladies [age five]) | HOUESS | (houses) |

The same children use -*s* for voiceless endings, too, of course.

| SOKS | (socks) | RABITS | (rabbits) |
|---|---|---|---|
| STMPS | (stamps) | | |

In fact, *s* stands for phonetic [z] and [s] in inherent segments as well as in inflections.

| CLOWSD | (closed) | BEECOS | (because) | SESTR | (sister) |
|---|---|---|---|---|---|
| WUS | (was) | KUS | ('cause) | SAND | (send) |

In general, *z* occurs rarely and only in positions such as initial pre-vocalic segments, where the occurrence of voicing is not predictable, as in ZIP.

The phonetic difference between [s] and [z] is not as great in final position, at least for some speakers, as in other positions.[26] It may be important, then, to ask whether the children represent the difference medially, where the phonetic contrast is greater and where voicing is also sometimes predictable.[27] (Leaving aside many details, voicing is assimilative, so that [s] occurs in voiceless consonant clusters, but [z] occurs elsewhere.) Evidence is less plentiful, but what there is clearly supports the conclusion that the children ignore the phonetic contrast. Compare, for instance,

| RASIS | (races) | SUSE | (Susie) |
|---|---|---|---|
| SESTR | (sister) | CLOWSD | (closed) |
| PANSEL | (pencil) | PRESINS | (presents) |

That the children do not distinguish [s] and [z] in their spelling can be explained in three quite different ways. First, the children may not generally perceive the two sounds as distinct. This result would be a clear counter-instance to the general conclusion that the children perceive fine phonetic differences, including other voicing contrasts, as in the [t]-[d]-[D] alterations, for instance. However, children of even three and a half years can usually answer questions involving pairs that differ only in voicing, such as *sip/zip*, *racer/razor*, and *bus/buzz*.[28] Accordingly, I believe that this explanation is untenable.

Second, considering the reversals of letters in children's writing, it is conceivable that the visual distinction between *s* and *ƶ* is too difficult for the children to make consistently; so they settle on one, the more common *s,* as the representation for both. This hypothesis does not deny that the children can make the phonetic discrimination. I am inclined to reject this view for a number of reasons: first, on this supposition one would expect the spelling distinction to reappear among children who make a very angular *z* but a curved *s*, or among children of European background who write a barred *ƶ*, or among children who learn to typewrite (as three of those discussed here did), and who therefore can rely on a positional as well as a shape difference. As far as I can judge, none of these expectations is correct. Furthermore, these children had no serious difficulty with other pairs of letters that are mirror-images or inversions, such as *b/d*, *w/m*, and *u/n*. There are occasional reversed letters, as in all children's printing, but not nearly enough to cause any of these other distinctions to collapse, nor is the reversal entirely in one direction.

A third interpretation is that the children distinguish [s] and [z] quite early and, perhaps even before beginning to write, conclude that their occurrence is predictable, so that spelling can be abstract from this difference without loss of information. This conclusion would be another over-generalization, but not for plurals, the most common examples. If this hypothesis is correct, we have another, and much earlier example of a typical process: the child has fairly narrow phonetic perceptions, but abstracts from these in systematic ways in spelling. In this case the abstraction is from a voicing contrast, just as in the case of the past-tense inflections and the rapid development of *T* for intervocalic flaps. Under this interpretation, the problem is to explain why this treatment of [s] and [z] emerges much earlier than these similar spellings for stops.

Adopting this view, we find evidence about a question raised by Berko in her classic study of children's acquisition of morphology. Having shown that pre-school children can form the appropriate [s] or [z] plural of even nonsense forms, and thus that they have acquired knowledge of a rule that extends to new instances, Berko questions whether the rule is morphological or phonological in nature, and notes, "It would be interesting to find out what the child thinks he is saying—if we could in some way ask him the general question, 'How do you make the plural?' "[29] We might look upon the invented spellings as embodying an answer to this general question, namely that the children regard these plural alternants as a single form at the level relevant to spelling—just as adults do, in fact.

Accordingly, a pedagogical orthography, such as i.t.a., that employs distinct symbols for the voiced and voiceless plurals may be introducing phonetic detail that a pre-school child can readily, even spontaneously, learn to abstract away from. Considering the abstract nature of children's invented spellings, we find that phonemic accuracy in pedagogical spellings may be an inappropriate goal. The question is really deeper: which phonetic facts are relevant in the child's own phonological system as he begins to read and write?

## Conclusion

We have seen evidence that children tacitly recognize certain phonetic contrasts and similarities, in that they represent these in their original spelling. For systematic reasons, standard English spelling does not reflect these same relationships. The contrasts, such as that between the first segments of *tuck* and *truck,* are predictable in context and therefore irrelevant to meaning and its representation in spelling. The similarities, such as that between tense and lax vowels, are not represented directly in standard spelling because of its abstract lexical character. Perhaps as a result of knowledge of this system, most adults do not recognize these phonetic relations; they have to learn, or re-learn, them in order to understand the children's judgments. What the children do not know is the set of lexical representations and the system of phonological rules that account for much of standard spelling; what they do know is a system of phonetic relationships that they have not been taught by their parents and teachers.

We have seen that the children choose representations in terms of phonetic properties, such as nasality, syllabicity, backness, height, and affrication. These are some of the terms in which the rules of English phonology must be stated. The contrary result would have been entirely possible; the children might have recognized no relation between the "flap" in *water* and the [d] of *waddle,* or between the vowels of *bite* and *pot,* although these share the properties of voicing and backness, respectively. In fact, the children might not have judged the segmentation of English words as they did; for example, that DIKTR (doctor) has five segments that need to be represented.

Finally, we have seen that children treat certain relationships as more basic than others in their spelling. Backness is preserved in place of tenseness and height for the vowels; affrication and place-of-articulation predominate over nasality and voicing for the consonants. On these bases, the children's spelling is systematically abstract from perceived phonetic detail. This characteristic is particularly notable in the abstraction from nasality, syllabicity, and voicing in certain contexts. These choices are not required by any lack of symbols, since in other contexts the children use letters (M,N,G,E,D, and Z) that represent these qualities. Evidently the children abstract on the basis of their tacit analysis to phonological features (as in distinguishing [r,l,m, and n] from other consonants in syllabic contexts) and possibly the predictability of certain details of pronunciation (such as the voicing of [t] between vowels). In general, the children treat sounds, not as unanalyzed wholes, but as items related by their constituent properties, and modified in regular, hence irrelevant, ways by their contexts. This result conflicts with the assumption that children are necessarily limited to matching spellings with phonemes defined on superficial taxonomic grounds. The children who created their own spellings arrived at a deeper analysis of English phonology a year or more before beginning school.

It would be easy but, I believe, incorrect to disregard the evidence presented here as having been produced by exceptional children. In that they began to spell and, often, to read early, these children were exceptional. Some, but not all, appeared to be independent and creative beyond the average, but their creativity was sometimes a result of their spelling accomplishments. Most of them came from relatively privileged middle-class families, with professional and academic parents, but this fact may have been a result of the informal procedure by which I located young spellers. Within this limitation, the families were quite diverse in beliefs and backgrounds. The one characteristic that all the parents had in common was a willingness to accept the child's own spelling efforts, to provide simple materials (first blocks and other elementary alphabet toys, then paper and pencil), and to answer questions. A cluster of unfortunate attitudes prevalent in our society may suppress this willingness in many parents: a fear that the child's own efforts will lead to "bad habits," a belief that English spelling is bizarre, and a corresponding reliance on the expertise of professional teachers or on sometimes complex educational devices that bear the stamp of expert approval. All of the parents provided just the information that any inexpert literate adult could provide: the names of the letters and answers to such questions as, "How do you spell 'chuh'?" They did not coax or expect their children to spell; most were surprised, in fact. There were no unusual educational devices relevant to spelling in any of the homes, and although the parents may have had inner qualms about "bad habits," their manner was relaxed and non-didactic. All of the children now in the primary grades and above have readily mastered standard spelling, with none of the laborious re-training that the notion of "habits" implies. Learning to spell need not be a process of acquiring habits, apparently.

In any case, to attribute the children's accomplishment *a priori* to exceptional general intelligence or an exceptional environment merely begs the important question. The children had tacitly acquired a knowledge of phonological relations of which their parents were themselves unaware. What the children had learned was not related in any obvious way to what they had heard or seen. The important theoretical question is how pre-school children can learn abstract relations of this sort. Until we have serious evidence bearing on this question, we can not assume that general intelligence must be the major factor in acquiring the knowledge that makes spelling possible. Even if it were true that all young spellers are exceptionally intelligent, the statistical observation by itself would not account for the occurrence of the spelling, nor, more important, for the specific and uniform character of what they all learned. Whatever variations there may be in individual development, the crucial conclusion remains that children can (and to some degree, must) make abstract inferences about the sound system of their language before they learn to read and write.

The educational importance of this conclusion seems clear enough, at least in general. We can no longer assume that a child must approach reading and writing as an untrained animal approaches a maze—with no discernible prior conception of its structure. We can not assume, in the essentially digestive metaphor that Paulo Freire rightly ridicules,[30] that the child is an empty vessel, mentally inert although physically so dynamic, waiting to be filled with adult spellings. Evidently, a child may come to school with a knowledge of some phonological categories and relations; without conscious awareness, he may seek to relate English spelling to these in some generally systematic way. If this inference is correct, some long-neglected questions turn out to be crucial for understanding and facilitating the process of learning to read: what levels of phonological analysis do individual children tacitly control at various stages of development; how do these analyses relate to the lexical representations that generally correspond to standard spelling; and how can reading instruction build on this relationship, while encouraging children to extend and deepen their notion of the sound system of the language? Detailed answers to these questions are not at all obvious; in fact, it is difficult to devise means of acquiring some answers, since children's phonological judgments are rarely explicit, as they are in the invented spellings. So far, we have evidence that at least some children do not attend to statistical associations between spellings and autonomous phonemes, which have been the subject of much research in reading. Rather, the children pair spellings with segments abstractly categorized in terms of a hierarchy of articulatory features.

In the classroom, an informed teacher should expect that seemingly bizarre spellings may represent a system of abstract phonological relations of which adults are quite unaware. Until we understand this system better, we can at least respect it and attempt to work with it, if only intuitively. A child who wants to spell *truck* with a *ch-* will not be enlightened by being told that *ch-* spells "chuh," as in *chicken*. He already knows that; in fact, the relation between the first segments of *truck* and *chicken* is exactly what he wants to represent. Nor will exaggerated (or exasperated) pronunciation of *truck* help much, for monolingual adult speakers of English are usually limited to pronouncing the two possibilities that our phonology allows. We will either insert a false vowel after the [t], which does away with the affrication at the cost of distorting the word, or we will exaggerate that very quality which the child wishes to represent. Drill and memorization of words with *tr-* and *dr-* may help the child to learn such cases, but these techniques suggest that spelling is arbitrarily related to speech and can only be memorized. This suggestion is not true of either standard spelling or the child's own invention. Better, it would seem, to say something like, "Yes, *truck* sounds like *chicken* at the beginning, but it is also like the first sound of *toy*, and that's what we show by using a *t*." Similarly for the child who spells *pen* with an *a* (or *dent* without an *n*, *brother* without an *e*, *liked* with a *t*, or *butter* with a *d*). Such a child needs to be told, in effect, that his phonological judgments are not wrong (though they may seem so to most adults), and that it is reasonable, indeed necessary, to categorize abstractly what he hears.

However, he must also learn that standard spelling reflects a system somewhat different from his own. He will have acquired the basis for this adult system only when he has tacitly learned rules such as affrication and vowel shift that make the standard spellings systematically accurate.[31] Then he can learn to read and spell on the principle that the written form corresponds to an abstract (lexical) form, not directly to what he hears. He is on his way when he begins to abstract from phonetic variations, as the spontaneous spellers did in their pre-school development. It may be particularly important to recognize when his own efforts are too abstract, or abstract in the wrong direction, and to suggest, at least implicitly, that he is using the right principle, even if in the wrong place. We cannot teach him this principle if we ourselves continue to believe that to learn to spell is to get in the "habit" of associating sounds with letters, or phonemes with graphemes. For at least some children, to learn standard spelling is to learn to broaden and deepen their preschool phonological analysis, which may already be abstract enough that phonemegraphene correspondences are indirect outcomes of an intricate system.

Our understanding of children's phonology is still shallow and fragmentary at best. The reasonable conclusion to be drawn from this work at this time is not that old dogmas should be replaced with new, but that we now have good reason to look more carefully at children's judgments of English phonology and spelling. In the meantime, we must assume that learning to read and write are matters of knowledge rather than habit, to use the terms of an old but honorable distinction.

## Notes

1. Noam Chomsky and Morris Halle, *The Sound Pattern of English* (New York: Harper & Row, 1968). The phonological analysis assumed in this article is largely that of this work.
2. Carol Chomsky, "Reading, Writing, and Phonology," *Harvard Educational Review,* XL (Spring 1970), 287–309. This includes a helpful discussion of the lexicon. See also Noam Chomsky, "Phonology and Reading," *Basic Studies on Reading,* ed. H. Levin and J. Williams (New York: Basic Books, 1970); Chomsky and Halle, 54–55 *et passim;* Wayne O'Neil, "The Spelling and Pronunciation of English," *The American Heritage Dictionary of the English Language,* ed. Wm. Morris (Boston: Houghton Mifflin, 1969), xxxv–xxxvii.
3. Noam Chomsky, *Aspects of the Theory of Syntax* (Cambridge, Mass.: M.I.T. Press, 1965), ch. 1; Jerry A. Fodor, *Psychological Explanation* (New York: Random House, 1968).
4. I do not intend the term "conventional" to suggest that English spelling is conventional in the sense of "arbitrary." The references of footnote 2 discuss some bases of standard spelling.
5. Idiosyncrasies of a child's pronunciation do not always affect his spelling. Some of these children had well-known non-standard articulations of sibilants, interdentals, and liquids; in some cases, they nevertheless spelled these sounds in the same way as other children. Nor was the parents' speech necessarily a model for spelling, in the case of parents with dialects different from their children's, especially a few non-native speakers of English. The evidence is too limited for any confidence, but it may be that children can abstract away from any one pronunciation in creating their spellings, at least for certain features.
6. (Broad) phonetic transcriptions will appear in square brackets; phonological representations, in slashes. The invented spellings will be entirely upper-case; standard spellings and individual letters will be italicized. Ages will be stated as, for example, 5.3 (five years, three months).
7. As in italicized positions in *thin, then, ship, mea*sure, *go, sing,* and *have.*
8. Vowels are described in terms of the position of the tongue during articulation—front or back, high, mid or low. Tenseness and laxness of vowels refer to a complex of articulatory properties. The vowel of *bite* is back, but unrounded.
9. See the references of footnote 2 for a further discussion of this issue.
10. Roman Jakobson, *Child Language, Aphasia, and Phonological Universals* (The Hague: Mouton & Co., 1968), p. 75. First published in 1941, this is the seminal work in this field.
11. Chomsky and Halle, p. 410.
12. In principle, the Initial Teaching Alphabet (i.t.a.) is based on this criticism. See ch. 5 of my *Children's Perceptions of the Sounds of English* (unpublished Ph.D. dissertation, Harvard University, 1970).
13. Further evidence that the children can analyze the letter-names occurs in the front vowels, not only for lax forms, but also in spellings like PLEYS (please), where the glide has been made explicit.
14. See Chomsky and Halle, pp. 178–87, for a discussion of the rules relating these pairs. See Carol Chomsky, "Reading, Writing, and Phonology," for a less technical discussion of the alternations and their spelling.
15. The adult spelling includes a final "silent" *e* in some of the tense cases. This is not simply a discontinuous digraphic spelling but has an independent function in lexical representations. Chomsky and Halle, pp. 147–50.
16. See chapter 2 of the dissertation referred to in footnote 12.

17. As there would be if words like *Christmas, chrome,* and *chronic* were pronounced with a first segment like that of *chop,* for instance.
18. There is no question, incidentally, that the children perceive the nasality that they do not represent—that they hear a distinctive difference between *wet* and *went,* for instance. An independent test with such pairs confirmed this point. The question is where they think the difference lies.
19. A. Malécot, "Vowel Nasality as a Distinctive Feature in American English," *Language,* XXXVI (1960), 222–29.
20. I am indebted to Wayne O'Neil for these observations about OE alliteration and folk-rhyme. They are reported in his paper, "The Reality of Grammars: Some Literary Evidence" (unpublished).
21. See Chomsky and Halle, pp. 85–89, for a discussion of such a rule and an independent justification of a lexical representation that omits syllabicity.
22. See Chomsky and Halle, pp. 353–55, for a discussion of a classificatory framework that makes this distinction in terms of a feature called *syllabic.*
23. Furthermore, there is little evidence that the children distinguish between lexical and predictable vowels in syllabic positions. There are, however, the spellings MANTIN (mountain) and ANE-MEL (animal) where the vowels explicitly represented must be lexical because they remain in non-syllabic positions, as in *mountainous* and *animality.*
24. The children apply this principle even in the use of H [ēyč] to spell [č], as in the first-grader's spelling of the initial sound of *try, train,* etc. A parallel example is the use of Y [wāy] to spell [w], as in YUTS (once). This came from a child, 4.6, whose parents often urged her to use the letter that seemed closest when she asked about spelling.
25. She was not the only child who marked inflections. Another girl, Pammie, went from LOOK, T (also NURS, T; CALL, D; NAME, D; etc.) at age seven to LOOK'D, etc. at age eight.
26. This was pointed out to me by Emmon Bach. Where it applies, it is perhaps a minor reflection in English of a general tendency toward de-voicing of final obstruents, as is the rule in German, for instance.
27. Some problems remain in the exact formulation. See Chomsky and Halle, pp. 228–29 and 232–33.
28. See chapter 3 of the dissertation referred to in footnote 12.
29. Jean Berko, "The Child's Learning of English Morphology," in *Psycholinguistics,* ed. Sol Saporta (New York: Holt, Rinehart and Winston, 1961), p. 373.
30. Paulo Freire, "The Adult Literacy Process as Cultural Action for Freedom," *Harvard Educational Review,* XL (Spring 1970), 208.
31. See Carol Chomsky, "Reading, Writing, and Phonology," for some suggestions as to how this process may be facilitated.

# 3
# Stages in Language Development and Reading Exposure

CAROL CHOMSKY
*Harvard University*

*Carol Chomsky emphasizes the need for a linguistically stimulating curriculum for elementary school children. She argues that the degree of sophistication in language acquisition is reflected in the ability to understand grammatically complex sentences. Her research examines elementary school children's language development and discusses its relation to reading. Chomsky's first study focuses on thirty-six children's linguistic competence in relation to complex aspects of English syntax. In spite of diverse individual differences in the rate of acquisition, the results clearly demonstrate that children pass through a developmental sequence of five linguistic stages in constructing implicit grammatical rules. A second study reveals a strong correlation between the rate of linguistic development and a variety of reading exposure measures, such as the amount and complexity of reading.*

This article summarizes a study of linguistic development in elementary school children. We investigated children's knowledge of specific aspects of the syntax of English by testing their comprehension of a number of complex structures. Thirty-six children between the ages of six and ten were in the experiment.

Because the study deals with only a few structures, it does not attempt a general description of children's grammar within the age group. Rather it traces the acquisition of specific structures, revealing interesting aspects of the children's construction of implicit grammatical rules. In addition, the results demonstrate a common order of acquisition of syntactic structures among the different children though there is

The work reported on here was performed under Office of Education Grant No. OEG-1-9-090055-0114 (010), Project No. 9-A-055, while the investigator was a Scholar at the Radcliffe Institute. This article was prepared from the final report to the Office of Education. The full report, "Linguistic Development in Children from 6 to 10," is available through the Educational Resources Information Center (ERIC) Document Reproduction Service.

*Harvard Educational Review*   Vol. 42   No. 1   February 1972, 1–33

considerable variation in age of acquisition. This shared order of acquisition of structures defines a developmental sequence of linguistic stages through which all of the children apparently pass. The ages at which different children reach the stages vary, but the sequence of stages appears to be the same for all.

A second aspect of the study investigated the children's exposure to the written language through independent reading and through listening to books read aloud. We examined the relation between rate of linguistic development and exposure to written materials as a source of complex language inputs. Our results show a strong correlation between a number of the reading exposure measures and language development. A description of the reading study is presented in the second half of this paper, along with a discussion of the relations between language development, the reading measures, IQ, and socioeconomic status (SES).

This article is a brief and fairly condensed description of a detailed study of several years' duration, and it attempts to present only the highlights of the methods employed and the experimental results.

## Framework for the Linguistic Study

The approach and methods of the linguistic study, described in detail in an earlier work,[1] demonstrate the feasibility of dealing with the learning of complex syntactic structures in children beyond age five through psycholinguistic experimentation. This is the period of life when a major portion of the task of language acquisition has already been accomplished. The child of six exhibits competence with his* native language that appears to approach adult competence. Discrepancies between his grammar and adult grammar are rarely revealed in spontaneous speech.

Our purpose is to explore areas in which the six-year-old's knowledge of his language falls short of adult knowledge, and to gain information about the course of the acquisition of this knowledge as the child matures. In order to deal with these questions, we must first characterize what we mean by knowing one's language. In effect, we must answer the question, "What is the nature of the information that is acquired by the child?"

Clearly, speakers of a language do not draw from a memorized list of all possible sentences in their language each time they wish to say something. Rather, they can understand and produce sentences they have never before heard. Indeed, a major portion of language usage consists of sentences that have never been spoken or written before, for example, this sentence or the closing sentence of any article in today's *New York Times*.

Given any sequence of words we care to devise, speakers can recognize whether or not the sequence constitutes a sentence in their language. This creative aspect of language use rests on the fact that we have learned the system of rules for making sentences. This system is called the grammar of the language.

---

*The masculine form of pronoun is used for convenience; children of both sexes were included in the study. [Ed.]

Our knowledge of these rules is implicit. We are not taught them, and we would be hard put to state even the smallest fraction of them. Yet they govern our speech.

Because these rules are implicit, they cannot be observed directly. While the linguist is interested in the speaker's *competence* (the underlying system of rules), he has access only to a speaker's *performance* (the way he uses the rules). Thus, various aspects of performance are used to reveal the nature of underlying competence.

What the child learns, then, as he acquires his language is a complex system of rules that enables him to understand and produce the sentences of his language. He internalizes these rules from what he hears by a process of active construction as yet little understood. His earliest utterances, even at the stage when he begins to put two words together to make sentences, are innovative and rule-governed. The evidence shows he is not just repeating fragments of sentences he has heard, but is creating his own sentences according to grammatical rules that he continually constructs and revises. The acquisition of syntax, then, means developing the rule system, restructuring it with increasing maturity as new evidence is added, and eventually producing an internalized grammar which accords with the facts of the language.

How do we employ this framework in studying knowledge of syntax in children between six and ten? The problem is that by age six, a child's grammar, as revealed in his spontaneous speech, does not appreciably differ from adult grammar. In order to identify areas in which child and adult grammar are different, we must actively probe the child's linguistic performance. We can do this by selecting complex grammatical structures—structures that we consider difficult and, therefore, likely to be acquired relatively late. Children's comprehension and interpretation of these complex structures yield evidence of the syntactic rules employed and the way in which these rules diverge from adult grammar. As we gain information about these child/adult discrepancies, we may contribute to existing notions about language complexity.

On the basis of current linguistic work we are able to select a variety of complex structures that appear to be likely candidates for late acquisition. Potential structures would include those "which deviate from a widely established pattern in the language, or whose surface structure is relatively inexplicit with respect to grammatical relationships, or even simply those which the linguist finds particularly difficult to incorporate into a thorough description." . . .[2] Some candidate structures turn out to be difficult for the children; some do not.

In order to be useful in this study, a structure must also lend itself to testing with young children. We must be able to devise an operational test of comprehension that even six-year-olds can handle. This requirement sharply limits the selection. The structures and tests finally decided upon are the result of much planning and revision, a good bit of pilot testing, and many discards.

Altogether, we tested nine structures with the children. Of these, only the five that turned out to be relevant to an overall developmental sequence will be discussed here. The other four were either too easy (all the children knew them), too hard (known by only one or two of the children), or they elicited scattered responses not relevant to the sequence. Almost twice as many structures were tested as turned out to be relevant to the developmental sequence. Thus, we proceeded by collecting a range of structures, testing them all, and leaving it up to the experimental results to reveal a sequence, if any.

   We did have some theoretical and practical guidelines to aid in selecting structures. For example, the relation between two structures, *promise* and *ask*, is such that a given order of acquisition is implied on theoretical grounds. *Promise* is simpler than *ask* along a particular scale of complexity, and ought therefore to be acquired first. And, in fact, evidence of this predicted order was found in an earlier experiment with *promise* and *ask*.[3] These two structures, then, were useful to include because of their strong potential for yielding developmental data. Another construction, *easy to see*, is recognized as a good indicator of grammatical development from the work of several different researchers[4] although no experimental work has yet suggested a relationship to other constructions in terms of order of acquisition. This construction was included because of its stability as a measure. Use of the measure led to identical conclusions in three separate experiments. Beyond considerations of this sort, there was little to go on. In fact all of the constructions tested with children for the first time here resulted from a fortuitous intersection of complex structures and experimental techniques that could measure them.

   Our experimental procedure elicited information from the children by direct interview. By age six, the children are willing to be questioned, play games, carry out tasks, manipulate toys, identify pictures, and engage in conversation. The interview was carried out informally and, for the children, was interesting play.

   Our test group ranged in age from five years old, when many of the children gave evidence of not yet knowing the constructions, up to ten years old, when a number of the children exhibited an adult command of the structures. For some structures there was considerable variation in age of acquisition in different children. Of particular interest is that this variation in *age* of acquisition does not seem to affect *order* of acquisition of different structures. For the structures reported here, the evidence is that linguistic development, whether it occurs earlier or later, nevertheless proceeds along similar paths. This has been a basic and repeated finding of longitudinal studies with younger children at earlier stages of language development. It is encouraging that the same principle is demonstrable on the basis of cross-sectional studies with older children at much later stages of linguistic development.

   We drew children from an elementary school in Cambridge, Massachusetts, which is predominantly middle-class, but has nevertheless some range in the socioeconomic background of the children. Thirty-six children from kindergarten through fourth grade were selected to ensure a representative sample in terms of age and reading level. The children were interviewed individually at school by the author and an assistant over a period of several months in the fall of 1969, with each interview lasting about a half hour.

## The Test Constructions

1.  The construction *Easy to See* in the sentence *"The doll is easy to see"*

   In this interview we tested the child's ability to determine the grammatical relations which hold among the words in sentences of the form *The doll is easy to see*.

The complexity of this construction derives from the fact that the grammatical relations among its words are not expressed directly in its surface structure. Of the two constructions

(a) The doll is eager to see.
(b) The doll is easy to see.

which look alike on the surface, only (a) retains in its surface structure the relations of subject and verb which are implicit in the meaning of the sentence; i.e., not only is *doll* the subject of sentence (a), but it is also the implicit subject of the complement verb *see*. The surface structure of (a) expresses this by normal word order of subject precedes verb. In (b), however, the word order is misleading. *Doll* is actually the implicit *object* of the complement verb *see*, for in (b) it is easy for someone else to see the doll. The implicit subject of *see* is omitted in (b)'s surface structure, and the listener must fill it in for himself as "someone else." The child who has not yet learned to recognize the underlying difference in structure of these two superficially similar sentences will interpret them both according to surface structure, and report that in (b), as well as (a), it is the doll who is doing the seeing. Such a child would interpret (b) incorrectly to mean "It is easy for the doll to see," instead of "It is easy for someone else to see the doll."

The interview was opened by placing a doll, with eyes that close, lying down with eyes closed on a table in front of the child. The child was then asked to say whether the doll was easy to see or hard to see. After responding, he was asked the question "why?" Then he was asked to make the doll either easy to see or hard to see, depending on his response to the first question.

The child who interprets the sentence correctly will answer that the doll is easy to see and support this interpretation when asked by answering that the doll is right there in front of him. When asked to make the doll hard to see he will hide the doll under the table or cover his own eyes or make a similar meaningful response.

The child who misinterprets the sentence and answers that the doll is hard to see will support this interpretation by indicating that her eyes are closed so she can't see and when asked to make her easy to see will open the doll's eyes.

This construction was fairly easy for the children. Everyone over age 7.1[5] succeeded with it, and below this age there was mixed success and failure. Five of the children below 7.1 failed, approximately half of this age group. Our sample did not include children young enough for us to observe onset of acquisition. Below we will see that lack of competence in this construction constitutes Stage 1 in our developmental sequence.

2.   The construction *Promise* as in
   *"Bozo promises Donald to stand on the book."*

Here we examined the child's knowledge of a particular syntactic structure associated with the word *promise*. His ability to identify the missing subject of a complement verb following *promise* was tested, a task which is relatively complex for the following reasons. Consider the sentences

(a) Bozo promised Donald to stand on the book.
(b) Bozo told Donald to stand on the book.

In these sentences the subject of the verb *stand* is not expressed, but must be filled in by the listener. Although the two sentences are superficially alike, differing only in their main verbs *promise* and *tell,* in (a) it is Bozo who is to stand on the book, and in (b) it is Donald who is to stand on the book. Since this information is not given anywhere in the surface structure of these sentences, the listener must, in order to interpret them differently, draw on his underlying knowledge of the verbs *promise* and *tell* and the structures associated with them.

Sentence (b) is a very common structure in English. The missing subject of a complement verb is almost always the first noun phrase preceding it. If Bozo tells Donald to stand on the book, it is Donald who is to do the standing. This is true for almost all verbs in English that can substitute for *tell* in this sentence, for example, *persuades, urges, expects, wants, orders, hires, likes,* etc. We learn this rule early and we learn it well. *Promise,* however, is an exception. With *promise* the missing subject is not the closest noun phrase, but a noun phrase farther away. This is a rare construction in English found with only a very few verbs. In order to interpret sentence (a) correctly, we must have learned in dealing with *promise* to discard the general rule and to substitute the special rule for *promise.*

Our expectation was that children who have not yet learned this exceptional feature of the verb *promise* will use their well-learned general principle and interpret sentence (a) according to the structure of (b). They will report that in (a) it is Donald who is to stand on the book; Bozo promises Donald that he, Donald, can stand on the book. In a previous experiment carried out by this writer, this was found to be the case; some children still misinterpreted the construction up to the age of eight and one-half, and uniform success was achieved only above this age.[6]

To test knowledge of this construction we had the child manipulate two toy figures to illustrate the action of a series of test sentences. The figures used were Bozo the Clown and Donald Duck, and a book was provided for them to stand on.

First it was determined that the child knew the meaning of the word *promise* by asking questions such as: Can you tell me what you would say to your friend if you promise him that you'll call him up this afternoon? What do you mean when you make somebody a promise? What's special about a promise?

Then the child was asked to name the two figures. Practice sentences were given to familiarize the child with the actions and with the "intentional" nature of the test sentences. The child has to illustrate how the stated intention of the sentence is carried out because in "Bozo promises Donald to stand on the book," the child shows who stands on the book. The practice sentences introduce this notion: Bozo wants to do a somersault—Make him do it. Bozo wants Donald to do a somersault—Have him do it. Donald decides to stand on the book—Make him do it.

This was followed by five test sentences of the form "Donald promises Bozo to hop up and down—Make him hop."

In general the children easily understood what they were to do, and appeared to enjoy the task. The sentences were repeated freely for those children who required repetitions or who seemed to hesitate.

The children who interpreted the sentences correctly selected the more distant noun phrase as subject of *stand*. For "Bozo promised Donald to stand on the book—Make him do it," they picked up Bozo and placed him on the book. The children who misinterpreted the construction selected the closest noun phrase as subject of *stand*. In response to this same sentence, they picked up Donald and placed him on the book.

We found the children to be highly consistent in their responses. The most common response was to assign the missing subject the same way in all five sentences, whether correct or incorrect, and to do so rapidly and with assurance. Only a very few children varied their responses, and generally these were the ones who hesitated and appeared confused.

Our results indicate that this construction was relatively easy for the children. Criterion for success was four correct out of five. Two thirds of the thirty-six children succeeded with the construction. The failers, with one exception, were all under eight years old, with failure being the rule for the five-year-olds, as likely as success for the six-year-olds, and the exception for the seven-year-olds. Lack of competence in this construction with the verb *promise* distinguishes children in Stage 2 in our developmental sequence from those in Stage 3.

3.  The construction *Ask* as in
    *"The girl asked the boy what to paint."*

This interview examined the child's knowledge of a particular syntactic structure associated with the verb *ask*. This construction, or the child's handling of the verb *ask* in general, proves to be a particularly good indicator of syntactic development. The child must identify the missing subject of a verb following *ask* in a complement clause, introduced by a question word such as *when* or *what*, for example, the subject of *paint* in
The girl asked the boy what to paint.
The verb *ask* breaks a general structural rule of English as does *promise*. The nature of the complexity of this construction has been treated at length elsewhere,[7] and will be reviewed only briefly here.

Consider the sentences

(a)  The girl asked the boy what to paint.
(b)  The girl told the boy what to paint.

The missing subject of *paint* in (a) is *the girl*. The correct paraphrase of (a) is *The girl asked the boy what she should paint.* In (b), as in most other sentences of this form in

English, the missing subject is *the boy,* that is *the girl told the boy what he should paint.* Since the weight of evidence in the language as a whole favors the (b) interpretation, children who have not yet learned this exceptional feature of the verb *ask* will interpret sentence (a) according to the structure of (b). They will report that in (a) the girl is asking the boy what he is going to paint. This interpretation persists in some children until age ten or later.

The actual interview consisted of a conversational portion and a picture identification test. In the conversational portion, two children who knew each other well carried out a number of tasks according to instructions. Only one child was being tested, the second child serving as a conversational partner. The two children were seated at a table on which were placed toy food, and figures of Donald Duck, Pluto Pup, and Bozo. We explained to the child that he was going to play some games with the things on the table; he would feed the dog, for example, and so on.

The instructions themselves were then given. *Ask* instructions were interspersed with *tell* instructions, but the opening instruction was always *ask.* The interview proceeded as follows:

Interviewer:  Ask Bruce what to feed the dog.
Child:        THE HAMBURGER.
Interviewer:  Tell Bruce what food to put back in the box.
Child:        THE HOT DOG.
              etc.

The interview was carried out in an informal conversational manner, with repetitions, extra instructions at the child's point of difficulty, discussion of confusions and inconsistencies, and with special attempts to draw the child's attention to his "errors." Maximum help was given the child to express what he knew.

Errors were of two kinds. Some children told their partner what to do in response to an *ask* instruction, rather than asking him. *The hamburger* above would be a correct response if the instruction had been "Tell Bruce what to feed the dog." Children who respond in this manner have failed to interpret *ask* as requiring a question response, and respond as if instructed to tell. This response error indicated the least competence with the verb *ask.*

When making the other error, children asked their partner a question, but assigned the wrong missing subject to the key verb, responding to "Ask Bruce what to feed the dog" with "What are you going to feed the dog?" The child who answers in this manner understands that he is to ask a question, but has not yet learned that *ask* signals an exception to his well-learned general rule of English for picking missing subjects. He picks his missing subject incorrectly, according to the general rule, which says to choose your partner rather than yourself. He may ask a variety of questions, all with the subject *you* following *ask;* for example,

What do you want to feed the dog? or
What are you going to feed the dog?

This response indicates greater competence with *ask* than the preceding response, but still reveals lack of knowledge of *ask* as signalling an exceptional structure.[8]

Only one third of the children were able to give the correct response, asking a question and assigning the correct subject to the key verb, responding to "Ask Bruce what to feed the dog," with the question "What should I feed the dog?" This response indicates mastery of the construction, and was the only one accepted as correct for our purposes. Criterion for success was correct response to at least four-fifths of the instructions given.[9]

After the conversational portion of the interview was concluded, the partner left, and the subject was shown two pairs of pictures (Figs. 1 and 2). For Pair 1 he was asked: "Which picture shows the girl asking the boy what to paint?" and "What is she saying to him?"; for Pair 2 he was asked: "Which picture shows the boy asking the girl what shoes to wear?" and "What is he saying to her?" The child was instructed to look at both pictures of a pair before deciding on an answer. In each case, the correct choice is Picture a. For Picture 1a, the girl should be quoted as saying, "What should I paint?" and for Picture 2a, the boy should be quoted as saying, "What shoes should I wear?"

Here again, we find the same two kinds of error as with the conversational test of *ask*. Some children choose the wrong picture (b), giving a quote in which one child *tells* the other what to do, e.g., "Wear those shoes." This would be a correct response if the cue had been "Which picture shows the girl telling the boy what shoes to wear?" As before, children who respond in this manner have failed to interpret *ask* as

1a. *Correct interpretation*    1b. *Incorrect interpretation*

FIGURE 1
*Test Pictures 1a and 1b.*
*Test sentence: The girl asks the boy what to paint.*
*Subject is shown both pictures simultaneously and asked*
*1. Which picture shows the girl asking the boy what to paint?*
*2. What is she saying to him?*

*2a. Correct interpretation*    *2b. Incorrect interpretation*

FIGURE 2
*Test Pictures 2a and 2b.*
*Test sentence: The boy asks the girl which shoes to wear.*
*Subject is shown both pictures simultaneously and asked*
*1. Which picture shows the boy asking the girl which shoes to wear?*
*2. What is he saying to her?*

requiring a question response. They respond as if instructed to tell. This response indicates the least competence with the verb *ask*.

The second error is to choose the wrong picture, quote the picture child as asking a question, but the wrong question: "What are you going to paint?"; "What shoes are you going to wear?" Again, the child who answers in this manner understands that he is to ask a question, but has not yet learned the exceptional nature of *ask*. He picks his missing subject incorrectly and proceeds to choose a picture and question consistent with his hypothesis. As before, this response indicates greater competence with *ask* than the preceding response, but falls short of total mastery.

In each of the above errors the picture choice and quoted command or question are consistent with each other. Given the way the child interprets the cue sentence, his response is logical and "correct." He is not confused nor is he guessing. This was true also for the conversational test, where the child's actions supported his words in almost all cases. He is operating successfully according to rule; it is just that his rule differs from the standard. This is a common observation in this type of linguistic testing, where children are often confident when operating with well-entrenched, though inappropriate, rules. Indeed, confusion or hesitation, or recognition that a construction is problematic, may signal progress on the child's part, usually indicating that he has begun the process of restructuring his rule system.

An interesting feature of the results is that the picture test for *ask* was easier for some children than the conversational test. Five children succeeded with the pictures and failed the conversational test, and only one child reversed this pattern. Criterion for success with the *ask* construction as a whole was success with both the pictures and the conversation test.[10]

An analysis of our results showed that this construction was considerably more difficult for the children than our preceding ones, and exhibited strong variability in age of acquisition. Only one third of the children, ranging in age from 7.2 years to 10.0, succeeded at both the conversational interview and the picture test. The ages of those who failed ranged from 5.9 to 9.9. No child under 7.2 succeeded. From 7.2 up, we find the children fairly evenly divided among passers and failers. The mean age of the failers was six months under that of the passers, 8.2 as compared to 8.8.

The striking feature of these results is the high variability in age of acquisition of the structure, and the persistence of lack of knowledge right up to the top age in our sample. Clearly after age seven, individual rate of development is a stronger factor than is age in acquisition of the *ask* construction. Below we will see that knowledge of this construction distinguishes Stage 3 from Stage 4 in our developmental sequence.

It is interesting that the ability to assign a missing subject correctly following *ask* appears later in the child than the ability to carry out what appears to be the same task with the verb *promise*. Both verbs require that a general rule of subject assignment be broken and replaced with a rule specific to these two words. If the specific rule is the same for both *ask* and *promise*, why then does the child consistently learn to apply it first with *promise*?

The answer appears to lie in the greater simplicity of the verb *promise* as compared to *ask*. *Promise* is a consistent verb, whereas *ask* evidences inconsistency when used in two different senses as follows. Consider (a) Seymour asked Gloria to leave, (b) Seymour asked Gloria when to leave. In (a) Gloria is to leave; *ask* behaves as the majority of verbs in English. In (b) Seymour is to leave; *ask* behaves according to the special rule. The child must learn conflicting rules for these two structures with *ask*, whereas no such problem exists with *promise*. *Promise* always requires the special rule—there is no structure such as (a) to complicate matters.

4.   Constructions following *And* and *Although*

Here we tested the children's ability to identify a missing verb differently in two sentences which differ only in the use of *and* and *although* as clause introducers. Consider the sentences:

   (a) Mother scolded Gloria for answering the phone, and I would have done the same.
   (b) Mother scolded Gloria for answering the phone, although I would have done the same.

These sentences do not say what I would have done; the listener must fill it in for himself. There are two candidate verbs preceding *done the same* which might serve as referent: *scolded* and *answered*. Following *and*, the referent is *scolded*; following *although*, the referent is *answered*; in (a) I would have scolded Gloria, and in (b) I would have answered the phone.[11]

No careful experimental technique was devised for testing these constructions. We simply read the sentences to the children and asked for each one: "What does this sentence say I would have done?" There was some question in our minds about the effectiveness of this direct approach, but it appears to have been adequate in this case. The results show interesting developmental patterns, and they fit in very well with the rest of our data.

The examples mentioned above were used as well as the sentences: "The cowboy scolded the horse for running away, and I would have done the same—What would I have done?" "The cowboy scolded the horse for running away, although I would have done the same—

What would I have done?"

These sentences were usually read several times to the children, particularly the younger children, before they were able to formulate an answer. Those who could read were given the sentences typed on cards to follow as we read aloud.

We determined in an earlier portion of the interview that all of the children could correctly interpret the shorter sentence, "The cowboy scolded the horse for running away—Who ran away?" None of the children had any trouble assigning *horse* as subject of *running away*.

We also determined earlier in the interview session which children were competent in the use of *although* in simpler sentences where no deletions were involved. All but eight of the children performed successfully on an oral sentence-completion task with sentences such as "Although my favorite TV program was on, I . . ." and "I wore a heavy jacket although. . . ." Those who failed were under seven years of age, and not among the passers of our *and* and *although* test.

This experiment turned out to be more interesting than anticipated. During the planning stage we considered the *although* sentences to be the difficult ones, and had included *and* sentences only for contrast. As it turned out, not only was the *although* construction very difficult for the children (only four children succeeded with it), but the *and* sentence, surprisingly enough, proved to be interesting in its own right. Unexpectedly, twenty-three children failed the *and* sentence. Whereas we had set out to test *although, and* itself proved to be a useful test construction as discussed below.

Scoring was as follows. In the *although* sentences the child had to choose the referent of *done the same* from two candidate verbs preceding it in the sentence: *scolded*, the far candidate, and *answering*, the near candidate. The correct choice is the near candidate, *answering*. Scoring, however, requires caution, for some children will choose the near candidate from lack of knowledge. As we have seen in the constructions of *promise* and *ask*, the child tends to always choose the *near* candidate to fill in a deletion when he works from general principles of English. In our test sentence the near candidate (*answering*) is the correct one, the one the child would choose also from specific knowledge of the *although* construction. Since both general principles and specific knowledge of *although* yield the same answer, how can we determine on what basis the child is choosing? Fortunately, our *and* sentence provides the means for distinguishing. It presents what appears to be the same construction differing only in the replacement of *although* by *and,* and requires the *far* candidate, *scolded,* as referent of *done the same.*

By correctly choosing the far candidate *(scolded)* for *and,* the child shows that he has learned to discard general principles in dealing with this surface structure. When this child then chooses the near candidate for *although* we can assume that he does so not from general principles but because he recognizes the different function of *although* in the sentence.

And indeed we find a pattern of development which supports this hypothesis. The younger children selected the near candidate for both *and* and *although;* apparently they worked from general principles for both words. As age increases children began to select the far candidate for both words; they have learned the exceptional nature of the surface structure, but not the specific *although* rule. In the most advanced stage, children have also learned the specific *although* rule and distinguish the two cases.

The criterion for success with *although,* then, was choosing the near candidate verb as referent of *done the same,* while at the same time choosing the far candidate verb for *and.* Children were scored correct only if all four test sentences were judged correctly. Only four children, ages 7.6, 8.3, 8.11, and 9.9. achieved this success. Clearly age is a poor predictor of success with this construction, and knowledge of it is strongly dependent on individual rate of development.

The relation between our simple use of *although* in the sentence completion task and its more complex use with verb deleted shows the expected course of development. There are children who know neither construction, children who know both, and many intermediate children who know the simple construction but not the complex one. No children reverse this order, and know the complex construction without knowing the simple one.

In summary, all children seven and older succeeded with *although* in its simple construction. The more complex *although* construction was very difficult for the children and only four succeeded at it. Knowledge of the simple construction precedes knowledge of the complex one.

This *although* construction was the most difficult of the constructions reported here, and we will see below that success at it constitutes the highest stage in our developmental sequence.

Considered separately, the *and* construction yielded interesting results. Above we pointed out that the youngest children dealt with *and* according to general principles of English and selected the near candidate to fill in the missing verb.

The parallel of these *and* results with our results for *ask* is remarkably close. Their main feature is the high variability in age of acquisition of the structure, and the fact that we find children up to the oldest failing. After age seven, age is less of a factor in acquisition of the construction than individual rate of development. We will see below that, with only minor exceptions, the same children succeeded with both *ask* and *and*. Accordingly, joint knowledge of *ask* and *and* serves to distinguish Stage 3 from 4 in our developmental sequence.

## Overall Developmental Sequence

By measuring children's competence in dealing with individual grammatical constructions, we gain information about patterns of acquisition characteristic of the different constructions. If we are fortunate this information may shed some light on the nature of the constructions themselves. It is far more interesting, however, to deal with a number of related structures. With a variety of structures, we hope to observe developmental sequences in the acquisition of the different constructions.

Thus, for a set of related constructions, with the verb *ask*, for example, we find that an individual child's successes and failures on test questions always assume the same pattern. Consider for the moment two separate *ask* constructions, the one discussed earlier and another, simpler one: (a) Ask Harry what time it is; (b) Ask Harry what to feed the dog.

Sentence *a* is simpler than *b* in that there is no missing subject in the clause—all information is given and nothing has to be filled in by the listener. To interpret (a) or (b) correctly, the child must recognize that *ask* signals a question. To interpret (b) correctly, the child must, in addition, select the missing subject correctly. In effect, the child must carry out the following three tasks:

1. Recognize that *ask* signals a question before the simple construction (a);
2. Recognize that *ask* signals a question before the complex construction (b);
3. Assign a correct missing subject in the complex construction (b).

Now when we test children on these two structures, we find the following pattern of successes and failures: Task (3) implies (2), which in turn implies (1).[12]

Given this pattern, we conclude that the children attain competence on these tasks in the order listed. The grammatical development is observed to take place in an orderly fashion, from simple to complex, according to an invariant sequence.

That we can find such sequences when testing closely related structures is not very surprising. Sometimes, however, we find a stage we did not expect (such as the first two lines of Table 1 above). This is more interesting because we have learned something about how individual syntactic rules are adjusted in children's grammatical systems as their linguistic competence increases and they approach the adult linguistic system. This is the heart of the matter in linguistic work of this sort, for in this way we find out what the rules look like, how they change, what steps the child has to go through, what progress actually looks like step by step, what is hard and what is easy.

It is most interesting of all, of course, when structures that are related to each other only loosely reveal this same orderly developmental sequence. The five structures discussed exhibit this sequential relationship, in the order presented: *easy to see, promise, ask, and,* and *although*.

TABLE 1
*Stages in Acquisition of Ask Constructions*

|  | Task 1 | Task 2 | Task 3 |
|---|---|---|---|
| Stage A | – | – | – |
| Stage B | + | – | – |
| Stage C | + | + | – |
| Stage D | + | + | + |

+ Success

– Failure

TABLE 2
*Developmental Stages in Children's Acquisition of Five Test Structures*

|  |  | Easy to See | Promise | Ask | And | Although |
|---|---|---|---|---|---|---|
| STAGE 1: | age 5.9–7.1 n = 4 | – | – | – | – | – |
| STAGE 2: | age 5.9–9.5 n = 9 | + | – | – | – | – |
| STAGE 3: | age 6.1–9.9 n = 12 | + | + | – | – | – |
| STAGE 4: | age 7.2–10. n = 7 | + | + | + | + | – |
| STAGE 5: | age 7.6–9.9 n = 4 | + | + | + | + | + |

+ Success

– Failure

These structures appear to be quite divergent, and one would not ordinarily group them together as candidates for a developmental sequence, nor predict a specific order of acquisition. Yet our results show that they are acquired in the order listed. The children's performance on these constructions divides them into five stages as shown in Table 2.

Children who fail all five constructions are at Stage 1; Stage 2 children pass *easy to see* and fail the others; Stage 3 children pass *easy to see* and *promise* and fail the others; Stage 4 children pass all but *although;* Stage 5 children pass all five constructions.

What is interesting in the data is the uniformity of the results. The amount of divergence from this sequence of acquisition is extremely small, the children's individual responses deviating from the observed pattern at the rate of 4 responses per 100.[13]

How do we account for this striking orderliness in the children's acquisition of these seemingly diverse structures? A closer look at the structures themselves reveals that they do have one feature in common. They all require the listener to fill in a missing item in order to understand the sentence. The surface form of these sentences lacks either a noun phrase or a verb phrase which is crucial to its understanding, and the listener must know how to fill it in if he is to understand the sentence correctly. In each case it has to be filled in in a manner at variance with the general tendency of the language, which accounts for the difficulty. More technically, the listener, given only the surface structure of the sentence, must recreate its underlying form. To do this he has to know, among other things, the rules governing deletions from underlying to surface structure. If a child has not yet mastered the rules for these constructions, he will make mistakes in filling in the missing items, and end up with wrong interpretations.

The general rule in English for filling in deletions such as in the above constructions is to choose the nearest preceding candidate item in the sentence. The child has learned this as a general principle of the language very early on. These five constructions, though very different from each other, all require that this principle be abandoned. They require instead the rather unusual principle: don't choose the nearest preceding candidate items in the sentence, keep looking. In a sense the child has to be freed from a deeply entrenched constraint in order to interpret each one of these constructions. He has specifically to learn in each of the above cases that his general principle does not apply. Evidently the relative complexities of these five structures are such that children tend to master them in the order listed, with surprisingly little variation.

Table 3 summarizes our test constructions. It illustrates the five structures, with the correct and incorrect interpretations given. Children who do not know a construction respond with the incorrect interpretation (near candidate); those who know the construction respond with the "other" candidate.

Several interesting observations may be noted in connection with the sequence of acquisition outlined here.

First, *easy to see*, which was tested along with *promise* and *ask* by the author in an earlier experiment[14] did not precede *promise* in that experiment as it does in this one. The reason for this may be faulty experimental technique in the first experiment,

## TABLE 3
*Correct and Incorrect Interpretations of 5 Test Structures*

|  | To Be Filled In | Near Candidate Incorrect | Other Candidate Correct |
|---|---|---|---|
| EASY TO SEE | subject of *see* | doll | somebody else |
| PROMISE | subject of *lie down* | Donald | Bozo |
| ASK | subject of *paint* | boy | girl |
| AND | referent of *done the same* | answered the phone | scolded |
| ALTHOUGH | referent of *done the same* | scolded* | answered the phone |

*likely candidate by analogy with AND sentence, once learned

STRUCTURES: EASY TO SEE: The doll is easy to see.
PROMISE: Bozo promises Donald to lie down.
ASK: The girl asks the boy what to paint.
AND: Mother scolded Gloria for answering the phone, and I would have done the same.
ALTHOUGH: Mother scolded Gloria for answering the phone, although I would have done the same.

which introduced extraneous cues and made the construction too difficult for the children. The current experiment, with improved technique, may reflect the children's competence more accurately.

Second, *promise* precedes *ask* in this experiment as in the 1969 experiment, confirming the earlier results. Only the final stage in the acquisition of *ask* (Table 1, Stage D) is relevant to this overall developmental sequence.

And finally, *and* and *ask* appear to "come in" together if *ask* is scored from both the conversational portion of the interview and the picture test. Apparently the child learns the *and* construction at about the time he masters *ask;* if this result is borne out by future experimentation, it would suggest that the two constructions are of approximately the same degree of complexity.

In summary, the five constructions tested in this study can be ordered in a Guttman scale, indicating a developmental sequence in children's acquisition of these structures. The five structures, though quite diverse, all require that the child apply a specific principle of sentence analysis that is uncommon in English. Apparently, the child's ability to apply this principle progresses in a regular fashion from simple structures to more complex ones.

## Reading

A second portion of this study surveyed the children's reading background and current reading activity. We wished to consider the relation of the amount and complexity of what children read to rate of linguistic development, along with other factors such as IQ and SES. To do this we used the five linguistic stages outlined above as the measure of rate of linguistic development and a variety of information on reading and listening.

Reading information was gathered through questionnaires to both children and parents, and through daily records kept at home of all reading (and listening to books read aloud) engaged in by the child over a one-week period. We calculated amount and complexity of independent reading (and listening), background in children's literature, and recall and recognition of books read and heard. In order to judge the extent of the children's reading at different complexity levels, we applied our own formula for measuring syntactic complexity to the books and magazines reported by the children in their week's record of day-to-day reading.

Our records thus contain a variety of measures of each child's reading exposure which together yielded a general picture of some interest. We have information on books read over a week's time, books that the child named in the course of a half-hour interview, parent reports of reading aloud, and so on. By assessing how much and what is read to him, and how much and what he reads on his own, we attempted to characterize each child's independent reading and get a picture of how reading functions in his background and current life. As mentioned above, both the amount read and the complexity of the material were taken into consideration.

Our concern is not so much with the child's level of reading ability as it is with the reading that he actually engages in. That is, the mechanical skill that he has acquired is of interest for our purposes primarily in the way he puts it to use. The written language is potentially of a more complex nature than speech, both in vocabulary and syntax. The child who reads (or listens to) a variety of rich and complex materials benefits from a range of linguistic inputs that is unavailable to the non-literary child. It is this exposure that we wish to examine for its relation to rate of linguistic development.[15]

In the following section we present some of our reading results and discuss their relation to linguistic development.

## Relations of Reading Measures to Linguistic Stages

One excellent measure used in our reading survey was Huck's *Taking Inventory of Children's Literary Background*.[16] This multiple-choice quiz tests a child's knowledge of the content of sixty widely-read books, poems, and stories from children's literature. Scores on the Huck inventory are positively related to linguistic stage. In other words, the higher the Huck score is, the higher, in general, is the child's linguistic stage in our data.

This can be seen from Table 4, line 1. Each of the Huck scores is the *average* for all children in the stage listed at the head of the column in Table 4.[17]

Other reading measures, developed by the author, also show a positive relation with linguistic stage. Like the Huck score, they appear as within-stage averages in Table 4. The data from which these measures were derived came from three sources:

1. *Master Book List.* This list contained the titles of some 400 children's books and was left in the home for the child and parent to complete jointly by checking off the titles of books with which the child was familiar. The number of books checked off that were at the top level of syntactic complexity was one positive measure and is presented in Table 4, line 6. The *total* number of books checked off on the Master Book List was also a good measure, though not quite as good as the top level count.

2. *Parent Interview.* One of the child's parents—in all but one case, the mother—

TABLE 4

*Average Scores at Each Linguistic Stage on a Variety of Reading and Other Measures*

|  | Stage 1 | Stage 2 | Stage 3 | Stage 4 | Stage 5 |
|---|---|---|---|---|---|
| *Measures good at all stages* | | | | | |
| 1. Huck *Inventory of Literary Background* | 23 | 31 | 38 | 39 | 43 |
| 2. Numerical scores from Child Interview | 37 | 50 | 55 | 56 | 59 |
| 3. Numerical scores from Parent Interview | 45 | 55 | 58 | 61 | 64 |
| 4. Weighted total books named—Parent Interview | 21 | 30 | 42 | 47 | 49 |
| 5. Average level books named—Parent Interview | 1.4 | 2.1 | 2.4 | 2.9 | 3.0 |
| 6. Master Book List—top level count | 2.3 | 3.9 | 4.9 | 5.0 | 6.3 |
| 7. IQ (WPPSI, WISC) full scale | 105 | 118 | 123 | 129 | 138 |
| 8. IQ—verbal | 105 | 119 | 122 | 129 | 141 |
| 9. IQ—performance | 104 | 114 | 120 | 123 | 129 |
|  | n = 4 | n = 9 | n = 13 | n = 6 | n = 4 |

was interviewed at home. Questions in the interview centered around the child's reading habits, library trips, reading aloud to the child, favorite books, time spent in independent reading, etc. Special attention was given to eliciting from the parent as many titles as possible of books and magazines that the child had encountered over the years.

Three measures from this interview were found to relate positively to linguistic stage as shown in Table 4: a) average complexity level of books named by the parent (line 5); b) the total number of books named, weighted by complexity levels of the individual books (the raw total was not a distinguishing measure) (line 4); and c) the total numerical score from the interview, calculated from questions with numerical answers such as time spent reading to the child during the early years, the amount of time the child spends reading now, frequency of public library visits, average number of books borrowed from the library each visit, and so on (line 3).

3. *Child Interview.* An interview was held with each child at school. Roughly the same information was sought as in the parent interview. The measure which correlated positively with linguistic stage from this interview was, as in the parent interview, numerical score. This score reflected the child's answers to questions concerning library trips (What books do you have out this week? How many of the books that you take out do you generally read?), favorite books and authors, books reread many times, time spent reading daily or weekly, TV watching (credit given inversely to amount of time spent watching TV), number of people at home who read to you, now or formerly, and so on. This numerical score measure for the child interview appears in Table 4 (line 2).

In addition to demonstrating a positive relation with linguistic stages displayed in Table 4, the five reading measures all relate positively to the Huck score. Four of the correlations were significant beyond the .001 level: Master Book List top level book count, average complexity level and weighted total of books from the parent interview, and the numerical score from the child interview. The Pearson product-moment correlations were .564, .577, .392, and .631 respectively. The numerical score from the parent interview was also positively correlated with the Huck score ($r = .462$, $p = .003$). With a sample of only thirty-six, these correlations indicate a high degree of association.

Given the positive relation of these five measures with linguistic stages in Table 4 (evidenced also by positive Kendall rank order correlations significant at least at the .013 level)[18] and the positive and significant Pearson correlations of these five measures with the Huck score, we conclude that the relation between reading exposure and linguistic stage is not due to a peculiarity of one of the reading measures. To assume otherwise, since the measures are largely non-overlapping, would lead us to claim that each measure has some unique peculiarity that causes it to produce a positive relation with linguistic stage that in fact has little or nothing to do with the child's reading exposure. Experience tells us that concentrating on six such unique measures is unlikely. Therefore, we conclude that a valid relation between reading exposure and linguistic stages exists.

It is worth noting that the Huck Inventory, a direct and easily obtainable measure, apparently functions as an excellent single measure of reading exposure to which linguistic stages are related. We may speculate that the Inventory refines the notion of exposure to written materials by incorporating not just the amount read but internalization and retention of the material as well.

## Relationship of Other Measures to Linguistic Stages

One other measure, IQ, is positively related to linguistic development across all stages.

The Wechsler Preschool and Primary Scale of Intelligence (WPPSI) test was given to the six children in the study who were under 6.2 years of age at testing time. The remaining thirty children (ages 6.5 and over) were given the Wechsler Intelligence Scale for Children (WISC) test. IQ's ranged from 98 to 142 and the average scores within each linguistic stage are presented in Table 4, lines 7–9. Not only do the full scale IQ scores increase with linguistic stage but so do the verbal and performance subtests of the test.

The Kendall rank order correlations of linguistic stage with IQ, with each of the IQ subtests, with age, and with grade were all significant at the .001 level while the Pearson correlation of linguistic stage with the Census Bureau measure of SES, whose range is 01–99, was significant at the .02 level.

It is not surprising that SES was highly correlated with IQ but not with age or grade. However, the correlations of SES with reading vocabulary and with reading comprehension grade level scores from standardized tests were also nonsignificant while the correlation of SES with IQ was significant at the .001 level. Moreover, the Pearson correlations of SES with all measures of books from the parent interview, child interview and Master Book List were significant at the .001 level.

What inferences can be drawn from this correlational information? First, if our five stages reflect an underlying developmental sequence, we would expect variables like age, grade, reading grade level scores, and IQ to be positively and significantly correlated with linguistic stage. They are.

Second, it is reasonable to speculate that the various IQ and reading exposure measures are not mere substitutes for the age measure; the exposure measures play an independent role in influencing linguistic stage. This follows because the IQ score and its components are age corrected[19] and are therefore uncorrelated with age. Also, the sample was stratified by age (young, medium, old) and by reading grade level score (low, medium, high). This stratification would lead at most to a negligible correlation between age and reading grade level score.

Third, given the pattern of significant and nonsignificant correlation of SES with various measures, *if* SES acts upon linguistic stage placement through any of the measures included in this study it is through general ability or the reading environment of the child. Statistical techniques for studying this question exist, but a new and larger sample should be drawn.

### *Relationship of Listening Measures to Linguistic Stages*

A calculation was made of the amount of time spent reading aloud to the children and the complexity of the books read to them at home during a one-week period.

As might be expected, listening to books read aloud decreases sharply after first grade as the children's own reading begins to replace their listening. Even in the first grade independent reading is beginning to predominate for the more able readers.

Among the pre-readers, listening to books read aloud is positively related to linguistic stage. As the next section will show, those pre-readers in higher linguistic stages are read to by more people and hear more books per week, at higher complexity levels than children at lower linguistic stages.

In summary, the measures which discriminate the whole linguistic range of stages include IQ, memory of content of books read (Huck), book counts weighted by complexity level, and questionnaire replies. In addition, certain measures work well at lower linguistic stages, and others at higher linguistic stages. Several of the book counts (number of books recalled and recognized) appear to discriminate best at the lower linguistic stages, and word counts (number of words read during the recorded week) discriminate best at the higher stages. Reading complex materials quite strikingly characterizes the top linguistic stage.

## Mini-Comparisons: Uniform Age and IQ, Different Linguistic Stages

A natural question, given the type of data collected here, is: What factors differentiate children in different linguistic stages, who are of roughly the same age and IQ? If we control for age and IQ, do any of the various measures that we used serve to distinguish children in lower linguistic stages from those in higher stages?

The small number of children tested precludes a statistical answer to this question. At most we can compare individual children who meet the requirement of same age and IQ and different linguistic stage. The results are not uninteresting, however. We were able to select three such sets of children, one from among the youngest in the sample, one from the mid-age group, and one from the oldest. In each group there were three children of comparable age and IQ, who were nevertheless at different linguistic stages.

Such a procedure of "mini-comparisons" clearly has its limitations, but we are able in each age group to note a number of factors that vary as does linguistic stage. The overall picture shows that at each age, reading or hearing books read is a strong factor, with many different individual measures of reading exposure contributing to this trend. Interestingly enough, SES appears as a factor most strongly in the youngest group (5.9–6.1), where many of the reading measures vary directly with SES. It is hardly news that higher SES parents read to their young children more; what is interesting is that SES is less of a differentiating factor among the older children. In the middle and oldest group, the children share a relatively high SES. For these children (particularly the oldest group where SES varies least), it is their own activity, not SES differences, that varies with linguistic stage. This suggests the following speculation, which might be interesting to test further: given a high SES, once a child can read, he's on his own. His linguistic progress at this age may well turn out to reflect what he does with his time.

The tables which follow (Mini-comparisons 1, 2, 3) present the individual differ-entiating measures in each mini-comparison. Only the significant measures are in-cluded at each age, although all questions were asked of all children.

Notice that three items appear in all three age groups: the number of books named by the child in the course of his interview (child and parent in the youngest group), the average number of books taken out on regular visits to the public library, and, interestingly, the number of books that the mother cited from her own childhood that she has enjoyed reading to the child. This third item, though somewhat of a surprise at first, makes sense once its implications are considered. The mother who recalls certain books with pleasure from her own childhood may well transmit this enjoyment to her child very early on when she reads to him. We may speculate that this child learns to assign a special role to reading, for what his mother enjoys doing with him, he quite naturally comes to enjoy and recognize as a valued activity.

## Conclusions

What status can we ascribe to the five linguistic stages observable in our data on the basis of the constructions tested? Given the small sample size and the fact that most of these relationships were observed for the first time here, they clearly should be considered as only suggestive. Further testing with larger groups of children, or at least replication with small groups, would be necessary if one wished to substantiate the order of emergence of the structures. My guess is that the distinction between

TABLE 5

*Mini-comparison 1 Measures that Vary as Linguistic Stage in Three Young Children of Uniform Age and IQ*

| | Ling. Stage 1 | Ling. Stage 2 | Ling. Stage 3 |
|---|---|---|---|
| age of child | 5.9 | 5.9 | 6.1 |
| grade in school | K | K | K |
| IQ (WISC) | 118 | 120 | 118 |
| SES (Census Bureau scale 01–99) | 63 | 89 | 93 |
| father's occupation score (Census Bureau scale 01–99) | 80 | 80 | 99 |
| father's years of education | 12 | 16 | 20 |
| WISC comprehension subtest | 13 | 14 | 18 |
| books named on parent and child questionnaires, weighted total | 14 | 40 | 111 |
| books named on parent and child questionnaires, average level | 1 | 1 | 3 |
| reading to child in experimental week, total number words read | 0 | 6,700 | 17,500 |
| reading to child in experimental week, number words read multiplied by complexity factor | 0 | 17,700 | 62,500 |
| Reported on parent questionnaire: | | | |
| books named by parent, weighted total | 12 | 40 | 62 |
| numerical score on parent's questionnaire | 27 | 37 | 60 |
| number of people at home who read to child | 1 | 2 | 2 |
| amount of time child is read to per week at home | ½ hr. | ½ hr. | >2 hrs. |
| average level of books cited by parent as reread to child many times | 1 | 1 | 2 |
| does child visit public library? | no | no | yes |
| average number public library books taken out each visit | — | — | 3 |
| subscriptions to children's magazines | 0 | 0 | 1 |
| years nursery school attendance | 0 | 0 | 1 |
| number books from mother's own childhood cited as read to child | 0 | 2 | 1 |

TABLE 6

*Mini-comparison 2 Measures that Vary as Linguistic Stage in Three*
*Mid-age Children of Uniform Age and IQ*

| | Ling. Stage 2 | Ling. Stage 4 | Ling. Stage 5 |
|---|---|---|---|
| age of child | 7.10 | 8.6 | 8.3 |
| grade in school | 2 | 3 | 2 |
| Reading grade score (school record) | voc: 5.2 | voc: 7.1 | voc: 4.8 |
| | compr: 5.1 | compr: 7.0 | compr: 5.4 |
| IQ (WISC) | 138 | 136 | 136 |
| SES (Census Bureau scale 01–99) | 81 | 93 | 91 |
| father's occupation score (Census Bureau Scale 01–99) | 68 | 94 | 92 |
| child's reading in experimental week, total number words read | 22,100 | 114,400 | 322,000 |
| child's reading in experimental week, number words read multiplied by complexity factor | 46,700 | 626,600 | 2,826,300 |
| | | | |
| Reported on child's questionnaire: | | | |
| books named by child, weighted total | 23 | 25 | 40 |
| average number public library books taken out each visit | 1 | 2 | 3 |
| recent books read, number named | 1 | 1 | 5 |
| average level of books cited as recently read | 2 | 2 | 5 |
| average time TV watched per day | >1 hr. | 1 hr. | <½ hr. |
| | | | |
| Reported on parent questionnaire: | | | |
| reads long books to child (now or formerly), continued from day to day | no | yes | yes |
| average level of long books named | — | 3 | 4 |
| rereads favorite books many times to child (now or formerly) | no | yes | yes |
| average level favorite books reread | — | 3 | 4 |
| frequency of child's visits to public library | irreg. | biweekly | > weekly |
| average number public library books taken out each visit | 1 | 2 | 4 |
| years nursery school attendance | 1 | 2 | 2 |
| number books from mother's own childhood cited as read to child | 0 | 2 | 7 |

Stages 3 and 4 would hold up under additional testing, since it has a good theoretical base and was observed here for the second time. The other stages may or may not be borne out by future experimentation. This has been only a first trial, in no sense definitive. It is important to stress that the interest of results such as these lies not so much in the particular structures dealt with as in the confirmation of the continuing and orderly course of language acquisition among older children. The structures are more interesting as means to this end than in themselves.

In this vein, I would like to caution against considering these constructions relevant for practical purposes such as diagnostic procedures or for teaching to children. In interpreting results such as these it is important to recognize that the choice of structures is highly arbitrary as far as children are concerned. The selection reflects more the state of knowledge in the field of linguistics than the field of language acquisition, for knowledge of child grammar is as yet far too rudimentary to guide such a choice. Further, our particular experimental requirements impose certain constraints. Thus our findings with regard to complexity of structure should not be interpreted to mean that because a child of eight does not know a particular construction, therefore we should attempt to teach it to him. All in all, our constructions

TABLE 7
*Mini-comparison 3 Measures that Vary as Linguistic Stage in Three
Older Children of Uniform Age and IQ*

|  | Ling. Stage 3 | Ling. Stage 4 | Ling. Stage 5 |
|---|---|---|---|
| age of child | 9.4 | 10.0 | 9.9 |
| grade in school | 4 | 4 | 4 |
| reading grade score (school record) | voc: 6.8 | voc: 6.7 | voc: 5.6 |
|  | compr: 6.6 | compr: 6.5 | compr: 6.3 |
| IQ (WISC) | 135 | 129 | 136 |
| SES (Census Bureau scale 01–99) | 93 | 96 | 96 |
| father's occupation score (Census Bureau scale 01–99) | 88 | 96 | 96 |
| father's years education | 16 | 16 | 20 |
| Reported on child's questionnaire: |  |  |  |
| books named by child, total number | 6 | 10 | 14 |
| books named by child, weighted total | 14 | 32 | 39 |
| numerical score on child's questionnaire | 50 | 56 | 69 |
| average number public library books taken out each visit | — | — | 6 |
| number library books out now | 0 | 0 | 4 |
| number favorite books named | 1 | 2 | 3 |
| are you in the middle of a book now? | no | yes | yes |
| child named last book read | no | yes | yes |
| level of last book read | — | 2 | 3 |
| do you ever read when you get home from school? | no | no | yes |
| average time spent reading | twice/wk. | daily <½ hr. | daily >½ hr. |
| average number books read per week | — | 2 | 3 |
| Reported on parent questionnaire: |  |  |  |
| average time child was read to when small | 1 hr./wk. | daily >15 min | daily >15 min. |
| average time child spends reading now | 1 hr./wk. | 15 min./day | >15 min./day |
| number books named by parent as read recently by child | 1 | 1 | 7 |
| average level of books recently read by child | 2 | 2 | 3 |
| number books from mother's own childhood cited as read to child | 2 | 2 | 3 |

may have little to do with what is important in children's knowledge and may tell virtually nothing about gaps that might be worth trying to fill in terms of enhancing development. Very likely they do reflect the extent of children's knowledge, but attempting to introduce these arbitrary structures artificially cannot be expected to have much effect on the total range of that knowledge.

What then are the practical implications of work of this sort, and what potential educational significance does it have? It seems to me that its relevance may lie in the continuing language acquisition that it reveals in school age children, and in the connections noted between this language development and reading. These results may have implications with regard to language programs in the elementary schools, and the philosophy underlying curriculum design and selection of materials.

We know very little about the actual processes by which children learn language, but there has been an increasing awareness over the past few years of just how much the child brings to the task by way of his own internal organization and innate human characteristics. He certainly is not "taught" language in any formal sense, but acquires it naturally, so to speak, in the course of maturing and developing in an environment where he is adequately exposed to it. Interestingly enough, we now see that this natural process of acquisition continues actively into the early school years, and perhaps beyond. The variety of linguistic material that the child is still learning on his own during the elementary school years must certainly be extensive, if our few, rather arbitrarily chosen examples (arbitrary from the point of view of language acquisition) uncovered this continuing acquisition so readily.

What results of this sort indicate is that the child enters the classroom equipped to learn language and able to do so by methods of his own. This suggests that perhaps the best thing that we might do for him in terms of encouraging this learning would be to make more of it possible, by exposing him to a rich variety of language inputs in interesting, stimulating situations. The question is how.

Our reading results indicate that exposure to the more complex language available from reading does seem to go hand in hand with increased knowledge of the language. This would imply that perhaps wider reading should find a place in the curriculum. The child could be read to, stimulated to read on his own, not restricted to material deemed "at his level" but permitted access to books well "above his level" to get out of them whatever he may. Perhaps he should be encouraged to skim when he reads, to skip uninteresting portions and get to the "good parts" instead of concentrating at length on controlled texts. In general it may be that the effort should be towards providing more and richer language exposure, rather than limiting the child with restrictive and carefully programmed materials. In this way the child would be permitted to derive what is accessible to him from a wide range of inputs, and put it to use in his own way. This approach would seem to be more closely in accord with the nature of language acquisition as we are coming to understand it.

These remarks are, of course, speculative. Their purpose is to emphasize that the potential relevance of work of this sort to language curricula will lie in its suggestiveness for effective use of classroom time, rather than in its relation to the specifics of grammar teaching.

## Notes

1. C. Chomsky, *The Acquisition of Syntax in Children from 5 to 10* (Cambridge, Mass.: M.I.T. Press, 1969).
2. Chomsky, p. 4.
3. Chomsky, p. 6.
4. R. F. Cromer, " 'Children are nice to understand': Surface Structure Clues for the Recovery of a Deep Structure." *British Journal of Psychology,* 61, 1970, pp. 397–408; F. S. Kessel, "The Role of Syntax in Children's Comprehension from Ages Six to Twelve," *Monographs of the Society for Research in Child Development,* Ser. no. 139, 35, (September, 1970); C. Chomsky, 1969.
5. 7.1 is used to indicate 7 years, 1 month.
6. Chomsky.
7. Chomsky.
8. The children's performance with *ask* in general reveals a number of levels of competence, which the present discussion only touches on. Since the various degrees of competence short of total mastery do not contribute to our developmental sequence, they are referred to only peripherally here.
9. The actual number of instructions given varied from child to child because of the informal nature of the interview.
10. This scoring procedure simplifies the stages of our developmental sequence, and was adopted

for this reason. Separating the children who passed only the picture test would add one stage to the sequence, which might be useful for some purposes but seemed superfluous here.

11. This interesting and rather unusual aspect of the word *although* was brought to the author's attention by Adrian Akmajian.

12. Children who can do Task 3 can always do 2 and 1, and children who can do 2 can always do 1. There are no children who break this pattern, who can do 3, for example, and not 2 and 1; or who can do 2 without being able to do 1; or 1 and 3 without 2. On the other hand we do find children who can do 1 but not 2 or 3; and children who can do 1 and 2, but not 3. When our data are of this sort, when the operations can be arranged into a Guttman scale such that 3 presupposes 2 which in turn presupposes 1, then we have information about order of acquisition. Although we have not observed children over time as they progress from 1 to 2 to 3, we can nevertheless conclude that this is the order of acquisition and that we have an invariant developmental sequence.

13. When the stages are considered as a Guttman scale, the coefficient of reproducibility is .96.

14. Chomsky.

15. From the point of view of exposure to the written language, it may matter little whether the child has the book read to him, as would be the case with the younger children in our study, or reads it himself, as do the older children. It is possible, perhaps even likely, that in both situations the contents, style, and language usage of the book are made available to the child with little difference in effectiveness.

16. Charlotte S. Huck, *Taking Inventory of Children's Literary Background* (Glenview, Ill.: Scott, Foresman, 1966).

17. For example, 23 is the average Huck score for all children in Stage 1. The notation "n = 4" at the foot of the first column tells you that four children are at Stage 1.

18. Kendall rank-order correlations for these measures are:

| | | |
|---|---|---|
| Master Book List—top level count | .328 | (.002) |
| Average Level books named—parent | .409 | (.001) |
| Weighted total books named—parent | .274 | (.009) |
| Numerical score—parent | .258 | (.013) |
| Numerical score—child | .327 | (.002) |

19. $IQ = \dfrac{\text{Mental Age}}{\text{Chronological Age}} \times 100$

# 4
# Trends in Second-Language-Acquisition Research

KENJI HAKUTA, *Stanford University*
HERLINDA CANCINO *San Francisco State University*

*Kenji Hakuta and Herlinda Cancino explore four theoretical approaches to second-language acquisition—contrastive, error, performance, and discourse analyses. Closely following the shifts among these methodologies with the change of the times, the authors critically examine the advantages and disadvantages of each. They also show how different methodological techniques reflect changes in conceptions of language acquisition and the nature of learners, from the behaviorist view of a first-language habit interfering with a second-language habit to the generative grammar view of active hypothesis testing. The authors, emphasizing the influence of first-language-acquisition research on studies of second-language acquisition, theorize an interplay of two possible factors: (1) language acquisition toward a universal order, and (2) native language transfer. Hakuta and Cancino conclude their discussions by predicting the future direction of research on second-language acquisition.*

Language provides one of the most readily accessible windows into the nature of the human mind. How children acquire this complex system with such apparent ease continues to fascinate the student of human language. The last quarter of a century in particular has witnessed a qualitative leap in our knowledge of the language-acquisition process in young children. In recent years researchers have begun extending their scope of inquiry into the problem of second-language acquisition. The motivation underlying this new endeavor is two-fold: first, it provides an added perspective on human language, and second, interest in second-language teaching and bilingual education has resulted in a greater need to understand the mechanisms

We would like to thank Helen Tager Flusberg, Bella DePaula, Steven Pinker, and Ellen Winner for helpful comments on this paper. We especially thank Roger Brown and Bruce Fraser for extensive written comments. Preparation of this manuscript was supported in part by Grant BNS 73-09150 from the National Science Foundation to Dr. Roger Brown.

*Harvard Educational Review*   Vol. 47   No. 3   August 1977, 294–316

underlying second-language acquisition. The focus of analysis has undergone distinct shifts in perspective as a function of our changing conceptualizations of what language is and also what the learner brings to the learning situation.

To anticipate the various approaches to be reviewed in this paper, let us entertain some ways in which one might proceed in analyzing the process of second-language acquisition. Assume that we had in our possession a year-long record of all the conversations of a second-language learner since initial exposure to the target language. One way to analyze the data, if we knew the grammars of both the native and the target languages, would be through a *contrastive* analysis of the two language structures. Where the two languages differ we would expect errors, and our predictions could be tested against the acquisition data. Another way to proceed in the analysis would be to catalogue all the systematic deviations—the *errors*—in the learner's speech from the target-language norm. These deviations, or errors, could be classified into whatever categories our theory might dictate. If we want more specific information than that provided by error data, we could examine *performance* on particular linguistic structures (such as negatives and interrogatives) and look for both the distributional characteristics of errors and correct usage of those structures. Or, we could look not just at linguistic structure but at *discourse* structure as well. For example, we could ask how linguistic forms might be derived from the way in which they are used in conversation.

Over the past thirty years second-language-acquisition research has passed through the four phases outlined above: *contrastive analysis, error analysis, performance analysis,* and *discourse analysis.* (For a review of earlier studies in this area see McLaughlin, 1977.) In this article, we summarize and critically review each of these research traditions. In addition, we discuss reasons for the transition from one form of analysis to the next, particularly that due to the influence of first-language-acquisition research.

## Contrastive Analysis

From the early 1940s to the 1960s, teachers of foreign languages were optimistic that the problems of language teaching could be approached scientifically, with the use of methods derived from structural linguistics. Essentially, the goal of structural linguistics was to characterize the syntactic structure of sentences in terms of their grammatical categories and surface arrangements. Fries (1945/1972) was explicit about the implications of this approach for foreign language teaching. He claimed that "the most effective materials are those that are based upon a scientific description of the language to be learned, carefully compared with a parallel description of the native language of the learner" (p.9).

Claims like Fries's were reinforced by informal observations of learners' systematic errors, which seemed to reflect the structure of their native language. Although many of the errors were phonological in nature, as illustrated by the native speaker of Japanese who consistently fails to distinguish between /r/ and /l/, others clearly originated at the syntactic and morphological levels. Consider a native speaker of Spanish who says "Is the house of my mother." The Spanish equivalent would be

"Es la casa de mi madre." The English utterance contains two errors, whose sources can be clearly traced back to Spanish. Spanish allows subject pronouns to be deleted. When this rule is transferred to English, "This is" or "It is" simply becomes "Is." Also, Spanish uses the possessed-possessor order; thus we have "the house of my mother" ("la case de mi madre"). It appeared, then, that the foreign-language learner's difficulties could be predicted from the differences in the structures of the two languages. Contrastive analysis was the label given to this comparative approach.

Principles such as imitation, positive and negative transfer, reinforcement, and habit strength were borrowed from the academic psychology of learning and incorporated into the contrastive analysis view of second-language acquisition. Presupposing that language development consisted of the acquisition of a set of habits, errors in the second language were seen as the result of the first-language habits interfering with the acquisition of the habits of the second. In classroom practice the principles of habit formation and interference led to the use of pattern drills in the audio-lingual method of second-language learning. On the basis of contrastive analysis, difficult patterns were predicted and consequently emphasized in the drills. For the interested reader the assumptions underlying the audio-lingual method are carefully examined and evaluated in an important book by Rivers (1964).

The comparison of the structures of languages continues to be a respectable activity within contrastive linguistics (Alatis, 1968) and has come to be conducted within the framework of transformational generative grammar. Its status as a psychological approach to the investigation of the second-language-acquisition process, however, fell into disrepute for several reasons. One reason was the unfortunate association of contrastive analysis with the behaviorist view of language acquisition, an account whose theoretical adequacy came to be seriously questioned, most notably by Chomsky (1959). In our view a more devastating reason was that contrastive analysis fared quite poorly once researchers, instead of relying on anecdotal impressions from the classroom, began collecting data in more systematic ways (Oller & Richards, 1973). From these data, analyses of learners' errors soon showed that a large proportion were not predictable on the basis of contrastive analysis. In fact, many of these errors, such as rule simplification (as in "Mommy eat tapioca") and over-generalization (as in "He wrote me a letter") exhibited a striking resemblance to those made by children acquiring a first language. Moreover, learners did not in fact make all the errors predicted by contrastive analysis (Nickel, 1971; Stockwell, Bowen, & Martin, 1965). When the inadequacy of contrastive analysis as a predictive model became apparent, Wardhaugh (1970) drew the useful distinction between strong and weak versions of the approach. The strong version claimed to predict errors, while the weak versions simply accounted for errors that occurred. Contrastive analysis survives only in its weak form with an obvious shortcoming; it gives an incomplete representation of the second-language-acquisition process since it can account only for some, not all, of the errors. Recently it has been incorporated into the more general approach of error analysis (Schumann & Stenson, 1975), which analyzes all systematic deviations of the learner's language from the target-language norms.

## Error Analysis

Chomsky's (1957) formulation of language as a powerful set of transformational rules was received with enthusiasm by many psychologists, and its impact on the study of language acquisition was almost immediate. By the early 1960s researchers began reporting the regularities in the speech of young children and showed that these regularities could be characterized by a set of rules, a grammar (Brown & Bellugi, 1964b). What motivated much of this research was the assumption that the end state of the developmental process is a transformational grammar. Strictly speaking, however, the grammars that were written to describe children's speech were not transformational. Nevertheless, the system of rules reflected in children's utterances was most impressive, particularly some rules for which no adult model seemed to exist. Many of the regularities were morphological in nature, such as "wented" and "hisself," but others were syntactic, for example, "Where he can go?" Although such utterances are errors from the viewpoint of adult grammar, their systematic occurrence in protocols from children gave convincing support to the notion that they were part of each child's developing grammar or linguistic system. The child's errors, rather than being considered products of imperfect learning, came to be regarded as inevitable results of an underlying, rule-governed system which evolved toward the full adult grammar. From this new perspective the child, in the eyes of researchers, gained the status of an active participant in the acquisition of language.

The influence of early first-language-acquisition research on second-language-acquisition research can be found in the error-analysis approach, best represented in collections by Oller and Richards (1973), Schumann and Stenson (1975), and Svartvik (1973). Many investigators noted similarities between the types of errors reported in the first-language-acquisition literature and the errors made by second-language learners. These errors could not be accounted for within the contrastive analysis framework. On the basis of this similarity, researchers speculated that the processes of first- and second-language acquisition are essentially the same (Corder, 1967; Dulay & Burt, 1972; Richards, 1973). Like children learning their first language, second-language learners were characterized as proceeding through a series of intermediate grammars (Corder, 1971; Nemser, 1971; Selinker, 1972). At any given time the learner was credited with having an "interlanguage," a genuine language in the sense that it consists of a set of systematic rules that can be described in a grammar. An interlanguage incorporates characteristics of both the native and the target language of the learner. Today, the goals of error analysis are twofold: to describe, through the evidence contained in errors, the nature of the interlanguage in its developmental stages and to infer from these descriptions the process of second-language acquisition.

The majority of studies in error analysis attempt to classify the errors made by learners. Generally, errors are divided into two categories: interference (or *inter*lingual) errors and *intra*lingual errors. Interference errors, those errors whose sources can be traced back to the native language of the learner, are the ones that contrastive analysis addressed. An important difference, however, is that within the framework of error analysis these errors are not interpreted as products of the first-language habit interfering with the second-language habit. Since the language-acquisition process is seen as active hypothesis testing on the part of the learner, interference errors are interpreted as a manifestation of the learner's hypothesis that the new language is just like the native language (Corder, 1967). Unlike interference errors, intralingual errors arise from properties of the target language and can be found among children learning it as their first language. Their errors include errors of simplification as well as overgeneralization.

Several researchers have investigated the extent to which learners make errors of each type. In two widely cited papers Dulay and Burt (1973, 1974b) report a study in which they considered two competing hypotheses about the nature of second-language acquisition. The first was that second-language acquisition was essentially the same as first-language acquisition. The alternative hypothesis was the one embodied in contrastive analysis, which viewed second-language acquisition as the acquisition of habits (Lado, 1957). Dulay and Burt's implicit assumptions were that intralingual errors constituted evidence for the first hypothesis, while interference errors were evidence for the alternative hypothesis. Notice that their interpretation of interference errors differed from other workers in error analysis. Using an elicitation device called the Bilingual Syntax Measure (BSM), Dulay and Burt collected speech samples from 179 Spanish-speaking children learning English with varying amounts of English-as-Second-Language instruction in three different areas in the United States. They tallied errors that could be "unamibiguously" classified as being either interference, intralingual (defined as similar to those reported in the first-language literature), or unique (neither of the two). The results were dramatic and straightforward: of the 513 unambiguous errors, only about 5 percent were interference, while 87 percent were intralingual, and the remainder were classified as unique. Dulay and Burt interpreted this finding as evidence that "children do not use their 'first language habits' in the process of learning the syntax of their new language" (1974b, p. 134).

Dulay and Burt's results can be interpreted in at least two ways. If we accept their assumption that interference errors constitute evidence for a habit-formation hypothesis, their data make an overwhelming argument against this explanation of second-language acquisition. On the other hand, if we take the viewpoint that interference errors are not products of habit formation but rather a form of active hypothesis testing and language transfer (Corder, 1967), a different conclusion emerges. Dulay and Burt's data might be interpreted as evidence that very little language transfer occurs—that is, the learning of the first language has very little influence on the learning of the second.

Whatever theoretical perspective one might take, however, two underlying assumptions in the study make both of the above interpretations questionable: 1) that an error is an appropriate unit of analysis, and 2) that equal weighting should be given to interference and intralingual errors. These assumptions are seriously called into question when one considers that all omissions of grammatical morphemes—including noun and verb inflections and other high-frequency morphemes such as the verb *be*—were classified as intralingual errors. Although Dulay and Burt do not provide the exact figures, there were many instances of these kinds of errors. Since interference errors generally involve either larger constituents or changes in word order, the two types of errors appear to originate from sources whose relative opportunities for occurrence are significantly different. Furthermore, interference errors may appear in the speech of learners only at specific points in development, and a cross-sectional sample might not capture learners at critical developmental levels.

Other studies in error analysis attempt to compare the proportions of interference and intralingual errors in adult learners. Corder (1975), citing Duskova (1969), reports that there is a larger proportion of interference errors for adults than Dulay and Burt (1973, 1974b) found for children. Duskova (1969) analyzed errors made in English composition by adult Czechoslovakians and reported that roughly 30 percent of the 1,007 errors collected were interference and the remainder intralingual. A closer look at the breakdown of her data, however, reveals that many interference errors were omissions of articles, a part of speech for which Czech does not have an equivalent. In the Dulay and Burt analysis, omissions of articles were considered intralingual errors, since children learning English as their first language also omit articles. When one tallies the interference errors according to Dulay and Burt's criteria, the proportion in Duskova's study is reduced to 5 percent. Despite differences both in the ages of the subjects and in the data collection instruments (speech versus composition), this figure is comparable to the Dulay and Burt results.

However, our earlier qualification still holds for the interpretation of the results of these studies of adult learners. The theoretical significance attached to interlingual and intralingual processes should not be considered proportionate to the number of the respective error types found in the learner's speech. An analogy with studies of first-language learners serves to illustrate this point. Children overgeneralize rules as in "I go*ed* home," and they simplify their speech into telegraphic form as in "Fraser come Tuesday" (Brown & Bellugi, 1964a). In total speech output there is probably a far greater proportion of oversimplification errors. Yet, no one would argue on this basis that simplification is the more important of the two processes in language acquisition. In fact the errors of overgeneralization in first-language learning are fine examples of the child's rule-governed behavior. Similarly, interference errors in second-language learning are fine examples of language transfer and should be regarded as such in their own right. Such errors strongly point to areas of dynamic interplay between the two languages.

Other studies of errors are taxonomic, generally classifying errors as interference, overgeneralization, and simplification. Such studies include Politzer and Ramirez's (1973) and Cohen's (1975) analyses of the speech of Mexican-American children learning English and a fine paper by Selinker, Swain, and Dumas (1975) analyzing errors in French made by English-speaking children in a language-immersion program (see Swain, 1974). A similar approach in adult studies was used by Jain (1974), Richards (1973), and Taylor (1975).

To summarize thus far, research in error analysis has revealed evidence for three general taxonomic categories of errors: interference, overgeneralization, and simplification. Of these error types, interference errors do not appear with strikingly high frequency. Second-language learners make a large number of overgeneralization and simplification errors; they bear a striking resemblance to errors made by first-language learners. And finally, there appear to be errors which are unique to second-language learners. These findings are of interest because they suggest the reality of distinct processes resulting in the respective types of errors. It is difficult, however, to see how the extent to which these error types occur would be of any empirical value until they are weighted according to their relative opportunities for occurrence. Such attempts, and also attempts at classifying errors with respect to their gravity (James, 1974), should prove informative.

All of the studies cited above used cross-sectional samples; very few studies have followed Corder's (1967) suggestion that errors should be studied longitudinally. Such analyses are needed to tell us whether specific types of errors might be prevalent at specific points in the course of development and whether errors in a learner's speech disappear abruptly or gradually. One of the few studies examining the pattern of interference errors over time was carried out by Cancino (Note 1). Her subject, Marta, a five-year-old Puerto Rican girl, was acquiring English through natural exposure to the speech of English-speaking peers. The data consisted of biweekly, spontaneous speech samples of two hours each, obtained over a period of eight months. In her analysis Cancino classified all instances of possessives (excluding possessive pronouns and adjectives) as being one of the following five types:

1) possessor-possessed order, with *'s* supplied, e.g., "Freddie's frog,"
2) possessor-possessed with *'s* omitted, e.g., "Freddie frog,"
3) possessed-possessor order, with preposition *of* supplied, e.g., "Frog of Freddie,"
4) same as (3) except with *of* omitted, e.g., "Frog Freddie," or
5) possessed-possessor order, with Spanish preposition *de* supplied, e.g., "Frog de Freddie."

The distribution for each category, displayed in Table 1, reveals a clear pattern of development.

First, the Spanish word *de* is used in producing English utterances (Type 5). Next, word order indicates the appearance of obligatory contexts for the English form *'s*—that is, contexts in which adult norms clearly require the form (Type 2). After that, *of* replaces *de* (Type 3) and finally *'s* is gradually supplied in obligatory contexts (Type 1). As far as we are aware, this is one of the clearest empirical illustrations of an interplay between the native language and the target language. Two points should be made here. Interference errors, at least for the possessive form, appear primarily in the earliest stages of acquisition. If, for example, Marta's speech had been sampled at a later point in development as part of a cross-sectional study, interference errors

TABLE 1
*Distribution of Possessives used by Marta. Samples are Bi-weekly.*

| Sample | 's Supplied | 's Omitted | of Supplied | of Omitted | de |
|---|---|---|---|---|---|
| 1 | | | | | 7 |
| 2 | | 3 | | | 8 |
| 3 | | 1 | | | 1 |
| 4 | | 1 | | | |
| 5 | | 5 | | | |
| 6 | | 7 | 3 | | |
| 7 | | 2 | 6 | | 1 |
| 8 | 2 | 1 | | | |
| 9 | 5 | 1 | | | |
| 10 | 7 | | | | |
| 11 | 9 | | | | |
| 12 | 8 | 1 | 1 | | |
| 13 | 7 | | 1 | | |
| 14 | 5 | | 1 | | 1 |
| 15 | 5 | 1 | | | |

Source: Cancino (Note 1).

might not have been found. In addition, errors do not seem to disappear abruptly. On the contrary, use of the correct forms appears to be quite variable, and development is gradual.

The pattern of gradual acquisition can be illustrated graphically. Figure 1 plots curves for several grammatical forms acquired by Uguisu, a five-year-old Japanese girl learning English in a natural setting, who was observed over a fifteen-month period (Hakuta, 1976). The graph plots over time the percentage of instances when a given form was supplied in obligatory contexts. In terms of errors, each curve represents the complement of errors of omission for a given morpheme. It is clear in this case that for each linguistic item errors disappear slowly and gradually. This pattern, which is characteristic of first-language acquisition (Brown, 1973), may very well hold for second-language learners' acquisition of any sort of linguistic item (Cazden, Cancino, Rosansky, & Schumann, 1975; Hakuta, 1975). Such variability in the usage of linquistic forms, even for a single learner at a given point in development, makes it difficult, if not impossible, to write grammars for corpora of utterances.

The above studies examined errors in production, but it is possible that learners might simply avoid certain linguistic structures on which they would be likely to make errors. Perhaps learners avoid particular structures due to differences between their native language and the target language. Error analysis cannot detect this type of language transfer. Schachter (1974) has provided some convincing evidence of such avoidance by looking at relative-clause construction in the English compositions of adult learners. Using contrastive analysis, Schachter predicted positive transfer of such construction interference for one group and negative transfer for the other. Surprisingly, the negative-transfer group made fewer errors than the positive-transfer group, which suggests that there was no interference. This counter-intuitive result, however, can be accounted for by the simple fact that the group for which

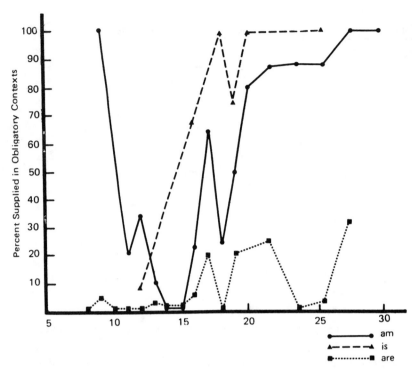

**FIGURE 1**
*Acquisition curves for the three allomorphs of* be (am, is, are) *as the auxiliary to the verb* gonna *(e.g., I'm gonna eat this one) in Uguisu, plotted as percentage supplied in obligatory contexts over time. Each sample represents a two-week interval.*
Source: Hakuta, 1975

positive transfer was predicted produced twice as many relative-clause constructions as the group for which negative transfer was predicted. The negative-transfer group made fewer errors because they were avoiding such constructions, a fact that the traditional method of error analysis would have obscured. Recently, Kleinmann (1976) found that groups of adult Arabic and Spanish speakers learning English avoided producing a variety of constructions (passives, infinitival complements, direct-object pronouns, and present progressives) for which contrastive analysis predicted difficulties. Hakuta (1976) compared relative-clause constructions in the spontaneous speech of his subject, Uguisu, with those of Cancino's subject, Marta, and found that, as predicted by contrastive analysis, Marta produced more relative clauses. Other writers have also suggested that avoidance may account for some of their data at both the syntactic (Swain, Note 2) and the lexical levels (Tarone, Frauenfelder, & Selinker, 1976).

Contrastive analysis was, in effect, consumed by error analysis because the evidence of interference errors it used failed to account for the learner's non-interference errors. Along similar lines, error analysis does not appear to provide a methodology with adequate sensitivity to detect phenomena such as structural avoidance. With increasing sophistication in the methods available to infer knowledge from performance, error analysis is currently in the process of being incorporated within an attempt to describe the learner's overall performance, not necessarily restricting the scope of analysis to errors alone. This line of work, *performance analysis* (Svartvik, 1973), once again bears the marks of work in first-language acquisition.

## Performance Analysis

At the time that researchers of second-language acquisition were focusing on error analysis, first-language-acquisition researchers were beginning to provide rather elegant descriptions of the development of linguistic structures in children. Two studies in particular have had a profound influence in shaping the direction of second-language acquisition research: Klima and Bellugi's (1966) study on the acquisition of negation and Brown's (1973) study on the acquisition order of grammatical morphemes. Both studies based their analyses of performance on longitudinal spontaneous-speech samples from three children—Adam, Eve, and Sarah—learning English as their first language. The studies were important in that they were longitudinal, and documented regularities across children in the acquisition of grammatical morphemes and negation. For the first-language-acquisition researcher these findings were appealing because they hinted at universal aspects in first-language-acquisition processes. For the second-language-acquisition researcher the studies provided norms against which to compare the acquisition of the same structures in second-language learners of English. The research also provided the motivation and methodology to search for universal orders of acquisitions of structures across second-language learners. This method was a novel way of testing for the role of language transfer.

Within the framework of performance analysis there has been considerable research on the acquisition of negation and grammatical morphemes in second-language learners of English. We restrict our review to these two types of structures. Less studied, but equally interesting for analysis are *prefabricated utterances*, utterances that are learned as wholes without knowledge of internal structure but that have high functional value in communications. We will end our discussion of performance analysis with a consideration of such prefabricated utterances.

### Negation

Klima and Bellugi (1966) described characteristics of three stages in the development of English negation among first-language learners. In Stage I children's negation consists of a negative particle—generally, "no"—placed outside the sentence nucleus to produce such utterances as "No Mommy go" and "no eat." In Stage II the negative element moves into the sentence nucleus and takes forms such as "can't," "not," and "don't" (as in "Mommy don't like tapioca"). However, these negative elements are not full auxiliary verbs, since they lack inflection and flexibility. In Stage III the full form with inflection for tense and number is used.

Among studies of the development of negation in second-language learners, Milon's (1974) report on Ken, a five-year-old Japanese boy learning English in Hawaii, has attracted considerable attention in the literature. Milon claimed that it was possible to apply Klima and Bellugi's (1966) stages for the development of negation in first-language learners in order to summarize Ken's development. He therefore concluded that Ken acquired the English negation system in the same way as first-language learners. Milon's application of Klima and Bellugi's stages to his data involved dividing the protocols into three periods roughly corresponding to the first-language stages. In his tables he reports the percentage of utterances within each of these periods that are accountable by the rules for each of the first-language stages.

In order for Milon's claim to be justified, there must be a majority of utterances within each of Ken's periods to be accounted for by the rules of the corresponding first-language stage. Even a cursory examination of Milon's published tables, however, indicates that this is not the case. The Stage I rule, which involves placing the negative particle outside the sentence nucleus, accounts for well over half the utterances not only for Ken's period I, but also for periods II and III as well. In addition, only 9 percent of the utterances within Ken's Stage III are accounted for by Klima and Bellugi's Stage III rules.

Cazden et al. (1975) conducted a rigorous descriptive study of negation in the acquisition of English by six native speakers of Spanish: two adults, two adolescents, and two children. For each sample they calculated the proportion of occurrence for each of four utterance types and their relative frequency over time. Each of these utterances "peaked" in usage at a certain point in acquisition. Although some subjects never attained the more advanced forms, the order in which the forms emerged was the same for all subjects. In the first form of negation to appear, "no" preceded the verb, such as in "Carolina no go to play." Notice that this form corresponds to Klima and Bellugi's Stage II rule in that the negative element is internal to the sentence (*no + verb*). There was no evidence that these second-language learners went through anything resembling Klima and Bellugi's Stage I, where the negative element is external to the sentence nucleus. The next acquired form was characterized by utterances in which "don't" preceded the verb, such as "He don't like it." The third form, *aux-neg*, included all negative auxiliaries, such as "can't" and "won't," but not the inflected forms of "don't." The final form, which Cazden and colleagues called *analyzed don't*, was essentially the full adult system. For illustrative purposes we include the graph of one of their subjects, Marta, in Figure 2.

Cazden et al. (1975) argue on the basis of their data that the *no + verb* forms represent "the Spanish speakers' first hypothesis . . . that negation in English is like negation in Spanish, hence the learners place *no* in front of the verb" (p. 32). This finding would easily have been obscured had the researchers simply classified learners' utterances according to Klima and Bellugi's stages, since *no + verb*, *don't + verb*, and *aux-neg* all correspond to their Stage II, and *analyzed don't* occurs in Stage III.

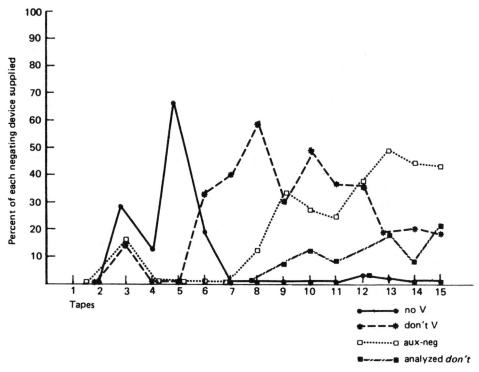

**FIGURE 2**
*Development of negation in Marta showing proportion of each negating device to total negatives in each sample.*
Source: Cazden et al., 1975.

This might have forced the conclusion that there was no transfer from Spanish. Other studies have also noted *no + verb* utterances in Spanish speakers learning English (Adams, 1974; Butterworth, 1972; Wong-Fillmore, 1976).

There is an alternative explanation for the *no + verb* construction other than as the product of transfer from Spanish. Klima and Bellugi (1966), Bloom (1970), and Lord (1974) have all reported such forms in the speech of first-language learners. Perhaps it is not necessary to invoke transfer from Spanish to explain these utterances. Data from Gillis and Weber's (1976) two Japanese children and from Uguisu (Hakuta, 1976), however, suggest the transfer interpretation to be the correct one. None of the three children produced the *no + verb* construction, thus making this form likely to be unique to speakers of Spanish. Milon (1974) reports the construction of his Japanese subject, Ken, but there is a simple explanation: Ken was exposed to Hawaiian Creole English, which has this form of negation.

Where does this leave us with respect to the development of negation? We now feel confident that *no + verb*, due to language transfer, is a common developmental step in Spanish speakers learning English. It is worth emphasizing once again that if Cazden et al. (1975) had simply tried to categorize their data into Klima and Bellugi's stages for first-language learners, this finding would not have been revealed. Their conclusion would have been that the learners went through Klima and Bellugi's Stages II and III. Indeed, this conclusion appears to be consistent with all the studies reported above, but it is too general to be of any value. All it tells us is that at first the auxiliary verb (e.g., "don't," "isn't") is unmarked for person or tense, and later that it becomes fully marked. There is no evidence for Stage I, which is theoretically the most interesting stage.

Before closing this section on negation, it should be pointed out that the universality of Klima and Bellugi's stages has been questioned even in first-language learners. Bloom (1970) and Lord (1974), for example, failed to find evidence for Stage I in their subjects. It is easy to overlook the fact that research in first-language acquisition is also still in its infancy. Owing to the tentative nature of the first-language findings, the second-language researcher needs to approach the task of comparing the two processes with extreme caution.

*Grammatical Morphemes*

With the exception of work by Cazden et al. (1975) the first- and second-language studies mentioned above were distributional, but not in a rigorously quantitative sense. If we are to obtain more accurate descriptions of learner performance, quantitative studies are particularly important. Grammatical morphemes, which include the articles *(a, the)*, the copula and auxiliary *be*, and the noun and verb inflections, lend themselves to quantitative analyses. They afford a particular advantage to the researcher because of their high frequency, which is generally independent of the topic of discourse. Furthermore, contexts where they are obligatory (i.e., clearly required according to adult standards) are easily identifiable. For example, "two book" clearly requires the plural morpheme-*s*.

Brown (1973) analyzed fourteen morphemes in data collected longitudinally from three unacquainted native speakers, Adam, Eve, and Sarah. Defining acquisition as the point at which a given morpheme occurred in more than 90 percent of obligatory contexts for three consecutive samples, he found that they were acquired in a roughly invariant order. De Villiers and de Villiers (1973) substantiated this finding in a larger, cross-sectional first-language sample. When Brown (1973) analyzed these morphemes according to semantic complexity and transformational cumulative complexity, he found that both factors predicted the obtained order but that they could not be separated.

Since the findings on first-language learners were so dramatic and the method was easily applicable to second-language speech samples, a plethora of performance studies on second-language learners has been carried out in the last three years. Some have been longitudinal (Hakuta, 1974a, 1976; Gillis, 1975; Rosansky, 1976; Cancino, Note 1; Mulford, Note 3) and others cross-sectional (Bailey, Madden, & Krashen, 1974; Dulay & Burt, 1973, 1974a, 1974c; Larsen-Freeman, Note 4). Longitudinal second-language studies generally have determined the order of acquisition of grammatical morphemes according to Brown's 90 percent criterion described above. In the cross-sectional research the standard procedure is to rank-order the morphemes according to the performance of the entire group. The latter procedure, of course, assumes that all individuals in the sample exhibit the same acquisition order. After obtaining a rank order in either longitudinal or cross-sectional studies, a comparison can be made across learners with different native languages.

Dulay and Burt (1974a) compared the order of acquisition of eleven morphemes for a group of Chinese and Spanish children learning English. They found the order of acquisition to be nearly identical between the two groups, although it was quite different from that established for children learning English as a first language (Brown, 1973; de Villiers & de Villiers, 1973). This similarity in the orders is a striking result in light of the differences between Chinese and Spanish. For example, Chinese, unlike Spanish, has no linguistic marking equivalent to English articles, but both groups performed equally well in supplying these morphemes. A more astonishing result has been obtained from adults receiving formal instruction in English as a second language. The order obtained was again approximately the same as the order found by Dulay and Burt, despite the fact that these adults spoke various native languages (Bailey, Madden, & Krashen, 1974; Larsen-Freeman, Note 4).

Complicating the results in the above studies is the fact that the speech samples were not spontaneous but were elicited with a device called the Bilingual Syntax Measure )BSM) (Burt, Dulay, & Hernandez-Chavez, 1973). One BSM procedure involves asking the subject in the pretest to point to each object in a set of cartoon pictures with the request, "Show me the——." Perhaps the reason why articles are easy in this task is that they are modeled for the subjects. Thus, the test itself may have influenced the outcome. A pilot investigation by Porter (Note 5) of children learning English as their first language buttresses this idea. Porter administered the BSM with these children and found their order resembled the second-language-learner's order more than it did the order found by Brown!

Rosansky (1976) questioned whether results obtained from a cross-sectional study would correlate well with a longitudinally derived acquisition order. Using longitudinal data from Jorge, a native Spanish-speaking adolescent, she compared the order of acquisition of the morphemes (longitudinal) with the relative accuracy of the use of the morphemes at a given point in development (cross-sectional). Rosansky found that Jorge's longitudinal order did not correlate with his cross-sectional order, and thus she concluded that cross-sectional orders could not be assumed to be the same as longitudinal orders.

However, there are two problems with Rosansky's results. First, she was able to compare the order of only six morphemes, since Jorge did not attain the 90 percent criterion longitudinally for the other morphemes studied. Second, Jorge was supplying all six morphemes in well over 90 percent of their obligatory contexts by the time of the cross-sectional sample. Since grammatical morphemes in general tend to fluctuate within the range between 90 and 100 percent once they attain the 90 percent criterion, Rosansky's failure to find a correlation with the longitudinal order could have been the result of this random fluctuation.

If we compare the order of acquisition of grammatical morphemes for Rosansky's subject, Jorge, with the order obtained in the Dulay and Burt study, the Spearman rank-order correlation coefficient (rho) is +.91. Cancino (Note 1) found that the longitudinal order for Marta compared favorably with Jorge's (rho = +.88) and correlates highly with that of Dulay and Burt's subjects as well (rho = +.93). Another piece of evidence comes from Mulford (Note 3), who studied the longitudinal-acquisition order for Steinar, an Icelandic boy. The correlation coefficients of Steinar's order with the orders of Jorge, Marta, and Dulay and Burt's subjects respectively are +.90, +.85, and +.82. Thus it might seem that there exists a universal order for acquisition of these morphemes.

The existence of a universal order, however, is not supported by analyses of Uguisu's longitudinal order (Hakuta, 1974a, 1976). Resembling none of the above orders, Uguisu's development indicates some interference from Japanese which does not have articles and plurals. A comparison of Uguisu's order with those of two Japanese children studied longitudinally by Gillis (1975) reveals that the three children's orders all differ and that none of them correlates with Dulay and Burt's subjects' order either. One reason for this lack of similarity may be that Gillis (1975) only reports on the verb-related morphemes and excludes some morphemes such as articles and plurals. Nevertheless, if there indeed is a universal order, the results should not vary according to the particular items chosen for investigation.

We can probably conclude, though, that among all second-language learners of English there may be a tendency to acquire morphemes in a certain order, determined by factors such as their frequency of occurrence (Larsen-Freeman, 1976) and their perceptual salience or distinctiveness (Wagner-Gough & Hatch, 1976). For example, the progressive *-ing* may be acquired early because of its high salience and high frequency, while the regular third-person indicative *-s* (as in "she comes") with its low frequency and low salience is acquired relatively late.

Another factor influencing acquisition, semantic complexity of the morphemes (Brown, 1973), may vary depending on the learner's native language. For example, the English articles *a* and *the* ("a book" versus "the book"), require rather sophisticated semantic discriminations for their proper use (Brown, 1973; Maratsos, 1971). If a native language makes those contrasts, as Spanish and French do, the learner may already possess the semantic discriminations necessary for using English articles. On the other hand, a native speaker of Japanese or Chinese does not make those discriminations and must learn them in order to make the definite/indefinite contrast. That articles in English have the highest frequency of all grammatical morphemes and appear in a highly predictable position, before nouns, also affects their acquisition. Thus articles may appear early even in Japanese or Chinese learners but with confusions along the definite/indefinite dimension.

Although articles appeared early in her speech, Uguisu had great difficulty with the definite/indefinite contrast, as evidenced by many errors (Hakuta, 1976). Marta and Jorge, on the other hand, acquired articles early and had little difficulty with the definite/indefinite distinction. Their greatest problem appeared to be within the indefinite category, where they initially used *one* rather than *a*, reflecting transfer from the Spanish indefinite articles *un* or *una*. Frauenfelder (1974), who studied the acquisition of gender marking among English-speaking children in a French immersion program, found that although the children made many errors in gender on articles, they never confused the definite/indefinite contrast. That Dulay and Burt found their Chinese learners acquiring articles so early might be attributed to the scoring method: they did not differentiate between *a* and *the*. Finally Fathman (Note 6), who administered an oral-production task (SLOPE) to Korean- and Spanish-speaking children, found a generally similar ordering on various grammatical forms for these two groups. A close look at her data, however, shows a very large discrepancy in the children's performance on articles: the Korean children, whose language has no article equivalents, performed poorly.

Thus, we conceive the order of acquisition of English grammatical morphemes as resulting from an interplay of at least two factors. One factor, consisting of variables such as frequency and salience, seems to direct the order of acquisition toward a universal order. But a second factor, transfer from the native language, modulates the order so as to produce differences between learners of different language backgrounds.

## Routine Formulas and Prefabricated Utterances

Since grammatical rules operate on units or constituents within a sentence, it was only natural for researchers interested in grammatical structure to focus on those utterances that indicated the learner's knowledge of individual constituents. In so doing, they excluded from their analysis utterances that seemed to be routine formulas (such as "What's this?" and "I don't know") learned as wholes through imitation. Huang (1971) related a delightful anecdote about the use of such a routine formula. Paul, a Taiwanese boy, used his first English utterance, "Get out of here," as a formula in roughly appropriate situations for warding off unwanted company. Another example is one of Uguisu's first utterances, "Not in particular!" which was used for the purpose of turning down offers of food. Variants of routine formulas are prefabricated patterns (Hakuta, 1974b), sentences such as "This is ———," where nouns can be inserted into the slots. Most investigators have reported in passing the existence of either routines or prefabricated patterns (Adams, 1974; Butterworth, 1972; Cazden et al., 1975). These patterns have not received close attention, because the central focus of study has been on grammatical structure. This lack of emphasis on prefabricated forms was reinforced by the apparent failure of the process of imitation to account for language acquisition (Chomsky, 1959; Ervin-Tripp, 1964; but see Bloom, Hood, & Lightbown, 1974).

If language were to be viewed from the perspective of communication, however, prefabricated utterances take on an added theoretical significance (Hakuta, 1976).

Huang (1971) found a considerable amount of prefabricated utterances in Paul's speech. This led him to postulate imitation as an important process, although it was considered to be less important than, and independent of, the process of rule-formation. Uguisu's speech, particularly in the early stages, also contained many prefabricated patterns (Hakuta, 1974b). Such patterns may have value in sustaining second-language learners' motivation by enabling them early on to express a variety of meanings. Since the "breakdown" of these forms is gradual and similar to the acquisition of grammatical rules, the use of prefabricated patterns may motivate the learner to search for internal structure (Hakuta, 1976).

In a recent dissertation on English acquisition by five Spanish-speaking children, Wong-Fillmore (1976) found that over half of the children's utterances contained prefabricated forms. She argued that through the gradual analysis of such forms, later linguistic structure developed: "All of the constituents of the formula become freed from the original construction, [and] what the learner has left is an abstract structure consisting of a pattern or rule by which he can construct like utterances" (p. 645). For example, Wong-Fillmore's subject Nora learned the question, "How do you do dese?" early in development and used only this form. During the next period she attached a noun or prepositional phrase to this form, and created such questions as "How do you do dese flower power?" and "How do you do dese in English?" Later she learned to slot other verbs into the pattern "How do you——?" and produced such forms as "How do you like to be a cookie cutter?" Nora then began alternating "How do you ——" with "How did you ——." In the last period of observation, she was constructing utterances like "How you make it?" and "How will take and paste?" Although Fillmore's examples are provocative, the principles used by the learner to analyze the prefabricated forms need to be specified; the traditional problem of the emergence of syntax remains to be solved.

## Discourse Analysis

The focus of research in both first- and second-language acquisition has shifted only recently to language in the social context. It would be somewhat unfair, however, to claim that earlier researchers did not pay attention to the role of discourse in the language acquisition. Brown (1968), for example, succinctly stated:

> It may be as difficult to derive a grammar from unconnected sentences as it would be to derive the invariance of quantity and number from the simple look of liquids in containers and objects in space. The changes produced by pouring back and forth, by gathering together and spreading apart are the data that most strongly suggest the conservation of quantity and number. The changes produced in sentences as they move between persons in discourse may be the richest data for the discovery of grammar. (p. 288)

Current work on discourse analysis can be roughly divided into two approaches (de Villiers & de Villiers, in press). Researchers employing the first approach (Garvey, 1975; Keenan, 1975) investigate rules of discourse, such as turn taking in dialogue.

Discourse rules are considered to be another aspect of language that the child must master more or less independently of syntax. The second approach (Antinucci & Parisi, 1975; Bates, 1976) assumes fundamentally that all language is pragmatic, obeying "rules governing the use of language in context" (Bates, 1976, p. 420). Researchers operating in this vein have investigated the emergence of various pragmatic functions, such as declaratives and imperatives, in very young children. They claim that syntax and semantics can ultimately be seen as derivatives of pragmatics, although it is difficult at this point to envision the specific process of derivation.

In the case of the second-language learner, we certainly would not expect to be able to study the emergence of the various pragmatic functions, since they are by definition universal and, presumably, acquired at a very early age. An interesting approach, however, would be to analyze a given pragmatic function over time. Tracing the development of the linguistic forms that the learner uses for the expression of a function might well reveal orderly and lawful patterns. In addition, such an analysis might reveal interesting differences across native speakers whose languages differ in the linguistic forms chosen for the same pragmatic act. In a sense, this approach would be a contrastive analysis of the way different languages map pragmatic functions onto linguistic forms. We believe this would be an extremely fruitful line of investigation, but it has not been pursued. What is sorely lacking before any such inquiry is an explicitly spelled out theory of pragmatics (Fraser, Note 7). The few studies on discourse reported in the literature have made only preliminary attempts at outlining the structure of discourse and the mechanisms underlying its regulation.

Hatch (1978) found that Huang's (1971) subject Paul initiated discourse by first identifying the topic, waiting for the other person to attend or speak, and then making some further comment. Repetition of the other speaker's previous utterance (Hatch, 1978; Keller-Cohen, 1978) has received some attention. We suspect that this is the major way in which prefabricated forms (Hakuta, 1974b; Wong-Fillmore, 1976) enter the learner's speech repertoire. A variant on the process of repetition is incorporation (Wagner-Gough, 1975; Wagner-Gough & Hatch, 1976), as illustrated in the following dialogue with Homer, an Iranian child:

Adult:    Where are you going?
Homer:   Where are you going is house.
(Wagner-Gouch & Hatch, 1976, p. 304)

Hatch (1978) has noted that a topic is broken into parts dictated by the constraints of conversation. The following example taken from a Japanese child, Takahiro, shows the learner taking apart and reassembling these various parts in the course of dialogue (Hatch, 1978).

Takahiro:   this
            broken

| Adult: | broken |
| Takahiro: | broken |
| | This /iz/ broken. |
| | broken |
| Adult: | Upside down. |
| Takahiro: | upside down |
| | this broken |
| | upside down |
| | broken |

Based on such examples, Hatch speculates that "one learns how to do conversation, one learns how to interact verbally, and out of this interaction syntactic structures are developed." This is essentially the same argument made by Wong-Fillmore (1976) for the emergence of syntax, and it is subject to the same criticism: the ultimate question of how exactly this happens has not been addressed. Furthermore, accounting for interference errors remains problematic, since such errors are aspects of the internal organization of language.

Implicit in studies of discourse is the importance of input. Unfortunately, rigorous empirical studies of the characteristics of input to the learner are nowhere to be seen in the second-language literature. The pedagogical implications of such studies would be powerful, since classroom instruction is essentially the manipulation of input variables. Although first-language-learning research has greatly influenced second-language research, the numerous studies on mother-to-child speech in first-language acquisition (DePaulo & Bonvillian, in press; Snow & Ferguson, in press) have not generated similar studies in second-language acquisition. In an exploratory second-language-learning study, Hatch, Shapira, and Wagner-Gough (Note 8) reinforce the need for future input studies. Anecdotally comparing the input for children with that for adults, they found that the speech addressed to children by native speakers resembled mother-to-child speech reported in the first-language literature: it was simple, short, grammatical, and restricted to here-and-now topics. The speech to adults, on the other hand, possessed many of the characteristics of "foreigner talk": the omission of inflections, an abundance of pauses, and many complex sentence forms (Ferguson, 1977). Furthermore, the topic of conversation often referred to something neither immediate nor present. Whatever the determining sociolinguistic factors, these observations by Hatch and his coworkers should encourage further research in this area. Such investigations may ultimately help explain the difficulty that adults have in acquiring a second language.

## The Future

Each of the four trends covered in this paper can be seen as successive attempts by researchers to create an adequate representation of the second-language-acquisition process. We began by describing contrastive analysis, which required only a comparison of the linguistic structures of the two languages. We end with the most recent trend, discourse analysis, in which the learner's status as a social being occupies center stage. Although it may take years of hard work before we develop a rigorous and sophisticated methodology for discourse analysis, the rewards will be great. For the results would create a solid link between the observed acquisition of the linguistic structures of the second language and the yet-to-be-determined variables involved in discourse.

Schumann (1975, 1976) has recently argued that there is a correlation between social factors and the degree to which one acquires a second language. These social variables rest at the heart of second-language acquisition; they determine the circumstances requiring people to acquire a second language. Along similar lines, Gardner and his colleagues (Gardner & Lambert, 1972; Gardner, 1973) have extensively explored the relationships of attitudes and motivation to degree of proficiency in a second language. While it may be difficult to see a direct relationship between these social factors and their supposed effects on the second-language-acquisition process, it is not difficult to imagine social factors influencing the types of discourse in which learners engage. This relationship is rigorously definable. Thus, we see discourse analysis as an empirical bridge to our next potential level of analysis, which might be called *sociolinguistic analysis*. Analysis at this level, we believe, would give greater acknowledgment to the complexity of the second-language-acquisition process.

## Notes

1. Cancino, H. *Grammatical morphemes in second language acquisition—Marta.* Unpublished manuscript, 1976. (Available from Harvard University, Graduate School of Education, Cambridge, Mass.).
2. Swain, M. *Changes in error: Random or systematic?* Paper presented at the Fourth International Congress of Applied Linguistics, Stuttgart, August 1975.
3. Mulford, R. Personal Communication, December 15, 1976.
4. Larsen-Freeman. D. *The acquisition of grammatical morphemes by adult ESL students.* Paper presented at the Ninth Annual TESOL Convention, Los Angeles, April 1975.
5. Porter, J. *A cross-sectional study of morpheme acquisition in first language learners.* Unpublished manuscript, 1975. (Available from Department of Psychology and Social Relations, Harvard University, Cambridge, Mass.).
6. Fathman, A. *Language background, age, and the order of English structures.* Paper presented at the Ninth Annual TESOL Convention, Los Angeles, April 1975.
7. Fraser, E. *On requesting: An Essay in pragmatics.* Book in preparation, 1977.
8. Hatch, E., Shapira, R., & Gough, J. *Foreigner-talk discourse.* Unpublished paper, 1975. (Available from English Department, University of California at Los Angeles, Los Angeles, Calif.).

## References

Adams, M. *Second language acquisition in children: A study in experimental methods: Observations of spontaneous speech and controlled production tests.* Unpublished master's thesis, University of California at Los Angeles, 1974.

Alatis, J. *Nineteenth annual round table meeting on linguistics and language studies: Contrastive linguistics and its pedagogical implications.* Washington, D.C.: Georgetown University Press, 1968.

Antinucci, F., & Parisi, D. Early semantic development in child language. In E. H. Lenneberg & E. Lenneberg (Eds.), *Foundations of language development: A multidisciplinary approach* (Vol. 1). New York: Academic Press, 1975.

Bailey, N., Madden, C., & Krashen, S. Is there a "natural sequence" in adult second language learning? *Language Learning*, 1974, **24**, 233–243.

Bates, E. Pragmatics and sociolinguistics in child language. In D. Morehead & A. Morehead (Eds.), *Normal and deficient child language.* Baltimore, Md.: University Park Press, 1976.

Bloom, L. *Language development: Form and function in emerging grammars.* Cambridge, Mass.: M.I.T. Press, 1970.

Bloom, L., Hood, L., & Lightbown, P. Imitation in language development: If, when and why? *Cognitive Psychology,* 1974, **6**, 380–420.

Brown, R. The development of Wh questions in child speech. *Journal of Verbal Learning and Verbal Behavior,* 1968, **7**, 279–290.

Brown, R. *A first language: The early stages.* Cambridge, Mass.: Harvard University Press, 1973.

Brown, R., & Bellugi, U. Three processes in the acquisition of syntax. *Harvard Educational Review,* 1964, **34**, 133–151. (a)

Brown, R., & Bellugi, U. The acquisition of language. *Monographs of the Society for Research in Child Development,* 1964, **29** (No. 1). (b)

Burt, M. K., Dulay, H. C., & Hernandez-Chavez, E. *Bilingual syntax measure.* New York: Harcourt Brace Jovanovich, 1973.

Butterworth, G. *A Spanish-speaking adolescent's acquisition of English syntax.* Unpublished master's thesis, University of California at Los Angeles, 1972.

Cazden, C., Cancino, H., Rosansky, E., & Schumann, J. *Second language acquisition sequences in children, adolescents, and adults.* Cambridge, Mass.: Harvard University, Graduate School of Education, 1975. (ERIC Document Reproduction Service No. ED 123 873).

Chomsky, N. *Syntactic structures.* The Hague: Mouton, 1957.

Chomsky, N. A review of *Verbal Behavior* by B. F. Skinner. *Language,* 1959, **35**, 26–59.

Cohen, A. D. *A sociolinguistic approach to bilingual education: Experiments in the American Southwest.* Rowley, Mass.: Newbury House, 1975.

Corder, S. P. The significance of learners' errors. *International Review of Applied Linguistics,* 1967, 5, 161–170.

Corder, S. P. Idiosyncratic dialects and error analysis. *International Review of Applied Linguistics,* 1971, **9**, 147–160.

Corder, S. P. Error analysis, interlanguage, and second language acquisition. *Language Teaching and Linguistics,* 1975, **14**, 201–218.

DePaulo, B., & Bonvillian, J. The effect on language development of the special characterization of speech addressed to children. *Journal of Psycholinguistic Research,* in press.

de Villiers, J., & de Villiers, P. A cross-sectional study of the acquisition of grammatical morphemes in child speech. *Journal of Psycholinguistic Research,* 1973, **2**, 267–278.

de Villiers, J., & deVilliers, P. Syntax and semantics in the first two years: The output of form and function and the form and function of the input. In L. L. Lloyd & F. Minifie (Eds.), *Communicative & cognitive abilities: Early behavioral Assessment* (NICHD Mental Retardation Research Series). Baltimore: University Park Press, 1978.

Dulay, H., & Burt, M. Goofing: An indicator of children's second language learning strategies. *Language Learning,* 1972, **22**, 235–252.

Dulay, H., & Burt, M. Should we teach children syntax? *Language Learning,* 1973, **23**, 245–258.

Dulay, H., & Burt, M. Natural sequences in child second language acquisition. *Language Learning,* 1974, **24**, 37–53. (a)

Dulay, H., & Burt, M. Errors and strategies in child second language acquisition. *TESOL Quarterly,* 1974, **8**, 129–136. (b)

Dulay, H., & Burt, M. A new perspective on the creative construction process in child second language acquisition. *Language Learning,* 1974, **24**, 253–278. (c)

Duskova, L. On sources of errors in foreign languages. *International Review of Applied Linguistics,* 1969, **7**, 11–36.

Ervin-Tripp, S. Imitation and structural change in children's language. In E. Lenneberg (Ed.), *New directions in the study of language.* Cambridge, Mass.: M.I.T. Press, 1964.

Ferguson, C. A. Toward a characterization of English foreigner talk. In C. E. Snow & C. A. Ferguson (Eds.), *Talking to children: Language input and acquisition.* Cambridge, Eng.: Cambridge University Press, 1977.

Frauenfelder, U. *The acquisition of French gender in Toronto French immersion school children.* Unpublished senior honors thesis, University of Washington, 1974.

Fries, C. *Teaching and learning English as a foreign language.* Ann Arbor: University of Michigan Press, 1972. (Originally published, 1945)

Gardner, R. C. Attitudes and motivation: Their role in second language acquisition. In J. Oller & J. Richards, *Focus on the learner: Pragmatic perspectives for the language teacher.* Rowley, Mass.: Newbury House, 1973.

Gardner, R. C., & Lambert, W. *Attitudes and motivation in second language learning.* Rowley, Mass.: Newbury House, 1972.

Garvey, C. Requests and responses in children's speech. *Journal of Child Language,* 1975, **2**, 41–63.

Gillis, M. *The acquisition of the English verbal system by two Japanese children in a natural setting,* Unpublished master's thesis, McGill University, 1975.

Gillis, M., & Weber, R. The emergence of sentence modalities in the English of Japanese-speaking children. *Language Learning,* 1976, **26**, 77–94.

Hakuta, K. A preliminary report on the development of grammatical morphemes in a Japanese girl learning English as a second language. *Working Papers on Bilingualism,* 1974, **3**, 18–43. (a)

Hakuta, K. Prefabricated patterns and the emergence of structure in second language acquisition: *Language Learning,* 1974, **24**, 287–297. (b)

Hakuta, K. Learning to speak a second language: What exactly does the child learn? In D. P. Dato (Ed.), *Developmental psycholinguistics: Theory and application.* Washington, D.C.: Georgetown University Press, 1975.

Hakuta, K. Becoming bilingual: A case study of a Japanese child learning English. *Language Learning,* 1976, **26**, 321–351.

Hatch, E. Discourse analysis. In E. Hatch (Ed.), *Studies in second language acquisition: A book of readings.* Rowley, Mass.: Newbury House, 1978.

Huang, J. *A Chinese child's acquisition of English syntax.* Unpublished master's thesis, University of California at Los Angeles, 1971.

Jain, M. Error analysis: Source, cause and significance. In J. Richards (Ed.), *Error analysis: Perspectives on second language acquisition.* London: Longman, 1974.

James, C. Linguistic measures for error gravity. *AVLA Journal,* 1974, **12**, 3–9.

Keenan, E. Conversational competence in children. *Journal of Child Language,* 1975, **2**, 163–183.

Keller-Cohen, D. Repetition in the non-native discourse: Its relation to text unification and conversational structure. In O. Freedle (Ed.), *Discourse processing: A multidisciplinary approach.* Hillsdale, N.J.: Ablex Publishing Co., 1978.

Kleinmann, H. *Avoidance behavior in adult second language acquisition.* Unpublished doctoral dissertation. University of Pittsburgh, 1976.

Klima, E., & Bellugi, U. Syntactic regularities in the speech of children. In J. Lyons & R. Wales (Eds.), *Psycholinguistic papers.* Edinburgh: Edinburgh University Press, 1966.

Krashen, S., Madden, C., & Bailey, N. Theoretical aspects of grammatical sequencing. In M. Burt & H. Dulay (Eds.), *New directions in second language learning, teaching and bilingual education.* Washington, D.C.: TESOL, 1975.

Lado, R. *Linguistics across cultures.* Ann Arbor, Mich.: University of Michigan Press, 1957.

Larsen-Freeman, D. An explanation for the morpheme acquisition order of second language learners. *Language Learning,* 1976, **26**, 125–134.

Lord, C. Variations in the acquisition of negation. *Papers and Reports on Child Language Development,* 1974, **8**, 78–86.

Maratsos, M. *The use of definite and indefinite reference in young children.* Unpublished doctoral dissertation, Harvard University, 1971.

McLaughlin, B. Second-language learning in children. *Psychological Bulletin,* 1977, **84,** 438–459.

Milon, J. The development of negation in English by a second language learner. *TESOL Quarterly,* 1974, **8,** 137–143.

Nemser, W. Approximative systems of foreign language learners. *International Review of Applied Linguistics,* 1971, **9,** 115–123.

Nickel, G. Problems of learners' difficulties in foreign language acquisition. *International Review of Applied Linguistics,* 1971, **9,** 219–227.

Olivier, D. *Stochastic grammars and language acquisition devices.* Unpublished doctoral dissertation, Harvard University, 1968.

Oller, J., & Richards, J. (Eds.). *Focus on the learner: Pragmatic perspectives for the language teacher.* Rowley, Mass.: Newbury House, 1973.

Politzer, R., & Ramirez, A. An error analysis of the spoken English of Mexican-American pupils in a bilingual school and a monolingual school. *Language Learning,* 1973, **23,** 39–61.

Richards, J. A non-contrastive approach to error analysis. In J. Oller & J. Richards (Eds.). *Focus on the learner: Pragmatic perspectives for the language teacher.* Rowley, Mass.: Newbury House, 1973.

Rivers, W. *The psychologist and the foreign language teacher.* Chicago: University of Chicago Press, 1964.

Rosansky, E. *Second language acquisition research: A question of methods.* Unpublished doctoral dissertation, Harvard University, Graduate School of Education, 1976.

Schachter, J. An error in error analysis. *Language Learning,* 1974, **24,** 205–214.

Schumann, J. Affective factors and the problem of age in second language acquisition. *Language Learning,* 1975, **25,** 209–235.

Schumann, J. Social distance as a factor in second language acquisition. *Language Learning,* 1976, **26,** 135–143.

Schumann, J., & Stenson, N. (Eds.). *New frontiers in second language learning.* Rowley, Mass.: Newbury House, 1975.

Selinker, L. Interlanguage. *International Review of Applied Linguistics,* 1972, **10,** 219–231.

Selinker, L., Swain, M., & Dumas, G. The interlanguage hypothesis extended to children. *Language Learning,* 1975, **25,** 139–152.

Snow, C. E., & Ferguson, C. A. (Eds.). *Talking to children: Language input and acquisition.* Cambridge, Eng.: Cambridge University Press, 1977.

Stockwell, R., Bowen, J., & Martin, J. *The grammatical structures of English and Spanish.* Chicago: University of Chicago Press, 1965.

Svartvik, J. *Errata: Papers in error analysis.* Lund, Sweden: Gleerup, 1973.

Swain, M. French immersion programs across Canada. *Canadian Modern Language Review,* 1974, **31,** 117–130.

Tarone, E. Some influences on interlanguage phonology. *Working Papers on Bilingualism,* 1976, **8,** 87–111.

Tarone, E., Frauenfelder, U., & Selinker, L., Systematicity/variability and stability/instability in interlanguage systems: More data from Toronto French immersion. In H. Brown (Ed.), *Papers in second language acquisition.* Ann Arbor, Mich.: *Language Learning,* 1976.

Taylor, B. The use of overgeneralization and transfer strategies by elementary and intermediate univeristy students learning ESL. In M. Burt & H. Dulay (Eds.), *New directions in second language learning, teaching and bilingual education.* Washington, D.C.: TESOL, 1975.

Wagner-Gough, J. Comparative studies in second language learning. *CAL-ERIC/CLL Series on Languages and Linguistics,* 26. Arlington, Va.: Center for Applied Linguistics, 1975.

Wagner-Gough, J., & Hatch, E. The importance of input data in second language acquisition studies. *Language Learning,* 1976, **25,** 297–308.

Wardhaugh, R. The contrastive analysis hypothesis. *TESOL Quarterly,* 1970, **4,** 123–130.

Whitehurst, G., Ironsmith, E., & Goldfein, M. Selective imitation of the passive construction through modelling. *Journal of Experimental Child Psychology,* 1974, **17,** 288–302.

Williams, L. *Speech perception and production as a function of exposure to a second language.* Unpublished doctoral dissertation, Harvard University, 1974.

Wong-Fillmore, L. *The second time around: Cognitive and social strategies in second language acquisition.* Unpublished doctoral dissertation, Stanford University, 1976.

# Essay Review

## Toward a Realistic Theory of Language Acquisition

JAMES PAUL GEE
*University of Southern California*

LANGUAGE LEARNABILITY AND LANGUAGE DEVELOPMENT
by Steven Pinker.
*Cambridge: Harvard University Press, 1984. 435 pp.*

Roger Brown, one of the founders of the modern study of child language, refers to Steven Pinker's *Language Learnability and Language Development* as "a landmark of psychological science." Though this remark undoubtedly partakes of some typical dust-jacket hyperbole, there is a sense in which Pinker is in at the beginning of something new. While studies of child language have been for the most part descriptions of what children do, Pinker proposes a theory of language acquisition that explicitly accounts for how children acquire language. That is, he makes a distinction between the study of child language and the study of language acquisition. Although one could argue with almost every proposal Pinker makes, the importance of his book lies not in the degree to which it is right or wrong but in the task he has begun.

Pinker's book is one that anyone interested in child language development ought to know about, though perhaps only a few need read it. Learnability theory represents a new discipline that, if successful, will change the character of the field of child language. It will do this in much the way that Chomsky's work changed the area of language study, even for those who knew little of or disagreed with it, by giving linguistics a formal foundation and by setting new goals and questions for the field. Learnability is in that unique stage of a discipline where anyone could easily read its entire literature, one that generative grammar and the modern study of child language were in not all that long ago. This stage will not last long if "learnability" works, in the sense of giving to the area of language acquisition a new formal foundation and a new set of goals and questions.

While Pinker's book is much less technical than the other major length study in learnability (Wexler & Culicover, 1980), it still requires a fair bit of sophistication in linguistics. Those seriously interested will find it one of the best places to start; others

*Harvard Educational Review* Vol. 56 No. 1 February 1986, 52–68

may want to wait for the more accessible treatments that will undoubtedly follow should learnability theory fulfill its promise.[1] In this review I will concentrate on the historical and intellectual developments leading to the birth of learnability theory. In turn, I hope to place Pinker's book in part of its historical and logical context and then discuss some of its leading claims in terms of this context.

## Chomsky's Contribution to Language Acquisition

If Chomsky gave rise to a revolution in linguistics, it was because he made "the logical problem of language acquisition" the key problem in linguistic theory (Chomsky, 1965). He insisted that linguistic theory had to go beyond "descriptive adequacy." It is important, therefore, to recognize the limitations of it. For Chomsky, descriptive adequacy meant that linguistic theory could supply a descriptively correct grammar for every natural language, that is, a grammar that correctly describes the native speaker's intuitions about the linguistic properties of the sentences of their language. The problem is that many different but equally good descriptions are available for each language. To take an example that we will return to later, consider the well-known English Dative Alternation. With many different verbs, such as *give, send, tell, bring,* and others that mean roughly "to transfer something," one can use either of two orderings of the direct object and the indirect object. One can order the direct object (the thing transferred) before the indirect object (the person receiving the object) as in 1a, or one can use the reverse order, placing the person receiving the transferred entity first, as in 1b. Thus, there are two nearly synonymous ways to use these verbs.

1a. Mary told the magic words [entity transferred] to John [recipient].
1b. Mary told John [recipient] the magic words [entity transferred].

Somewhat paradoxically, however, other verbs that also appear to mean "transfer" will not alternate this way, for instance *donate* or *say.*

2a. Mary said the magic words to John.
2b. *Mary said John the magic words.[2]

There are any number of ways to formally describe these facts. One is the classic transformational approach. We set up a deep or underlying structure for the basic, "unmarked," normal sentence type, example 2a in this case. This underlying structure is exemplified in 3a by a "phrase structure tree," which is simply a way to formally represent the syntactic structure of a sentence. This tree is "generated" by a set of phrase structure rules together with a lexicon (dictionary) as in 3b. Phrase structure rules are formal rules that stipulate the structure of possible sentences, or, in other words, parse a sentence (the sort of thing one did in grammar school on the blackboard). For instance, the first rule in 3b says that a sentence in English is made up of a noun phrase (NP)(its subject) and a very phrase (VP)(its predicate). This VP is in turn made up of a verb followed optionally by an object and a prepositional phrase (PP)(for example, "Give the book to the boy"), while an NP can be made up of a

noun optionally preceded by an article (ART) and adjective (ADJ) and optionally
followed by a prepositional phrase.

3.a

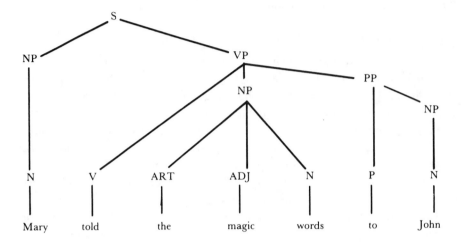

3b.

S   → NP VP
VP  → V (NP) (PP)
NP  → (ART) (ADJ) N (PP)
PP  → P NP

LEXICON: *tell* =

| | Verb |
|---|---|
| | Must be followed by an NP (Direct Object) and can optionally also be followed by a PP headed by *to* |
| | Pronunciation: /tɛl/ |
| | Meaning: "tell" |

*to* = Preposition

We then set up a transformational rule, known as the Dative Transformation, that
will change the tree in 3a into an appropriate tree for "Mary told John the magic
words" (see 3c). What we are doing, in basic terms, is stipulating that the order
represented in 3a, "Mary told the magic words to John," is the basic one, and that
the language contains a general rule that stipulates that this basic order can be

changed or transformed into another less basic or more special purpose order, namely, the order represented in 3c.

3c.

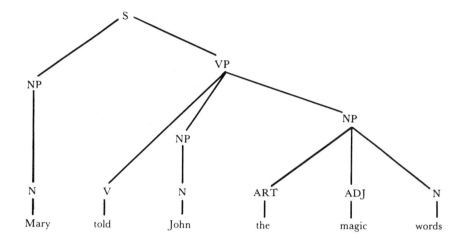

Transformations are stated in a formal notation (which we can ignore here) that stipulates exactly how one tree can be changed into another. Under this approach, verbs that do not undergo the Dative Transformation, such as *donate* and *tell*, will be marked in the lexicon as negative exceptions to the rule of Dative (as [− Dative]). Thus, the rule will not operate on sentences that contain these verbs and they will appear in only one ordering.

But there is another way to describe the same data. This is the problem with seeking descriptive adequacy only; we have too many ways to describe the same thing without being able to choose between the competing descriptions. We have to list in the lexicon, for each verb, its privileges of occurrence. For instance, we have to say that a transitive verb such as *love* requires an object ("John loves Mary" but not "John loves"), and an intransitive verb like *die* does not allow an object ("John died" but not "Mary died John"). Thus, why not stipulate in the lexical entries for verbs like *tell* or *give* that they allow either a following NP and PP (as in 1a) or a following NP NP (as in 1b). No need for a transformation. One might say, however, that we were missing the generalization that many verbs meaning "transfer," but not all, have these two possibilities. To capture this generalization we set up a lexical redundancy rule. Just as English allows many, but not all, adjectives to add *un* and mean "not adjective" (for example, *happy* and *unhappy*, but *silly*, though not *unsilly* [see 4a]), so we add a word formation rule to the lexicon that says that there is one version of many verbs meaning "transfer" that is followed by NP PP and another version, related to it, that is followed by NP NP (see 4b).

4a. Lexical rule: For many adjectives, you can prefix "un" and get an adjective meaning "not adjective."

4b. Lexical rule: For many verbs meaning "transfer," which have the possibility of being followed by NP PP, you can add another verb just like it in sound and meaning that can be followed by NP NP.

The actual lexical entries will, of course, have to say whether rule 4a or 4b is true for that word, since they are true of many but not all words they could apply to. Rules 4a and 4b just express tendencies or limited generalizations in the language. The two accounts of the Dative Alternation already provided are both perfectly good descriptions of English as far as they go. They are both descriptively adequate, and it would be a matter of splitting hairs to choose between them. In fact, there are many other such descriptions. The two I have given both use syntactic terms such as NP and PP. Accounts are possible that use semantic terms like *agent* and *patient*, and alternative accounts are available that use discourse terms like *topic, new information*, and *old information* (Givon, 1984). As far as description goes, there are no gounds, apart from particular uses we might make of the descriptions, on which to choose one or the other of the alternatives. Similarly, in mathematics there are many different ways to mathematize a problem (such as in terms of different branches or kinds of mathematics), all equally correct, apart from the particular purposes one might have on particular occasions.

Chomsky demanded more of a linguistic theory than descriptive adequacy. He demanded "explanatory adequacy"; in so doing, he construed explanatory adequacy to be the "logical problem of language acquisition" (Baker & McCarthy, 1981; Chomsky, 1965, 1984). To gain explanatory adequacy, linguistic theory must select one and only one descriptively adequate grammar for each human language on the basis of "primary linguistic data," which are the data available to a child in the early stages of language acquisition.

Let me say first what it means to call this a "logical problem." Chomsky ignored the real-world fact that children acquire language over time, perhaps going through certain stages (much as Galileo ignored the fact of friction in formulating a law of falling bodies). He conceived of the problem of language acquisition in abstract and logical terms. A child is born with some initial state of tacit or unconscious knowledge about language; perhaps this state is zero (as a rigid empiricist might argue), perhaps it is relatively rich (as a linguistic rationalist might argue). Call this state $S_{INITIAL}$. The child is exposed to certain finite data about the language, the "primary linguistic data." On the basis of these data and whatever is known at state $S_{INITIAL}$, the child induces a grammar of the language to which she is exposed; where this grammar represents a final state of knowledge of the language, call it $S_{FINAL}$.[3] (This is what the adult knows about the language if we ignore the fact that people continue to learn about language throughout their lives, and concentrate on the fact that even older children have an immense mastery of language that far exceeds what they had as younger children.) The problem for linguistic theory, then, is to supply not just a descriptively adequate grammar but the unique grammar that the child arrives at when exposed to the primary data—$S_{FINAL}$—given whatever knowledge is in $S_{INITIAL}$.

If children just memorized the data and $S_{INITIAL}$ was empty, then $S_{FINAL}$ could be a memorized list of the sentences of the language, and the problem would be trivial. But, of course, they cannot do this given the fact that there are an infinite number of possible sentences. At a slightly less trivial level, we might assume that the child memorizes not sentences but patterns, and draws analogies. Thus, $S_{INITIAL}$ would be empty, save perhaps for some very general knowledge about similarity and difference. This doesn't work either, of course. For example, from the occurrence of both *sleepy* and *sleeping* before nouns ("the sleepy girl" and "the sleeping girl"), the child should draw the correct conclusion that they are both adjectives; then from the equally correct observation that *sleepy* occurs after the verb *seems* ("The girl seems sleepy"), the child should draw the conclusion, by analogy, that "The child seems sleeping" is grammatical. But it isn't. From the correct observation that *happen* and *seems* occur in similar syntactic environments ("The girl seems to be sleepy." "The girl happens to be sleepy"), and the observation that one can say "The girl seems sleepy," the child by analogy should conclude that "The child happens sleepy" is grammatical. But it isn't. Analogies based on recognized patterns are a poor basis on which to acquire a language.

One of Chomsky's most important contributions to linguistics was to show that the logical problem of language acquisition is nontrivial (in fact, solving it may be beyond human science-forming abilities). In order even to approximate a solution, one must make fairly rich assumptions about the initial state $S_{INITIAL}$ which amounts to making substantive assumptions about the human biological capacity for language or, put in other terms, about the innate knowledge children bring to the language acquisition task.

Let me give an example which contains the sorts of assumptions about $S_{INITIAL}$ we might have to make and which is also indicative of one type of research methodology in theoretical linguistics. Everything in the primary linguistic data that any child is exposed to would indicate that the Content Question Rule below is true of English (Ross, 1967), though it turns out in fact to be false. That is, if all that children paid attention to were the data they are exposed to in the course of language acquisition, they ought to grow up using this rule. They do not, however, because they "know" (in some sense) that it is wrong. Then the question is, Where did this knowledge come from?

> CONTENT QUESTION RULE: One can form a grammatical content question from any declarative sentence by changing any one of its NPs into a question word or phrase and placing it at the front of the sentence (plus inverting its first helping verb, or adding a form of "do" if no helping verb is present, when one has questioned anything but the subject). For example:

5a. John likes *Mary*. → *Who(m)* does John like?
5b. *John* likes Mary. → *Who* likes Mary?
5c. John thinks Bill likes *Mary*. → *Who(m)* does John think Bill likes?
5d. John thinks *Bill* likes Mary. → *Who* does John think likes Mary?
5e. *John* thinks Bill likes Mary. → *Who* thinks Bill likes Mary?

Nothing in the primary data (nothing, in fact, that any English speaker—child or adult—has ever said or heard) contradicts this statement. Nonetheless, as 6a and 6b show, it is false, since not just any NP can be questioned.

6a.  John recognized the truck that hit *Mary*. →
6b.  *\*Who(m)* did John recognize the truck that hit?

Since nothing in the primary data can explain why 6b is ungrammatical, that is, why adults in $S_{FINAL}$ know that it is ungrammatical, then we must attribute some knowledge to the $S_{INITIAL}$ to account for this fact (since all we have to play with, to account for $S_{FINAL}$, is $S_{INITIAL}$ and the primary data). Let us say we attribute to $S_{FINAL}$ the knowledge that relative clauses (such as "that hit Mary" in 6a) are islands— nothing can "leave" them. Nothing in a relative clause can move to form a question in English because to do so would be to take something out of the relative clause (for example, the object of *hit* in 6a) and move it to the front of the sentence (in the form of *who* in 6b). Talk of movement here is merely a way of representing the fact that English word order is, in the normal case, subject-verb-object, while if we pose a question about the object it appears at the front of the sentence. Since $S_{INITIAL}$ is the state of the human being prior to language acquisition, it is the same for all humans, regardless of what language they are acquiring. Thus, when we attribute something to $S_{INITIAL}$, as in this case, we are tacitly making predictions about language universals: If a language has relative clauses and if it has any rules that *move* things, then it cannot move them out of relative clauses. Thus, we can check our hypothesis about $S_{INITIAL}$ by looking at other languages, and in turn refine the hypothesis.[4] If our hypothesis is confirmed, the correct grammar for English is one that has the Content Question Rule as part of it (which is all that could have been learned from the primary data of English). The restriction displayed in 6a and 6b is part of the innate knowledge the child brings to the task of language acquisition ($S_{INITIAL}$) and thus also a language universal (not part of the grammar of English alone).

The approach to language acquisition that Chomsky gave rise to, then, was one which, for purposes of scientific theory building, ignored the real-world circumstances of language acquisition and assumed that language was acquired simultaneously on the basis of the primary data. This was done in order to formally demonstrate that the logical problem of language acquisition is not solvable solely by induction from the primary data, that the solution involves nontrivial assumptions about $S_{INITIAL}$, and thus about biology. This is, in itself, an important result. Indeed, all science involves such idealizations. (For example, the law of gravitation says that all bodies fall at an equal rate. This, however, is false unless we ignore friction caused by air particles in our atmosphere. If we ignore friction we get an elegant and general law that holds not only in our world but throughout the universe.) It is possible, of course, that the idealization we have made is wrong in the sense that the problem would have a quite different solution if we added back the real-world variables. This is not true for the law of gravitation. Many have claimed, however, that Chomsky's idealization is wrong, although no one has come close to showing this. Moreover, Chomsky has always assumed that $S_{INITIAL}$ must be knowledge-specific to *language*, not knowledge—however rich—about learning, problem solving, or processing in general. Again, though many have claimed that this is wrong, no one has come close to showing convincingly that it is (see Piatelli-Palmarini, 1980).[5]

One can, however, go beyond the logical problem of language acquisition and ask, Can the grammar arrived at by a linguistic theory in search of explanatory adequacy (for example, English) be successfully incorporated into *realistic* models of language acquisition, comprehension, and production? ("Realistic" here means a model that does not ignore or put to one side the actual circumstances of language acquisition, language production, and language perception.) This is something like asking what happens to the law of gravity when we consider its operation in a world with friction. Chomsky (1965) referred to this problem as the question of feasibility.

Psycholinguistics initially had little success in incorporating generative-transformational grammars (based on the so-called *standard theory* of Chomsky, 1965) in realistic "on-line" (real-time) models of language production and processing (Fodor, Bever, & Garrett, 1974). For instance, linguistics once proposed that a sentence like "Wouldn't John be hurt by that remark?" was derived from an underlying structure for a sentence like "That remark would not hurt John" by a series of transformations that progressively deformed a structure for the latter sentence into one for the former: Passive ("John would not be hurt by that remark"), Negative Contraction ("John wouldn't be hurt by that remark"), and Question Formation ("Wouldn't John be hurt by that remark?"). It was then hypothesized by psycholinguists that the more transformations that applied in the derivation of a particular sentence, the longer it would take to comprehend it (on the theory that one had to "unwrap" the transformations to recover the deep structure, the level of the grammar that determined semantic representation). This turned out to be false, as shown by experimental research. In addition, it turned out to be difficult to assign any role at all to transformations in the process of actually producing or comprehending a sentence, though they did capture nicely the static knowledge native speakers had about the ways various types of sentences were related to each other (for example, "John would be hurt by that remark" is the passive of "That remark would hurt John").

Linguists responded to this problem in several different ways. One response was the development of nontransformational generative grammars that were constructed, in part, with an eye to their possible incorporation into realistic models of language production and comprehension. The most successful of these responses to date is the theory of Lexical Functional Grammar (LFG) developed by Bresnan (1982) and her colleagues. On the other hand, Chomsky and his colleagues never accepted the psycholinguists' interpretation of transformations. They stressed that generative grammar was meant to capture the knowledge native speakers had about their language, not how that knowledge actually was put to use. They insisted that their principles would have to be supplemented with various additional psychological principles to handle the way speech is produced and comprehended. Chomsky and his colleagues have, however, made the theory of generative-transformational grammar progressively more abstract. They have argued for a model of science in which the relationship between principles in a theory and the data they attempt to explain is quite abstract, often requiring a long deductive chain of reasoning to relate them. This has led to a theory with a much more constrained use of transformations (Chomsky, 1981, 1984), but one that is also much less accessible than Chomsky's earlier work. The theory, called Government and Binding (GB), is, in fact, probably no less a candidate than Bresnan's for incorporation into a realistic model of language processing though little such work has been done to date.

The concern with incorporating grammatical theory in a realistic model of language acquisition is fairly new. It received its impetus from Hamburger, Wexler, and Culicover's pioneering work on formal learnability theory (Hamburger & Wexler, 1975; Wexler & Culicover, 1980), and, for many linguists, was given a big push by Baker (1979). To see some of the issues that arise, let us consider the Dative Alternation again. When we consider language acquisition in a realistic setting, we discover that there are a number of problems with the primary data, apart from the fact that they are finite. The biggest problem is the lack of "negative evidence." Children can assume that, more often than not, sentences they hear in the primary data are grammatical, but they receive no useful indication of what count as ungrammatical sentences. Children are not, in general, corrected when they make errors, and it is certain that they can acquire language in the absence of any overt correction (see Baker, 1979, for a discussion of this point and citations of the relevant literature). On the other hand, children hear errors in the primary data (speech disfluencies, repetitions, self-corrections, false starts, and so forth), but they are not told that these are errors. More generally, many ungrammatical sentences are never exemplified in the data, and children are never explicitly told that these sentences are ungrammatical. Consider in this light the transformational view of the Dative Alternation (see 3a–c). A child could learn that there was a Dative Alternation for verbs like *tell, send,* and *give,* simply by hearing both sorts of sentences in the data. But how would a child learn that the rule does not apply in the case of similar verbs such as *say, donate,* and *report,* and therefore that these verbs have to be marked in the lexicon as [ − Dative]? The child is never told that these verbs are ungrammatical in the NP NP construction ("Mary reported John the story") and is not corrected if she uses such a construction. At this point in the story there is some debate about the empirical facts. Some (for example, Baker, 1979) claim that children never overgeneralize the dative, that is, say things like "He said me the magic words." Then the question becomes, Why don't they? since they do overgeneralize in other cases (saying *foots* for *feet* or making up novel causatives like "Mommy sweater me"). Others claim that children do overgeneralize the dative (p. 312). Then the problem becomes,

How do they ever recover from the overgeneralization? Why wouldn't they just add this verb to the dative rule and change the language? Such things do happen. For instance, *bead* used to mean *prayer,* but children, seeing monks "saying their beads" while handling a rosary, took *beads* (prayers) to mean *beads* (rosary). Further, adults will accept innovations like "I'll xerox you a copy of the paper."

Obviously the problem of language acquisition is even more acute than we had assumed. In the case of the ungrammatical content question in 6b, there was absolutely nothing in the data to indicate that it was ungrammatical; we simply had to assume a piece of innate knowledge at work. Yet in the case of the Dative Alternation rule, there is evidence for it in the primary data, but the rule still does not look learnable since there is no way for the child to learn its limits. Further, it is hard to see what innate constraint could be in operation here. We are forced to talk about an actual procedure which a child could use to acquire the language in this case, not about an abstract constraint on the operation of a rule.

The second, lexical approach to the Dative Alternation we described above can be the basis of such an account, if in fact children do not overgeneralize the dative rule. When a child hears a sentence such as 1a, she will add to her lexicon the information that *tell* can occur in the environment [___ NP to NP]; when she hears a sentence such as 1b, she will add the additional information that it can occur in an environment like [___ NP NP]. Since for *say* children will only hear sentences like 2a, they will only add [___ NP to PP] to that entry, and never [___ NP NP]. This is essentially to say that children are conservative learners, at least in this case. Of course, it still does not account for the overgeneralizations of the Dative Alternation that some children do appear to make, nor does it explain how they recover from them. This in fact makes the problem nearly intractable. It does demonstrate, however, that considerations about learnability in real time have implications for the shape of grammars.

## Pinker's Contribution to Language Acquisition

Pinker's goal is the construction of a theory of acquisition that is realistic—in the sense that it considers language acquisition under the sorts of conditions in which it actually takes place—but still retains the ground Chomsky has won through his formal approach to the logical problem of language acquisition. In addition, his project moves beyond formal (mathematical) proofs that a particular grammar is learnable and attempts to state in explicit step-by-step terms the procedures children use to acquire specific aspects of the language. One of the most illuminating things about such an enterprise is the way it exposes substantive assumptions that are normally tacit in the traditional child language literature.

Let me sketch some of the crucial and highly controversial assumptions Pinker makes prior to his first significant proposal about an actual learning mechanism:

1. The learning theory is stated in terms of several submechanisms that are each

built to acquire a particular class of rules in the grammar. This means Pinker has to pick a particular theory of grammar to work with since different theories postulate different rule types (LFG has no transformations, for example, whereas GB does). Pinker picks LFG, though he never offers a convincing argument that GB would not work as well. The point is that one has to pick a theory. This differentiates learnability theories from almost all extant work in child language, where no formal theory is assumed.

2. He also accepts Chomsky's central assumption that the child has substantive innate language-specific knowledge. Thus, Pinker assumes that the child knows, prior to language acquisition, such task-specific knowledge as the overall structure of the grammar, the formal nature of the sorts of rules it contains, and the primitives from which these rules may be composed (such as *noun* and *verb*). This assumption is obviously controversial, but task-general learning theories for language are nowhere to be found, and theories that assume no innate knowledge (whether language-specific or not) are ruled out by the logical problems of language acquisition above.[6]

3. Under the rubric of what he calls the *continuity assumption*, Pinker assumes that the cognitive and grammatical mechanisms of the child are qualitatively the same as those of the adult (p.7). That is, at any stage of development, the child's grammar is stated in the same formal terms as the adult's. This assumption rules out qualitative maturational changes in the course of linguistic development. It rules out, for instance, the possibility that at the beginning stages of acquisition the child has linguistic rules that are stated in purely semantic terms (agent, patient, instrument, and so on) and that later, through some maturational growth, the child's grammar is stated in syntactic terms (noun, verb, noun phrase, verb phrase, and so forth). Since the adult's rules are statable only in syntactic terms (accepting this as shown by Chomsky), then the child's rules at all stages must also be stated in these terms.

This assumption—that the child's cognitive and linguistic mechanisms are qualitatively the same as the adult's—immediately rules out, for example, Piaget's approach to language development, where the child goes through qualitatively different stages (for example, a stage in which a certain cognitive schema is stated in motoric terms and later in formal operational terms). As Pinker points out, the burden of proof falls on those who would deny the continuity assumption. So far, no one has shown how we would know that underlying mechanisms were significantly different at different stages, and, worse, how the child gets from one set of mechanisms as a whole to another. In Pinker's theory the child simply changes pieces of rules or adds rules to a system already in place. Surely this is the more parsimonious assumption, though one has to admit that the biological world is full of examples of qualitative change in physical development. Without the continuity assumption, a theory of acquisition is probably not attainable given the current state of our knowledge.

4. Finally, Pinker assumes that a child, even when she does not know the structure of a sentence, can infer the meaning of adults' utterances from their physical and discourse contexts and from the meanings of individual words in the sentence. He

actually makes some quite specific assumptions about what semantic knowledge a child has prior to the acquisition of syntax: a child can extract the meanings of predicates and their associated arguments (nominals); the relations of these arguments to the predicate; the potentially grammatically relevant semantic features of the sentence participants (their number, person, gender, and so forth) and of the proposition as a whole (tense, aspect, modality, and so forth); and the discourse features of the speech act (whether it is, for example, declarative, interrogative, exclamative, negative, or emphatic). This is tantamount to assuming a *language of thought* that essentially has its own structure *(grammar).* It renders the learnability question one of how a child "translates" from this language of thought to the language she is learning. In context, a child might understand that certain "pieces of meaning" are being talked about—for instance, that an action of throwing is being talked about, and that throwing involves an animate agent, an action, and a patient. She knows that such meaningful features as the animateness, personhood, number, and sex of the participants may be linguistically relevant (the sort of thing that languages can encode). She knows that languages have nouns and verbs, and, from context, she knows that a statement is being made, not a question asked.

But, even knowing all this beforehand, and even assuming that a child can segment the speech stream, how does she figure out what pieces in a string of words (such as "They boy threw the rock") encode the various pieces of meaning she has recognized to be relevant from context? It does no good to know that an action of throwing is being talked about if you do not know which word encodes this concept. It does no good to know that languages have nouns if you do not know which are the nouns in the incoming speech stream. This, then, is the first problem. To solve it, Pinker (following Grimshaw, 1981; Macnamara, 1982) proposes his first acquisition mechanism. In adult grammar there is no one-to-one correspondence between semantic categories and syntactic ones. Not all nouns name persons, places, or things *(honesty, a throw, dizziness);* not all verbs name actions or changes of state *(know, see);* not all subjects are agents and not all objects are patients (for example, in "John received a blow on the head," "John" is the patient). However, let's assume that the child makes the assumption that syntactic categories *do* match semantic ones one-for-one *until proven otherwise.* Thus the child has a scheme that says, for instance, that the prototypical noun names a person or thing, the prototypical verb names an action or change of state, the prototypical subject names an agent or causer, the prototypical object names a patient. Then the child simply has to find some instances in the input of sentences where these correspondences hold (and can ignore the rest for the time being). Faced with a string of words such as "The boy threw the rock," the child can assign syntactic categories and grammatical relations through these prototypicality schemes. Although in the earliest stages of acquisition children ignore function words such as articles (the indefinite article *a* and the definite article *the*), for the sake of simplicity we will assume that the child has a prototypicality scheme that associates definiteness in discourse with the category ART (a device which actually comes into play later in acquisition).

| Given from context and child's semantic knowledge: | Definite | Agent | Action | Definite | Patient |
|---|---|---|---|---|---|
| | the | boy | threw | the | rock |
| Assigned grammatical relations and syntactic categories, on the basis of prototypicality: | ART | N(Subj) | VERB | ART | N(Obj) |

Pinker calls this procedure *semantic bootstrapping* (see also Grimshaw, 1981; Macnamara, 1982). It is essentially a way into the system. As a next step, we assume that the theory of phrase structure is part of the child's innate linguistic knowledge. This tells the child that languages have phrases, that each type of phrase (noun phrase, verb phrase, adjective phrase) is headed by (organized around) a matching grammatical category (noun, verb, adjective), and that phrases can contain certain other sorts of units beside their heads (noun phrases can contain ARTs, for example). The child, of course, doesn't know what order words will have in phrases because this differs across languages. Using this knowledge about phrase structure, and the representation the child has induced from semantic bootstrapping, the child can now induce some of the phrase structure rules of the language, assigning a tree to the input and storing phrase structure rules that will make predictions about other possible sentences. Additionally, she can add certain words to her lexicon (see 7a and 7b below). In LFG, phrase structure rules are annotated with symbols for grammatical relations.

7a.                                                    7b.

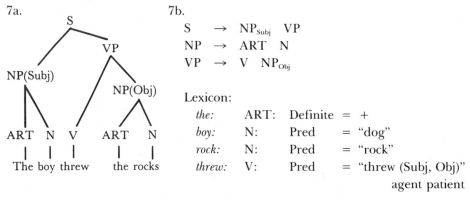

$$S \rightarrow NP_{Subj} \; VP$$
$$NP \rightarrow ART \; N$$
$$VP \rightarrow V \; NP_{Obj}$$

Lexicon:

| | | | |
|---|---|---|---|
| *the:* | ART: | Definite | = + |
| *boy:* | N: | Pred | = "dog" |
| *rock:* | N: | Pred | = "rock" |
| *threw:* | V: | Pred | = "threw (Subj, Obj)" |
| | | | agent patient |

Once a basic scaffolding of semantically induced rules and lexical items is in place, semantically neutral (nonprototypical) items and rules can be learned by observing their distribution within the known structures. For example, hearing a sentence such as "The situation frightened John," the child could learn that *situation* is a noun and that it heads noun phrases because it patterns in the same way as the previous class of prototypical nouns. Pinker refers to this process as *structure-dependent distributional learning.*

The role of semantic bootstrapping can be seen in another way. Syntactic notions, such as *subject,* in reality stand for a correlated set of phenomena. For instance, across languages, subjects tend to display a variety of correlated properties: (a) they can stand for an agent, whatever else they can stand for (that is, all languages will allow an agent to be the subject of a sentence, some will allow other semantic relations to be the subject—as in "John received a blow," where the patient is the subject—while others allow only agents to be subject; (b) they can stand for a topic, whatever else they can stand for; (c) they can trigger agreement on the verb; (d) they can be unexpressed in complements ("John wanted ____ to win"); (e) they are never expressed as reflexives (*Himself loves John); (f) they can be unexpressed in conjoined clauses ("John likes soup and ____ hates meat"); and (g) they can be relativized, even if nothing else in the language can ("the boy who died"), and so on. In fact, this is how a linguist identifies subjects across languages. Pinker's bootstrapping hypothesis assumes that the child knows, prior to language acquisition, this clustering of properties and that, in order to start the acquisition process, she looks for a prototypical agent, identifies this as a subject, sets up the phrase structure rule for subjects (fixes word order), and then predicts that all of the properties of subjects will follow (until proven otherwise in a particular language). Notice that the claim is *not* that *subject* is a semantic notion nor that the grammar contains rules that are purely semantic (S→ Agent + Action + Patient) at any point. The child uses semantic knowledge to break into a formal system. Once in, the child knows what other formal properties can cluster with this semantic property.

It may seem counterintuitive to attribute to young children who utter only two- and three-word combinations (as in Brown's Stage I, 1973, for example), syntactic rules which will generate much more complicated structures. Because of the restricted sorts of sentences young children utter, it has been claimed that children's early rules ought to be stated in semantic terms (Sentence → Agent + Action) or that subject and objects are not drawn from a unitary syntactic category (NP) but rather are different entities (Sentence → Pronoun or Animate Noun + Verb + Inanimate Noun). Pinker's bootstrapping hypothesis claims that children use actionhood as a cue that a word is a verb, and agenthood and patienthood as cues to determine which NP is its subject (the agent) and which its object (the patient). Thus, he predicts that children's earliest (at least first) verbs will indeed denote actions whose subjects and objects are agents and patients respectively. However, this semantic pattern will not continue past the earliest utterances, since it is merely a key into the formal system. Through a close study of the available developmental data, Pinker shows that children do not restrict their grammars in semantic terms. Early grammars are not restricted to animate preverbal elements (subjects) and inanimate postverbal ones (objects)—children produce enough of the opposite possibilities to demonstrate that they have grammars that can generate the full range of possibilities (grammars that must appeal, then, to a unitary formal notion like *noun phrase*). Pinker shows that postverbal elements are expanded using all the same structural combinations (noun, pro, art + noun, adj + noun, poss + noun) regardless of the semantic role they are playing (patient, object of experience, predicate nominal, locative). Furthermore, Pinker cites work by Brown which shows that children at Brown's Stages I and II produce virtually all the possible combinations of elements that a simple phrase structure grammar would predict (with the same structural possibilities for subject and object, that is, NP), though only in strings of less than five words.[7]

Pinker concludes that the fragmentary nature of early speech is due to performance factors (how the child uses rules) and not the rule system the child has. While many have found it "obvious" that children's grammars must be stated in semantic or pragmatic terms, Pinker demonstrates that this is not obvious. If, in fact, it is true that only purely formal (syntactic) rules can account for the full range of children's early language production, then Pinker's case that children have syntactic rules from the start, and the case for a universal grammar statable in structural terms, is strengthened.

Let us return to the sorts of problems raised by the Dative Alternation. We saw that many verbs alternate between sentences like "Mary told the magic words to John" and "Mary told John the magic words" but that it is hard to account for how a child learns just which verbs do this and which do not. Here we will discuss, however, a different syntactic structure (causatives), one where the issues are somewhat more tractable, at least in Pinker's framework (pp. 324–347). In English, lexical causatives (cases where the language has a word that includes causation as part of its meaning, as in 8a) can be used in cases of direct or immediate physical causation. Periphrastic causatives (cases where we need to use a verb like *cause* or *make* to express causation) are used for indirect causation (see 8b). Moreover, lexical causation requires that the agent, manner, and goal of causation be conventional or stereotypical for the relevant action. Thus, there are no lexical causatives for verbs such as *laugh* or *vomit*, which lack conventional direct means of causation (see 8c).

8a. John broke the window.
8b. John caused/made the window break.
8c. *John laughed Harry.

Children overgeneralize lexical causatives, producing sentences such as "Sweater me" and "Don't giggle me" that violate the conventionality constraint above or sentences such as "I come it closer so it won't fall," where the adult would use a periphrastic construction ("Make it come closer"). The question, then, is how children come to learn the constraints noted above and to remove the overgeneralized forms they have created, all in the absence of negative evidence (that is, in the absence of being corrected or told that certain cases are ungrammatical).

Pinker offers an interesting solution to this problem, one that is fairly indicative of his overall approach. Somewhat surprisingly, he relates the problem to that of learning "paradigms." For example, in a language that has case markers on its nouns, each noun has a paradigm of forms (in Latin, for instance: *puella* = subject; *puellam* = object; *puellae* = dative; *puellae* = genitive). In these cases, Pinker assumes that while the child may initially use one form *(puella)* for all cases, eventually she realizes that in the data the noun keeps varying in form. At this point the child has to hypothesize about what is causing this variation. Pinker further assumes that the child initially considers only hypotheses available in universal grammar, and perhaps in some order of likelihood also specified by universal grammar. In a similar vein, Pinker claims that children also learn the various syntactic constructions in which a verb can occur as paradigms. The cells of the paradigm could include active, passive, causative, reflexive, double-object dative, inchoative, middle, and so on, differing somewhat from language to language but drawn from a small universal set.[8] A child would form such a paradigm for each verb and fill in each cell with an entry corresponding to it which is learned from positive evidence. Below is part of a word-specific paradigm for *open* that may have been formed by a child at a certain stage (*theme* refers to the name of the semantic role of the entity that moves or changes state or location in a sentence; patients are a subclass of themes).

*Open*

| Intransitive | | | Causative | | | | | Passive | | | |
|---|---|---|---|---|---|---|---|---|---|---|---|
| Subj | V | | Subj | V | Obj | | | Subj | V | by | NP |
| Theme | | | Agent | | Theme | | | Theme | | | Agent |
| | | | | | | | | | | | |
| The door opened | | | John | opened | the door | | | | | | |
| | | | | | | | | The door | was opened | by | John |
| | | | Subj | cause | Subj | V | Obj | | | | |
| | | | Causer | | Agent | | Theme | | | | |
| | | | Bill | made | John | open | the door | | | | |

Throughout his book Pinker assumes the *unique entry principle:* no construction can be realized by more than one lexical form. The paradigm for *open* violates this principle since the causative cell is realized in two ways. A child can resolve this violation by searching for a new dimension that distinguishes between the two competing forms of the causative. She does this by focusing on context-specific features evident in future usages of one of the forms. For instance, she may notice on a particular occasion that the lexical causative is being used to denote an act of direct physical causation (or conversely, she may notice that the periphrastic form is being used to denote an act of indirect causation) and hypothesize that this is the relevant distinction. This hypothesis will not suffer from disconforming instances and will yield a new paradigm with a cell for direct causation and one for indirect causation. We still have to account for how the child who has overgeneralized (to "Giggle me," for example) will be able to expunge this entry from her lexicon. Pinker assumes that any entries that have been created by generalizing from the data, and not from direct positive evidence, bear a mark of "preemptability." When the child discovers constraints such as those above, she will remove any items that bear the preemptability mark and that break the constraint. If some item not only had no such mark but also broke the constraint, it would be viewed as a legitimate exception and noted as such. Notice that this proposal has the effect of significantly blurring the line between learning syntax (constructions like the periphrastic causative) and learning morphology (word paradigms like *puella, puellam*).

This is an insightful move. A theory of acquisition must account for how the child learns any language, not just English. And across languages we find that what one language does syntactically (for instance, the periphrastic causative in English) another language does morphologically (for instance, many languages have affixes that are added to a verb to signal indirect causation; they use lexical forms like *open* for direct causation; see Comrie, 1981). If the learning mechanism is the same in both cases, we not only account for how the child learns in both cases but begin to account for this sort of variation across languages. The most important implication of Pinker's enterprise is, I believe, the realization that without explicit proposals about learning mechanisms which explain what the child is learning and how exactly she is doing it, attributions to the child are meaningless. For instance, it is possible to collect a large body of data showing that children are sensitive to discourse properties such as topic, focus, new information, and old information. This fact in itself tells us very little. It leaves open many possibilities about what the child's grammar looks like and, thus, amounts to "descriptive adequacy" at best. Pinker demands more—namely, explicit assumptions about the child's grammar and learning mechanisms that explain why the data look the way they do and still render the purely formal, syntactic part of language learnable. He is thus proposing that the study of child language move beyond "descriptive adequacy" and on to "explanatory adequacy." Perhaps it is too early for this demand or perhaps not. Only time will tell. Until then we can only hope that we begin to reach this goal before we are crushed by mountains of data.

## Notes

1. Pinker (1979) is an excellent though somewhat technical survey of various formal models of language learning; Pinker's unpublished study (n.d.) is an equally excellent nontechnical discussion. Pinker (1982) is an earlier, fairly technical treatment of the material in his book. While the book represents a number of advances on the article, many readers will find it quite sufficient to give them a feeling for the basic approach. Pinker (1985) is a new and less technical discussion that is probably at this point the best and most accessible place for the interested reader to turn. Slobin has also done extremely important work relevant to learnability theory. It is less technical because not tied to any particular linguistic theory (though less easy to falsify, perhaps, for this same reason). Slobin (1982, in press), among others, is essential reading for anyone interested in language acquisition, as well as learnability.
2. The * in 2b means the sentence is ungrammatical. Notice that this is a structural fact since one can perfectly well figure out what 2b means. Furthermore, there is nothing particularly deviant about this meaning since it is not all that different from the meaning of the grammatical sentence in 1b.
3. I will use the feminine pronominal forms *she* and *her* for the generic pronoun form.
4. Perhaps *relative clause* is not the right term; see, for example, Chomsky (1981).
5. Piatelli-Palmarini (1980) is the record of a fascinating debate between Chomsky and Piaget and their respective followers. Chomsky has made two substantive claims that psychologists have disputed: (1) no one can account for the acquisition of language without making substantive and rich assumptions about innate tacit knowledge somehow encoded in the brain; and (2) that this innate knowledge is specifically germane to language, and not other areas of cognition, and thus we must assume a specially evolved capacity of the mind (somehow represented in the brain) for the acquisition of language. One can accept (1) and still reject (2) by giving an account of language acquisition that draws on innate knowledge relevant to a wide range of domains—for example, perception of the physical world, the construction of space and time, mathematical concepts, systems of social behavior, problem solving, and so forth—and not just language. One can deny both assumptions by constructing a general learning theory that shows how a full range of human knowledge, including language, is acquired by principles that store and process data but does

not assume substantive innate knowledge about any of these domains. The task for Chomsky's critics is fairly clear—and his positions are readily falsifiable. For instance, if anyone could account for how all adult speakers know 6b (*Who(m) did John recognize the truck that hit?) is ungrammatical without appealing to any purely linguistic innate knowledge, they would have falsified assumption (1) in this case, and if they could do so without appealing to any innate knowledge at all they would have falsified (2). No one, as far as I can see, has come remotely close to doing so. Notice also that their account would have to explain why it is the case that whatever blocks this sentence in English blocks the same sort of sentence in other languages, since sentences like this one are indeed also ungrammatical cross-linguistically. One should, however, bear in mind that Chomsky's current account of these matters is much more abstract and covers a far wider range of cases than I have indicated here.

6. "Task-general" learning theories are theories that would appeal only to innate principles relevant to a wide range of domains, not just language. They would deny not that humans have innate knowledge but that they have any innate knowledge germane only to one area of cognition, such as language. For instance, they may claim that humans have innately specified principles germane to problem solving generally and that they use these principles to acquire language as well as solve other sorts of cognitive problems; see n. 3.

7. Stage I and II are the first two of Brown's five stages of language acquisition. Brown's stages were defined in terms of mean length of utterance (MLU). Stage I children have an MLU of 1.75 words per utterance with an upper bound of 5, while Stage II children have an MLU of 2.5 with an upper bound of 7. Pinker has gone carefully through Brown's copious data to test his claims against what children actually do.

8. Some examples of the constructions named *Active:* John sold the book to Mary; *Passive:* The book was sold to Mary by John; *Causative:* John made Herman sell the book to Mary; *Reflexive:* John sold himself to Mary; *Double-Object Dative:* John sold Mary the book; *Inchoative:* The book came to be sold to Mary; and *Middle:* Books sell easily. One should keep in mind that other languages have different verb forms for several or all of these constructions, that is, *sell* would change its shape or have a morpheme added to it in each use rather than simply adding new words to the sentence as a whole (like *was* or *made* or *himself*), or changing word order. For example, *yomaserareta* in Japanese is a complex word made up of several parts meaning "was made to read": *yom* (read) *sase* (cause) *rare* (passive) *ta* (past). This verb is a passive causative, realizing in one word what English needs several words for. Thus, we cannot clearly separate learning morphology (the ordering of the different morphemes in complex words) from syntax (the ordering of words in sentences).

## References

Baker, C. L. (1979). Syntactic theory and the projection problem. *Linguistic Inquiry, 10,* 533–581.

Baker, C. L., & McCarthy, J. J. (Eds.). (1981). *The logical problem of language acquisition.* Cambridge: MIT Press.

Bresnan, J. W. (Ed.). (1982). *The mental representation of grammatical relations.* Cambridge: MIT Press.

Brown, R. (1973). *A first language: The early stages.* Cambridge: Harvard University Press.

Chomsky, N. (1965). *Aspects of the theory of syntax.* Cambridge: MIT Press.

Chomsky, N. (1981). *Lectures on government and binding.* Dordrecht, Netherlands: Foris.

Chomsky, N. (1984). *Knowledge of language: Its nature, origin, and use.* Unpublished manuscript, Massachusetts Institute of Technology, Cambridge.

Comrie, B. (1981). *Language universals and linguistic typology.* Chicago: University of Chicago Press.

Fodor, J. A., Bever, T. G., & Garrett, M. F. (1974). *The psychology of language: An introduction to psycholinguistics and generative grammar.* New York: McGraw-Hill.

Givon, T. (1984). *Syntax: A functional-typological introduction.* (Vol. 1). Amsterdam/Philadelphia: John Benjamins.

Grimshaw, J. (1981). Form, function, and the language acquisition device. In C. L. Baker & J. J. McCarthy (Eds.), *The logical problem of language acquisition* (pp. 165–182). Cambridge: MIT Press.

Hamburger, H., & Wexler, K. (1975). A mathematical theory of learning transformational grammar. *Journal of Mathematical Psychology.* 12, 137–177.

Macnamara, J. (1982). *Names for things: A study of child language.* Cambridge: Bradford Books/MIT Press.

Piattelli-Palmarini, M. (Ed.). (1980). *Language and learning: The debate between Jean Piaget and Noam Chomsky.* Cambridge: Harvard University Press.

Pinker, S. (1979). Formal models of language learning. *Cognition, 1,* 217–283.

Pinker, S. (1982). A theory of the acquisition of lexical interpretive grammars. In J. W. Bresnan (Ed.), *The mental representation of grammatical relations.* (655–726). Cambridge: MIT Press.

Pinker, S. (1985). Language learnability and children's language: A multidisciplinary approach. In K. Nelson (Ed.), *Children's language* (Vol. 5). Hillsdale, NJ: Erlbaum.

Pinker, S. (n.d.). *Recent advances in the study of the acquisition of grammar.* Unpublished manuscript, Massachusetts Institute of Technology, Dept. of Psychology and Center for Cognitive Science, Cambridge.

Ross, J. R. (1967). *Constraints on variables in syntax.* Unpublished doctoral dissertation, Massachusetts Institute of Technology, Cambridge.

Slobin, D. I. (1982). Universal and particular in the acquisition of language. In E. Wanner and L. R. Gleitman (Eds.), *Language acquisition: The state of the art* (pp. 128–170). Cambridge: Harvard University Press.

Slobin, D. I. (Ed.). (in press). *The crosslinguistic study of language acquisition.* Hillsdale, NJ: Erlbaum.

Wexler, K., & Culicover, P. (1980). *Formal principles of language acquisition.* Cambridge: MIT Press.

# Book Review

ROBERT W. KOPFSTEIN
*Saddleback College, Mission Viejo, California*

STAGES OF READING DEVELOPMENT
by Jeanne S. Chall.
*New York: McGraw-Hill, 1983. 293 pp.*

In an earlier book, *Learning to Read: The Great Debate* (1967), Jeanne Chall explored the differing perspectives of reading theoreticians and practitioners and examined one of the key areas of debate: reading comprehension. What is it? How does it work? What is the best way to teach it? Why do some students learn to read well at a rapid pace while others are late bloomers or, worse yet, fail to bloom at all? Chall's most recent work, *Stages of Reading Development,* offers plausible answers to these questions and proposes a six-stage model to describe the reading process. These stages describe the act of reading from the prereading period (birth to age six, or Stage 0), to the often highly sophisticated critical reading skills necessary for academic success in high school and college (Stages 4 and 5).

The development of a model of reading stages is not unique to Chall. Her text outlines the corresponding schemes of other researchers, including Gray (1925), Gates (1947), Russell (1949), and Rozin and Gleitman (1977). The clarity and conciseness of this historical perspective makes *Stages of Reading Development* a valuable resource for any teacher seeking a solid overview of the progression of reading skills in students. In fact, this presentation of the theoretical background helps to reinforce and validate Chall's own model, which is characterized by its clearly defined steps, its connection to age and grade levels, and its practicality for use by the classroom teacher.

In one chapter Chall outlines evidence from four disciplines that support the validity of reading stages: psychology, linguistics, neuroscience, and education. She also includes additional findings from these fields in Appendix A. However, Chall is careful to point out that her evidence is not intended to be all-encompassing.

> The literature on reading alone is vast, with several thousand books and articles published every few years. We searched, instead, for those theories, research findings, and practices that relate to reading development and to our proposed

reading states. . . . I am mindful that evidence of validity for a scheme such as the one proposed here will ultimately require many observations and experiments and the cooperation of many scholars. But they can do this only after the scheme is made available to them. (pp. 59–60)

The evidence Chall does include covers a forty-year span of research, and all of the studies indicate that neurological and linguistic development seems to occur in graduated steps which tend to become increasingly complex as they progress. There appears to be little disagreement among the researchers that the human organism exhibits behaviors which build and interact with one another to produce new behaviors that tend to become more and more sophisticated.

In reading, stage theory is not new. In Appendix B, Chall extensively outlines other stage models proposed by Gray (1925, 1937), Gates (1947), Russell (1949, 1961), Ilg and Ames (1950), and Rozin and Gleitman (1977). Her analysis of the relative merits of each of the theories is not only interesting but illustrates an overall progression of thought on the idea of a stage model.

Chall stresses—and rightfully so—the necessary links between research and its practical application in the classroom. Educators have traditionally lamented the gap between theory and applied teaching. Often this gap exists because the teacher cannot see the immediate use of the findings. Chall addresses this problem directly by aiming her material at teachers, the audience who can best use it. The book's format is clear, and even after a casual reading, the premises underlying the six stages, as well as the stages themselves, are relatively easy to grasp and to remember.

## The Six Stages

To Chall, Stage 0, the prereading stage from birth to age six, probably represents the period of most rapid growth in the child's acquisition of language. Although researchers continue to debate the relative importance of environment and experience versus individual characteristics (such as sex, race, IQ), there is general agreement that all these factors are important. One characteristic of Chall's Stage 0 is that the child may pretend to read books. Chall generally regards television programs oriented toward this age group, such as *The Electric Company* and *Sesame Street,* as positive factors in sparking the child's early interests in reading and writing, and she cites these two programs several times throughout the book. While there is no doubt that the *intent* of the programs is admirable, there are teachers from kindergarten to third grade who feel that they simply cannot compete with the razzle-dazzle of Kermit the Frog and Big Bird when it comes to reading instruction in the classroom. These teachers feel that the rapid-fire, slick entertainment format of many "kidvid" shows may actually hinder the child's ability to maintain concentration in school.[1] Chall herself points out that, in later reading stages, the material now used in basal readers is perhaps geared more toward narrative entertainment than toward solid content.

Does this mean that Mr. Gradgrind's school of Dickens' *Hard Times* is about to make a comeback? Probably not. Rather than extolling the dubious virtues of a just-the-facts-and-nothing-but-the-facts approach, Chall argues that if the act of reading is to be carried out to its fullest development, the germs of the processes which come into play in the final stages must also be present at the beginning. This need for a simultaneity of skills is probably most obvious to teachers of adult reading students.

In Chall's scheme, decoding the printed word or letter characterizes Stage 1 reading. According to a study by Biemiller (1970), there are likely substages embedded within Stage 1 in which the reader shows an ever-increasing concern with graphic correctness, even at the expense of semantic acceptability. In other words, as the beginning reader becomes more adept at phonics skills, his or her errors or miscues in reading tend to have a closer resemblance to the actual printed word, even though semantically the substitution may not "fit" the meaning of the passage. For example, when a reader mistakes the word "because" for "before," he or she is focusing on the similarity in the first two letters and last letter, rather than on any semantic similarity. In the very beginning phase of Stage 1, the miscue substitutions are likely to be more syntactically and semantically appropriate, even though graphically they are farther removed from the printed word. Thus, Biemiller's findings seem to run counter to the psycholinguistic model of reading in which readers who are actually at a later stage of development could be considered less skillful than those at an earlier stage because they are more dependent on the print of a given passage than on its sense.

Chall sees the main difference between Stages 1 and 2 as the process of "ungluing" from the printed page. In Biemiller's model this represents a synthesis between his first two phases of early reading skills. Not only is the beginning reader aware of the overall meaning of the passage, but he or she is also sensitive to what the printed words look and sound like. Chall concludes that

> in one sense, beginning and very mature readers seem to behave in a similar manner toward print: they do not stick too closely to it, focusing instead on the meaning. Yet mature readers can stick to the print if they want to or need to. Going beyond it is a conscious choice for them, one based on knowledge. . . . To advance, to build up the skill for making choices, beginners have to let go of pseudo-reading. They have to engage, at least temporarily, in what appears to be less mature reading behavior glued to the print—in order to achieve real maturity later. They have to know enough about the print in order to leave the print (pp. 17–18)

In Stage 2 the reader gains fluency and, in the process of reading material which is highly predictable, there is a built-in confirmation of what the reader already knows. This fluidity is accomplished between grades two and three, at approximately age seven or eight. But it is also at Stage 2 that adult basic literacy programs here and abroad begin to falter. According to Chall:

> Although most adults can get through Stage 1, they begin to falter at Stage 2. Reading a newspaper or pamphlet containing new agricultural information, which requires at least Stage 3 reading, is difficult or impossible for most. The following explanation may prove useful. After the literacy classes complete their

> Stage 1 programs, there are not enough readable materials available—material
> that is familiar in its use of language and content—for the new literates to gain
> the fluency of Stage 2. Nor is there usually a compelling need to keep on reading.
> (p. 19)

Anyone who has taught functionally illiterate adults can easily identify with the
frustrations generated by this problem: at the end of the class the adult students can
"read," but they cannot *read.*

More than sixty-five years ago, Thorndike (1917) asserted that reading is a thinking
activity, and being able to process the ideas put forth by the author is what counts
in reading successfully, not just the ability to relate symbol to sound. Stage 3 (grades
four to eight) begins the phase of reading to learn. While Stages 1 and 2 concentrate
primarily on relating print to speech, and the texts tend to be conversational in
nature, Stage 3 reading involves an ever-increasing number of abstract and technical
terms. Sentences become longer and syntactically more complex.

Chall divides Stage 3 into two phases. In 3A (grades four to six, ages nine to
eleven), readers begin to read about "conventional knowledge of the world," and in
so doing they become less egocentric in their language development. In 3B (grades
seven to eight, ages twelve to fourteen) readers are able to read at a general adult
level, including popular magazines, local newspapers, and some adult fiction. Chall
contends that

> as readers move from the first to the second phase of Stage 3, they also grow
> in their ability to analyze what they read and react critically to the different
> viewpoints they meet. Much can be done here in reading critically, but it is better
> and more consistently done in Stage 4 when more of what is read is known and
> the reader's critical abilities are more developed. (pp. 22–23)

While this point is certainly defensible, there are at least two problems associated
with reserving the teaching of critical reading skills (such as making inferences and
judgments, drawing conclusions, and formulating analysis) until Stages 4 and 5. The
first is that, in teaching functionally illiterate adults, the critical skills are already
there and need at least to be reckoned with in the earlier stages, and, secondly,
current research indicates that there are benefits in teaching critical reading skills
at *all* levels.[2] Many publishers (Jamestown, Barnell-Ioft, and others) are now including
critical reading questions even in their lowest-level materials.

Stage 4 (high school, ages fourteen to eighteen) is what Chall refers to as the
Multiple Viewpoints Stage. Readers are now confronted with the task of sorting out
the various—and often equally reasonable—points of view which they encounter in
texts, reference books, newspapers, and magazines. In order to achieve this goal
successfully, readers must have the background acquired either through experience
or Stage 3–type reading. Often Stage 4 reading adds layers of facts and ideas to
concepts which readers have previously encountered. At Stage 5 (college, age eighteen), readers achieve a level of critical skills in which they can synthesize information.
Chall calls this the "Construction and Reconstruction Stage," "a struggle to balance
one's comprehension of the ideas read, one's analysis of them, and one's own ideas

on them" (p. 24). This stage is characterized by a search for generalizations based on abstract ideas and an evaluative process which weighs the reader's perceptions of the world against the perceptions of others.

One of the goals of our educational system is to produce graduates who are not simply able to read but who are able to perceive the complexities of the world around them, to think and to express themselves logically and clearly. Recent studies and discussions of our schools indicate that we are doing a better than average job up to grade four—then something happens.[3] Copperman (1979) outlines the problem and lays the blame for students' poor academic performance and their subsequent lack of interest in school subjects on the deemphasis of phonics. Given Chall's model, the problem is obviously more complex; the transition to Stage 3 and beyond requires the ability to decode, but there is a broader dimension of skills involved as well. According to her theory, "sophisticated reading is not just a mechanical skill, it demands artful thinking as well as phonics. The teacher of reading is at the same time a teacher of a broad range of cognitive skills."

The model of reading stages presented in *Stages of Reading Development* could have potentially broad application at the classroom level. It could also give teachers a more precise scale for judging the theoretical basis of their reading programs. For researchers, this book provides fertile ground for further investigations into the model and how it could apply to critical reading, beginning readers, adult readers, and the reading-disabled. Throughout the book Chall stresses that her proposal is just that— a proposal. She cautions that further investigation and testing of the model are necessary; the model itself is not intended to be a confining or rigidly applied standard. Used judiciously, Chall's six-stage model could be a useful tool in sorting out some of the muddle that has developed in the ongoing debate among educators over the literacy issue.

## Notes

1. For a brief overview of the concerns of many psychologists on the effect of television as a whole on children, see *Newsweek* ("Kid-vid," 1977); and for a more in-depth treatment of the neuro-physiological effects of television on perception and communication in children, see Mander (1977) and Winn (1972).
2. See Lapp and Flood (1978, chap. 9) for a concise discussion of the critical reading process. Since publication of Bloom's handbook (1956) there have been several refinements of the theory. Instead of viewing levels of comprehension—literal, inferential, critical—in a strictly linear progression of increasing difficulty, subsequent research has indicated a model of reading comprehension in which the components interact with one another at all levels (Frederiksen, 1977; Trabasso, 1972).
3. The National Commission on Excellence in Education (1981) also issued a lengthy report on the strengths and weaknesses of student academic performance in America today. The K-6 grades were generally praised in the report, while grades 7–12 were criticized, especially for neglecting basic skills for students who were college bound. More recently, Sizer (1984) has written a book critical of the American high schools.

## References

Biemiller, A. (1970). The development of the use of graphic and contextual information as children learn to read. *Reading Research Quarterly, 6,* 75–96.

Bloom, B. (1956). *Taxonomy of educational objectives, Handbook I: Cognitive domain.* New York: McKay.

Chall, J.S. (1967). *Learning to read: The great debate* (1st ed.). New York: McGraw-Hill.

Copperman, P. (1979). *The literacy hoax.* New York: Morrow.

Frederiksen, C.H. (1977, March). *Inference and the structure of children's discourse.* Paper presented at the Symposium on the Development of Processing Skills, at the meeting of the Society for Research in Child Development, New Orleans.

Gates, A.I. (1947). *The improvement of reading.* New York: Macmillan.

Gray, W.S. (1925). Reading activities in school and in social life (pp. 1–8). Essential objectives of instruction in reading (pp. 9–19). A modern program of reading instruction for the grades and for the high school (pp. 21–73). In *24th yearbook of the NSSE: Report of the National Committee on Reading: Part I.* Bloomington, IL: Public School Publishing.

Gray, W.S. (1937). The nature and types of reading (pp. 23–40). The nature and organization of basic instruction in reading (pp. 65–132). In *36th yearbook of the NSSE: The teaching of reading: A second report: Part I.* Bloomington, IL: Public School Publishing.

Ilg, F.I., & Ames, L.B. (1950). Developmental trends in reading behavior. *Journal of Genetic Psychology.* **76,** 261–312.

Kid-vid: What TV does to kids. (1977, February 21). *Newsweek,* pp. 63–70.

Lapp, D., & Flood, J. (1978). *Teaching reading to every child.* New York: Macmillan.

Mander, J. (1977). *Four arguments for the elimination of television.* New York: Morrow.

National Commission on Excellence in Education (1981). *A nation at risk: The imperative for educational reform.* Washington, DC: U.S. Government Printing Office.

Rozin, P., & Gleitman, L. (1977). The structure and acquisition of reading, II. In A.S. Reber & D.I. Scarborough (Eds.), *Toward a psychology of reading.* Hillsdale, NJ: Erlbaum.

Russell, D.H. (1949). Reading and child development. In *48th yearbook of the NSSE: Reading in the elementary school:* Part II (pp. 11–32). Chicago: University of Chicago Press.

Russell, D.H. (1949). *Children learn to read.* Boston: Ginn.

Sizer, T.R. (1984). *Horace's compromise: The dilemma of the American high school.* Boston: Houghton Mifflin.

Thorndike, E.L., Reading as reasoning: A study of mistakes in paragraph reading. *Journal of Educational Psychology,* **8,** 323–332.

Trabasso, T. (1972). Mental operations in language comprehension. In J.B. Carroll & R.D. Freedle (Eds.) *Language comprehension and the acquisition of knowledge.* Washington, DC: Winston.

Winn, M. (1972). *The plug-in drug.* New York: Viking.

# Book Review

KENJI HAKUTA
*Stanford University*

LANGUAGE AND LEARNING: THE DEBATE BETWEEN
JEAN PIAGET AND NOAM CHOMSKY
edited by Massimo Piattelli-Palmarini.
*Cambridge, MA: Harvard University Press, 1980. 409 pp.*

Most of us who have received training in psychology, linguistics, or education in the last twenty years would undoubtedly like to have been at Abbaye de Royaumont in France in October 1975. Jean Piaget and Noam Chomsky, two great minds in the modern field of cognition, met there for the first and only time. Flanked by distinguished scholars from a variety of disciplines—ranging from anthropology to artificial intelligence, from philosophy to biology—Chomsky the specialist and Piaget the generalist debated the assumptions, achievements, and goals of their respective research programs.

The present volume is a documentation of that historic occasion. There are twelve chapters comprising the debate proper, six chapters of afterthoughts on the debate, and three separate appendices that discuss tangential issues. The editor, Massino Piattelli-Palmarini, has made the proceedings not only palatable, but exciting. He has written a preface and an epilogue for most chapters, placing the issues in perspective and integrating the book's three sections. Howard Gardner's excellent foreword lays the groundwork for the relative novice to the field. In the closing chapter, Jacques Mehler provides a fitting tribute to these two great scholars by setting their achievements in historical perspective.

Two central tensions characterize the debate. The first concerns the nature of development: what is development the development of? For Piaget, the biologist-turned-genetic epistemologist, cognitive development consists of the elaboration of sensorimotor schemes into logico-mathematical structures through interaction with the environment. While rejecting empiricism as an explanation for development, Piaget is equally opposed to nativism as an explanation; the elaborate cognitive structures that are the end product of development cannot be the result of random mutation and selection. A nativistic stand, he argues, would have to "go back as far

*Harvard Educational Review* Vol. 51 No. 3 August 1981, 437–439

as protozoa and viruses" (p. 26) to locate the origins of these structures. Piaget's familiar position is constructivism, whereby new concepts are formed through the interaction of a limited set of innate mechanisms with the external world. His favorite biological metaphor for genetic-environmental interaction is a mollusk, which takes different forms when raised in different environments. The resulting forms, Piaget contends, cause a change in genotype, a contention challenged by renowned biologist Francois Jacob (pp. 61–62). For Piaget, there is no clear-cut distinction to be drawn between what is innate and what is acquired.

Chomsky, on the other hand, characterizes development as the "successive maturation of specialized hardware" (p. 73), a phrase he borrowed during the debate from Guy Cellerier, who, in fact, was a colleague of Piaget at the latter's International Center for Genetic Epistemology. Drawing on some simple examples from his own research, which show the dependency of certain linguistic rules on abstractly specified structures (and not on their surface, linear properties), Chomsky argues that there could be no relevant experiences that would lead to the "construction" of such linguistic knowledge. The theory of universal grammar posits a set of abstract specifications that is powerful enough to account for both adult linguistic competence and the variations observed across languages. Chomsky proposes that this universal grammar is innate—a claim, he argues, that is subject to empirical disconfirmation. He opposes Piaget's contention that a structure of such complexity as universal grammar cannot be innately specified on biological grounds. For example, we cannot at present explain the biological evolution of physical organs, yet no one doubts that their properties are genetically determined.

The debate dwells at some length on the nature of the "fixed nucleus," the genetically determined structure from which cognitive structures are derived. For Chomsky, the properties of universal grammar must be present in the fixed nucleus. The child, therefore, has all possible representations of language available at the initial stage of language acquisition, and development consists of eliminating properties that do not correspond to the target language. Piaget attributes considerably less structure to the fixed nucleus and accounts for later complexity with his theory that "any structure at all is going to create others by the possibilities it raises" (p. 157). Chomsky and the philosopher Jerry Fodor vehemently criticize this basic premise of constructivism, arguing on purely logical grounds that it is impossible for higher-order logics to be generated from lower-order ones; properties of the final state must be present in some form in the initial state.

While it is difficult to identify the individual participants with either camp, both Piaget and Chomsky had their supporters. For example, Piaget received enthusiastic endorsement from Seymour Papert, who cited examples from research in artificial intelligence in which computers have been programmed to set up and test hypotheses based on relatively simple structures. Chomsky found sympathy among the biologists, particularly Jacob. Other participants, most notably neurobiologist Pierre Changeux, suggested compromise theories. Changeux's notion of a "genetic envelope" posits that the genetic component dictates a range of developmental possibilities for structures. While Piaget is appreciative of such attempts at compromise (p. 278), Chomsky characteristically maintains his radical position. The difference between Chomsky's and Piaget's models appears sharpest on the question: does the environment influence the creation of new structures in any substantive way?

A second tension in the debate concerns the extent to which different cognitive capacities should be treated as independent of each other. Once again, the debate centers on the specificity of language. Chomsky uses his familiar biological metaphor of language as a mental organ and focuses on its distinctive characteristics. To Piaget, on the other hand, language is only a subset of the general semiotic system; he rejects Chomsky's claim that it is qualitatively different from other cognitive capacities. However, when challenged by Chomsky to propose structures in other domains analogous to abstract linguistic structures, Piaget and his supporters, notably Papert, manage to come up with only broad arguments for a general developmental mechanism; they can make no specific counterproposals. Chomsky's skill as a debater is exemplary.

Aside from elucidating the two central tensions described above, the book contains many intellectual nuggets of more than passing interest. David Premack offers a lucid summary of current knowledge about representational capacities in chimpanzees. His unique approach characterizes chimpanzee intelligence as an end in itself and not simply as a way to explore whether language can be learned only by humans. For example, Premack demonstrates that chimpanzees have "the very critical psychological capacity of being able to recognize representations of one's own behavior" (p. 222), speculating that this capacity is shared by all primates. While Premack delineates the necessary conditions of language and demonstrates their presence in chimpanzees, his interpretation, in respect to the nature of learning, is consistent with that of Chomsky/Fodor: "the main thing human training is doing here for the chimpanzee is disclosing capacities that are present" (p. 222). Given the interdisciplinary nature of the conference participants, the ensuing discussion is lively.

Hilary Putnam and Chomsky/Fodor engage in a lengthy exchange on the concept of innatism and the value of arguing for innateness of specific capacities such as language versus general intelligence. In the appendix, there is additional discussion reflecting the truly interdisciplinary implications of the Piaget-Chomsky debate.

Since the book documents a debate, one is tempted to ask, "Who won?" This is a simplistic question with complex answers, and one to be answered by each reader. Personally, I find the book to be an excellent projective test for my own biases. Its appearance at this particular point in the history of developmental psychology seems quite timely. In cognitive development, the theory of stages is coming under increasingly severe criticism. There is enormous interest in early manifestations of cognitive skills, such as the number concept. The kinds of questions asked by developmental psychologists are beginning to change. For example, after a period of intense interest in communicative and semantic aspects of language development, researchers are again beginning to ask the question that motivated the field initially: how can we account for the observed regularities in syntactic development in children? A reading of the Piaget-Chomsky debate, even by those most jaded by these issues, will help clarify the basic questions of developmental psychology and cognition. As for those relatively unfamiliar with the works of Piaget and Chomsky, yet with even a passing interest in cognition, language, and development, the book should be at the top of their reading agenda. For specialists and nonspecialists alike, these issues on the nature of language and learning will be a topic of debate for years to come.

# Book Review

JOHN B. CARROLL
*University of North Carolina, Chapel Hill*

THOUGHT AND LANGUAGE
by Lev Semenovich Vygotsky; edited and translated by
Eugenia Hanfmann and Gertrude Vakar.
*Published jointly by MIT Press and John Wiley, 1962.*
[With (separately published) *Comments* by Jean Piaget. 14 pp.]

The name of Vygotsky, a Russian psychologist who lived from 1896 to 1934, has been known in the English-speaking world in two ways: first as the author of two singularly perceptive articles, one on language and thought in children, and one on schizophrenic language, which had been translated and published in American medical periodicals, and second, as the originator of the "Vygotsky test," a high-level concept formation test adapted for clinical use in 1937 by Hanfmann and Kasanin. It was known, however, that Vygotsky had left much more to posterity than only these things—the pity was that his writings were in Russian. His major work, *Myshlenie i rech' (Thought and Language)* was not published until a few months after his death. We are told that this work was not very well organized; even though Vygotsky had attempted to combine several previously written essays into a coherent whole, it was written in haste and in an involved style, contained much unnecessary polemical discussion, and was unsystematic in its use of references.

The present translation remedies all these defects. What we have is a book written in admirable English, every page of which presents something meaty and striking—whether it be a theoretical discussion, a critique of another's position, or a report of experimental findings. The seven chapters, even though recognizably originating from separate essays, can be read in a continuous sequence, indeed must be read in that way. For this transformation (it is much more than a translation), we have to thank Eugenia Hanfmann and Gertrude Vakar, the former a well-known psychologist of Russian birth who has resided in the U.S. since 1930, and the latter a professional translator.

Why, after twenty-eight years, bring out a translation of a work originally published in 1934? For one thing, a work of the character of Vygotsky's does not become

*Harvard Educational Review* Vol. 33 No. 2 May 1963, 246–251

obsolete in twenty-eight years, and perhaps not even in eighty-eight. The Soviet Union saw fit to republish Vygotsky's work in 1956, after long years of suppression or neglect, and Vygotsky's thinking is today a major influence in Soviet psychology. But further, it can be said that Vygotsky's approach to problems of language and thought was far ahead of his time even at the first posthumous publication both in the Soviet Union and in other parts of the Western world. In the United States, psychology was still mightily under the domination of stimulus-response theories (Vygotsky would have called them reflexological), and even the Gestaltist and Freudian positions did not readily admit the kind of cognitive theory espoused by Vygotsky. Only in the last decade has Western psychology turned its attention squarely in the direction of problems of thought and knowing; only in the last five years has the establishment of an organization with a title like the Center for Cognitive Studies not seemed slightly quixotic. The appearance of the Hanfmann-Vakar redaction, therefore, is timely. The book is a challenge to solve what Vygotsky calls the "focal issue of human psychology" (p. xxi)—the interrelation of thought and language.

Not all of Vygotsky's thought is still novel, of course, for it is not as though nothing had been accomplished in the psychology of thought and language in the intervening years. We hardly need to be supplied with the further "experimental evidence that word meanings undergo evolution during childhood" (p. xx) that Vygotsky offers as one of his major contributions. For whether we mean by "word meaning" the institutionalized correspondence between a symbol and some class of referents, or the "mediational process" that is said by some psychologists to occur in the individual in response to a word, we know rather clearly, at least in principle, the conditions under which word meanings change. In point of fact, Vygotsky does not report in any detail his experimental evidence to the effect that word meanings change. One of the keenly disappointing things about the book is that it offers little information concerning the experiments that Vygotsky and his students did to support their conclusions. The style of writing in Russian psychology, then as now, shows little of the kind of concern with the exact particulars of methodology on which American behavioral science lays so much stress. We must be content, therefore, with the often striking and provocative formulations of Vygotsky, many of which are essentially hypotheses awaiting experimental check.

If I were asked to epitomize Vygotsky's point of view, I think I could hardly do better than to quote the final sentence in the book: "A word is a microcosm of human consciousness." (p. 153) Early in the book, the author had been at pains to indicate that his "unit of analysis" was the *word*—the total constellation embracing both the sound and the meaning. He avoided any breaking down of the word into "elements" such as sounds and aspects of meaning. The meaning of a word or expression, in his view, is not to be equated to a referent or thing to which it refers, because the same referent can be symbolized with different expressions like "the victor at Jena" or "the loser at Waterloo." "There is but one category of words," he writes, "—proper names—whose sole function is that of reference." (p. 73) A major part of his exposition is devoted to an explication of *meaning*; the treatment is almost philosophical in manner. Word meaning is the "internal aspect of the word" (p. 5), and in word meaning, thought and speech unite to form a "verbal thought." The basic problem of language and thought is to describe how thought and speech interact in the verbal thought unit, and to study how these units develop and function.

Thought and speech are viewed by Vygotsky as independent processes, each with its own life and growth. We may accept Vygotsky's demonstration (Chapter IV) that there can be pre-linguistic thought activity (both in animals and in children) and also pre-intellectual speech activity (in children). Thought and speech nevertheless interact; at times, one is ahead of the other in development, while at other times, the positions are reversed. But "at a certain point these lines meet, whereupon thought becomes verbal and speech rational." (p. 44) This statement is not to be taken quite literally, however, for "fusion of thought and speech, in adults as well as in children, is a phenomenon limited to a circumscribed area." (p. 48) It must exclude cases like reciting a poem without thinking of its meaning or speaking "lyrically" under the influence of emotion.

The formal analysis of Vygotsky's exposition runs into a certain difficulty when we try to distinguish between word meaning as a "unit of verbal thought," and the *concept*. Although there are places (e.g., p. 5) where word meaning is spoken of as a "generalization," or where the term *concept* is used in connection with words (p. 7: "children often have difficulty in learning a new word not because of its sound but because of the concept to which the word refers," and p. 120, "The meaning of every word is a generalization or a concept"), the treatment of the term *concept* is carried out independently of the treatment of word meaning. Indeed, whereas Vygotsky supplies numerous definitional statements for the term *meaning*, he gives no formal definition of the term *concept*. We are thus left to infer the meaning of the term from Vygotsky's treatment of it. Such inferences as I have been able to draw are not wholly satisfactory, and thus the somewhat informal organization of Vygotsky's writing becomes at times lamentable. It is more to be regretted because some of the most interesting and provocative materials in this book are those having to do with the development of concepts.

*Concept* seems to be a developmental term for Vygotsky. In the studies of concept formation carried out by his colleague Sakharov (whose name perhaps ought to be attached to the famous "Vygotsky" block test), "true" concepts were not formed until the period of adolescence—"seldom at first, then with increasing frequency." (p. 79) Earlier, the responses showed primitive syncretic forms of thinking, then "thinking in complexes," followed by the use of "potential" concepts before the "true" concept was attained. To be sure, the Sakharov block test uses "artificial" rather than "real" concepts; that is to say, it uses concepts based on contrived combinations of attributes like "small and tall" or "big and thin." But the same developmental phenomena are said to occur for "real" concepts such as those found in the teaching of "science" (actually, *social* science; Vygotsky's experiments often dealt with whether children could understand concepts like "exploitation").

Vygotsky borrows Piaget's contrast between "spontaneous" and "non-spontaneous" or "scientific" concepts—the former being the concepts formed naturally by the child on the basis of everyday experience, the latter being the concepts which the child is likely to acquire on the basis of specific, directed instruction. Thus, the child may acquire for himself concepts like those represented by the words "brother" and "flower," but he is unlikely to acquire concepts like "Planned economy is possible in the U.S.S.R. because there is no private property . . ." without specific instruction. For Vygotsky, a "concept" is something essentially in the realm of thought, not words: apprehending a concept is apprehending a thought "behind" the word, and not at all identical with it. In this particular example, what he is concerned with is whether the child apprehends the relation indicated by the conjunction "because." He reports that children are often better able to complete sentences ending in *because* when the setting is "scientific" (i.e., social science) than when the setting is non-scientific and deals with "spontaneous" concepts, as "A boy fell and broke his leg because. . . ." In the latter case, the child is likely not to be aware of the concept of "because" and will supply something like "he was sick" or "he went to the hospital." It is on the basis of this kind of evidence that Vygotsky makes the interesting suggestion that practice with "scientific" concepts transfers to "non-scientific" concepts in such a way as to accelerate their development. Thus, conceptualization in the non-spontaneous domain tends to run ahead of that in the spontaneous domain.

A hard-nosed reaction to this evidence would be to ask whether the results could not be explained on the basis of the increased verbal practice given in the "scientific" instruction as compared to wholly fortuitous amounts of practice with spontaneous concepts. Vygotsky's experiments deserve to be repeated with more adequate controls.

Like so many other treatments of the problem of language and thought, Vygotsky tends to get bogged down because of the failure to define terms precisely and op-erationally. If the term "concept" cannot be used consistently to mean the same thing, or if there are insufficient qualifications associated with its use, we cannot derive a series of unequivocal propositions about it. Vygotsky juggles with a number of di-mensions—the degree to which a concept is part of a system of thought, the degree to which it is within awareness and under conscious control, the degree to which it is formed as a result of instruction, and the degree to which it conforms to a "mature" or adult form, but he never clearly indicates to what extent "concepts" can be re-garded as corresponding to "word meanings," and indeed, there is little consideration of the influence of language in the formation of concepts. This, to be sure, is a topic that has been taken up by a number of later Russian investigators, e.g., Luria, and Liublinskaya, as one may learn by reading Simon's *Psychology in the Soviet Union* (Stanford University Press, 1957) or Luria and Yudovich's *Speech and the Development of Mental Processes in the Child* (London, 1959). As far as his basic views on language and thought are concerned, Vygotsky offers not a fully-formed theory but some interesting components of a theory.

Let us turn, therefore, to some of the more interesting ideas that can be found in this work.

Although at times Vygotsky seems to espouse the kind of notion put forward by

Piaget that there are natural constitutional limits to development, represented perhaps by a series of age-timed steps, he is much more willing that Piaget (both the Piaget of the early 'twenties—the one known by Vygotsky—and the Piaget of today) to allow the possibility of accelerating or at least strengthening the course of the child's conceptual development. What Vygotsky has to say about instruction (and he calls it that unabashedly) will be of interest and use to educators.

> Instruction is one of the principal sources of the schoolchild's concepts and is a powerful force in directing their evolution; it determines the fate of his total mental development. (p. 85)

He reviews, and rejects, three theories of the relation of instruction to development: (1) that instruction must hobble along after development, waiting for certain stages of development to begin or to be completed before it can do its work; (2) that development and instruction are identical, since development is nothing more than the accumulation of conditioned reflexes; and (3) that development has two interdependent aspects, maturation and learning. In connection with the last of these, he feels that Thorndike's critique of formal discipline "did not touch its valuable kernel" because Thorndike ignored qualitative differences between lower and higher functions of the mind. In Vygotsky's view, "the ability to gauge the length of lines may not affect the ability to distinguish between angles, but the study of the native language—with its attendant sharpening of concepts—may still have some bearing on the study of arithmetic." (p. 97) In this year 1963, we do not even yet have sufficient evidence positively to confirm or to deny this view, but it still seems reasonable if transfer takes place through identical elements. Indeed Thorndike's later writings show that he would probably have accepted Vygotsky's opinion.

Vygotsky's own "tentative" theory is stated by him as follows: "The only good kind of instruction is that which marches ahead of development and leads it: it must be aimed not so much at the ripe as at the ripening function." (p. 104) This entirely reasonable idea emerges, we are told, from four series of empirical investigations, described all too briefly, in the teaching of various school subjects. Only one of these series will be mentioned here—the one that examined the levels of development of the "psychic functions" requisite for learning the school subjects—reading and writing, arithmetic, and natural science. This investigation disclosed, for example, that in writing (that is, composing, not merely handwriting) it is the abstract quality of written language that is the main stumbling block—not poor motor coordination or the like. The author also states, without citing evidence, that "our analysis clearly showed the study of grammar to be of paramount importance for the mental development of the child," apparently because it forces the child to become aware of grammatical concepts and to get them under conscious control.

To a few close students of the subject, Vygotsky's critique of Piaget's conception of the function of egocentric speech (in which the child "talks to himself") was already familiar from a brief translated article published in the journal *Psychiatry* in 1939. Vygotsky had suggested that egocentric speech, far from representing a transition

131

from autistic speech to socialized speech, is rather a stage on the way to the interiorization of speech, "inner speech," or "silent speech." The evidence was ingeniously derived. It was shown that at a certain stage of development, egocentric speech normally occurred only when the child was in the presence of other children; in the absence of other children, it could be assumed that whatever thinking processes were occurring were accompanied by interiorized speech. "Egocentric speech" could occur under another condition: a child sitting alone and performing some activity like drawing would normally not speak, but if his task was interrupted, or if some difficulty were interposed, egocentric speech would appear. Again, the interpretation was that in the silent period inner speech was occurring, but that when a difficulty presented itself the child would regress, so to speak, to the use of overt speech.

It is interesting now to find that Piaget himself, having had an opportunity to examine Vygotsky's postulations on egocentric speech, is completely willing to entertain them. His only reservation is that Vygotsky may have failed to recognize the parallel existence of another type of egocentric speech in which the child is truly talking "for himself," or perhaps (to take the suggestion of the French child psychologist Zazzo) "according to himself" *(selon lui)*, a stage in which he has not truly learned to take full account of his audience. Piaget has a number of reservations, too, about other parts of Vygotsky's theory, but we shall not consider them here. Like Piaget, we can only close with an affirmation of our genuine respect for the extraordinary grasp of his subject and the penetrating insights exhibited by Vygotsky in this fascinating book.

# Part II
*Literacy as a Social Product:*
*A Sociocultural Approach*

# 5

# The Nature of Literacy: An Historical Exploration

DANIEL P. RESNICK, *Carnegie Mellon University*
LAUREN B. RESNICK, *University of Pittsburgh*

*Daniel and Lauren Resnick examine three major historical models for literacy development and discuss the implications of these models with regard to the present educational situation. The authors argue that these literacy models, which are based on French and U.S. models before the twentieth century, were established in order to attain high levels of literacy not for the entire population, but only for a small number of elites. They argue that, in contrast to past educational goals, the goal of contemporary education is to achieve high levels of literacy for the entire population. Emphasizing the uniqueness of the present situation, they suggest that historical models of literacy are inapplicable to current educational practice. To achieve the contemporary goal of mass literacy, the Resnicks present an alternative model as a possible solution to the unique issues facing educators in the 1990s.*

Reports of low literacy achievement and widespread reading difficulties have lent strength to a still inchoate "back to basics" movement in education. The apparent suggestion is that methods of instruction that succeeded in the past can remedy many of our present problems. Looking backward for solutions, however, can succeed only when social conditions and educational goals remain relatively stable. Only by a serious examination of our history can we determine the extent to which older educational practices are likely to succeed in today's environment, for today's purposes. This paper begins such an examination by exploring selected European and

This paper was written during our stay at the Center for Advanced Study in the Behavioral Sciences at Stanford University. Lauren Resnick was supported there by a fellowship from the Spencer Foundation. The work was also supported in part by Contract #400-75-0049 of the National Institute of Education with the Learning Research and Development Center, University of Pittsburgh.

*Harvard Educational Review*   Vol. 47   No. 3   August 1977, 370–385

American historical models of literacy standards and training in order to assess the degree to which the goals and practices of earlier times are relevant to our present needs.

Our research suggests that there has been a sharp shift over time in expectations concerning literacy. With changed standards come changed estimates of the adequacy of a population's literacy. To illustrate, if writing one's name were what was meant by literacy, we would not be worried that illiteracy was a national problem. Yet the signature was not always a demand easy to satisfy. Until well into the nineteenth century, the capacity to form the letters of one's signature was not a skill shared by the majority of the population, even in the more developed nations of Europe.[1] Even a somewhat more stringent literacy criterion would not force recognition of a major problem. If the ability to read aloud a simple and well-known passage were the measure, America would have a few "illiterates" but hardly a crisis. If we expected people to demonstrate after reading this simple passage, that they had registered its content at some low level, perhaps by saying who a story was about or what a named character did, we would probably find a low percentage of illiterates in our adult population.

But the number would start to rise, perhaps quite sharply, if unfamiliar texts were to be read and new information gleaned from them. And, if inferential rather than directly stated information were to be drawn from the text, we would probably announce a true crisis in literacy. If we used as a literacy criterion the ability to read a complex text with literary allusions and metaphoric expression and not only to interpret this text but to relate it sensibly to other texts, many would claim that only a tiny fraction of our population is "truly literate," a charge not infrequently made in discussions about standards of literacy at the university level.

We think that this nation perceives itself as having an unacceptable literacy level because it is applying a criterion that requires, at a minimum, the reading of new material and the gleaning of new information from that material. We shall argue in this paper that this high literacy standard is a relatively recent one as applied to the population at large and that much of our present difficulty in meeting the literacy standard we are setting for ourselves can be attributed to the relatively rapid extension to large populations of educational criteria that were once applied to only a limited elite. The result of this rapid extension is that instructional methods suitable to large and diverse populations rather than small and selected ones have not yet been fully developed or applied. Further, not all segments of our population have come to demand literacy skills of the kind that educators, members of Congress, and other government officials think necessary.

Our argument is that the standards currently applied to mass literacy have been with us for at most three generations. To examine the proposition that the current definition of literacy is a relatively new one, we have undertaken a selective review of published material on standards of literacy in various historical settings and on the social and political conditions under which these standards were applied. Some of the less commonly cited historical models seem especially instructive because of either the large size of the literate population, the high standards of literacy, or the democratic ideology. We will elaborate three major historical models for literacy development before the twentieth century: the Protestant-religious, the elite-technical, and the civic-national. To illustrate these models, we will describe literacy training and examinations in seventeenth-century Sweden, elite scientific and technical education in France since the eighteenth century, and schooling among the French peasants during the last century. In so doing, we shall try to relate particular kinds of literacy standards and instructional approaches to changing social needs and conditions. Finally, we will trace the changes in literacy standards that occurred in the first part of this century in the United States.

Having examined these historical cases, we will be in a position to consider the degree of fit between certain persisting traditions of education and present-day literacy standards. We shall also note a remarkable match between our conclusions and certain current theories of reading development that are based on observation of the stages through which individuals pass as they gain competence with the written word. In concluding we will consider various implications of our historical and theoretical analysis for current educational policy.

## Models from the Historical Experience

### Protestant-Religious Education

Historians have come to view the efforts of Protestant communities to bring their members into personal contact with biblical history and the Christian message as very important for the growth of literacy.[2] These efforts have also been recognized as significant in affecting social and economic development.[3] With respect to American development, Bernard Bailyn and Lawrence Cremin have described colonial literacy as so profoundly transforming that its development constituted a break with traditional attitudes.[4]

More recently, the connection between literacy and socioeconomic shifts has been called into question. Kenneth Lockridge has argued that literacy was of little significance for the shaping of modern social values in Protestant colonial New England.[5] The absence of such a relationship between schooling and economic development in Lancashire before the mid-nineteenth century has been one of the themes in the revisionist work of Michael Sanderson.[6] However, even for those who have been skeptical about its causal relationship to attitudes, the early modern Protestant experience with literacy has been seen as a watershed because of the great numbers of people who shared in that experience. In colonial New England, Lockridge estimates that male literacy, which was well above 60 percent for the generation born around 1700, became nearly universal by the end of the century;[7] in Scotland, Lawrence Stone found that the rate of literacy among adult males went from 33 percent around 1675 to almost 90 percent by 1800;[8] and in Sweden, Egil Johansson found that the number of males "able to read" in the parishes of Skelleftea went from half the population to 98 percent in the period from 1645 to 1714.[9]

The question of what kinds of knowledge defined literacy in these Protestant experiments has not been directly addressed by historians concerned with the relationship of literacy to economic and social development. We are able to respond to the question by considering the Swedish case, which represents the first instance of systematic record keeping relative to reading. To cite one example, the oldest extant registers of Möklinta parish in central Sweden, for the years from 1656 to 1669, offer columns to note whether or not minimum competency had been met in each of five areas.[10] The first involved the actual words to the text of the *Little Catechism;* the second, Luther's explanations of the words of the text; the third, the Confession of Sin; the fourth, morning and evening prayers; the fifth, prayers said at the table.[11] Questions on Lutheran creed and practice were apparently posed by the pastor on each of these topics. The examination assumed the availability of a printed catechism and prayer book in every home and prior discussion of these materials at catechetical meetings, attendance at which was to be checked off in a final column of the register.

No formal column for the capacity to read, as such, is to be found in this register (although one would be introduced in its successor), but all the questions assume the capacity to read, review, memorize, and recall familiar material. A second register, used during the period from 1686 to 1705, includes a corroborating column for "literacy," which was understood as the ability to read to the satisfaction of the examiner. An analysis of this material indicates that, while only one-fourth of the parish residents born in the early part of the seventeenth century were described as literate, the percentage grew to three-fourths for those born at the end of the century.

From the standpoint of current expectations, the literacy criterion that yielded these figures is a limited one. No unfamiliar material was given to the examinee. No writing was expected. No application of knowledge to new contexts was demanded. And no digressions from the text of the catechism and prayers were expected or permitted. The result was an exercise in the reading and memorizing of familiar material, to be recalled upon demand. Nevertheless, the Swedish experience, like the less controlled systems of early Protestant education in Scotland and the American colonies, represents more than simply a baseline of low literacy expectation. Instead, subsequent pedagogic efforts in literacy were heavily influenced by early religious activities.

### The Elite-Technical Schools

A quite different tradition of literacy, one aimed at an elite, is represented by the growth of higher technical education in France. This system had its beginnings in the *collèges* and private academies of the Old Regime. The schools were run by such religious orders as the Oratorians and Jesuits, largely for sons of the aristocracy and bourgeoisie, although a few extremely able sons of the poor were accepted. Boys could enter at age seven and could stay until age seventeen or eighteen for an extended period of formal schooling. From these schools young men could enter a variety of state technical and professional schools that prepared their graduates for careers in civil and military public service.

By the eighteenth century, mathematics had become established as the touchstone of elite education. At all levels mathematics was stressed as the key to effective reasoning. For La Chalotais, in his *Plan d'éducation nationale* of 1763, it was "very possible and very common to reason badly in theology, or in politics; it is impossible in arithmetic and in geometry; if accuracy of mind is lacking, the rules will supply accuracy and intelligence for those who follow them." For Diderot, geometry was "the best and simplest of all logics, and it is the most suitable for fortifying the judgment and the reason."[12] But mathematics was deemed more than a better way to reason; it was central to the curriculum not only because of its alleged utility for developing young minds, but also because of its perceived usefulness to the state. It was essential for military purposes, civil engineering, and the monarchy's "civilizing" action in architecture, surveying, standard measures, and public finance.

In this context, literacy necessarily meant the acquisition of theoretical knowledge and the development of problem-solving capacities. But this criterion was thought to be applicable not to the whole population but only to a small elite. Competitive examinations restricted entry to the best state schools from the time of their establishment during the Old Regime; and the École Polytechnique, created during the Revolution, maintained the same standards of competitive entry.

The Revolution in no way challenged the definition or state support of this elite training at either the secondary or the graduate level. Established in 1795, the *écoles centrales* continued at the secondary level the scientific tradition of the *collèges* and academies of the Old Regime. The *écoles centrales* were succeeded by the *lycées*, which came to place greater emphasis on Latin than on mathematics. Despite this change in subject matter, a strong and visible place was maintained within secondary education for students who were preparing for the *grandes écoles*.[13]

Higher technical training was enshrined in the educational program of France and thus became—and continues to be—the distinguishing mark of the French graduate elite. Strong on theory and arrogant about their ability to apply knowledge to a variety of situations, these graduates have only recently found a world of technical literacy in which they feel comfortable despite the limits of their training. As Charles Kindleberger has argued, "Excessively deductive, Cartesian, geometric, mathematical, theoretical by nineteenth century standards, the system is coming into its own in a world of scientific sophistication."[14]

## Civic-National Schooling

While elites continued to attend specialized academies, responsibility for mass education gradually shifted from religious communities to public bodies. We again consider France as an example. The French system of primary education has been credited with breaking new ground in secularizing education, universalizing schools, and fostering patriotism. From 1789 to 1914, this system of primary education increased the number of people with basic literacy from less than half to more than 90 percent of the French population.[15]

Primary education became a public commitment during the French Revolution. When the Revolutionary government introduced the first plan for national education in France in 1795, its major interest was military: the preservation of schools and training routes for those entering technical and military careers was considered essential. (Similarly, Napoleon's system of secondary education, the *lycée*, was focused on providing personnel for the nation's military and technical needs.) The 1795 plan contained only the outlines of a system for primary education. It neither provided funding for primary schools nor created a sufficient number to serve the predominantly rural public.[16]

Before legislation abolished the religious orders' endowments and their right to receive public and private contribution, these orders had played a major role in providing basic education. The restrictive measures of the Revolution, in combination with wartime activity, drove many of the clergy underground or abroad. This effectively dismantled the church system of primary education that had functioned at the village level.

However, even in those areas where public primary schools were established, it was difficult to separate primary education from religious instruction. The attempt to do so initially generated much hostility in conservative areas. For this and other reasons the separation between religious and public education was far from complete. Without public funding for school textbooks, religious materials continued to serve as beginning reading matter for children. The personnel of the old church primary schools also tended to reappear in the new secular ones.

Literacy levels appear to have remained fairly stable across the Revolutionary divide, despite the undermining of the church-run primary schools. There was no important growth in literacy, as measured by signatures on marriage contracts, in any department during the thirty years after the opening of the Revolution. Only one-quarter of the French departments had growth rates of more than one percent, in the male capacity to sign, and almost all of that growth was in the range of one to two percent. Twelve departments showed declines in the male capacity to sign during this period, but all were of less than one percent.[17]

The literacy expectations in the primary schools that did function before the 1830s remained modest. This is hardly surprising since primary education was largely a catch-as-catch-can affair for the first two post-Revolutionary generations in rural France. Children usually attended school for only the winter months, since the demands of family and farm had priority, and even then they did so irregularly. Those who attended generally left between the ages of ten and twelve after confirmation in the Church. Communions were held rather early, to coincide roughly with the end of the primary-school course.[18]

In addition to irregular school attendance, poorly prepared teachers may also have contributed to low levels of literacy. Teachers were not professionally trained before the 1830s, even though efforts to impose professional standards for their certification were first made in 1816.[19] The minimum standard was a demonstrated ability to read, write, and use simple figures, yet even this standard was not always met. For example, even after 1830, teachers who hired themselves out by the season at fairs in eastern France reportedly placed one, two, or three feathers in their caps to indicate what subject or subjects they knew how to teach: the first stood for reading, the second for arithmetic, and the third for Latin. In arithmetic, moreover, those who could only add and subtract far outnumbered those who could multiply and divide as well. One teacher, Sister Gandilhon, who ran a school at Selins (Cantal) in the 1840s, taught "prayers, the catechism and the first two rules of arithmetic." According to a contemporary, "she had heard of a third but never learned it."[20] The teaching of arithmetic was further complicated by the use of regional units for weights and measures, like the *pouce* and the *toise*, which had no relationship to the metric system introduced by the Revolution.[21]

The methods of reading instruction were equally primitive. Before the 1840s, the teaching of reading was characterized by instruction in the names of the letters ("ah, bay, say, day. . . ."), independent of any relationship to other vowels and consonants. From the pronunciation of letters, students moved directly to the pronunciation of words.[22] A study of a village in western France noted that one teacher, much respected, read aloud sentences from the children's readers and then had children repeat the sentences. According to a resident of the village:

> The children were not required to make any effort to understand the words or to attempt to associate the shapes with sounds and meanings. They merely repeated what had been said to them and gradually discovered . . . by the place on the page or the approximate shape of what they were being given to read the sounds they were required to emit to avoid being beaten.[23]

It is hardly surprising, given these methods, that many pupils did not learn how to read at all. Further, those who did manage to read generally worked only on religious books and simple readers.

Mastery may also have been rare because the language of instruction did not always match the vernacular of the region. Most of France was a nation of *patois*, and in many regions Provençal, German, Italian, or Catalan was the major language. Since the language of instruction during most of the nineteenth century was almost universally French, the result was predictable. Even when students were able to read the written language fluently, inspectors in Brittanny noted, "No child can give account of what he has read or translate it into Breton; hence there is no proof that anything is understood."[24]

### Persisting Limits of the Civic-National Model

School attendance rose sharply throughout France as a result of two major reforms of the primary system of public education, the first in 1833 and the second in 1881–82.[25] Steps were taken under Ministers of Education Guizot and Ferry to democratize the system by increasing the number of primary schools, by reducing school fees, and by increasing the number of training colleges for teachers. These measures, in varying degrees, increased school attendance and contributed to the professionalization of teachers. However, despite these efforts toward democratization, primary schooling remained clearly distinct from the elite-secondary program.

Public schooling, moreover, did not for some time abandon its preoccupation with religious principles. Although in the field of education a civic religion of nationalism ultimately replaced traditional Catholic beliefs, schoolmasters remained dependent on local religious authorities for the nearly fifty years between the two reforms.[26] In 1833 the education minister attempted to make peace with the parish religious authorities in order to convince parents of the value of public primary schooling. "It is on the preponderant and united action of Church and State that I rely to establish primary instruction," Guizot told the legislature.[27] In practice this meant the responsibilities of the primary teacher included encouraging attendance at Mass, teaching prayers and biblical lore, and assisting the priest as needed. Reports from the 1840s and 1850s cite many examples of schools in which an alphabet book in Latin or a fifteenth-century *Life of Christ* served as the reading text.[28]

This educational alliance with the Church was broken by the Ferry reforms of 1881–82. The catechism was eliminated from the school reading program. Every *commune* was required to support a schoolmaster and a public school for girls as well as boys. A policy of free tuition, though not one of free books, replaced the earlier program of limited scholarships. For the first time school attendance was made compulsory, and the primary program was extended to age fourteen.[29] Finally, the national education ministry began a massive program of school construction.

Instruction was not designed to enlarge the skills of the literate or to encourage critical approaches to reading; rather, it was meant to cultivate a love of the familiar. History and geography texts were introduced to promote love of country.[30] The purpose of history instruction, for example, was unabashedly identified as patriotic. When questioned about the role of history in education, nearly 80 percent of the candidates for a *baccalauréat* in 1897 answered with statements about the "need to exalt patriotism."[31] Thus, despite the new curriculum, many of the criteria for literacy embedded in seventeenth- and eighteenth-century religious instruction were allowed to persist.

By the time of World War I, the successes of public primary schooling were clearly visible. Almost every child in the nation had relatively easy access to schools, and nearly all fourteen-year-olds by then had attended schools for seven years. Teachers were generally graduates of special training colleges located in each *département*. Attendance was increasingly regular for those enrolled in the schools, and students did not leave with the passing of winter. Inability to pay did not directly bar students' access to school. French was clearly the national language, and the metric system had triumphed over local measures. Statistics compiled by the Ministry of Education on years of schooling as well as the dramatic rise in the proportion of military recruits capable of signing their own names[32] are further evidence of these successes.

However, these facts do not inform us about the quality of education or the growth of individual capacity, and on these issues the evidence is mixed. Thabault observed that, while fewer than one-fifth of the inhabitants of his village knew how to form the letters of their names in 1833, more than half were able to do so thirty years later. Nevertheless, "the amount of knowledge that most of them had acquired did not make them very different from the completely illiterate."[33] By the eve of World War I, there had been considerable improvement in the knowledge of history, geography, and the French language. The inculcation of this knowledge took the form of a civic education, a new catechism based on patriotic devotion and civic duty. Eugen Weber has argued that this system, along with the army and improved transportation in the years from 1876 to 1914, contributed to the modernization of the attitudes and behavior of the French peasantry. But acculturation and adaptation do not necessarily produce generalized understanding, transferable learning, or reasoning skills.

## Teaching Methods and Literacy Criteria in America

American methods of teaching reading were influenced initially by approaches developed in Europe. The classic method, as we have seen in the French system, was alphabetic. Children were first drilled on the letter names and then on syllables. No attempt was made to select meaningful syllables or to emphasize comprehension; rather, accurate and fluent pronunciation was emphasized. The following description of reading instruction in the Sessional School in Edinburgh, Scotland, was reported to American educators in 1831. This account suggests the dominant goal of literacy instruction in the United States as well as in Scotland:

> English reading, according to the prevailing notion, consists of nothing more than the power of giving utterance to certain sounds, on the perception of certain figures; and the measure of progress and excellence is the facility and continuous fluency with which those sounds succeed each other from the mouth of the learner. If the child gather any knowledge from the book before him, beyond that of color, form and position of the letters, it is to his own sagacity he is indebted for it, and not to his teacher.[34]

Pedagogical reforms that had been introduced in Britain, Germany, and France during the eighteenth and nineteenth centuries later influenced instructional practice in the United States. The Prussian educator Friedrich Gedike[35] had introduced a "word method" of reading instruction which used words as the starting point for teaching the alphabet and spelling. Other reformers substituted the use of sounds, or "powers," of the letters for their names in the initial teaching of the alphabet. Although these reforms improved the teaching of fluent oral reading, they did not imply any new or greater concern for students' ability to understand what was read.

In the United States many forward-looking educators recognized that a greater emphasis on meaning would enliven instruction and make it more palatable to children. Putnam, in 1836, stressed the need for comprehension while criticizing the dominant instructional practice:

> A leading object of this work is to enable the scholar, while learning to *read*, to *understand*, at the same time, the *meaning* of the words he is reading. . . . if, for

example, when the pupil is taught to read, he is enabled, at the same time, to discover the *meaning* of the words he repeats, he will readily make use of the proper inflections, and place the emphasis where the sense demands it. The monotonous sing-song mode of reading, which is common in schools and which is often retained in after life, is acquired from the exercise of reading what is not understood.[36]

Nearly fifty years later, Farnham voiced similar concern when proposing his sentence method of reading instruction:

It is important that this two-fold function of reading should be fully recognized. The first, or silent reading, is the fundamental process. . . . The second, oral reading, or "reading aloud," is entirely subordinate to silent reading. While oral expression is subject to laws of its own, its excellence depends upon the success of the reader in comprehending the thought of the author.[37]

Although these educators laid the groundwork for new methods and standards in literacy, their ideas did not become common educational practice until much later. Fundamental change in the standards applied to reading instruction came early in the twentieth century with the advent of child-centered theories of pedagogy, which stressed the importance of intrinsic interest and meaningfulness in learning, and the introduction of standardized group testing during World War I.

The American entry into the war highlighted a national literacy problem. Under the leadership of Robert Yerkes, then president of the American Psychological Association, a group of psychologists prepared and validated group-administered forms of a general intelligence test.[38] This test had two forms—Army Alpha for literate recruits and Army Beta for recruits unable to take the Alpha form. The tests were administered in 1918 to 1.7 million men, and it was noted with dismay that nearly 30 percent could not understand the Alpha form because they could not read well enough. This discovery evoked the following comment by an American educator, May Ayres Burgess:

[I]f those [men] examined were fairly representative of all, there must have been over one million of our soldiers and sailors who were not able to write a simple letter or read a newspaper with ease.

[A]lthough one-fourth of the men could not read well enough to take tests based on reading, this deficiency was not caused by their never having learned to read. The fact is that an overwhelming majority of these soldiers had entered school, attended the primary grades where reading is taught, and had been taught to read. Yet, when as adults they were examined, they were unable to read readily such simple material as that of a daily newspaper.[39]

After army intelligence tests had alerted people to defects in reading instruction, the growth in the 1920s of graded and standardized achievement testing gave educators tools for evaluating their efforts. The development of testing was stimulated in part by the successes of the army testing program and by the growing receptivity of school administrators to what they regarded as scientific tools of management.[40] The army program had demonstrated the practicality and validity of group-administered psychological tests. Because group-administered reading tests required silent reading rather than oral, the ability to answer questions or follow directions based upon a simple text became the most typical test of reading competence. This focus on deriving the meaning of a text fit well with what the most forward-looking educators had already been advocating. The ability to understand an unfamiliar text, rather than simply declaim a familiar one, became the accepted goal of reading instruction and the new standard of literacy.

This newer standard, previously applied only to the programs of elite institutions, required the ability to gain information from reading and use that information in new contexts. The 1920s marked the first time in history that such a rigorous standard had been applied in the United States. This emphasis on deriving meaning from text bolstered the cause of those educators advocating changes in reading instruction. With this change in the criterion of literacy, national aspirations also rose for the portion of the population expected to meet this new standard.

Patterns of school attendance in this century best illustrate these radical changes. Reviewing data from several American cities, Leonard Ayres reported in 1909 that of one hundred children who were in school at age seven, ninety would still be there at age thirteen, fifty at age fourteen, and only thirteen of the original one hundred would remain in school at age sixteen.[41] Equally important were the large numbers of students not promoted; attendance at school for six or seven years by no means assured passage into the sixth or seventh grade. In general, Ayres found that, from any given grade level, 20 percent would not be promoted—if they returned to school at all.[42] Ayres's statistics clearly demonstrate that only a limited percentage of the population completed elementary school in the early part of this century. Whatever the eighth-grade level of reading competence may have been, only half of those attending school ever completed that grade. The literacy level that came closer to being universal was the fifth-grade level, which was comparable to that attained at the completion of primary schooling in nineteenth-century France. Although we cannot estimate exactly the functioning level of literacy at the beginning of the century, it seems fair to conclude that it did not approach present standards.

## The Growth of Literacy Expectations

This article documents changes in literacy standards and teaching methods in the United States and some European countries, chiefly France, during the past several centuries. Our evidence suggests a rough progression in literacy expectation and performance. Expectations for popular literacy appeared after a long period in which the general population could not read. The earliest mass-literacy effort, Protestant-religious instruction, was intended to develop not a generalized capacity to read but only the mastery of a very limited set of prescribed texts. Although civic-national public schooling introduced a slightly broadened set of texts, students were not expected to use their reading skills to acquire new information but only to become fluent oral readers. Nonetheless, some individuals did learn to read for information and even to engage in critical and inferential reading similar to that demanded by elite schools.

It is only during the present century that the goal of reading for the purpose of gaining information has been applied in ordinary elementary schools to the entire population of students. Today, the term "functional literacy" has come to mean the ability to read common texts such as newspapers and manuals and to use the information gained, usually to secure employment.[43] The objectives of functional literacy may seem limited, yet this mass-literacy criterion is stronger than that of any earlier period of history. Achieving universal literacy as it is now defined poses a challenge not previously faced. We estimate that literacy standards in the United States in the 1990s will be both more demanding and more widely applied than any previous standard. The accompanying Figure 1 permits a schematic comparison between the aspirations which we have projected for the United States and standards met by earlier literacy movements. Depending on how the figure is read we are either attempting to increase by a significant degree the quality of literacy competence in our population, or to increase, also very significantly, the portion of our population to which an already established criterion is to apply.

The historical development of ever more demanding criteria for literacy mirrors to some extent a model for individual development of reading competence that has recently been proposed by Jeanne Chall.[44] In this sense, social phylogeny seems to reflect ontogeny. Chall points out that at successive stages in reading development,

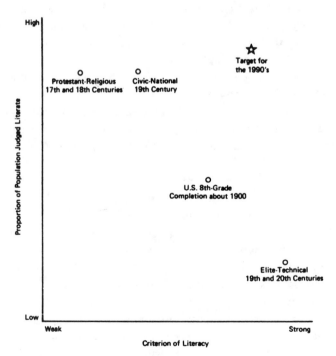

FIGURE 1
*Schematic Representation of Shifts in Literacy Standards*

"the reader is doing essentially 'different' things in relation to printed matter, although the term reading is used to describe each of these stages." Further, "the successive stages are characterized by growth in the ability to read language of greater complexity, rarity, technicality, and abstractness, and with a change in how such materials are viewed and used."

Chall proposes five stage of reading. After a prereading period the first stage is initial reading or decoding. The essential aspect here "is the learning of the arbitrary set of letters and associating these with the corresponding parts of spoken words. . . ." The second stage is confirmation and fluency: "Essentially reading at this stage is a consolidation. . . . By reading familiar stories, smoothness and fluency are gained." Chall points out that at one time the Bible and religious tracts were familiar texts. The congruence between Chall's earlier stages and the literacy standards of the religious and civic-national periods is striking. During these periods reading instruction centered on mastering print, associating letters with words, and reading aloud. Chall's stage of confirmation and fluency seems parallel to the practice, highly valued in the nineteenth century, of public reading of texts. Chall's third stage, "reading for learning the new," is the first point at which mastering the ideas conveyed comes to be the dominant goal. For a long time, reading for new information was not expected of many, and it is only now becoming a nearly universal standard.

## Implications for Policy

Our review of the Protestant-religious, civic-national, and elite-technical educational efforts has been very selective, but it nonetheless suggests the novelty of our present situation. Educational leaders often argue as if "real literacy" is compromised by an acceptance of functional-literacy standards tied to very practical demands of work and citizenship such as filing tax returns and reading technical manuals. On the contrary, our findings suggest that the serious application to the entire population of the contemporary standard of functional literacy would represent a real and important increase in literacy. This is not to deny the ultimate possibility and desirability of seeking a still higher literacy criterion, but forms of pedagogy will almost surely have to change to accommodate the changes in both the literacy criterion and target population.

This discussion of changes in literacy standards has implications for the growing "back to basics" movement. Although the claim is frequently made that a return to basics would improve our educational system, the consequences of such a program are not clear. Presumably, proponents of basic education want schools to stress skills of literacy and mathematics more than certain recent additions to the curriculum. This much is reasonable. But, unless we intend to relinquish the criterion of comprehension as the goal of reading instruction, there is little to go *back* to in terms of pedagogical method, curriculum, or school organization. The old tried and true approaches, which nostalgia prompts us to believe might solve current problems, were designed neither to achieve the literacy standard sought today nor to assure successful literacy for everyone. Whatever the rhetoric of the common school, early dropping out and selective promotion were in fact used to escape problems that must now be addressed through a pedagogy adequate to today's aspirations. While we may be able to borrow important ideas and practices from earlier periods, there is no simple past to which we can return.

## Notes

1. For the use of signatures in public oaths and as a source on literacy in seventeenth- and eighteenth-century England, see Roger S. Schofield, "The Measurement of Literacy in Pre-Industrial England," in *Literacy in Traditional Societies*, ed. Jack R. Goody (Cambridge, Eng.: Cambridge Univ. Press, 1968), pp. 311–25; and Richard T. Vann, "Literacy in Seventeenth-Century England: Some Hearth-Tax Evidence," *Journal of Interdisciplinary History*, 5 (1974), 287–93. The uses of signatures for retrospective literacy assessment in France are discussed in François Furet and Vladimir Sachs, 'La Croissance de l'alphabétisation en France (XVIIIe-XIXe siècles)," *Annales: Économies, Sociétés, Civilisations*, 29 (1974), 714–37.
2. Lawrence Stone, "Literacy and Education in England, 1640–1900," *Past and Present*, No. 42 (1969), esp. pp. 77–83, examines the relationship of Protestantism to the development of literacy.
3. For samples of current work exploring the effect of education on economic growth in different contexts, see Roger S. Schofield, "Dimensions of Illiteracy, 1750–1850," *Explorations in Economic History*, 10 (1973), 437–54; and David McClelland, "Does Education Accelerate Economic Growth?" *Economic Development and Cultural Change*, 14 (1966), 257–78. For the effect of education on personality change, see Howard Schuman, Alex Inkeles, and David Smith, "Some Social and Psychological Effects and Non-Effects of Literacy in a New Nation," *Economic Development and Cultural Change*, 16 (1967), 1–14.
4. See Bernard Bailyn, *Education in the Forming of American Society: Needs and Opportunities for Study* (Chapel Hill: Univ. of North Carolina Press, 1960), esp. pp. 48–49; and Lawrence Cremin, *American Education: The Colonial Experience, 1607–1783* (New York: Harper & Row, 1970), pp. 545–70. The counterargument by Kenneth Lockridge, *Literacy in Colonial New England: An Inquiry into the Social Context of Literacy in the Early Modern West* (New York: Norton, 1974), pp. 28–29 and nn., overstates Cremin's position but not the thrust of his argument.
5. On the failure of colonial wills to offer evidence of nontraditional social behavior, see Lockridge, pp. 33–35.
6. See Michael Sanderson, "Literacy and Social Mobility in the Industrial Revolution in England," *Past and Present*, No. 56 (1972), esp. pp. 89–95, and the later exchange with Thomas Laqueur in "Debate," *Past and Present*, No. 64 (1974), pp. 96–112.
7. Lockridge, *Literacy in Colonial New England*, pp. 13, 87–88.
8. For Scotland, see Stone, "Literacy and Education in England," pp. 79–80, 82–83, 123–24, 126–27, 135–36.
9. Egil Johansson, "Literacy Studies in Sweden: Some Examples," in *Literacy and Society in a Historical Perspective: A Conference Report*, ed. E. Johansson, Educational Reports Umeå (Umeå, Sweden: Umeå Univ. and School of Education, 1973), p. 49. We would like to thank Professor Kjell Härnqvist for his assistance in pursuing this investigation.
10. This discussion is based on Johansson, "Literacy Studies in Sweden," pp. 41–50, which includes reproductions of two pages from the registers.
11. The Little Catechism of Luther, translated into Swedish, with officially published "Explanations," functioned as did the Bible in Cromwellian England as a source of religious authority. One of the reasons for this was the failure of various projects to translate the Bible in its entirety into Swedish. The era of cheap Bibles opened in Sweden only at the beginning of the nineteenth century. See Michael Roberts, "The Swedish Church," in *Sweden's Age of Greatness*, ed. M. Roberts (New York: St. Martin's Press, 1973), pp. 138–40. Those who had not learned the Little Catechism were forbidden by law in 1686 to marry. See Claude Nordmann, *Grandeur et liberté de la Suède (1660–1792)* (Paris and Louvain: Béatrice-Nauwelaerts, 1971), p. 118.
12. See François de la Fontainerie, ed. and trans., *French Liberalism and Education in the Eighteenth Century: The Writings of La Chalotais, Turgot, Diderot and Condorcet on National Education* (New York and London: McGraw-Hill, 1932), pp. 95, 230, quoted in Frederick B. Artz, *The Development of Technical Education in France, 1500–1850* (Cambridge, Mass.: M.I.T. Press, 1966), pp. 68, 71. The centrality of mathematics is also discussed in Roger Hahn, *The Anatomy of a Scientific Institution: The Paris Academy of Sciences, 1666–1803* (Berkeley: Univ. of California Press, 1971), esp. pp. 95–97. For efforts to apply mathematics to social questions, see Keith Michael Baker,

*Condorcet: From Natural Philosophy to Social Mathematics* (Chicago: Univ. of Chicago Press, 1975), esp. pp. 332–42.

13. For the struggle between humanist classicists and scientists for direction of the secondary-school program, see Antoine Prost, *Histoire de l'enseignement en France, 1800–1967* (Paris: A. Colin, 1968), pp. 55–58.

14. Charles Kindleberger, "Technical Education and the French Entrepreneur," in *Enterprise and Entrepreneurs in Nineteenth- and Twentieth-Century France,* ed. Edward C. Carter, II, Robert Forster, and Joseph N. Moody (Baltimore: Johns Hopkins Press, 1976), pp. 26–27.

15. For eighteenth-century growth rates in literacy, as estimated by marriage-contract signatures, see Furet and Sachs, "La Croissance de l'alphabétisation," 726–27.

16. For primary and secondary schooling during the Revolutionary and Napoleonic years, see Maurice Gontar, *L'Enseignement primaire en France de la Révolution à la loi Guizot (1789–1833)* (Paris: Belles Lettres, 1959); Louis Liard, *L'Enseignement supérieur en France, 1789–1893,* 2 vols. (Paris: A. Colin, 1888–94); and Robert R. Palmer, ed. and trans., *The School of the French Revolution: A Documentary History of the Collège Louis-le-Grand . . . 1762–1814* (Princeton, N.J.: Princeton Univ. Press, 1975).

17. Furet and Sachs in "La Croissance de l'alphabétisation," 722–37, argue that the Revolution accelerated trends in progress. The South continued to "catch up," the difference between male and female literacy rates narrowed, and the rate of literacy progress, within a narrow band, slowly moved forward. This argument will be developed further by them in a forthcoming volume. Evidence of some newly appreciated continuities in secondary education over the period from 1780 to 1836 are analyzed in the revisionist work of Dominique Julia and Paul Pressly, "La Population scolaire en 1789," *Annales: Économies, Sociétés, Civilisations,* 30 (1975), 1516–61.

18. See Eugen Weber, *Peasants into Frenchmen: The Modernization of Rural France, 1870–1914* (Stanford, Calif.: Stanford Univ. Press, 1976), p. 319, for an example of this relationship as late as the 1860s.

19. For a discussion of these standards in the context of the 1816 rulings, see Gontard, *L'énseignement primaire,* pp. 300–306.

20. For the contemporary sources, see Weber, *Peasants into Frenchmen,* pp. 305–6.

21. On the metric system, made the only legal measure in 1840, see Weber, pp. 30–35.

22. On the nineteenth-century pedagogy, see the observations of Prost, *Histoire de l'enseignement,* pp. 119–24, 276–82.

23. Roger Thabault, *Education and Change in a Village Community: Mazières-en-Gâtine 1848–1914* (New York: Schocken Books, 1971), p. 61.

24. Cited in Weber, *Peasants into Frenchmen,* p. 306.

25. A table of legislation affecting French education at all levels, 1794–1967, may be found in Prost, *Histoire de L'Enseignement,* pp. 501–11.

26. For the preprofessional dependence of the French primary school teacher on local religious authority during the early nineteenth century, see Peter V. Meyers, "Professionalization and Societal Change: Rural Teachers in Nineteenth-Century France," *Journal of Social History,* 9 (1976), 542–46.

27. F. Guizot, *Mémoires,* III, 69–70, cited in Gontard, *L'Enseignement primaire,* pp. 495–96.

28. See Weber, *Peasants into Frenchmen,* pp. 305–6 and nn. In arguing the laicization of French education by the mid-nineteenth century, Michalina Clifford-Vaughn and Margaret Archer, *Social Conflict and Educational Change in England and France, 1789–1848* (Cambridge, Eng.: Cambridge Univ. Press, 1971), p. 202, have not presented a convincing argument.

29. Prost, *Histoire de L'Enseignement,* pp. 192–203. Legislation in 1886 was designed to eliminate the religious from a teaching role in public schools.

30. For an excellent discussion of the role of Ernest Lavisse in creating the "civic" and "national" history texts, see William R. Keylor, *Academy and Community: The Foundation of the French Historical Profession* (Cambridge, Mass.: Harvard Univ. Press, 1975), pp. 92–100.

31. From Charles-Victor Langlois and Charles Seignobos, *Introduction aux études historiques* (Paris: Hachette et Compagnie, 1898), pp. 288–89, cited in Keylor, p. 99, and Weber, *Peasants into Frenchmen,* p. 333. On the relationship of this kind of instruction to nation-building, see Karl Deutsch, *Nationalism and Social Communication: An Inquiry into the Foundations of Nationality* (Cambridge, Mass.: M.I.T. Press; and New York: Wiley, 1953), pp. 92–99, 155.

32. A graph showing the rise in literacy measured by the capacity to sign in the years from 1830 to 1910 is offered in Prost, *Histoire de l'enseignement,* p. 96. Also given (p. 98) is a graph showing the number and distribution of students in primary schooling from 1810 to 1890.

33. Thabault, *Education and Change,* p. 64. The relationship between capacity to sign and capacity to read is discussed by Schofield, "The Measurement of Literacy in Pre-Industrial England,"

p. 324; Furet and Sachs, "La Croissance de l'alphabétisation," esp. 715–16, 720–21; and Stone, "Literacy and Education in England," pp. 98–99.

34. From Mitford Mathews, *Teaching to Read: Historically Considered* (Chicago: Univ. of Chicago Press, 1966), p. 55.
35. For an assessment of Gedike's work, see Mathews, pp. 37–43.
36. Samuel Putnam, *The Analytical Reader* (Portland, Maine: Wm. Hyde, 1836), cited in Charles C. Fries, *Linguistics and Reading* (New York: Holt, Rinehart & Winston, 1963), p. 10.
37. George Farnham, *The Sentence Method* (Syracuse, N.Y.: C. W. Bardeen, 1881), cited in Fries, p. 11.
38. Clarence S. Yoakum and Robert M. Yerkes, *Army Mental Tests* (New York: Henry Holt, 1920), p. 2; and Lewis M. Terman, "Methods of Examining: History, Development and Preliminary Results," in *Psychological Examining in the United States Army*, ed. Robert M. Yerkes, Memoirs of the National Academy of Sciences, Vol. 15, Part 2 (Washington, D.C.: Government Printing Office, 1921), 299–546.
39. May Ayres Burgess, *The Measurement of Silent Reading* (New York: Russell Sage Foundation, 1921), pp. 11–12.
40. See Raymond E. Callahan, *Education and the Cult of Efficiency* (Chicago: Univ. of Chicago Press, 1962); and David B. Tyack, *The One Best System: A History of American Education* (Cambridge, Mass.: Harvard Univ. Press, 1974), pp. 198–216.
41. Leonard P. Ayres, *Laggards in Our Schools: A Study of Elimination and Retardation in City School Systems* (New York: Russell Sage Foundation, 1909). This book was prompted by concern with the large number of schoolchildren who were older than they should have been for their assigned grade level.
42. Ayres, pp. 20, 38, 66.
43. On functional illiteracy, see David Harman, "Illiteracy: An Overview," *Harvard Educational Review*, 40 (1970), 226–30. The United States Census Bureau, however, uses the completion of six years of schooling as the standard for literacy. For a review of the relationship of six years of schooling to selected measures of reading ability, see John R. Bormuth, "Reading Literacy: Its Definition and Assessment," in *Toward a Literate Society: The Report of the Committee on Reading of the National Academy of Education*, ed. John B. Carroll and Jeanne S. Chall (New York: McGraw-Hill, 1975), pp. 62–63.
44. Jeanne S. Chall, "The Great Debate: Ten Years Later, with a Modest Proposal for Reading Stages," in *Theory and Practice of Early Reading*, I, ed. Lauren B. Resnick and Phyllis Weaver (Hillsdale, N.J.: Erlbaum Associates, 1979).

# 6

# *From Utterance to Text: The Bias of Language in Speech and Writing*

DAVID R. OLSON
*Ontario Institute for Studies in Education*

*David Olson attempts to reframe a variety of issues related to language, such as linguistic theory, language learning, comprehension, reasoning, and reading. According to Olson, controversies over these issues stem from two opposing assumptions: (1) meaning is negotiated through the shared intentions between interlocutors and is thus situated, and (2) meaning is independently indicated in the text itself. Tracing the history from the invention of the Greek alphabet to the British essayist technique, the author delineates a transition from oral language statements of "utterances" to explicit, written prose statements of "texts." He further claims that as the representation of meaning becomes more unambiguous and autonomous, the evolution progressed culturally as well as developmentally from the utterance to the text. Olson concludes that one of the major roles of schooling is to facilitate children's smooth mastery of this "language as text."*

The faculty of language stands at the center of our conception of mankind; speech makes us human and literacy makes us civilized. It is therefore both interesting and important to consider what, if anything, is distinctive about written language and to consider the consequences of literacy for the bias it may impart both to our culture and to people's psychological processes.

An early version of this paper was presented to the Epistemics meeting at Vanderbilt University, Nashville, Tenn., in February 1974 and will be published in R. Diez-Guerrero & H. Fisher (Eds.), *Logic and Language in Personality and Society*. New York: Academic Press, 1978.

I am extremely grateful to the Canada Council, the Spencer Foundation, and the Van Leer Jerusalem Foundation for their support at various stages of completing this paper. I am also indebted to the many colleagues who commented on the earlier draft, including Roy Pea, Nancy Nickerson, Angela Hildyard, Bob Bracewell, Edmund Sullivan, and Frank Smith. I would also like to thank Mary Macri who assisted with the clerical aspects of the manuscript and Isobel Gibb, Reference Librarian at OISE, who assisted with the reference editing.

*Harvard Educational Review*   Vol. 47   No. 3   August 1977, 257–281

The framework for examining the consequences of literacy has already been laid out. Using cultural and historical evidence, Havelock (1973), Parry (1971), Goody and Watt (1968), Innis (1951), and McLuhan (1964) have argued that the invention of the alphabetic writing system altered the nature of the knowledge which is stored for reuse, the organization of that knowledge, and the cognitive processes of the people who use that written language. Some of the cognitive consequences of schooling and literacy in contemporary societies have been specified through anthropological and cross-cultural psychological research by Cole, Gay, Glick, and Sharp (1971), Scribner and Cole (1973), Greenfield (1972), Greenfield and Bruner (1969), Goodnow (1976), and others.

However, the more general consequences of the invention of writing systems for the structure of language, the concept of meaning, and the patterns of comprehension and reasoning processes remain largely unknown. The purpose of this paper is to examine the consequences of literacy, particularly those consequences associated with mastery of the "schooled" language of written texts.

In the course of the discussion, I shall repeatedly contrast explicit, written prose statements, which I shall call "texts," with more informal oral-language statements, which I shall call "utterances." Utterances and texts may be contrasted at any one of several levels: the linguistic modes themselves—written language versus oral language; their usual usages--conversation, story-telling, verse, and song for the oral mode versus statements, arguments, and essays for the written mode; their summarizing forms—proverbs and aphorisms for the oral mode versus premises for the written mode; and finally, the cultural traditions built around these modes—an oral tradition versus a literate tradition. My argument will be that there is a transition from utterance to text both culturally and developmentally and that this transition can be described as one of increasing explicitness, with language increasingly able to stand as an unambiguous or autonomous representation of meaning.

This essay (a word I use here in its Old French sense: *essai*—to try) begins by showing that theoretical and empirical debates on various aspects of language—ranging from linguistic theories of meaning to the psychological theories of comprehension, reading, and reasoning—have remained unduly puzzling and polemical primarily because of different assumptions about the locus of meaning. One assumption is that meaning is in the shared intentions of the speaker and the hearer, while the opposite one is that meaning is conventionalized in a sentence itself, that "the meaning is in the text." This essay continues by tracing the assumption that the meaning is in the text from the invention of the alphabetic writing system to the rapid spread of literacy with the invention of printing. The consequences of that assumption, particularly of the attempts to make it true, are examined in terms of the development and exploitation of the "essayist technique." The essay then proceeds to re-examine the linguistic, logical, and psychological issues mentioned at the outset; it demonstrates that the controversies surrounding these issues stem largely from a failure to appreciate the differences between utterances and texts and to understand that the assumptions appropriate for one are not appropriate for the other.

## The Locus of Meaning

The problem at hand is as well raised by a quotation from Martin Luther as by any more contemporary statement: scripture is *sui ipsius interpres*—scripture is its own interpreter (cited in Gadamer, 1975, p. 154). For Luther, then, the meaning of Scripture depended, not upon the dogmas of the church, but upon a deeper reading of the text. That is, the meaning of the text is in the text *itself*.[1] But is that claim true; is the meaning in the text? As we shall see, the answer offered to that question changed substantially about the time of Luther in regard not only to Scripture but also to philosophical and scientific statements. More important, the answers given to the question lie at the root of several contemporary linguistic and psychological controversies. Let us consider five of these.

In linguistic theory, an important controversy surrounds the status of invariant structures—structures suitable for linguistic, philosophical, and psychological analyses of language. Are these structures to be found in the deep syntactic structure of the sentence itself or in the interaction between the sentence and its user, in what may be called the understanding or interpretation? This argument may be focused in terms of the criterion for judging the well-formedness of a sentence. For Chomsky (1957, 1965) the well-formedness of a sentence—roughly, the judgment that the sentence is a permissible sentence of the language—is determined solely by the base syntactic structure of the sentence. Considerations of comprehensibility and effectiveness, like those of purpose and context, are irrelevant to the judgment. Similarly, the rules for operating upon well-formed base strings are purely formal. For Chomsky the meaning, or semantics, of a sentence is also specified in the base grammatical structure. Each unambiguous or well-formed sentence has one and only one base structure, and this base structure specifies the meaning or semantic structure of that sentence. Hence the meaning of a sentence relies on no private referential or contextual knowledge; nothing is added by the listener. One is justified, therefore, in concluding that, for Chomsky, the meaning is in the sentence per se.[2]

The radical alternative to this view is associated with the general semanticists led by Korzybski (1933), Chase (1954), and Hayakawa (1952). They claim that sentences do not have fixed meanings but depend in every case on the context and purpose for which they were uttered. Chafe (1970) offers a more modest alternative to Chomsky's syntactic bias, asserting that the criterion for the well-formedness of a sentence is determined by the semantic structure: a sentence is well-formed if it is understandable to a listener. This semantic structure is necessarily a part of language users' "knowledge of the world," and language can serve its functions precisely because such knowledge tends to be shared by speakers. Thus comprehension of a sentence involves, to some degree, the use of prior knowledge, contextual cues, and nonlinguistic cues.

In his philosophical discussion of meaning, Grice (1957) makes a distinction that mirrors the difference between the views of Chomsky and Chafe. Grice points out that one may analyze either "sentence meaning" or "speaker's meaning." The sentence per se may mean something other than what a speaker means by the sentence. For example, the speaker's meaning of "You're standing on my toe" may be "Move your foot." In these terms Chomsky provides a theory of sentence meaning in which the meaning of the sentence is independent of its function or context. Chafe, in contrast, offers a theory of intended meaning that encompasses both the intentions of the speaker and the interpretations the hearer constructs on the bases of the sentence, its perceived context, and its assumed function.

But these theories differ not only in the scope of the problems they attempt to solve. My suggestion is that these linguistic theories specify their central problems differently because of differing implicit assumptions about language; Chomsky's assumption is that language is best represented by written texts; Chafe's is that language is best represented by oral conversational utterances.

Psychological theories of language comprehension reflect these divergent linguistic assumptions. Psycholinguistic models of comprehension such as that of Clark (1974) follow Chomsky in the assumption that one's mental representation of a sentence depends on the recovery of the unique base syntactic structure underlying the sentence. Hence, a sentence is given the same underlying representation regardless of the context or purposes it is ultimately to serve. Similarly, Fodor, Bever, and Garrett (1974) have claimed that the semantic properties of a sentence are determined exclusively and automatically by the specification of the syntactic properties and the lexical items of the sentence. The assumption, once again, is that the meaning, at least the meaning worth psychological study, is in the text.

Conversely, a number of researchers (Anderson & Ortony, 1975; Barclay, 1973; Bransford, Barclay, & Franks, 1972; Bransford & Johnson, 1973; Paris & Carter, 1973) have demonstrated that sentence comprehension depends in large part on the context and on the prior knowledge of the listeners. In one now famous example, the sentence, "The notes were sour because the seams were split," becomes comprehensible only when the listener knows that the topic being discussed is bagpipes. Bransford and Johnson (1973) conclude, "What is understood and remembered about an input depends on the knowledge structures to which it is related" (p. 429).

Differing assumptions as to whether or not the meaning is in the text may also be found in studies of logical reasoning. Logical reasoning is concerned with the formulation and testing of the relations that hold between propositions. Such studies are based on models of formal reasoning in which it is assumed that the rules of inference apply to explicit premises to yield valid inferences. Subjects can be tested on their ability to consistently apply these formal rules to various semantic contents, and development can be charted in terms of the ability to apply the rules consistently to the meaning in the text (Neimark & Slotnick, 1970; Piaget, 1972; Suppes & Feldman, 1971).

Studies have shown, however, that formal propositional logic is a poor model for ordinary reasoning from linguistic propositions. Some researchers (Taplin & Staudenmayer, 1973) have suggested that logic and reasoning are discontinuous because "the interpreted meaning of a sentence is usually not entirely given by the denotative meaning in the linguistic structure of the sentence" (Staudenmayer, 1975, p. 56); factors such as prior knowledge and contextual presuppositions are also important. Analyzing the protocols of graduate students solving syllogisms, Henle (1962) found that errors resulted more often from an omission of a premise, a modification of a premise, or an importation of new evidence than from a violation of the rules of inference. If logic is considered to be the ability to draw valid conclusions from explicit premises—to operate upon the information in the text—then these students were reasoning somewhat illogically. However, if logic is considered to be the ability to operate on premises as they have been personally interpreted, then these students were completely logical in their operations. The critical issue, again, is whether or not the meaning is assumed to be fully explicit in the text.

Theories of language acquisition also reflect either the assumption that language is autonomous—that the meaning is in the text—or that it is dependent on nonlinguistic knowledge. Assuming that language is autonomous and independent of use or context, Chomsky (1965) and McNeill (1970) have argued that an innate, richly structured language-acquisition device must be postulated to account for the child's remarkable mastery of language. Hypothesized to be innate are structures that define the basic linguistic units (Chomsky, 1972) and the rules for transforming these units. Independent of a particular speaker or hearer, these transformations provide the interpretation given to linguistic forms. For example, at the grammatical level, "John hit Mary" is equivalent to "Mary was hit by John," and at the lexical level, "John" must be animate, human, male, and so on. These conclusions seem plausible, indeed inescapable, as long as it is assumed that language is autonomous and the meanings are in the sentences themselves.

Most recent research on language acquisition has proceeded from the alternative assumption that an utterance is but a fragmentary representation of the intention that lies behind it. Thus the meaning of the utterance comes from shared intentions based upon prior knowledge, the context of the utterance, and habitual patterns of interaction. The contextual dependence of child language was emphasized by de Laguna (1927/1970) and Buhler (1934). De Laguna (1927/1970) claimed, "Just because the terms of the child's language are in themselves so indefinite, it is left to the particular context to determine the specific meaning for each occasion. In order to understand what the baby is saying, you must see what the baby is doing" (pp. 90-91).

Recent studies extend this view. Bloom (1970) has shown, for example, that a young child may use the same surface structure, "Mommy sock," in two quite different contexts to represent quite different deep structures or meanings: in one case, the mother is putting the sock on the child; in the other, the child is picking up the mother's sock. The utterance, therefore, specifies only part of the meaning, the remainder being specified by the perceived context, accompanying gestures, and the

155

like. Moreover, having established these nonlinguistic meanings, the child can use them as the basis for discovering the structure of language (Brown, 1973; Bruner, 1973; Macnamara, 1972; Nelson, 1974). In other words, linguistic structures are not autonomous but arise out of nonlinguistic structures. There is no need, then, to attribute their origins to innate structures. Language development is primarily a matter of mastering the conventions both for putting more and more of the meaning into the verbal utterance and for reconstructing the intended meaning of the sentence per se. In de Laguna's terms, "The evolution of language is characterized by a progressive freeing of speech from dependence upon the perceived conditions under which it is uttered and heard, and from the behavior that accompanies it. The extreme limit of this freedom is reached in language which is written (or printed) and read" (1927, 1970, p. 107). Thus the predominant view among language-acquisition theorists is that while the meaning initially is not in the language-acquisition itself, it tends to become so with development.

Finally, theories of reading and learning to read can be seen as expressions of the rival assumptions about the locus of meaning. In one view the meaning is in the text and the student's problem is to find out how to decode that meaning (Carroll & Chall, 1975; Chall, 1967; Gibson & Levin, 1975). In fact, the majority of reading programs are based upon the gradual mastery of subskills such as letter recognition, sound blending, word recognition, and ultimately deciphering meaning. The alternative view is that readers bring the meaning to the text, which merely confirms or disconfirms their expectations (Goodman, 1967; Smith, 1975). Thus if children fail to recognize a particular word or sentence in a context, their expectations generate substitutions that are often semantically appropriate. Again, the basic assumption is that the meaning is—or is not—in the text.

To summarize, the controversial aspects of five issues—the structure of language, the nature of comprehension, the nature of logical reasoning, and the problems of learning to speak and learning to read—can be traced to differing assumptions regarding the autonomy of texts. Further, the distinction between utterances and texts, I suggest, reflects the different assumptions that meaning is or is not in the sentence per se.

## The Beginnings of a Literate Technology

Let us consider the origin of the assumption that the meaning is in the text and the implications of that assumption for language use. The assumption regarding the autonomy of texts is relatively recent and the language conforming to it is relatively specialized. Utterance, language that does not conform to this assumption, is best represented by children's early language, oral conversation, memorable oral sayings, and the like. Text, language that does conform to that assumption, is best represented by formal, written, expository prose statements. My central claim is that the evolution both culturally and developmentally is from utterance to text. While utterance is universal, text appears to have originated with Greek literacy and to have reached a most visible form with the British essayists. My argument, which rests heavily on the seminal works of Havelock (1963), McLuhan (1962), and Goody and Watt (1968), is that the invention of the alphabetic writing system gave to Western culture many of its predominant features, including an altered conception of language and an altered conception of rational man. These effects came about, in part, from the creation of explicit, autonomous statements—statements dependent upon an explicit writing system, the alphabet, and an explicit form of argument, the essay. In a word, these effects resulted from putting the meaning into the text.

*Meaning in an Oral Language Tradition*

Luther's statement, that the meaning of Scripture depended not upon the dogmas of the church, but upon a deeper reading of the text, seems a simple claim. It indicates, however, the profound change that occurred early in the sixteenth century in regard to the presumed autonomy of texts. Prior to the time of Luther, who in this argument represents one turning point in a roughly continuous change in orientation, it was generally assumed that meaning could not be stated explicitly. Statements required interpretation by either scribes or clerics. Luther's claim and the assumption that guided it cut both ways: they were a milestone in the developing awareness that text could explicitly state its meaning—that it did not depend on dogma or interpretive context; more importantly, they also indicated a milestone in the attempt to shape language to more explicitly represent its meanings. This shift in orientation, which I shall elaborate later in terms of the "essayist technique," was one of the high points in the long history of the attempt to make meaning completely explicit. Yet it was, relatively speaking, a mere refinement of the process that had begun with the Greek invention of the alphabet.

Although the Greek alphabet and the growth of Greek literacy may be at the base of Western science and philosophy, it is not to be assumed that preliterate people were primitive in any sense. Modern anthropology has provided many examples of theoretical, mythical, and technological systems of impressive sophistication and appropriateness. It has been established that a complex and extensive literature could exist in the absence of a writing system. In 1928, Milman Parry (1971) demonstrated that the *Iliad* and the *Odyssey,* usually attributed to a literate Homer, were in fact examples of oral composition composed over centuries by preliterate bards for audiences who did not read. In turn, it was recognized that large sections of the Bible possessed a similar oral structure. The books of Moses and the Prophets, for example, are recorded versions of statements that were shaped through oral methods as part of an oral culture.

To preserve verbal statements in the absence of a writing system, such statements would have to be biased both in form and content towards oral mnemonic devices such as "formalized patterns of speech, recital under ritual conditions, the use of drums and other musical instruments, and the employment of professional remembrances" (Goody & Watt, 1968, p. 31). Language is thus shaped or biased to fit the requirements of oral communication and auditory memory (see, for example, Havelock, 1973, and Frye, 1971). A variety of oral statements such as proverbs, adages, aphorisms, riddles, and verse are distinctive not only in that they preserve important cultural information but also in that they are memorable. They tend, however, *not* to be explicit or to say exactly what they mean; they require context and prior knowledge and wisdom for their interpretation. Solomon, for example, introduced the *Book of Proverbs* by saying: "To understand a proverb and the interpretations; the words of the wise and their dark sayings" (Chapter I:6). Maimonides, the twelfth-century rabbi, pointed out in his *Guide of the Perplexed* that when one interprets parables "according to their external meanings, he too is overtaken by great perplexity!" (1963, p. 6).

The invention of writing did not end the oral tradition. Some aspects of that tradition merely coexist with the more dominant literate traditions. Lord (1960) in his *Singer of Tales* showed that a remnant of such an oral culture persists in Yugoslavia. Even in a predominantly literate culture, aspects of the oral tradition remain. Gray (1973) suggested that Bob Dylan represents the creative end of such an oral tradition in Anglo-American culture; the less creative aspects of that tradition show up in the stock phrases and proverbial sayings that play so large a part in everyday conversational language.

With the introduction of writing, important parts of the oral tradition were written down and preserved in the available literate forms. The important cultural information, the information worth writing down, consisted in large part of statements shaped to fit the requirements of oral memory such as the epics, verse, song, orations, and since readers already knew, through the oral tradition, much of the content, writing served primarily for the storage and retrieval of information that had already been committed to memory, not for the expression of original ideas.

Scripture, at the time of Luther, had just such a status. It consisted in part of statements shaped to the requirements of oral comprehension and oral memory. Scripture had authority, but since the written statements were shorn of their oral contexts, they were assumed to require interpretation. The dogma of the Church, the orally transmitted tradition, had the authority to say what the Scripture meant. In this context Luther's statement can be seen as profoundly radical. Luther claimed that the text supplied sufficient context internally to determine the meaning of the passage; the meaning was in the text. What would have led Luther to make such a radical claim? My suggestion is that his claim reflected a technological change—the invention of printing—one in a series of developments in the increasing explicitness of language, which we shall now examine.

*Alphabetic Writing—Making Meanings Explicit*

Significant oral-language statements, to be memorable, must be cast into some oral, poetic form. Consequently, as we have seen, these statements do not directly say what they mean. With the invention of writing, the limitations of oral memory became less critical. The written statement, constituting a more or less permanent artifact, no longer depended on its "poetized" form for its preservation.

However, whether or not a writing system can preserve the meanings of statements

158

depends upon the characteristics of the system. An elliptical or nonexplicit writing system, like nonexplicit statements, tends to rely on prior knowledge and expectancies. An explicit writing system unambiguously represents meanings—the meaning is in the text. It has a minimum of homophones (seen/scene) and homographs (lead/ lead) at the phonemic and graphemic levels, few ambiguitites at the grammatical level, and few permissible interpretations at the semantic level.

The Greek alphabet was the first to approach such a degree of explicitness and yet to be simple enough to provide a base for mass literacy. Gelb (1952) differentiated four main stages in the development of writing systems. The first stage, which goes back to prehistory, involves the expression of ideas through pictures and pictographic writing. Such writing systems have been called ideographic in that they represent and communicate ideas directly without appeal to the structure of spoken language. While the signs are easily learned and recognized, there are problems associated with their use: any full system requires some four or five thousand characters for ordinary usage; their concreteness makes the representation of abstract terms difficult; they are difficult to arrange so as to produce statements (Gombrich, 1974); and they tend to limit the number of things that can be expressed.

The next stage was the invention of the principle of phonetization, the attempt to make writing reflect the sound structure of speech. In an attempt to capture the properties of speech, early phonetic systems—Sumerian, Egyptian, Hittite, and Chinese—all contained signs of three different types: word signs or logogens, syllabic signs, and auxiliary signs.

The third stage was the development of syllabaries which did away both with word signs and with signs representing sounds having more than one consonant. Whereas earlier syllabaries had separate signs for such syllables as *ta* and *tam*, the West Semitic syllabaries reduced the syllable to a single consonant-vowel sequence, thereby reducing the number of signs. However, since these Semitic syllabaries did not have explicit representations for vowels, the script frequently resulted in ambiguities in pronunciation, particularly in cases of writing proper names and other words which could not be retrieved from context. Semitic writing systems thus introduced phonetic indicators called Matres Lectionis (literally: "mothers of reading") to differentiate the vowel sounds (Gelb, 1952, p. 166).

The final stage in the invention of the alphabet, a step taken only by the Greeks, was the invention of a phonemic alphabet (Gelb, 1952; Goody & Watt, 1963). The Greeks did so, Gelb suggests, by using consistently the Matres Lectionis which the Semites had used sporadically. They discovered that these indicators were not syllables but rather vowels. Consequently the sign that preceded the indicator also must not be a syllable but rather a consonant. Havelock (1973) comments: "At a stroke, by this analysis, the Greeks provided a table of elements of linguistic sound not only manageable because of its economy, but for the first time in the history of *homo sapiens,* also accurate" (p. 11).

The faithful transcription of the sound patterns of speech by a fully developed alphabet has freed writing from some of the ambiguities of oral language. Many sentences that are ambiguous when spoken are unambiguous when written—for example, "il vent toujours a sept heures" ("he always comes at seven o'clock") versus "il vient toujours a cette heure" ("he always comes at this hour") (Lyons, 1969, p. 51). However, a fully developed alphabet does not exhaust the possibilities for explicitness of a writing system. According to Bloomfield (1939) and Kneale and Kneale (1962), the remaining lack of explicitness necessitated the invention of the formal languages of logic and mathematics.

To summarize, we have considered the extent to which meaning is explicitly represented in a statement. Oral language statements must be poetized to be remembered, but in the process they lose some of their explicitness; they require interpretation by a wise man, scribe, or cleric. Written statements bypass the limitations of memory, but the extent to which a writing system can explicitly represent meaning depends upon the nature of the system. Systems such as syllabaries that represent several meanings with the same visual sign are somewhat ambiguous or nonexplicit. As a consequence, they again require interpretation by some authority. Statements can become relatively free from judgment or interpretation only with a highly explicit writing system such as the alphabet. The Greek alphabet, through its ability to record exactly what is said, provided a tool for the formulation and criticism of explicit meanings and was therefore critical to the evolution of Greek literacy and Greek culture.

*Written Text as an Exploratory Device*

Writing systems with a relatively lower degree of explicitness, such as the syllabaries, tended to serve a somewhat limited purpose, primarily that of providing an aid to memory. Havelock (1973) states:

> When it came to transcribing discursive speech, difficulties of interpretation would discourage the practice of using the script for novel or freely-invented discourse. The practice that would be encouraged would be to use the system as a reminder of something already familiar, so that recollection of its familiarity would aid the reader in getting the right interpretation. . . . It would in short tend to be something—tale, proverb, parable, fable and the like—which already existed in oral form and had been composed according to oral rules. The syllabic system in short provided techniques for recall of what was already familiar, not instruments for formulating novel statements which could further the exploration of new experience. (p. 238)

The alphabet had no such limits of interpretation. The decrease in ambiguity of symbols—for example, the decrease in the number of homographs—would permit a reader to assign the appropriate interpretation to a written statement even without highly tuned expectations as to what the text was likely to say. The decreased reliance upon prior knowledge or expectancies was therefore a significant step towards making meaning explicit in the conventionalized linguistic system. The technology was sufficiently explicit to permit one to analyze the sentence meaning apart from the speaker's meaning. Simultaneously, written language became an instrument for the formulation and preservation of original statements that could violate readers' expectancies and commonsense knowledge. Written language had come free from its base in the mother tongue; it had begun the transformation from utterance to text.

The availability of an explicit writing system, however, does not assure that the statements recorded in that language will be semantically explicit. As previously mentioned, the first statements written down tended to be those that had already been shaped to the requirements of oral production and oral memory, the Greek epics being a case in point. Over time, however, the Greeks came to fully exploit the powers of their alphabetic writing system. In fact, Havelock (1973) has argued that the Greeks' use of this invention was responsible for the development of the intellectual qualities found in classical Greece:

> And so, as the fifth century passes into the fourth, the full effect upon Greece of the alphabetic revolution begins to assert itself. The governing word ceases to be a vibration heard by the ear and nourished in the memory. It becomes a visible artifact. Storage of information for reuse, as a formula designed to explain the dynamics of western culture, ceases to be a metaphor. The documented statement persisting through time unchanged is to release the human brain from certain formidable burdens of memorization while increasing the energies available for conceptual thought. The results as they are to be observed in the intellectual history of Greece and Europe were profound. (p. 60)

Some of the efforts of the Greeks' utilization of the alphabetic writing system are worth reviewing. First, as Goody and Watt (1968) and a number of other scholars have shown, it permitted a differentiation of myth and history with a new regard for literal truth. When the Homeric epics were written down, they could be subjected to critical analysis and their inconsistencies became apparent. Indeed, Hecataeus, faced with writing a history of Greece, said: "What I write is the account I believe to be true. For the stories the Greeks tell are many and in my opinion ridiculous" (cited in Goody & Watt, 1968, p. 45). Second, the use of the alphabetic system altered the relative regard for poetry and for prose. Prose statements were neither subtle nor devious; they tended to mean what they said. Havelock (1963) has demonstrated that Plato's *Republic* diverged from the tradition of the oral Homeric poets and represented a growing reliance on prose statements.

Third, the emphasis on written prose, as in Aristotle's *Analytics* (see Goody & Watt, 1968, pp. 52–54), permitted the abstraction of logical procedures that could serve as the rules for thinking. Syllogisms could operate on prose premises but not on oral statements such as proverbs. Further, the use of written prose led to the development of abstract categories, the genus/species taxonomies so important not only to Greek science but also to the formation and division of various subject-matter areas. Much of Greek thought was concerned with satisfactorily explaining the meaning of terms. And formulating a definition is essentially a literate enterprise outside of the context of ongoing speech—an attempt to provide the explicit meaning of a word in terms of the other words in the system (see, for example, Bruner & Olson, in press; Goody & Watt, 1968; and Havelock, 1976).

The Greeks, thinking that they had discovered a method for determining objective truth, were in fact doing little more than detecting the properties implicit in their native tongue. Their rules for mind were not rules for thinking but rather rules for using language consistently; the abstract properties of their category system were not true or unbiased descriptions of reality but rather invariants in the structure of their language. Writing became an instrument for making explicit the knowledge that was already implicit in their habits of speech and, in the process, tidying up and ordering that knowledge. This important but clearly biased effort was the first dramatic impact of writing on knowledge.

The Greeks' concern with literacy was not without critics. Written statements could not be interrogated if a misunderstanding occurred, and they could not be altered to suit the requirements of listeners. Thus Socrates concluded in *Phaedrus:* "Anyone who leaves behind him a written manual, and likewise anyone who takes it over from him, on the supposition that such writing will provide something reliable and permanent, must be exceedingly simple minded" (*Phaedrus,* 277c, cited in Goody & Watt, 1968, p. 51). In the *Seventh Letter,* Plato says: "No intelligent man will ever be so bold as to put into language those things which his reason has contemplated, especially not into a form that is unalterable—which must be the case with what is expressed in written symbols" (*Seventh Letter,* 341 c-d, cited in Bluck, 1949, p. 176).

### The Essayist Technique

Although the Greeks exploited the resources of written language, the invention of printing allowed an expanded and heterogeneous reading public to use those resources in a much more systematic way. The invention of printing prompted an intellectual revolution of similar magnitude to that of the Greek period (see McLuhan, 1962, and Ong, 1971, for fascinating accounts). However, the rise of print literacy did not merely preserve the analytic uses of writing developed by the Greeks; it involved as well, I suggest, further evolution in the explicitness of writing at the semantic level. That is, the increased explicitness of language was not so much a result of minimizing the ambiguity of words at the graphemic level but rather a result of minimizing the possible interpretations of statements. A sentence was written to have only one meaning. In addition, there was a further test of the adequacy of a statement's representation of presumed intention: the ability of that statement to stand up to analysis of its implications. To illustrate, if one assumes that statement X is true, then the implication Y should also be true. However, suppose that on further reflection Y is found to be indefensible. Then presumably statement X was not intended in the first place and would have to be revised.

This approach to texts as autonomous representations of meaning was reflected in the way texts were both read and written. A reader's task was to determine exactly what each sentence was asserting and to determine the presuppositions and implications of that statement. If one could assume that an author had actually intended what was written and that the statements were true, then the statements would stand up under scrutiny. Luther made just this assumption about Scripture early in the sixteenth century, shortly after the invention and wide utilization of printing. One of the more dramatic misapplications of the same assumption was Bishop Usher's inference from biblical genealogies that the world was created in 4004 B.C.

The more fundamental effect of this approach to text was on the writer, whose task now was to create autonomous text—to write in such a manner that the sentence was an adequate, explicit representation of the meaning, relying on no implicit premises or personal interpretations. Moreover, the sentence had to withstand analysis of its presuppositions and implications. This fostered the use of prose as a form of extended statements from which a series of necessary implications could be drawn.

The British essayists were among the first to exploit writing for the purpose of formulating original theoretical knowledge. John Locke's *An Essay Concerning Human Understanding* (1690/1961) well represents the intellectual bias that originated at that time and, to a large extent, characterizes our present use of language. Knowledge was taken to be the product of an extended logical essay—the output of the repeated application in a single coherent text of the technique of examining an assertion to determine all of its implications. It is interesting to note that when Locke began his criticism of human understanding he thought that he could write it on a sheet of paper in an evening. By the time he had exhausted the possibilities of both the subject and the new technology, the essay had taken twenty years and two volumes.

Locke's essayist technique differed notably from the predominant writing style of the time. Ellul (1964) says, "An uninitiated reader who opens a scientific treatise on law, economy, medicine or history published between the sixteenth and eighteenth centuries is struck most forcibly by the complete absence of logical order" (p. 39); and he notes, "It was more a question of personal exchange than of taking an objective position" (p. 41). In his introduction to *Some Thoughts Concerning Education* (Locke, 1880), Quick reports that Locke himself made similar criticisms of the essays of Montaigne. For Locke and others writing as he did, the essay came to serve as an exploratory device for examining problems and in the course of that examination producing new knowledge. The essay could serve these functions, at least for the purposes of science and philosophy, only by adopting the language of explicit, written, logically connected prose.

This specialized form of language was adopted by the Royal Society of London which, according to its historian Sprat (1667/1966), was concerned "with the advancement of science and with the improvement of the English language as a medium of prose" (p. 56). The society demanded a mathematical plainness of language and rejected all amplifications, digressions, and swellings of style. This use of language made writing a powerful intellectual tool, I have suggested, by rendering the logical implications of statements more detectable and by altering the statements themselves to make their implications both clear and true.

The process of formulating statements, deriving their implications, testing the truth of those implications, and using the results to revise or generalize from the original statement characterized not only empiricist philosophy but also the development of deductive empirical science. The result was the same, namely the formulation of a small set of connected statements of great generality that may occur as topic sentences of paragraphs or as premises of extended scientific or philosophical treatise. Such statements were notable not only in their novelty and abstractness but also in that they related to prior knowledge in an entirely new way. No longer did general premises necessarily rest on the data of common experience, that is, on commonsense intuition. Rather, as Bertrand Russell (1940) claimed for mathematics, a premise is believed because true implications follow from it, not because it is intuitively plausible. In fact, it is just this mode of using language—the deduction of counterintuitive models of reality—which distinguishes modern from ancient science (see Ong, 1958).

Moreover, not only did the language change, the picture of reality sustained by language changed as well; language and reality were reordered. Inhelder and Piaget (1958) describe this altered relationship between language and reality as a stage of mental development:

> The most distinctive property of formal thought is this reversal of direction between reality and possibility; instead of deriving a rudimentary theory from the empirical data as is done in concrete inferences, formal thought begins with a theoretical synthesis implying that certain relations are necessary and thus proceeds in the opposite direction. (p. 251)

The ability to make this "theoretical synthesis," I suggest, is tied to the analysis of the implications of the explicit theoretical statements permitted by writing.

Others have made the same point. Ricoeur (1973) has argued that language is not simply a reflection of reality but rather a means of investigating and enlarging reality. Hence, the text does not merely reflect readers' expectations; instead, the explicitness of text gives them a basis for constructing a meaning and then evaluating their own experiences in terms of it. Thus text *can* serve to realign language and reality. N. Goodman (1968), too, claims that "the world is as many ways as it can be truly described" (p. 6).

This property of language, according to Popper (1972), opens up the possibility of "objective knowledge." Popper claims that the acquisition of theoretical knowledge proceeds by offering an explicit theory (a statement), deriving and testing implications of the theory, and revising it in such a way that its implications are both productive and defensive. The result is a picture of the world derived from the repeated application of a particular literary technique: "science is a branch of literature" (Popper, 1972, p. 185).

Thus far I have summarized two of the major stages or steps in the creation of explicit, autonomous meanings. The first step toward making language explicit was at the graphemic level with the invention of an alphabetic writing system. Because it had a distinctive sign for each of the represented sounds and thereby reduced the ambiguity of the signs, an alphabetic system relied much less on readers' prior knowledge and expectancies than other writing systems. This explicitness permitted the preservation of meaning across space and time and the recovery of meaning by the more or less uninitiated. Even original ideas could be formulated in language and recovered by readers without recourse to some intermediary stage.

The second step involved the further development of explicitness at the semantic level by allowing a given sentence to have only one interpretation. Proverbial and poetic statements, for example, were not permissible because they admitted more than one interpretation, the appropriate one determined by the context of utterance. The attempt was to construct sentences for which the meaning was dictated by the lexical and syntactic features of the sentence itself. To this end, the meaning of terms had to be conventionalized by means of definitions, and the rules of implication had to be articulated and systematically applied.

The Greeks perfected the alphabetic system and began developing the writing style that, encouraged by the invention of printing and the form of extended texts it permitted, culminated in the essayist technique. The result was not an ordinary language, not a mother tongue, but rather a form of language specialized to serve the requirements of autonomous, written, formalized text. Indeed, children are progressively inducted into the use of this language during the school years. Thus formal schooling, in the process of teaching children to deal with prose texts, fosters the ability to "speak a written language" (Greenfield, 1972, p. 169).

## The Effects of Considerations of Literacy on Issues of Language

Let us return to the linguistic and psychological issues with which we began and reconsider them in the light of the cultural inventions that have served to make language explicit, to put the meaning into the text.

### Linguistic Theory

The differences between oral language and written text may help to explain the current controversy between the syntactic approach represented by Chomsky and the semantic approach represented by Chafe. Several aspects of Chomsky's theory of grammar require attention in this regard. For Chomsky, the meaning of language is not tied to the speaker's knowledge of the world but is determined by the sentence or text itself. The meaning of a sentence is assigned formally or mechanically on the basis of the syntactic and lexical properties of the sentence per se and not on the basis of the expectancies or preferred interpretations of the listener (Chomsky, 1972, p. 24). Chomsky's theory is fundamentally designed to preserve the truth conditions of the sentence, and permissible transformations are ones that preserve truth. To illustrate, an active sentence can be related to a passive sentence by means of a set of transformations because they are assumed to share a common base or underlying structure. The equivalence between active and passive sentences is logical meaning: one sentence is true if and only if the other is true (see Harman, 1972; Lakoff, 1972).

My conjecture is that Chomsky's theory applies to a particular specialization of language, namely, the explicit written prose that serves as the primary tool of science and philosophy. It can serve as a theory of speech only when the sentence meaning is a fully adequate representation of the speaker's meaning. In ordinary conversational language this is rarely the case. The empirical studies mentioned earlier have

165

provided strong evidence that experimental subjects rarely confine their interpretations to the information conventionalized in text. Rather, they treat a sentence as a cue to a more elaborate meaning.

As we have seen, other linguistic theories treat language as a means of representing and recovering the intentions of the speaker. The general semanticists and, to a lesser extent, Chafe, have argued that the linguistic system is not autonomous. The meaning of a sentence is not determined exclusively by the lexical and syntactic properties of the sentence itself; rather, the sentence is an indication of the speaker's meaning. While this assumption seems appropriate to the vast range of ordinary oral language, it overlooks the case in which the intended meaning is exactly represented by the sentence meaning as is ideally the case in explicit essayist prose.

We may conclude, then, that the controversy between the syntacticists and the semanticists is reducible to the alternative assumptions that language is appropriately represented in terms of sentence meanings or in terms of speaker's meanings. The latter assumption is entirely appropriate, I suggest, for the description of the ordinary oral conversational language, for what I have called utterances. On the other hand, I propose that Chomsky's theory is not a theory of language generally but a theory of a particular specialized form of language assumed by Luther, exploited by the British essayists, and formalized by the logical positivists. It is a model for the structure of autonomous written prose, for what I have called text.

## On Comprehension

The comprehension of sentences involves several different processes. Ordinary conversational speech, especially children's speech, relies for its comprehension on a wide range of information beyond that explicitly marked in the language. To permit communication at all, there must be wide agreement among users of a language as to phonological, syntactic, and semantic conventions. A small set of language forms, however, maps onto an exceedingly wide range of referential events; hence, ambiguity is always possible if not inevitable. Speakers in face-to-face situations circumvent this ambiguity by means of such prosodic and paralinguistic cues as gesture, intonation, stress, quizzical looks, and restatement. Sentences in conversational contexts, then, are interpreted in terms of the following: agreed-upon lexical and syntactic conventions; a shared knowledge of events and a preferred way of interpreting them; a shared perceptual context; and agreed-upon prosodic features and paralinguistic conventions.

Written languages can have no recourse to shared context, prosodic features, or paralinguistic conventions since the preserved sentences have to be understood in contexts other than those in which they were written. The comprehension of such texts requires agreed-upon linguistic conventions, a shared knowledge of the world, and a preferred way of interpreting events. But Luther denied the dependence of text on a presupposed, commonsensical knowledge of the world, and I have tried to show that the linguistic style of the essayist has systematically attempted to minimize if not eliminate this dependence. This attempt has proceeded by assigning the information carried implicitly by nonlinguistic means into an enlarged set of explicit linguistic conventions. In this way written textual language can be richer and more explicit than its oral language counterpart. Within this genre of literature, if unconventionalized or nonlinguistic knowledge is permitted to intrude, we charge the writer with reasoning via unspecified inferences and assumptions or the reader with misreading the text.

Comprehension, therefore, may be represented by a set of procedures that involves selectively applying one's personal experiences or knowledge of the world to the surface structure of sentences to yield a meaning. In so doing, one elaborates, assimilates, or perhaps "imagines" the sentence. And these elaborative procedures are perfectly appropriate to the comprehension of ordinary conversational utterances. In turn, the sentence becomes more comprehensible and dramatically more memorable, as Anderson and Ortony (1975), Bransford and Johnson (1973), and Bransford, Barclay, and Franks (1972) have shown.

The price to be paid for such elaboration and assimilation is that the listener's or reader's meaning deviates to some degree from the meaning actually represented in the sentence. Such interpretation may alter the truth conditions specified by the statement. To illustrate, using Anderson and Ortony's sentence, if the statement "the apples are in the container" is interpreted as "the apples are in the basket," the interpretation specifies a different set of truth conditions than did the original statement. We could legitimately say that the statement had been misinterpreted. Yet that is what normally occurs in the process of understanding and remembering sentences; moreover, as we have shown in our laboratory, it is what preschool children regularly do (Olson & Nickerson, 1977; Pike & Olson, 1977; Hildyard & Olson, in press). If young children are given the statements, "John hit Mary" or "John has more than Mary," unlike adults, they are incapable of determining the direct logical implications that "Mary was hit by John" or "Mary has less than John." If the sentence is given out of context, they may inquire, "Who is Mary?" Given an appropriate story or pictorial context, children can assimilate the first statement to that context and then give a new description of what they now know. If the sentence cannot be assimilated to their knowledge base, they are helpless to arrive at its implications; children are unable to apply interpretive procedures to the sentence meaning, the meaning in the text. They can, however, use sentences as a cue to speaker's meaning if these sentences occur in an appropriate context. Literate adults are quite capable of treating sentences in either way. What they do presumably depends on whether the sentence is too long to be remembered verbatim, whether it is written and remains available for repeated consultation, or, perhaps, whether the sentence is regarded as utterance or text.

*On Reasoning*

Extending the argument to reasoning tasks, it is clear that solutions may be reached in either of two quite different ways. Relying on the processes usually involved in the comprehension of spoken language, one may interpret a premise in terms of previous knowledge of the world, operate on that resulting knowledge, and produce an answer other than that expected on a purely formal logical basis. Such reasoning, based on an intrusion of unspecified knowledge, is not a logical argument but an enthymeme. Nevertheless, it is the most common form of ordinary reasoning (Cole, Gay, Glick, & Sharp, 1971; Wason & Johnson-Laird, 1972).

Logical reasoning, on the other hand, is the procedure of using conventionalized rules of language to draw necessary implications from statements treated as text. For such reasoning, the implications may run counter to expectancies or may be demonstrably false in their extension; however, it matters only that the conclusion follows directly from the sentence meaning, the conventionalized aspects of the statement itself. The fact that most people have difficulty with such operations indicates simply their inability or lack of experience in suspending prior knowledge and expectancies in order to honor the sentence meaning of statements. In fact, Henle (1962) has noted that in reasoning tasks subjects often have difficulty in distinguishing between a conclusion that is logically true, one that is factually true, and one with which they agree. According to the analysis offered here, in the first case the conclusion logically follows from the text—the meaning is restricted to that explicitly represented or conventionalized in the text and to the implications that necessarily follow; in the second case the conclusion follows from unstated but shared knowledge of the world; in the third case the conclusion follows from unspecified and unshared personal knowledge. I would argue that in neither of the latter cases are we justified in calling the reasoning logical.

Logical reasoning as defined here assumes that fully explicit, unambiguous statements can be created to serve as premises. This is a goal that consistently evades ordinary language use. It is extremely difficult if not impossible to create statements that specify all and only the necessary and sufficient information for drawing logical inferences.[3] Hence, formal reasoning has led to a reliance, where possible, on the use of symbols related by a logical calculus. To illustrate the difficulties, I will use three studies from our laboratory. Bracewell has shown that the simple propositional statement employed by Wason and Johnson-Laird (1970), "If p is on one side, then q is on the other," is ambiguous in at least two ways: "one side" may be interpreted as referring to "the showing side" or to "either the showing side or the hidden side"; "if . . . then" may be interpreted as a conditional relation or as a biconditional relation.[4] Differences in subjects' performance can be traced to different interpretations of the proposition. In a similar vein, Hidi has shown that if a simple proposition such as "if you go to Ottawa, you must travel by car" is understood as describing a temporal event, subjects draw quite different inferences than if it is treated purely as a logical statement.[5] In a developmental study, Ford (1976) has shown that, given a disjunctive statement, children (and adults in natural language contexts) treat "or" as posing a simple choice between mutually exclusive, disjoint alternatives (for example, "Do you want an apple *or* an orange?" "An apple"). When children of five or six years of age are presented with "or" commands involving disjoint events as well as overlapping and inclusive events—the latter being involved in Piaget's famous task "Are there more rabbits *or* animals?"—Ford found that children's logical competence breaks down only when the known structure of events runs counter to the presuppositions of the language. Rather than revise their conception of events—rabbits and animals are not disjoint classes—children misinterpret or reject the sentence. They say, for example, "There are more rabbits because there are only two ducks!"

There are, then, at least two aspects to the study of logical reasoning. The first stems from the fact that statements are often ambiguous, especially when they occur out of context. Thus failures in reasoning may reflect merely the assignment of an interpretation that, although it is consistent with the sentence meaning explicit in the text, is different from the one intended by the experimenter. Second, logical development in a literate culture involves learning to apply logical operations to the sentence meaning rather than to the assimilated or interpreted or assumed speaker's meaning. Development consists of learning to confine interpretation to the meaning explicitly represented in the text and to draw inferences exclusively from that formal but restricted interpretation.

Whether or not all meaning can be made explicit in the text is perhaps less critical than the belief that it can and that making it so is a valid scientific enterprise. This was clearly the assumption of the essayists, and it continues in our use of language for science and philosophy. Explicitness of meaning, in other words, may be better thought of as a goal rather than an achievement. But it is a goal appropriate only for the particular, specialized use of language that I have called text.

## On Learning a Language

The contrast between language as an autonomous system for representing meaning and language as a system dependent in every case upon nonlinguistic and paralinguistic cues for the sharing of intentions—the contrast between text and utterance—applies with equal force to the problem of language acquisition. A formal theory of sentence meaning, such as Chomsky's, provides a less appropriate description of early language than would a theory of intended meanings that admitted a variety of means for realizing those intentions. Such means include a shared view of reality, a shared perceptual context, and accompanying gestures, in addition to the speech signal. At early stages of language acquisition the meaning may be specified nonlinguistically, and this meaning may then be used to break the linguistic code (Macnamara, 1972; Nelson, 1974). Language acquisition, then, is primarily a matter of learning to conventionalize more and more of the meaning in the speech signal. This is not a sudden achievement. If an utterance specifies something different from what the child is entertaining, the sentence will often be misinterpreted (Clark, 1973; Donaldson & Lloyd, 1974). But language development is not simply a matter of progressively elaborating the oral mother tongue as a means of sharing intentions. The developmental hypothesis offered here is that the ability to assign a meaning to the sentence per se, independent of its nonlinguistic interpretive context, is achieved only well into the school years. It is a complex achievement to differentiate and operate upon either what is actually said, the sentence meaning, or what is meant, the speaker's meaning. Children are relatively quick to grasp a speaker's intentions but relatively slow, I suggest, to grasp the literal meaning of what is, in fact, said.

Several studies lend plausibility to these arguments. For example, Olson and Nickerson (1977) examined the role of story or pictorial context on the detection of sentence implications. Five-year-old children were given a statement and asked if a second statement, logically related to the first, was true. For instance, they were told, "John was hit by Mary," then asked, "Did Mary hit John?" The ability of these five-year-olds to answer such a question depended on how much they knew about the characters and context mentioned in the sentences. If they did not know who John and Mary were or why the experimenter was asking the question, they could not assign a full semantic interpretation to the sentence. This and other studies suggest that children, unlike adults, assign a speaker's meaning to a simple sentence if that sentence is contextually appropriate and directly assimilable to their prior knowledge, but they have difficulty assigning a meaning to the statement alone (Carpenter & Just, 1975; Clark, 1974; Olson & Filby, 1972; Hildyard & Olson, Note 1). But by late childhood, at least among schooled children, meanings are assigned quite readily to the sentence per se. Children come to see that sentences have implications that are necessary by virtue of sentence meaning itself. They become progressively more able to exist in a purely linguistically specified, hypothetical world for both purposes of extracting logical implications of statements and of living in those worlds that, as Ricoeur (1973) notes, are opened up by texts. This, however, is the end point of development in a literate culture and not a description of how original meanings are acquired in early language learning.

## On Reading

The relations between utterances and texts become acute when children are first confronted with printed books. As I have pointed out, children are familiar with using the spoken utterance as one cue among others. Children come to school with a level of oral competence in their mother-tongue only to be confronted with an exemplar of written text, the reader, which is an autonomous representation of meaning. Ideally, the printed reader depends on no cues other than linguistic cues; it represents no intentions other than those represented in the text; it is addressed to no one in particular; its author is essentially anonymous; and its meaning is precisely that represented by the sentence meaning. As a result, when children are taught to read, they are learning both to read and to treat language as text. Children familiar with the use of textlike language through hearing printed stories obviously confront less of a hurdle than those for whom both reading and that form of language are novel.

The decoding approach to reading exploits both the explicit nature of the alphabet and the explicit nature of written prose text. Ideally, since the meaning is in the text, the programmatic analysis of letters, sounds, words, and grammar would specify sentence meaning. But, as I have indicated, it is precisely with sentence meaning that children have the most difficulty. Hence, the decoding of sentence meaning should be treated as the end point of development, not as the means of access to print as several writers have maintained (Reid, 1966; Richards, 1971).

## On Language and Meaning: Summary and Conclusions

Clearly some aspects of meaning must be sufficiently conventionalized in the language to permit children and adults to use it as an all-purpose instrument. Thus, children must learn grammatical rules and lexical structure to use language in different contexts for different purposes. However, the degree to which this linguistic knowledge is conventionalized and formalized need not be very great in oral contexts since the listener has access to a wide range of information with which to recover the speaker's intentions. Generally, nonlinguistic cues appear to predominate in that if the speaker is elliptical or even chooses the wrong word or grammatical form, we can successfully recover the speaker's intention.

To serve the requirements of written language, however, all of the information relevant to the communication of intention must be present in the text. Further, if the text is to permit or sustain certain conclusions, as in the essayist technique, then it must become an autonomous representation of meaning. But for this purpose the meanings of the terms and the logical relations holding between them must be brought to a much higher degree of conventionalization. Words must be defined in terms of other words in the linguistic system, and rules of grammar must be specialized to make them suitable indications of the text's underlying logical structure. Once this degree of conventionalization is achieved, children or adults have sufficient basis for constructing the meaning explicitly represented by the text. Written text, I am suggesting, is largely responsible for permitting people to entertain sentence meaning per se rather than merely using the sentence as a cue to the meaning entertained by the speaker.

The differences between utterances and texts may be summarized in terms of three underlying principles: the first pertains to meaning, the second to truth, and the third to function. First, in regard to meaning, utterance and text relate in different ways to background knowledge and to the criteria for successful performance. Conventional utterances appeal for their meaning to shared experiences and interpretations, that is, to a common intuition based on shared commonsense knowledge (Lonergan, 1957; Schutz & Luckmann, 1973). Utterances take for content, to use Pope's words, "What oft was tho't but ne'er so well expressed" (cited in Ong, 1971, p. 256). In most speech, as in poetry and literature, the usual reaction is assent— "How true." Statements match, in an often tantalizing way, the expectancies and experiences of the listener. Because of this appeal to expectancies, the criterion for a successful utterance is understanding on the part of the listener. The sentence is not appropriate if the listener does not comprehend. A well-formed sentence fits the requirements of the listener and, as long as this criterion is met, it does not really matter what the speaker says—"A wink is as good as a nod."

Prose text, on the other hand, appeals to premises and rules of logic for deriving implications. Whether or not the premise corresponds to common sense is irrelevant. All that is critical is that the premises are explicit and the inferences correctly drawn. The appeal is formal rather than intuitive. As a consequence, the criterion for the success of a statement in explicit prose text is its formal structure; if the text is formally adequate and the reader fails to understand, that is the reader's problem. The meaning is in the text.

Second, utterance and text appeal to different conceptions of truth. Frye (1971) has termed these underlying assumptions "truth as wisdom" and "truth as correspondence." Truth in oral utterance has to do with truth as wisdom. A statement is true if it is reasonable, plausible, and, as we have seen, congruent with dogma or the wisdom of elders; truth is assimilability to common sense. Truth in prose text, however, has to do with the correspondence between statements and observations. Truth drops its ties to wisdom and to values, becoming the product of the disinterested search of the scientist. True statements in text may be counter to intuition, common sense, or authority. A statement is taken to be true not because the premises from which it follows are in agreement with common sense but rather because true implications follow from it, as Russell (1940) pointed out in regard to mathematics.

Third, conversational utterance and prose text involve different alignments of the functions of language. As Austin (1962) and Halliday (1970) argue, any utterance serves at least two functions simultaneously—the rhetorical or interpersonal function and the logical or ideational function. In oral speech, the interpersonal function is primary; if a sentence is inappropriate to a particular listener, the utterance is a failure. In written text, the logical or ideational functions become primary, presumably because of the indirect relation between writer and reader. The emphasis, therefore, can shift from simple communication to truth, to "getting it right" (Olson, 1977). It may be this realignment of functions in written language that brings about the greater demand for explicitness and the higher degree of conventionalization.

The bias of written language toward providing definitions, making all assumptions and premises explicit, and observing the formal rules of logic produces an instrument of considerable power for building an abstract and coherent theory of reality. The development of this explicit, formal system accounts, I have argued, for the predominant features of Western culture and for our distinctive ways of using language and our distinctive modes of thought. Yet the general theories of science and philosophy that are tied to the formal uses of text provide a poor fit to daily, ordinary, practical, and personally significant experience. Oral language with its depth of resources and its multitude of paths to the same goal, while an instrument of limited power for exploring astract ideas, is a universal means of sharing our understanding of concrete situations and practical actions. Moreover, it is the language children bring to school. Schooling, particularly learning to read, is the critical process in the transformation of children's language from utterance to text.

## Notes

1. I am indebted to Frank Smith for pointing out that I use the phrase "the meaning is in the text" as a metaphor for describing language in which the meaning is fully conventionalized.
2. The hypothesis of autonomous meaning of sentences, that is, the assumption that the meaning is in the text, may simply reflect the presupposition that linguistics, as a discipline, is autonomous.
3. This question touches upon the important epistemological issue of the formal adequacy of the methods of science. The most common argument is that almost any important theory can be shown to be formally inadequate (see Gellner, 1975).
4. Bracewell, R. J. *Interpretation factors in the four-card selection task.* Paper presented to the Selection Task Conference, Trento, Italy, April 1974.
5. Hidi, S. *Effects of temporal considerations in conditional reasoning.* Paper presented at the Selection Task Conference, Trento, Italy, April 1974.

## References

Anderson, R. C., & Ortony, A. On putting apples into bottles: A problem of polysemy. *Cognitive Psychology,* 1975, **7,** 167–180.

Austin, J. L. *How to do things with words.* (J. O. Urmson, Ed.). New York: Oxford University Press, 1962.

Barclay, J. R. The role of comprehension in remembering sentences. *Cognitive Psychology,* 1973, **4,** 229–254.

Bloom, L. *Language development: Form and function in emerging grammars.* Cambridge, Mass.: M.I.T. Press, 1970.

Bloomfield, L. *Linguistic aspects of science.* Chicago: University of Chicago Press, 1939.

Bluck, R. S. *Plato's life and thought.* London: Routledge & Kegan Paul, 1949.

Bransford, J. D., Barclay, J. R., & Franks, J. J. Sentence memory: A constructive versus interpretive approach. *Cognitive Psychology,* 1972, **3,** 193–209.

Bransford, J. D., & Johnson, M. K. Consideration of some problems of comprehension. In W. Chase (Ed.), *Visual information processing.* New York: Academic Press, 1973.

Brown, R. *A first language: The early stages.* Cambridge, Mass.: Harvard University Press, 1973.

Bruner, J. S. From communication to language: A psychological perspective. *Cognition,* 1973, **3,** 255–287.

Bruner, J. S., & Olson, D. R. Symbols and texts as the tools of intellect. In *The Psychology of the 20th Century, Vol. VII: Piaget's developmental and cognitive psychology within an extended context.* Zurich: Kindler, in press.

Buhler, K. *Sprachtheorie.* Jena, Germany: Gustav Fischer Verlag, 1934.

Carpenter, P., & Just, M. Sentence comprehension: A psycholinguistic processing model of verification. *Psychological Review,* 1975, **82,** 45–73.

Carroll, J. B., & Chall, J. S. (Eds.) *Toward a literate society.* New York: McGraw-Hill, 1975.

Chafe, W. *Meaning and the structure of language.* Chicago: University of Chicago Press, 1970.

Chall, J. S. *Learning to read: The great debate.* New York: McGraw-Hill, 1967.

Chase, S. *The power of words.* New York: Harcourt, Brace, 1954.

Chomsky, N. *Syntactic structures.* The Hague: Mouton, 1957.

Chomsky, N. *Aspects of a theory of syntax.* Cambridge, Mass.: M.I.T. Press, 1965.

Chomsky, N. *Problems of knowledge and freedom.* London: Fontana, 1972.

Clark, E. Non-linguistic strategies and the acquisition of word meanings. *Cognition, 1973,* **2,** 161–182.

Clark, H. H. Semantics and comprehension. In T. A. Sebeok (Ed.), *Current trends in linguistics, Vol. 12: Linguistic and adjacent arts and sciences.* The Hague: Mouton, 1974.

Cole, M., Gay, J., Glick, J., & Sharp, D. *The cultural context of learning and thinking.* New York: Basic Books, 1971.

de Laguna, G. *Speech: Its function and development.* College Park, Md.: McGrath, 1970. (Originally published, 1927.)

Donaldson, M., & Lloyd, P. Sentences and situations: Children's judgments of match and mismatch. In F. Bresson (Ed.), *Current problems in psycholinguistics.* Paris: Editions du Centre National de la Recherche Scientifique, 1974.

Ellul, J. *The technological society.* New York: Vintage Books, 1964.

Fodor, J. A., Bever, T. G., & Garrett, M. F. *The psychology of language.* Toronto: McGraw-Hill, 1974.

Ford, W. G. *The language of disjunction.* Unpublished doctoral dissertation, University of Toronto, 1976.

Frye, N. *The critical path.* Bloomington: Indiana University Press, 1971.

Gadamer, H. G. *Truth and method.* New York: Seabury Press, 1975.

Gelb, I. J. *A study of writing.* Toronto: University of Toronto Press, 1952.

Gellner, E. Book review of *Against Method* by P. Feyerabend. *British Journal for the Philosophy of Science,* 1975, **26,** 331–342.

Gibson, E. J., & Levin, H. *The psychology of reading.* Cambridge, Mass.: M.I.T. Press, 1975.

Gombrich, E. The visual image. In D. R. Olson (Ed.), *Media and symbols: The forms of expression, communication and education.* (The 73rd Yearbook of the National Society for the Study of Education). Chicago: University of Chicago Press, 1974.

Goodman, K. S. Reading: A psycholinguistic guessing game. *Journal of the Reading Specialist,* 1967, **6,** 126–135.

Goodman, N. *Languages of art: An approach to a theory of symbols.* Indianapolis: Bobbs-Merrill, 1968.

Goodnow, J. The nature of intelligent behavior: Questions raised by cross-cultural studies. In L. Resnick (Ed.), *New approaches to intelligence.* Potomac, Md.: Erlbaum and Associates, 1976.

Goody, J., & Watt, I. The consequences of literacy. In J. Goody (Ed.), *Literacy in traditional societies.* Cambridge, Eng.: Cambridge University Press, 1968.

Gray, M. *Song and dance man: The art of Bob Dylan.* London: Abacus, 1973.

Greenfield, P. Oral and written language: The consequences for cognitive development in Africa, the United States, and England. *Language and Speech,* 1972, **15,** 169–178.

Greenfield, P., & Bruner, J. S. Culture and cognitive growth. In D. A. Goslin (Ed.), *Handbook of socialization: Theory and research.* Chicago: Rand-McNally, 1969.

Grice, H. P. Meaning. *Philosophical Review,* 1957, **66,** 377–388.

Halliday, M. A. K. Language structure and language function. In J. Lyons (Ed.), *New horizons in linguistics.* New York: Penguin Books, 1970.

Harman, G. Deep structure as logical form. In D. Davidson & G. Harman (Eds.), *Semantics of natural language.* Dordrecht, Holland: Reidel, 1972.

Havelock, E. *Preface to Plato.* Cambridge, Mass.: Harvard University Press, 1963.

Havelock, E. Prologue to Greek literacy. *Lectures in memory of Louise Tatt Semple, second series, 1966–1971.* Cincinnati: University of Oklahoma Press for the University of Cincinnati Press, 1973.

Havelock, E. *Origins of western literacy.* Toronto: Ontario Institute for Studies in Education, 1976.

Hayakawa, S. I. *Language in thought and action.* London: Allen and Unwin, 1952.

Henle, M. On the relation between logic and thinking. *Psychological Review,* 1962, **63,** 366–378.

Hildyard, A., & Olson, D. R. *On the mental representation and matching operation of action and passive sentences by children and adults,* in preparation.

Inhelder, B., & Piaget, J. *The growth of logical thinking.* New York: Basic Books, 1958.

Innis, H. *The bias of communication.* Toronto: University of Toronto Press, 1951.

Korzybski, A. *Science and sanity: An introduction to non-Aristotelian systems and general semantics.* Lancaster, Pa.: Science Press, 1933.

Kneale, W., & Kneale, M. *The development of logic.* Oxford: Clarendon Press, 1962.

Lakoff, G. Linguistics and natural logic. In D. Davidson & G. Harman (Eds.), *Semantics of natural language.* Dordrecht, Holland: Reidel, 1972.

Locke, J. *An essay concerning human understanding.* (J. W. Yolton, Ed.). London: Dent, 1961. (Originally published, 1690.)

Locke, J. *Some thoughts concerning education.* (Introduction and Notes by R. H. Quick). Cambridge, Eng.: Cambridge University Press, 1880.

Lonergan, B. J. F. *Insight: A study of human understanding.* New York: Philosophical Library, 1957.

Lord, A. B. *The singer of tales* (Harvard Studies in Comparative Literature, 24). Cambridge, Mass.: Harvard University Press, 1960.

Lyons, J. *Introduction to theoretical linguistics.* Cambridge, Eng.: Cambridge University Press, 1969.

Macnamara, J. The cognitive basis of language learning in infants. *Psychological Review,* 1972, **79,** 1–13.

Maimonides, M. [*Guide of the perplexed*] (S. Pines, trans.). Chicago: University of Chicago Press, 1963.

McLuhan, M. *The Gutenberg galaxy.* Toronto: University of Toronto Press, 1962.

McLuhan, M. *Understanding media: The extensions of man.* Toronto: McGraw-Hill, 1964.

McNeill, D. *The acquisition of language.* New York: Harper & Row, 1970.

Neimark, E. D., & Slotnick, N. S. Development of the understanding of logical connectives. *Journal of Educational Psychology,* 1970, **61,** 451–460.

Nelson, K. Concept, word, and sentence: Interrelations in acquisition and development. *Psychological Review,* 1974, **81,** 267–285.

Olson, D. R. The languages of instruction. In R. Spiro (Ed.), *Schooling and the acquisition of knowledge.* Potomac, Md.: Erlbaum and Associates, 1977.

Olson, D. R., & Filby, N. On the comprehension of active and passive sentences. *Cognitive Psychology,* 1972, **3,** 361–381.

Olson, D. R., & Nickerson, N. The contexts of comprehension: Children's inability to draw implications from active and passive sentences. *Journal of Experimental Child Psychology,* 1977, **23,** 402–414.

Ong, W. J. *Ramus, method and the decay of dialogue.* Cambridge, Mass.: Harvard University Press, 1958. (Reprinted by Octagon Books, 1974.)

Ong, W. J. *Rhetoric, romance and technology: Studies in the interaction of expression and culture.* Ithaca: Cornell University Press, 1971.

Paris, S. G., & Carter, A. Y. Semantic and constructive aspects of sentence memory in children. *Developmental Psychology,* 1973, **9,** 109–113.

Parry, M. The making of Homeric verse. In A. Parry (Ed.), *The collected papers of Milman Parry.* Oxford: Clarendon Press, 1971.

Piaget, J. Intellectual evolution from adolescence to adulthood. *Human Development,* 1972, **15,** 1–12.

Pike, R., & Olson, D. R. A question of *more* or *less. Child Development,* 1977, **48,** 579–586.

Popper, K. *Objective knowledge: An evolutionary approach.* Oxford: Clarendon Press, 1972.

Reid, J. F. Learning to think about reading. *Educational Research,* 1966, **9,** 56–62.

Richards, I. A. Instructional engineering. In S. Baker, J. Barzun, & I. A. Richards (Eds.), *The written word.* Rowley, Mass.: Newbury House, 1971.

Ricoeur, P. Creativity in language: Word, polysemy and metaphor. *Philosophy Today*, 1973, **17,** 97–111.

Russell, B. *An inquiry into meaning and truth.* London: Allen and Unwin, 1940.

Scribner, S., & Cole, M. Cognitive consequences of formal and informal education. *Science,* 1973, **182,** 553–559.

Schutz, A., & Luckmann, T. [*The structures of the life world*] (R. Zaner, & H. Engelhardt, trans.) Evanston, Ill.: Northwestern University Press, 1973.

Smith, F. *Comprehension and learning.* Toronto: Holt, Rinehart & Winston, 1975.

Sprat, T. *History of the Royal Society of London for the improving of natural knowledge.* (J. I. Cope and H. W. Jones, Eds.). St. Louis: Washington University Press, 1966. (Originally published, London, 1667.)

Staudenmayer, H. Understanding conditional reasoning with meaningful propositions. In R. J. Falmagne (Ed.), *Reasoning, representation and process.* Hillsdale, N.J.: Erlbaum and Associates, 1975.

Strawson, P. F. *Meaning and truth: An inaugural lecture delivered before the University of Oxford.* Oxford: Clarendon Press, 1970.

Suppes, P., & Feldman, S. Young children's comprehension of logical connectives. *Journal of Experimental Child Psychology,* 1971, **12,** 304–317.

Taplin, J. E., & Staudenmayer, H. Interpretation of abstract conditional sentences in deductive reasoning. *Journal of Verbal Learning and Verbal Behavior,* 1973, **12,** 530–542.

Wason, P. C., & Johnson-Laird, P. N. A conflict between selecting and evaluating information in an inferential task. *British Journal of Psychology,* 1970, **61,** 509–515.

Wason, P. C., & Johnson-Laird, P. N. *The psychology of reasoning.* London: B. T. Batsford, 1972.

# 7
# Literacy and the Oral Foundations of Education

KIERAN EGAN
*Simon Fraser University*

*Reviewing the classical literature on orality versus literacy and the related issues, Kieran Egan delineates the rich oral forms of expression that have been used in nonliterate societies since the beginning of the ancient Greek period. Exploring how orality has historically accounted for a vast amount of intellectual resources and mental strategies, he argues that: (1) although sometimes undervalued in Western culture, orality is neither a deficit nor a lack of literacy, and that (2) the developmental path should be understood as the transition from orality to a combination of orality and literacy. In discussing the implications of orality for early childhood education, the author not only emphasizes the importance of correctly understanding children's orality but also advocates appropriate curriculum development so that orality can serve as the solid foundation for the later development of literacy.*

We have inherited from the ancient Greeks the notion of a deep-cutting distinction between rational and irrational thinking. The word they commonly used for "reason" was *logos*, which was also the term used for "word" or "speech." For the Greeks of the Platonic tradition, then, taking a rational view enabled one to give an articulate account of something: "We have a rational grasp of something when we can *articulate* it; that means, distinguish and lay out different features of the matter in perspicuous order" (Taylor, 1982, p. 90). Rationality entails trying to perceive things as they are, despite our hopes, fears, or intentions regarding them. One may achieve such a view by *theoria* (sight, speculation, contemplation): theoretical understanding results from taking a disengaged perspective. Only the knowledge that results from this kind of intellectual activity, Plato argued in *Timeus* and *The Republic*, is true knowledge. The manner in which Plato distinguished rational thinking and its product—true knowl-

I would like to thank the Editorial Board of the *Harvard Educational Review*, and especially Polly Steele, for their most helpful comments and criticisms; they have much improved this article.

*Harvard Educational Review*   Vol. 57   No. 4   November 1987, 445–472

edge (*episteme*)—from irrational thinking and its various products—confusion, superficial plausibility, mere opinion (*doxa*)—involved setting up a number of enduring conceptual associations. Among these associated ideas, and of particular interest in this article, was that of adulthood with the attainment of *episteme* and childhood with *doxa*.[1] This rational theoretic understanding, Plato and his pupil Aristotle argued, gives a superior view of reality. Those who violate the basic standards of the articulation of this theoretical understanding are, in this view, irrational, and they fail to articulate what is real and true.

With the "rediscovery" of classical Greece by nineteenth-century European scholars, and the growing sense of Greece's cultural superiority over the classical Roman models that had dominated European intellectual and artistic life during the previous century, the distinction between rational and irrational thinking began a new career. It proved a convenient tool for dismissing from serious comparison with Western forms of thought those forms of "primitive" thought that expanding colonial empires, early anthropological studies, and travelers' tales were bringing increasingly to the attention of Europeans and North Americans (Jenkyns, 1980; Turner, 1981). When combined later in the century with the extensions of evolutionary theory, the distinction between "rational" and "irrational" thinking helped to generate theories about the development of human societies from irrational beginnings to the refined rationality of contemporary Western intellectual life. Frazer (1900), for example, argued that human thought always passes through a magical stage, to a religious stage, and finally to a rational scientific stage. This distinction has entered during this century into everyday language, finding varied, more or less casual, use in terms of approval or disparagement. At the same time, in the scholarly world, the distinction has come increasingly into question. Anthropologists such as E. E. Evans-Pritchard (1937), for example, have argued the rationality of witchcraft in particular cultural settings, and classicists such as E. R. Dodds (1951) have pointed to the irrationality of significant features of Greek life and thought. Vexed and problematic though the distinction is, it remains deeply embedded in Western cultural history and habits of thought (Hollis & Lukes, 1982; Putnam, 1981; Wilson, 1970).

The mental life of children has commonly been represented in terms influenced by this distinction. Children are assumed to begin life in irrational confusion and ignorance, and education is regarded as the process of inculcating both rationality and knowledge. In his allegory of the cave in *The Republic* Plato likens the process of education to unchaining prisoners in a dark cave; while chained, they can see on the cave wall only flickering shadows of what is happening outside, and, when released, they are led out to behold reality. Similarly, Christian ideas of education represented the child as beginning in sin and ignorance, able to progress only gradually and with great difficulty to virtue and knowledge.

Children and "savages" have often been assumed to lack access to certain forms of thought that are considered the hallmarks of rational adulthood. Attempts have been made to capture the perceived differences between the thought forms of people in oral cultures and those of literate Westerners in distinctions such as primitive/

developed, irrational or prerational/rational, mythic/historical, simple/complex, mythopoeic/logico-empirical, "cold"/"hot," traditional/modern, and so on (see Goody, 1977; Hollis & Lukes, 1982). Relatively recently, attempts have been made to break down these distinctions as applied wholesale to particular kinds of cultures. Jack Goody, for example, has argued that any distinction that suggests "two different modes of thought, approaches to knowledge, or forms of science" is inadequate, not least because "both are present not only in the same societies but in the same individuals" (1977, p. 148). That is, whenever we try to define precisely some distinctive feature of "our" thinking, we find examples of it in "their" cultures, and whenever we identify a distinctive feature of "their" thinking, we find cases in "our" culture. Robin Horton has shown that what have been regarded as distinctive features of scientific thinking are common in traditional cultures in Africa (1970, 1982); and it has now, post-Freud, become a cliché that certain central features of mythic thinking are common in Western cultures (Blumenberg, 1985). (One wonders, for example, whether Bronislaw Malinowski's [1922] outrage at the wastefulness of piles of rotting yams in the Trobriand Islands would be equally directed at the "mountains" of dairy foods and grains and "lakes" of wine that have accumulated in support of the farming policies of the European Economic Community.) "We" and "they" constantly exhibit thinking that is both rational and irrational, complex and simple, logico-mathematical and mythopoeic. We are "them" and they are "us." (See Lévi-Strauss, 1966; Goody, 1977.)

What about the evident differences, then, between modes of thinking used in oral societies and those used in complex industrial ones? While we may indeed recognize common features in forms of thought that were in the past considered entirely dissimilar, we need to recognize also that modern science, history, and mathematics are hardly identical with anything found in oral cultures. One can scarcely claim that differences do not exist. How do we account for them if we reject explanations involving "primitiveness" or deficiencies of mind or of language? And how do we characterize the dramatic changes in forms of thought and methods of inquiry made during the Greek classical period—changes that involved the birth of philosophy, critical history, and modern science? Goody (1977) maintains that the evident differences are best accounted for by technology, especially the technology of writing. His argument builds on and extends a growing body of work that is seeking to clarify how literacy affects strategies of thinking. The economy of the mind inclines us to theorize that members of oral cultures—in which what one knows is what one remembers—use particular mental strategies, and that some different mental strategies are used in literate cultures—in which various mental operations can be enormously enhanced by visual access to organized bodies of knowledge.

The path from orality to literacy is one that we want all children to take as they pass through our educational systems. Better understanding of what this movement entails might clarify some of our practical educational problems. It might, for example, help us find ways to reduce the rates of illiteracy in Western societies, and perhaps also to improve the quality and richness of literacy we can achieve. From the research that has so far drawn on our increasing knowledge of orality and of the transition to literacy, it is clear that any adequate conception of literacy must account for much more than simple encoding and decoding "skills" and must encompass significant features of rationality (Olsen, 1977, 1986). That is to say, even though there is considerable difficulty in characterizing rationality with precision, it is increasingly clear that the acquisition of literacy can have cognitive effects that have traditionally been considered features of rational thought—particularly those associated with "abstract" thinking. Considering oral cultures, then, may help us to understand better what is entailed in the transition of Western children from orality to literacy.

This is not to posit some mysterious evolutionary recapitulation process in the lives of our schoolchildren. There is a trivial sense in which an education involves the individual's recapitulating the development of his or her culture; in a matter of years we learn knowledge, skills, and ways of making sense of the world that were developed over millenia. Recapitulation theorists in Europe and North America have gone further, however, and have argued that the classroom curriculum should be designed so that children learn the central content of their cultures largely in the sequence in which that content was invented or discovered. Recapitulation schemes in schools have been based on notions of biological recapitulation, logical sequences in the development of knowledge, and/or psychological predispositions (Gould, 1977). In what follows, however, I will be considering the recapitulation of specific techniques used in thinking. By making children literate, for example, we are recreating, in each individual's case, the internalization of a technology that can have some quite profound and precise effects on cognitive processes and modes of communication. As Walter Ong has observed, "Technologies are not mere exterior aids but also interior transformations of consciousness" (1982, p. 82), and "Writing is a technology that restructures thought" (1986, p. 23).

*Technology* is a slightly aggressive term to use for writing, and "tools for thinking" is a handy but tendentious metaphor. One is led to assume that spades and computers have similar transforming powers over our manual and cognitive functions. That they have transforming powers is beyond doubt, but that these are the same as, or akin to, what internalizing literacy produces needs further evidence. I prefer to use a less aggressive term, coined, as far as I am aware, by Lévi-Strauss. In discussing the structural categories underlying totemic classification, he debunked the notion that totemic species are chosen because of their economic or culinary value; he argued they are not so much "*bon à manger*" (good for eating) as "*bon à penser*" (good for thinking with) (Lévi-Strauss, 1962). Literacy is a set of strategies that are not only utilitarian, but also *bon à penser*.

One purpose of this article is to explore oral practices that are also "good for thinking with." Orality, we shall see, is not a condition of deficit—to be defined simply as the lack of literacy. Regarding orality only in terms of literacy is (in Ong's neat simile) like regarding horses as automobiles without wheels (1982, p. 12). Orality entails a set of powerful and effective mental strategies, some of which, to our cost, have become attenuated and undervalued in many aspects of our Western cultures and educational systems. In the following pages I shall explore some of the effective strategies of thinking used in oral cultures, and then consider their relevance to education.

A word of caution is required. Any simplistic assumption that equates the thinking of adults in oral cultures with that of children in literate societies will be undermined in two ways. First, adults have the accumulated experience and cognitive development that children necessarily lack. Second, most children in Western cultures live in environments that presuppose literacy and its associated forms of thought: constant adult interactions with young children assume conventions that depend on literacy, and preliterate children are constantly encouraged to adopt forms of thinking and expression that are more easily achieved as a product of literacy.

My purpose is to focus on forms of thought that are *bon à penser* if one is not literate. Consequently, I will be *seeking* comparisons between forms of thought used by members of oral cultures and those used by modern Western children. The basis of the comparison, however, is neither knowledge content nor psychological development, but techniques that are required by orality. Keeping this idea to the fore will, I hope, allow us to avoid the kind of deprecatory ethnocentrism criticized above.

I shall not try to establish an exhaustive inventory of the intellectual strategies common in oral cultures. Further, I do not consider that the purpose of education in Western cultures is to preserve and delay such strategies uncritically. We are not in the business of preparing children to live in an oral culture—though it may be worth reiterating that we are preparing them for a literate-and-oral culture. Indeed, we see fast developing around us features of what Ong (1982) has called "secondary orality." The electronic media are its most energetic promoters, but even newspapers and journals are explicitly, and somewhat paradoxically, relying less and less on strategies of communication that draw on the skills of "high literacy" and their associated forms of thought (Ong, 1977). Although orality is not the end of our educational development, we might consider whether it is a necessary constituent of it, and whether the study of orality might be *bon à penser*, as we attempt to construct both a richer primary school curriculum and a fuller sense of how children might effectively learn its contents.

A central theme of this article might be summed up in Lévi-Strauss's observation:

> I think there are some things we have lost, and we should perhaps try to regain them, [but] I am not sure that in the kind of world in which we are living and with the kind of scientific thinking we are bound to follow, we can regain these things exactly as if they had never been lost; but we can try to become aware of their existence and their importance. (1978, p. 5)

I shall begin with a brief account of some of the overlapping branches of research in classical studies and anthropology that have helped to clarify the kinds of thinking that have proven effective in cultures that do not have writing. Next, I shall discuss some prominent features of orality—the poetics of memory, participation and conservation, and classification and explanation—that have proved *bon à penser*. I shall

181

conclude by discussing the possible implications of these features of orality for early childhood education. Central to this discussion is a reconsideration of what the foundations of education are when literacy and rationality are conceived as growing out of, rather than displacing, the oral culture of early childhood.

## The Rediscovery of Orality

The relatively recent rediscovery of orality by Western scholars is connected with some problems presented by Homer's epic poems. Thinkers could easily apply the influential late-Victorian evolutionary paradigm to the development of science, which was seen as a positive progression from myth to rationality to empirical science. When applied more generally to human cultures, however, this paradigm encountered the anomaly of Homer's literary achievements. Educated Victorians were more familiar with long-ago battles on the windy plains of Troy, the wooden horse, and the destruction of the topless towers of Ilium than with much of their own society. How, they asked, could such vividly powerful epics, with their richness of human insight, their technical sophistication and emotional force, and their overwhelming, engaging reality, be composed by and for what were in all other regards considered primitive people? "Primitive" mentality—supposedly a mess of irrationality and confusion—must, it would seem, have had the resources to create some great cultural achievements.

Two other complications arose. First, the story of the *Iliad*, long regarded as straightforward fiction, came to be seen as an account of events that actually occurred in the thirteenth century B.C. This historicity began to be established by Heinrich Schliemann's excavations at Troy and Mycaenae during the latter part of the nineteenth century and has gradually become fuller and clearer. (Recently, a persuasive picture of the period has been pieced together in Michael Wood's popular television series and book *In Search of the Trojan War* [1985]).

The second complication was the growing evidence that Homer and other poets in his tradition of wandering "singers of tales" were illiterate. As Berkley Peabody put it, "Despite the implications of its name, literature does not seem to have been the invention of literate people" (1975, p. 1). The master poet Homer lived about five hundred years after the events of which he sang, long after the kingdoms whose ships sailed for Troy had themselves been destroyed. Yet growing knowledge of the spread of literacy in Greece made it increasingly difficult for nineteenth-century scholars to imagine Homer—by tradition blind in any case—sitting at a table *writing* his poems.

But how could such technically complex poems, many thousands of lines long, be composed without writing? Surely no illiterate bard could make up such supple hexameters in a matter of hours while he sang, and then recall them word for word? Virgil, that other great epic poet of the ancient world, labored for years writing his *Aeneid* by hand. We know (Suetonius, *De Poetis*) that he revised it constantly and on his deathbed asked that it be destroyed; the highly literate Virgil believed that he had struggled in vain to match the power, vividness, and quality of Homer's work.

The story of the rediscovery of the Homeric methods of composition is itself an epic of scholarly ingenuity. In the 1920s, Milman Parry (1928), following a number of earlier scholars (Wolf, 1795/1884; Vico, 1744/1970), contended in his doctoral dissertation that the structure and distinctive stylistic features of the Homeric poems reflect directly the requirements of oral methods of composition (Burke, 1985; Griffin, 1980). Parry's analyses of the *Iliad* and the *Odyssey* showed that they were composed largely of verbal formulae—repeated morphemic clusters—whose form was dictated by the metrical requirements of the hexameter line. For example, Homer used a large number of adjectival epithets for most of the recurring nouns in the poems—for wine, the sea, ships, the major characters, and so on. The epithet chosen at any point is not necessarily the most apposite for the meaning of the line, but is dictated instead by its fit into the line's meter (Kirk, 1965, ch. 1). One-fifth of Homer's lines are repeated almost verbatim elsewhere in his poems; in about 28,000 lines there are about 25,000 repeated phrases (Parry, 1928).

The poet who performed orally did not memorize the poems, as we would have to do. Rather, the singer learned—through a long, *non-literate* apprenticeship—the particular metrical form of his tradition, until it was absorbed like a somatic rhythm, which habitually accompanied and shaped his thought (Lord, 1964). The content of the song was held together first by the poet's clear grasp of the overall story, and the meter determined the pattern of sounds. As Albert B. Lord wrote, "Man without writing thinks in terms of sound groups and not in words" (1964, p. 25). Traditional oral performance, then, does not involve repeated recitation of a memorized poem—the idea of a fixed text is a product of literacy. Rather, each performance is a new composition. It may be very like previous ones, and certain patterns will recur, but the singer is composing each time, not repeating something fixed in memory. It is, in Lord's words, "the preservation of tradition by the constant re-creation of it" (1964, p. 29).

These metrically arranged units of sound, then, accumulated line by line in the Homeric poems to repeat the heroic story. The poet "stitched" together the formulae to fit the metrical line, and the episodes to fit the story. The Greeks called singers "rhapsodes"—literally, "song-stitchers." It seems likely that Homer, as one of the greatest epic poets, represented the culmination of his tradition, and that he recited his poems to trained scribes.

In the early 1930s, Parry supplemented his arguments by studying methods of oral composition being used by contemporary singers of heroic tales in Yugoslavia. After his death, his work was supported and extended by Lord's studies (1964) of comparable singers in the Balkans. Lord has described in some detail the conditions of their intensive, and almost invariably non-literate, training, which cannot be very unlike Homer's (Lord, 1964, esp. ch. 2). This work has been further elaborated by Peabody's ingenious analysis of Hesiod's *Works and Days* (1975). Peabody has shown in still greater depth how the oral poet uses the techniques developed over uncountable generations to realize for the audience a kind of alternate reality. That is, the techniques of oral poetry are designed to discourage critical reflection on the stories and their contents, and instead to "enchant" the hearers, drawing them into the world of the story. I will describe these techniques below.

This process of enthralling the audience, of impressing upon them the reality of the story, is a central feature of education in oral cultures. Their social institutions are sustained in large part by sound, by what the spoken or sung word can do to commit individuals to particular beliefs, expectations, roles, and behaviors. Thus the techniques of fixing the crucial patterns of belief in the memory—rhyme, rhythm, formula, story, and so on—are vitally important. Education in oral cultures is largely a matter of constantly immersing the young in enchanting patterns of sound until their minds resonate to them, until they become in tune with the institutions of their culture.

The Homeric poems were called the educators of the pre-classical Greeks because they performed this social function. Poems were not listened to or learned solely because of their aesthetic value; that was incidental to their value as "a massive repository of useful knowledge, a sort of encyclopaedia of ethics, politics, history, and technology which the effective citizen was required to learn as the core of his educational equipment" (Havelock, 1963, p. 29). In the process of such an education a substantial amount of mental energy is spent memorizing the chief messages of the culture, because they can exist and survive only in people's memories. According to Eric Havelock, little mental energy is left for reflection on those messages, or analysis of them, because such activities would interfere with the need to sink them unquestioningly into every mind.

Havelock further extended Parry's and Lord's work. His *Preface to Plato* (1963), *Origins of Western Literacy* (1976), and *The Muse Learns to Write* (1986) help clarify the achievements of the early literate Greek philosophers, by offering a better understanding of the oral poetic culture that preceded it. In particular, they highlight Plato's reasons for wishing to exclude poets from his ideal state. Havelock read Plato's *Republic* as a program for educating people to discard the residues of oral culture and to embrace forms of thinking made possible by full literacy. In Havelock's interpretation, Plato says that the mind need no longer be immersed in the oral tradition, memorizing and copying the paradigmatic structures and patterns of the Homeric poems, but can be freed to engage its proper objects—what we might call abstract concepts, and what he called Forms or Ideas. Plato characterized this mode of thinking as opposed to the Homeric tradition; the Platonic scheme of education, as he saw it, brought the mind to reality, while Homer's crippled the intellect through its seductive illusions and distortions of reality.

The new forms of thinking made possible by literacy, early in our educational discourse, were represented as enemies of the oral techniques that were *bon à penser*: "Plato's target was indeed an educational procedure and a whole way of life" (Havelock, 1963, p. 45). There are clear ambivalences in Plato's reflections on the oral tradition (see the *Phaedrus* and the possibly apocryphal *Seventh Letter*) and on Homer, but in the end those earlier forms of thinking, education, and society had to be destroyed to make way for the new abstract forms of thought and whatever world they brought with them. Plato did not conceive his educational scheme as a structure built on the oral tradition, but as a replacement for it. His work, in Havelock's view, "announced the arrival of a completely new level of discourse which as it became perfected was to create in turn a new kind of experience of the world—the reflective, the scientific, the technological, the theological, the analytic. We can give it a dozen names" (1963, p. 267). Plato's influence is so strong in Western thought that it is extremely difficult for us now to imagine the kind of consciousness created in the oral tradition, and the kind of experience created for listeners by a singer of tales or teller of myths.

Havelock's description of the techniques of oral recitation in the ancient world shows that audiences received poems rather differently from the way we read the same texts today. A youth in an oral culture, whether Greek or Australian aborigine, needed to expend considerable mental resources to learn by listening to these foundations of his or her cultural institutions. But the messages of the professional singers were also repeated everywhere by their listeners. Proverbs and maxims and riddles uttered at meals, on rising or going to sleep, in the market or the field, are constantly repeated pieces of the great myths or epic poems of oral cultures. African children, for example, traditionally learn the practices and mores of their ethnic groups through riddles asked by their grandparents. In religious schools throughout the Muslim world, young students commit to memory phenomenally long passages of Koranic literature and law. It is likely that biblical stories were first repeated and handed on by singers and storytellers, as are the tales of African *griots* in many places today.

Learning the sustaining messages of an oral culture differs from the effort at accumulation of knowledge with which we are familiar in literate cultures. In oral cultures memorization is central, but it is not performed in the way that we might try to learn something by heart. For us memorization is usually an attempt to remember a text so that it is possible to repeat it verbatim on command; and our techniques are typically impoverished, involving largely repetition, some mnemonics perhaps, or saying words aloud with our eyes closed, and so on. In an oral culture, learning proceeds more somatically, with the whole body used to support the memorizing process. The Homeric singer, and singers throughout the world, usually use a simple stringed instrument, sometimes a drum, whose beat reinforces the rhythm of the telling and draws the hearer into the enchantment of the song. The audience does not so much listen to it, as we might listen to a play, as they are invited to live it. The acoustical rhythm created by the singer and his instrument is supported by the repetitive meter, rhythmic body movements, and by the pattern of formulae and the story, to set up conditions of enchantment that impress the message on the minds of the hearers. The techniques of the skilled performer generate a relaxed, half-hypnotized pleasure in the audience.[2]

This semi-hypnotized state is similar to that often described by anthropologists as the condition in which audiences receive the fundamental messages of their culture. Thus, Lévi-Strauss, in his study of mythology, aimed "to show, not how men think in myths, but how myths operate in men's minds without their being aware of the

185

fact" (1969, p. 12). He preferred to compare this process to a musical performance rather than to linguistic forms or texts: "The myth and the musical work are like conductors of an orchestra, whose audience becomes the silent performers" (p. 17). While no Western educator would wish to replicate all aspects of this phenomenon in our schools, it seems important to understand the nature of this receptive state. Anyone familiar with children's rapt attention to television broadcasts may recognize Lévi-Strauss's descriptions.

Similarly, Edmund Leach (1967) argued that the structural patterns of myths and their underlying messages are communicated powerfully and unambiguously by oral performances, despite considerable variation in the surface stories and settings:

> Whenever a corpus of mythology is recited in its religious setting, such structures are "felt" to be present, and convey meaning much as poetry conveys meaning. Even though the ordinary listener is not fully conscious of what has been communicated, the "message" is there in a quite objective sense. (Leach, 1967, p. 12)

According to Lévi-Bruhl, when a sacred myth is recited in the course of ritual settings or other situations characterized by heightened emotion, "what they [the participants] hear in it awakens a whole gamut of harmonics which do not exist for us" (1910/ 1985, p. 369). The written form of the myth that we can study "is but the inanimate corpse which remains after the vital spark has fled" (1910/1985, p. 369).

In his re-examination of orality, Goody (1977, 1986, 1987) has not only undermined traditional notions of the move from "primitive" to rational thought, and instead shown that the differences typically educed as evidence for such a shift are better understood as epiphenomena of the move from orality to literacy; he has also clarified some specific steps that accompanied the move from orality to literacy, and has detailed various consequences of literacy—for example, the development of Western scientific inquiry and abstract thought (Goody & Watt, 1968; Goody, 1986, 1987). (For the best current survey of this field, see Ong, 1982.)

In the following discussion of several techniques of oral expression common in non-literate cultures, my choice has been guided not by a desire to conduct a systematic survey, but primarily by educational relevance.

## *Oral Expressions:* Bon à penser

In listing certain features of oral cultures I do not mean to imply that such cultures are all alike; nor do I imply that they all use precisely the same sets of techniques for preserving their institutions. Clearly, there are enormous differences among the cultures of preclassical Greeks and those of the early twentieth-century Trobriand Islanders, Australian aborigines, and the indigenous peoples of the Americas before extensive contacts with literate peoples. In particular, their myths, and the range of techniques used to transmit them, differ significantly.

It is inevitably difficult for us to think of orality simply as a positive set of tactics that are *bon à penser;* the intellectual capacities and forms of communication that have been stimulated by literacy intrude upon our attempts to understand orally sustained forms of thought. But we need to see orality as an energetic and distinct set of ways of learning and communicating, not simply as an incomplete and imperfect use of the mind awaiting the invention of literacy. Orality is not at all the same as what we usually mean today by illiteracy in the Western cultural context. Illiteracy is perhaps best understood as a condition in which one has not acquired the positive capacities that either orality or literacy can provide.

*Poetics of Memory*

Let us begin considering orality by focusing on what seems to be the central reason it involves some different tactics of thinking from literacy: its need to rely on memory. If the preservation of the institutions of one's culture depends on the memories of its living members, then the techniques that most effectively impress the appropriate messages upon their minds and sustain them are vitally important. The Victorians, who judged members of oral cultures to be mentally "incapable" because of their supposed reluctance or inability to perform mental functions that are commonplace in literate Western cultures, often failed to recognize this fact at work in the intellectual "anomalies" of traditional societies they encountered. Lucien Lévi-Bruhl, writing in 1910, described various feats of memory that seemed to him prodigious, but to the oral peoples he studied, commonplace:

> This extraordinary development of memory, and a memory which faithfully reproduces the minutest details of sense-impressions in the correct order of their appearance, is shown moreover by the wealth of vocabulary and the grammatical complexity of the languages. Now the very men who speak these languages and possess this power of memory are (in Australia or Northern Brazil, for instance) incapable of counting beyond two and three. The slightest mental effort involving abstract reasoning, however rudimentary it may be, is so distasteful to them that they immediately declare themselves tired and give it up. (Lévi-Bruhl, 1910/1985, p. 115)

Lévi-Bruhl perceived there were no differences between his own capacities and those of his subjects on any simple scale of mental superiority or inferiority, but that the conditions of life in oral cultures stimulated different mental developments to deal with those conditions. The people he observed had a highly developed set of techniques for learning and remembering, and their apparent incapacity for "abstraction," as such, lay in the dissociation of the problems Lévi-Bruhl gave them from their lives. It may be helpful to remember this as we investigate the development of our children's capacities for abstract thinking (Hayek, 1969; Egan, in press).

Goody's experience with the LoDogaa of Ghana (1977, pp. 12–13) makes this clear. When he asked some tribesmen to count for him, they responded with the—to them—obvious question, "Count what?" The LoDogaa have not only an abstract numerical system, but also several sophisticated forms of counting that are chosen according to what is being counted: their methods for counting cows and for counting cowrie shells differ. "Abstract reasoning" is beyond no human mind; but abstraction that is very heavily dependent on writing is not available to people who do not write or read.

In describing the apparent anomaly of prodigious mental feats executed by the supposedly mentally deficient, Lévi-Bruhl (1910/1985) perceived that there were no differences between purely oral and literate peoples on any simple scale of mental superiority/inferiority, but that the conditions of life in oral cultures stimulated a difference in mental developments to deal with those conditions. He located a wide range of those differences precisely. The uses of memory in oral cultures, Lévi-Bruhl concluded, "are quite different because its contents are of a different character. It is both very accurate and very emotional" (1910/1985, p. 110).

Oral cultures engage the emotions of their members by making the culturally important messages event-laden, by presenting characters and their emotions in conflict in developing narratives—in short, by building the messages into stories. Lévi-Strauss pointed out that "all myths tell a story" (1962, p. 26), and Lord concluded that the story provides the firm structure for the constant reconstruction of heroic songs. The various linguistic structures in the end "serve only one purpose. They provide a means for telling a story. . . . The tale's the thing" (Lord, 1964, p. 68). The story form is one of the few cultural universals—everyone, everywhere, has told and enjoyed stories. They are one of the greatest cultural inventions for catching and fixing meaning. Perhaps "discovery" is a more appropriate term than "invention": some enormously creative person or people discovered that messages shaped into the distinctive form of the story were those best remembered, and they carried a charge of emotional identification that greatly enhanced social cohesion and control.

Myth stories also, of course, have what we would consider aesthetic value. But whereas we distinguish aesthetic from utilitarian values, for members of oral cultures these are bound up together (Durkheim, 1915, ch. 4; Cassirer, 1946). The story form has been one of the most powerful and effective sustainers of cultures across the world. Its great power lies in its ability to fix affective responses to the messages it contains and to bind what is to be remembered with emotional associations. Our emotions, to put it simply, are most effective at sustaining, and helping in the recall of, memories of events (Bartlett, 1932). This should not be a surprise if we reflect on the events of our lives that are most memorable. Almost invariably we find that they are accompanied by vivid emotional associations, and retain quite clearly a particular emotional tone. Most of the world's cultures and its great religions have at their sacred core a story, and indeed we have difficulty keeping the facts of our history from being shaped constantly into stories. It is likely that the simplified histories sanctioned in the schools of most nation states (Ravitch, 1983) have at least as much in common with the origin myths of oral cultures as they do with the austere ideals of historiography. The story form also has important implications for schooling. Its survival among oral peoples as a technique for sustaining culture speaks to its appropriateness for education, despite our recent tendencies to neglect it. There are many ways in which we might use this most powerful of communicative media in education today, especially in the primary school (Egan, 1985, in press).

Rhyme, rhythm, meter, repetition of formulae, redundancy, the use of visual imagery—figures of speech used to create enhancement in oral cultures throughout the world—are also among the techniques used in Western poetry, and the state of mind they induce is close to what we describe as poetic. Like the singer of heroic tales or the reciter of myths, the literate poet shapes sound to create particular emotional effects and fix particular meanings. The shaping of sound finds one outlet in poetry and another in rhetoric. These two, along with music, are perhaps the most evident and direct manifestations of the oral tradition that have survived in the literate world.

Metaphor, metonymy, and synecdoche are important among the linguistic tools that are *bon à penser*. In oral cultures, thinking moves according to the complex logic of metaphor, more readily than it follows the systematic logic of rational inquiry. As Ernst Cassirer notes, "It is a familiar fact that all mythic thinking is governed and permeated by the principle [of metaphor]" (1946, p. 92; see also Lévi-Strauss, 1966, esp. ch. 7). Although the logic of mythic thinking, with its reliance on metaphor, has been difficult for some Westerners to make sense of, we should appreciate and find readily accessible this metaphoric power, for it suffuses all languages. It is one of the foundations of all our mental activity, upon which our systematic logics of rational inquiry also rest, or—a better metaphor—the soil out of which they grow. Both myth and our everyday language, then, are permeated with metaphor; as Cassirer concluded, "The same form of mental conception is operative in both. It is the form which one may denote as *metaphorical thinking*" (1945, p. 84). Or, as Lévi-Strauss observes, "metaphor . . . is not a later embellishment of language but is one of its fundamental modes—a primary form of discursive thought" (1962, p. 102; see also Cooper, 1986).

The characteristics of oral literature that I have mentioned are generated by a people's need to memorize and be committed to their cultural institutions. We find these techniques to a greater or lesser degree in all oral cultures: "At different periods and in different cultures there are close links between the techniques for mental recall, the inner organization of the faculty (of memory), the place it occupies in the system of the ego, and the ways that men picture memory to themselves" (Vernant, 1983, p. 75; see also Finnegan, 1970, 1977).

We remain familiar with these tactics that are *bon à penser*, but usually in a much attenuated or altered form. Rhyme, for example, seems little more than fun for us now, a part of children's games, anachronistic and therefore ironic in modern poetry. We would hardly consider its systematic use a matter of vital social importance. We can write, so we do not need rhyme to sustain the memory of our institutions. These survivors of orality—rhyme, rhythm, meter, story, metaphor—serve largely (I am tempted to write "merely") aesthetic purposes for us. While metaphor and story may still seem to us culturally important in some imprecise way, we tend to think of rhyme and rhythm as only casual cultural survivors, anachronisms serving merely to entertain the literate—like the lords and ladies of a defeated civilization made into clowns and dancers. But art has a utilitarian purpose when it supports faith—whether in gods, in the validity of one's cultural institutions, in one's society, in one's sense of oneself. The origins of any of the tools of spoken language invented to create and sustain memory lie in the remarkable human ambition "to liberate the soul from time and open up a path to immortality" (Vernant, 1983, p. 95). All the world's amazing cultural and technological achievements since the development of literacy have been built on the efficacy of these oral tools of communication and the intellectual space they once did, and can still, generate. We would do well, therefore, to consider carefully their actual and potential roles in early childhood education.

## Participation and Conservation

An Ojibwa Indian observed: "The white man writes everything down in a book so that it will not be forgotten; but our ancestors married the animals, learned their ways, and passed on the knowledge from one generation to another" (Jenness, in Lévi-Strauss, 1966, p. 37). This sense of participation in the natural world, of having knowledge that is different from the kinds of propositions generated by rational inquiries, reflects a mental condition anthropologists have often tried to describe as a kind of oneness with nature; by comparison, our normal relationship with the natural world seems alienated. "The mainspring of the acts, thoughts, and feelings of early man was the conviction that the divine was immanent in nature, and nature intimately connected with society" (Frankfort, Wilson, & Jacobsen, 1949, p. 237). All the attempts to pinpoint the causes and character of this sense of participation in nature display a conviction that, despite their inadequacies when it comes to pragmatic control *over* the world, myth and consciousness in oral cultures somehow enable people to feel that they are comfortable participants *in* their life world. But it is not a simple condition, obviously, nor one we can feel unequivocally regretful of having largely lost. Ong describes it this way:

> The psyche of a culture innocent of writing knows by a kind of empathetic identification of knower and known, in which the object of knowledge and the total being of the knower enter into a kind of fusion, in a way which literate cultures would typically find unsatisfyingly vague and garbled and somehow too intense and participatory. (Ong, 1977, p. 18)

One of the cornerstones of Western rationality is knowing, as it were, where we end and the world begins: distinguishing the world from our feelings, hopes, fears, and so on. This form of thinking seems to be very largely a product of literacy. As Ong puts it, "Writing fosters abstractions that disengage knowledge from the arena where human beings struggle with one another" (1982, pp. 43–44), or, in Peabody's words: "The shift in medium from utterance to record affects the way such an institution works and tends to change what was an immediate, living, active agent into an increasingly distant, timeless, passive, authority" (1975, pp. 1, 2). In an oral culture the ear is most highly attuned to picking up cultural messages, supplemented by the eye. In our case it is usually the other way around.

Sound is alive and participatory. It is effective within only a short physical range. The hearer must be in the presence of the speaker—there are no carefully crafted memos from the president or manager. "The living word," as Socrates put it in Plato's *Phaedrus*, "has a soul . . . of which the written word is properly no more than an image" (Jowett, 1982, p. 279). The living word is the word in the arena of human interactions and conflicts. It is not the distanced and "cooled" word of the written text. Language use in an oral culture tends to be, in Ong's phrase, "agonistically toned" (1977, p. 113); it is charged with the direct energy of the speaker's body, and thus with the speaker's hopes, fears, wants, needs, and intentions. Oral heroic tales are full of bragging, elaborate abuse of adversaries, and exuberant praise of leaders or those from whom the speaker wants a favor. The tensions of daily struggles are felt face-to-face in an oral culture. These facts of oral life lead to a verbally highly polarized world, of good and evil, friends and enemies, fear and security. Ong points out that the mental life of oral cultures "is sure to carry a heavy load of praise and vituperation" (1977, p. 112), because "if one does not think formulary, mnemonically structured thoughts, how can one really know them, that is, be able to retrieve them, if the thoughts are even of moderate complexity?" (p. 104). Thus, because oral cultures "necessarily store knowledge largely in narrative concerned with interacting human or quasi-human figures" (1977, p. 112), there is a powerful pressure to polarize. The African Batomba, for instance, have two typically polarized paraphrastic names for White foreigners: "The white man, honored by all, companion of our chiefs" or, as occasion may demand, the pointed expression "You do not touch the poisonous caterpillar" (Ong, 1977, p. 112). In such societies the forms of verbal play also tend to be "agonistically toned"—riddles, tricks, and jokes are often characterized by a playful competitiveness or even aggressiveness.

In an oral culture "the meaning of each word is ratified in a succession of concrete situations, accompanied by vocal inflections and physical gestures, all of which combine to particularize both its specific denotation and its accepted connotative uses" (Goody & Watt, 1968, p. 306). As a result, words typically are not themselves objects of reflection, and thus oral cultures have no epistemology as we might define it. When words are closely tied into their context of reference, philosophical problems do not arise. People in oral cultures do not dissociate words from things to the point where they might wonder how short the legs of a small table have to be for it to be considered a tray. This feature of their thinking has nothing to do with "defects" or "inadequacies" of the mind, but is rather a function of the uselessness of many of our forms and techniques of thought in the conditions of most oral cultures.

In nearly all oral cultures, for example, time is reckoned in terms of the significant daily activities of the social group. An "abstract" or dissociated system for measuring time, such as we employ, is useful only when it is necessary to coordinate a large number of quite diverse kinds of activities. Such diversity does not exist in most oral cultures, where time measurement reflects the sequence of activities that constitute the rhythms of daily life.

In his studies of non-literate peasants in remote areas of the Soviet Union, Alexander Luria (1976) posed to them apparently simple problems, such as "In the far north, where there is snow, all bears are white. Novaya Zemlya is in the far north and there is always snow there. What colors are the bears around Novaya Zemlya?" His subjects, no doubt politely wishing to play their part in the conversation, would reply that they had never been to Novaya Zemlya and so didn't know, or that they had seen a black bear but never a white one, and so on. The rules and underlying forms of thought of the kind of conversation in which Luria tried to engage these non-literate people are familiar to us, but appeared bizarre to them. The point is not a concern with mental capacity, but with social utility, and the influence of the latter over cognition. Pragmatic thought in oral cultures participates more intimately in the life world; it does not treat the world and experience as objects distanced from people's emotional, aesthetic, and utilitarian needs. As such, it makes "no clear-cut distinction between subjective states and the properties of the cosmos" (Lévi-Strauss, 1969, p. 240).

Oral cultures have been described as being intellectually inclined toward home-ostasis, conservatism, and stability in ways that our modern literate cultures are not (see Geertz, 1973, esp. ch. 5). Such cultures, of course, undergo changes of many kinds—migration, disaster, invasion, merging with other groups—but the mental forms dominant in oral cultures strive to maintain verbal accounts of the culture's life that assert continuity and stability.

One striking difference between oral and literate cultures is in their different attitudes to the past; literate peoples have and value accurate historical accounts; oral societies cultivate what J. A. Barnes has called "structural amnesia"—systematic procedures for "forgetting," or wiping out from the oral records of the culture's past (Goody & Watt, 1968, p. 309). Although oral cultures often preserve the memory of particular historical events in stories or in memorized genealogies of leading families, it usually turns out that the record kept does not reflect past reality with complete accuracy. Rather, it is faithful to present social conditions and statuses. As conditions change, so do the accounts or genealogy. Malinowski (1954) showed this process at work among the Trobriand Islanders. As changes occurred in the structure and power relationships of their society, the myths of origin changed to reflect the current social structure; that is, historical changes were gradually effaced. Malinowski concluded that "myths serve to cover certain inconsistencies created by historical events" (1954, p. 125). The oral record, then, ensures that "the individual has little perception of the past except in terms of the present" (Goody & Watt, 1968, p. 310).

We find it hard to think of this structural amnesia as anything other than an unawareness of history, another difficulty resulting from the lack of literacy. It seems merely a way of making the best of things, or the only strategy manageable if the society cannot keep written records. But the positive value of such structural amnesia is that it tends to preserve a sense of stability and clarity. The social structure and its prevailing institutions are constantly supported by whatever sanction is contained in the myths, whether of sacred ancestors or gods, and are constantly renewed: "time is recorded only biologically without being allowed to become 'history'—that is, without its corrosive action being able to exert itself upon consciousness by revealing the irreversibility of events" (Eliade, 1959, pp. 74–75). One technique constantly used to achieve this end is the assertion of continual rebirth—rebeginning as the first beginning. We preserve a vague shadow of this sense of birth in our New Year festivals. Even if we, like Malinowski (1954), discount other functions of myth, we ought not to disregard the sense of intellectual security conferred by sloughing off the memory of events that are no longer relevant or useful to present life. This is indeed another way in which orality is *bon à penser*. While direct comparisons are difficult to make, this process may have relevance as we consider preliterate children's conceptions of time and the implications this may have for developing a history curriculum based on the telling of stories. We may wish to make better use of the children's imaginative lives as vividly lived in the present moment.

This emphasis on the preservation of stability through selective memory of events relevant to present social conditions leads to what is often characterized as a conservative frame of mind. It is indeed conservative, but in a radical sense. The pressure to preserve in memory the institutions of one's culture does not invite innovation or experimentation. Although some oral cultures are undoubtedly more resilient in this regard than others, on the whole anthropologists attest to the powerful sanctions against change. "The most apparently trifling innovation may lead to danger, liberate hostile forces, and finally bring about the ruin of its instigator and all dependent upon him" (Lévi-Bruhl, 1910/1985, p. 42). The cultural institutions support a limited stock of archetypal forms of appropriate behavior for each member of the society, and the repetition of these alone is sanctioned and validated by the myths. These are believed to be the behaviors of sacred ancestors or gods, which it is the human task to imitate: "The inhibition against new invention, to avoid placing any possible strain on the memory, continually encourage[s] contemporary decisions to be framed aş though they were the acts and words of the ancestors" (Havelock, 1963, p. 121) or, we might add, gods. As Mircea Eliade wrote, the individual in oral cultures "acknowledges no act which has not been previously posited and lived by someone else, some other being who was not a man. What he does has been done before. His life is a ceaseless repetition of gestures initiated by others" (1959, p. 15). In such a culture, "only the changeless is ultimately significant" (Frankfort, 1961, p. viii).

Although these generalizations may be somewhat less appropriate for some oral cultures than for others, they do point to further common ways in which their orality is, in their cultural context, *bon à penser*. The pressures against change and innovation serve stability, order, and intellectual security. One's familiar territory is intellectually mapped out, categorized, and under secure control. The resources of orality considered in this section help to provide intellectual security and a sense of persisting order in society despite historical changes. They also help to preserve a sense of participation in nature which users of literate forms of thought find somewhat alien. Not entirely alien, of course; attempts to recapture this sense of participation in nature find their most common literate expression in poetry. It is in the work of poets such as Wordsworth that the sense of participation in nature is most plausibly recaptured, and, significantly for my general argument about the cognitive effects of orality, it is in preliterate childhood that he most vividly locates it:

Blest the infant Babe . . .
No outcast he, bewildered and depressed.
Along his infant veins are interfused
The gravitation and the filial bond
Of nature that connect him with the world.
(*The Prelude*, Bk. II, 241–244)

*Classification and Explanation*

Members of oral cultures often have remarkably detailed knowledge of the flora and fauna of their environments, but their systems for classifying this knowledge tend to be very different from ours. Many anthropologists have commented on members of traditional societies who could give remarkably precise inventories of kinds of plants, trees, or weather conditions but had no words for "plant," "tree," or "weather." This phenomenon further supported their conclusions about such people's inability to "abstract." Yet, indeed, some purely oral languages use abstractions where speakers of English would prefer concrete terms (see Boas, 1911). For example, the proposition "The bad man killed the poor child" is rendered in Chinook: "The man's badness killed the child's poverty" (Lévi-Strauss, 1966, p. 1). A major difference between oral cultures and our own lies not in their incapacity for abstraction, but in our dissociation from the life world. This kind of dissociation is a product of the techniques of writing, not some property that some human minds possess and others lack: "Writing, and more especially alphabetic literacy, made it possible to scrutinise discourse in a different kind of way . . . this scrutiny favoured the increase in scope of critical activity, and hence of rationality, scepticism, and logic" (Goody, 1977, p. 37).

Among the common basic techniques of classification in oral cultures is the use of what Lévi-Strauss called "binary opposites": "All classification," he wrote, "proceeds by pairs of contrasts" (1966, p. 139). These are not necessarily opposites in any precise logical or empirical sense, but become used as such by serving as the basis for further discriminations: "The substance of contradictions is much less important than the fact that they exist" (p. 95).

Lévi-Strauss began his four-volume analysis of myths by identifying sets of binary opposites on which each myth was built. Although many of his critics have regarded this as a rather arbitrary procedure, he presents a compelling argument by demonstrating the prevalence of such oppositions giving structure to the contents of myths.

Attempts at classification are fundamental to rational thought. It makes little sense to consider people who develop sophisticated taxonomic schemes "irrational" (Lévi-Strauss, 1966, p. 15). The differences between classificatory schemes in oral cultures and those in our scientific culture commonly rest on the qualities of phenomena used as the basis for classification. Lévi-Strauss's study of myth is, as he puts it, an attempt "to prove that there is a kind of logic in [the] tangible qualities" of the concrete phenomena of everyday life—of the raw and the cooked, honey and ashes, and so on (1969, p. 1). While our children's constant classifications of their universe are necessarily less sophisticated, an understanding of the logic they use in forming them may help us understand their development of literacy.

The kinds of explanations offered in oral cultures about natural and cosmological phenomena often seemed to Victorian intellectuals perverse or crazy, and were taken as clear evidence of oral peoples' infirmities of mind. Unfamiliar medical practices were considered bizarre (although today a growing body of anthropology literature elucidates the physical or psychological efficacy of many traditional practices). Lévi-Strauss, however, pointed out that the mistake of earlier interpreters of such explanations "was to think that natural phenomena are *what* myths seek to explain, when they are rather the *medium through which* myths try to explain facts which are themselves not of a natural but a logical order" (1966, p. 95). We must, he said, attend to the form as well as the content of such explanations if we are to understand them.

For us, explanation is a central part of our efforts both to understand and control nature, to have practical effects. But its main purpose in oral cultures "is not a practical one. It meets intellectual requirements rather than or instead of satisfying needs" (Lévi-Strauss, 1966, p. 9). In serving such intellectual purposes it does not, like our logic, tie itself to the ways the world in fact works; indeed the "savage" mind "does not bind itself down, as our thought does, to avoiding contradictions" (Lévi-Bruhl, 1910/1985, p. 78). Certainly in the myths and medical lore of oral cultures, the literate, rationalistic concern with noncontradiction is not a prominent structuring feature. Underlying the surface of explanations that may seem bizarre to Western observers, however, is a quest for order in diversity whose motive should be familiar to us from the similar motive that drives our science (see Horton, 1970, pp. 131–171).

The mode of thought that directs the approaches of various oral cultures to classification and explanation is closely linked with the modes of expression discussed earlier. Malinowski observed of the Trobriand Islanders: "They never explain in any sense of the word; they always state a precedent which constitutes an ideal and a warrant for its continuance, and sometimes practical directions for the procedure" (1954, p. 110). What seem like explanations in oral cultures do not focus only on the relevant relationships among content features, but they mix in the whole equipment of the psyche—the explanation, that is, is cast in the form of a narrative in which characters, events, motives, and emotions carry the ideas forward—leading to what Goody calls the "personalization of theory" (1977, p. 42).

## Implications for Early Childhood Education

The research on orality sketched above has a number of implications for early childhood education; here I will consider just two. The first concerns the early childhood curriculum; the second concerns methods of teaching.

The implications turn on the validity of the connections that can be established between characteristics of orality and the thinking of young children in modern literate cultures. I started by noting the need for caution in making such connections. First, psychological developmental connections seem particularly inappropriate. For example, the fact that adults in oral cultures commonly cannot perform intellectual tasks such as properly concluding "disembedded" syllogisms or successfully achieving Piagetian conservations (Ashton, 1975; Buck-Morss, 1982), does not mean that they are psychologically or developmentally equivalent to children in Western literate cultures, nor does the fact that adults in Western literate cultures can commonly perform such tasks make them psychologically superior or intellectually more fully developed. It means only that Western adults have adapted to a cultural environment shaped by centuries of elaboration of the thinking techniques made possible by literacy. Second, it is inappropriate to seek connections in the *content* of thoughts between adults in oral cultures and children in Western cultures; the concern here is, rather, what they think *with*. The connections I am focusing on are in certain formal characteristics of thought, in the strategies and resources the human mind has available and has developed over countless centuries in oral cultures. As young children in Western literate cultures themselves inhabit an oral culture, they have access to the intellectual resources of early orality until such a time as literacy is internalized.

There are two ways in which we might hope to establish relationships between the resources available to thought in oral cultures and those deployed by modern Western children. The first is analytic. This focuses on the necessary requirements of thought in oral conditions, and on what is entailed by the need to memorize when written recording is not available. Such analytic work obviously goes forward most securely and fruitfully when combined with the second method, which is empirical. We can observe characteristic features of language and thought in oral cultures around the world, and see whether we find similar features in the language and thought of preliterate children in Western cultures; we may then be able to suggest some research issues that are worthy of further attention. The empirical observations alone can provide us only with correlations; it is the analytic work that can posit causal relationships between observed forms of language and the requirements of an oral environment.

The body of this article has outlined a variety of formal characteristics of thought inferred from observations in oral cultures. One obvious source of equivalent material about modern Western children is in ethnographic studies of their lore and language. Fortunately, there are a number of quite substantial studies of children's oral cultures, notably those made by the Opies (1959, 1969, 1985) in Britain, and the Knapps (1976) and Sutton-Smith (1981) in the United States.

Those techniques used in oral cultures to shape sound into more memorable forms we find also to be prominent in children's oral cultures. Rhyme, rhythm, meter, and the story form are ubiquitous. The prominence of rhyme in everyday speech will in all English-speaking countries elicit the response, "You're a poet and didn't know it" (Opie & Opie, 1959, p. 73). The strength of rhythm and meter is such that many children's songs are made up of parodies of well-known, usually solemn or sacred, songs carried on echoes of the same rhythms and meters. The Opies report variants of this practice all over Britain (1959, p. 108). A children's taunting rhyme recalls the lively competitiveness and moral core of many verbal games observed in oral cultures:

> Liar, liar, pants on fire!
> Nose as long as a telephone wire.
> (Knapp & Knapp, 1976, p. 11)

Children's easy use of metaphoric thinking is evident in their ability to understand the kinds of metaphors that fill all languages—"It's bitter cold," "He feels bouncy today"—and their easy perception of the distinction between literal and metaphoric usage—"Mom killed that plan!" In what might be expected to be the constraining circumstances of constructed tasks, Gardner et al. (1975) report that nursery school children are much more likely than older children to use a metaphor to complete a sentence of the form, "He looks as gigantic as ———." This ready grasp of metaphor and punning is prerequisite to an understanding of the jokes that are common in children's oral culture: "What did the quarter say when it got stuck in the slot?" "Money's very tight these days"; "Why does Fred work in the bakery?" "I guess he kneads the dough," and so endlessly on.

Children's sense of the story form seems to exist very early in life; it is clearly evident in the language of many children by age two (Applebee, 1978; Pitcher & Prelinger, 1963). Themes framed as binary opposites, too, are evident as the most prominent structuring elements in the classic folktales (Bettelheim, 1976) and in children's invented stories (Paley, 1981). The stories are particularized versions of the struggles between such moral concepts as good and evil, bravery and cowardice, fear and security, hope and despair, and so on.

Rhyme, metaphor, and stories are, of course, found in adult cultures as well. This in no way undermines their identification as prominent features of orality. In literate Western cultures we do not move from orality to literacy, but rather from orality to a combination of literacy and orality. The techniques that are *bon à penser* for oral peoples do not disappear with the acquisition of literacy; they may be attenuated, but even the most highly literate people are also dependent in many circumstances of their lives on some aspects of orality. In addition, literate adults use techniques of thinking encouraged specifically by literacy; the Western forms of rational inquiry and the standard written forms for reporting their results have developed in part by their exclusion of the techniques of orality. Attempts were made in the past to reach accommodation between the two in the field of rhetoric (see Ong, 1971; Todorov, 1982, ch. 3), but their clear separation, institutionalized by the dominance of positivistic science, is evident in the commonly dismissive use of the phrase "mere rhetoric." Previously, mingling the features of orality and literacy was not considered odd. Orality tends to survive, however, only in the daily lives of literate peoples; it is attenuated to the point of near invisibility in the cultures of positivistic science and technology, and in the realms of the most refinedly "literate" scholarship.

It is possible to take each of the characteristics of orality indicated in the body of this paper and find clear analogies in the oral culture of modern Western children

(Egan, forthcoming). That such empirical connections are unlikely to be merely coincidental is suggested by the analysis of orality and what it implies for linguistic forms and techniques of thinking—an analysis owed largely to the main authorities cited above; in particular, Goody, Havelock, and Ong. Let us provisionally assume that this kind of study of oral cultures throughout the world can yield a better understanding of orality and that an understanding of orality can help us better understand young children's minds in literate cultures.

Too often, I think, our perception of young children is clouded when we consider them illiterate and lacking in the skills of Western rationality. It is far better, I would argue, to regard them as oral in a positive sense: they have a distinctive culture of their own. While the image of young children as *tabulae rasae*, or empty vessels to be filled with knowledge, is no longer prominent in educational discourse, we persist in characterizing young children in terms of the absence of the development and knowledge that constitute the mature condition. Even otherwise liberating theories such as Piaget's, for example, represent the developmental process as the gradual accumulation of increasingly sophisticated capacities and their hierarchical integration (Inhelder & Piaget, 1969). Such theories, when used to reflect on education, focus attention on the sequence of capacities to be developed, helping further to define young children in terms of what they lack. In Piaget's scheme, for example, they are *pre*-operational. Developmental schemes focused on the acquisition of the forms of thought characteristic of literate cultures, such as Piaget's focus on logico-mathematical structures, show a gradually rising scale of achievements to adulthood. If we were to focus instead on the thinking techniques of oral peoples, we would surely produce a quite different "developmental" profile. If the techniques of orality are, as I suggested earlier, conducive to formation of the imagination, we might have cause to be very concerned about this.

Perhaps we need a *New Science* of childhood based on the insight that led Vico (1744/1970) towards a better understanding of the "irrational" thinking of early peoples: He argued that notions of irrationality were beside the point; rather, they were "poets who spoke in poetic characters. This discovery, which is the master key of this Science, has cost us the persistent research of almost all our literary life because with our civilized natures we cannot at all imagine and can understand only by great toil the poetic nature of these first men" (Vico, 1744/1970, p. 5).

Vico's thesis was that literacy and rational prose, and the forms of thought associated with them, which Westerners consider so fundamental to their "civilized natures," were late achievements in human thinking. He contended that they grew from, and on, our "poetic nature." If, instead of viewing children's transition from orality to literacy as unqualified progress, we were to view it as a trade-off made for obvious functional advantages in a literate culture, then we might gain a different view of what is entailed in early education. This might make us more wary of displacing orality with literacy, and more sensitive to how we might preserve some of the more valuable characteristics of orality. We cannot hope to preserve orality in children just as it existed before the achievement of literacy, with all its cultural consequences. But we can hope to preserve or regain some things we have been in danger of losing, or have lost, in the dominant conceptions of early childhood education. These conceptions, I would argue, focus primarily upon the absence of literacy and the skills of Western rationality, and fail to recognize the presence of positive orality.[3]

What are these valuable characteristics of orality, then, and how can we hope to preserve or regain them? They are the characteristics Vico summed up by calling people in oral cultures "poets"—in the sense of people whose culture relied on, and whose cultural environment stimulated the development of, the features of orality sketched above. (The poet in Western cultures is, of course, the person who most forcefully retains and deploys the resources of orality—the sensitivity to the sounds of words and their emotional effects, the precise use of metaphor, the arrangement of sound in metrical patterns, the use of rhyme, and so on.) The young child, as a "maker" of imaginative worlds, is a kind of poet, and is in command of some considerable intellectual resources developed and exercised by such imaginative work. It is worth remembering that in our attempts to create artificial intelligence in computers, the most refined mathematical and logical operations have proven the easiest to simulate, while we still have no idea how to simulate these sophisticated and complex "poetic" operations.

The need to remember led, in oral cultures, to the invention of particular techniques to convey and make memorable ideas and information. We saw as prominent among these techniques the story-shaping of narratives—myths—made up of vivid characters and events which carried those ideas and information. What we generally call the imagination is a mental capacity that is evoked, stimulated, and developed by the needs of orality. Its value for literate culture persists; yet we have been in danger of depreciating it. We would be wise to preserve it as fully as possible (Egan & Nadaner, in press). Valuable too is the fluent and flexible use of metaphor, as it is fundamental to language and thought, and is, along with the systematic logic of Western rationality, one of the tools of effective thinking (Cooper, 1986). In the education of modern children into literacy, then, we will want to ensure that fluency of metaphoric thinking is maintained and, if possible, increased. Similarly, the sense in which members of oral cultures see themselves as participants in nature, rather than as set off against it and "conquering" it, seems a valuable characteristic that we should try to preserve in children and regain for literate Western cultures. The development of this sensibility in some form may save us from destroying the natural world that sustains us.

What kinds of curricula will stimulate the development of young children's orality? Two main concerns will need to guide development of such programs. First, they must ensure the fullest possible development of the techniques of orality. This follows the recognition that associating literate/oral with the polarities of rational/irrational is inappropriate. Oral and literate are not opposites; rather, the development of orality is the necessary foundation for the later development of literacy. Second, it must be remembered that our school curricula are preparing children not for an oral culture, but for a literate one, with distinctive forms of thought and understanding. They must prepare children for particular kinds of scientific understanding, logic, and historical consciousness, among other things. During the early school years, children will also be learning to read and write with increasing sophistication. Stimulating orality is not incompatible with the early stages of acquiring the skills of literacy—indeed a sensitive program of instruction will use the child's oral cultural capacities to make reading and writing engaging and meaningful. I think one can plausibly argue that Western schools' relatively poor achievement in teaching literacy is due in significant part to the failure to recognize and stimulate the development of a rich orality in the first place, and then to use the capacities of orality to teach literacy. Following Ong (1982), I think the "transforming" effects of literacy do not begin to have significant impact on children's oral culture until literacy is fluently mastered, used for pleasure, and "internalized," a process that occurs around age seven or eight in most Western cultures.[4]

A useful guiding question for the curriculum developer considering how best to initiate children into science, logic and philosophy, or history would be, "What is the oral foundation of science, or of logic and philosophy, or of history?" Throughout, our focus has been not on knowledge content or psychological development, but on the *techniques* that are *bon à penser*. The question about oral foundations is not, therefore, about curriculum content; it does not lead us to magic, astrology, or myth, but to the forms of thought that undergird them. In history, for example, our aim is not to teach children myths, but to provide them with the foundations of historical understanding that underlie myth. This involves the sense of intellectual security that comes from knowing one's place in a wider context of human experience.

We might, for example, construct an early-childhood history curriculum that tells the story of Western culture as a struggle for freedom against tyranny, for peace against arbitrary violence, for knowledge against ignorance, for power against powerlessness, and so on. In the first year the overall story of Western culture, for example, might be taught as one such struggle of binary forces. In each of the next two or three years the overall story could be taught again using different binary organizers to illuminate further dimensions of the culture's history. In my view, such a curriculum would be more engaging, meaningful, and educationally valuable than the typical content of the social studies curriculum. Such a presentation of historical content need not falsify history, though, like all historiography, it must simplify it. And its problems of ideological bias are no different in kind from those of any historiography (Egan, 1982).

What are the oral foundations of science? Among the characteristics of orality noted above are a sense of participation in nature and a sense of inquiry about it. In oral cultures those inquiries might lead to magic, witchcraft, and forms of classification that seem strange to Western science. Yet if our elementary curriculum is concerned with providing foundations that will remain constituents of scientific understanding, we might consider how to encourage respect and appreciation for the natural world and our place in it.

One part of our elementary science curriculum, then, might involve children in close and systematic observation of some particular natural object or process—a tree, rain, a spider's web, a patch of grass. Each child would have his or her own object. It might become usual, for example, to see young children observing that object at length—say, for twenty-minute intervals three times a week. They might break off other activities to observe how a tree moves in winds of different intensities, how the leaves hang in the sun, or how rain water drips down. This would not be a matter of "training in observation skills," with checklists and reports. Rather, the activity would have no end beyond itself; the child would be encouraged to share the life of the tree, let his or her imagination flow into it, feel its branches and stretch with it toward the light, let stories form about it, converse or commune with it. This brief example may indicate how our conception of the range of human characteristics that are appropriately addressed by the curriculum is changed by a focus on the oral foundations of education. Such efforts might reinforce the sense of participation in nature that scholars have seen as characteristic of oral cultures.

Another capacity that tends to be very largely ignored in present curricula is the sense of humor. The early stimulation and development of the sense of humor, and even the sense of the absurd, seem to me to be ways of setting in place the foundations of logic and philosophy. Recognition of the categories deployed in arguing and thinking, and fluency in analyzing them, are integral to those disciplines. One of the arenas of oral culture in which fluency in manipulating categories occurs is the joke. Lewis Carroll was one logician who seemed keenly aware of this, and used such category-manipulating jokes extensively. His *Alice* adventures, which grew from stories invented aloud for children, contain many examples of the kinds of jokes that stimulate flexibility in the use of categories, and which highlight the limits of the grasp our categories have on reality. The beginnings of logic and philosophy, then, might involve encouraging each child to "see" jokes and become jokesters. From there we could move on to more sophisticated jokes, like Zeno's paradoxes, and later to consideration of paradoxes in the nature of knowledge, morality, art, and so on.

What implications follow for teaching? I will focus briefly on some that seem to follow from the prominence of the story form in oral cultures. We might think of teaching the curriculum as telling young children the great stories of their culture. In the case of Western culture these involve the stories of their history, mathematics, logic, arts, and sciences. They *are* terrific stories. At present, teachers are encouraged to plan by organizing the curriculum into sets of objectives to be attained. If we were to think of lessons and units as good stories to be told rather than (or in addition to) objectives to be attained, we might be able to organize our content in ways that make it more accessible and engaging to young children.

If we consider just a few features of the story form, we should be able to develop a technique for the planning and teaching of lessons and units that would offer an alternative to the now dominant objectives-content-methods-evaluation schemes derived from R. Tyler's model (1949). The selection of content for the class or unit to be planned would be determined by identifying what binary opposites best catch and expose its most important themes. A unit on heat, for example, might be planned around the dichotomy of heat-as-helper/heat-as-destroyer. A class on the Vikings might use survival/destruction as central story themes. We might recreate the terror induced by a Viking raid on a monastic community. We would not have to *explain* the value of manuscripts or sacred vessels, but instead would *show* their value through the horror felt by the monks at their destruction. Then we could select the remaining content according to the related criteria provided by the central binary conflict, to elaborate and develop the story. The conclusion of the lesson, or unit, would come with the resolution or mediation of the binary opposites whose conflict set the story in motion. Mediation might be sought, for example, by indicating the value of the constructive energy of the Vikings in the overall story of Western culture. Evaluation of such lessons or units might focus on children's understanding of the content in the context of the overall story, and on their coherent use of the content in stories of their own (Egan, 1985).

I recognize that the prominence of binary opposites here will seem a little odd to many people. Their use need not lead to extreme reductionism. My argument, made at length elsewhere (Egan, in press), is simply based on the prominence and utility of initially grasping the world in binary terms. Some (for example, Lévi-Strauss, 1966) argue that the use of binary opposites is simply a function of the structure of the human mind. I think one need not go so far in order to recognize their ubiquitousness in the forms of thought common in oral cultures and in the ways young children spontaneously make sense of the world and experience.

Some of the teaching and curriculum practices sketched above are, of course, already evident in some classrooms. If my description of orality is accurate and relevant to the education of young children, it would be surprising if many teachers had not shaped their lessons and teaching methods, in their own ways, to draw on some of the same observations about children—even though those observations might be articulated in different terms. I do not claim originality for these ideas on educational implications of orality; rather, I am concerned to establish a set of principles that might help us more systematically and routinely to achieve the kinds of success that good teachers manage daily.

The most general implication of this brief exploration is that we should consider children when they come to school as already in possession of some features of orality that are *bon à penser*. Their ability to think and learn is, in general, sophisticated, but structured according to norms significantly different from those of literate adult cultures. Two corollaries follow. First, clear understanding of children's orality is essential if we are to make what we want to teach engaging and meaningful; second, orality entails valuable forms of thought that need to be developed as the foundation for a sophisticated literacy and Western rationality. If we see the educational task as simply to put literacy in place, we risk undermining the very foundations on which a rich literacy must rest. Stimulating children's imaginations, metaphoric fluency, and narrative sophistication can become more prominent aims of early education. Such a view might help to resolve what is often seen as a conflict in early education between the need to establish the "skills" of literacy and rational thought and the wish to encourage more varied experience and imaginative development. This brief exploration should have shown that these are not competitors; rather, the fullest achievement of literacy requires the fullest achievement of oral capacities as well.

## Notes

1. See the parable of the line in *The Republic,* ed. Cornford, 1941, ch. 24. For a discussion of the sets of associations, see Simon (1978), pp. 164ff.
2. For a full discussion, see Havelock (1963), ch. 9, "The Psychology of Poetic Performance."
3. Referring to dominant conceptions in an area of such diversity as present educational discourse can leave some uncertainty about what is meant, and on what the impression of dominance is based. I mean here those conceptions of early childhood education that see the primary task as initiating the child into the basic skills of literacy and rational forms of inquiry, with little attention to the character and sophistication of children's orality and their imaginative lives. Such conceptions are evidenced in the practice of all too many classrooms, as reported, for example, in J. I. Goodlad's *A Place Called School* (1984). This bias may also be seen in curriculum guides in various subjects, in textbooks designed for pre-service and in-service teachers, and perhaps most vividly, in textbooks designed for children's use. To take more or less random examples of such general texts on early childhood education, which circulate widely in North America, one might cite Shepherd and Ragan (6th ed., 1982) and Broman (1982). Examples of textbooks intended for teachers include, for social studies, Michaelis (7th ed., 1985); for science, Gega (5th ed., 1986); and for mathematics, Troutman and Lichtenberg (1982). Children's text series that typify current practice include Addison-Wesley's *Mathematics,* Ginn's *Reading 700,* Rand McNally's *Elementary Science Study,* and Guinness's *Cultural Studies for Children.*
4. For a more extensive account of an "oral" curriculum, see Egan, in press.

## References

Applebee, A. N. (1978), *A child's concept of story.* Chicago: University of Chicago Press.

Ashton, P. T. (1975). Cross-cultural Piagetian research: An experimental perspective. *Harvard Educational Review, 45,* 475–506.

Bartlett, F. (1932). *Remembering, a study in experimental and social psychology.* New York: Cambridge University Press.

Bettelheim, B. (1976). *The uses of enchantment.* New York: Knopf.

Blumenberg, H. (1985). *Work on myth.* Cambridge: MIT Press.

Boas, F. (1911). *The mind of primitive man.* New York: Macmillan.

Broman, B. L. (1982). *The early years in early childhood education.* Boston: Houghton Mifflin.

Buck-Morss, S. (1982). Socio-economic bias in Piaget's theory and its implications for cross-cultural studies. In S. Modgil & C. Modgil (Eds.), *Jean Piaget: Consensus and controversy.* New York: Praeger.

Burke, P. (1985). *Vico.* New York: Oxford University Press.

Cassirer, E. (1946). *Language and myth* (S. K. Langer, trans.). New York: Harper.

Cooper, D. E. (1986). *Metaphor.* Oxford: Blackwell.

Cornford, F. M. (Ed.). (1941). *The Republic of Plato.* New York: Oxford University Press, ch. 26.

Dodds, E. R. (1951). *The Greeks and the irrational.* Berkeley and Los Angeles: University of California Press.

Douglas, M. (1966). *Purity and danger.* London: Routledge & Kegan Paul.

Durkheim, E. (1915). *The elementary forms of the religious life.* London: Allen & Unwin.

Egan, K. (1982, March). Teaching history to young children. *Phi Delta Kappan,* 439–441.

Egan, K. (1985). *Teaching as story-telling.* London, Ont.: The Althouse Press, and London: Methuen.

Egan, K. (in press). *Primary understanding.* London and New York: Routledge & Kegan Paul.

Egan, K., & Nadaner, D. (Eds.). (In press). *Imagination and education.* New York: Teachers College Press.

Eliade, M. (1959). *Cosmos and history.* New York: Harper & Row.

Evans-Pritchard, E. E. (1937). *Witchcraft, oracles and magic among the Azande.* New York: Oxford University Press.

Finnegan, R. (1970). *Oral literature in Africa.* New York: Oxford University Press.

Finnegan, R. (1977). *Oral poetry: Its nature, significance, and social context.* Cambridge: Cambridge University Press.

Frankfort, H. A. (1961). *Ancient Egyptian religion.* New York: Harper.

Frankfort, H. A., Wilson, J. A., & Jacobsen, T. (1949). *Before philosophy.* Harmondsworth, Eng.: Pelican.

Frazer, J. G. (1900). *The golden bough* (2nd ed.). London: Macmillan.

Gardner, H., Kircher, M., Winner, E., & Perkins, D. (1975). Children's metaphoric productions and preference. *Journal of Child Language, 2,* 125–141.

Geertz, C. (1973). *The interpretation of cultures.* New York: Basic Books.

Gega, P. C. (1986). *Science in elementary education.* New York: Wiley.

Goodlad, J. I. (1984). *A place called school.* New York: McGraw-Hill.

Goody, J. (1977). *The domestication of the savage mind.* New York: Cambridge University Press.

Goody, J. (1986). *The logic of writing and the organization of society.* New York: Cambridge University Press.

Goody, J. (1987). *The interface between the written and the oral.* New York: Cambridge University Press.

Goody, J., & Watt, I. (1968). The consequences of literacy. In J. Goody (Ed.), *Literacy in traditional societies* (pp. 304–345). New York: Cambridge University Press.

Gould, S. J. (1977). *Ontogeny and phylogeny.* Cambridge: Harvard University Press.

Griffin, J. (1980). *Homer.* New York: Oxford University Press.

Havelock, E. A. (1963). *Preface to Plato.* Cambridge: Harvard University Press.

Havelock, E. A. (1976). *Origins of Western literacy.* Toronto: Ontario Institute for Studies in Education.

Havelock, E. A. (1986). *The muse learns to write.* New Haven: Yale University Press.

Hayek, F. A. (1969). The primacy of the abstract. In Arthur Koestler and J. R. Smythies (Eds.), *Beyond reductionism.* New York: Macmillan.

Heath, S. B. (1983). *Ways with words.* Cambridge: Cambridge University Press.

Hollis, M., & Lukes, S. (Eds.). (1982). *Rationality and relativism.* Cambridge: MIT Press.

Horton, R. (1970). African traditional thought and Western science. In B. Wilson (Ed.), *Rationality* (pp. 131–171). Oxford: Blackwell.

Horton, R. (1982). Tradition and modernity revisited. In M. Hollis & S. Lukes (Eds.), *Rationality and relativism.* Cambridge: MIT Press, 201–260.

Huizinga, J. (1949). *Homo ludens.* London: Routledge & Kegan Paul.

Inhelder, B., & Piaget, J. (1969). *The early growth of logic in the child.* New York: Norton.

Jenkyns, R. (1980). *The Victorians and ancient Greece.* Cambridge: Harvard University Press.

Jowett, B. (1982). *The dialogues of Plato.* London: Macmillan.

Kirk, G. S. (1965). *Homer and the epic.* New York: Cambridge University Press.

Knapp, M., & Knapp, H. (1976). *One potato, two potato.* New York: Norton.

Leach, E. (1967). Genesis as myth. In J. Middleton (Ed.), *Myth and cosmos* (pp. 1–13). New York: Natural History Press.

Lévi-Bruhl, L. (1910/1985). *How natives think* (L. A. Clare, trans.; C. S. Littleton, Intro.). Princeton: Princeton University Press.

Lévi-Strauss, C. (1962). *Totemism.* New York: Merlin.

Lévi-Strauss, C. (1966). *The savage mind.* Chicago: University of Chicago Press.

Lévi-Strauss, C. (1969). *The raw and the cooked.* New York: Harper & Row.

Lévi-Strauss, C. (1978). *Myth and meaning.* Toronto: University of Toronto Press.

Lord, A. B. (1964). *The singer of tales.* Cambridge: Harvard University Press.

Luria, A. R. (1976). *Cognitive development: Its cultural and social foundations.* Cambridge: Harvard University Press.

Luria, A. R. (1979). *The making of mind.* Cambridge: Harvard University Press.

Malinowski, B. (1922). *Argonauts of the western Pacific.* London: Routledge & Kegan Paul.

Malinowski, B. (1954). *Magic, science and religion.* New York: Anchor.

Michaelis, J. (1985). *Social studies for children.* Englewood Cliffs, NJ: Prentice Hall.

Olsen, D. R. (1977). Oral and written language and the cognitive processes of children. *Journal of Communications, 17* (3), 10–26.

Olsen, D. R. (1986). Learning to mean what you say: Towards a psychology of literacy. In S. de Castell, A. Luke, & K. Egan (Eds.), *Literacy, society and schooling.* New York: Cambridge University Press.

Ong, W. J. (1971). *Rhetoric, romance, and technology.* Ithaca: Cornell University Press.

Ong, W. J. (1977). *Interfaces of the world.* Ithaca: Cornell University Press.

Ong, W. J. (1982). *Orality and literacy.* New York: Methuen.

Ong, W. J. (1986). Writing is a technology that transforms thought. In G. Baumann (Ed.), *The written word: Literacy in transition* (pp. 23–50). Oxford: Clarenden Press.

Opie, I., & Opie, P. (1959). *The lore and language of schoolchildren.* New York: Oxford University Press.

Opie, I., & Opie, P. (1969). *Children's games in street and playground.* New York: Oxford University Press.

Opie, I., & Opie, P. (1985). *The singing game.* New York: Oxford University Press.

Paley, V. G. (1981). *Wally's stories.* Cambridge: Harvard University Press.

Parry, M. (1928). *L'Epithète traditionelle dans Homère.* Paris: Société Editrice les Belles Lettres.

Parry, M. (1971). *The making of Homeric verse: The collected papers of Milman Parry* (A. Parry, Ed.). Oxford: Clarendon Press. (This includes the previous reference in English translation.)

Peabody, B. (1975). *The winged word.* Albany: State University of New York Press.

Pitcher, E. G., & Prelinger, E. (1963). *Children tell stories: An analysis of fantasy.* New York: International Universities Press.

Putnam, H. (1981). *Reason, truth and history.* New York: Cambridge University Press.

Ravitch, D. (1983). *The troubled crusade.* New York: Basic Books.

Shepherd, G. D., & Ragan, W. B. (1982). *Modern elementary curriculum.* New York: Holt, Rinehart & Winston.

Simon, B. (1978). *Mind and madness in ancient Greece: The classical roots of modern psychiatry.* Ithaca: Cornell University Press.

Spence, J. E. (1984). *The memory palace of Matteo Ricci.* New York: Viking Penguin.

Sutton-Smith, B. (1981). *The folkstories of children.* Philadelphia: University of Pennsylvania Press.

Taylor, C. (1982). Rationality. In M. Hollis & S. Lukes (Eds.), *Rationality and relativism* (pp. 87–105). Cambridge: MIT Press.

Todorov, T. (1982). *Theories of the symbol* (C. Porter, trans.). Ithaca: Cornell University Press.

Troutman, A. P., & Lichtenberg, D. K. (1982). *Mathematics: A good beginning.* Monterey, CA: Brooks/Cole.

Turner, F. M. (1981). *The Greek heritage in Victorian Britain.* New Haven: Yale University Press.

Tyler, R. (1949). *Basic principles of curriculum and instruction.* Chicago: University of Chicago Press.

Vernant, J. P. (1983). *Myth and thought among the Greeks.* London: Routledge & Kegan Paul.

Vico, G. (1744/1970). *The new science* (T. G. Bergin & M. H. Fisch, trans.). Ithaca: Cornell University Press.

Wilson, B. R. (Ed.). (1970). *Rationality.* Oxford: Blackwell.

Wolf, F. A. (1795/1884). *Prolegomena and Homerum.* Halle.

Wood, M. (1985). *In search of the Trojan War.* London: BBC.

# 8
# Literacy and Language: Relationships during the Preschool Years

CATHERINE E. SNOW
*Harvard University*

*Catherine Snow disconfirms the hypothesis that variations in the level of literacy in the home are responsible for social class differences in children's reading achievement. Snow argues instead that as the specific oral discourse style that middle-class families employ at home closely matches school language use, this, rather than literacy levels, accounts for the later literacy success of children from these homes. Citing recent research findings and using a case study of a young child's early social interactions with his mother, Snow presents many similarities between language and literacy in the early stages of their development. In addition, as common characteristics between these two processes, she points out and discusses social interactive factors, communicative needs in the early stages of development, and increasing freedom from contextual support.*

Twenty years ago it was something of a commonplace to suggest that working-class and minority children were deficient in language ability when compared to middle-class, mainstream children. During the last two decades, however, considerable effort has been expended to demonstrate that, although working-class and minority children may use language differently from middle-class children, they are not deficient in language ability. Their language is as complex and their mastery of language as complete as it is for middle-class children (Dittmar, 1976; Edwards, 1976; Miller, 1982).

The conclusion that working-class children are different, not deficient, has not, however, been extended from language ability to literacy. Social class differences in reading achievement are large and reliable (reviewed in Anastasiow, Hanes, & Hanes, 1982; Coleman, Campbell, Hobson, McPartland, Mood, Weinfeld, & York, 1966;

*Harvard Educational Review* Vol. 53 No. 2 May 1983, 165–189

DeStefano, 1978; Stubbs, 1980). They have not been eliminated by "Sesame Street," Headstart, Follow Through, or other interventions aimed at poor and minority populations (Carnoy, 1972; Kennedy, 1978; Rivlin & Timpane, 1975; Stearns, 1971), even though lasting effects of intervention on other aspects of school achievement and school competence have been found (Lazar & Darlington, 1982).

The persistence of social class differences in reading achievement is puzzling in light of (1) the widespread assumption that language and literacy are closely related skills (Cazden, in press; DeStefano, 1978; Loban, 1963; Simons, 1970; Shuy, 1981) and (2) the evidence that there are no social class differences in language skill. Clearly, reading is a form of language use. Reading ability is highly correlated with measures of language skill such as vocabulary (Davis, 1974; Farr, 1969; Spearitt, 1972; Thorndike, 1974–1975; Yap, 1979), tests of grammatical knowledge (Dale & Chall, in press; Simons, 1970), and a metalinguistic awareness, the ability to reflect upon and talk about linguistic forms (Menyuk & Flood, 1981; Salus, 1982). Why then, if there are no social class differences in language ability, do we find such differences in reading and other literacy skills?

The answer to this question might be that literacy and language, though related, are in fact very different skills, and thus differently distributed in the population. If literacy is sufficiently different from language that its course of development is subject to a different set of influences, then a much greater degree of variation in literacy skill than in language skill could result.

This article first will argue that such an explanation is not correct and that, in fact, literacy and oral language are very similar and closely related skills which are acquired in much the same way. This argument rests on a demonstration of the many similarities between language and literacy during their acquisition. The second section will examine the major alternative explanation for social class differences in reading achievement, that the level of literacy in the home predicts literacy skill, and will reject this argument as well. Finally, the third section will propose a reanalysis of the demands made on children during literacy activities, in an attempt to identify more exactly the nature of the failure of those children who do not progress in the acquisition of literacy.

## Language and Literacy Defined

The tendency in recent research on literacy (Olson, 1977; Scollon & Scollon, 1982; Tannen, 1982) is to emphasize the degree to which literacy is continuous with language, and to point out the ubiquity of literacy experiences in children's lives. Since this tendency has led to some blurring of the meaning of the terms "oral language" and "literacy," it is important to define these terms precisely. By literacy, I mean the activities and skills associated directly with the use of print—primarily reading and writing, but also such derivative activities as playing Scrabble or Boggle, doing crossword puzzles, alphabetizing files, and copying or typing. Oral language refers simply to all oral forms of communication, speaking, and listening. Thus, I would reject such formulations as Scollon and Scollon's literate two-year-old (1982) to refer to a child who uses orally some of the conventions normally associated with written stories, or Tannen's description of literate conversational styles (1982). It seems to me that such uses of the term "literate" confuse frequently co-occurring but noncriterial characteristics of literate activities with the crucial defining feature of literacy, the use of print.

## Parallels Between Language and Literacy in Development

### Complexity of the System

Learning to read and learning to talk are both challenging tasks, in part because the systems which must be acquired are complex. Furthermore, both domains require a complex mapping of form onto meaning. Expert levels of performance in both domains require the knowledge and ability to honor, purely for the sake of correctness, conventions which are not derived from the semantic or communicative system. That learning language and learning literacy are complex tasks is evident in the length of time it takes children to master them and in the amount of concentrated effort, investment of energy, and frustration at failure both tasks occasion.

### Maturational Limitations

No one could reasonably deny that the course of maturation plays a major role in the development of language and literacy. There is an age below which children have considerable difficulty learning to talk or to read—though for reading this age may be considerably lower than proponents of "reading readiness" are prepared to admit. The process of learning language is fairly slow and painful for the one-year-old and is considerably faster and easier for the older child (Snow & Hoefnagel-Höhle, 1978). Similarly, though it is clearly possible to teach a two-year-old to read, a six-year-old can be brought to the same level of reading skill in considerably less time. The finding that children with organic learning disabilities which slow the course of reading acquisition also show language disabilities (for example, Bannatyne, 1971) underlines the degree to which the state of the brain can influence the course of development of both language and literacy.

### Centrality of Social Interaction and Communicative Needs to Development

Ten years ago, it was commonly assumed that synctactic development could be treated independently of pragmatic and semantic development. Today, however, no one would deny that language development can be understood only as an aspect of the development of communication in general, and only in the context of the child's interactions.

Learning to read has traditionally been seen as a cognitive problem—something children have to solve on their own, inside their own heads. Only recently has reading been treated as a social phenomenon—one which often occurs by and in groups (Bloome, 1981), and which is intrinsically embedded in the culture of its users (Heath,

1980). Many examples could be given to demonstrate that the social nature of the reading process is especially potent during the earliest stages of its acquisition. This article presents a few examples from one child, Nathaniel, in interaction with his mother, which demonstrate the relevance of three characteristics of social interaction in literacy acquisition and training—semantic, contingency, scaffolding, and accountability procedures.[1]

It is well demonstrated (Cross, 1978; Wells, 1980) that a major facilitator of language acquisition is *semantic contingency* in adult speech. Adult utterances are semantically contingent if they continue topics introduced by the child's preceding utterances. Semantically contingent utterances thus include: (1) expansions, which are limited to the content of the previous child utterance; (2) semantic extensions, which add new information to the topic; (3) clarifying questions, which demand clarification of the child utterance; and (4) answers to child questions. Topic initiations by adult speakers and attempts to switch the topic from the one introduced by the child constitute semantically noncontingent speech, and the frequency of such utterances in parents' speech correlates negatively with children's gains in language ability.

The notion of semantic contingency can be applied to the literacy domain as well. Examples of semantic contingency to literacy behaviors would include answering questions about letter and number names, answering questions about words, reading out loud on request, answering questions about pictures in books, carrying on coherent conversations with children about the pictures and text in books, and giving help with writing when requested. Semantic contingency to literacy-related behaviors seems to be associated with early acquisition of literacy. All of these literacy-contingent behaviors are typical of middle-class families, and they have been identified (Clark, 1976; Durkin, 1966; Söderbergh, 1971) as instrumental in producing preschool readers.

Parts of the lengthy exchange between Nathaniel at 31 months and his mother presented in Table 1 demonstrate many of these characteristics of semantic contingency (marked with a +). National's mother had been proposing a trip to the playground but dropped that discussion when Nathaniel sat down at his playschool desk, picked up a magnetized plastic M, and said, "Put it on the board" (line 1). In the subsequent conversation his mother asked him to name the symbols he picked up (lines 6, 15, 18); repeated and confirmed his correct labels for symbols (lines 4, 22, 62, 80); corrected his errors (line 33); provided labels if he did not know them (lines 8, 33); and helped to accomplish tasks of finding letters (lines 42, 43, 44, 45, 47, 50, 52, 53, 54), finding number sequences (lines 72, 73, 75, 77, 78, 80), and creating letter sequences (lines 64–69). It is clear, though, that large chunks of Nathaniel's mother's speech in Table 1 are not semantically contingent. She introduced their major literacy task herself (spelling *Nathaniel*, line 34) and persisted with it rather than following his lead in other directions. In the conversation that continued from the one in Table 1 she twice even interrupted his concentration on the letters to clean out his ears!

TABLE 1

*Semantic Contingency in a Literacy-focused Interaction Between Nathaniel (31 Months) and His Mother*

| Line | Nathaniel | Mother |
|---|---|---|
| 1 | put it on the board | |
| 2 | | *what's that |
| 3 | Mmmmm | |
| 4 | | *Mmmmm |
| 5 | | *put the M on the board |
| | (*N picks up an 8*) | |
| 6 | | *what's that? |
| 7 | dat | |
| 8 | | *eight |
| 9 | eight | |
| 10 | | *that's a number |
| 11 | number | |
| 12 | rectangle | |
| 13 | | + a rectangle |
| 14 | | + that's a shape |
| | (*N picks up a 2*) | |
| 15 | | *what's that? |
| 16 | that? | |
| 17 | is it? | |
| 18 | | *what is it? |
| 19 | is it? | |
| 20 | | *have you forgotten that one? |
| 21 | a two | |
| 22 | | *two, that's right |
| | (*N hiccups*) | |
| 23 | | + you've got the hiccups |
| 24 | mommy have hiccups? | |
| 25 | stays up | |
| 26 | | + stays up, yeah |
| 27 | | + mommy gonna help, okay? |
| 28 | stays up | |
| 29 | | + stay up |
| 30 | there's Nathaniel (*pointing to number sequence*) | |
| 31 | | *where's Nathaniel? |
| 32 | there's Nathaniel | |
| 33 | | *that's not . . . this says # 1 2 3 4 5 6 7 8 9 10 |
| 34 | | *shall we make it say Nathaniel? |
| 35 | | *do you want it to say Nathaniel? |
| 36 | | *have to find the right letters |
| 37 | | *find me an A |
| 38 | enne find a Z | |
| 39 | find a Z | |
| 40 | | *is that a Z? |
| 41 | | *you gonna put the Z up? |
| 42 | | *okay, there's no Z in Nathaniel though let's see, here's an N and there's another N, Nathaniel, we need that |
| 43 | | here's an I |
| 44 | | here's a better I |
| 45 | | we need an E |
| 46 | need E | |
| 47 | | and we need a T and an H here's . . . here's an H |

*Continued on next page*

TABLE 1—*Continued*

| Line | Nathaniel | Mother |
|---|---|---|
| 48 | T | |
| 49 | H | |
| 50 | | and . . . there's an L |
| 51 | L | |
| 52 | | what else do we need? |
| 53 | | can we put this in, pretend this is an A? |
| 54 | | N A |
| 55 | this like that | |
| 56 | | *you want to put that like that? |
| 57 | | *okay |
| 58 | | *that's not part of Nathaniel, you understand. Well, Nathaniel, I can't find all the letters we need |
| 59 | | we need a T |
| 60 | | where's the T? |
| 61 | here's the T | |
| 62 | | *there's the T |
| 63 | | oh, you found one |
| 64 | | N A T H |
| 65 | | we need another pretend A |
| 66 | | here's another pretend A |
| 67 | | A N I E L |
| 68 | | spells Nathaniel |
| 69 | | isn't that good? |
| 70 | enne do it | |
| 71 | enne do 1 2 3 | |
| 72 | | *you can see where there's 1 2 3 |
| 73 | | *look, look, what does this say? |
| 74 | 1 2 3 | |
| 75 | | *4 5 6 |
| 76 | 4 1 2 3 more | |
| 77 | | *7 8 9 10 |
| 78 | | *right there it says that |
| 79 | enne do X | |
| 80 | | *X |

Note: + Semantically contingent response

    \* Semantically contingent response to a literacy-related behavior or utterance

Nathaniel's mother also demonstrates another commonly noted feature of language facilitation, *scaffolding*. Scaffolding (Bruner, 1978) refers to the steps taken to reduce the degrees of freedom in carrying out some task, so that the child can concentrate on the difficult skill he is in the process of acquiring. In interaction with younger children, for example, mothers may rearrange the pieces of a puzzle so they are right-side up or steady the bottom blocks in a tower so that the child can successfully continue the task. Nathaniel's mother extensively scaffolds the rather difficult task of spelling *Nathaniel* by reminding him of what they are doing, rejecting false starts (line 42), and guiding the letter search. She also rearranges the letters on the desk so he can find the required ones more easily.[2]

A more consistently semantically contingent interaction occurred between Nathaniel and his mother the evening of the same day (see Table 2), when he again sat down at his desk just after getting ready for bed. (At 31 months, Nathaniel was

TABLE 2
*Semantic Contingency Limited by Accountability Procedures*
*(Nathaniel, 31 months)*

| Line | Nathaniel | Mother |
|------|-----------|--------|
| 1 | wanna spell Lia | |
| 2 | | *you wanna what? |
| 3 | eh wanna spell Nathaniel | |
| 4 | | *you wanna spell Nathaniel |
| 5 | eh wanna spell Lia | |
| 6 | | *you wanna spell Lia |
| 7 | | *okay |
| 8 | | *what does Lia start with? |
| 9 | Lia starts with a N | |
| 10 | | *no, Nathaniel starts with an N |
| 11 | | *Lia starts with an L |
| 12 | Lia starts with a O | |
| 13 | | *no, with an L |
| 14 | | *not an O, an L |
| 15 | put the O up there de . . . | |
| 16 | | *okay, we don't need an O |
| 17 | | ?have to find an L |
| 18 | de eh T I need a T either | |
| 19 | | *don't need the T either, no |
| 20 | I need . . . I no moon | |
| 21 | | *no, we don't need a moon either, no |
| 22 | | ?let's see |
| 23 | | ?let's put these things up here that we don't need |
| 24 | | ?cuz we don't need those, and maybe we'll find an L |
| 25 | | ?while we're looking |
| 26 | looking | |
| 27 | | ?see if you can find an L |
| 28 | eh . . . there's a T for to put it up there | |
| 29 | | *no, we don't need a T |
| 30 | don't need the T | |
| 31 | | *don't need the T |
| 32 | don't need to need that | |
| 33 | | *what's that? |
| 34 | don't need that eiger | |
| 35 | don't need the big I | |
| 36 | | *don't need the big I |
| 37 | | *that's right |
| 38 | oh . . . dis doesn't work | |
| 39 | | +that doesn't work? |
| 40 | | +oh |
| 41 | | +there |
| 42 | that doesn't work up there | |
| 43 | | ?are you looking for an L, Nathaniel? |
| 44 | | ?can you see an L? |
| 45 | I o . . . I don't know eh that Nathaniel is | |
| 46 | | *you don't know what that is |
| 47 | | *that's a number |
| 48 | | *that says 4 |
| 49 | I don't de dat spell Lia with a 4 | |
| 50 | | *no, you don't spell Lia with a 4, that's right |
| 51 | | ?why don't you see if you can find the L |

*Continued on next page*

TABLE 2—*Continued*

| Line | Nathaniel | Mother |
|------|-----------|--------|
| 52 | iiii | |
| 53 | I find another 4 | |
| 54 | | *that's right, that is another 4 |
| 55 | | ?see any L's yet? |
| 56 | this uh . . . this uh . . . this a O | |
| 57 | | *that's an O |
| 58 | this uh . . . this uh . . . who's this? | |
| 59 | who de do like that(?) | |
| 60 | do dit on de dat | |
| 61 | | ?put your glasses on when you read, you can see better |
| 62 | | ?but we're looking for L's, Nathaniel |
| 63 | | ?we need the L's |
| 64 | | ?where are the L's? |
| 65 | where's the L's? | |
| 66 | | *see any L's? |
| 67 | this the L's | |
| 68 | | *ooohh |
| 69 | | *oh, there's an L |
| 70 | | *put an L up, for spelling Lia |
| 71 | | *very good |
| 72 | put the other L up spelling Lia with the other | |
| 73 | | ?now we need . . . we need an I, Nathaniel |
| 74 | | ?where's an I |
| 75 | eh enne need a other I | |
| 76 | | *put the I over there |
| 77 | | ?I, I and now we need an A |
| 78 | | *oh, you found it |
| 79 | | *put it right next |
| 80 | | *put it next to the I |
| 81 | that's an A | |
| 82 | | *that's an A |
| 83 | | ?put it next to the I |
| 84 | | ?the other side |
| 85 | | ?oh, Lia |
| 86 | | ?that spells Lia |
| 87 | enne spells Nathaniel now | |
| 88 | | listen, how do you spell Lia? you read it |
| 89 | (have to?) read de book te see Lia | |
| 90 | | what does that say? |
| 91 | read the book to Lia | |
| 92 | | it's just a letter, it's just a word |
| 93 | | you spell it L I A |
| 94 | | okay, Nathaniel, we're just going to spell Nathaniel, and then after that Nathaniel goes to bed |
| 95 | L O (?) | |
| 96 | | ?what do we need for Nathaniel? |
| 97 | enne need the S (*shaking head*) | |
| 98 | | *you don't need the S for Nathaniel, no |
| 99 | | ?what do you need |
| 100 | eh put dit up dere | |
| 101 | | *okay, what do you need for Nathaniel? |
| 102 | | *what letter? |
| 103 | enne need de N | |
| 104 | | *you do need the N, that's right |
| 105 | | *put the N up |
| 106 | | ?what else do we need for Nathaniel? |

*Continued on next page*

TABLE 2—*Continued*

| Line | Nathaniel | Mother |
|------|-----------|--------|
| 107 | need eh need de other I | |
| 108 | | *that's right, we do |
| 109 | | *you put that up there too |
| 110 | | ?what else do we need? |
| 111 | need the circle | |
| 112 | | +no |
| 113 | put the circle right there | |
| 114 | | ?here, we need this L |
| 115 | | ?put that L over there |
| 116 | put the put the L right there | |
| 117 | | *yeah, we put that L up there cuz we're gonna need that L |
| 118 | enne put the O right there | |
| 119 | | ?for spelling . . . |
| 120 | | ?but you don't need an O, Nathaniel |
| 121 | | ?don't need an O for spelling Nathaniel |
| 122 | | ?better take the O away |
| 123 | | ?okay, now we need an . . . here, we need this A |
| 124 | | ?and we need a T |
| 125 | | ?can you find a T? |
| 126 | enne find de other T | |
| 127 | | *can you find a T? |
| 128 | | *oh, very good |
| 129 | | ?you put that T right next to the A |
| 130 | | ?turn it upright . . . turn it right side up |
| 131 | | ?that's right |
| 132 | | ?and now we need an H |
| 133 | | ?can you find an H? |
| 134 | find de M | |
| 135 | | ?we don't need an M |
| 136 | that's an M | |
| 137 | | *yeah, but we don't need an M |
| 138 | | ?no M in Nathaniel |
| | (*puts down M*) | |
| 139 | | *that's right |
| 140 | | ?we need an H |
| 141 | | ?find an H |
| 142 | dere's de H dere's de H | |
| 143 | | *there's an H |
| 144 | | *can you put the H right next to the T? |
| | (*does so*) | |
| 145 | | *very good |
| 146 | | ?now we need another A, and that's a problem cuz we don't have another A |
| 147 | | ?but you know what we always use for that |
| 148 | eh use de N eh de dat | |
| 149 | | *no, we use a little triangle for an A |
| 150 | | ?okay, now we need another N |
| 151 | | ?see another? |
| 152 | see another N | |
| 153 | | *see another N? |
| 154 | | *look in your desk |
| 155 | see another N either | |
| 156 | | *well I think there's one if you look around |
| 157 | | *look in your desk |

*Continued on next page*

TABLE 2—*Continued*

| Line | Nathaniel | Mother |
|------|-----------|--------|
| 158 | this uh there's another N | |
| 159 | | *there's an N |
| 160 | | ?okay, you put that right next to the A over here |
| | *(does so)* | |
| 161 | | *that's right |
| 162 | | ?then we have the I, and we need the E right there |
| 163 | I need the other E | |
| 164 | | *oh, you've got the E right there |
| 165 | | *stick it right up between the I and the I |
| 166 | there's the other E | |
| 167 | | *yeah, there's an orange E |
| 168 | | *put that right up there next to the I |
| 169 | | *turn it around the right way |
| 170 | upside up | |
| 171 | | +upside up |
| 172 | | ?there |
| 173 | enne enne need the P | |
| 174 | | ?no, we don't need the P |
| 175 | | ?look, what does that say? |
| 176 | that say Nathaniel | |
| 177 | | *that says Nathaniel |
| 178 | enne put the put the M on it | |
| 179 | | ?no, if you put the end on the M (sic) it says Nathanielm and that's sort of silly |
| 180 | | ?okay, we just put these up, and then we close the desk and go to sleep |

*Note:* + Semantically contingent response

    * Semantically contingent response to a literacy-related behavior or utterance

    ? Utterance in which semantic contingency is unclear

well aware that literacy activities were better bets for postponing bedtime than other types of play.) This time he introduced the task of spelling *Nathaniel* (line 87) after completing his other chosen task of spelling *Lia*. His mother did not respond immediately to his switch to *Nathaniel* because she was intent on holding him accountable for completion of the prior task, insisting that he repeat the spelling of *Lia* and "read" *Lia* before moving on. It is interesting to note that Nathaniel did not understand "you read it" with reference to a word. He responded "(have to?) read de book te see Lia" and "read the book to Lia" (lines 89, 91), revealing his understanding of reading as an activity related to books, not to words.

Note in Table 2 the ambiguity in several cases about the status of maternal utterances as semantically contingent (marked with a ?). Many of the mother's comments fail to be semantically contingent to Nathaniel's immediately preceding remarks because she is persisting with the higher-order task of getting something spelled or read. The status of such deviations from utterance-by-utterance semantic contingency is unclear within Cross's (1978) or Wells's (1980) formulation of the semantic contingency hypothesis. However, Dore (in press) deals very well with such maternal behaviors within his two-by-two categorical split between positive/negative accountability/nonaccountability. In Dore's system, positive nonaccountability (or play) is the term given to the case where the mother follows the child's lead; and positive accountability (or teaching) refers to situations such as those in Table 2 where the mother demands that a task be completed. Such cases of positive accountability are also frequent in language-facilitating situations. Examples include a mother's refusing to answer her children's questions if she feels they know the answers, or demanding their most correct pronunciation of some word rather than a baby-talk form. Ninio and Bruner (1978) have referred to such behavior as "upping the ante," or requiring the most sophisticated behavior the child is capable of giving. Examples of such accountability procedures in Table 2 are the mother's insistence that Nathaniel find the *L* (lines 10 through 70); her demand after they succeed in finding and placing the *L, I,* and *A* that he read the letters to spell *Lia* (lines 88, 90); and her general unwillingness to let Nathaniel divert from the tasks of spelling *Lia* and *Nathaniel.*

These examples demonstrate that the three characteristics of adult-child interaction which facilitate language development—semantic contingency, scaffolding, and accountability procedures—are also characteristic of interactions around literacy materials and activities. It is obvious that such characteristics can also contribute to the development of literacy skill.

## Increasing Decontextualization

A well-documented aspect of language acquisition is children's initial limitation to talking about the concrete here-and-now, and the growth of their ability to discuss the remote and the abstract. Early utterances can be described as highly contextualized, both from the point of view of the child and from the point of view of the observer, who cannot make sense of the utterances without knowing the context in which they were uttered. Many different aspects of language development demonstrate increasing freedom from context; for example: (1) early words are used performatively (*brm-brm* while moving a car) or socially (*hi* and *bye-bye*), but later words can be used referentially as well, in order to talk about experience as well as to share experience (Nelson, 1981); (2) early utterances comment on physically present objects or current activities, and only later can children understand or make reference to absent objects or to past and future activities (Chapman, 1981); (3) early conversational competence relies on a familiar conversational partner who will ask the expected questions and give the expected answers, whereas older children can converse about familiar things with unfamiliar partners (Snow, 1978); and (4) young children often assume shared knowledge in their conversation, whereas later they can estimate what the listener is unlikely to know (Scollon & Scollon, 1982). All of these changes constitute decreasing reliance on the present or the historical context of interaction.

Full-blown adult literacy is the ultimate decontextualized skill. Even during the preschool years, children show a development from highly contextualized literacy skills to relatively decontextualized ones. For example, in addition to his own name the first words that Nathaniel could read were *Michigan* and *Go Blue* (printed on a football jersey which he wore frequently), *I Love NY* (printed on a t-shirt he was given as a present), and *Puerto Rico* (printed on a sweatshirt he wore). These words are not all phonetically simple or easily decodable, but their degree of contextualization supported their readability. Similarly, Nathaniel's early attempts to write or spell words all involved his own name or the names of good friends and favorite babysitters. Many examples are given in Mason's paper (1982) of the highly contextualized reading that young children do—*Stop and Shop* on the supermarket's sign, *Cheerios* on the cereal box, and *Gulf* at the gas station. Mason identifies contextualized print recognition as the first strand in prereading development. Moving from such highly contextualized reading (which many would deny is truly reading) to relatively de-contextualized reading, such as reading words in isolation or reading sentences in a book where the pictures cannot be mapped easily to elements within the text, involves a real transition.

Context is usually thought of as physical context; for example, a particularly salient visual display or encountering a particular word always in the same place. For the very young child the physical context is no doubt the most important support for language or literacy skill. Another important aspect of context, though, and one which becomes very useful to the child as young as two years old, is the "historical" context. By this I mean children's previous experience with some event, place, word, or text, which can support their current interpretation or reaction. Nathaniel's hy-pothesis in Table 2 (line 9) that "Lia starts with N" is clearly a product of his previous experience in this same situation, spelling *Nathaniel.* Reading *Winnie-the-Pooh* cannot be a physically contextualized experience in the same sense that reading *Gulf* on the gas station sign can be, but it can be historically contextualized if the child has heard the book read aloud many times before trying to read it himself. Memory provides the context that the physical environment cannot.

Other books popular with children do provide a physical context which can, in combination with the experience of being read to, support word reading. The Dr. Seuss books, for example, often provide a few graphically salient displays (*so so so so* printed diagonally across the page in *The Cat in the Hat,* 1956; *Sam I am* printed on the sign carried by Sam in *Green Eggs and Ham,* 1960) that identify the word physically. The first picture-word books, with single words printed under easily identifiable pictures, have the same effect. In these cases, historical context is much less necessary to the reading of the words; for most books, though, even the ones designed for very young children, the historical context of words is probably of much more help than the physical context in supporting reading.

Clearly, the young child would prefer a world in which print was contextualized, predictable, and nonarbitrary. Table 3 presents an example of Nathaniel's pre-sumption at 31 months that print would be both contextualized and nonarbitrary. He often played with a toy cargo truck on which was printed *KLM.* This toy was commonly referred to as the "airport truck." He recognized the print on the side of the truck as a word and could at this age read the letters *K, L,* and *M;* but he concluded nonetheless that the word on the truck could only be "airport truck." As

TABLE 3
*Nathaniel's Presumption that Literacy is Contextualized (31 months)*

| Line | Nathaniel | Mother |
|------|-----------|--------|
| | (*pointing to KLM on toy truck*) | |
| 1 | that say airport truck | |
| 2 | | no, that says KLM |
| | (*insistently*) | |
| 3 | that says de airport truck | |
| 4 | | KLM cargo |
| | (*more insistently*) | |
| 5 | that says airport truck | |
| | | (*patiently*) |
| | | In the airport the trucks have to carry the cargo from the planes to other planes, or into the city and that's what this truck does |
| | (*pointing to KLM*) | |
| 7 | who's this | |
| 8 | | where . . . |
| 9 | that says . . . de airport . . . | |
| | | (*interrupting*) |
| 10 | | KLM, Nathaniel, this says KLM |

his insistence reveals (see Table 3, lines 3, 5), he was firmly convinced that any writing on an object would be a label for that object—a conviction perhaps supported by his experience with cereal boxes and generic grocery labels, but one which probably emerged from a more general set of principles for dealing with the world.

An example of Nathaniel's increasing recognition of the existence of decontextualized text emerges from longitudinal analysis of his readings of one book (Scarry's *The Storybook Dictionary*, 1964) over the course of a year (Snow & Goldfield, 1982 and in press). In the early sessions, Nathaniel and his mother discussed the pictures and, through their conversations, jointly developed complex information structures about the characters and events. At 40 months Nathaniel started to resist conversing about the pictures. Rather than selecting a picture by pointing to it and asking a question about it, he pointed to the text and said, "Read this one." Although it was still possible to get him involved in a conversation about the pictures at 40 months, shortly thereafter he became quite insistent that he be read to out of this book and all others. He would still occasionally discuss the pictures but only after hearing the text.

*The Role of Routines*

Although responsiveness and semantic contingency are the aspects of parent-child interaction that are recognized facilitators of language development, another aspect of interaction which also contributes to language acquisition is parental use of routines (see Peters, in press; Snow, in press; Snow, deBiauw, & Dubber, 1982). Bruner refers to such routines as *formats* (in press, 1981) emphasizing the fact that they are neither rigid nor unexpandable, but are highly predictable and thus constitute ideal contexts for language acquisition.

Such routinized or formatted contexts could also contribute to literacy acquisition; in fact, the most studied format for language learning is book reading (Ninio, 1980a,

1980b; Ninio & Bruner, 1978; Snow & Goldfield, 1982; and in press) which can be seen to contribute to language and to literacy simultaneously. Book reading routines constitute occasions for vocabulary acquisition (Ninio, 1980b), for the acquisition of book-handling skills (Mason, 1982), for the discovery of print, for the recognition of words, and for the development of a story scheme which could ultimately contribute to reading comprehension (Snow & Goldfield, 1982).

A prime example of the exploitation of a format is given by traditional ABC books, with their standard, "A is for a--- B is for b---" form; their use of simple pictures corresponding to the least predictable item in the format; and their reliance on such a well-learned sequence as the alphabet. Tables 4 and 5 present excerpts from two sessions, two weeks apart, using two ABC books with Nathaniel. Comparisons of these conversations reveal how much he had learned about the format of ABC books in this short time, even though the particular book used at the later reading was unfamiliar to him. At 32 months, 4 days (Table 4) he treated the first ABC book much like any other book, identifying a picture or a letter when he could and talking about the pictures with his mother. By 32 months, 20 days (Table 5), Nathaniel had learned the "X is for X-word" format, as indicated even more clearly by his errors (lines 22, 27, 94) than by his correct use of the format.

Another effective exploitation of formats is exemplified by the Dr. Seuss books which use rhyme, rhythm, and nonsense words in ways that facilitate rote memorization. Rote learning of a text, with subsequent matching of the role-learned sequences to the visual display, is an effective way to learn to read—a method discovered spontaneously by some children in this society and used as the major pedagogical method in the Koranic schools of the Arab world (Wagner & Lofti, 1979). Table 6 exemplifies the relatively early stages of such rote learning and the changes over a short time, as revealed in Nathaniel's reading of *Hop on Pop* (Seuss, 1963) at 37 months, 6 days and 37 months, 26 days. During the earliest readings of this book, Nathaniel's contribution had been primarily imitative. At 37 months, 6 days he mixed imitation and memorized bits. Twenty days later, his contributions suggested that he had memorized a rather large portion of the book.

At the age of 5 years, 7 months, Nathaniel, who by this time had developed considerable decoding skills, was observed to read books of nursery rhymes and poems by scanning the pictures until he found a rhyme he knew by heart then reading those rhymes by sounding them out. He was quite capable of sounding out unfamiliar rhymes or of reciting the memorized ones fluently without any decoding, but chose to apply his decoding skills to familiar texts instead.

*Summary*

The acquisition of language and of literacy can be seen to be very similar to one another on a number of points: the complexity of the learning involved, the centrality of communicative needs to the early stages of acquisition, the nature of the social interactive factors that contribute to acquisition and the child's increasing ability to

TABLE 4

*Nathaniel (32 months, 4 days) and his Mother Reading an ABC Book*

| Line | Nathaniel | Mother |
|------|-----------|--------|
| 1 | wanna read dat . . . dat book dis book | |
| 2 | | wanna read that book? |
| 3 | | okay |
| 4 | read dis dat book | |
| 5 | | this is a Christmas book |
| 6 | ABC book | |
| 7 | | that's an ABC book how did you know that? |
| 8 | dat's a present | |
| 9 | | where's it say ABC? |
| 10 | dis eh A | |
| 11 | dat's a present | |
| 12 | | yeah, it was a present a long time ago |
| 13 | as a present day | |
| 14 | | this says A is for angel |
| 15 | | B is for bell |
| 16 | | C is for candle and carol as well |
| 17 | | D is for |
| 18 | donkey | |
| 19 | | E is for elf |
| 20 | | F is for fun |
| 21 | | filling Christmas itself |
| 22 | | G is for gifts |
| 23 | | what's a gift? |
| 24 | dat's a gift | |
| 25 | | gifts are the same thing as presents, Nathaniel |
| 26 | gifts are the same thing as present | |
| 27 | | right, gifts and presents are the same thing |
| 28 | | H is for holly |
| 29 | | I is for . . . ice cream |
| 30 | eh dis a I | |
| 31 | I for ice cream | |
| 32 | | which is the I? |
| 33 | dis is de I | |
| 34 | | I |
| 35 | E | |
| 36 | | no that's an I |
| 37 | dat's a I | |
| 38 | | and that's a little I |
| 39 | dat's a little I | |
| 40 | dis is E . . . dis is de little I | |
| 41 | | no this is a big I a big I |

TABLE 5

*Nathaniel (32 months, 20 days) and his Mother Reading an ABC book*

| Line | Nathaniel | Mother |
|------|-----------|--------|
| 1 | how 'bout dis book? | |
| 2 | | how 'bout this book? |
| 3 | how 'bout de banana | |
| 4 | wanna read dat . . . wanna read . . . | |
| 5 | how 'bout dat book? | |
| 6 | | how 'bout that book? |
| 7 | | this is an ABC book |
| 8 | eh eh dis eh banana | |
| 9 | | that's right |
| 10 | | and what's this? |
| 11 | das da dat's a banana peels | |
| 12 | | that's the B for . . . |
| 13 | dat's a banana | |
| 14 | | B for banana |
| 15 | B for banana | |
| 16 | | A for apple |
| 17 | A for apple | |
| 18 | | C for cup |
| 19 | C for cup | |
| 20 | | what's that say? |
| 21 | det | |
| 22 | C for plate | |
| 23 | | (*laughing*) no it's P for plate |
| 24 | P for plate | |
| 25 | C | |
| 26 | | C for . . . |
| 27 | A for plate | |
| 28 | | A for apple |
| 29 | A for apple | |
| 30 | dis eh banana | |
| 31 | | that's right |
| 32 | | B for banana |
| 33 | B for banana | |
| 34 | | what else begins with B? |
| 35 | b . . . B for . . . | |
| 36 | | bagel |
| 37 | B for bagel | |
| 38 | where's eh bagel? | |
| 39 | | we don't have a picture of a bagel |
| 40 | | C for cup |
| 41 | | C for coffee |
| 42 | c for de . . . C C for coffee | |
| 43 | | E for egg |
| 44 | E for egg | |
| 45 | | G for . . . |
| 46 | G for . . . uh | |
| 47 | | those what are those? |
| 48 | grapes | |
| 49 | | grapes, right |
| 50 | four | |
| 51 | | F for four |
| 52 | | that's right |
| 53 | hamburger | |
| 54 | | hamburger, right |

*Continued on next page*

TABLE 5—*Continued*

| Line | Nathaniel | Mother |
|------|-----------|--------|
| 55 | ice cream | |
| 56 | | ice cream |
| 57 | | what's this? |
| 58 | wha deh? | |
| 59 | | I think that's lollipop |
| 60 | one two three | |
| 61 | | three |
| 62 | dese are light en put up deh | |
| 63 | who dat? | |
| 64 | | that's a kettle for the tea |
| 65 | | to make tea |
| 66 | what dat? | |
| 67 | | what's that? |
| 68 | milk | |
| 69 | | milk, yes |
| 70 | | M for milk |
| 71 | M for milk | |
| 72 | | N for |
| 73 | dis eh nut en walnut | |
| 74 | | a walnut, right |
| 75 | | O for |
| 76 | O for | |
| 77 | ah ah | |
| 78 | | orange |
| 79 | orange | |
| 80 | | P for |
| 81 | P for plate | |
| 82 | | right |
| 83 | | Q for |
| 84 | for | |
| 85 | | quince |
| 86 | quince | |
| 87 | | R for |
| 88 | for | |
| 89 | | raspberry |
| 90 | raspberry | |
| 91 | | S for |
| 92 | S for spoon | |
| 93 | | T for |
| 94 | T for . . . apple | |
| 95 | | tomato |
| 96 | tomato | |
| 97 | dis eh dis? | |
| 98 | | that's a cake |
| 99 | | that's an upside down cake |
| 100 | upside down | |
| 101 | eh book upside down | |
| | | *(laughing)* |
| 102 | | oh no it doesn't mean |
| 103 | | you don't have to turn the book upside down |
| 104 | | well never mind |

TABLE 6
*Nathaniel's Development of Knowledge about a Single Text*

| Printed Text | Conversation at 37 months, 6 days | Conversation at 37 months, 26 days |
|---|---|---|
| | M: what is this book called? | |
| | N: steppin' an on . . . | |
| | dis one | |
| | step onnn | |
| | step on | |
| | M: it's called hop on . . . | |
| | N: hop on . . . top | N: eh I wanna read hop on top |
| *Hop on Pop* | M: hop on pop | |
| | by . . . | M: hop on pop |
| | N: by . . . | by . . . |
| by Dr. Seuss | M: Doctor | N: Doctor Seuss |
| | N: Seuss | |
| PAT PAT | M: Pat pat | M: Pat pat |
| They call him Pat. | they call him . . . | they call him pat |
| | N: Pat | |
| PAT SAT | M: Pat sat | Pat sat |
| Pat sat on hat. | Pat sat on a . . . | Pat sat on . . . |
| | N: hat | N: the hat |
| | M: this is a . . . | |
| | N: hat | |
| PAT CAT | M: Pat cat | M: Pat cat |
| Pat sat on cat. | Pat sat on a . . . | Pat sat on . . . |
| | N: cat | N: a cat |
| PAT BAT | M: Pat bat | M: Pat bat |
| Pat sat on bat. | Pat sat on a . . . | Pat sat on |
| | N: cat | |
| | M: bat | N: a bat |
| | N: bat | |
| NO PAT NO | M: no Pat no | M: no Pat no |
| | don't . . . | N: he sayin' no? |
| | | M: that's right |
| | | he's saying no Pat no, don't . . . |
| Don't sit on that. | N: sit on that | N: sit on that |
| THING THING | M: thing | M: thing thing |
| | N: thing | |
| What is that thing? | M: what is that . . . | what is that thing? |
| | N: thing | |
| THING SING | M: thing sing | thing sing |
| That thing can sing! | that thing can . . . | that thing can sing |
| | N: sing | |
| SONG LONG | M: song | song long |
| | N: song | |
| | M: long | |
| | N: long | |
| A long, long song. | M: A long long song | a long long song |
| | N: song long song | |
| Good-by, Thing. | M: good-by Thing | good-by Thing |
| You sing too long. | you sing too . . . | |
| | N: too long | N: you sing too long |
| FATHER MOTHER | M: father mother sister . . . | |
| SISTER BROTHER | N: brother | M: father mother sister brother |

*Continued on next page*

224

TABLE 6—*Continued*

| Printed Text | Conversation at 37 months, 6 days | Conversation at 37 months, 26 days |
|---|---|---|
| That one is | M: that one is . . . | that one . . . |
| my other brother. | N: my other brother | N: my other brother |
| My brothers read | M: my brothers read a little bit | M: my brothers read a little bit |
| a little bit. | little words like | little words like . . . |
| Little words like | N: it | N: bit and it |
| if and it. | M: and | |
| | N: hit | |
| My father can read | M: my father can read big words too | M: my father can read big words too |
| big words, too. | like . . . | |
| Like . . . | N: like . . . | N: like Consandople and Timbuctoo |
| CONSTANTINOPLE | M: Constantinople | |
| and | N: Constantinople | |
| TIMBUKTU | M: and | |
| | N: and | |
| | M: Tim . . . | |
| | N: Tim . . . | |
| | M: buk . . . | |
| | N: too | |

*Note:* M = mother; N = Nathaniel.

perform the tasks required without the support of social, physical, or historical context.

## Dissimilarities in the Development of Language and Literacy

Whereas the similarities between language and literacy acquisition are impressive, there are several points of dissimilarity as well. These will be discussed in this section and analyzed to determine if they constitute true or apparent differences.

### Teaching versus Learning

The most striking difference between the acquisition of language and the acquisition of reading is that the first occurs naturally whereas the second relies on formal instruction. This difference holds for the vast majority of children but constitutes a statistical rather than an absolute difference. Some children learn to read more or less on their own (for example, Durkin, 1966), at least without formal school instruction. I have argued that language acquisition, seemingly natural, is supported by patterns of interaction with adults which, if analyzed carefully, tend to be quite pedagogical. Thus, although most children are taught to read, the fact that some learn without formal instruction from precisely the same kinds of interactions that support language acquisition suggests a greater similarity than dissimilarity between the processes on this point.

### Universal Success versus High Risk for Failure

All children, barring extreme deprivation or organic damage, learn to talk; but a significant number of children, even those whose intelligence is in the normal or above-average range, fail at or have great difficulty in learning to read. The universal success of language acquisition is, of course, related to the fact that language need not be taught whereas literacy acquisition, a riskier venture, requires instruction. One explanation given for this difference is that literacy skills rely on higher metalinguistic functions than do language. The status of this distinction between literacy and language will be discussed further; here I will only outline the problem by making the distinction in this way: while it is true to say that most children learn to talk without explicit instruction, the language skills achieved naturally by children constitute the highly contextualized skills of communication, not the decontextualized uses of language such as presenting monologues, doing abstract verbal reasoning, and giving metalinguistic judgments.[3]

Reading and writing as normally used in school are two examples of decontextualized language use, and we might therefore expect considerable variability in the speed and ease with which they are acquired. An example of decontextualized language in the purely oral mode is giving metalinguistic judgments; for example, judging sentences as grammatical or ungrammatical, identifying ambiguity, and giving definitions. This is also an area in which enormous individual differences in ability are found, differences which correlate furthermore with educational level (Gleitman & Gleitman, 1970). This finding supports the suggestion (Scribner, 1977) that the process of education consists largely of training in decontextualized language use.

I would argue that the existence of individual differences in literacy skills does not differentiate literacy from language. Rather, any skill which must be acquired or plied in a decontextualized way—whether that be reading, writing, talking, or listening—will be difficult, require some instruction, and show individual differences. By their very nature, most literacy experiences are somewhat decontextualized. By the nature of Western schooling, most of our children's literacy experiences are highly decontextualized. If we were to compare moderately decontextualized literacy skills with equally decontextualized language skills, I predict we would find them to be of the same level of difficulty.

## Role of Practice in Acquisition

Basic tenets of reading and writing curricula are that practice makes perfect and that achieving higher levels of skill, especially for reading, requires having achieved a minimum speed and fluency at earlier levels through practice. Practice has never been suggested as a major factor influencing the speed of first-language acquisition, though it certainly can be demonstrated to have a positive effect on second language learning. Recent evidence, however, suggests that, at least at the level of articulatory skill and sentence production planning, children get better partly as a product of practice with talking. Here again, then, an apparent difference may be illusory.

## Imposition of Conventionality

Conventions, the "right way to do it," are important both in oral and in literate exchanges. Violations of conventions, such as using nonstandard speech forms or making spelling errors, reflect badly on the user, at least in some circumstances. Observing conventions in print is, however, more important to successful communication than in oral exchanges, partly because of print's greater decontextualization. Following the conventions helps to ensure effective communication even in situations where communicative repair is not possible. Face-to-face exchanges do not break down if an unconventional form is used because a speaker's meaning can be questioned and clarified. Defying convention in written communication is much riskier because one's communicative partner is at a distance and unavailable for checks and confirmation.

Purely conventional forms are infrequently required of young speakers though "May I please be excused?" and other such formulas are certainly not absent from their repertoires (see Gleason, Perlmann, & Greif, 1980), despite the fact that children seem to have an expectation that rote-learned utterances will be appropriate ways of dealing with certain communicative situations (see Snow, in press). Reading and writing require conventional forms from the very start though children who do spontaneous spelling are freed from even this demand. Interestingly, children who are more advanced in their understanding of the nature of literacy may well resist nonconventional spelling—they know that "there is a right way to spell it" and do not want to produce their own, incorrect forms (Giacobbe, 1982). For example, though Nathaniel at 4 years could be forced to provide his own spellings, he preferred to copy or be told how to spell things and asked after each letter in a spontaneously spelled word if it were correct. Part of his unwillingness to do spontaneous spelling derived from his knowledge of the arbitrariness of English spelling—he knew that he could not be sure, for example, if a *C* or an *S* spelled an /s/, if *C* or *K* was needed for /k/, or if *EA, EE* or *IE* was appropriate for /i/.

Nathaniel's interpretation of literacy tasks as ones where the conventions must be followed was also evident in the development of his book-reading routine with his mother. Although at 30 to 35 months he gladly discussed the pictures in the books being read, at about 3 years he discovered the text and reinterpreted "reading books" as "being read to." He became increasingly insistent on this as the correct book-reading activity and impatient with his mother's attempts to discuss the pictures.

It may thus be the case that the power of the convention is first discovered by many children in the context of literacy tasks rather than for oral language, though this difference between language and literacy acquisition is one of degree. The degree of difficulty most children have when asked to call a cow "ink" (Piaget, 1954) demonstrates their natural commitment to the notion that words are conventional. It would be surprising, then, if they had any particular difficulty with understanding this fact about written language.

*Summary*

The differences between language and literacy are differences more of degree than of absolutes. Reading requires more explicit teaching, is more susceptible to failure, may be more dependent on practice, and may be more limited by conventions. Nevertheless, none of these characteristics is entirely untrue of language during the early stages of its acquisition. Indeed, the more decontextualized the oral language task, the more these characteristics apply.

## Literacy in the Home

This review of the similarities and differences between language and literacy in the early stages of their development provides a picture of enormous similarity on several points and differences of degree rather than of kind. We are left, then, with the troublesome questions with which we began. Why do some children have so much trouble learning to read? If learning to read is supported by the same sorts of interactions which support language development and if all children learn to talk, we should expect that all will learn to read as well.

One answer which has been offered to this question is to invoke the degree of "literacy" of children's home cultures as a determining variable in their acquisition of school-literacy. Middle-class homes in which books are present familiarize children with the purpose of books and ways to use them, thus providing school-relevant skills very directly. However, recent studies of low-income preschool children (Heath, 1982; Miller, 1982) suggest that some of these children have considerable access to and experience with books. In fact, very low-income children studied in South Baltimore were socialized for school in quite direct and explicit ways by their mothers (Miller, Nemoianu, & DeJong, 1981). Thus, simple access to literacy materials probably does not explain the large differences between middle-class and working-class children in reading achievement. It has been argued, though, that in addition to experience with books, middle-class homes prepare children for written forms of literacy by providing literate features in oral discourse: that is, by telling or reading stories in which the author is impersonal, the setting is distanced, deictic contrasts have to be understood from the writer's or speaker's point of view, and relatively complex language forms are used. Such features show up in very young middle-class children's own oral stories (Scollon & Scollon, 1982) long before they learn to read or write.

Another feature of literate interaction in middle-class homes is the use of conversation to build "shared histories" between mother and child. The mother asks the child questions about past, shared events, thus providing the child with help in recounting and in building internal representations of those events (Schieffelin & Eisenberg, in press). Such establishment of shared, permanent histories is characteristic of the "literate" approach to information as stable and enduring, rather than the "oral" approach in which shared representations are reconstructed as needed. Since information is not made permanent by being written down in oral cultures, it does not endure except as synopsized by epigrams and proverbs.

Even classroom teachers have been described as giving children an "oral preparation for literacy" in the form of sharing-time (Michaels & Cook-Gumperz, 1979). Children are expected, during their sharing turns, to present information in much the same way it would be presented in a well-written paragraph: assume no prior knowledge on the part of the listener, present the topic in a topic sentence, include only information relevant to that topic in subsequent sentences, and be explicit. Children's difficulty in following these rules demonstrates how foreign the rules are to normal conversational exchange in which the listener and the speaker share considerable knowledge. High levels of explicitness in face-to-face interactions often constitute redundancy with information available from the nonverbal context.

## The Oral and the Literate: Separate Domains

The argument that some homes prepare children for literacy by giving them experience with "literate" oral discourse flirts with terminological confusion and obscures the nature of the experiences that are crucial to preparing children for literacy. The characteristics of oral discourse that have been identified as potentially facilitative for literacy are distance between sender and receiver, explicitness of reference, fictionalization of sender and of receiver, complexity of syntactic structures, permanency of information, autonomous rather than interactive establishment of truth, and high degree of cohesion (Tannen, 1982). These are the characteristics of decontextualized language use. Literacy is normally decontextualized, and literate activities normally show these features. But if oral discourse can have these characteristics and be used in a decontextualized way, so too can literate activities be context-bound. Prime examples of contextualized literacy are given by Scribner and Cole (1981) from their study of Vai literacy.[4] Vaiscript literates use their literacy skills primarily for two activities: writing letters intended for one reader and keeping personal diaries. Both of these uses of literacy are relatively contextualized because they rely on shared information between writer and reader.

Consider the literacy of the preschool child. The first part of this paper presented many examples of highly contextualized literacy skills—reading the words on shirts and cereal boxes, reading one's own name, reading well-memorized rhymes in a book. Somewhat older children's abilities to deal with tasks such as reading a note taped on the refrigerator, finding favorite programs listed in *TV Guide*, or selecting lunch from the menu at Burger King (see Bloome, 1981) similarly constitute positive evidence of children's ability to deal with literacy but no evidence about their ability to deal with decontextualized information.

Perhaps most children are not failing at reading and writing but at comprehending and producing decontextualized information. Cox and Sulzby (1982) have found a relationship between skills at producing monologues (one-person narratives and descriptions) and reading ability in kindergarteners and have hypothesized a direct connection between monologue skills and literacy skills. I suggest that they found this relationship because the reading tasks they used as an outcome measure conflate two sets of abilities—the strictly literate abilities involved in decoding and comprehending print and the decontextualization skills involved in using language without the support of conversational context.

By about fourth grade, many school literacy activities are highly decontextualized. Children are no longer asked just to fill in worksheets or read from books with pictures but are expected to read from textbooks and write clear paragraphs. Thus, the basic reason for children's failure in the middle grades may not be the difficulty of literacy but the problems associated with decontextualizing language use. It is clear that the academically successful twelve- or thirteen-year-old must have mastered skills of literacy and of decontextualization. These skills are at least theoretically separable, and Scribner and Cole's finding that literacy and schooling have differential effects on cognitive skills suggest that they are practically separable as well. Further, success at either set of skills can be related to experiences during the preschool years. It seems likely, though, that different sets of preschool experiences contribute to literacy skill and to skill in decontextualized language use.

Much research remains to be done in order to test the hypothesis that the development of literacy skills and of skills at decontextualized language use emerge from different ontogenetic roots. As difficult at these skills are to distinguish from one another in testing or in school performance, the interactive situations that facilitate their acquisition may be even more difficult to separate.

It is clear, though, that many of the experiences identified as contributing to preschool children's literacy development (such as, being told stories, being read to, receiving help in constructing descriptions of past events, being asked tutorial questions) contribute more to their ability to use language in a decontextualized, and even noncommunicative, way than to their literacy skills per se. The teaching built into "Sesame Street," "The Electric Company," and many prereading curricula, in contrast, provides hardly at all for skills of decontextualized language use. Children need both literacy and decontextualized language skills to succeed in school; but it may be that literacy skills are simple enough to be acquired at school, whereas developing the skill of using language in a decontextualized way relies more heavily on experiences only home can provide.

## Notes

1. Nathaniel, the first-born child of academic parents, was tape-recorded at home during everyday activities such as meals, dressing, undressing, and playtimes, between the ages of 18 and 36 months. Recordings were made approximately every other week, in one-half to 3 hour sessions. Reading books was among Nathaniel's favorite activities during this time, and many of his book-reading interactions were recorded.
2. Farr (1982) discusses how a teacher uses comments on a student's journal to scaffold the writing process for the child.
3. A related point has been made in the domain of second-language learning by Cummins (1979a, 1979b), who distinguishes between Basic Interpersonal Communicative Skill, acquired relatively quickly by most second-language learners, and Cognitive-Academic Linguistic Potential, required for academic success and acquired much more slowly.
4. See review of *The Psychology of Literacy* (Scribner & Cole, 1981) by Patricia Marks Greenfield, p. 333 of this book.—ED.

## References

Anastasiow, N., Hanes, M. L., & Hanes, M. *Language and reading strategies for poverty children.* Baltimore: University Park Press, 1982.
Bannatyne, A. D. *Language, reading and learning disabilities.* Springfield, Ill.: Thomas, 1971.
Bloome, D. *An ethnographic approach to the study of reading activities among black junior high*

*school students: A socio-linguistic ethnography.* Unpublished thesis, Kent State University, 1981.

Bruner, J. S. Learning how to do things with words. In J. S. Bruner and R. A. Garton (Eds.), *Human growth and development.* Oxford, U.K.: Oxford University Press, 1978.

Bruner, J. S. *The social context of language acquisition.* Keynote address, Sixth Annual Boston University Conference on Language Development, October, 1981.

Bruner, J. S. The acquisition of pragmatic commitments, In R. Golinkoff (Ed.), *The transition from prelinguistic to linguistic communication.* Hillsdale, N.J.: Erlbaum, in press.

Carnoy, M. Is compensatory education possible? In M. Carnoy (Ed.), *Schooling in a corporate society: The political economy of education in America.* New York: McKay, 1972.

Cazden, C. Literacy in school contexts. In *Proceedings of the International Symposium on New Perspectives on the Process of Reading and Writing.* Mexico City: Editorial, Siglo XXI, in press.

Chapman, R. Cognitive development and language: Comprehension in 10- to 21-month-olds. In R. Stark (Ed.), *Language behavior in infancy to early childhood.* New York: Elsevier, 1981.

Clark, M. *Young fluent readers.* London: Heinemann, 1976.

Coleman, J., Campbell, F., Hobson, C., McPartland, J., Mood, A., Weinfeld, F., & York, R. *Equality of educational opportunity.* Washington, D.C.: U.S. Government Printing Office, 1966.

Cox, B., & Sulzby, E. *Evidence of planning in dialogue and monologue by five-year-old emergent readers.* Unpublished manuscript, Northwestern University, 1982.

Cross, T. G. Mother's speech and its association with rate of linguistic development in young children. In N. Waterson & C. Snow (Eds.), *The development of communication.* London: Wiley, 1978.

Cummins, J. *Cognitive academic language proficiency, linguistic interdependence, the optimum age question, and some other matters* (Working Papers in Bilingualism, No. 19). Toronto: Ontario Institute for Studies in Education, November 1979. (a)

Cummins, J. Linguistic interdependence and the educational development of bilingual children. *Review of Educational Research,* 1979; **49,** 222–251. (b)

Dale, E., & Chall, J. *Readability.* New York: McGraw-Hill, in press.

Davis, F. B. Fundamental factors of comprehension in reading. *Psychometrika,* 1974, **9,** 185–197.

DeStefano, J. *Language: The learner and the school.* New York: Wiley, 1978.

Dittmar, N. *Sociolinguistics.* London: Edward Arnold, 1976.

Dore, J. Intentionality, accountability, and play: The intersubjective basis for language development. In R. Golinkoff (Ed.), *The transition from prelinguistic to linguistic communication.* Hillsdale, N.J.: Erlbaum, in press.

Durkin, D. *Children who read early.* New York: Teachers College Press, 1966.

Edwards, A. E. *Language in culture and class.* London: Heinemann, 1976.

Farr, M. *Learning to write English.* Paper presented at the meeting of the American Educational Research Association, New York, March, 1982.

Farr, R. *Reading—What can be measured.* Newark, Del.: International Reading Association, 1969.

Giacobbe, M. E. Personal communication, December, 1982.

Gleason, J. Berko, Perlmann, R., & Greif, E. *What's the magic word?: Learning language through politeness routines.* Paper presented at the meeting of the Southeast Regional Conference on Human Development, Alexandria, Va., April, 1980.

Gleitman, L., & Gleitman, H. *Phrase and paraphrase.* New York: Norton, 1970

Heath, S. B. The functions and uses of literacy: Literacy in a media world, *Journal of Communication*, 1980, **30**, 123–133.

Heath, S. B. What no bedtime story means: Narratives at home and school. *Language in Society*, 1982, **11**, 49–78.

Kennedy, M. Findings from the Follow Through planned variation study. *Educational Researcher*, 1978, **7**, 3–11.

Lazar, I., & Darlington, R. Lasting effects of early education: A report from the consortium for longitudinal studies. *Monographs of the Society for Research in Child Development*, 1982, **47**, (2–3, Serial No. 195).

Loban, W. *The language of elementary school children* (Research Report No. 1). Urbana, Ill.: National Council of Teachers of English, 1963.

Mason, J. *The acquisition of knowledge about reading: The preschool period.* Paper presented at the meeting of the American Educational Research Association, New York, March, 1982.

Menyuk, P., & Flood, J. Language development, reading/writing problems, and remediation. *Orton Society Bulletin*, 1981, **31**, 13–28.

Michaels, S., & Cook-Gumperz, J. A study of sharing time with first grade students: Discourse narrative in the classroom. *Proceedings of the Fifth Annual Meeting of the Berkeley Linguistics Society*, 1979, **5**, 647–660.

Miller, P. *Amy, Wendy and Beth: Learning language in South Baltimore.* Austin: University of Texas Press, 1982.

Miller, P., Nemoianu, A., & DeJong, J. *Early socialization for schooling in a working-class community.* Paper presented at the Ethnography in Education Research Forum, University of Pennsylvania, March, 1981.

Nelson, K. Acquisition of words by first-language learners. In H. Winitz (Ed.). *Native language and foreign language acquisition.* New York: New York Academy of Sciences, 1981.

Ninio, A. Picture book reading in mother-infant dyads belonging to two subgroups in Israel. *Child Development*, 1980, **51**, 587–590. (a)

Ninio, A. The ostensive definition in vocabulary teaching. *Journal of Child Language*, 1980, **7**, 563–573. (b)

Ninio, A., & Bruner, J. The achievement and antecedents of labelling. *Journal of Child Language*, 1978, **5**, 1–15.

Olson, D. From utterance to text: The bias of language in speech and writing. *Harvard Educational Review*, 1977, **47**, 257–281.

Peters, A. *The units of language acquisition.* New York and Cambridge, U.K.: Cambridge University Press, in press.

Piaget, J. *The construction of reality in the child.* New York: Basic Books, 1954.

Rivlin, A. M., & Timpane, P. M. (Eds.). *Planned variation in education: Should we give up or try harder?* Washington, D.C.: Brookings Institution, 1975.

Salus, M. *The syntax and metalinguistic skills of children who read early.* Unpublished doctoral dissertation, Boston University, 1982.

Scarry, R. *The storybook dictionary.* London: Hamlyn, 1964.

Schieffelin, B., & Eisenberg, A. Cultural variation in dialogue. In R. Schiefelbusch (Ed.), *Communicative competence: Acquisition and intervention.* Baltimore: University Park Press, in press.

Scollon, R., & Scollon, S. *Narrative, literacy and face in interethnic communications.* Norwood, N.J.: Ablex, 1982.

Scribner, S. Modes of thinking and ways of speaking: Culture and logic reconsidered.

In P. Johnson-Laird & P. Wason (Eds.), *Thinking: Readings in cognitive science.* New York and Cambridge, U.K.: Cambridge University Press, 1977.

Scribner, S., & Cole, M. *The psychology of literacy.* Cambridge, Mass.: Harvard University Press, 1981.

Seuss, Dr. [T. Geisel]. *The cat in the hat.* New York: Random House Beginner Books, 1956.

Seuss, Dr. [T. Geisel]. *Green eggs and ham.* New York: Random House Beginner Books, 1960.

Seuss, Dr. [T. Geisel]. *Hop on pop.* New York: Random House Beginner Books, 1963

Shuy, R. W. *Relating research on oral language function to research on written discourse.* Paper presented at the meeting of the American Educational Research Association, Los Angeles, April, 1981.

Simons, H. D. *The relationship between aspects of linguistic performance and reading comprehension.* Unpublished doctoral dissertation, Harvard University, 1970.

Snow, C. The conversational context of language acquisition. In R. Campbell & P. Smith (Eds.). *Recent advances in the psychology of language: Social and interactional factors* (Vol. 2). New York: Plenum, 1978.

Snow, C. Saying it again: The role of expanded and deferred imitations in language acquisition. In K. E. Nelson (Ed.), *Children's language* (Vol. 4). New York: Gardner Press, in press.

Snow, C., deBlauw, A., & Dubber, C. Routines in parent-child interaction. In L. Feagans & D. Farran (Eds.), *The language of children reared in poverty.* New York: Academic Press, 1982.

Snow, C., & Goldfield, B. Building stories: The emergence of information structure from conversation and narrative. In D. Tannen (Ed.), *Analyzing discourse: Text and talk.* Washington, D.C.: Georgetown University Press, 1982.

Snow, C., & Goldfield, B. Turn the page please: Situation specific language acquisition. *Journal of Child Language,* in press.

Snow, C., & Hoefnagel-Höhle. The critical period for language acquisition: Evidence from second language learning. *Child Development,* 1978, **49,** 1114–1128.

Söderbergh, R. *Reading in early childhood: A linguistic study of a Swedish pre-school child's gradual acquisition of reading ability.* Stockholm: Morssedt, 1971.

Spearitt, D. Identification of subskills of reading comprehension by maximum likelihood factor analysis. Reading Research Quarterly, 1972, **8,** 92–111.

Stearns, M. S. *Report on preschool programs: The effects of preschool programs on disadvantaged children and their parents.* Washington, D.C.: U.S. Government Printing Office, 1971.

Stubbs, M. *Language and literacy: The sociolinguistics of reading and writing.* London: Routledge & Kegan Paul, 1980.

Tannen, D. (Ed.). *Spoken and written language: Exploring orality and literacy.* Norwood, N.J.: Ablex, 1982.

Thorndike, R. Reading as reasoning. *Reading Research Quarterly,* 1974–75, **10,** 135–147.

Wagner, D., & Lofti, A. *Traditional Quranic education in contemporary Morocco.* Unpublished manuscript, University of Pennsylvania, 1979.

Wells, G. *Some antecedents of early educational achievement;* Edinburgh: British Psychological Society, 1980.

Yap, K. O. Vocabulary—Building blocks of comprehension. *Journal of Reading Behavior,* 1979, **11,** 49–59.

# 9
# *Literacy without Schooling:*
# *Testing for Intellectual Effects*

SYLVIA SCRIBNER*
MICHAEL COLE, *University of California, San Diego*

*There has been much discussion of the relationship between literacy and schooling. In these discussions, literacy, particularly in combination with schooling, is seen as an index and precipitator of intellectual development. Sylvia Scribner and Michael Cole challenge many of the generalizations made about the consequences of literacy and advocate examining the use of literacy in different social contexts. Through the observation of unschooled but literate adults, the Vai of Liberia, a people who have invented a syllabic writing system to represent their own language, Scribner and Cole consider the effects of becoming literate separately from the effects of attending school.*

In most discussions of schooling and literacy, the two are so closely intertwined that they are virtually indistinguishable. Yet intellectual consequences have been claimed for each as though they were clearly independent of one another. For several years we have been studying the relation between schooling and literacy, particularly the psychological consequences of each and the extent to which they substitute for each other. Our research among the Vai, a West African people for whom schooling and the acquisition of literacy are separate activities, has led us to reconsider the nature of literacy and its intellectual effects.

Over the centuries and across disciplines, there has been remarkable agreement that the written word has its own peculiar psychological properties. Its relationship to memory and thinking is claimed to be different from that of the spoken word, but conceptions of this relationship are as diverse as the perspectives brought to bear on the question.

Plato considered the issue within the context of basic educational goals and values,

*Until her death in July 1991, Sylvia Scribner was Professor of Psychology at the City University of New York.

The preparation of this paper was made possible by support from the Ford Foundation.

*Harvard Educational Review*   Vol. 48   No. 4   November 1978, 448–461

suggesting that the relationship of writing to intellect be considered problematic, rather than taken at face value. To the claim that letters would give men better memories and make them wise, Socrates replied that, on the contrary, letters would create forgetfulness. Learners would not use their memories but rely instead on external aids for "reminiscence." Disciples of the written word would "have the show of wisdom without the reality" (Plato, p. 323). Plato, on the other hand, was suspicious of education that relied solely on the oral mode of the Homeric tradition. Oral thinking in this context was considered the enemy of logic (Havelock, 1963).

The view that the relationship between writing and mental abilities is problematic has given way to the dominant belief that literacy leads inevitably to higher forms of thought. Oral and literate thought are often contrasted in a modern version of the old dichotomy of primitive and civilized thought. Increasingly, literacy instruction is justified not only as a means to material advancement for the individual and society but also as a means of transforming minds. The UNESCO Secretary-General has recently urged the acceleration of world-wide literacy programs to overcome the deep psychological differences between oral and literate thought (UNESCO, 1965). Similar arguments are made in pedagogical discussions here in the United States (Farrell, 1977).

Debates about the cognitive consequences of literacy play a role in determining priorities for national investments in education and in defining outcomes of schooling. Moreover, the claims for consequences themselves have consequences. If, for example, we believe that literacy is a precondition for abstract thinking, how do we evaluate the intellectual skills of nonliterate people? Do we consider them incapable of participating in modern society because they are limited to the particularistic and concrete? If we believe that writing and logical thinking are always mutually dependent, what do we conclude about the reasoning abilities of a college student who writes an incoherent essay? Is this an automatic sign of defective logic? Answers to these questions have implications for social and educational policies that are at least as profound as those questions that concerned Plato.

To examine some of these implications, we will consider recent work in experimental psychology that brings an empirical perspective to these questions. We will analyze how different investigators specify the relationships between literacy and intellectual skills. Oversimplifying, we will contrast two perspectives: one represented by the metaphor of literacy as development, and the other, by literacy as practice. The developmental framework is an established theoretical tradition. Its presuppositions implicitly or explicitly inform the great majority of literacy and instructional writing programs. The framework of practice, or function, is our own attempt at systematizing the knowledge we gained while investigating literacy without schooling among the Vai. Although the two perspectives start from similar questions, we will intentionally sharpen their contrasting features to bring out their different implications for research and educational policy. The differences lie both in the nature of the evidence considered crucial for developing hypotheses about literacy and in the procedures for relating evidence to theory. Our purpose is not to pose them as entirely antagonistic or to argue for the one best model. Rather we advocate an approach to literacy that moves beyond generalities to a consideration of the organization and use of literacy in different social contexts.

## Literacy as Development

In the 1960s Greenfield and Bruner (1966) put forward the thesis that writing promotes cognitive development. This was derived largely from Greenfield's (1966) studies in Senegal, comparing the performance of schooled and unschooled Wolof children on experimental cognitive tasks. In one task, children were required to sort pictures or objects into groups of things that belonged together and to explain the basis of their sorting. The items could be exhaustively grouped by form, function, or color. Three aspects of performance were considered especially indicative of levels of abstract thinking. First, school children more often shifted the basis of their grouping from one attribute to another over trials. For example, if they sorted by color on the first trial, on the second trial they might sort by function or form. Second, when asked to explain the basis of their sorting, school children tended to state their reasons in sentences with predication, saying, for example, "these *are* red," instead of using a label "red" or a phrase "this red," such as unschooled children tended to do. Finally, school children could easily answer questions about why they thought items were alike whereas unschooled children had difficulty doing this. Greenfield interpreted these performance characteristics as measures of a general ability for context-independent, abstract thinking that only school children displayed.

Greenfield (1972) suggested that oral language relies on context for the communication of messages and is, therefore, a context-dependent language. In contrast, written language requires that meaning be made clear, independent of the immediate reference. If one assumes that context-dependent speech is linked with context-dependent thought, and context-dependent thought is the opposite of abstract thought, it follows that abstract thought fails to develop in an oral culture. Put the other way around, societies with written language provide the means for decontextualized abstract thinking; and since schooling relies primarily on written language, those attending school get a greater push toward abstract thought than those not going to school (Bruner, Olver, Greenfield, Hornsby, Kemey, Maccoby, Modiano, Mosher, Olson, Potter, Reisch, & Sonstroem, 1966, p. 318).

Bruner has presented the most general form of this argument—namely that technologies available in a given culture determine the level and range of abilities in its members. Environments with such symbolic technologies as a written language "push cognitive growth better, earlier and longer than others" (Greenfield & Bruner, 1966, p. 654).

Olson also believes that literacy and education push cognitive growth. In recent essays (1975, 1977, 1977) he contends that a unique form of logical competency is linked to literacy. This competency involves the mastery of the logical functions of language apart from its interpersonal functions. According to Olson, literate individuals come to regard meaning as residing in the text. An example is the ability to derive from the sentence "John hit Mary" the logical implication that "Mary was hit by John." Another is drawing logical conclusions from propositions solely from their linguistic evidence and without considering their factual status. Such logical abilities are not universal, Olson (1977) maintains, but are the endpoint of development in literate cultures. To secure evidence for literacy-related logical processes, Olson and his colleagues (for example, Olson & Filby, 1972) have conducted experimental studies of sentence comprehension and reasoning, comparing the performance of preliterate, preschool youngsters with school children of varying ages and with educated literate adults. Olson's speculations about how literacy develops these abilities come from historical analyses of the cultural changes accompanying the invention of the alphabet and the printing press. Both these inventions, Olson says, increase the explicitness of language, biasing cultures toward the development of explicit formal systems and accounting for distinctive modes of thought in Western societies.

This brief summary fails to do justice to the full argument of these psychologists but it does permit us to focus on what we conceive to be certain limitations and difficulties of the developmental perspective. This work is important and innovative, but we wish to caution against the notion that this evidence of the effects of literacy can provide a foundation for educational programs and that it offers a model strategy for future research.

A defining characteristic of the developmental perspective is that it specifies literacy's effects as the emergence of general mental capacities—abstract thinking, for example, or logical operations—rather than specific skills. These abilities are presumed to characterize the individual's intellectual functioning across a wide range of tasks. Thus, based on a limited sample of performance in experimental contexts, the conclusion has been drawn that there is a great divide between the intellectual competencies of people living in oral cultures and those in literate cultures.

From this perspective the capacities generated by literacy are seen not merely as different, but as higher-order capacities because they resemble the abilities that psychological theories attribute to later stages in development. For decades, developmental inquiry has been organized around the notion that children's thinking progresses from the concrete to the abstract. Olson specifically links literacy-related logical operations to Piaget's final stage of formal operational thought. It is within this framework that statements are made about arrested mental growth in cultures without literacy. Since this research compares children of different ages as well as children and adults, a developmental interpretation seems to have some validity. Can it be extrapolated, without further evidence, to characterize changes in the intellectual operations of adolescents and adults? Whether or not these changes are developmental, in a transformational sense, should at the very least be considered an open question.

Perhaps the most serious problem with this work is its vagueness about the mechanisms by which literacy promotes new intellectual capacities. Both Greenfield and Olson present plausible hypotheses about how literacy achieves its effects, but they offer a multitude of possibilities and no systematic theory for selecting the most fruitful for further exploration. Greenfield (1972) variously attributes the effects of literacy to the structure of the written language, to the school-based uses of language, or to growing up in a literate culture and speaking a written language. Olson (1977) stresses the effects on mental skills of the properties of an alphabetic script, of the exposure to the school language of written text, or of the acquisition of bodies of written knowledge. The ways in which these alleged antecedents exert their effects, however, are neither specified nor linked to the observed behaviors. Piaget (1976) has recently pointed out the limitations of this perspective: "To explain a psychological reaction or a cognitive mechanism . . . is not simply to describe it, but to comprehend the process by which it is formed. Failing that, one can but note results without grasping their meaning" (p. vi).

These empirical studies do not clarify the specific contribution of any of these experiences. None tested literacy as such. In all research, literacy was confounded with schooling; yet students are engaged in many learning experiences in school besides learning how to read and write. And we are all aware today that some children spend many years in school without learning how to read and write. There is little guidance here for educational policies and programs. To set educational goals and to plan curricula, research is needed that relates particular kinds of experiences with written language to the development of particular skills.

A final observation is that the developmental perspective supports an "inevitability" interpretation of literacy. It assumes that various components of literacy—say, an alphabetic script or an essayist text—are likely to have the same psychological consequences in all cultures irrespective of the contexts of use or of the social institutions in which literacy is embedded. In reality, however, the developmental model has been elaborated in terms of institutions and technologies specific to our own society. It has been restricted to literacy as practiced in the schools. In addition, confusion stems from failure to differentiate the consequences of literacy over the course of human history from its consequences for the individual in present-day societies. It is a big jump from intellectual and cultural history to a theory of ontogenetic development in any present-day society.

## A Functional Approach to Schooling and Literacy

We have long been interested in cultural influences on the development of thought, particularly the influence of literacy (Scribner, 1968) and formal schooling (Scribner & Cole, 1973); however, we have been skeptical about the usefulness of applying current developmental theory to these problems. Some of our doubts arose from the observation of unschooled nonliterate adults in other societies, some from experiments comparing schooled and unschooled individuals on cognitive tasks. We concluded from these data that the tendency of schooled populations to generalize across a wide range of problems occurred because schooling provides people with a great deal of practice in treating individual learning problems as instances of general classes of problems. Moreover, we did not assume that the skills promoted by schooling would necessarily be applied in contexts unrelated to school experience. This orientation led us to concentrate on the actual practices of literacy that hypothetically produced behavioral changes, looking for likely causal mechanisms. We needed a way to examine the consequences of literacy apart from schooling under conditions that made literate practices most accessible to observation.

The Vai are a traditional society on the northwest coast of Liberia who are well known in that area for their invention of a syllabic writing system to represent their own language. Preliminary reports (for example, Stewart, 1967) and our own observations indicated that between 20 and 25 percent of Vai men could read and write using their own script, which was invented approximately 150 years ago and transmitted from one generation to another without schooling or professional teachers. The mere existence of an indigenous writing system was enough to arouse our curiosity, but we were interested in the Vai for two additional reasons. First, except that they are predominantly Muslim, the Vai, according to ethnographies of Liberia, are virtually indistinguishable from their neighbors in terms of ecology, social organization, economic activities, and material culture. Second, their writing and reading are not activities separate from other daily pursuits, nor does learning to read and write require a person to master a large body of knowledge that is unavailable from oral sources. These two characteristics of Vai literacy provided an extremely interesting, if not unique, opportunity to investigate the effects of becoming literate separately from the effects of attending school or becoming educated, an inquiry that had heretofore eluded social science.

A detailed description of this work is beyond the scope of this article; however, we will briefly describe its major phases to explain what we mean by a functional approach to the study of literacy and thinking. To begin with, we gave questionnaires and tests to more than 700 Vai adults. Our survey included a variety of tasks based on previous research showing the effects of formal schooling among tribal Liberians. These tasks were included to determine if cognitive performance that was improved by schooling was similarly influenced by indigenous Vai literacy. The test battery also contained sorting and verbal reasoning tasks similar to those used by Greenfield and Olson as the basis for speculations about literacy effects. Results were clearcut. As in previous research, improved performance was associated with years of formal schooling, but literacy in the Vai script did not substitute for schooling. Vai literates were not significantly different from nonliterates on any of these cognitive measures, including the sorting and reasoning tasks that had been suggested as especially sensitive to experience with a written language.[1]

In the next phase of our work we moved down one level of generality in the kinds of hypotheses we tested. Instead of looking for improvements in general cognitive performance associated with literacy, we concentrated on the hypothesis that literacy promotes metalinguistic skills—the idea that in acquiring literacy skills an individual acquires the ability to analyze language (Goody, 1977). One task tested nominal realism, the identification of name and object; other items tested the ability to specify the nature of grammatical rules, to reason from evidence provided by a syllogism, and to define words.

This series of studies showed that Vai literacy was associated with small increments in performance for some of the tasks (for example, increased ability to specify the nature of a grammatical error in spoken Vai) but there was no across-the-board evidence of enhanced performance associated with this unschooled literacy. Furthermore, and most damaging to the metalinguistic hypothesis, our results showed virtually no correlations among performances on the various probes of metalinguistic ability.

At the end of our first year of fieldwork, we had not made much progress in illuminating literacy skills among the Vai by administering standard laboratory tasks whose theoretical status with respect to literacy was uncertain. We decided to take a different approach. Instead of working down from developmental theories, we began to work up from actual observations of how literacy was socially organized and used by the Vai. We decided to base our experimental activities on our ethnographic observations—to let our fieldwork generate specific hypotheses and suggest appropriate tasks.

Reading and writing are not prominent activities in the villages; still, the knowledge and use of the script by Vai literates are manifest in many ways. For one thing, the arrival of a taxi often brings letters, written in Vai, from relatives and business associates in other areas of Vai country and other parts of Liberia. We found that Vai literates write and receive between one and forty letters a month, depending upon a number of factors, including the kinds of economic enterprises in which they are involved and the location of the town in which they live. Funerals are a ubiquitous feature of life in a Vai village, where the infant mortality rate exceeds 50 percent and life expectancy is low. Funerals attract relatives and acquaintances from many parts of the country, each of whom is obligated to bring gifts in money or kind that must be reciprocated. Consequently, recording the names of donors and their gifts at funerals, as well as a variety of other administrative activities such as listing political contributions, are features of Vai life in which literacy plays a central and visible role. Some religious and fraternal organizations maintain records in Vai script, and we have documented at least one case in which a Muslim association was governed by a constitution and by-laws written in Vai script (Goody, Cole, & Scribner, 1977). Farmers and craftsmen use the script for business ledgers and technical plans. A few who might qualify as Vai scholars write family and clan histories, keep diaries, and record maxims and traditional tales in copybooks.

Despite test results, we know that Vai literacy functions in the society and that Vai people seem to feel that it functions well since literates are accorded high status. We began to look carefully at the specific skills these literacy activities seemed to involve: what did it require to write a letter, record contributions to a funeral feast, or list contributions to a religious society? We made functional analyses of the skills involved in these activities. Then, on the basis of these analyses, we designed tasks with different content but hypothetically similar skills to determine if prior practice in learning and use of the script enhanced performance.

Since letter-writing is the most common use of the Vai script, we closely studied the cognitive consequences of letter-writing. In the psychological literature, written communication is said to impose cognitive demands not encountered in face-to-face oral communication. In writing, meaning is supposed to be carried entirely by the text; thus, effective written communication requires sensitivity to the informational needs of the reader and skill in the use of elaborative linguistic techniques. We speculated that Vai literates' experience in writing and reading letters would contribute to the development of these skills, especially because the ability to communicate in writing with people from different places signifies successful completion of the study of the script.

To test this proposition, we adapted a communication task used in previous research (Flavell, Botkin, Fry, Wright, & Jarvis, 1968). Individuals were taught to play a simple board game with little verbal explanation; they were then asked to explain the game, without the materials of the game present, to a listener unfamiliar with it. In addition, we asked subjects to dictate a letter explaining the game to someone far away who had never seen it before.

The game involves two players taking turns racing their counters on a board of eight colored stripes. A counter's movements are governed by the color of the chip selected from a cup on each turn (Flavell et al., 1968). Board games are familiar to the Vai, who play a game called "ludo," which has a similar racing format.

We coded the transcribed protocols for the amount of game-related information they contained and for the presence of statements describing the materials of the game. On both of these measures of quality of communication, we found that men literate in the Vai script were far superior to nonliterates, and that this pattern was apparent in both the face-to-face explanation and the dictated letter. We also analyzed the protocols to see whether they reflected characteristics of Vai literates' style of communication in their day-to-day letter-writing practices.

Over the years, Vai letters have evolved certain stylized formats. Here is a sample:

> 17/7/1964
> Vaitown
>
> This letter belongs to Pa Lamii in Vonzuan. My greeting to you, and my greeting to Mother.
>
> This is your information. I am asking you to do me a favor. The people I called to saw my timber charged me $160.00. I paid them $120.00 and $40.00 still needed, but business is hard this time. I am therefore sending your child to you to please credit me amount of $40.00 to pay these people. Please do not let me down.
>
> I stopped so far.
>
> I am Moley Doma
> Vaitown

The statements "This is your information. I am asking you to do me a favor." are examples of what we call the contextualization of the communication. They tell the recipient what the communication is all about and what information to expect. This aspect of an affective communication was well understood by Vai literates and clearly explained to us in some of our interviews. In one discussion on what makes a good letter, a middle-aged farmer told us, "You must first make the person to understand that you are informing him through words. Then he will give his attention there. It is the correct way of writing the Vai script." When we examined game instructions for this characteristic we found that Vai literates almost always contextualized their communication by giving some general characterization of the game—for example, "This is a game I am coming to tell you about where two people take a race and one of them wins."

A second set of studies tested for the transfer of skills needed to read Vai text. Our observations of Vai literates deciphering letters from friends and coping with mundane reading indicated that decoding the script is extraordinarily difficult because of special properties of the Vai writing system. Vai script characters map the consonant-vowel syllabic structure of the language in a systematic manner; however, this does not produce a direct one-to-one correspondence between the visual symbols and the units of sound. Vowel tone, a phonological feature that is semantically crucial in the spoken language, is not marked in the script. In addition, because the script is not standardized, the representation of vowel length, another semantically distinctive feature of the language, varies considerably from one script-writer to another. Finally, the script is written without division into words or other language units; a string of syllabic characters runs across the page without spacing or segmentation. Each character, depending on its semantic function, may represent a single-syllable word, one of several such words differentiated by tone, or a component unit of a polysyllabic word.

How does a literate Vai resolve these ambiguities? From observations of men reading letters we found that a common technique is what we have called experimentation in pronunciation—saying strings of syllables aloud recursively, varying vowel tones and lengths until they click into meaningful units. Readers must keep separate syllables in mind until they can be integrated into words or phrases. We supposed that this experience might foster skills in language analysis and integration and that these skills might apply in language contexts that did not involve the script. To test this idea we devised a listening task. Each person listened to tape recordings in which a native speaker of Vai slowly read meaningful Vai sentences. Sentences were segmented either into word units or syllable units. The listener was simply asked to repeat the sentence and answer a comprehension question about it. On sentences containing word units, there was no superiority for individuals with experience in Vai script; but, on sentences composed of syllable units, Vai literates with advanced reading skills outdistanced all others, including those with fewer years of practice in reading.

These two tasks, and the remainder of our research, demonstrate that skills involved in literacy behaviors are indeed transferable to behaviors unrelated to literacy. The effects reported—analyzing oral speech and giving clearer instructions—are neither self-evident nor trivial. Speech perception and instruction have real utility. These studies provide the first direct evidence that what an individual does with text, or with pencil and paper, can promote specific skills that are available to support other behaviors. In terms of the concerns with which the research began, we believe it important that these skills are associated with literacy, not with schooling—they are not byproducts of general learning experiences in the classroom. Although our demonstration of literacy-related skills is limited by the range of literacy practices in Vai society, it stands as the first clear-cut evidence in a present-day society that personal engagement in reading and writing does have psychological consequences. These consequences, however, are all highly specific to activities with the Vai script.

The metaphor of literacy as a practice will help us put the Vai research in a more general framework. By combining several dictionary definitions, we can state what we mean by "a practice." A practice may be considered to be the carrying out of a goal-directed sequence of activities, using particular technologies and applying particular systems of knowledge. It is a usual mode or method of doing something— playing the piano, sewing trousers, writing letters. This definition shares certain features with the notion of practice in educational psychology—repeated performance of an act in order to acquire proficiency or skill. How does this apply to literacy? Consider a goal-directed sequence of activities such as letter-writing. This involves a technology—a particular script and particular writing materials. It also requires knowledge of how to represent oral language in script and of the conventional rules of representation. One must know the form and style suitable for writing personal letters as well as what the intended reader knows about the subject of the message and how the new information will fit into the old. A variety of skills at different levels is required to perform this complex act. As one writes more letters, these skills should become more efficiently organized, less dependent on content, and more transferable to new contents and contexts. We did indeed find transfer of these skills in our game-instruction task but the range of transfer was narrow. In summary, our results show that certain literacy practices among the Vai produced intellectual outcomes closely tied to those practices.

Our negative findings are an equally important part of the story. We did not find that literacy in the Vai script was associated in any way with generalized competencies such as abstraction, verbal reasoning, or metalinguistic skills. The tasks used in North American research as alternative measures of these capacities simply did not show consistency of performance in any group except the schooled group. Furthermore, we did not find that either literacy or schooling had an all-or-none effect; on all experimental tasks, including those showing the strongest effects of Vai literacy, some nonliterates achieved high scores and displayed the same skills as literates.

The results of our research among the Vai present us with two apparently contrasting conclusions about the effects of literacy. The literacy as development view would have us believe that literacy, in combination with schooling, produces generalized changes in the way people think. Our functional perspective suggests that the effects of literacy, and perhaps schooling as well, are restricted—perhaps to the practice actually engaged in or generalized only to closely related practices. These extreme alternatives echo an educational debate that began at the turn of the century.

Thorndike and Woodworth (1901) suggested that learning is specific and transfer from one task to another will occur only when both tasks shared identical elements. Their antagonists believed that education, through mental discipline, strengthens the mind in general. (For a summary of the arguments at that time, see Thorndike, 1969, p. 357). However, no theory guided the search for identical elements and no theory gave substance to the mental discipline position. After seventy-five years of debate and data accumulation, the issue of the effects of practice has not been resolved. We have no illusions that our skimpy data with respect to literacy will resolve the discrepancies between these two viewpoints, but our framework may help us think about literacy and its effects in a way that does not get us lost in unsupported generalities or insignificant particulars.

The specific outcomes that we observed in our studies of Vai literacy confirm earlier observations that certain cognitive skills show little generalizability across experimental tasks among traditional adults. The situation with respect to Vai writing and reading is similar to that of other skilled practices—such as weaving (Childs & Greenfield, in press) or pottery-making (Bunzel, 1953)—in nontechnological societies, in which highly organized, complex skills are applied to a limited set of problems. Previously, we argued that generalized skills might not arise when common operations are applied to a limited set of tasks (Scribner & Cole, 1973). If the uses of writing are few and limited, skills should be applied to each use in a more or less original way. As the repertoire of functions expands, the operations necessary for each may be applied across a range of tasks and contexts. For example, an individual might write a letter to distribute proceeds from a funeral feast—two functions that are usually separate. This example represents the upper limit of typical Vai writing practices because each individual's practices are restricted.

As the technology of any society becomes more complex, the number and variety of tasks to which literacy skills must be applied increases as well. A task might include some mix of a common core of skills like decoding, for example, with new skills or more complicated versions of old skills, as when Vai tradesmen begin to write to people they have never met before because business practice makes this necessary. If our argument that specific uses promote specific skills is valid, we might expect to find the outcomes that Olson or others predict, but only under conditions evoking these skills. Carrying out critical analyses of text, for example, might promote certain analytic operations with language, whereas rote learning from the same text, or reading it for some other purpose, is not likely to do so. Writing poetry is likely to have different consequences for language skills than preparing a letter to a department store requesting a refund for damaged goods.

As practice in any activity continues, we would expect that skills would extend to a wide range of tasks and materials and when the skill systems involved in literacy are many, varied, complex, and widely applicable, the functional and general ability perspectives will converge in their predictions of intellectual outcomes. Whether we choose to interpret these acquired functional skill systems developmentally is a matter of theoretical predilection, the discussion of which lies outside the argument of this article.

Although we do not advocate a single approach to the complex issues of the psychology of literacy, we believe that the strategy of functional analysis emerging from the Vai research may have particularly useful implications for educational research in our own society. It suggests that different literacy activities need to be analyzed independently. If, as we have demonstrated, particular skills are promoted by particular kinds of literacy practices, we need to know a great deal more about just how literacy is practiced. Studies of the range of reading and writing activities carried out in school, including those outside the official curriculum, would be a useful extension of work such as that done by Martin, D'Arcy, Newton, and Parker (1976). We have far fewer precedents, however, for an equally important research task: finding out what people in various communities and walks of life do with literacy—how they use their knowledge of reading and writing, to what tasks they apply it, and how they accomplish these tasks. Such analyses should help us understand the differences between school-based literacy practices and literacy practices unrelated to schooling as well as their possibly different implications for intellectual outcomes. Although attempts to arrive at some overall measures of literacy competencies may be useful for certain comparative purposes, the conceptualization of literacy as a fixed inventory of skills that can be assessed out of the contexts of application has little utility for educational policies.

We need to acknowledge, however, that we are a long way from having the methods, techniques, and theories required to make a systematic analysis of the component skills involved in reading and writing. Considerable progress has been made in identifying components in decoding activities and, more recently, in the higher-level intellectual skills involved in controlled reading tasks under laboratory-like or highly constrained classroom conditions. (See especially the reports of The Center for the Study of Reading, 1975–1978). Sticht, Fox, Hauke, and Zapf (1977) have used the skills-analysis approach to reading activities outside the classroom and have distinguished between reading-to-do and reading-to-learn activities. The long-range objective is to devise methods for an adequate description and analysis of skills in out-of-school literacy practices that can be coordinated with the micro-level analyses of laboratory studies.

Both educational practice and research might benefit from a recognition of the complex interrelationships between mental skills and literacy activities. Terms that refer to oral and literate modes of thought, although historically significant, are not useful characterizations of the mental abilities of nonliterate and literate adults in American society; in fact, most research with adults in traditional societies confirms their inappropriateness for any contemporaneous culture. Thus research does not support designing adult literacy programs on the assumption that nonliterates do not think abstractly, do not reason logically, or lack other basic mental processes. In each case, the skills available for learning how to read and write or for improving rudimentary literacy abilities need to be assessed with respect to the accomplishments nonliterates display in other activities—for example, disputation, hypothetical reasoning, or oral narrative. To the question posed at the beginning of this paper—"Is a college student's incoherent essay symptomatic of faulty reasoning?"—our answer would be, "No, it is not a symptom; it is a sign to be evaluated."

If different literacy activities are linked to different intellectual outcomes, a second implication of our research is that reading and writing activities need to be tailored to desired achievements. These outcomes can be defined in terms of the literacy competencies required for participation in our highly technological society, but they need not be defined in narrowly pragmatic terms, reflecting merely the current demand for job security or advance. A skills approach might make it possible to identify a common core of skills that will enable an individual to master more intellectually demanding reading and writing tasks after completing the school curriculum or literacy program. If the educational objective is to foster analytic logical reasoning, that objective should guide the choice of instructional program. It should not be assumed that these skills will follow inevitably from practice in writing essays. Writing essays may be helpful, as may oral practices. This is undoubtedly the common wisdom of the classroom and the educational planner. But it would be helpful to ally this wisdom with the psychological literature on literacy so that the broad conceptual framework informs teaching practice and practice informs the theory.

We realize that the kind of program implied by our discussion may seem difficult to attain. The comments of the Soviet psychologist Vygotsky (1934/1978) some fifty years ago on the status of the specific-skill versus mental-development argument of his day offer useful guidance for our research choices today: "Such a matter cannot be dealt with by a single formula of some kind, but rather suggests how great is the scope for extensive and varied experimental research" (p. 34).

## Notes

1. Any effects reported as significant refer to regression analyses in which the variable in question entered the equation at the .05 level of significance or better.

## References

Bruner, J., Olver, R., Greenfield, P., Hornsby, J., Kemey, H., Maccoby, M., Modiano, N., Mosher, F., Olson, D., Potter, M., Reisch, L., & Sonstroem, A. *Studies in cognitive growth*. New York: Wiley, 1966.

Bunzel, R. Psychology of the Pueblo potter. In M. Mead & N. Calas (Eds.)., *Primitive heritage*. New York: Random House, 1953.

Center for the Study of Reading. *Technical reports 1–102*. University of Illinois at Champaign-Urbana, 1975–1978.

Childs, C., & Greenfield, P. Informal modes of learning and teaching: The case of Zinacanteco weaving. In N. Warren (Ed.), *Advances in cross-cultural psychology*, vol. 2. London: Academic Press, in press.

Farrell, T. Literacy, the basics, and all that jazz, *College English*, 1977, 38, 443–459.

Flavell, J., Botkin, P., Fry, C., Wright, J., & Jarvis, P. *The development of role-taking and communication skills in children*. New York: Wiley, 1968.

Goody, J. *The domestication of the savage mind.* Cambridge, Eng.: Cambridge University Press, 1977.

Goody, J., Cole, M., & Scribner, S. Writing and formal operations: A case study among the Vai. *Africa,* 1977, **47,** 289–304.

Greene, W. The spoken and the written word. *Harvard Studies in Classical Philology,* 1951, **60,** 23–59.

Greenfield, P. On culture and equivalence. In J. Bruner, et al. (Eds.), *Studies in cognitive growth.* New York: Wiley, 1966.

Greenfield, P. Oral or written language: The consequences for cognitive development in Africa, the United States and England. *Language and Speech,* 1972, **15,** 169–178.

Greenfield, P., & Bruner, J. Culture and cognitive growth. *International Journal of Psychology,* 1966, **1,** 89–107.

Havelock, E. *Preface to Plato.* Cambridge, Mass.: Harvard University Press, 1963.

Martin, N., D'Arcy, P., Newton, B., & Parker, R. *Writing and learning across the curriculum 11–16.* London: Ward Lock Educational, 1966.

Olson, D. Review of *Toward a literate society,* ed. J. Carroll & J. Chall. In *Proceedings of the National Academy of Education,* 1975, **2,** 109–178.

Olson, D. From utterance to text: The bias of language in speech and writing. *Harvard Educational Review,* 1977, **47,** 257–281.

Olson, D. The language of instruction. In R. Anderson, R. Spiro, & W. Montague (Eds.). *Schooling and the acquisition of knowledge.* Hillsdale, N.J.: Erlbaum and Associates, 1977.

Olson, D., & Filby, N. On the comprehension of active and passive sentences. *Cognitive Psychology,* 1972, **3,** 361–381.

Piaget, J. Foreword. In J. Piaget, B. Inhelder, & H. Chipman (Eds.), *Piaget and his school.* New York: Springer-Verlag, 1976.

Plato. Phaedrus. In I. Edman (Ed.), *The works of Plato.* New York: Modern Library, 1928.

Scribner, S. *The cognitive consequences of literacy.* Unpublished manuscript, Albert Einstein College of Medicine, 1968.

Scribner, S., & Cole, M. Cognitive consequences of formal and informal education. *Science,* 1973, **182,** 553–559.

Stewart, G. Notes on the present-day usage of the Vai script in Liberia. *African Language Review,* 1976, **6,** 71–74.

Sticht, T., Fox, L., Hauke, R., & Zapf, D. *The role of reading in the navy* (NPRDC TR 77–40). San Diego, Calif.: Navy Personnel Research and Training Center, 1977.

Thorndike, E. *Educational Psychology,* vol. 2. New York: Arno Press, 1969.

Thorndike, E., & Woodworth, R. The influence of improvement in one mental function upon the efficiency of other functions. *Psychological Review,* 1901, **8,** 247–261.

UNESCO: World Congress of Ministers of Education on the Eradication of Illiteracy, Teheran, 8–19, September 1965. Inaugural speeches, messages, closing speeches. Paris: Author, 1965.

Vygotsky, L. Learning and mental development at school age. In B. Simon, & T. Simon (Eds.), *Educational Psychology in the USSR.* London: Routledge & Kegan Paul, 1963. See also L. Vygotsky, Learning and development. In M. Cole, V. John-Steiner, S. Scribner, & E. Souberman (Eds.), *Mind in society: The development of higher psychological processes.* Cambridge, Mass.: Harvard University Press, 1978.

# 10
# The Adult Literacy Process as Cultural Action for Freedom

PAULO FREIRE
*Advisor to São Paulo City Government*

*Brazilian educator Paulo Freire presents his theory of literacy and argues for educational practice based on authentic dialogue between teachers and learners as equally knowing subjects. Recognizing that nonliterate people are oppressed in a highly literate society, he states that the literacy education should focus on empowering these people, thus functioning as a form of cultural action. Freire, a leading theorist of critical literacy, rejects the idea that becoming literate results from the simple, mechanical increase of vocabulary. Instead, drawing on his experience with nonliterate farmers in Latin America, he advocates an adult literacy education that promotes knowledge through the critical examination of existing social conditions as an integral part of the curriculum.*

## Every Educational Practice Implies a Concept of Man and the World

Experience teaches us not to assume that the obvious is clearly understood. So it is with the truism with which we begin: All educational practice implies a theoretical stance on the educator's part. This stance in turn implies—sometimes more, sometimes less explicitly—an interpretation of man and the world. It could not be otherwise. The process of men's orientation in the world involves not just the association of sense images, as for animals. It involves, above all, thought-language; that is, the

This article is part of a longer essay by Paulo Freire, *Cultural Action for Freedom,* Harvard Educational Review Monograph Series, No. 1 (Cambridge, Mass.: Harvard Educational Review, 1970). Copyright © 1970 by Paulo Freire.
   The author gratefully acknowledges the contributions of Loretta Slover, who translated this essay, and João da Veiga Coutinho and Robert Riordan, who assisted in the preparation of the manuscript.

*Harvard Educational Review*   Vol. 40   No. 2   May 1970, 205–225

possibility of the act of knowing through his praxis, by which man transforms reality. For man, this process of orientation in the world can be understood neither as a purely subjective event, nor as an objective or mechanistic one, but only as an event in which subjectivity and objectivity are united. Orientation in the world, so understood, places the question of the purposes of action at the level of critical perception of reality.

If, for animals, orientation in the world means adaptation to the world, for man it means humanizing the world by transforming it. For animals there is no historical sense, no options or values in their orientation in the world; for man there is both an historical and a value dimension. Men have the sense of "project," in contrast to the instinctive routines of animals.

The action of men without objectives, whether the objectives are right or wrong, mythical or demythologized, naive or critical, is not praxis, though it may be orientation in the world. And not being praxis, it is action ignorant both of its own process and of its aim. The interrelation of the awareness of aim and of process is the basis for planning action, which implies methods, objectives, and value options.

Teaching adults to read and write must be seen, analyzed, and understood in this way. The critical analyst will discover in the methods and texts used by educators and students practical value options which betray a philosophy of man, well or poorly outlined, coherent or incoherent. Only someone with a mechanistic mentality, which Marx would call "grossly materialistic," could reduce adult literacy learning to a purely technical action. Such a naive approach would be incapable of perceiving that technique itself as an instrument of men in their orientation in the world is not neutral.

We shall try, however, to prove by analysis the self-evidence of our statement. Let us consider the case of primers used as the basic texts for teaching adults to read and write. Let us further propose two distinct types: a poorly done primer and a good one, according to the genre's own criteria. Let us even suppose that the author of the good primer based the selection of its generative words[1] on a prior knowledge of which words have the greatest resonance for the learner (a practice not commonly found, though it does exist).

Doubtlessly, such an author is already far beyond the colleague who composes his primer with words he himself chooses in his own library. Both authors, however, are identical in a fundamental way. In each case they themselves decompose the given generative words and from the syllables create new words. With these words, in turn, the authors form simple sentences and, little by little, small stories, the so-called reading lessons.

Let us say that the author of the second primer, going one step further, suggests that the teachers who use it initiate discussions about one or another word, sentence, or text with their students.

Considering either of these hypothetical cases we may legitimately conclude that there is an implicit concept of man in the primer's method and content, whether it is recognized by the authors or not. This concept can be reconstructed from various angles. We begin with the fact, inherent in the idea and use of the primer, that it is the teacher who chooses the words and proposes them to the learner. Insofar as the primer is the mediating object between the teacher and students, and the students are to be "filled" with words the teachers have chosen, one can easily detect a first important dimension of the image of man which here begins to emerge. It is the profile of a man whose consciousness is "spatialized," and must be "filled" or "fed" in order to know. This same conception led Sartre, criticizing the notion that "to know is to eat," to exclaim: *"O philosophie alimentaire!"*[2]

This "digestive" concept of knowledge, so common in current educational practice, is found very clearly in the primer.[3] Illiterates are considered "undernourished," not in the literal sense in which many of them really are, but because they lack the "bread of the spirit." Consistent with the concept of knowledge as food, illiteracy is conceived of as a "poison herb," intoxicating and debilitating persons who cannot read or write. Thus, much is said about the "eradication" of illiteracy to cure the disease.[4] In this way, deprived of their character as linguistic signs constitutive of man's thought-language, words are transformed into mere "deposits of vocabulary"—the bread of the spirit which the literates are to "eat" and "digest."

This "nutritionist" view of knowledge perhaps also explains the humanitarian character of certain Latin American adult literacy campaigns. If millions of men are illiterate, "starving for letters," "thirsty for words," the word must be *brought* to them to save them from "hunger" and "thirst." The word, according to the naturalistic concept of consciousness implicit in the primer, must be "deposited," not born of the creative effort of the learners. As understood in this concept, man is a passive being, the object of the process of learning to read and write, and not its subject. As object his task is to "study" the so-called reading lessons, which in fact are almost completely alienating and alienated, having so little, if anything, to do with the student's socio-cultural reality.[5]

It would be a truly interesting study to analyze the reading texts being used in private or official adult literacy campaigns in rural and urban Latin America. It would not be unusual to find among such texts sentences and readings like the following random samples:[6]

> *A asa é da ave*—"The wing is of the bird."
> *Eva viu a uva*—"Eva saw the grape."
> *O galo canta*—"The cock crows."
> *O cachorro ladra*—"The dog barks."
> *Maria gosta dos animais*—"Mary likes animals."
> *João cuida das arvores*—"John takes care of the trees."

> *O pai de Carlinhos se chama Antonio. Carlinhos è um bom menino, bem comportado e estudioso*—"Charles's father's name is Antonio. Charles is a good, well-behaved, and studious boy."

> *Ada deu o dedo ao urubu? Duvido, Ada deu o dedo a arara. . . .* [7]

> *Se você trabalha com martelo e prego, tenha cuidado para nao furar o dedo.*—"If you hammer a nail, be careful not to smash your finger."[8]

・ ・ ・

"Peter did not know how to read. Peter was ashamed. One day, Peter went to school and registered for a night course. Peter's teacher was very good. Peter knows how to read now. Look at Peter's face. [These lessons are generally illustrated.] Peter is smiling. He is a happy man. He already has a good job. Everyone ought to follow his example."

In saying that Peter is smiling because he knows how to read, that he is happy because he now has a good job, and that he is an example for all to follow, the authors establish a relationship between knowing how to read and getting good jobs which, in fact, cannot be borne out. This naiveté reveals, at least, a failure to perceive the structure not only of illiteracy, but of social phenomena in general. Such an approach may admit that these phenomena exist, but it cannot perceive their relationship to the structure of the society in which they are found. It is as if these phenomena were mythical, above and beyond concrete situations, or the results of the intrinsic inferiority of a certain class of men. Unable to grasp contemporary illiteracy as a typical manifestation of the "culture of silence," directly related to underdeveloped structures, this approach cannot offer an objective, critical response to the challenge of illiteracy. Merely teaching men to read and write does not work miracles; if there are not enough jobs for men able to work, teaching more men to read and write will not create them.

One of these readers presents among its lessons the following two texts on consecutive pages without relating them. The first is about May 1st, the Labor Day holiday, on which workers commemorate their struggles. It does not say how or where these are commemorated, or what the nature of the historical conflict was. The main theme of the second lesson is *holidays*. It says that "on these days people ought to go to the beach to swim and sunbathe . . ." Therefore, if May 1st is a holiday, and if on holidays people should go to the beach, the conclusion is that the workers should go swimming on Labor Day, instead of meeting with their unions in the public squares to discuss their problems.

Analysis of these texts reveals, then, a simplistic vision of men, of their world, of the relationship between the two, and of the literacy process which unfolds in that world.

*A asa é da ave, Eva viu a uva, o galo canta,* and *o cachorro late,* are linguistic contexts which, when mechanically memorized and repeated, are deprived of their authentic dimension as thought-language in dynamic interplay with reality. Thus impoverished, they are not authentic expressions of the world.

Their authors do not recognize in the poor classes the ability to know and even create the texts which would express their own thought-language at the level of their perceptions of the world. The authors repeat with the texts what they do with the words, i.e., they introduce them into the learners' consciousness as if it were empty space—once more, the "digestive" concept of knowledge.

Still more, the a-structural perception of illiteracy revealed in these texts exposes the other false view of illiterates as marginal men.[9] Those who consider them marginal must, nevertheless, recognize the existence of a reality to which they are marginal—not only physical space, but historical, social, cultural, and economic realities—i.e., the structural dimension of reality. In this way, illiterates have to be recognized as beings "outside of," "marginal to" something, since it is impossible to be marginal to nothing. But being "outside of" or "marginal to" necessarily implies a movement of the one said to be marginal from the center, where he was, to the periphery. This movement, which is an action, presupposes in turn not only an agent but also his reasons. Admitting the existence of men "outside of" or "marginal to" structural reality, it seems legitimate to ask: Who is the author of this movement from the center of the structure to its margin? Do so-called marginal men, among them the illiterates, make the decision to move out to the periphery of society? If so, marginality is an option with all that it involves: hunger, sickness, rickets, pain, mental deficiencies, living death, crime, promiscuity, despair, the impossibility of being. In fact, however, it is difficult to accept that 40% of Brazil's population, almost 90% of Haiti's, 60% of Bolivia's, about 40% of Peru's, more than 30% of Mexico's and Venezuela's, and about 70% of Guatemala's would have made the tragic *choice* of their own marginality as illiterates.[10] If then, marginality is not by choice, marginal man has been expelled from and kept outside of the social system and is therefore the object of violence.

In fact, however, the social structure as a whole does not "expel," nor is marginal man a "being outside of." He is, on the contrary, a "being inside of," within the social structure, and in a dependent relationship to those whom we call falsely autonomous beings, inauthentic beings-for-themselves.

A less rigorous approach, one more simplistic, less critical, more technicist, would say that it was unnecessary to reflect about what it would consider unimportant questions such as illiteracy and teaching adults to read and write. Such an approach might even add that the discussion of the concept of marginality is an unnecessary academic exercise. In fact, however, it is not so. In accepting the illiterate as a person who exists on the fringe of society, we are led to envision him as a sort of "sick man," for whom literacy would be the "medicine" to cure him, enabling him to "return" to the "healthy" structure from which he has become separated. Educators would be benevolent counsellors, scouring the outskirts of the city for the stubborn illiterates, runaways from the good life, to restore them to the forsaken bosom of happiness by giving them the gift of the word.

In the light of such a concept—unfortunately, all too widespread—literary programs can never be efforts toward freedom; they will never question the very reality which deprives men of the right to speak up—not only illiterates, but all those who are treated as objects in a dependent relationship. These men, illiterate or not, are, in fact, not marginal. What we said before bears repeating: They are not "beings outside of"; they are "beings for another." Therefore the solution to their problem is not to become "beings inside of," but men freeing themselves; for, in reality, they are not marginal to the structure, but oppressed men within it. Alienated men, they cannot overcome their dependency by "incorporation" into the very structure responsible for their dependency. There is no other road to humanization—theirs as well as everyone else's—but authentic transformation of the dehumanizing structure.

From this last point of view, the illiterate is no longer a person living on the fringe of society, a marginal man, but rather a representative of the dominated strata of society, in conscious or unconscious opposition to those who, in the same structure, treat him as a thing. Thus, also, teaching men to read and write is no longer an inconsequential matter of *ba, be, bi, bo, bu,* of memorizing an alienated word, but a difficult apprenticeship in naming the world.

In the first hypothesis, interpreting illiterates as men marginal to society, the literacy process reinforces the mythification of reality by keeping it opaque and by dulling the "empty consciousness" of the learner with innumerable alienating words and phrases. By contrast, in the second hypothesis—interpreting illiterates as men oppressed within the system—the literacy process, as cultural action for freedom, is an act of knowing in which the learner assumes the role of knowing subject in dialogue with the educator. For this very reason, it is a courageous endeavor to demythologize reality, a process through which men who had previously been submerged in reality begin to emerge in order to re-insert themselves into it with critical awareness.

Therefore the educator must strive for an ever greater clarity as to what, at times without his conscious knowledge, illumines the path of his action. Only in this way will he truly be able to assume the role of one of the subjects of this action and remain consistent in the process.

## The Adult Literacy Process as an Act of Knowing

To be an act of knowing the adult literacy process demands among teachers and students a relationship of authentic dialogue. True dialogue unites subjects together in the cognition of a knowable object which mediates between them.

If learning to read and write is to constitute an act of knowing, the learners must assume from the beginning the role of creative subjects. It is not a matter of memorizing and repeating given syllables, words, and phrases, but rather of reflecting critically on the process of reading and writing itself, and on the profound significance of language.

Insofar as language is impossible without thought, and language and thought are impossible without the world to which they refer, the human word is more than mere vocabulary—it is word-and-action. The cognitive dimensions of the literacy process must include the relationships of men with their world. These relationships are the source of the dialectic between the products men achieve in transforming the world and the conditioning which these products in turn exercise on men.

Learning to read and write ought to be an opportunity for men to know what *speaking the word* really means: a human act implying reflection and action. As such it is a primordial human right and not the privilege of a few.[11] Speaking the word is not a true act if it is not at the same time associated with the right of self-expression and world-expression, of creating and re-creating, of deciding and choosing and ultimately participating in society's historical process.

In the culture of silence the masses are "mute," that is, they are prohibited from creatively taking part in the transformations of their society and therefore prohibited from being. Even if they can occasionally read and write because they were "taught" in humanitarian—but not humanist—literacy campaigns, they are nevertheless alienated from the power responsible for their silence.

Illiterates know they are concrete men. They know that they do things. What they do not know in the culture of silence—in which they are ambiguous, dual beings—is that men's actions as such are transforming, creative, and re-creative. Overcome by the myths of this culture, including the myth of their own "natural inferiority," they do not know that *their* action upon the world is also transforming. Prevented from having a "structural perception" of the facts involving them, they do not know that they cannot "have a voice," i.e., that they cannot exercise the right to participate consciously in the socio-historical transformation of their society, because their work does not belong to them.

It could be said (and we would agree) that it is not possible to recognize all this apart from praxis, that is, apart from reflection and action, and that to attempt it would be pure idealism. But it is also true that action upon an object must be critically analyzed in order to understand both the object itself and the understanding one has of it. The act of knowing involves a dialectical movement which goes from action to reflection and from reflection upon action to a new action. For the learner to know what he did not know before, he must engage in an authentic process of abstraction by means of which he can reflect on the action-object whole, or, more generally, on forms of orientation in the world. In this process of abstraction, situations representative of how the learner orients himself in the world are proposed to him as the objects of his critique.

As an event calling forth the critical reflection of both the learners and educators, the literacy process must relate *speaking the word* to *transforming reality,* and to man's role in this transformation. Perceiving the significance of that relationship is indispensable for those learning to read and write if we are really committed to liberation. Such a perception will lead the learners to recognize a much greater right than that of being literate. They will ultimately recognize that, as men, they have the right to have a voice.

On the other hand, as an act of knowing, learning to read and write presupposes not only a theory of knowing but a method which corresponds to the theory.

We recognize the indisputable unity between subjectivity and objectivity in the act of knowing. Reality is never just simply the objective datum, the concrete fact, but is also men's perception of it. Once again, this is not a subjectivistic or idealistic affirmation, as it might seem. On the contrary, subjectivism and idealism come into play when the subjective-objective unity is broken.[12]

The adult literacy process as an act of knowing implies the existence of two interrelated contexts. One is the context of authentic dialogue between learners and educators as equally knowing subjects. This is what schools should be—the theoretical context of dialogue. The second is the real, concrete context of facts, the social reality in which men exist.[13]

In the theoretical context of dialogue, the facts presented by the real or concrete context are critically analyzed. This analysis involves the exercise of abstraction, through which, by means of representations of concrete reality, we seek knowledge of that reality. The instrument for this abstraction in our methodology is codification,[14] or representation of the existential situations of the learners.

Codification, on the one hand, mediates between the concrete and theoretical contexts (of reality). On the other hand, as knowable object, it mediates between the knowing subjects, educators and learners, who seek in dialogue to unveil the "action-object wholes."

This type of linguistic discourse must be "read" by anyone who tries to interpret it, even when purely pictorial. As such, it presents what Chomsky calls "surface structure" and "deep structure."

The "surface structure" of codification makes the "action-object whole" explicit in a purely taxonomic form. The first stage of decodification[15]—or reading—is descriptive. At this stage, the "readers"—or decodifiers—focus on the relationship between the categories constituting the codification. This preliminary focus on the surface structure is followed by problematizing the codified situation. This leads the learner to the second and fundamental stage of decodification, the comprehension of the codification's "deep structure." By understanding the codification's "deep structure" the learner can then understand the dialectic which exists between the categories presented in the "surface structure," as well as the unity between the "surface" and "deep" structures.

In our method, the codification initially takes the form of a photograph or sketch which represents a real existent, or an existent constructed by the learners. When this representation is projected as a slide, the learners effect an operation basic to the act of knowing; they gain distance from the knowable object. This experience of distance is undergone as well by the educators, so that educators and learners together can reflect critically on the knowable object which mediates between them. The aim of decodification is to arrive at the critical level of knowing, beginning with the learner's experience of the situation in the "real context."

Whereas the codified representation is the knowable object mediating between knowing subjects, decodification—dissolving the codification into its constituent elements—is the operation by which the knowing subjects perceive relationships between the codification's elements and other facts presented by the real context—relationships which were formerly unperceived. Codification represents a given dimension of reality as individuals live it, and this dimension is proposed for their analysis in a context other than that in which they live it. Codification thus transforms what was a way of life in the real context into "objectum" in the theoretical context. The learners, rather than receive information about this or that fact, analyze aspects of their own existential experience represented in the codification.

Existential experience is a whole. In illuminating one of its angles and perceiving the inter-relation of that angle with others, the learners tend to replace a fragmented vision of reality with a total vision. From the point of view of a theory of knowledge, this means that the dynamic between codification of existential situations and de-codification involves the learners in a constant re-construction of their former "ad-miration" of reality.

We do not use the concept "ad-miration" here in the usual way, or in its ethical or esthetic sense, but with a special philosophical connotation.

To "ad-mire" is to objectify the "not-I." It is a dialectical operation which char-acterizes man as man, differentiating him from the animal. It is directly associated with the creative dimension of his language. To "ad-mire" implies that man stands over against his "not-I" in order to understand it. For this reason, there is no act of knowing without "ad-miration" of the object to be known. If the act of knowing is a dynamic act—and no knowledge is ever complete—then in order to know, man not only "ad-mires" the object, but must always be "re-ad-miring" his former "ad-miration." When we "re-ad-mire" our former "ad-miration" (always an "ad-miration *of*") we are simultaneously "ad-miring" the act of "ad-miring" and the object "ad-mired," so that we can overcome the errors we made in our former "ad-miration." This "re-ad-miration" leads us to a perception of an anterior perception.

In the process of decodifying representations of their extrinsic situations and perceiving former perceptions, the learners gradually, hesitatingly, and timorously place in doubt the opinion they held of reality and replace it with a more and more critical knowledge thereof.

Let us suppose that we were to present to groups from among the dominated classes codifications which portray their imitation of the dominators' cultural models—a natural tendency of the oppressed consciousness at a given moment.[16] The dom-inated persons would perhaps, in self-defense, deny the truth of the codification. As they deepened their analysis, however, they would begin to perceive that their apparent imitation of the dominators' models is a result of their interiorization of these models and, above all, of the myths of the "superiority" of the dominant classes which cause the dominated to feel inferior. What in fact is pure interiorization appears in a naive analysis to be imitation. At bottom, when the dominated classes reproduce the dominators' style of life, it is because the dominators live "within" the dominated. The dominated can eject the dominators only by getting distance from them and objectifying them. Only then can they recognize them as their antithesis.[17]

To the extent, however, that interiorization of the dominators' values is not only an individual phenomenon, but a social and cultural one, ejection must be achieved by a type of cultural action in which culture negates culture. That is, culture, as an interiorized product which in turn conditions men's subsequent acts, must become the object of men's knowledge so that they can perceive its conditioning power. Cultural action occurs at the level of superstructure. It can only be understood by what Althusser calls "the dialectic of overdetermination."[18] This analytic tool prevents us from falling into mechanistic explanations or, what is worse, mechanistic action.

An understanding of it precludes surprise that cultural myths remain after the infrastructure is transformed, even by revolution.

When the creation of a new culture is appropriate but impeded by interiorized cultural "residue," this residue, these myths, must be expelled by means of culture. Cultural action and cultural revolution, at different stages, constitute the modes of this expulsion.

The learners must discover the reasons behind many of their attitudes toward cultural reality and thus confront cultural reality in a new way. "Re-ad-miration" of their former "ad-miration" is necessary in order to bring this about. The learners' capacity for critical knowing—well beyond mere opinion—is established in the process of unveiling their relationships with the historical-cultural world *in* and *with* which they exist.

We do not mean to suggest that critical knowledge of man-world relationships arises as a verbal knowledge outside of praxis. Praxis is involved in the concrete situations which are codified for critical analysis. To analyze the codification in its "deep structure" is, for this very reason, to reconstruct the former praxis and to become capable of a new and different praxis. The relationship between the *theoretical context,* in which codified representations of objective facts are analyzed, and the *concrete context,* where these facts occur, has to be made real.

Such education must have the character of commitment. It implies a movement from the *concrete context* which provides objective facts, to the *theoretical context* where these facts are analyzed in depth, and back to the *concrete context* where men experiment with new forms of praxis.

It might seem as if some of our statements defend the principle that, whatever the level of the learners, they ought to reconstruct the process of human knowing in absolute terms. In fact, when we consider adult literacy learning or education in general as an act of knowing, we are advocating a synthesis between the educator's maximally systematized knowing and the learners' minimally systematized knowing— a synthesis achieved in dialogue. The educator's role is to propose problems about the codified existential situations in order to help the learners arrive at a more and more critical view of their reality. The educator's responsibility as conceived by this philosophy is thus greater in every way than that of his colleague whose duty is to transmit information which the learners memorize. Such an educator can simply repeat what he has read, and often misunderstood, since education for him does not mean an act of knowing.

The first type of educator, on the contrary, is a knowing subject, face to face with other knowing subjects. He can never be a mere memorizer, but a person constantly readjusting his knowledge, who calls forth knowledge from his students. For him, education is a pedagogy of knowing. The educator whose approach is mere memorization is anti-dialogic; his act of transmitting knowledge is inalterable. For the educator who experiences the act of knowing together with his students, in contrast, dialogue is the seal of the act of knowing. He is aware, however, that not all dialogue is in itself the mark of a relationship of true knowledge.

Socratic intellectualism—which mistook the definition of the concept for knowledge of the thing defined and this knowledge a virtue—did not constitute a true pedagogy of knowing, even though it was dialogic. Plato's theory of dialogue failed to go beyond the Socratic theory of the definition as knowledge, even though for Plato one of the necessary conditions for knowing was that man be capable of a "*prise de conscience,*" and though the passage from *doxa* to *logos* was indispensable for man to achieve truth. For Plato, the "*prise de conscience*" did not refer to what man knew or did not know or knew badly about his dialectical relationship with the world; it was concerned rather with what man once knew and forgot at birth. To know was to remember or recollect forgotten knowledge. The apprehension of both *doxa* and *logos,* and the overcoming of *doxa* by *logos* occurred not in the man-world relationship, but in the effort to remember or rediscover a forgotten *logos.*

For dialogue to be a method of true knowledge, the knowing subjects must approach reality scientifically in order to seek the dialectical connections which explain the form of reality. Thus, to know is not to remember something previously known and now forgotten. Nor can *doxa* be overcome by *logos* apart from the dialectical relationship of man with his world, apart from men's reflective action upon the world.

To be an act of knowing, then, the adult literacy process must engage the learners in the constant problematizing of their existential situations. This problematizing employs "generative words" chosen by specialized educators in a preliminary investigation of what we call the "minimal linguistic universe" of the future learners. The words are chosen (a) for their pragmatic value, *i.e.,* as linguistic signs which command a common understanding in a region or area of the same city or country (in the United States, for instance, the word *soul* has a special significance in black areas which it does not have among whites), and (b) for their phonetic difficulties which will gradually be presented to those learning to read and write. Finally, it is important that the first generative word be tri-syllabic. When it is divided into its syllables, each one constituting a syllabic family, the learners can experiment with various syllabic combinations even at first sight of the word.

Having chosen seventeen generative words,[19] the next step is to codify seventeen existential situations familiar to the learners. The generative words are then worked into the situations one by one in the order of their increasing phonetic difficulty. As we have already emphasized, these codifications are knowable objects which mediate between the knowing subjects, educator-learners, learner-educators. Their act of knowing is elaborated in the *circulo de cultura* (cultural discussion group) which functions as the theoretical context.

In Brazil, before analyzing the learners' existential situations and the generative words contained in them, we proposed the codified theme of man-world relationships in general.[20] In Chile, at the suggestion of Chilean educators, this important dimension was discussed concurrently with learning to read and write. What is important is that the person learning words be concomitantly engaged in a critical analysis of the social framework in which men exist. For example, the word *favela* in Rio de

Janeiro, Brazil, and the word *callampa* in Chile, represent, each with its own nuances, the same social, economic, and cultural reality of the vast numbers of slum dwellers in those countries. If *favela* and *callampa* are used as generative words for the people of Brazilian and Chilean slums, the codifications will have to represent slum situations.

There are many people who consider slum dwellers marginal, intrinsically wicked and inferior. To such people we recommend the profitable experience of discussing the slum situation with slum dwellers themselves. As some of these critics are often simply mistaken, it is possible that they may rectify their mythical clichés and assume a more scientific attitude. They may avoid saying that the illiteracy, alcoholism, and crime of the slums, that its sickness, infant mortality, learning deficiencies, and poor hygiene reveal the "inferior nature" of its inhabitants. They may even end up realizing that if intrinsic evil exists it is part of the structures, and that it is the structures which need to be transformed.

It should be pointed out that the Third World as a whole, and more in some parts than in others, suffers from the same misunderstanding from certain sectors of the so-called metropolitan societies. They see the Third World as the incarnation of evil, the primitive, the devil, sin and sloth—in sum, as historically unviable without the director societies. Such a manichean attitude is at the source of the impulse to "save" the "demon-possessed" Third World, "educating it" and "correcting its thinking" according to the director societies' own criteria.

The expansionist interests of the director societies are implicit in such notions. These societies can never relate to the Third World as partners, since partnership presupposes equals, no matter how different the equal parties may be, and can never be established between parties antagonistic to each other.

Thus, "salvation" of the Third World by the director societies can only mean its domination, whereas in its legitimate aspiration to independence lies its utopian vision: to save the director societies in the very act of freeing itself.

In this sense the pedagogy which we defend, conceived in a significant area of the Third World, is itself a utopian pedagogy. By this very fact it is full of hope, for to be utopian is not to be merely idealistic or impractical but rather to engage in denunciation and annunciation. Our pedagogy cannot do without a vision of man and of the world. It formulates a scientific humanist conception which finds its expression in a dialogical praxis in which the teachers and learners together, in the act of analyzing a dehumanizing reality, denounce it while announcing its transformation in the name of the liberation of man.

For this very reason, denunciation and annunciation in this utopian pedagogy are not meant to be empty words, but an historic commitment. Denunciation of a dehumanizing situation today increasingly demands precise scientific understanding of that situation. Likewise, the annunciation of its transformation increasingly requires a theory of transforming action. However, neither act by itself implies the transformation of the denounced reality or the establishment of that which is announced. Rather, as a moment in an historical process, the announced reality is already present in the act of denunciation and annunciation.[21]

That is why the utopian character of our educational theory and practice is as permanent as education itself which, for us, is cultural action. Its thrust toward denunciation and annunciation cannot be exhausted when the reality denounced today cedes its place tomorrow to the reality previously announced in the denunciation. When education is no longer utopian, *i.e.*, when it no longer embodies the dramatic unity of denunciation and annunciation, it is either because the future has no more meaning for men, or because men are afraid to risk living the future as creative overcoming of the present, which has become old.

The more likely explanation is generally the latter. That is why some people today study all the possibilities which the future contains, in order to "domesticate" it and keep it in line with the present, which is what they intend to maintain. If there is any anguish in director societies hidden beneath the cover of their cold technology, it springs from their desperate determination that their metropolitan status be preserved in the future. Among the things which the Third World may learn from the metropolitan societies there is this that is fundamental: not to replicate those societies when its current utopia becomes actual fact.

When we defend such a conception of education—realistic precisely to the extent that it is utopian—that is, to the extent that it denounces what in fact is, and finds therefore between denunciation and its realization the time of its praxis—we are attempting to formulate a type of education which corresponds to the specifically human mode of being, which is historical.

There is no annunciation without denunciation, just as every denunciation generates annunciation. Without the latter, hope is impossible. In an authentic utopian vision, however, hoping does not mean folding one's arms and waiting. Waiting is only possible when one, filled with hope, seeks through reflective action to achieve that announced future which is being born within the denunciation.

That is why there is no genuine hope in those who intend to make the future repeat their present, nor in those who see the future as something predetermined. Both have a "domesticated" notion of history: the former because they want to stop time; the latter because they are certain about a future they already "know." Utopian hope, on the contrary, is engagement full of risk. That is why the dominators, who merely denounce those who denounce them, and who have nothing to announce but the preservation of the status quo, can never be utopian nor, for that matter, prophetic.[22]

A utopian pedagogy of denunciation and annunciation such as ours will have to be an act of knowing the denounced reality at the level of alphabetization and post-alphabetization, which are in each case cultural action. That is why there is such emphasis on the continual problematization of the learners' existential situations as represented in the codified images. The longer the problematization proceeds, and the more the subjects enter into the "essence" of the problematized object, the more they are able to unveil their "essence." The more they unveil it, the more their awakening consciousness deepens, thus leading to the "conscientization" of the situation by the poor classes. Their critical self-insertion into reality, *i.e.*, their conscientization, makes the transformation of their state of apathy into the utopian state of *denunciation* and *annunciation* a viable project.

One must not think, however, that learning to read and write precedes "conscientization," or vice-versa. Conscientization occurs simultaneously with the literacy or post-literacy process. It must be so. In our educational method, the word is not something static or disconnected from men's existential experience, but a dimension of their thought-language about the world. That is why, when they participate critically in analyzing the first generative words linked with their existential experience; when they focus on the syllabic families which result from that analysis; when they perceive the mechanism of the syllabic combinations of their language, the learners finally discover, in the various possibilities of combination, their own words. Little by little, as these possibilities multiply, the learners, through mastery of new generative words, expand both their vocabulary and their capacity for expression by the development of their creative imagination.[23]

In some areas in Chile undergoing agrarian reform, the peasants participating in the literacy programs wrote words with their tools on the dirt roads where they were working. They composed the words from the syllabic combinations they were learning. "These men are sowers of the word," said Maria Edi Ferreira, a sociologist from the Santiago team working in the Institute of Training and Research in Agrarian Reform. Indeed, they were not only sowing words, but discussing ideas, and coming to understand their role in the world better and better.

We asked one of these "sowers of words," finishing the first level of literacy classes, why he hadn't learned to read and write before the agrarian reform.

"Before the agrarian reform, my friend," he said, "I didn't even think. Neither did my friends."

"Why?" we asked.

"Because it wasn't possible. We lived under orders. We only had to carry out orders. We had nothing to say," he replied emphatically.

The simple answer of this peasant is a very clear analysis of "the culture of silence." In "the culture of silence," to exist is only to live. The body carries out orders from above. Thinking is difficult, speaking the word, forbidden.

"When all this land belonged to one *latifundio*," said another man in the same conversation, "there was no reason to read and write. We weren't responsible for anything. The boss gave the orders and we obeyed. Why read and write? Now it's a different story. Take me, for example. In the *asentamiento*,[24] I am responsible not only for my work like all the other men, but also for tool repairs. When I started I couldn't read, but I soon realized that I needed to read and write. You can't imagine what it was like to go to Santiago to buy parts. I couldn't get orientated. I was afraid of everything—afraid of the big city, of buying the wrong thing, of being cheated. Now it's all different."

Observe how precisely this peasant described his former experience as an illiterate: his mistrust, his magical (though logical) fear of the world; his timidity. And observe the sense of scrutiny, with which he repeats, "Now it's all different."

"What did you feel, my friend," we asked another "sower of words" on a different occasion, "when you were able to write and read your first word?"

"I was happy because I discovered I could make words speak," he replied.

Dario Salas reports,[25] "In our conversations with peasants we were struck by the images they used to express their interest and satisfaction about becoming literate. For example, 'Before we were blind, now the veil has fallen from our eyes'; 'I came only to learn how to sign my name. I never believed I would be able to read, too, at my age'; 'Before, letters seemed like little puppets. Today they say something to me, and I can make them talk.'

"It is touching," continues Salas, "to observe the delight of the peasants as the world of words opens to them. Sometimes they would say, 'We're so tired our heads ache, but we don't want to leave here without learning to read and write.' "[26]

The following words were taped during research on "generative themes."[27] They are an illiterate's decodification of a codified existential situation.

"You see a house there, sad, as if it were abandoned. When you see a house with a child in it, it seems happier. It gives more joy and peace to people passing by. The father of the family arrives home from work exhausted, worried, bitter, and his little boy comes to meet him with a big hug, because a little boy is not stiff like a big person. The father already begins to be happier just from seeing his children. Then he really enjoys himself. He is moved by his son's wanting to please him. The father becomes more peaceful, and forgets his problems."

Note once again the simplicity of expression, both profound and elegant, in the peasant's language. These are the people considered absolutely ignorant by the proponents of the "digestive" concept of literacy.

In 1968, an Uruguayan team published a small book, *You Live as You Can (Se Vive como se Puede),* whose contents are taken from the tape recordings of literacy classes for urban dwellers. Its first edition of three thousand copies was sold out in Montevideo in fifteen days, as was the second edition. The following is an excerpt from this book.

### THE COLOR OF WATER

Water? Water? What is water used for?
"Yes, yes, we saw it (in the picture)."
"Oh, my native village, so far away. . . ."
"Do you remember that village?"
"The stream where I grew up, called Dead Friar . . . you know, I grew up there, a childhood moving from one place to another . . . the color of the water brings back good memories, beautiful memories."
"What is the water used for?"
"It is used for washing. We used it to wash clothes, and the animals in the fields used to go there to drink, and we washed ourselves there, too."
"Did you also use the water for drinking?"
"Yes, when we were at the stream and had no other water to drink, we drank from the stream. I remember once in 1945 a plague of locusts came from somewhere, and we had to fish them out of the water . . . I was small, but I

remember taking out the locusts like this, with my two hands—and I had no others. And I remember how hot the water was when there was a drought and the stream was almost dry . . . the water was dirty, muddy, and hot, with all kinds of things in it. But we had to drink it or die of thirst."

The whole book is like this, pleasant in style, with great strength of expression of the world of its authors, those anonymous people, "sowers of words," seeking to emerge from "the culture of silence."

Yes, these ought to be the reading texts for people learning to read and write, and not "Eva saw the grape," "The bird's wing," "If you hammer a nail, be careful not to hit your fingers." Intellectual prejudices and above all class prejudices are responsible for the naive and unfounded notions that the people cannot write their own texts, or that a tape of their conversations is valueless since their conversations are impoverished of meaning. Comparing what the "sowers of words" said in the above references with what is generally written by specialist authors of reading lessons, we are convinced that only someone with very pronounced lack of taste or a lamentable scientific incompetency would choose the specialists' texts.

Imagine a book written entirely in this simple, poetic, free, language of the people, a book on which inter-disciplinary teams would collaborate in the spirit of true dialogue. The role of the teams would be to elaborate specialized sections of the book in problematic terms. For example, a section on linguistics would deal simply, thought not simplistically, with questions fundamental to the learners' critical understanding of language. Let me emphasize again that since one of the important aspects of adult literacy work is the development of the capacity for expression, the section on linguistics would present themes for the learners to discuss, ranging from the increase of vocabulary to questions about communication—including the study of synonyms and antonyms, with its analysis of words in the linguistic context, and the use of metaphor, of which the people are such masters. Another section might provide the tools for a sociological analysis of the content of the texts.

These texts would not, of course, be used for mere mechanical reading, which leaves the readers without any understanding of what is real. Consistent with the nature of this pedagogy, they would become the object of analysis in reading seminars.

Add to all this the great stimulus it would be for those learning to read and write, as well as for students on more advanced levels, to know that they were reading and discussing the work of their own companions. . . .

To undertake such a work, it is necessary to have faith in the people, solidarity with them. It is necessary to be utopian, in the sense in which we have used the word.

## Notes

1. In languages like Portuguese or Spanish, words are composed syllabically. Thus, every non-monosyllabic word is, technically, *generative,* in the sense that other words can be constructed from its de-composed syllables. For a word to be authentically generative, however, certain conditions must be present which will be discussed in a later section of this essay. [At the phonetic level the term *generative word* is properly applicable only with regard to a sound-syllabic reading

methodology, while the thematic application is universal. See Sylvia Ashton-Warner's *Teacher* for a different treatment of the concept of generative words at the thematic level.–Editor]

2. Jean Paul Sartre, *Situations I* (Paris: Librairie Gallimard, 1947), p. 31.

3. The digestive concept of knowledge is suggested by "controlled readings," by classes which consist only in lectures; by the use of memorized dialogues in language learning; by bibliographical notes which indicate not only which chapter, but which lines and words are to be read; by the methods of evaluating the students' progress in learning.

4. See Paulo Freire, "La alfabetizacion de adultos, critica de su vision ingenua; compreension de su vision critica," in *Introduction a la Acción Cultural* (Santiago: ICIRA, 1969).

5. There are two noteworthy exceptions among these primers: (1) in Brazil, *Viver e Lutar*, developed by a team of specialists of the Basic Education Movement, sponsored by the National Conference of Bishops. (This reader became the object of controversy after it was banned as subversive by the then governor of Guanabara, Mr. Carlos Lacerda, in 1963.) (2) in Chile, the ESPIGA collection, despite some small defects. The collection was organized by Jefatura de Planes Extraordinarios de Educación de Adultos, of the Public Education Ministry.

6. Since at the time this essay was written the writer did not have access to the primers, and was, therefore, vulnerable to recording phrases imprecisely or to confusing the author of one or another primer, it was thought best not to identify the authors or the titles of the books.

7. The English here would be nonsensical, as is the Portuguese, the point being the emphasis on the consonant *d*.—Editor

8. The author may even have added here, " . . . If, however, this should happen, apply a little mercurochrome."

9. [The Portuguese word here translated as *marginal man* is *marginado*. This has a passive sense: he who has been made marginal, or sent outside society; as well as the sense of a state of existence on the fringe of society.—Translator.]

10. UNESCO: La situación educativa en América Latina, Cuadro no. 20, page 263 (Paris, 1960).

11. Paulo Freire, "La alfabetizacion de adultos."

12. "There are two ways to fall into idealism: The one consists of dissolving the real in subjectivity; the other in denying all real subjectivity in the interests of objectivity." Jean Paul Sartre, *Search for a Method*, trans. Hazel E. Barnes (New York: Vintage Books, 1968), p. 33.

13. See Karel Kosik, *Dialectica de lo Concreto* (Mexico: Grijalbo, 1967).

14. [*Codification* refers alternatively to the imaging, or the image itself, of some significant aspect of the learner's concrete reality (of a slum dwelling, for example). As such, it becomes both the object of the teacher-learner dialogue and the context for the introduction of the generative word.—Editor]

15. [*Decodification* refers to a process of description and interpretation, whether of printed words, pictures, or other "codifications." As such, decodification and decodifying are distinct from the process of decoding, or word-recognition.—Editor.]

16. Re the oppressed consciousness, see: Frantz Fanon, *The Wretched of the Earth* (New York: Grove Press, 1968); Albert Memmi, *Colonizer and the Colonized* (New York: Orion Press, 1965); and Paulo Freire, *Pedagogy of the Oppressed* (New York: Seabury Press, 1970).

17. See Fanon, *The Wretched*; Freire, *Pedagogy*.

18. See Louis Althusser, *Pour Marx* (Paris: Librairie François Maspero, 1965); and Paulo Freire, *Annual Report: Activities for 1968, Agrarian Reform, Training and Research Institute ICIRA, Chile*, trans. John Dewitt, Center for the Study of Development and Social Change, Cambridge, Mass., 1969 (mimeographed).

19. We observed in Brazil and Spanish America, especially Chile, that no more than seventeen words were necessary for teaching adults to read and write syllabic languages like Portuguese and Spanish.

20. See Paulo Freire, *Educacao como Pratica da Liberdade* (Rio de Janeiro: Paz e Terra, 1967). Chilean Edition (Santiago: ICIRA, 1969).

21. Re the utopian dimension of denunciation and proclamation, see Leszek Kolakowski, *Toward a Marxist Humanism* (New York: Grove Press, 1969).

22. "The right, as a conservative force, needs no utopia; its essence is the affirmation of existing conditions—a fact and not a utopia—or else the desire to revert to a state which was once an accomplished fact. The Right strives to idealize actual conditions, not to change them. What it needs is fraud not utopia." Kolakowski, *Toward a Marxist Humanism*, pp. 71–72.

23. "We have observed that the study of the creative aspect of language use develops the assumption that linguistic and mental process are virtually identical, language providing the primary means for free expansion of thought and feeling, as well as for the functioning of creative imagination." Noam Chomsky, *Cartesian Linguistics* (New York: Harper & Row, 1966), p. 31.

24. After the disappropriation of lands in the agrarian reform in Chile, the peasants who were

salaried workers on the large latifundia become "settlers" (*asentados*) during a three-year period in which they receive varied assistance from the government through the Agrarian Reform Corporation. This period of "settlement" (*asentamiento*) precedes that of assigning lands to the peasants. This policy is now changing. The phase of "settlement" of the lands is being abolished, in favor of an immediate distribution of lands to the peasants. The Agrarian Reform Corporation will continue, nevertheless, to aid the peasants.

25. Dario Salas, "Algumas experiencias vividas na Supervisao de Educacao basica," in *A alfabetizacao funcional no Chile*. Report to UNESCO, November, 1968, Introduction: Paulo Freire.

26. Dario Salas refers here to one of the best adult education programs organized by the Agrarian Reform Corporation in Chile, in strict collaboration with the Ministry of Education and ICIRA. Fifty peasants receive boarding and instruction scholarships for a month. The courses center on discussions of the local, regional, and national situations.

27. An analysis of the objectives and methodology of the investigation of generative themes lies outside the scope of this essay, but is dealt with in the author's work, *Pedagogy of the Oppressed*.

# Essay Review

## The Legacies of Literacy: From Plato to Freire through Harvey Graff

JAMES PAUL GEE
*University of Southern California*

THE LEGACIES OF LITERACY: CONTINUITIES AND
CONTRADICTIONS IN WESTERN CULTURE AND SOCIETY
by H. G. Graff.
*Bloomington: Indiana University Press, 1987. 494 pp.*

> The most revolutionary event in the history of writing came with the introduction of signs correlated not with things or ideas or even whole words, but with individual sounds, thereby enabling men easily to transcribe speech. Our alphabet is a product of this revolution. . . . (Pattison, 1982, p. 35)

> The introduction of the Greek letters into inscription somewhere about 700 B.C. was to alter the character of human culture, placing a gulf between all alphabetic societies and their precursors. The Greeks did not just invent an alphabet; they invented literacy and the literate basis of modern thought. (Havelock, 1982, p. 82)

> Oral cultures indeed produce powerful and beautiful verbal performances of high artistic and human worth, which are no longer even possible once writing has taken possession of the psyche. Nevertheless, without writing, human consciousness cannot achieve its fuller potentials, cannot produce other beautiful and powerful creations. . . . There is hardly an oral culture or a predominantly oral culture left in the world today that is not somehow aware of the vast complex of powers forever inaccessible without literacy. . . .

> Without writing, the literate mind would not and could not think as it does, not only when engaged in writing but normally even when it is composing its thoughts in oral form. More than any other single invention, writing has transformed human consciousness. (Ong, 1982, pp. 14–15, 78)

A note before we start in earnest: What follows is a reflection of the history of literacy, a reflection that stems from a consideration of Harvey Graff's new book, *The Legacies of Literacy: Continuities and Contradictions in Western Culture and Society.* Graff (1979, 1981a, 1981b, 1986, 1987a, 1987b; Graff & Arnove, 1987) has become a leading figure in current work on literacy which seeks to reappraise, from a variety of perspectives (sociocultural, historical, and cognitive), the significance and role of

*Harvard Educational Review*   Vol. 58   No. 2   May 1988, 195–212

literacy and schooling. (A very small and selective sample includes Bourdieu & Passeron, 1977; Bowles & Gintis, 1976; Cazden, 1987; Clanchy, 1979; Cook-Gumperz, 1986; Eagleton, 1984; Gee, 1986a, 1986b, 1987, in press; Giroux, 1983; Heath, 1983; Hymes, 1980; Lemke, 1986; Michaels, 1981; Ohmann, 1976; Scollon & Scollon, 1981; Scribner & Cole, 1981; Street, 1984; Willis, 1981.) Though I will take Graff's *Legacies of Literacy* as my focus, I should point out that readers will find much of the same material, in more digestible form, in his collection of articles that appeared at the same time, *The Labyrinths of Literacy: Reflections on Literacy Past and Present* (1987b). In this latter book, the force of Graff's explanatory framework emerges more clearly, less hidden by the wealth of historical detail which is the hallmark of *Legacies*, a book which Graff (1987b, p. 6) describes as his "culminating interpretive synthesis." Finally, let me point out that the remarks in this paper should be read as proposing a problem/ question, not as supplying an answer. I attempt to make the case that the problem/ question must be taken quite seriously and requires an answer from each reader in the form of his or her own "theory of literacy." As the reader will see, given where I start (Plato) and where I end (Freire), I am on unsafe ground indeed if I propose anything other than a dialogue with the reader (if this is in fact possible in writing, which is part of the problem/question).

To begin, then. Literacy leads to logical and analytic modes of thought; general and abstract uses of language; critical and rational thought; a skeptical and questioning attitude; a distinction between myth and history; the recognition of the importance of time and space; complex and modern governments (with separation of church and state); political democracy and greater social equity; economic development; wealth and productivity; political stability; urbanization; and contraception (lower birth rate). It leads to people who are innovative, achievement oriented, productive, cosmopolitan, politically aware, more globally (nationally and internationally) and less locally oriented, who have more liberal and humane social attitudes, are less likely to commit a crime, and more likely to take education and the rights and duties of citizenship seriously. The common popular and scholarly conception that literacy has such powerful effects as these constitutes what Graff refers to as a "literacy myth."

Graff clearly demonstrates that there is precious little historical evidence for the literacy myth. And where such evidence does exist, the role of literacy is always more complex and contradictory, more deeply intertwined with other factors, than the literacy myth allows. As the final products of nearly four thousand years of an alphabetic literacy, we all tend to believe strongly in the powerful and redeeming effects of literacy, especially in times of complex social and economic crises (Goody, 1977, 1986; Goody & Watt, 1963; Havelock, 1963, 1982, 1986; Olson, 1977; Ong, 1982). Graff seeks both to take away our "crutch," and to reconceptualize the role of literacy in history and in society. In the United States today, we are once again in the midst of a widely proclaimed "literacy crisis" (Hirsch, 1987; Kozol, 1985), with virtual calls to arms in a war against illiteracy nationally and internationally (Graff points out that such "crises" are a recurrent motif in the history of literacy). While those waving the banners are fervent adherents of the literacy myth, I would argue in this article, as Graff does in much of his work, that, at least in academic circles, the literacy myth is on its last legs. The center of attention is shifting, in much current work, to the often ignored language and literacy skills of non-mainstream people and to the ways in which mainstream, school-based literacy often serves to perpetuate social inequality while claiming, via the literacy myth, to mitigate it (see, for example, the papers in Cook-Gumperz, 1986). In fact, it may be that the current fears and alarms over illiteracy mask deeper, more complex, and less socially acceptable fears. Consider, for instance, that within the next decade the total number of young adults aged 21–25 will shrink from around 21 million to roughly 17 million and will comprise a significantly larger proportion of persons of color, who will perforce be able to demand a much more significant social and economic role in the society (Kirsch & Jungeblut, 1986).

Graff, though a leader, is but one in the forefront of the current battle against the simplifications in the literacy myth. The first shot in the battle was fired a bare three hundred years or so after the invention of alphabetic literacy. And in many ways the first shot was the best. It was, at any rate, rife with implications for the thousands of years of literacy that have followed it. If the Greeks invented the basis of Western literacy, Plato was the first great literate in Western culture (in fact, his dialogues were both great literature and great discursive, expository writing). Plato also has the distinction of being the first writer to attack writing in writing, primarily in his brilliant dialogue, the *Phaedrus* (Rowe, 1986; see also Burger, 1980; Derrida, 1972; De Vries, 1969; Griswold, 1986). To start with, Plato thought writing led to the deterioration of human memory and to a view of knowledge which was both facile and false. Given writing, knowledge no longer had to be internalized, made "part of oneself." Rather, writing allowed, perhaps even encouraged, a reliance on the written text as an "external crutch" or "reminder." For Plato, one knew only what one could reflectively defend in face-to-face dialogue with someone else. The written text tempted one to take its words as authoritative and final because of its illusory quality of seeming to be explicit, clear, complete, closed, and self-sufficient— that is, "unanswerable" (precisely the properties which, under the rubric of "the decontextualized nature of written language," have been seen as the hallmarks of the essay and so-called "essayist literacy"; see Scollon & Scollon, 1981).

In addition to these flaws in writing, two others were far more important to Plato. To cite the dialogue, the first of these follows:

> *Socrates:* I think writing has this strange feature, which makes it like painting. The offspring of painting stand there as if alive, but if you ask them something, they preserve a quite solemn silence. Similarly with written words: you might think that they spoke as if they had some thought in their heads, but if you ever ask them about any of the things they say out of a desire to learn, they point to just one thing, the same thing each time. (275d4–275e1)

Socrates goes on immediately to the second charge:

> And when once it is written, every composition is trundled about everywhere in the same way, in the presence both of those who know about the subject and

of those who have nothing at all to do with it, and it does not know how to address those it should address and not those it should not. When it is ill-treated and unjustly abused, it always needs its father to help it; for it is incapable of defending or helping itself. (275e1–275e6)

These charges are connected. What writing can't do is defend itself; it can't stand up to questioning. For Plato, true knowledge comes when one person makes a statement and another asks, "What do you mean?" Such a request forces the speaker to "re-say," that is, to say in different words, what he or she means. In the process he sees more deeply what he means, and responds to the perspective of another voice/viewpoint. In one sense, writing can only respond to the question, what do you mean? by repeating what it has said (the text). At this juncture of the argument Plato extends his charges against writing to an attack also on rhetoricians and politicians (he referred to both as "speech writers"). They sought in their writing and speeches to forestall questioning altogether, since their primary interest was to persuade (through language that claimed to be logically complete and self-sufficient, standing in no need of supplement or rethinking, authoritative in its own right), not to discover the truth in mutual dialogue.

There is a sense, however, in which writing *can* respond to the question, what do you mean? It can do so when the reader re-says, in *his or her own* words, what the text means. But this is a problem for Plato. It is, in fact, part of what he has in mind when he says that writing "does not know how to address those it should address and not those it should not." By its very nature writing can travel in time and space away from its author (for Plato, its "father") to be read by just anyone, interpreted however they will, regardless of the reader's training, effort, or ignorance (witness what happened to Nietzsche in the hands of the Nazis; to the Bible in the hands of those who have used it to justify wealth, racism, imperialism, war, and exploitation). The voice behind the text cannot respond or defend itself. And it cannot vary its substance and tone to speak differently to different readers based on their natures and contexts.

Plato was too sophisticated to make a crude distinction between speech and writing, orality and literacy. He extended his attack to the poets, and in particular to Homer, the great representative of the flourishing oral culture that preceded Greek literacy. The oral culture stored its knowledge, values, and norms in great oral epics (such as the *Iliad* and the *Odyssey*), passed down from generation to generation. To ensure that these epics, and with them the cultural knowledge and values they stored, were not lost to memory, they had to be highly memorable. Thus, they were highly dramatic (built around action) and rhythmical (a species of song), features that fa-cilitate human memory. That is, they had to be a form of poetry (Havelock, 1963; Ong, 1982). But, Plato argued, the oral tradition via its very drama and poetry lulled the Greeks to sleep and encouraged them to "take for granted" the contents of the epics, thus allowing them to accept uncritically the traditional values of their culture. The oral epic also could not stand up to the question, what do you mean? Such a question was a request to the poet to re-say his or her words in a different form, to take them out of poetry and put them into prose, thus causing the words to lose the power which had lulled the Greeks into a "dream state" (Havelock, 1963). Here, writing *facilitated* the critical process. Once written down, the epics could be scanned at leisure, various parts of the text could be juxtaposed, and in the process contradictions and inconsistencies were easier to find, no longer hidden under the waves of rhythm and the limitations of human aural memory (Goody, 1977, 1986; Havelock, 1963; Ong, 1982).

Plato's deeper attack, then, is against any form of language or thought that cannot stand up to the question, what do you mean? That question tries to unmask attempts to persuade (whether by poets, rhetoricians, or politicians) based on self-interested claims to authority or traditionalism, and not on a genuine disinterested search for truth. In this regard, he reminds one of the currently popular (and fashionable) Russian writer, Mikhail Bakhtin (1981; see also Clark & Holquist, 1984; Todorov, 1984):

> Bakhtin continually sought and found unexpected ways to show that people never utter a final word, only a penultimate one. The opportunity always remains for appending a qualification that may lead to yet another unanticipated dialogue.
>
> . . .
>
> Perhaps the sudden and dramatic interest in Bakhtin arises from his emphasis on debate as open, fruitful, and existentially meaningful at a time when our theoretical writings have become increasingly closed, repetitive, and "professional."
>
> Genuine dialogue always presupposes that something, but not everything, can be known. "It should be noted," Bakhtin wrote " . . . that both relativism and dogmatism equally exclude all argumentation, all authentic dialogue, by making it either unnecessary (relativism) or impossible (dogmatism)." (Morson, 1986, pp. vii–viii)

Plato, then, considered only dialogic thought, speaking, and writing authentic, with the proviso that writing was inherently prone to anti-dialogic properties. Plato's own resolution to this conflict, as a writer, was to write dialogues and to warn that writing of any sort should never be taken too seriously. It should never be taken as seriously as the "writing" that is "written together with knowledge in the soul of the learner, capable of defending itself, and knowing how to speak and keep silent in relation to the people it should" (276a5–276a8). For Plato, authentic uses of language were always educational in the root sense of "drawing out" of oneself and others what was good, beautiful, and true.

All this may make Plato sound like a progressive, modern educator defending "open classrooms" and "process" approaches to writing and speaking. He was no such thing. Plato's concerns about writing had a darker, more political side, one pregnant for the future of literacy. Both Socrates and Plato were opponents of the traditional order of their societies, and in that sense, revolutionaries. In the *Republic*, Plato drew a blueprint for a utopian, "perfect" state that he wished to put in place of the current order. (See Havelock, 1963; for a consideration of Plato's *Republic* in the context of the history of political thought in Western culture, see Leo Strauss's article on Plato in Strauss & Cropsey, 1987, as well as the other articles in this volume.) Plato's perfect state was based on the view that people are by and large born for a particular place in a naturally given hierarchy, with "philosopher-kings" (that is, Plato or people like him) at the top (or at least given differential access to higher places in society based on inherent characteristics and various tests.) The philosopher-kings rule in the best interests of those below them, many of whom have no actual say in government, the philosopher-king knowing their interests better than they do. In this light, Homer, the rhetoricians, and the politicians can be seen as Plato's political opposition, competitors in the philosopher-king's assertion to power. As long as Greek culture was swept away in rhapsody by Homer's epic verse, its members were not listening either to the oral or written dialogues of Plato. Plato's tactic (originated by Socrates) of confronting the poets with the question, what do you mean?—forcing them into prose—was both an intellectually and a politically motivated attempt to break the power base of Homer and traditional culture (Havelock, 1963). This question had a related effect when asked of the politicians, speechwriters, and lawgivers who controlled the new Greek literacy. It was a request for them to say what they had just said over again, but in less rhetorically persuasive language. Stripped of its "rhetoric," their language revealed power seeking, lack of critical thought, and self-interest. And in the process they were also rendered vulnerable to a political assault by Plato's dialectic and its assumptions about what is right and just (in other words, the invitation to "dialogue" with Plato, given his skills, was not likely to show the politicians and rhetoricians to their best advantage).

With this understanding, Plato's attack on writing takes on additional meaning. His objection that the written text can get into the wrong hands, that it cannot defend itself, is an objection to the fact that the reader can freely interpret the text without the author ("authority") being able to "correct" that interpretation; that is, to stipulate the correct interpretation. In this sense, Plato wants the author to stand as a voice behind the text not just to engage in responsive dialogue, but to enforce canonical interpretations. And these canonical interpretations are rendered correct by the inherently higher nature of the philosopher-king, backed by the advantages (which the *Republic* ensures) of socially situated power and state-supported practice in verbal and literacy skills. As a writer, Plato also had a resolution to the problem of how to enforce "correct" interpretation. First, he believed that his writings should be restricted mainly to his own inner circle of students and followers. Second, it appears he may not have written his most serious thoughts, but only spoken them (none of his dialogues contains a discussion between two mature philosophers). And, finally, he invested his written dialogues with layers of meaning, so that they announce their deeper message only to those readers skilled enough to find it, a skill tied to being trained (or "initiated") to interpret the way one is "supposed" to (Griswold, 1986, p. 221). The same strategy is used in many sacred writings; for example, in the New Testament (see Kermode, 1979). His ultimate solution, however, would have been the instantiation of the society delineated in the *Republic,* where the structure of the state and its institutions would have ensured "correct" interpretations. As we will see, this last solution is the one that has in fact been realized most often in history (though not by states realizing all the other aspects of the *Republic*).

There is a contradiction here. In Plato we see two sides to literacy: literacy as liberator and literacy as weapon. Plato wants to ensure that a voice behind the spoken or written "text" can dialogically respond, but he also wants to ensure that this voice is not overridden by respondents who are careless, ignorant, lazy, self-interested, or ignoble. One must somehow empower the voice behind the text, privilege it, at least to the extent of ruling out some interpretations and some interpreters (readers/listeners). And such a ruling-out will always be self-interested to the extent that it must be based on some privileged view of what the text means, what correct interpretations are, and who are acceptable readers (where acceptable readers will perforce include the one making the ruling). The ruling is also self-interested in that it has a political dimension, an assertion to power, a power that may reside in institutions that seek to enforce it (whether modern schools and universities or Plato's governing classes in the *Republic*). But then we are close to an authority that kills dialogue by dictating who is to count as a respondent and what is to count as a response. There is, however, no easy solution: if all interpretations (re-sayings) count, then none do, as the text then says everything and therefore nothing. And if it takes no discipline, experience, or "credentials" to interpret, then it seems all interpretations *will* count. If they can't all count, then someone has to say who does and who does not have the necessary credentials to interpret. A desire to honor the thoughtful and critical voice behind the text, to allow it to defend itself (often coupled with a will to power), leads us to Plato's authoritarianism. In fleeing it, we are in danger of being led right into the lap of Plato's poets, speechwriters, and politicians. For them, all that counts is the persuasiveness or cunning of their language, its ability to capture the reader, to tell him or her what he or she wants to hear, to validate the status quo (and therefore the views the reader in all likelihood already holds and which form the basis for his or her interpretations). Their interest is decidedly not in the capacity of their language to educate the reader or listener in the root sense discussed above.

There have been many facile attempts to get out of Plato's dilemma. But there is no easy way out. Claude Lévi-Strauss (1978) has argued that what creates and energizes mythology is the existence of a real contradiction that cannot be removed (for example, life and death, nature and culture, God and human), but simply reworked continually by the imagination in an ultimately vain, but temporarily satisfying, attempt to resolve it. Plato's contradiction is real, and the literacy myth can be seen as a response to it.

Although Graff devotes but a single paragraph to Plato (p. 24), he places the notion of contradiction at the center of his study. Virtually every aspect of the history of literacy that he surveys can be read as a real-world commentary on Plato's thoughts. The central contradiction that emerges from Graff's book is the disparity between the claims in the literacy myth and the actual history of literacy (much of it produced by people who firmly believed in the literacy myth). Let us take one particularly revealing snapshot from the history of literacy: Sweden. Sweden was the first country in the West to achieve near-universal literacy, having done so before the end of the eighteenth century. Women had equality with men in literacy (an equality that does not exist even now in most of the world). By the tenets of the literacy myth, Sweden should have been an international example of modernization, social equality, economic development, and cognitive growth. In fact, however, it was not. Sweden's remarkable achievement took place in a land of widespread poverty, for the most part without formal institutional schooling, and it neither followed from nor stimulated economic development. Sweden achieved its impressive level of reading diffusion without writing, which did not become a part of popular literacy until the mid-nineteenth century. And, furthermore, the quality of the literacy was far behind its quantity. Graff reports that even in the nineteenth century, more than a hundred years after Sweden's achievement:

> according to reading and comprehension tests, good reading ability did not relate strongly to the ability to understand. Popular skills tested well in assessments of oral reading and in memorization. They were, however, much less useful when it came to comprehension. . . .
> Even near-universal Swedish literacy was stratified. . . . Not surprisingly, members of the high-ranking and wealthy families scored highest on reading tests. . . . (p. 310)

How did Sweden manage the feat of universal literacy? The Swedish literacy campaign, one of the most successful in the Western world, was stimulated by the Reformation and Lutheran Protestantism. Teaching was done on a household basis (hence the emphasis on the literacy of women), supervised and reinforced by the parish church and clergy, with regular compulsory examinations:

> people were persuaded to learn to read by means of an actual campaign initiated for political and religious reasons. . . . The social pressure was enormous. Everybody in the household and in the village gathered once a year to take part in examinations in reading and knowledge of the Bible. The adult who failed these examinations was excluded from both communion and marriage. (Egil Johansson, 1977; cited in Graff, p. 149)

The goal of literacy in Sweden was the promotion of Christian faith and life, the promotion of character and citizenship training in a religiously dominated state. The campaign was based not just on compulsion, but on the individual's felt religious need, a need internalized in village reading and family prayers. Religious, social, and political ideologies were transmitted to virtually everyone through literacy learning. The Church Law of 1686 stated that children, farmhands, and maid-servants should "learn to read and see with their own eyes what God bids and commands in His Holy Word" (p. 150). Note the phrase "with their own eyes": literally they see it with their own eyes, but figuratively they see it through the eyes of the state church that dictates how it is to be seen. Plato's dilemma haunts us. The people are given the text for themselves, but then something must ensure that they see it "right," from the perspective of an authoritative institution that delimits correct interpretations. The individual reader does not need deep comprehension skills and surely doesn't need to write.

This problem—that people might not see the text in the right way—plagued both

Protestant and Catholic countries, but the two hit on somewhat different solutions. Catholic-dominated countries were much more reluctant to put the Bible and other sacred texts into the hands of the people, for fear they would not interpret them correctly (for example, using them as the basis for political or religious dissent). They preferred to leave interpretation to the oral word of Church authorities. When the Catholic Church did allow sacred texts into the hands of the people:

> The authorities perceived the dangers of print and of individual, unmediated access to the Holy Writ. Their answer was to make the text safe; that was attempted by wrapping it in orthodox exposition, in which the Jesuits were especially active. They attempted to fix the meaning of devotional works by accompanying them with standardized religious illustrations. Catholic people were permitted an increasing amount of spiritual literature "in which the eye was guided by exposition and illustration." (p. 147)

As a result of these attitudes, Catholic countries tended to be less literate than areas of intense Protestant piety (such as Sweden, lowland Scotland, New England, Huguenot French centers, and places within Germany and Switzerland). But we should ask: Is there any essential difference between the sort of literacy in eighteenth- and nineteenth-century Sweden and in a country with quantitatively more restricted literacy, but equally dominant modes of interpretation ensconced in its powerful religious and civil institutions? Some would argue that there is a difference and that the difference is in the *capacity* of literacy to give rise to dissent and critical awareness (Plato's liberating, dialogic side to language), not in the *actual* reality of eighteenth- and nineteenth-century Catholic France and Protestant Sweden, for instance.

The *capacities* of literacy are the heart of the matter. The example of Sweden, among others discussed by Graff, raises deep questions about the literacy myth. But we are still left with the question: What good does (could?) literacy do? I would argue that Sweden is actually the historical analog of a well-known, nonhistorical assault on the literacy myth—the work of Sylvia Scribner and Michael Cole (1981) on the cognitive effects of literacy. It has been assumed for centuries that literacy gives rise to higher-order cognitive abilities, to more analytic and logical thought than is typical of oral cultures (see Musgrove, 1982, for a modern version of the argument at its fullest). This almost commonsense assumption is disputed by Scribner and Cole in their groundbreaking work on the Vai in Liberia found in *The Psychology of Literacy* (1981). Among the Vai, literacy and schooling don't always go together. There are three sorts of literacy among the Vai: English literacy acquired in formal school settings; an indigenous Vai script (syllabic, not alphabetic) transmitted outside institutional settings (that is, among peers and family) and with no connection with Western-style schooling; and, finally, a form of literacy in Arabic. Each of these literacies is tied to a particular context of use: English literacy is associated with government and education; Vai literacy is used primarily for keeping commercial and personal records and for letters; Arabic literacy is used for reading, writing, and memorizing the Qur'an. (Many Arabic literates do not know Arabic, but have memorized and can recite large sections of the Qur'an.) Since some Vai are versed in only one of these forms of literacy, others in two or more, and still others are nonliterate altogether, Scribner and Cole could disentangle various effects of literacy from effects of formal schooling (which affected only the English literates).

Scribner and Cole examined subjects' performance on categorization and syllogistic reasoning tasks, and their results call into question much work on the cognitive consequences of literacy. Neither syllabic Vai script nor Arabic alphabetic literacy was associated with what have been considered higher-order intellectual skills. Neither of these types of literacy enhanced the use of taxonomic skills, nor did either contribute to a shift toward syllogistic reasoning. In contrast, literacy in English, the only form acquired through formal schooling, was associated with some types of decontextualization and abstract reasoning. However, after English literates had been out of school a few years, they did better than nonliterates only on verbal explanation tasks ("talking about" tasks); they did no better on problem-solving tasks (categorization and abstract reasoning tasks). The effects of schooling on task performance, not just task explanation, are transitory, unless they are repeatedly practiced in people's daily lives, as Scribner and Cole conclude: " . . . school fosters abilities in expository talk in contrived situations" (pp. 242–243). This is not at all a bad definition of what Plato called "speech writing," a term of abuse for him. In the Scribner and Cole study, literacy in and of itself led to no grandiose cognitive abilities; instead, formal schooling led to quite specific abilities that are useless without institutions (such as schools, courts, and bureaucracies) which reward "expository talk in contrived situations."

Scribner and Cole's work, demonstrating the rather particular contribution of schooling, should not tempt us to replace the literacy myth with an "education myth." Graff's book is full of examples showing that widespread education does not necessarily lead to all the good things formerly attributed to literacy. In fact, the transitory effect of school on-task performance, coupled with its more long-term effect on "expository talk in contrived situations," is interesting if we consider the relationship between education and jobs in the West. Ivar Berg's (1971) work, discussed by Graff (p. 384), found no historically increasing link between education and occupation in the twentieth century. Education in the West has expanded more rapidly than changes in skill requirements. Berg did, however, find self-fulfilling prophecies of the value of education for occupational requirements rampant among managers and employers. Not only did he find overeducation for job requirements, but he found little, if any, relationship between changes in educational levels and changes in output per worker. Education may predict initial salary and job title, but not promotion or productivity. In professional and managerial positions, Berg found, educational achievement, rather than performance, was rewarded. In work that broadens the impact of Berg's, Fry (1981), studying 140 nations, found that educational expansion bore little relationship to changing patterns of inequality or economic development: "It appears that greater equality does not result from the expansion of schooling, but rather from fundamental structural changes that reduce dependency on foreign capital" (Fry, cited in Graff, p. 384). As Graff writes:

> According to the "literacy myth," education is supposed to do many things: stimulate economic development, provide a foundation for democracy, and expose people to common values, institutions, and languages to unite and integrate them. But "despite much higher educational attainment rates today than fifteen or twenty years ago, there is still little democracy [or economic development, or social equality] in Africa, Asia, or Latin America, and the optimism that there ever will be is fading." Education and literacy change, but the presumed consequences do not follow. (p. 384; see Levin, 1981, for inserted quote)

Any discussion of jobs and education brings us immediately to the question of the purposes of education. Graff's book clearly shows that, throughout history, education has not, for the most part, been directed primarily at vocational training or personal growth and development. Rather, it has stressed behaviors and attitudes appropriate to good citizenship and moral behavior, largely as these are perceived by the elites of the society. And this has often meant, especially over the last century, different sorts of behaviors and attitudes for different classes of individuals: docility, discipline, time-management, honesty, and respect, for the lower classes (suiting them for industrial or service jobs); verbal and analytical skills, "critical thinking," discursive thought and writing, for the higher classes (suiting them for management jobs). There is ample evidence that, in contemporary U.S. schools, tracking systems, which are pervasive, have exactly this effect. In a massive study of tracking in junior and senior high schools across the United States, Jeannie Oakes (1985) found that a student's race, class, or family-based access to knowledge about college and career routes has a larger effect on the track he or she ends up in than does his or her inherent intelligence or actual potential. Once in a lower track, however, a child almost always stays there and eventually behaves in ways that appear to validate this placement. Oakes cites a number of typical interview responses on the part of students and teachers to questions about the teaching and learning that go on in classes of various tracks. These responses eloquently speak to the shaping of social inequality in schools. They demonstrate clearly the way two quite different sorts of literacy are being taught, one stressing thinking for oneself, suitable to higher positions in the social hierarchy, and the other stressing deference, suitable for lower positions. Some examples, taken from Oakes's book (pp. 79–83, 85–89), follow:

> What are the . . . most critical things you [the teacher] want the students in your class to learn?
>
> —Deal with thinking activities—Think for basic answers—essay-type questions. (High-track English—junior high)
>
> —To think critically—to analyze—*ask* questions. (High-track Social Science—junior high)
>
> —Ability to use reading as a tool—e.g., how to fill out forms, write a check, get a job. (Low-track English—junior high)
>
> —To be able to work with other students. To be able to work alone. To be able to follow directions. (Low-track English—junior high)
>
> What is the most important thing you [the student] have learned?

—To know how to communicate with my teachers like friends and as teachers at the same time. To have confidence in myself other than my skills and class work. (High-track English—junior high)

—I have learned to form my own opinion on situations. I have also learned to not be swayed so much by another person's opinion but to look at both opinions with an open mind. I know now that to have a good solid opinion on a subject I must have facts to support my opinion. Decisions in later life will probably be made easier because of this. (High-track English—senior high)

—I have learned about many things like having good manners, respecting other people, not talking when the teacher is talking. (Low-track English—junior high)

—In this class, I have learned manners. (Low-track English—junior high)

The most striking continuity in the history of literacy that emerges from Graff's book is the way literacy has been used, in age after age, to solidify the social hierarchy, empower elites, and ensure that people lower in the hierarchy accept the values, norms, and beliefs of the elites, even when it is not in their self-interest (or "class interest") to do so. In fact, the concept of "hegemony" (associated with Gramsci's work; see Bobcock, 1986) underlies "the analytic and interpretive framework" of Graff's book (1987, p. 11):

> Gramsci noted that only weak states rely on force for their power and control. Stronger states and institutions rule and cohere through hegemony. Literacy is not a likely technique for domination or coercion; for hegemony, however, it has proved a much more viable option and often a successful tool. "Schooling," in common values, attitudes, and norms, as well as in skills and common languages, has long been grasped as especially useful. . . .
>
> Typically, the process of schooling has sought, in Gramsci's conception, to develop assimilation and control. Since the Reformation, schooling and analogous hegemonic activities have sought to secure the *consent* of the masses in response to "the direction imposed on social life by the dominant fundamental group." Hegemony derives from consent, "the spontaneous loyalty that any dominant social group obtains from the masses by virtue of its social and intellectual prestige and its supposedly superior function in the world of production." (Graff, pp. 11–12)

The work of the sociolinguists, starting with William Labov (1966, 1972; Milroy, 1980, 1987; Milroy & Milroy, 1985), has shown clearly how hegemony works at a detailed linguistic level. In a speech community (such as New York City), speakers of all classes accept the same norms for "correct speech" (for example, not dropping "r's" in words like "car," among myriad other linguistic features). This norm represents, by and large, the way the middle classes behave in their more or less casual speech. Lower-class speakers show their tacit acceptance of this norm by dropping less prestigious pronunciations and adopting the prestige forms more and more as they speak in more formal styles (for example, job interviews or school-based tasks). Lower-class speakers often perceive themselves as *always* using the prestige pronunciations, claim to do so, and condemn those who use less prestigious forms (for example, Labov reports that they say they would not hire such a person even for a lower-level job), when in reality they use the low-prestige forms regularly in their own casual speech. Thus, they "police themselves," applying the standards of another class's behavior to their own. The situation is rendered worse when, as sociolinguists point out, lower-class speakers use non-prestige forms, however unconsciously, as markers of solidarity with their own local community and peers (Milroy & Milroy, 1985). Thus, their condemnation of their own behavior is a condemnation of their own social network. Of course, such behavior could be taken to demonstrate loyalty to a national set of values and norms when speaking in the "public sphere" (that is, in more formal contexts), a loyalty that in this context takes precedence over more localized or community-based values. Nonetheless, the fact that these national norms more closely match the local or community-based behavior of the middle class than they do those below them on the social scale favors the former against the latter. Furthermore, the process whereby lower-class speakers condemn their own community-based behaviors as compared to these national norms undergirds the myth that these norms are somehow natural and God-given, when in fact they represent merely the historical empowering of one set of localized, community-based conventional behaviors over other sets. The concept of hegemony argues that this model applies to a range of behaviors and attitudes well beyond language.

In reading Graff's book one feels almost like an eavesdropper on a "grand debate" that runs through history. On the one side are elites (whether social, religious, economic, or hereditary), arguing that the lower classes should not be given literacy because it will make them unhappy with their lot, politically critical and restive, and unwilling to do the menial jobs of society. On the other side are elites who argue that literacy will not have this effect. Rather, they argue, if literacy is delivered in the right moral and civil framework, one that upholds the values of the elites, it will make the lower classes accept those values and seek to behave in a manner more like the middle classes (that is, they will become more "moral" and "better citizens"). This debate (carried out in quite explicit terms) goes on well into the nineteenth century and the beginning of the twentieth. The latter camp was clearly right. Just as lower-class New Yorkers will drop a significant number of "r's" while claiming that people who do so aren't fit for society's lesser jobs, so too, throughout the Western world, non-elites are prone to accept uncritically middle-class norms of behavior as natural, God-given, and right. They are often not raised in homes that habitually practice such behaviors and attitudes (in language and social interaction), however, and they have less access to schools and school experiences that fully habituate them to such behaviors and attitudes. Thus, they often fail to replicate such behavior and attitudes perfectly. Then, they (and others) may use their failure to fully emulate middle-class norms (norms they accept) to explain and justify their position in society and to see the social structure as fair, giving an equal chance to all. Graff's book shows clearly that an old contrast in society between literate elites and the nonliterate masses has become a highly stratified social ranking based not on literacy per se, but on the degree to which one controls a certain type of school-based literacy (in speech and behavior, as well as in writing) associated with the values and aspirations of the middle classes.

Up to this point, I have built a somewhat one-sided case, concentrating on the authoritarian side of Plato's dilemma. But there is another side, the liberating side of the dilemma—that is, the use of an emancipatory literacy for religious, political, and cultural resistance to domination:

> Literacy was one of the core elements of England's centuries-old radical tradition. In the context of a complex interweaving of political, cultural, social, and economic changes, an essentially new element in literacy's history was formed: the association of literacy with radical political activities, as well as with "useful knowledge," one of the many factors in the making of an English working class. . . .
>
> Reading and striving for education helped the working class to form a political picture of the organization of their society and their experience in it. (Graff, p. 324)

No name is more closely associated with emancipatory literacy than that of Paulo Freire (1970, 1973, 1985). Like Bakhtin, and to a certain extent like Plato, Freire believes that literacy empowers people only when it renders them active questioners of the social reality around them:

> Reading the world always precedes reading the word, and reading the word implies continually reading the world. . . . In a way, however, we can go further and say that reading the word is not preceded merely by reading the world, but by a certain form of writing it or rewriting it, that is, of transforming it by means of conscious, practical work. For me, this dynamic movement is central to the literacy process. (Freire & Macedo, 1987, p. 35)

In a chapter entitled "The People Speak Their Word: Literacy in Action" in his recent book with Donaldo Macedo (1987), Freire discusses and cites material from learner workbooks he helped design for a national literacy campaign in the republic of São Tomé and Principe, a nation that had recently freed itself from "the colonial yoke to which it was subjected for centuries" (p. 65). He calls attention to the way "the challenge to the critical perception of those becoming literate gradually grows, page by page." (p. 72). The second *Workbook* begins by "provoking a debate" (p. 76) and goes on to say to the learner: "To study is not easy, because to study is to create and re-create and not to repeat what others say" (p. 77). The *Workbook* tells the learner that education is meant to develop "a critical spirit and creativity, not passivity" (p. 91). Freire says that in these materials "one does not particularly deal with delivering or transferring to the people more rigorous explanations of the facts, as though these facts were finalized, rigid, and ready to be digested. One is concerned with stimulating and challenging them" (p. 78). All this sounds open and liberating, much as Plato initially did, and in not dissimilar terms. But there is another note here as well. Freire comes up square against Plato's problem: what is to ensure that when people read (either a text or the world) they will do so "correctly"? Thus, the second *Workbook* also reads:

> When we learn to read and write, it is also important to learn to think correctly. To think correctly we should think about our practice in work. We should think about our daily lives. (p. 76)

> Our principal objective in writing the texts of this Notebook is to challenge you, comrades, to think correctly. . . . (p. 87)

> Now try to do an exercise, attempting to think correctly. Write on a piece of paper how you see this problem: "Can the education of children and adults, after the Independence of our country, be equal to the education that we had before Independence?" (p. 88)

> Let's think about some qualities that characterize the new man and the new woman. One of these qualities is agreement with the People's cause and the defense of the People's interests. . . . The correct sense of political militancy, in which we are learning to overcome individualism and egoism, is also a sign of the new man and the new woman.
>     To study (a revolutionary duty), to think correctly, . . . all these are characteristics of the new man and the new woman. (p. 92)

It is startling that a pedagogy that Freire says is "more a pedagogy of question than a pedagogy of answer," that is radical because it is "less certain of 'certainties' " (p. 54), in fact knows what it is to *think* correctly. The student is told not to repeat what others say, but then the problem becomes that in re-saying what the student reads for him- or herself, he or she may say it wrong, that is, in conflict with Freire's or the state's political perspective. Thus, the literacy materials must ensure that he or she thinks correctly, that is, re-says or interprets both the text and the world "correctly." Freire is well aware that no literacy is politically neutral, including the institutionally based literacy of church, state, and school that has and continues to undergird the hegemonic process in Western society. Freire has his *Republic* too. There is no way out of Plato's dilemma. Literacy always comes with a perspective on interpretation that is ultimately political. One can hide that perspective the better to claim it isn't there, or one can put it out in the open. Plato, Sweden, and Freire—each has a perspective, and a strong one.

   In the end, we might say that, contrary to the literacy myth, *nothing* follows from literacy or schooling. Much follows, however, from what comes *with* literacy and schooling, what literacy and schooling come wrapped up in; namely, the attitudes, values, norms, and beliefs (at once social, cultural, and political) that always accompany literacy and schooling. These consequences may be work habits that facilitate industrialization, abilities in "expository talk in contrived situations," a religiously or politically quiescent population, radical opposition to colonial oppressors, and any number of other things. A text, whether written on paper, on the soul (Plato), or on the world (Freire), is a loaded weapon. The person, the educator, who hands over the gun, hands over the bullets (the perspective), and must own up to the consequences. There is no way out of having an opinion, an ideology, and a strong one—as did Plato, as does Freire. Literacy education is not for the timid.

## Conclusion

The "loaded weapon" metaphor with which I have closed the main discussion of this paper raises several questions. Graff's work makes clear the ways literacy has been used as a weapon for the oppression of nondominant groups or for maintaining a societal status quo which has often had much the same oppressive effect. Graff's work is less clear in confronting the question of whether and how literacy can be used as a weapon for significant, long-term social change: as a tool for liberation. The very militaristic connotations of my metaphor ("loaded weapon") raise another important question: Can truly emancipatory literacy and literacy education evolve in a society without a prior or concomitant social revolution, the sort of revolution that has rarely in history been without violence and major social upheaval?

In neither of his books does Graff devote much space to the historical manifestations of resistance to oppression or the uses of literacy as a tool of liberation (Apple, 1986; Giroux, 1983). He does not deal with the question of whether or how history holds out hope for serious change, whether in the creation of truly democratic states or the creation of schools that challenge rather than maintain the status quo of highly inequitable societies (Zinn, 1980). In fact, since Graff does not address the question directly, it is not clear whether he would view this failing as his or history's. Graff's work has shaped the way I have developed my interpretation of literacy, and I believe it is already helping to shape the way other literacy theorists construct their theories (see a number of the papers in deCastell, Luke, & Egan, 1986). Thus, it is not surprising that I am left at the end of this paper with the same questions that, unanswered, confront Graff at the end of his work.

And this brings us back to Freire. Consider the following objection to my remarks above about Freire's "correct way of thinking": There is a difference between "correct way of thinking" as a universal dilemma in the interpretation of texts and "correct way of thinking" as an individual's process of attempting to think clearly *for him/ herself* in the specific context where he or she is learning to throw off the internalized voice of the oppressor. While this objection misses my point, it actually gets us to the heart of the matter. It is clear in the material I cited above that any thoughts which do not fit "the new man and the new woman," which do not agree with "the People's cause," will count as "misinterpretations," as the internal voice of the oppressor, and thus, as false. But this is, I have argued, the *normal* case with any literacy practice, whatever our politics: any literacy (any practice of interpretation) comes with built-in perspectives and assumptions that serve as a test of whether one is correctly practicing that literacy. There is no honest way to evade "owning up" to our perspectives and assumptions (which in one sense constitute "politics"); to leave them implicit is to pretend they don't exist and to allow them to serve our political purposes covertly. Indeed, much of the literature on school-based literacy makes just this point: the perspectives, values, and assumptions built into school-based literacy practices are often left implicit, thus empowering those mainstream children who already have them and disempowering those children who do not and for whom they are never rendered visible, save in the negative evaluations they constantly receive (Cazden, 1987; Cook-Gumperz, 1986; Heath, 1983).

The phrase "think for oneself" is the culprit here. It obscures the *social* nature of interpretation. Whether the words are written on paper, on the soul/mind, or on the world, every text is of a certain *type* (consider newspapers, political tracts, literature, lectures, political speeches, religious texts, comic books, schoolbooks and lessons, and so on through hundreds of varieties). And each type of text can be read in several different ways; meaning can be given to or taken from the text at a variety of levels (one can "read" the text more or less deeply; see Gee, 1987, in press). Types of texts and the various ways of reading them do not flow full-blown from the individual soul (or biology); they are the social and historical inventions of various groups of people. One always and only learns to interpret texts of a certain type in certain ways through having access to, and ample experience in, social settings where texts of that type are read in those ways. One is socialized or enculturated into a certain *social practice*. In fact, each of us is socialized into many such groups and social institutions (consider social institutions like churches, banks, schools, government offices; or groups defined around certain interests, whether politics, comic books, or the environment; or groups defined around certain places like the local bar, community centers, the courts, or, for certain adolescent peer groups, the street). One doesn't think for oneself; rather, one always thinks for (really *with* and *through*) a group—the group which socialized one into that practice of thinking. And, of course, one "thinks for" different groups in different contexts. Thus, the study of literacy ultimately requires us to study the social groups and institutions within which we are socialized to interpret certain types of words and worlds in certain ways (Bruner, 1986). Since the literacy practices of these groups are always fully embedded in their whole repertoires of social practices, going well beyond language and literacy per se, we must study these groups as wholes. Ultimately, there is no autonomous linguistics in this regard, no study that is just a study of literacy. After Graff, that is the sort of history we need; and a large number of scholars are just beginning to write its foundations (Apple, 1986; Cazden, 1987; Cook-Gumperz, 1986; Heath, 1983; Scribner & Cole, 1981; Street, 1984; Trueba, 1987), work which Graff acknowledges briefly in an epilogue (pp. 373–398).

The question, then, as to whether literacy can be used as a tool for liberation is in reality not a question about literacy, at least as traditionally conceived. The question comes down to whether the social groups and institutions that underwrite various types of texts and ways of interpreting them can be changed. There is a sense in which schools—at least in much of the Western world—are the chief such social institution. In school each of us is socialized into practices which go beyond the home and peer group and initiate us into the "public sphere" (Gee, 1987; Eagleton, 1984; Sennett, 1978). Schools *mediate* (Vygotsky, 1978) between what we might call "community-based" social institutions (and their literacies) and public institutions (and their literacies). The question then reduces to this: Can schools be changed? I don't have the answer, but let me end where Michael Apple (1986) does; namely with Raymond Williams:

> It is only in a shared belief and insistence that there are practical alternatives that the balance of forces and chances begins to alter. Once the inevitabilities are challenged, we begin gathering our resources for a journey of hope. If there are no easy answers there are still available discoverable hard answers, and it is these that we can now learn to make and share. This has been, from the beginning, the sense and the impulse of the long revolution. (Williams, 1983, pp. 268–269)

What we need now are hope and hard answers.

## References

Apple, M. W. (1986). *Teachers and texts: A political economy of class & gender relations in education.* New York: Routledge & Kegan Paul.

Bakhtin, M. M. (1981). *The dialogic imagination.* (M. Holquist, Ed.). Austin: University of Texas Press.

Berg, I. (1971). *Education and jobs.* Boston: Beacon Press.

Bobcock, R. (1986). *Hegemony.* New York: Tavistock/Ellis Horwood/Methuen.

Bourdieu, P., & Passeron, J. F. (1977). *Reproduction in education, society, and culture.* Beverly Hills, CA: Sage.

Bowles, S., & Gintis, H. (1976). *Schooling in capitalist society.* New York: Basic Books.

Burger, R. (1980). *Plato's Phaedrus: A defense of a philosophic art of writing.* Tuscaloosa: University of Alabama Press.

Bruner, J. (1986). *Actual minds, possible worlds.* Cambridge: Harvard University Press.

Cazden, C. (1987). *Classroom discourse: The language of teaching and learning.* Portsmouth, NH: Heinemann.

Clanchy, M. (1979). *From memory to written record 1066–1307.* London: E. Arnold.

Clark, R., & Holquist, M. (1984). *Mikhail Bakhtin.* Cambridge: Harvard University Press.

Cook-Gumperz, J. (1986). *The social construction of literacy.* Cambridge: Cambridge University Press.

deCastell, S., Luke, A., & Egan, K. (Eds.). (1986). *Literacy, society, and schooling: A reader.* Cambridge: Cambridge University Press.

Derrida, J. (1972). La pharmacie de Platon. In *La dissemination* (pp. 69–198). Paris: Seuil.

De Vries, G. J. (1969). *A commentary on the Phaedrus of Plato.* Amsterdam: Adolf M. Hakkert.

Eagleton, T. (1984). *The function of criticism: From the Spectator to post-structuralism.* London: Verso.

Freire, P. (1970). *Pedagogy of the oppressed.* New York: Seabury Press.

Freire, P. (1973). *Education for critical consciousness.* New York: Seabury Press.

Freire, P. (1985). *The politics of education.* South Hadley, MA: Bergin & Garvey.

Freire, P., & Macedo, D. (1987). *Literacy: Reading the word and the world.* South Hadley, MA: Bergin & Garvey.

Fry, G. W. (1981). Schooling, development, and inequality: Old myths and new realities. *Harvard Educational Review, 51,* 107–116.

Gee, J. P. (1986a). Literate America on illiterate America: An essay review of *Illiterate America* by Jonathan Kozol. *Journal of Education, 168,* 126–140.

Gee, J. P. (1986b). Orality and literacy: From *The Savage Mind to Ways with Words, TESOL Quarterly, 20,* 719–746.

Gee, J. P. (1987). What is literacy? *Teaching and Learning, 2,* 3–11.

Gee, J. P. (in press). Discourse systems and aspirin bottles. *Journal of Education.*

Giroux, H. A. (1983). *Theory and resistance in education.* South Hadley, MA: Bergin & Garvey.

Goody, J. (1977). *The domestication of the savage mind.* Cambridge: Cambridge University Press.

Goody, J. (1986). *The logic of writing and the organization of society.* Cambridge: Cambridge University Press.

Goody, J., & Watt, I. P. (1963). The consequences of literacy. *Comparative Studies in History and Society, 5,* 304–345.

Graff, H. J. (1979). *The literacy myth: Literacy and social structure in the 19th century city.* New York: Academic Press.

Graff, H. J. (ed.). (1981a). *Literacy in history: An interdisciplinary research bibliography.* New York: Garland Press.

Graff, H. J. (1981b). *Literacy and social development in the West: A reader.* Cambridge: Cambridge University Press.

Graff, H. J. (1986). The legacies of literacy: Continuities and contradictions in Western society and culture. In S. deCastell, A. Luke, & K. Egan (Eds.), *Literacy, society, and schooling: A reader* (pp. 61–86). Cambridge: Cambridge University Press.

Graff, H. J. (1987a). *The legacies of literacy: Continuities and contradictions in Western culture and society.* Bloomington: University of Indiana Press.

Graff, H. J. (1987b). *The labyrinths of literacy: Reflections on literacy past and present.* New York: The Falmer Press.

Graff, H. J, & Arnove, R. (Eds.). (1987). *National literacy campaigns in historical and comparative perspectives.* New York: Plenum.

Griswold, C. L. (1986). *Self-knowledge in Plato's Phaedrus.* New Haven: Yale University Press.

Havelock, E. A. (1963). *Preface to Plato.* Cambridge: Harvard University Press.

Havelock, E. A. (1982). *The literate revolution in Greece and its cultural consequences.* Princeton: Princeton University Press.

Havelock, E. A. (1986). *The muse learns to write: Reflections on orality and literacy from antiquity to the present.* New Haven: Yale University Press.

Heath, S. B. (1983). *Ways with words: Language, life and work in communities and classrooms.* Cambridge: Cambridge University Press.

Hirsch, E. D. (1987). *Cultural literacy: What every American needs to know.* Boston: Houghton Mifflin.

Hymes, D. (1980). *Language in education: Ethnolinguistic essays.* Washington, DC: Center for Applied Linguistics.

Johansson, E. (1977). *The history of literacy in Sweden.* Umeaa, Sweden: Umeaa University Press.

Kermode, F. (1979). *The genesis of secrecy: On the interpretation of narrative.* Cambridge: Harvard University Press.

Kirsch, I., & Jungeblut, A. (1986). *Literacy: Profiles of America's young adults, Final Report* (Report No. 16-PL-01). Princeton: National Assessment of Educational Progress.

Kozol, J. (1985). *Illiterate America.* Garden City: Anchor Press/Doubleday.

Labov, W. (1966). *The social stratification of English in New York City.* Washington, DC: Center for Applied Linguistics.

Labov, W. (1972). *Sociolinguistic patterns.* Philadelphia: University of Pennsylvania Press.

Lemke, J. L. (1986). *Using language in classrooms.* Victoria, Australia: Deakin University Press.

Levin, H. (1981). The identity crisis of educational planning, *Harvard Educational Review*, *51*, 85–93.

Lévi-Strauss, C. (1978). *Myth and meaning*. New York: Schocken Books.

Michaels, S. (1981). "Sharing time": Children's narrative styles and differential access to literacy. *Language in Society*, 10, 423–442.

Milroy, L. (1980). *Language and social networks*. Oxford: Basil Blackwell.

Milroy, L. (1987). *Observing and analysing natural language*. Oxford: Basil Blackwell.

Milroy, J., & Milroy, L. (1985). *Authority in language: Investigating language prescription and standardisation*. New York: Routledge & Kegan Paul.

Morson, G. S. (Ed.). (1986). *Bakhtin: Essays and dialogues on his work*. Chicago: University of Chicago Press.

Musgrove, F. (1982). *Education and anthropology: Other cultures and the teacher*. New York: Wiley.

Oakes, J. (1985). *Keeping track: How schools structure inequality*. New Haven: Yale University Press.

Ohmann, R. (1976). *English in America*. Oxford: Oxford University Press.

Olson, D. R. (1977). From utterance to text: The bias of language in speech and writing. *Harvard Educational Review*, 47, 257–281.

Ong, W., S. J. (1982). *Orality and literacy: The technologizing of the word*. London: Methuen.

Pattison, R. (1982). *On literacy: The politics of the word from Homer to the age of rock*. Oxford: Oxford University Press.

Rowe, C. J. (1986). *Plato: Phaedrus (translation and commentary)*. Warminster, Wilts., Eng: Aris & Philips.

Scollon, R., & Scollon, S.B.K. (1981). *Narrative, literacy and face in interethnic communication*. Norwood, NJ: Ablex.

Scribner, S., & Cole, M. (1981). *The psychology of literacy*. Cambridge: Harvard University Press.

Sennett, R. (1978). *The fall of public man: On the social psychology of capitalism*. New York: Vintage Books.

Strauss, L. (1987), Plato. In L. Strauss & J. Cropsey (Eds.), *History of political philosophy*, 3rd ed. (pp. 33–89). Chicago: University of Chicago Press. (Original edition 1963).

Street, B. (1984). *Mikhail Bakhtin: The dialogical principle*. Minneapolis: The University of Minnesota Press.

Trueba, H. T. (Ed.). (1987). *Success or failure: Learning and the language minority student*. New York: Newbury House.

Vygotsky, L. S. (1978). *Mind in society*. Cambridge: Harvard University Press.

Willis, P. (1981). *Learning to labor*. New York: Columbia University Press.

Williams, R. (1983). *The year 2000*. New York: Pantheon Books.

Zinn, H. (1980). *A people's history of the United States*. New York: Harper & Row.

# Essay Review

## Culture or Canon? Critical Pedagogy and the Politics of Literacy

PETER L. McLAREN
*Miami University, Ohio*

LITERACY: READING THE WORD AND THE WORLD
by Paulo Freire and Donaldo Macedo.
*South Hadley, MA: Bergin & Garvey, 1987. 184 pp.*

A major debate has emerged in the United States over the question of what constitutes literacy, who has access to it, and what values and practices are legitimated by it. The parameters of this debate are no longer constrained by what it means to be occupationally literate; rather, the more pressing question today is what kind of knowledge learners must acquire in order to participate in society as active, informed citizens. Literacy has ceased to be treated solely as a technical discourse for entrance into the world of work. In fact, the use of the term has changed dramatically in recent years. Once restrictively defined as providing students with specific technical skills related to reading, writing, and speaking, the term literacy has also come to mean educating students to be culturally literate; that is, to be bearers of certain meanings, values, and views.

That the concept of literacy has entertained nearly constant debate during recent years is not surprising, given the various reactions to current reform efforts which are attempting to bring "excellence" back to American education. In addition to generating antipathy among various groups of critics, these efforts have yielded to an inexorable process of narrowing and technicizing the concept of literacy. Within the last decade three positions have come to characterize the politics and pedagogy of literacy. These positions generally break down into the following: functional literacy, cultural literacy, and critical literacy. Functional literacy refers primarily to the technical mastery of particular skills necessary for students to decode simple texts such as street signs, instruction manuals, or the front page of a daily newspaper. Definitions of functional literacy vary, but generally include the ability to read somewhere between the fourth- and eighth-grade levels on standardized reading tests.[1]

*Harvard Educational Review*   Vol. 58   No. 2   May 1988, 213–234

Cultural literacy refers to the acquisition of a broad range of factors which accompany functional literacy, such as a familiarity with particular linguistic traditions or bodies of information. More specifically, it means acquiring a knowledge of selected works of literature and historical information necessary for informed participation in the political and cultural life of the nation. Two radically different positions characterize cultural literacy. The first advances the establishment of a cultural index or a cultural canon of literary works prescribed for all students and also insists upon a required form of English usage; the second advocates using the language standards and cultural information students bring into the classroom as legitimate and important constituents of learning. Critical literacy, on the other hand, involves decoding the ideological dimensions of texts, institutions, social practices, and cultural forms such as television and film, in order to reveal their selective interests. The purpose behind acquiring this type of literacy is to create a citizenry critical enough to both analyze and challenge the oppressive characteristics of the larger society so that a more just, equitable, and democratic society can be created. Each of these perspectives on literacy has its exponents, proponents, and detractors; and each category has become a buzz-word in the lexicon of the current debate over excellence in education.

## Functional Literacy

Recent revelations by Jonathan Kozol and others that the functionally and marginally illiterate population of the United States may now exceed 60 million has provoked widespread concern both in the public domain and across the educational system.[2] While this estimate has been the focus of some dispute among literacy researchers, it remains the case that only about 4 million adults nationwide are being helped through currently available literacy programs, including volunteer programs (such as Literacy Volunteers of America and Laubach Literacy Volunteers) as well as competency-based and community-based programs.[3] Together, all federal, state, municipal, and private literacy programs in the United States reach a maximum of 4 percent of the illiterate population.[4] In an even less salutary light, the current literacy crisis has helped heighten the moral panic—no doubt fueled by a growing xenophobia—surrounding the rapidly expanding Hispanic population. A movement is now in progress, headed by former California senator S. I. Hayakawa, to devalue bilingual education programs and to make English the official language of the United States.

Mainstream theories of literacy conceive of being literate as possessing only that requisite fund of knowledge—that privileged form of linguistic currency—necessary for students to succeed materially in an industrialized capitalist society. This perspective still informs most school-based literacy programs across the United States. In this view, the nonstandard literacies of minority groups and the poor (that is, different dialects, nonstandard English) are regarded as deficits or deprivations rather than differences. Some research suggests that many of today's illiterates are dropouts of reading programs that demand strongly analytic/auditory reading styles as distinct from whole-language approaches to teaching reading.[5]

## Cultural Literacy

Although approaches to literacy continually suffer the conflictual relationships of opposing groups and theoretical perspectives, a more critical consensus on what literacy means is beginning to take shape. Theorists are starting to acknowledge the difficulty in separating cultural literacy from reading and writing in general. In fact, some argue that reading and writing are relatively futile and empty exercises *unless accompanied by at least some form of cultural knowledge.*[6] For example, Ivan Illich has recently begun to theorize about the relationship between "scribal literacy," the ability to read and write, and "lay literacy," the set of pervasive competencies and cultural knowledge that is required to participate in a literate society.[7]

In her 1985 American Educational Studies Association Butts Lecture entitled "Literacy and Learning in the Making of Citizens," Shirley Brice Heath emphasizes the indissoluble link between literacy, context, and meaning. She notes:

> Unless accompanied with cultural knowledge, personal drive, political motivation, or economic opportunity, literacy does not lead the writer to make the essential leap from literacy to being literate—from knowing what the words say to understanding what they mean. Readers make meaning by linking the symbols on the page with real-world knowledge and then considering what the text means for generating new ideas and actions not explicitly written or "said" in the text. The transformation of literacy skills into literate behaviors and ways of thinking depends on a community of talkers who make the text mean something. For most of history, such literate communities have been elite groups, holding themselves and their knowledge and power apart from the masses.[8]

Among the exponents of "cultural literacy," two polar positions seem apparent that reflect both liberal and conservative orientations in the cultural literacy perspective. The "prescriptivists" argue that students' success in the North American marketplace depends upon their successful entrance into the academy. This generally means being taught from a prescribed canon of literary works and acquiring a standard form of English. The "pluralists," on the other hand, argue for the legitimacy of a broader range of discursive practices which reflect more closely the language practices, values, and interests of racially and economically diverse groups of students.[9] The pluralists attempt to affirm and legitimize the cultural universes, knowledge, and language practices that students bring into the classroom. Both these orientations reflect an understanding of literacy which incorporates, along with the mastery of technical skill, the explicit recognition of the importance of some form of shared cultural knowledge.

Figures most frequently associated with the recent debate over "what every American needs to know"—E.D. Hirsch, Allan Bloom, and Secretary of Education William J. Bennett—have raised the stakes appreciably with respect to the kind of knowledge students should be taught, and in what manner.[10] Their widely publicized positions on literacy and the virtues of higher learning focus directly on which knowledge should be dispensed to students, which virtues should be reflected in student character and behavior, and who should be the credentializing agents for this process.

Bennett's ideological recipe for a national curriculum reflects the positions of both Hirsch and Bloom. In his attack on the fragmented curriculum, Hirsch argues for cultural uniformity—a "traditional literate culture" consisting of a common prescribed content which will supposedly give students access to mainstream economic and political life (and thus by implication become a key avenue to social and economic justice for minority students).

Bloom's concept of literacy is more sweeping. Unlike Hirsch, who incorporates information from both mainstream and elite cultures, Bloom seeks to instill, among the worthiest of students, high-status knowledge based on Platonic principles and virtues which treat knowledge as pristine, transhistorical, universal, and context free. What Hirsch, on the other hand, would like to prescribe for present and future generations of students (despite his claim to be a "descriptivist" and not a "prescriptivist") is cultural information based on some 4,700 items which include facts, dates of battles, authors of books, figures from Greek mythology, and the names of past presidents of the United States. These qualify not so much as information from elite culture but as items familiar to "literate" Americans, although authorities may cavil with respect to which particular pieces of information should be included in Hirsch's index.

While the work of Hirsch and Bloom contains many ideological affinities, it is as difficult to imagine what a common curriculum would look like based on their writings as it is to imagine the game of Trivial Pursuit being played in Plato's Republic. What the work of Hirsch and Bloom means for prescriptivists like Bennett is first of all specifying *the shared prior knowledge* necessary for students to succeed in the discourse community of literate Americans (for Bloom this becomes the discourse community within the hallowed halls of the academy) and then developing a pedagogical strategy for teaching this knowledge (preferably codified in texts) *prescriptively* to those who are assumed to be culturally deficient. The prescriptivists' call for a nationally endorsed cultural canon—a "republic of letters" of sorts that would be capable of encoding our culture with a selective history, world view, and epistemology—is tantamount to calling for the construction of a national identity. Accordingly, students become accredited as culturally literate to the degree that they accept this national identity inscribed on the tablet of Western high culture.

## Critical Literacy

Lately some participants in the literacy debate have become critical of the prevailing conceptualizations of what it means to be literate and have begun vigorously to challenge the previously sacrosanct positions. These critics are not the inevitable dissenting minority in any discipline but include many recognized leaders in the field, such as Paulo Freire, Harvey Graff, Kenneth Goodman, Yetta Goodman, and Henry Giroux. As the theoretical limitations of the old functional and cultural literacy models become more evident, the focus on formal standards of English is giving way to an exploration of the social construction of knowledge and the ideological processes involved in the reading of texts. In recent years literacy critics have become much more aware of the centrality of "relations of power" to the domain of literacy, which would not normally have been included under the rubric of conventionally defined "politics." What this suggests is that if the process of becoming literate is, in large part, a struggle for voice and the reclamation of one's history, then there is also a critical sense in which literacy itself must be politically defined.[11]

At a time when popularizers of cultural literacy are prescribing a literary canon to pry open the "closed minds" of an American youth putatively on the path to intellectual and moral decline, radical critics, armed with a welter of ethnographic evidence, are attempting to draw our attention to the gendered, racial, and socio-economic contexts of literacy and the challenge that these new conceptualizations represent.[12] This challenge, which is presently being undertaken on the dual fronts of pedagogy and popular culture, has manifested itself as a struggle over what counts as legitimate educational knowledge, who has the power to define it as such, and the instructional means by which it should be taught to learners.

Those who argue for critical literacy maintain that an uncritical enthusiasm for making individuals functionally literate conceals the substantive issue of what it means to be truly literate behind the imperatives of linguistic mastery. To couch the process of literacy mainly in terms of linguistic competency is to remove the process from the varied context in which literacy is achieved—a context that includes the experiences students bring to the reading act, as well as the contingencies of history, culture, and politics. Exponents of critical literacy generally regard the prescriptivist models of cultural literacy to be a form of cultural imposition undertaken by the guardians of academic discourse communities and the dominant social classes with which they are associated. Advocates of critical literacy avoid espousing a view of cultural knowledge in which meaning derives from a unitary and fixed essence—inherited knowledge and formulations which have been sedimented by the impersonal force of history into the wisdom of the ages. Rather, they conceptualize the production of cultural knowledge as a struggle over competing discourses, the history of which has been swathed in ambiguities and contradictions. In this view, the value of cultural and literary texts resides not in their collective currency as the heralded virtues of society or disinterested ideals of truth, but in the manner in which they have been constructed out of a web of relationships shaped by different gendered, racial, economic, and historical contexts. It is wrong to assume that individual women and men from different social classes read texts in a similar manner, just as it is wrong to assume that the context of reading a work of literature remains undifferentiated through time. As historically produced subjects, readers of texts are governed by different social and ideological formations which may or may not correspond to the formations present when the text was originally produced. Critical literacy focuses, therefore, on the interests and assumptions that inform the generation of knowledge itself. From this perspective all texts, written, spoken or otherwise represented, constitute ideological weapons capable of enabling certain groups to solidify their power through acts of linguistic hegemony. This can be seen in the ways in which mainstream schooling has stressed the cultural capital of certain speech communities that make up the dominant culture. It is to the issue of the school's complicity in maintaining a "culture of silence" in which inequality is produced among groups on the basis of race, class, and gender that the work of Paulo Freire becomes so significant for American audiences.

## Critical Literacy: A Freirean Perspective

*Literacy: Reading the Word and the World* is the third book by Paulo Freire to appear in the United States in the past three years. It is the second book translated by, and with the participation of, Donaldo Macedo, although Macedo's contribution is much greater in the present book.

Freire's work has become almost synonymous with the project of literacy. Born in 1921 in Recife, Brazil, a large port city and capital of the northeastern state of Pernambuco, Freire spent his early life in poverty, as underdevelopment and world-wide economic crisis of 1929 saw his family lose its middle-class status and be forced into poverty. Experiencing firsthand the listlessness and apathy of the poor, Freire soon realized that the education system was a primary vehicle in maintaining this "culture of silence." Dedicating his life to the struggle against poverty, Freire spent nearly three decades exploring how the culture and consciousness of illiterate peasants have been shaped by the language and values of the "colonizer," or the dominant culture.

As Professor of History and Philosophy at the University of Recife in the early 1960s, Freire worked with peasants in the Brazilian Northeast during that country's national literacy campaign. At that time he evolved a theory of literacy which is based on the conviction that every human being is capable of critically engaging the world in a dialogical encounter with others. In 1964 Freire was arrested, jailed, and later sent into exile after the military seized control of the Brazilian government. His theory of literacy and empowerment culminated in 1970 in the release of his now classic treatise, *Pedagogy of the Oppressed,* which stressed building upon the learners' indigenous language as the basis for developing reading and writing. Subsequent years were tumultuous and productive: a five-year stay in Chile as a UNESCO consultant with the Agrarian Reform Training and Research Institute in programs for adult education; an appointment in 1969 as Fellow of Harvard University's Center for the Study of Development and Social Change; a move to Switzerland in the same year as consultant and Special Advisor in Education to the Office of Education of the World Council of Churches, where he developed literacy programs for Tanzania and Guinea-Bissau; and the establishment of the Instituto de Acción Cultural in Geneva. Freire's influence was strongly felt in the literacy campaigns of Nicaragua, Cuba, Portugal, Chile, and Angola.

Today his influence extends beyond the domain of literacy and includes developments in social work, education, sociology, participatory research, and critical pedagogy. Freire returned to Brazil in June of 1980, after an amnesty was declared in 1979. He is now Professor of Philosophy of Education at the Pontifícia Universidade Católica de São Paulo and the public Universidade de Campinas in São Paulo.

The participation of Donaldo Macedo, a Cape Verdean-born sociolinguist who now teaches in the Department of English at the University of Massachusetts at Boston, brings a complementary and critical voice both to the theoretical and practical aspects of Freirean pedagogy. In particular, Macedo's familiarity with the critical sociological tradition in education helps to clarify some of Freire's positions on the pedagogical implications and applications of his work. In addition, Macedo's own brand of radical educational politics assists in both situating and extending the more recent advances of Freire's work within the critical educational tradition in the United States.

Ann Berthoff's pithy foreword provides an illuminating discussion of the philosophical roots of Freire's pedagogy, which she terms "a pedagogy of knowing." Following this is a theoretically detailed preface by Henry A. Giroux, which could have functioned equally as an afterword, since it extends many of the ideas discussed throughout the book. A longtime exponent of Freire's work in the United States, Giroux establishes a critical context that provides an invaluable conceptual basis for engaging the text. He provides readers with three primary—and in many ways original—categories for approaching the concept of literacy: literacy as cultural politics; literacy as liberating remembrance; and literacy as narrative.

Giroux's use of the category "cultural politics" draws attention to the social, cultural, political, and economic dimensions of everyday life and illustrates how these must become the major contexts for both language acquisition and usage. The concept of "liberating remembrance" highlights the fundamental importance of history to the process of becoming critically literate. History, argues Giroux, can provide educators with the possibility of establishing both a referent for and a critique of injustice and oppression. Critical readings of history can enable students to recover and reconstruct the "radical potential of memory," investigating historical sources of human suffering so that they can never be repeated. Such "liberating remembrance" will also enable the educator to seize whatever images of hope these events might offer to the present. Giroux's third category—literacy as a form of narrative—draws attention to the fact that literacy is always about somebody's story. As a story *by* somebody and *for* somebody, knowledge is invariably informed by a set of underlying interests that structure how a particular story is told through such factors as the organization of knowledge, social relations and cultural values, reader reception, and forms of assessment. As a form of narrative, critical literacy becomes a struggle over whose "stories" will prevail as a legitimate object of learning and analysis. The conceptual framework Giroux provides helps to enlarge the range of critical possibilities for examining Freire and Macedo's work.

The book itself takes a somewhat disjointed form: three extensive dialogues between Macedo and Freire; a letter written by Freire to Mario Cabral, Minister of Education of Guinea-Bissau; a portion of the texts of *Practice to Learn* and other workbooks prepared for the "culture Circles" of São Tomé and Principe; two essays by Freire; and an essay coauthored by Freire and Macedo. The generative themes involve the act of reading, an updated version of a previously published article; adult literacy and popular libraries, adapted from a talk Freire presented at the Eleventh Brazilian Congress of Library Economy and Documentation in 1982; rethinking literacy, which takes the form of a dialogue between Freire and Macedo; literacy in action, a detailed and practical exposition by Freire of his "Popular Culture Notebooks"; a critical exchange between Freire and Macedo to clarify Freire's controversial involvement in the literacy campaign in Guinea-Bissau; a dialogue between Freire and Macedo on literacy in the United States; and a coauthored essay in which Freire and Macedo link the concept of literacy to that of critical pedagogy.

Positioning Freire and Macedo's work within the foregoing perspectives on literacy highlights some of the problematic assumptions which inform them. Moreover, it sheds some critical light on current approaches in the United States designed to rescue the nation's "illiterates" through the establishment of a requisite cultural knowledge for all who wish to participate as American citizens. A frequently enunciated thesis of Freire and Macedo states that approaches to literacy, regardless of the country in which they take place, must constitute more than simply the "alphabetization" of the so-called illiterate student. That children have linguistic and communicative skills outside the school which often go unrecognized in the classroom is the first consideration that must be addressed in any critical literacy program. No text can be taught to students in antiseptic isolation from their life and culture. Freire underscores this point when he remarks:

> If adult literacy was once treated and realized in an authoritarian way, centered on the magical understanding of the word, a word bestowed by the educator on the illiterate, and if the texts generally offered students once hid much more than they revealed of reality, now literacy as an act of knowledge, as a creative act and as a political act, is an effort to read the world and the word. Now it is no longer possible to have the text without context. (p. 43)

Freire and Macedo significantly enrich our understanding of literacy by helping us essentially to see it as socially constructed forms of cultural and communicative practices. Viewing literacy in this manner shifts our attention away from the dominant concept of literacy as the ability to read, write, and speak. Instead, by demonstrating how culturally different minorities use oral and literate modes to interact in the home, community, and classroom, they bring us closer to understanding literacy as a form of cultural politics.

Stressing that the language of subordinate groups is as linguistically rule-governed and sophisticated as the language of dominant groups, Freire notes: "What they [sociolinguists] show is that, scientifically, all languages are valid, systematic, rule-governed systems, and that the inferiority/superiority distinction is a social phenomenon" (p. 53). However, Freire and Macedo are quick to point out that regardless of the equality of language forms, the notion that cultures are simply different but equal is a gross mystification perpetuated by dominant theories of literacy. We are constantly reminded throughout the book that subordinate groups are located within social relations marked by the unequal distribution of power. Since the dominant culture generally functions in the interests of certain groups over others on the basis of race, age, class, and gender, subordinate groups are often denied access to the power, knowledge, and resources that could allow them to become critically literate. Macedo draws a parallel between this aspect of American society and public schooling, remarking that "When curriculum designers ignore important variables such as social-class differences, when they ignore the incorporation of the subordinate cultures' values in the curriculum, and when they refuse to accept and legitimize the students' language, their actions point to . . . inflexibility, insensitivity, and rigidity . . . " (p. 124). Linguistic- and racial-minority students are the hardest hit by the educational system, which has systematically evaluated their school performance and revealed it to be inferior to that of mainstream students in English. This has been done, however, without fully considering "their struggle against racism, educational tracking, and the systematic negation of their histories" (p. 154). This dilemma has been brought about, according to Freire and Macedo, because of a general failure by American educators to link school performance to the structural relations of the wider society:

> Educators, including the present secretary of education, William J. Bennett, fail to understand that it is through multiple discourses that students generate meaning of their everyday social contexts. Without understanding the meaning of their immediate social reality, it is most difficult to comprehend their relations with the wider society. (p. 154)

Mainstream approaches to literacy, which too often concentrate on the sheer mechanics of reading and writing, fail to take seriously enough the learner's sociocultural context—his or her own social reality—in which meaning is actively constructed. All too frequently the social reality of the learner is assumed to correspond to reality as it is defined by the dominant culture—to what Freire refers to as the "schooling class."[13] Speaking on this issue, Freire comments:

> This large number of people [in the United States] who do not read and write and who were expelled from school do not represent a failure of the schooling class; their expulsion reveals the triumph of the schooling class. In fact, this misreading of responsibility reflects the schools' hidden curriculum. (p. 121)

Freire goes on to interpret the so-called "illiteracy" among students as their reaction "to a curriculum and other material conditions in schools that negate their histories, cultures, and day-to-day experiences" (p. 121). He explains that illiteracy, as it is treated within the dominant perspective, refers to reading and writing skills which are inadequate to the task of carrying out efficiently and productively the actions required by dominant social groups to secure established social relations of production. Potential labor power is therefore wasted among "illiterates," and this adversely affects the economic and technological expansion of the wider society. Freire and Macedo consider this dominant view of illiteracy to pose a real threat to democracy, since the possibilities for making choices and intervening in reality are all but foreclosed when the social, political, and economic consequences of reading and writing are tied to the logic of the marketplace. The dominant model of literacy not only ignores the learner's creative capacity but also encourages a passive acceptance of the status quo. On the contrary, critical literacy always implies a political reading of the world, accompanied by a transformation of the oppressive relations which constitute that world. In a powerfully moving response to a question posed by Macedo, Freire states:

> Your question reminds me of my dream of a different society, one in which saying the word is a fundamental right and not merely a habit, in which saying the word is the right to become part of the decision to transform the world. To read the word that one says in this perspective presupposes the reinvention of today's society. The reinvention of society, on the other hand, requires the reinvention of power. (p. 55)

## Critical Literacy and the Canon

When placed beside Freire and Macedo's conception of critical literacy, the flaws in the prescriptivists' positions become more obvious. For instance, the arguments for the establishment of a literary canon fail to address the ways in which dominant texts constitute an articulation of the societies that produced them. That is, those in favor of teaching a canon of prescribed works rarely draw attention to the importance of understanding the ideological dimensions of such works—an understanding which challenges the interests and values of the societies in which these works were generated. Read collectively, the arguments of the prescriptivists sound like a rallying cry to bring back a bogus past in which teachers were required to act "with statute" and students slavishly venerated school escutcheons, crests, cups, honor boards, badges, pennants, and school ties—the standard supporting insignia during the days when Mr. Gradgrind cracked you on the knuckles for failing to memorize your ten lines of Cicero.

Strands of elite Western culture, those that encode primarily the triumph of White males, constitute a significant portion of this canon. Culture in this view is presented as a sacred pool of cultural information—a cultural index, if you will—the mastery of which will usher the student into the forum of national literacy. While prescriptivists consider prior knowledge important, just as pluralists do, prescriptivists tend not to acknowledge the social contexts which shape this prior knowledge. Prescriptivists who favor the development of a national canon of literary works in higher education are more likely to identify with Bloom's position over that of Hirsch. Bloom's perspective tends to naturalize among subordinate groups the idea that the classic works of literature are not only constitutive of a high status incompatible with the social standing of those groups but partake of a certain quality of understanding for the most part inaccessible to their "closed minds"; such high-status knowledge is therefore better off left to be consumed by those students who have "earned" entrance to the top Ivy League schools. In a similar fashion, Bloom's perspective reinforces the idea among privileged groups that the classics bear a natural allegiance to their more culturally nourished, inherently superior, and vastly more "open" minds.

The most compelling argument in favor of this canon is its harkening back to the civilizing influence of the Great Tradition, much like the clarion call sounded by the Leavisites throughout the pages of their journal, *Scrutiny*, and in their valorization of the works of Austen, Eliot, James, Conrad, and Lawrence. Such a yearning for past virtue may produce a temporary surge of adrenalin in those who "man" the ivory towers of contemporary America, but ultimately rings hollow for those who hold that great literature should have emancipatory social consequences and be able to empower individuals to redress the structural inequalities that plague the social order. The argument which claims that a return to the Great Tradition will re-civilize illiterate America and purge it of the dross accumulated by the current cultural barbarism is contradicted by the pretensions which structure its own discourse— pretensions which lead us to believe that literature can transcend the forces of history, material relations, and the multiplicity of responses that it evokes in its readers. In Bloom's quest for a literary canon, knowledge is monumentalized, sanctified, and held up self-consciously and reverently as the guardian of those souls seeking virtue and those minds in search of eternal wisdom. Bloom's agenda for educational reform asserts the contradiction between what is and what should be based on a romantic distortion of what once was; on the other hand, Freire and Macedo build their case for educational reform by seeking utopian possibilities within the social forms of the present historical juncture based on what could be, while at the same time challenging the oppressive characteristics of those social forms.

This literary canon will always remain a form of cultural invasion as long as the interests which inform it are not uncovered to reveal their political locus, their real social and ideological weight. As long as knowledge is posited as eternal wisdom, educators will be discouraged from becoming self-reflective about the internal as- sumptions which legitimate such knowledge. This canon also implies a pedagogy of submission. From the prescriptivists' perspective, little is relevant outside the stric- tures of the required curriculum. From a Freirean position, this approach extin- guishes independent thinking and critical human action. We are left with a traditional discourse dressed up for the current generation and prescribed without a precise knowledge of the rules of its own formation.

While prescriptivists argue that the cultural heritage of the United States should be taken seriously, they do so in a way that conceals its socially derivative status and cloaks the selective interests which this inherited agenda serves in the mantle of eternal principles of justice, equality, and fraternity. They fail to acknowledge that ideology shadows the steps of all knowledge—inherited or not. In other words, they fail to take into account the relationship between knowledge and power. This failing is readily apparent in the epistemological premises set forth in the work of E. D. Hirsch. Here knowledge is equivalent to sharing a body of information, and teaching is reduced to transmitting this information. Hirsch's view of how students become culturally literate reifies culture as a museum of events frozen in time and shrouded in the classical quest for performance. Pedagogy in this view is reduced to sharing the "facts," and the role of the teacher becomes that of the curator of the national heritage. Rarely are attempts made to destabilize the reified conceptualizations of cultural "facts" or to defamiliarize the domesticating myths which often serve to legitimate existing relations of power and privilege in the larger social order. Culture in this view becomes essentialized outside the forces of power and history rather than analyzed as a fluid and contestatory site where power works to favor certain forms of knowledge and where a multiplicity of discourses war for dominance. In order to draw attention to this relationship between knowledge and power, Freire poses the following questions: *"in favor of whom and what* (and thus against whom and what) do we promote education? And *in favor of whom and what* do we develop political activity?" (p. 38). On this matter, Freire is unwavering:

> Only those who have power . . . can define what is correct or incorrect. Only those who have power can decide what constitutes intellectualism. Once the intellectual parameters are set, those who want to be considered intellectuals must meet the requirements of the profile dictated by the elite class. To be intellectual one must do exactly what those with the power to define intellec-tualism do. (p. 122)

Hirsch's argument for the cognitive superiority of standard English, which attributes intellectual advancement to the formal structure of the symbol system, steadfastly ignores the social situatedness and ideological nature of language. That is, he avoids attending to the cultural and political significance attached to mastering dominant discourses. Macedo points out that different English dialects, such as Black English, "decode different world views" (p. 127) and that "the semantic value of specific lexical items belonging to black English differs radically, in some cases, from the reading derived from the standard, dominant dialect" (p. 127). While affirming Black English does not, in Freire's words, "preclude the need to acquire proficiency in the linguistic code of the dominant group," it does mean that Black English can become, in Macedo's terms, "a powerful tool demystifying the distorted reality prepackaged for them by the dominant curriculum" (p. 128). Whereas Hirsch believes the infor-mation processing of standard English is necessary to be able to transcend cultural and historical contingencies, Freire and Macedo understand literacy to inhere in the sociopolitical context of the subjects themselves. Freire makes this clear when he suggests that educators in the United States "need to use their students' cultural universe as a point of departure, enabling students to recognize themselves as pos-sessing a specific and important cultural identity" (p. 127). In a similar manner, works of literature cannot be detached from their social origins.[14] What Freire and Macedo take seriously, and prescriptivists do not, is the means by which history has granted certain texts canonical status and excluded the local cultural canons of sub-jugated groups. In other words, history is often written by the powerful, and the literary texts most likely to be found on a list of prescribed works are those which rarely threaten the social and economic stability of the established order. Works by writers who have been marginalized because they happen to be female or members of minority groups, or works that constitute political perspectives inhospitable to the dominant culture, are not likely to be admitted to the national canon. The text, from the perspective of a critical literacy, never ceases to be open to the world or to history.

Even purportedly high culture is shot through with history and steeped in the meanings that the dominant culture has given it.[15]

Any perspective which advocates the incontestable superiority of the Great Books, in which teachers are required to transmit the praiseworthy aspects of our cultural heritage, is inherently problematic from a Freirean standpoint. Such a strident, demanding manifesto rests on the neoclassical notion that culture exists as a receptacle for ideas and somehow "contains" knowledge (as distinct from the concept that knowledge is socially constructed). Granted, to deny students access to the great intellectual and aesthetic works our culture has to offer is a grave injustice. But it is important to recognize that great works do not speak for themselves. To claim that they do is to argue erroneously that they transcend history and the contextual specificity of the discourses which generated them and to additionally argue that these works deserve to be universally consumed regardless of the particular characteristics of the students whom the curriculum is intended to serve. The prescriptivists do not seriously consider the question of whose interests, values and stories are affirmed and legitimated by the canon. From Freire and Macedo's point of view, such an approach to cultural literacy is sectarian and paternalistic, and represents a form of cultural domination in which the socially constitutive nature of both readers and texts is all but ignored. This non-ideological view of literacy, which presents knowledge as inexorably given and self-justified by its academic valorization through the ages, becomes a "magical view" of the written word based on its status as ideologically uncontaminated information. Freire underscores this position in the following passage:

> To avoid misinterpretation of what I'm saying, it is important to stress that my criticism of the magical view of the written word does not mean that I take an irresponsible position on the obligation we all have—teachers and students—to read the classic literature in a given field seriously in order to make the texts our own and to create the intellectual discipline without which our practice as teachers and students is not viable. (p. 34)

What is disquieting in the prescriptivists' position is that the high-status knowledge of classic literary works becomes the only kind of knowledge deemed immutable and sacred enough to warrant its inclusion in the curriculum. The subjugated knowledge of economically disadvantaged groups, women, and minorities is insistently denigrated in the prescriptivists' view of what should be taught, how it should be taught, and to whom.[16] For instance, in Bloom's sanctified universe it would be scandalous to include in the pantheon of great literary masters the figures of Richard Wright, James Baldwin, Ralph Ellison, or Alice Walker—writers whose brilliant vernacular ascriptions, writing "degree zero," and carnivalesque discourse have broken down the time and space of the conventional aesthetic theory of the "white male Brahmins."[17] It is here that the fixity of classical thought and the exclusionary practices of racist elites impose interpretive shackles on the literary possibilities of the "other," which include writers who are Black, female, or belong to minority groups. Addressing the matter of elitism, Freire writes:

> From the authoritarian, elitist, reactionary point of view, the people's incompetence is almost natural. The people need to be defended because they are incapable of thinking clearly, incapable of abstracting, knowing, and creating; they are eternally "of lesser value"; and their ideas are permanently labeled exotic. Popular knowledge does not exist. The memory of their struggles needs to be forgotten, or those struggles related in a different way; the "proverbial inculture" of the people does not permit them to participate actively in the constant reinvention of their society. (p. 44)

The issue here is not necessarily to add oral literatures, minority literatures, and other noncanonical works to the canon, but to study canonical and noncanonical works comparatively, with an eye to the historical and ideological reasons why some works are canonized and others are not and the interests such works promote within power and knowledge junctures constructed in wider institutional and social contexts.

The disdain of many prescriptivists (especially those influenced by Bloom) for the prosaic plane of the popular or "vulgar" offers little room for a critical understanding of more contemporary cultural formations, such as radio, video, and film genres, and how they operate in today's world to help construct student subjectivities. But it is precisely in the understanding of how the everyday and the popular intersect with the larger social order that the success of critical literacy rests. That is, for critical literacy to be effective, it must be embedded in the concrete conditions of the students themselves.[18] For instance, to ignore or dismiss as barbaric popular cultural forms such as rock music or music videos is to erroneously deny the relationships which obtain among popular culture, student experience, and the construction of ideological codes governing reader reception. Further, it is to willfully dismiss as unimportant or insignificant the connection between student alienation from classical texts and new narrative forms currently being constructed in the domain of the popular. From this vantage point, the idea of a national canon of literary works reeks with intellectual elitism,[19] constitutes an "anti-dialogical" theory of action, and encourages educators to ignore both popular culture and the cultural integrity of the student. Simply to attempt to inculcate a set of eternal virtues in students by transmitting a prescribed body of so-called wisdom—as if such wisdom transcends social contexts and the local ideological agendas to which they give rise—is virtually to anesthetize consciousness in Freirean terms; it is to adapt students to become pliable and docile members of the world as it exists rather than as it might become.[20] Rather than encouraging students to become ambassadors of the status quo, Freire and Macedo invite them to take part in a critically active transformation of the larger social order. Once the student is able to "depedestal" the literary tradition of Great Works, he or she can begin to gauge the importance of popular texts and "local knowledge" in establishing the grounds for a critical literacy. From a Freirean perspective, Bloom's agenda for educational reform is co-opted by the very conditions it attempts to analyze because it does not challenge the premises which structure the logic of its own mode of inquiry.

Freire and Macedo argue against the "banking" form of pedagogy often implied in prescriptivist models of cultural literacy. The authors argue that simply to deposit into the memory banks of students tidings from the most esteemed minds of Western culture inhibits the development of a critical consciousness.[21] Freire makes this position clear in the following remarks:

> He who "immobilizes" knowledge and transfers it to students, whether in primary schools or universities; he who bears only the echo of his own words, in a kind of oral narcissism; he who believes it insolvent for the working class to recover its rights; he who thinks the working class is uncultured and incompetent and, thus, needs to be liberated from top to bottom—this type of educator does not really have anything to do with freedom or democracy. On the contrary, he who acts and thinks this way, consciously or unconsciously, helps to preserve the authoritarian structures. (p. 40)

Brushing against the grain of the prescriptivists' quest for a literary canon is Freire and Macedo's rallying cry to make the content of the curriculum relevant to the transformation of the sociopolitical reality and life situations of learners. They assert that students become active, knowing subjects not by being fed cultural information but through the process of *conscientization,* that is, through learning to perceive social, political, and economic contradictions in the social world in order to transform one's lived social relations and the larger, macrosocial order.[22] Freire and Macedo know that their primary matrix as educators is coextensive not with the logic of capitalism but with the suffering of the oppressed. A critical literacy situates itself in the intersection of language, culture, power, and history—the nexus in which the subjectivities of students are formed through incorporation, accommodation, and contestation. The struggle is one that involves *their* history, *their* language, and *their* culture, and the pedagogical implications are such that students are given access to a critical discourse or are conditioned to accept the familiar and self-evident as the inevitable. Worse still, they are denied a voice with which to be present in the world; they are made invisible to history and rendered powerless to shape it. Critical literacy in Freire's terms is a transgressive act of reading the word and the world that embodies an attack on dominant signifying practices and calls into question the moribund scruples of the bourgeois humanist text, placing them in a wider social and temporal context. Any Freirean approach to the canon must therefore make clear the fact that texts are products of the interests that inform dominant social and cultural groups, and that educators must assuredly probe the canon for what it does not say—for its "structured silences," its "present absences," its exclusionary politics— as well as for what it actually does say. Freire and Macedo deny a privileged status to claims that knowledge finds its quintessential expression in classical discourse. Rather than arguing for a cultural canon of inherited texts, Freire advocates the creation of what he calls the "popular library." A popular library would serve as a cultural aid and learning center "and not just a silent depository of books" (p. 45). The purpose of constructing a network of popular libraries would be to "stimulate educational or popular culture programs (in the fields of adult literacy, health education, research, theatre, technical training, and religion), programs that respond to the popular demands provoked by an effort of the popular, wherein it becomes an active process of dialogical engagement between teachers and students. What emerges from a collaborative pedagogy between teachers and students is a knowledge that is generated dialectically from cultural ingredients that could be—and often are—both canonical and non-canonical. The idea of the popular library as set forth by Freire differs from the common cultural index advocated by Hirsch, in that Hirsch pays little attention to the sociopolitical context which frames the act of knowing. Also lacking in Hirsch's work is an understanding of the power/knowledge junctures in which pedagogy is practiced and learning takes place. If, on the other hand, we are to make a clear distinction between cultural literacy as advocated by Freire and Macedo, we would have to say that the former position transforms high culture into a form of currency made up of essentially inert ideas culled from the selective tradition of classic literature, which are to be deposited among the uncultured as timeless truths. The Freirean position, on the other hand, invites an understanding of culture as the lived relation of individuals to historical conditions and material circumstances. Literacy is something that grows out of these lived relations as part of the dynamics of everyday life.

We could thus say that literacy in Freire and Macedo's view is language that is enfleshed; that is, language consisting of many tissues of meaning which have been constructed not only through a rational engagement with the cultural world but through an engagement in this world by the learner's own body. All discourse, spoken or written, is caught in the net of the body. Literacy, therefore, is an act of the body. Language not only organizes and legitimates our world on a rational basis but resonates with and constructs our "felt" needs, desires, and values. Literacy divorced from the lived situations of the learner is a form of disembodied knowledge, severed from the interests, values, and concerns of the learner. What makes literacy "critical," in Freire and Macedo's view, is its ability to make the learner aware of how relations of power, institutional structures, and models of representation work on and through the learner's mind and body to keep him or her powerless, imprisoned in a culture of silence.

In fact, a critical perspective demands that the very ideological process of language construction itself be interrogated. Individually and collectively we produce language, yet the social reality which language constructs, conveys, and objectifies also produces us, its users, by providing us with subject positions from which to speak and consequently from which to be spoken to. As a social practice, language is constituted by material and social reality which informs both its codes and the subjectivities of its users. Language provides us with tools with which to shape meaning from a universe of indeterminate signs; yet the very tools we use to cobble meaning have been fired in the same crucible of historical and discursive struggle from which we have forged the linguistic weapons for our crusades of cultural domination.

## Conclusion

Freire and Macedo argue that the fundamental structural principle of a pedagogy

301

of critical literacy is the need for pedagogical practices that will provide students with the opportunity to use their own reality, including the language these students bring into the classroom, as the basis of literacy. However, Freire and Macedo also make clear that while educators "should never allow the students' voice to be silenced by a distorted legitimation of the standard language" (p. 152), they should, none-theless, "understand the value of mastering the standard dominant language of the wider society" (p. 152). This perspective goes directly against the claim made by William Bennett that *only* English "will ensure that local schools will succeed in teaching non-English-speaking students English so that they will [enjoy] access to the opportunities of the American society" (p. 155). Bennett's claim also contradicts the theoretical and research literature which argues that literacy skills acquired through linguistic interaction in one language (such as Spanish) play a major role in making input in another language (such as English) comprehensible.[23]

Mainstream approaches to pedagogy, as advocated by Bennett and others, are unable to develop a critical literacy because, in Freire's view, they violate the basic structuring principle of emancipatory pedagogy, which focuses on empowerment. Empowerment in this instance refers to the process of helping students acquire modes of critical analysis which will provide them with both the theoretical ability and more incentive to transform, rather than merely serve, the dominant social order. In any pedagogy of critical literacy, certain values must be made concrete. These include the values of "solidarity, social responsibility, creative discipline in the service of the common good, vigilance, and critical spirit" (p. 156), all of which are to be linked pedagogically to the overall goal of "national reconstruction." Freire and Macedo understand that, as a form of political empowerment, critical literacy represents both a theory of pedagogy and a pedagogy of theory.[24] It constitutes a theory of pedagogy in that students are taught to analyze critically how culture functions within asym-metrical relations of power to give certain groups an advantage over others on the basis of race, class, and gender. It serves as a pedagogy of theory because it recognizes that only when theory transforms itself into praxis and engages in a project of possibility does it truly enter the world of emancipatory teaching. That is, only when theory becomes transformed into a political act can it realize its socially transformative potential.

Freire and Macedo read the problem of illiteracy in American education primarily as one of resistance to a dehumanizing and alienating culture of silence, as well as an act of self-affirmation. Ironically, this perspective turns the act of resistance into an exercise of critical literacy:

> The many people who pass through school and come out illiterate because they resisted and refused to read the dominant word are representative of self-affirmation. This self-affirmation is, from another point of view, a process of literacy in the normal, global sense of the term. That is, the refusal to read the word chosen by the teacher is the realization on the part of the student that he or she is making a decision not to accept what is perceived as violating his or her world. (p. 123)

For Americans besieged by the relentless logic of consumerism and privatization, it is no wonder that illiteracy thrives as a means of resistance—of refusing to be part of the cultural nightmare. What is needed to meet the crisis of literacy is a critical theory that frames reading, writing, and the performance of public discourse in terms of moral and political decisionmaking. Literacy in this view is not linked to learning to read advertisements in order to become a better consumer, to escaping into the pages of a romance novel or spy thriller, or to engaging a classical work of literature in order the learn to meaning of "the good" or "the true" so that one can live "the virtuous life." Rather, a critical literacy links language competence to the acquisition of a public discourse in which empowered individuals are capable of critically engaging the social, political, and ethical dimensions of everyday life. To be literate in this instance means not only being able to understand and engage the world but also to be able to exercise the kind of moral courage needed to change the social order when necessary. Such a perspective of literacy astutely recognizes that language is that sociolinguistic territory in which history both rehearses its nightmares and dreams its liberating possibilities. Language may be used to affirm the voices of the marginalized and disaffected or to silence them. Critical literacy acknowledges the importance of constructing "dangerous memories"—depictions of events of human suffering and courage—through excavating, rescuing, and affirming the voices of those who have been silenced and marginalized by the dominant culture. In this regard, critical literacy becomes an expression of both protest and hope that leads to political action.

The solution to achieving critical literacy in the classroom rests, according to Freire, "in a full understanding of the ideological elements that generate and sustain linguistic, racial, and sex discrimination" (p. 155). Only by approaching literacy as a form of ideological critique can knowledge be made critically relevant to students and eventually lead to a reinvention of society through a transformation of the oppressive power relations which structure society. It is precisely in this emphasis on an ideological unveiling of the oppressive features of social reality that Freire and Macedo tend to repeat themselves, thereby limiting possibilities for further theoretical advancement. Too often they refrain from being explicit about the connections between critical literacy and critical pedagogy, although this link is discussed thoroughly in Giroux's preface. While the authors have argued for the importance of student experience in developing a critical pedagogy, they sometimes fail to articulate how popular culture—especially in the context of the United States—enables as well as constrains the development of student subjectivity. Consequently, the authors have neglected to build into their critical pedagogy those life-affirming dimensions of popular culture which could point to potentially liberating forms of social relations, of ways to create meaning, and of ways of representing ourselves, our relations to others, and our relation to the environment—in short, possibilities not yet realized. This criticism should not, however, detract from the overwhelming strength and brilliance of this book.

Some readers of *Literacy: Reading the Word and the World* may be disappointed by its lack of a technically articulated model of educational change. This criticism has been anticipated and rejected outright by Freire and Macedo in one of their dialogues. Making very clear that he disdains "texts that primarily give recipes," Freire announces his "[refusal] to write such texts, because [his] political convictions are opposed to the ideology that feeds such domestication of the mind" (p. 134). While some readers may view this as a deliberate attempt to avoid being pinned down theoretically or perhaps even pedagogically, Freire would consider such criticism to be consistent with that aspect of North American ideology which reveres the logic of quick fixes. This is the same logic that, when embodied by educators, shrinks their capacity to comprehend critically the contextual conditions of Freire's own work and to investigate these conditions in their own classrooms. The tacit injunction, "don't criticize something unless you have a blueprint of the solution," seeks to freeze knowledge in its instrumental moment, refuses to address the dialectical tension between theory and practice, and refrains from acknowledging the provisional nature of truth itself. Those more familiar with or sympathetic towards Freire's work will clearly see the redemptive logic in Freire's idea that education is primarily about problem-posing rather than answer-giving. Once old problems have been resolved, new problems must be formulated. Freire and Macedo implicitly recognize that the struggle over knowledge is one that can never be won, or pedagogy stops.[25]

One of the great strengths of *Literacy: Reading the Word and the World* is that it refuses to reduce critical educational theory to a blueprint for educational transformation, while at the same time challenging readers with a wide array of sensitizing constructs, critically articulated and passionately advocated, with which to rethink their educational priorities. Such an accomplishment cannot be overlooked, especially during an era in which the nature of critical knowledge is increasingly being redefined, codified for mass consumption, and imposed on teachers in a top-down fashion, irrespective of the class, gender, and racial characteristics of the vast numbers of students whom such knowledge is intended to serve. In the final instance, Freire and Macedo are able to illustrate what could be called radical hope. Radical hope is always multivocal, and carries with it a surplus of meaning. Like language, radical hope signifies beyond its own significance. Moreover, it resists the fixity of interpretation that could turn it into despair, and refuses to abandon the moral principles which generate it, thus preventing it from becoming merely "wishful thinking."

*Literacy: Reading the Word and the World* provides an articulate and courageous response to current questions arising from the literacy debate. It extends beyond the question of how language functions to the critical issue of how it should function. Freire and Macedo offer readers an ethical imperative designed to assist them in taking responsibility for their linguistic practices. In the final instance, *Literacy: Reading the Word and the World* establishes a framework for literacy which succeeds in insuring the diversity of culture and providing for the transformation of oppressive social practices. Like Bakhtin, Freire and Macedo remind us that we are all always authors, every time we speak or listen, read or write, and that ultimately we must assume the moral obligation for our dialogue with the world.[26]

## Notes

1. If one defines illiteracy as being able to read only the simplest texts and street signs, then about 27 million adults would be considered illiterate. If one includes the ability to read the local newspaper or articles in digest magazines, then about 45 million adults would be classified as illiterate. If the standards are closer to a high school level, then 72 million Americans would be classified as illiterate. Adults who are functionally literate read somewhere between fourth- and eighth-grade levels. See Jeanne S. Chall, Elizabeth Heron, and Ann Hilferty, "Adult Literacy: New and Enduring Problems," *Phi Delta Kappan, 69* (1987), 190–196.
2. Jonathan Kozol, *Illiterate America* (New York: Anchor Press/Doubleday, 1985), p. 4.
3. Chall, Heron, and Hilferty, "Adult Literacy," p. 192. For a comparison between the Laubach and Freirean approaches, see Michael Holzman, "A Post-Freirean Model for Adult Literacy Education," *College English, 50* (1988), 177–189.
4. Kozol, *Illiterate America*, p. 5.
5. Marie Carbo, "Deprogramming Reading Failure: Giving Unequal Learners an Equal Chance," *Phi Delta Kappan, 69* (Nov. 1987), 197–202. Colin Lankshear has undertaken an excellent critique of literacy programs based on the model of functional literacy. Lankshear claims that conventional models of functional literacy are actually dysfunctional for the disadvantaged illiterate adult and functional for those whose interests are best served by maintaining the economic, political, and cultural status quo. His radical alternative model of functional literacy is very similar to the position of critical literacy, although Lankshear prefers to keep the term "functional literacy" because it enjoys widespread support and financial affirmation. Based on the ideas of Freire, Lankshear's model is grounded in a dialectic between literacy and empowerment that is linked to a transformation of dehumanizing social structures. See Colin Lankshear, "Humanizing Functional Literacy: Beyond Utilitarian Necessity," *Educational Theory, 36* (1986), 375–387.
6. Shirley Brice Heath, "Literacy and Learning in the Making of Citizens," 1985 Butts Lecture. In *Civic Education, Pluralism and Literacy,* published jointly by *AESA News and Comment* and The Center for the Studies of Citizenship and Public Affairs, Syracuse University, August, 1986, p. 16.
7. Ivan Illich, "A Plea for Research on Lay Literacy," *Interchange, 18* (1987), 9–22.
8. Heath, "Literacy and Learning," p. 16.
9. Patricia Bizzell, "Cultural Literacy," unpublished paper. I am greatly indebted to this paper for providing me with some of the primary categories used in my analysis. A published version of this paper has recently appeared. See Patricia Bizzell, "Arguing about Literacy," *College English, 50* (1988), 141–153.
10. The works of these individuals include E. D. Hirsch, Jr., "Restoring Cultural Literacy in the Early Grades," *Educational Leadership, 45* (December 1987/January 1988), 63–70; E. D. Hirsch, Jr., *Cultural Literacy: What Every American Needs to Know* (New York: Houghton Mifflin, 1987); E. D. Hirsch, Jr., "Cultural Literacy," *American Scholar, 52* (1982–83), 159–169; E. D. Hirsch, Jr., "Culture and Literacy," *Journal of Basic Writing, 3* (1980), 27–47; E. D. Hirsch, Jr., *The Philosophy of Composition* (Chicago: University of Chicago Press, 1977); Allan Bloom, *The Closing of the American Mind: How Higher Education Has Failed Democracy and Impoverished the Souls of Today's Students* (New York: Simon & Schuster, 1987); and the views of William Bennett, which were published when he was chairman of the National Endowment for the Humanities and which were summarized in " 'To Reclaim a Legacy':Text of Report on Humanities in Education," *Chronicle of Higher Education,* November 28, 1984, pp. 16–21. Closely resembling Bennett's view on cultural literacy is *What Do Our 17-Year-Olds Know?* (New York: Harper & Row, 1988), written by Diane Ravitch and Chester Finn, Jr., which follows the lead of E. D. Hirsch in substituting the mindless teaching of skills with the mindless teaching of content. See also the review by Deborah Meier and Florence Miller in *The Nation,* January 9, 1988, pp. 25–27.
11. Simply labeling one in five American adults functionally illiterate masks the fact that a large proportion of these individuals are not fluent in English, and that more than half of them are women. Literacy in this view is treated as though it occurs in a vacuum. Kathleen Rockhill writes that mainstream literacy programs, which emphasize reading and writing in the dominant language, conceal under the banner of equality the ethnocentrism, racism, and sexism inherent in literacy policies. Thus, the presumed neutrality of becoming literate enshrouds the interests of entrenched groups. Rockhill reports that within most literacy approaches learners are treated as the same, but symbolically are dichotomized as literate or illiterate—that is, learners or non-learners—and literacy is established as an isolated, measurable, uniform "thing," a skill or commodity that can be acquired if one only has the necessary motivation to participate in learning

opportunities or literacy programs. That is, literacy is treated as though it is outside the social and political relations, ideological practices, and symbolic meaning structures in which it is embedded. See Kathleen Rockhill, "Gender, Language and the Politics of Literacy," *British Journal of Sociology of Education, 8* (1987), 153–167. See also Kathleen Rockhill, "Literacy as Threat/Desire: Longing to be SOMEBODY," unpublished paper.

12. Many important advances in the field of literacy over the last decade have been achieved primarily by researchers working in discourse linguistics and the ethnography of communication. As a result of their efforts, it has become clear that educators can no longer ignore the gap between formal school literacy and the oral tradition of the student's family, home, and community. See J. Cook-Gumperz, ed., *The Social Construction of Literacy* (London: Cambridge University Press, 1986); Adrian T. Bennett, "Discourses of Power, the Dialectics of Understanding, the Power of Literacy," *Journal of Education, 165* (1983), 53–64; and Michelle Sola and Adrian T. Bennett, "The Struggle for Voice: Literacy and Consciousness in an East Harlem School," *Journal of Education, 167* (1985), 88–110. See also James Donald, *Language, Literacy and Schooling* (London: Open University Press, in press).

13. Donald, *Language, Literacy and Schooling.* See also Henry A. Giroux and Peter McLaren, "Teacher Education and the Politics of Democratic Life: Beyond the Reagan Agenda in the Era of " 'Good Times,' " in *Schools as Conduits: Educational Policymaking During the Reagan Years,* ed. Carol Camp Yeakey and Gladys Styles Johnson (New York: Praeger, in press); Peter McLaren, "No Light But Rather Darkness Visible: Language and the Politics of Criticism," *Curriculum Inquiry,* in press. It should be made clear here that even the more radical theories of resistance, while romanticizing the culture of the poor without considering how it also has been colonized by the dominant ideology replete with its differences and contradictions, have failed to analyze how power is lived in everyday, practical experience. Theories of resistance often miss the connection between literacy and sexuality and the manner in which sexual domination reproduced as literacy is lived through the gendered practices of the family and society (Rockhill, "Gender, Language and the Politics of Literacy"; see also Rockhill, "Literacy as Threat/Desire").

14. The problem, as some critics see it, is not with the idea of preserving our cultural heritage, a surely laudable end in itself, but with preserving a heritage which is too homogeneous and narrow in scope. As John Sisk notes: "We are confronted once again with the question of whether it is more characteristic of Americans to fear that they are losing their heritage, or to fear that the heritage they are supposed to be afraid of losing has been too narrowly constructed." See John P. Sisk, "What Is Necessary," *Salmagundi, 72* (Fall 1986), 145.

   The narrowness of vision inscribed in this view of the canon stems, in part, from the uncritical assumption that humanistic texts are—and should be—essentially ideologically neutral. Robert Scholes criticizes William Bennett for being upset that the humanities are sometimes used by educators to present certain social perspectives. Scholes writes:

   > He [Bennett] wants the classroom to be exciting and value free, and he believes the great humanistic texts to be exciting and value free also, as if Dante, Virgil, Karl Marx and T. S. Eliot (to name four from his list of classics) were ideological innocents, sharing a common humanistic view of the world. Mr. Bennett is not innocent either, and nowhere is this more apparent than in his taking the hotly debated question of the ideological component of humanistic texts as a matter already settled to the effect that they have none—or if they do it should not influence our regard for them. (Robert Scholes, "Aiming a Canon at the Curriculum," *Salmagundi, 72* [Fall 1986], 110.)

   In his call for a return to a classics-oriented core curriculum for the universities, Bennett has recently criticized scholars who are trying to include works by women and members of minority groups into the canon as "trendy lightweights." (See *The Chronicle of Higher Education,* February 17, 1988, pp. 1, 16). Of course, Bennett's concept of the canon, as Rockhill points out, is also linked to his drive to establish "moral literacy" as a fundamental teaching of schools and colleges. The argument being leveled at the exponents of the illiberal canon by critics such as Scholes is not so much a greater call for more relevance (for example, the inclusion of folk culture or popular culture) as much as it is a call for rendering official culture problematic; that is, they are concerned not with the canon itself (although they would like to see it broadened to include works by subjugated groups such as women and minority writers) but with the pedagogical strategy used to teach the canon. See reference to Bennett in the *New York Times,* September 30, 1986, p. 25, as cited in Rockhill, "Gender, Language and the Politics of Literacy," p. 157.

15. Patricia Bizzell, "Arguing about Literacy," *College English, 50* (1988), 141–153. According to Bizzell, Hirsch believes that the academic canon "has been granted by history the power to transcend and hence to control local canons" (p. 147); furthermore, "Hirsch assumes that history has granted the academic canon the right to exercise this power over other cultures, through

establishing canonical ways of thinking and of using language, canonical values, verbal styles, and mindsets as the " 'most important' to our national culture" (p. 147). In adopting a deterministic view of history, Hirsch's use of the term "history" is reduced to "a cover term, concealing not only the process whereby certain texts achieve canonical status but also the process whereby attitudes towards the very existence of any canon, and its function in society, become ingrained" (p. 148).

16. According to Elizabeth Fox-Genovese, the canon is profoundly bound by gender, race, and class. At the same time, she argues that some kind of canon is necessary, if not inevitable, and the present one need not be completely rewritten. If social transformation is to take place, two things must happen. First, the established canon must be reinterpreted from the perspectives of history, race, class, and gender. Second, the canon must be expanded. She writes:

> We can, with little difficulty, select texts by standard canonical authors that address issues of gender, race, and class. We can, in the spirit of contemporary theory, view teaching as an exercise in hermeneutics: We reread our texts from the perspective of contemporary concerns. In addition, we can transform the entire focus of conventional courses by the themes we select. . . . Modern criticism reminds us that even a reactionary text may raise contradictions that it imperfectly resolves. (Fox-Genovese, "The Claims of a Common Culture: Gender, Race, Class and the Canon," *Salmagundi, 72* [Fall 1986], 141–142.)

For an excellent critical analysis of some "great books," see Terry Eagleton, *William Shakespeare* (New York: Basil Blackwell, 1986). Eagleton is able to show how the search for identity undertaken by many of Shakespeare's characters is historically bound up with the exchange economy of commodity production.

17. Houston A. Baker, Jr., *Blues, Ideology, and Afro-American Literature: A Vernacular Theory* (Chicago: University of Chicago Press, 1984), pp. 150–151. Baker's work constitutes a brilliant discussion of Afro-American culture and literary history, particularly in relation to Afro-American expressive culture.

18. To become literate is always to engage the world as a continuous, deep penetration of cultural and historical experience. Becoming literate can never occur in antiseptic isolation from the world. Furthermore, criticisms of mainstream literacy programs in schools have been based on the charge that they have been reduced to a process which encourages students to learn sanitized facts stripped of ambiguity and contradiction and therefore do not necessarily lead students to be critically minded or acquire a significant amount of social, political, or intellectual empowerment. As Mikhail Bakhtin has so presciently shown us, becoming literate is a form of "philosophical anthropology" in which literacy becomes the most empowering precisely when it becomes the most social and contextually interactive. See Mikhail Bakhtin, *Speech Genres and Other Late Essays* (Austin: University of Texas Press, 1986).

19. Terry Eagleton reflects the perspective of Freire and Macedo by drawing attention to the ideological formations into which works of literature are inserted and valorized. He writes:

> Texts are *constituted* as "literary," in the normative sense, because they are judged to exemplify certain peculiar uses of language, to evoke certain significant responses, to communicate certain valued meanings. . . . Literature helps to secure our present social relations, not in the first place by apologizing for capitalism, but by being Literature. It is already relevant to class divisions that there exists a privileged body of discourse, sharply demarcated from "popular" modes, enshrined and disseminated, as valuable cultural capital, to future members of the dominant social class. . . . To construct . . . a tradition demands a practice which will select, reconstitute, process and "correct" certain pieces of writing so that they compose an imaginary unity, one responsive to the demands of a ruling ideology. (Eagleton, *Critical Quarterly, 20* [1978], 66 )

20. Radical critics of this "value neutral" position pose the question of who decides what text will be chosen, and which individuals will be selected to engage this privileged text. Hirsch, Bloom, and Bennett fail, in these critics' view, to link the concept of cultural literacy to the empowerment of a language of public life, one that resonates with the lived experiences of a heterogeneous population. See Henry A. Giroux, *Schooling and the Struggle for Public Life: Critical Pedagogy in the Modern Age* (Minneapolis: University of Minnesota Press, in press). See also Peter McLaren, "Foreword: Critical Theory and the Meaning of Hope," in *Teachers as Intellectuals: Toward a Pedagogy of Practical Learning* by Henry A. Giroux (South Hadley, MA: Bergin & Garvey, in press); Peter McLaren, "Postmodernism and the Death of Politics: A Brazilian Reprieve," *Educational Theory, 36* (1986), 389–401; Peter McLaren, *Life in Schools: An Introduction to Critical Pedagogy in the Social Foundations of Education* (New York: Longman, in press); and Laurie McDade, "The Deficit-Difference Debate: Theoretical Smokescreen for a Conservative Am-

bush," paper presented at the meeting of the Ohio Valley Philosophy of Education Society, Lexington, Kentucky, October 16, 1987.

21. Critics of this view of cultural transmission argue against the position that the meanings of great works are forever fixed, and assert instead that the very act of reading a text subjects the reader to the textual strategies of the writing in question and its attempt to position readers as subjects and to extend to them its values and view of the world. Feminist critics of this version of cultural literacy argue that it is possible to trace the formative power of patriarchal, class, and racial interests not just in modes of reading and the constitution of the canon, but in what is available to be read at all. See Chris Weedon, *Feminist Practice and Poststructuralist Theory* (New York: Basil Blackwell, 1987), pp. 169–170. We gain a key insight into Hirsch's epistemology and pedagogy from his early work, *Validity in Interpretation* (New Haven: Yale University Press, 1967), which is concerned with how meaning is communicated. According to Hirsch, meanings can be shared and truth thus preserved because the objects of understanding have a unitary, fixed, or ideal essence. Meanings are determinate, possess boundaries and self-identity, and can be directly transferred from the consciousness of one person to that of another. This makes it possible for a number of persons to hold the same meaning or to share similar interpretations of events. In Hirsch's view, individuals are the authors of their own meanings: they claim actual ownership over their meanings. Thus, people can share in other people's meanings quite readily. Meanings are stable and determinant and escape the contingency and indeterminacy of individual consciousness. In this account, Hirsch's epistemology is very traditional and stands in direct opposition to more recent influences within the domain of critical pedagogy made by deconstruction and postmodern social theory. For Hirsch, meanings can be willed by individuals who fix the contexts of their messages. To share somebody's meaning, we must become subservient to the will or unified with the intentionality of the author of that meaning. In contrast, deconstruction attacks the concept of rational volition and the law of identity, as do recent manifestations of poststructuralism, continental philosophy, and postfeminism. The concepts of the "decentered subject" and the radical discontinuity and fragmentation of the ideal object—which are taken seriously in these recent theories of discourse—have important implications for developing a pedagogy of literacy. By purging concepts of their unequivocal metaphysical foundations (foundations which Hirsch seeks to preserve at all costs), the concepts of truth and meaning become, in the poststructuralist view, contingent on the contexts of culture, language, history, and the material forces of production. This formulation of meaning shatters the concept of the *ideal wholeness of meaning* which undergirds the epistemology of Hirsch. Freire and Macedo, in contrast to Hirsch, are in partial sympathy with the poststructuralist position on meaning in that they recognize its contingency and ideological dimensions, which they argue must be probed by a radical doubt. Freire and Macedo are not denying that meanings may be intended and communicated by an author; rather, they suggest that meanings cannot be essentialized outside of the experiences readers bring to those meanings, the cultural contexts in which those meanings are generated, and the historical juncture in which text and reader meet. Language, in this view, is structurally open and may be detached from the intention of its user. That is, there always exists the possibility that language may position both author and reader ideologically within relations of power according to the contextual specificities of race, class, and gender. These contexts must be understood and addressed if we are to become critically literate. Hirsch, however, assumes that meanings, as fixed and shareable, may be transferred from text to reader independent of the messy web of ideological ingredients that might throw doubt on or alter the substance of what the author of the text intended. Freire and Macedo do not assume that meanings can be deposited in readers' minds as fixed essences, for in their view, meanings inscribed by language are always subject to the contextual specificity of their generation and reception. Meanings, in other words, are always dependent upon who interprets them and the experiences brought to the act of interpretation. For instance, neither women's nor men's experiences as readers are homogeneous. The same is true for White women and Black women, White men and Black men, middle-class students and economically disenfranchised students. For a discussion of Hirsch's epistemology in relation to the theories of Wittgenstein and Derrida, see Henry Staten, *Wittgenstein and Derrida* (Lincoln: University of Nebraska Press, 1984). pp. 139–145.

22. Adrian Bennett has enlarged our understanding of the politics of literacy by recognizing that students do not simply communicate sociolinguistically through various "participant structures" (that is, restricted or elaborate codes, oral or literate modes, literary practices), but also engage in what he calls "participant struggles." Bennett uses this term to underscore his observation that students frequently question the contradictions inherent in the ideologies voiced by the teacher, very often without recognizing it. Bennett formulates illiteracy as an act of refusal, one in which students engage in a struggle over the ways in which conflicting interpretations of the

social world are considered valid by both students and teachers alike. In this view, becoming literate, or refusing to be literate, involves a sociopolitical struggle over whether the teacher's interpretation of the world is to prevail and over how much serious accord will be given the voices of the students. Acquiring literacy is thus fundamentally linked to the model of social life students and teachers use to articulate their ideas in their interaction with each other, and to what degree these models are tied to specific social, political, and economic interests. The crucial question that is immediately raised by this insight is: What are the social conditions that construct the framework out of which students and teachers "read" particular forms of knowledge? See Adrian T. Bennett, *The Struggle for Voice: Literacy and Consciousness in an East Harlem School* (South Hadley, MA: Bergin & Garvey, in press). See also Peter McLaren, *Schooling as a Ritual Performance* (New York: Routledge & Kegan Paul, 1986).

23. See S. Krashen and D. Biber, *Bilingual Education in California,* report prepared for the California Association for Bilingual Education, 1987. See also Jim Cummins, *Bilingualism and Special Education: Issues in Assessment and Pedagogy* (Clevedon, Eng.: Multilingual Matters, 1984, copublished in the United States by College-Hill Press, San Diego); Jim Cummins, "Empowering Minority Students: A Framework for Intervention," *Harvard Educational Review, 56* (1986), 18–36; and Jim Cummins, *Empowering Minority Students* (Albany: State University of New York Press, in press).

24. See David Lusted, "Why Pedagogy?" *Screen, 27* (1986), 4–5.

25. See Magda Lewis and Roger I. Simon, "A Discourse Not Intended for Her: Learning and Teaching within Patriarchy," *Harvard Educational Review, 56* (1986), 457–472. See also Henry A. Giroux and Roger Simon, "Ideology, Popular Culture and Pedagogy," *Curriculum and Teaching* (in press).

26. Gary Saul Morson, "Preface: Perhaps Bakhtin," in *Bakhtin: Essays and Dialogues on His Work,* ed. Gary Saul Morson (Chicago: University of Chicago Press, 1986), p. x.

# Essay Review

## The Voices of Communities and Language in Classrooms

HAROLD ROSEN
*University of London Institute of Education*

WAYS WITH WORDS
by Shirley Brice Heath.
*Cambridge, Eng.: Cambridge University Press, 1983. 448 pp.*

The reputation of Shirley Brice Heath's book will have marched triumphantly ahead of this review, not, I hasten to add, because of a voguish novelty in its content, not because it is ethnography-on-the-doorstep, but rather because it represents a unique blend of cultural-linguistic analysis with a resolute intention to intervene positively in the world she describes. We have not been short of analyses in the human sciences which purport to offer, and on occasion actually provide, illumination to teachers. Heath's huge endeavor to present the texture and meaning of the daily goings-on and of the talk, as we say, of "ordinary folk" is complemented by a readiness, notoriously rare, to work alongside teachers in the construction of programs and practices. These are then informed by an awareness of the language and culture she has come to know as "ethnographer learning." For all her expertise she stays a learner, offering the teachers and students ways of understanding but also learning from them.

Trackton and Roadville are the two small communities at the heart of Heath's study. They are, you might say, exotic little places as remote—culturally speaking—from the lives of most contemporary city dwellers or farming communities as the Trobriand Islands described by Bronislaw Malinowski.[1] Why, then, should we follow with the closest attention the inhabitants' daily doings on porches or in the plaza, and eavesdrop on their chatter? We must admit that we often have a voyeuristic taste for scenes from the lives of those who in space, time, or culture seem distantly bizarre. There are academic studies which pander, wittingly or unwittingly, to these desires in peeping-Tom mainstreamers. Heath's book, however, is never in danger of being one. Heath proposes that (a) there are more Roadvilles and Tracktons than we recognise and know about, even if they are a stone's throw away, and (b) that

*Harvard Educational Review*   Vol. 55   No. 4   November 1985, 448–456

schools which address themselves to formulating a culture-sensitive curriculum must be, in a sense, ethnographic centers. Her book, then, is no travelogue for the fireside but a sharp challenge to everyone concerned with schooling, teachers in particular.

Heath is a rare figure, an academic who does not see her role as a chastener of the ignorant. We do not have to hear yet again how teachers have got it all wrong, are victims of their cultural prejudices, and are irredeemably class-bound, linguistically naive, and politically impotent. She operates amongst them as a colleague who shares their dilemmas and strategies. It can be put very simply: she is not seeking the accolades of the academy but intends, when her ethnography is put to work, to help students to learn.

Back then to Roadville and Trackton in the Piedmont Carolinas. We might have called these two tiny collections of houses industrial villages. Almost—for they lack the communal amenities we associate with the term "village," except for churches, which are shown to play a major role in the people's lives. Trackton is black and Roadville is white. They are both dependencies of the textile mill, the major source of employment for these working-class people. They are both off the beaten track and some way from Gateway, a small town which Heath sees as the embodiment of mainstream values. Until she takes us fully into their lives, the people and their towns seem fragile, marginalized in a society which has passed them by. Vulnerable encampments, microghettos. It is here—in these towns and in Gateway—that Heath installs herself with the solid advantage that she grew up in Piedmont and has personal acquaintances in both Roadville and Trackton. *And she pursues her work for ten years:* watching infants grow up and enter school and get jobs; witnessing marriages, departures, deaths. Ten years, I say again, from 1969 to 1978.

In an uncompromising prologue, Heath lays out the context and theoretical starting-points of her study. The context was the concern felt by "black and white teachers, parents, and mill personnel," about communication, the "effects of the preschool home and community environment on the learning of those language structures and uses which were needed in classrooms and job settings" (p. 2). At this point, let me pause to say that the citation of the "concern" felt by certain significant people does not make clear whether Heath subscribed to that view or is merely tendering it for the record. I had the same difficulty at certain critical points in the text. The concern of millowners baffles me, too, for right down at the end of the book we are told that the mill offers "almost no opportunities to write, few chances to read, and almost no occasions when their uses of oral language are critical for success" (p. 365).

Heath sets out, nevertheless, to satisfy a "need for a full description of the primary face-to-face interactions of children from community cultures other than [the] mainstream one" (p. 3) which would meet the above concerns and in the end "help working-class black and white children learn more effectively" (p. 4). At this stage in the text certain terms begin to glow provocatively. I take it that here "working class" is being contrasted with "mainstream." What then does "mainstream" imply? Middle class? There is the suggestion here of a norm. Sure enough, tucked away in the notes to a later chapter is an attempt to face up to the difficulty (p. 392, n. 2), but it raises more questions than it answers: What are the *fundamental* determinants of class? How do the practices of everyday life relate to them? Who are the "middle class" and to what extent it is a homogeneous stratum? Yet her allegiance is clear and explains how it was that she became, through her collaboration with teachers, an "associate, colleague, aide, and sometime-coauthor of curricular materials" (p. 4).

The aspirations are familiar enough—more effective learning by students through deeper understanding of the culture by teachers—yet we know these aspirations have been repeatedly challenged; mainstream school culture has been criticized as promoting shoddy or even pernicious values; it has been contended that schools are class institutions which internally regulate their diet for different clients; it has been said that mainstream culture does not exist, for there is no such homogeneous thing in our society, and so on. The relationship between schools and jobs is never a simple one, and the proposition that certification and high test scores will lead into the Promised Land is a plain and painful delusion. I think Heath knows all this and is content at the outset to pretend a certain innocence. The key lies in her tart and brief rejection of certain bleak, radical views at the very end of the book:

> It is easy to claim that a radical restructuring of society or the system of education is needed for the kind of cultural bridging reported in this book to be large scale and continuous. I have chosen to focus on the information and bridging skills needed for teachers and students as individuals to make changes which were for them radical, and to point to ways these cultural brokers between communities and classrooms can perhaps be the beginning of larger changes. (p. 369)

Heath is no political innocent: she has read her Bowles and Gintis (see p. 369, n. 5), and much more besides; and she may be reassured, because at a period of intense attack from the Right on the best hopes of schools, teachers, and students (recorded in a moving section of the epilogue), it no longer looks so radical to join in the attack.[2]

Moreover, Heath makes clear that she has rejected totally the well-known scientific model of "experiments" and research design. Instead she offers a record of "the natural flow of community and classroom life over nearly a decade . . . actual processes, activities, and attitudes involved in the enculturation of children in Roadville and Trackton" (p. 8). It should be noted that Gateway gets nothing like the "thick description" which is lovingly devoted to Trackton and Roadville (the ratio is approximately seven to one, the townspeople getting one chapter of twenty-six pages). Perhaps the assumption is that her most likely readers all swim in the mainstream one way or another, or have at least gazed at it long enough from the bank, but it does raise some problems. More of that later. For the moment let us emphasize that she is content to let her case rest in the hands of her readers, who must be the judges of how scientific her work is. This reviewer-reader's assessment is that, if anything, she might have probed further, in her own chosen manner, certain aspects of the lives of the communities which for me remain shrouded in mystery. But before pursuing that, I have to say without equivocation that I applaud her stance. Whether the research watchdogs bark or not, I cannot imagine anyone honestly concerned with the complex interpretation of community, language, and schooling who would not choose to become caught up in the fates of the infants, young people, and old folk who are brought to life with deep but unsentimental respect in her text. No research training of any type could by itself produce her eye and her voice. These must emerge from values which we are left to deduce less from explicit intellectual propositions than from our perceptions of her conduct. I defy any reader to exorcise Heath from her account, to distinguish the dancer from the dance. The result is not an egocentric display but a subtle refusal to disappear behind the foliage of research lingo. She openly acknowledges a role, openly intervenes, and finally goes for total immersion in a bold collaboration with teachers and students. The "neutral observer" becomes a sorry figure in comparison. Listen to the infants of Trackton talking to Heath about some wooden blocks she had brought for them to play with and we get a glimpse of how involved they are with her. " 'Dese Shannon's blocks?' 'You buy dese?' 'Can I keep dese?' 'What you do wid 'em?' 'How'd dat git dere/*pointing to the glue/*?' " (p. 107).

One more insistence: the book represents an unwavering case for looking at the social and cultural context in a particular kind of way rather than constructing an edifice of discrete data ("input," as she says witheringly). We know about context these days. A lot of people vote for it. We know too the acrimonious battles fought in the field of linguistics (compare Halliday to Chomsky).[3] It seems almost strange that Heath should have to underline its importance. However, her warm acknowledgment of Dell Hymes as her teacher should remind us that, as he has so persuasively argued, only a profound awareness of who and what our students are and the accommodation of that awareness in the ways schools conduct themselves can take us forward.[4] But there are those who bitterly dispute this idea. Here in Britain there are those who argue that it is none of our business. Schools must deliver the national culture, whatever that is, to students, whoever they are. For Heath, culture includes history. Obvious again? Not at all. There are sociological studies, including sociolinguistic studies, which assume that the working class has no history, that it is no more than "the murmur of societies," "a multitude of qualified heroes who lose their names and faces while becoming the mobile language of calculations and rationalities."[5] Teachers, schools, curricula have histories too. Heath is as good as her word. Her book begins with a history of workers in the mills of Piedmont. Yet this readiness to inscribe history into ethnography creates its own vulnerability.

Rich and intimate as it is, Heath's description cannot be total; telling how it is means telling how it seems through a prism which foregrounds the significant and does not register what seems insignificant. Consider this: "Any reader who tries to explain the community contrast in this book on the basis of race will miss the central point of the focus of culture as learned behavior and on language habits as part of that shared learning. Children in Roadville and Trackton came to have different ways of communicating, because their communities had different social legacies" (p. 11).

I was distressed by this evasion, especially as it runs counter to some of the deepest *implicit* awarenesses of the book. A second reading (my first was almost uncritically rapturous) revealed a persistent refusal to confront the issue of race. I do not trust Heath's apparent naivete; at best it is an astute calculation of political possibilities. Throughout the text we are made aware that Roadville is white and Trackton is black. Why bother? Yes, indeed, communities have different social legacies. A major component of this legacy must be the experience of racism and *its continued existence.* Why has Heath chosen to warn us off? Black English is the expression and negotiation of black experience. Racism does no more than lurk in the shadows of this text, raising questions which are not posed by Heath. The historical chapter firmly announces, "The Civil Rights Movement forced the breaking of the color barrier on hiring, and blacks began to assume production line jobs in the mills" (p. 27). In the rest of the book there is scarcely a whiff of the continuation of that struggle. Are Trackton people so "lumpen" that none of their "ways with words" are affected? One way of cleansing the book of such awkward considerations is to avoid (a) analyzing talk in black and white encounters and (b) probing further the implications of what momentarily pops up in the text. From the description of Gateway, homogeneously "mainstream," there peeps out the existence of black suburbs. Suddenly we hear someone in Roadville declaring, "When the niggers (pause) uh, the blacks, you know, started comin' in, I knew that wasn't for me. I wasn't ever gonna work for no nigger" (p. 39). These almost subliminal moments make one aware of a kind of self-denying ordinance or self-censorship operating in the ethnography.

By the same token, Heath's history tells how "workers began to show signs of an independent and unbiddable spirit when strikes claimed the lives of some of their leaders" (p. 25). Does nothing of that remain in either Roadville or Trackton? Apparently not. In speaking of Trackton, Heath writes that "they do not themselves take part in any aspect of the political process . . ." (p. 62). Of white Roadville no such comment is made, though it seems to apply equally. For them "the sun shines on the chimneys of the mill" (p. 47). On the job in both Roadville and Trackton, "workers look for no reasons for the task, nor do they give their opinion of the role of their task in the whole. . . . The topics of their talk rarely include their work" (p. 365). I find it odd, but it is perhaps true. Are they unionized or not? Do they never talk about their working conditions and attempt to change them? Is it all harmony, or resignation? Do blacks and whites occupy the same kinds of posts, and is this never a theme of anyone's conversation? What is the significance of the fact that "most households [in Trackton] have a double portrait of Coretta and Martin Luther King" (p. 55)?

Gateway's townspeople, we are told, are mainstreamers divided into two groups— "old-timers" and "newcomers." From thousands of miles away I remain skeptical. I cannot believe they are all economically and professionally successful, that there are no sharp divisions and clashes based on ethnicity and class. Nor can I envisage a town of 50,000 inhabitants without its "lower orders"—garage mechanics, truck drivers, workers in small enterprises, street cleaners, hospital employees, school ancillary staff, minor government employees, and so forth.

I have a feeling that there is a calculated strategy behind this, for, as I have indicated, Heath is highly conscious of these matters and how they have been debated. Yet she treads very warily round them. The reason eludes me. The book is far, far richer ethnographically than, for example, Paul Willis's *Learning to Labour*,[6] but far weaker politically. However, nothing I have said would lead anyone to be in doubt about the unique qualities of this book. Indeed, I suspect that it is constructed in order to provoke my kind of response.

Let us now see how Heath imposed order on what must have been one of the most daunting piles of accumulated material ever to have confronted a researcher at the moment of writing-up. Part 1 begins by taking us into the two communities, sampling their day-to-day living and their notions of "getting-on." Armed with this awareness, we are led into a presentation of "learning how to talk" in Trackton and "teaching how to talk" in Roadville, which simultaneously compares early language development in the two communities and enlarges our view of how life is conducted. It is a credit to Heath that there is no way of summarizing the density of her descriptions. All is alive and enacted. But at carefully selected moments a very legible signpost appears. In black Trackton, for example, "babies are in the midst of nearly constant human communication . . . which flows about them" (pp. 74, 75). In white Roadville: "At both individual and group levels, the belief in and practice of using 'the right word' help structure the cognitive patterns which children draw of the world, i.e. what they come to know, and their notion of how to show what they know. Rigidly prescribed oral performance . . . is the way to prove learning" (p. 144).

Yet it is the voices, scenes, and episodes which command our attention and stir our thinking. In what for me is the most memorable transcript in the book, Annie Mae of Trackton, "the community cultural broker," delivers her sociolinguistic analysis and language development curriculum:

> He gotta learn to *know* 'bout dis world, can't nobody tell 'im. Now just how crazy is dat? White folks uh hear dey kids say sump'n, dey say it back to 'em, dey aks 'em 'gain 'n 'gain 'bout things, like dey 'posed to be born knowin'. You think I kin tell Teegie all he gotta know to get along? He just gotta be keen, keep his eyes open, don't he be sorry. Gotta watch hisself by watchin' other folks. Ain't no use me tellin' 'im: 'Learn dis, learn dat. What's dis? What's dat?' He just gotta learn, gotta know; he see one thing one place one time, he know how it go, see sump'n like it again, maybe it be de same, maybe it won't. He hafta try it out. If he don't he be in real trouble; he get lef out. Gotta keep yo' eyes open, gotta feel to know. (p. 84)

> Watcha *call* it ain't so important as whatcha *do* with it. That's what things 'n people are for, ain't it? (p. 112)

I can see myself and others interpreting that text, knowing that in the process I am telling Annie Mae what she means, and in the stiff cadences, our stock-in-trade, losing its nuances and fervor.

Compare the do-it-yourself Headstart program of white Roadville as Peggy sees it.

> I figure it's up to me to give 'im a good start. I reckon there's just some things
> I know he's gotta learn, you know, what things are, and all that. 'n you just don't
> happen onto doin' all that right. Now, you take Danny 'n Bobby, we, Betty 'n
> me, we talk to them kids all the time, like they was grown-up or something, 'n
> we try to tell 'em bout things, 'n books, 'n we buy those educational toys for 'em.
> (pp. 127–128)

Always, Heath by her uncanny ear makes her choices jump from the page at you, and the invitation is to understand before we rush to deliver verdicts or pigeonholed complex utterances in neatly polarized concepts (restricted/elaborated; universalistic/ particularistic).

The story continues. We move on to consider oral traditions in Roadville and Trackton and then literate traditions. I shall single out one central aspect of oral traditions—narrative—and let it stand as a paradigm for all that is best in this book. Since I hold that narrative is a touchstone of oral tradition, I believe that Heath's account should become a point of reference for all discussion of spontaneous oral story telling.[7] Moreover, Heath's work on literacy in the community was being cited widely before the appearance of this book.[8]

In Roadville there are criteria for story telling which establish a clear framework, firmly excluding some possibilities and making very clear the principles of inclusion. Stories must be accounts of actual events, free from hyperbole, "an expression of social unity, a commitment to maintenance of the norms of the church and the roles within the mill community's life" (p. 150). Above all, they require a moral or summary message. The induction of children into story telling constitutes a dramatic apprenticeship to this tradition: "Children in Roadville are not allowed to tell stories, unless an adult announces that something which happened to a child makes a good story and invites a retelling. When children are asked to retell such events, they are expected to tell non-fictive stories which 'stick to the truth'" (p. 158).

Fictive stories are lies. Roadville stories are moral episodes, and the monitoring of their narrations ensures that the model is thoroughly learned.

*Sue:*     Why did you drop your eggs? What did Aunt Sue tell you 'bout climbing
on that thing?

*Wendy:*   We better be careful.

*Sue:*     No, 'bout eggs 'n climbing?

*Wendy:*   We better not climb with our eggs, else 'n we'd drop 'em. (p. 158)

To turn to Trackton's stories is to enter another narrative universe. In Trackton, "Good story-tellers . . . may base their stories on an actual event, but they creatively fictionalize the details surrounding the real event, and the outcome of the story may not even resemble what indeed happened" (p. 166).

Stories do not contain didactic highlighting to guide or control moral conduct. The stories must be dramatic, and therefore storytellers frequently resort to dialogue, which in itself opens up a source of mimicry, humor, narrative point. The free expression of feeling generates word-play and word-artistry which Heath is quick to pounce on (see twelve-year-old Terry's tale on p. 181 in which fantasy and reality are inextricably intertwined). She sums up her detailed examination and comparison with a bold contrast: "In short, for Roadville, Trackton's stories would be lies; for Trackton, Roadville's stories would not even count as stories" (p. 189). All this is laid out beautifully and delicately for us: the participants, the settings, the microdramas of the tellings and their subtexts. To all this are added some very detailed inspections of the storyteller's art in both communities, rounded off with a more general and distanced view. However, to demur a little again, there is no attempt to tell us *why* such divergent cultural practices have arisen, nor to see their roots in the social and economic experience of the narrator. Black and white again?

Part 2 is the knight's move, for it contains an account of the collaboration between the author and the schools, a maneuver of high risk not only in its execution but even more in its being recorded here in cold print. The project, as I have indicated, is "to make accessible to teachers an understanding of the differences in language and culture their students bring to their classrooms" (p. 265), and then to engage in the development of programs and practices in the light of that understanding. The goal is success in school for everyone. Heath recounts in detail the endeavors of the teachers. It would be easy to dismiss much of what the teachers do as familiar curriculum practice—familiar, that is, to anyone conversant with the curriculum reforms of the last twenty years—for example, what came to be regarded as "good practice" before the current fierce dismantling process got under way. Mrs. Gardner, having been allocated a class of nineteen black first-grade students designated potential failures, opens up her classroom and engages in her now-despised "activity methods." Her children tell stories and there is lots of talk. That old standby, the grocery store, is set up in another class. In a fifth-grade science class, consisting again of black boys with a low reading level, an ethnographic project on local agricultural practices is mounted, involving the youngsters in work in the community. To say we've heard all this before is to miss the point. It is the nature and consequences of the process of change which are significant, and if they include reinventing the wheel (a much maligned practice!), so be it. The contrast is between, on the one hand, teachers and students actively engaged in changing their ways of learning and teaching and, on the other, uniform programs emanating from above which presume that teachers are mere docile transmitters and that learners are uniform and culture-free in their needs. I feel it both irrelevant and impertinent, therefore, to scrutinize closely the language teaching described in this section. In any case, there are better things to do than snigger at one teacher's enthusiasm for topic sentences or another's insistence on "a school-accepted format" (p. 320) for written work. But, of course, this puts Heath in a difficult position. She too rejects the role of judge and jury, but her respect for the teachers and children leaves us to guess, though not without clues and nudging, where her preferences lie. The science-cum-ethnography project is described with scarcely concealed delight, but it includes amongst its goals the mastery of "the language of science" and making "acceptable scientific statements" (p. 325). It would appear that this includes, "avoid telling stories about their knowledge: be able to discuss an item or event for its own sake, not in terms of their direct experiences with it" (p. 325). Do those suspect goals receive Heath's imprimatur? I give her the benefit of the doubt, for she must know the philosophical and linguistic debate on these matters. I never understand what it means to do something for "its own sake." And what has Heath been doing for the previous three hundred pages but telling stories about her knowledge, and not for their own sake but for ours?

Picking her way judiciously through the innovations, Heath makes very clear that the teachers did not see themselves as launching basic changes in content, nor abandoning established classroom methods (basal readers, for example). The criteria for "school success" in the end remain unchanged, and the core of mainstream values is not tampered with: "students learned to share the goals and methods of the classroom" (p. 340). There is not a hint that black and white students in the Carolinas studying in the same classrooms might raise some tricky issues in history and social studies and in the job-getting aspects of some of their work. What Heath has chosen to do is to present all that seems most positive in the teachers' work and to imply that ethnicity did not affect the basic processes. Yet, the introduction of teachers—and later, students—to ethnographic ways of studying surreptitiously their own and their community's practices does in fact erode the old curriculum. New *ways* of learning constitute new learning. How else can one begin? As Heath observes, "Students now provided information for the teacher to question—the reverse of the usual classroom practice of the teacher presenting the information and questioning students on their knowledge" (p. 342). Furthermore, she offers: "Critical in the thinking of these teachers was that their approach was not a remedial one designed for poor learners. Instead, they felt that the attention given to different ways of talking and knowing, and the manipulation of contexts and language benefited all students" (p. 355).

The principles do not in themselves constitute a complete apparatus for changing the role of language in the curriculum, but they have a huge potential if pushed to their logical conclusion. They could be extended into a critical examination of the language of textbooks or the ways in which communities are linked to and shaped by influential forces in society, including the ways in which language is used in the media, by politicians and others, to affect daily lives. Finally, there is the question of how Roadville and Trackton students are to develop their own voices so that they can articulate a critical view of society and act more powerfully in it. Ethnography cannot by itself achieve these ends. To assert this is not to diminish the courageous work of the teachers; it is only to sketch out its essentially initiatory character and its vulnerability.

And vulnerable it proved to be. In a sad but all too familiar phrase, we learn that "in the Piedmont of today, the methods used by these teachers have all but disappeared" (p. 356). The bureaucracy of tests has taken over and, as one teacher says, "there's no joy left in teaching now" (p. 359). This defeat is known on both sides of the Atlantic. To reverse it requires acting outside the classroom.

Heath writes in her last pages of "a recognition and a drive to use language as a source of power," but an indication of limits she sets herself is registered in the way that the sentence tails off into a circumscribed notion of power and its source: "for access to and maintenance of expanded types and places of work" (p. 363). The source of the power is much more than the job market.

In the end, teachers can defend successfully the enclaves they have constructed only if they have won the parents and community to their methods and can invoke their support in sustaining them. And those are "ways with words" which have to be learned too. They constitute the language of political participation. If all of us do not learn this way with words, we shall go on placing wreaths on the tombstones of projects all over the world, overcome with sadness and impotence.

Whatever we do or fail to do in resisting the conversion of our schools into brutally frank machines for social control, in the end thousands of teachers must encounter millions of students daily in classrooms. Heath's book suggests to us a new way of looking at that encounter. Ethnographers are the heroes of her text. There are other kinds of heroes whom we need to acknowledge, but that should not prevent us from saluting the ethnographers—and Shirley Brice Heath in particular.

## Notes

1. Malinowski, *Coral Gardens and Their Magic*, vol. 2 (London: Allen & Unwin, 1935).
2. See, for example, Henry Giroux's *Theory and Resistance in Education* (Portsmouth, NH: Heinemann, 1983).
3. See M. A. K. Halliday, *Language as Social Semiotic* (London: Edward Arnold, 1978); and Noam Chomsky, *Language and Responsibility* (Sussex: Harvester Press, 1979).
4. For a rich elaboration of Dell Hymes's ideas, see Hymes, *Language in Education: Ethnolinguistic Essays* (Washington, DC: Center for Applied Linguistics, 1980); and Hymes, *Ethnolinguistic Study of Classroom Discourse*, Final Report to the National Institute of Education (ERIC, 1982. ED 217–710). The thesis he elaborates is summed up in the latter document:

   > Educational linguistics requires a theoretical groundwork of its own. What is now called "theoretical linguistics" leaves out of account too much of what educational linguistics must consider. The teacher interpreting the verbal behavior of children must take into account intonation, classroom context, personal histories, community background. The teacher must always take into account abilities, means, and intentions that can be operating in the context in question. This set is likely to be less than the formally imaginable ideal set of the language as a whole, on the one hand, and is likely to include possibilities not taken into account by the formal models. (p. 22)

   Hymes also provides an example very relevant to Heath's approach: "Narrative behavior, the telling of stories in class that seem disorderly to us because of our own assumptions about narrative order, may actually express an order of its own, coming from another set of cultural understandings as to what it is to report experience, tell a story, make a speech, and the like" (p. 23).
5. See Michel De Certeau, "On the Oppositional Practices of Everyday Life," *Social Text, 1* (1980), 3–43.
6. Willis, *Learning to Labour* (Westmead, Eng.: Saxon House, 1977).
7. See Rosen, *Stories and Meanings* (Sheffield, Eng.: National Association for the Teaching of English, 1984).
8. See, for example, "Protean Shapes in Literacy Events," in *Spoken and Written Language: Exploring Orality and Literacy,* ed. Deborah Tannen (Norwood, NJ: Ablex, 1982).

# Essay Review

## The Cultural Organization of Teaching and Learning

E R I C  B R E D O, *University of Virginia*
M A R Y  H E N R Y, *Washington State University*
R. P. McDERMOTT, *Stanford University*

CLASSROOM DISCOURSE: THE LANGUAGE OF TEACHING
AND LEARNING
by Courtney B. Cazden.
*Portsmouth, NH: Heinemann, 1988. 230 pp.*

Courtney Cazden's *Classroom Discourse* is a "progress report" that attempts to summarize and synthesize what has been discovered about how teachers and children
can, do, and even should talk with each other in classrooms. Cazden attempts to
distill the results of classroom studies from anthropology, linguistics, social psychology, and psychology. Some of the research is based on her own teaching in a
second- and third-grade classroom, which she and Hugh Mehan videotaped and
reviewed for clues to the nature of classroom language.[1] The book moves easily from
Cazden's personal experiences as a teacher to examples of classroom talk drawn from
one or another study to more abstract conceptualizations of classroom events. Each
chapter can be seen as a short lesson for teachers on key concepts and empirical
research relating to a particular topic in classroom discourse.

Cazden's volume is distinctive because it is grounded in ethnographic research,
using many examples drawn from the moment-to-moment lives of real teachers
around the country, and because it locates many of the problems faced by minority
children and their teachers in cultural differences in the communicative skills they
bring to school. After briefly discussing these two aspects of the book, we describe

We want to thank Anneke Bredo for her helpful suggestions for this review.

*Harvard Educational Review*  Vol. 60  No. 2  May 1990, 247–258

its contents in some detail, offer a number of points of appreciation, and conclude with some questions raised by the book's approach.

## Ethnographic Perspective

To her early training in psycholinguistics Cazden brought social concerns about how to deliver equal education to all children. These concerns developed side-by-side with a growing focus on communication in both linguistics and ethnography. In the 1960s, Dell Hymes[2] was urging anthropologists to focus their ethnographies on the details of how people talk with each other, and William Labov[3] was showing how racial and class divisions separating Black and White Americans could be described by attending to the phonological details of the talk of people from different communities in different situations. Cazden helped relate this developing ethnographic and linguistic research to the problem of equal education.[4]

A major step in bringing this focus on communication to bear on educational issues was the publication in 1972 of the book *Functions of Language in the Classroom.*[5] This volume, edited by Cazden, Vera John, and Dell Hymes, brought together a variety of research papers documenting the difficulties that children and teachers have in communicating with each other using the language and dialects of their various communities. It made abstract communicative concerns more specific and concrete for educators, while also presenting examples of research in culturally varied settings. Educational research had been dominated by approaches that, in the name of rigor, were in danger of killing the phenomena they set out to study,[6] and the Cazden volume helped show the viability of an ethnographic approach as an alternative.

Cazden's latest book also draws on ethnographic research, which is inherently local in focus. As Clifford Geertz noted, ethnographers do not study cultures, they study *in* cultures.[7] Despite this local focus, ethnographers may then use data from a single event to address issues at different levels of analysis. Depending on how data are handled, events from a single classroom can be used to address issues in the lives of the particular children in the class or in the wider community that brought the children together; issues facing all members of American society or indeed any country with a school system in a modern economy. It is as though one were looking at a small piece of a much larger and intricately patterned carpet. This piece can be used to help see patterns of many different sizes. This is true in the study of social interaction in particular, since smaller scale or shorter run events are constructed with reference to conceptions of broader and longer run events.[8] Among these various possibilities, Cazden focuses in detail on the classroom level itself, rather than on broader features of American culture or society or the institutional structure of schooling.

In bringing ethnographic research to teaching and learning, Cazden has also contributed to an emerging intellectual dialogue between psychology and anthropology. At the same time that Hymes, Labov, and Cazden were bringing linguistics and ethnography to the classroom, Michael Cole was criticizing the standard assumptions implicit in psychological theory and research and trying to carve out an ethnographic approach to psychology.[9] Criticism of traditional psychological approaches to thinking and learning, which take roles and goals as predefined rather than negotiated and discovered, has continued, and is reflected in the current interest in a theory of practical cognition. We now have a number of studies of "situated," "everyday," or "practical" thinking and learning, giving us, perhaps, the beginnings of some theory in this area.[10] This new interest, to which Cazden's latest book can be seen as a contribution, seems promising both for revitalizing overly decontextualized and fragmented academic research and for providing a more realistic understanding of educational processes.

## Normative Perspective

It may be helpful to consider as well the normative underpinnings of Cazden's book. Books for teachers often rest on unstated assumptions about the problems to be found in classrooms. By framing problems in a particular way, they focus attention on a certain set of possible solutions and neglect others. One common orientation is the "cultural deficit" view, in which the researcher or practitioner implicitly looks down upon minority cultures from the standpoint of the majority or dominant culture, viewing failing children from minority cultures as deprived and disabled by their own experiences. This was once an easily taken for granted position, and despite being under attack in academic circles for the past twenty years, it lives on in many commonsense accounts of schooling, such as those that view difficulties of minority students as due to their limited "intelligence." In this view at its worst, groups whose members tend to fail are blamed for their own condition, with the implication that they should change themselves or expect to be justifiably weeded out.

A more recently popular position in the educational research community is the "cultural difference" view, whereby another culture is regarded as equally valuable and sensible, and school failure is examined in terms of the communicative misunderstanding that develops between minority group children and majority group teachers. Cazden appears, in general, to adopt this view, at times explicitly and at other times implicitly, arguing that differences in school performance stem from interference between home cultures and school culture (pp. 3, 4). "When children fail to meet a teacher's expectations," she notes, "the cause will be sought in the complexities of the child's task, or cultural differences in our expectations, rather than in deficiencies in the children themselves" (p. 25). Furthermore, " . . . responsibility for doing everything possible to break into this circle of reciprocity remains with the teacher" (p. 94). The sensitivity of the sociolinguistic stand is in direct opposition to the "cultural deficit" approach. Any careful look at the language deficits of supposedly deprived children, for example, reveals a contextually competent and articulate speaker. For its insensitivity, Cazden calls the deficit approach "colonial."

Cazden's implicit position also differs from a more skeptical "cultural dominance" view, of which critical theory is an example.[11] From this standpoint one looks up at a dominant, institutionalized ideology, which represents a partial view that is self-interested and distorts understanding, because it is taken for the whole or only view. The ways schools identify and highlight cultural deficits and differences are seen as political acts that serve to legitimize inequality and division. While these distinctions may or may not be accepted by those they place at a disadvantage, they are often consciously or unconsciously resisted.[12] Loaded categories distinguishing between types of children (Black, White), types of action (school-relevant, street-wise), and types of performance (smart, dumb) may be tacitly imposed, and treated as if they are neutral descriptions. To overcome this falseness, it must be first recognized as such, and then changes made so that schools are not in the position of offering hope to groups or classes for whom there are few opportunities and whose failure must then be justified. Cazden does not directly criticize this approach but does note, "outside the scope of this book are analyses of school culture from the perspective of Marxist 'resistance theory' " (p. 155). For her focus on teaching, Cazden apparently finds the cultural difference approach most useful.

## Formal, Informal, and Expressive Talk

*Classroom Discourse* is divided into three main sections, "Talk with the Teacher," "Talk with Peers," and "Ways of Talking." The first focuses on the tacit cultural demands of the classroom: how these differ from those with which students are familiar at home and how such differences may affect learning. This is the longest section and represents the central focus of the book; it is also the one we emphasize. The second section is about informal talk among students in the classroom and what they may learn from interacting with one another, and the third is about the expressive use of talk by teachers and students, as they use different language "registers" and other means to convey their feelings and comment on their relationships. These three sections may be seen as loosely focusing on the propositional, social, and expressive functions of discourse that Cazden identifies in the beginning of the book, although each is also about other matters.

## The Hidden Demands of the Classroom: The Structure of Classroom Lessons

In school lessons, as in other stable social activities, the relational aspects tend to be taken for granted. In thinking about a lesson we tend to remember what was said or the teacher's emotional tone, quickly forgetting the underlying social-interactional pattern.

Cazden's aim in analyzing the interactional structure of classroom lessons is to make the hidden cultural demands of the classroom more visible to teachers, so that they may better understand the problems of students unprepared for these demands—although these same students may be well prepared for others. Carefully analyzing the interactional structure of a classroom lesson helps make its implicit demands explicit. Indeed, for Cazden, a structural description of these patterns is "a claim, or hypothesis, about the communicative competence (required) of both teacher and students" (p. 45).

Since it is by no means self-evident how to analyze patterns of social interaction fruitfully, Cazden attempts to provide tools that will help. She looks at lessons as rule-governed activities with an inner grammar of their own, specifying which kinds of social acts are culturally expected to follow which others. Two aspects of the social organization of lessons are highlighted: their selectional and sequential structures.[13] Just as a pianist must select a combination of keys to play, and play this combination at just the right point in a sequence, so too teachers or students must select a type of social action to take (such as asking a question, making a statement, or giving a command) and fit this selection into an appropriate point in the conversational sequence. The structure of conversations can be analyzed by looking at their organization in terms of the alternative types of actions that can be selected and the types of sequences that can be constructed when conversing in culturally appropriate ways.

For an analysis of the sequential pattern of interaction in lessons, Cazden primarily uses Hugh Mehan's careful description of her own classroom teaching.[14] Mehan found that lessons often have an instrumental pattern; the basic sequence includes a teacher Initiative followed by a student Response, which is in turn followed by a teacher Evaluation (in total, an "IRE" sequence).[15] This basic sequence may be then combined into larger, more complex sequences, ultimately forming a whole lesson. In effect, Mehan developed a way to formally analyze the pattern of social interaction evident in "recitational" teaching as well as to show how different levels of lesson structure are nested inside one another. Cazden also considers the selectional structure of discourse, drawing upon John Sinclair and Richard Coulthard's[16] analysis of the culturally appropriate types of alternative actions available at a given point in a sequence, to suggest some of the implications of selecting one or another form of expression at a particular time.

Cazden's discussion of these two aspects of the structure of lessons provides some helpful tools for systematically analyzing and reflecting upon the tacit cultural demands of the classroom. It helps to bring to light the instrumental and individualistic aspects of American classrooms. In some Asian cultures, for instance, the sequence of interaction during lessons better fits a rote learning pattern, rather than the instrumental learning pattern implicit in the IRE sequence. Likewise, in some cultures it is more appropriate for students to help each other in constructing an answer rather than placing a single individual on the spot as in recitational teaching. Seeing how these patterns are interactionally constructed helps show that the classroom environment is not simply a given, external object, but a socially generated pattern in whose maintenance and construction students play a part.

This analysis of Mehan and Cazden documents an important difference between classroom discourse and that of everyday life. For example, if you ask someone on the street, "What time is it?" and they reply, "Nine o'clock," then an appropriate response would be "Thank you." If a teacher asks the same question of a child in the classroom and receives the same answer, then the teacher's response is more likely to be something like "Very good." In passing street encounters one receives a simple appreciation for answering questions; in many second grades one is more likely to be evaluated. Indeed, though evaluation is unwelcome in most everyday encounters, it is at the heart of many (if not most) school events.

Cazden also considers the relationship between interactional patterns and the type of knowledge or subject being taught. She suggests that a recitational lesson structure

> is an interactional format that fits knowledge that is factual and can be evaluated as right or wrong, and can be subdivided into short units for demonstration in short student answers . . . some school content is like that—arithmetic facts and geographical information, for example. But [other contents, such as] . . . children's conceptions of fairness . . . are different kinds of knowledge that require a different kind of discourse structure [such as discussion]. (pp. 59–60)

At other points Cazden questions the notion that interactional arrangements should be fitted to the subjects being taught, noting that "we have to ask why the lesson-recitation form is more common in some schools than others" and "have to be alert to the danger that too much of the curriculum—especially for some children—is being reduced to the "algorithmic and the factual" (p. 51). For instance, some studies find that teachers tend to teach different subjects differently, such as by using more whole class instruction, instructional grouping, or individualized desk-work in one subject as compared to another.[17] Cazden recognizes that the constraints of the subject interact with those of the social pattern of talk, and presumably does not want to make either one a fixed constraint to which the other is summarily fitted. Teachers are urged to move beyond the mundane IRE structure in their classrooms and to more flexibly utilize other patterns, such as discussion.

## Sources of Trouble: Cultural Differences and Differential Treatment

Cazden next uses the analysis of tacit demands of the classroom to help understand how some students may have special difficulties at school. As she puts it, "For some children, there will be greater cultural discontinuity, greater sociolinguistic interference, between home and school" (p. 68). If we can better understand the sources of difficulty, then we can, presumably, also better remove them.

One can draw various inferences about cultural interference from the studies Cazden reviews, such as Susan Philip's study of classroom interaction on the Warm Springs Indian reservation,[18] Shirley Brice Heath's study of the "ways with words" of working-class Blacks and Whites in Appalachia,[19] and Kathryn Au's research on reading groups in the Kamehameha Early Education Program in Hawaii.[20] Warm Springs children may not be accustomed to being singled out to speak in front of others at the teacher's command; Black children from the town of Trackton are not used to direct questions for which the questioner already knows the answer; the Hawaiian children are not used to answering individually and separately from others' collaborative and overlapping contributions. In each case, the underlying hypothesis is that difficulty arises because of "incompletely shared awareness or acceptance of the norms of interaction" (p. 74). Conflict in cultural norms leads teachers to perceive student actions as socially inappropriate and deficient, rather than understanding them as complying with different standards.

The flip side of cultural difference is differential treatment, which Cazden considers in a review of research on how teachers treat high- versus low-achieving students in reading. She arrives at a more interesting interpretation of the data than the usual view that teachers are engaging in outright favoritism—namely, that teachers sacrifice meaning for mechanics when dealing with low-achieving students. Teachers of lower-track children are more likely to correct responses that have the correct meaning but are otherwise inappropriate, to pounce quickly on technical errors, and to fail to pick up on student initiatives, thereby interrupting the flow of meaning. To put the matter bluntly, those who fail to fit easily into the flow of social activity are all-too-often treated as though they are deficient, rather than as though they are trying to make sense of things in their own, possibly different, way. Cazden concludes that "It is unfortunate if attention to understanding larger meaningful units of text is more neglected during instruction for the very children who may need it most" (p. 89).

This pattern of differential treatment for students in different ability level groups is reinforced by practices of instructional tracking and the dualistic learning theories that justify it. For instance, behavioristic rote learning is used with the "learning disabled," while cognitive problem-solving approaches are applied to the "gifted." In effect, this justifies teaching some children merely to follow routines while others learn to think. Cazden argues that efficient reading for everyone involves the co-ordinated use of both top-down (deductive, problem-solving) and bottom-up (inductive, rote) processes, rather than exclusively one or the other.

Cazden's review of research on cultural differences and differential treatment, though clear and useful, leaves unanswered the question of which cultural differences make a difference. Which of all the possible differences are likely to be seized upon as particularly glaring or egregious? Furthermore, people often get over their differences or even celebrate them, rather than making an issue of them, so "what makes ethnic differences become ethnic borders?"[21] Cazden asks this question, but does not pursue it, perhaps because it would lead her to a consideration of the broader social and political relations between groups, and away from the classroom focus. The reason the issue is important is that differences in the ways people think or act, barring blatant prejudice, are generally not so problematic in and of themselves; they only become actively problematic when people interfere with each other's goals or undercut each other's valued identities. And these goals and identities, as well as particular sensitivities to their frustrations, often have roots outside of the classroom. The problem may not be that people do not understand each other, but that their "misunderstandings" are often motivated and made consequential by wider political circumstances as well as narrower personal ones.[23]

## Solutions: Scaffolding and Recontextualization

Having diagnosed the problems of particular students as arising from cultural interference and differential treatment, Cazden turns to ways to improve teaching. She draws primarily on Lev Vygotsky's sociohistorical approach to individual development to suggest how classroom contexts may be more supportive and growth-enhancing for students.[23] One of Vygotsky's key assumptions is that concepts have their origins in social practices, rather than simply being "in one's head." As a result, learning a new concept is not so much a psychological as a social matter, like learning a new part in a game. In working out the relationship between verbal interaction and learning, Cazden begins to fill a significant gap in much of the work on cultural interference in the classroom, which has made it clear how interactional difficulties may arise, but has often neglected to make explicit the connections between interactional problems and learning difficulties.

Cazden's analysis of how teaching can be improved is organized in terms of two key concepts for a social-interactional view of learning: scaffolding and recontextualization. She explains the concept of scaffolding as follows:

> The adult so structures the game that the child can be a successful participant from the beginning; then, as the child's competence grows, the game changes so that there is always something new to be learned and tried out, including taking over what had been the adult's role. Bruner's term scaffold has become a common caption for the adult's role in these games, and it is a good name if we remember that this is a very special kind of scaffold—one that self-destructs gradually as the need lessens and the child's competence grows. (p. 104)

In other words, by scaffolding, the teacher or adult adaptively changes his or her participation in an interactive activity or game so that children may successfully participate, however minimally, in a whole activity, while continuing to be challenged and encouraged to contribute more fully as the activity becomes more manageable. Such sensitive adaptation on the part of a teacher to what a student can actually handle contrasts with the common practice of blaming students for not being able to play the "game" and assigning them to remediation (as in the pattern of differential treatment considered above).

Whereas scaffolding refers to changes in interactional roles within a given game, recontextualization (Cazden also terms it "reconceptualization") refers to a shift in the "game" being played.[24] It takes old moves and places them in new domains of activity. For instance, parents respond to their children's utterances by expanding on them as though they have a variety of additional meanings. Similarly, teachers respond to student expressions in ways that place them in new types of contexts, giving them meanings beyond those the student initially imagined. In effect, parents and teachers are pointing out additional possibilities for meaning latent in a given action. They may also use recontextualization as a corrective, helping to place wayward actions back in the contexts to which they are thought to properly belong.

When done with proper sensitivity, recontextualization can help give actions new and more manifold meanings. Cazden suggests that for many students, however, classroom discourse is *de*contextualized rather than *re*contextualized. Classroom talk often presupposes a context formed by the words of oral or written texts that may not be so universally shared as the immediate physical situation. Decontextualization on the part of the teacher involves the implicit use of contexts with which students are unfamiliar, and is often accompanied by ritual degradation and blaming of students for not catching the allusion.

Scaffolding and recontextualization are two aspects of a social-interactional theory of learning generally consistent with a cultural-difference view.[25] Dynamic matching of teacher-created environments to patterns of student interactive behavior is emphasized rather than insensitive imposition, discontinuity, and blame. The practical implications for teaching involve teachers learning how to adapt sensitively to different social-interactional patterns, so that they may more deftly make their own contributions to the interactional duet. As Cazden asks (quoting Dennis Searle), "Who's building whose building?" She suggests that one's position depends on one's educational values and asserts her own values: "We have to ask not just whose scaffold but whose world view. Here, in the domain of knowledge . . . imposition by authority should be questioned. Reconceptualization should add alternative meanings without denying the validity of meanings students bring to school" (p. 118).

The need for such sensitivity is the central message of the book, and is indeed a necessity for any competent pedagogy. Cazden has suggested many new ways for teachers to understand and hence better teach children. Yet her particular focus necessarily leaves some of the complexity of the subject partially unexplored.

## Further Questions

*Classroom Discourse* is an excellent summary and integrates a great deal of linguistic research at the classroom level; it will aid learning about a wide range of linguistic concepts and their practical application to education. Cazden shows that real progress has been made getting inside the cultural organization of teaching and learning, rather than treating this organization as taken for granted or nonexistent. Cazden's use of many studies and her success in placing them in a personal and scholarly context make her book a good introduction, particularly for those with teaching experience and an interest in sociolinguistics.

With its classroom focus, the book is particularly relevant to teachers. However, it does raise some issues of concern. By looking primarily at the classroom, other areas of attention are downplayed, such as a consideration of individual children in their immediate behavioral contexts, the organizational and institutional structures of schools, and the sociocultural structures in which they all exist. Consideration of each of these may also be important in guiding classroom teaching. Clarifying constraints at other levels of analysis is important—for even if teachers followed Cazden literally and completely, cultural inequalities would not disappear. There might be more local equality in the classroom, but troubles in discourse may also point elsewhere—to individuals, to schools, or to broader social, political, or economic conditions. Take the case of South Africa as an example, where members of the Black majority have often wanted to be instructed in English rather than Afrikaans, since the latter is seen as the language of an oppressor and a way of limiting their future opportunities. It would be very surprising if classroom reactions to use of one language or the other were not inflamed by their resonance with this broader political issue. Philip Cusick documents a similar interplay between racial tensions in an American community and classroom events.[26] Although one can certainly focus on discourse in the classroom itself, its significance often lies as much outside the classroom as within it.

It is important to take seriously Cazden's call to equip teachers with all the sensitivity they will need to understand the talk of the many kinds of children that will arrive at their doors. But the children will be more than just culturally different. An increasing number will be poor, alienated, and resistant. They will be troubled, not just because they are misunderstood, but because they understand all too well that things are stacked against them. The teachers facing such a challenge will need sociolinguistic detail, but much more, as well.

In focusing on students as representatives of different cultural groups, conflicts that arise from divided loyalties to different communities can also be overlooked, as can students' unique biographies and strategies for handling such situations.[27] Taking cultural differences too literally may even help create social barriers by overemphasizing exclusive membership in particular social groups and deemphasizing individual differences within a group. Groups only exist sometimes, and even then individuals only sometimes participate. Teachers have to walk a thin line between being culturally sensitive and reinforcing unfortunate stereotypes.

Classroom events may also be as much a product of organizational decisions regarding classroom composition, curriculum, schedule, and objectives, as of teacher insensitivity. Who is assigned to one classroom or school as opposed to another, which subjects are studied and which materials used, the times available in the class schedule, the kind of spaces available, and the objectives expected of the class as a whole can have a great effect on the ability of teachers to match their teaching to pupil needs.[28] School-wide patterns of age-grading, tracking, subject specialization, and promotion have a great deal to do with how differences between groups are likely to be handled. While Cazden suggests that "We have to be sympathetic to pressures on teachers to get through their lesson plans and cover the curriculum" (p. 194), her analysis could leave the burden of change on teachers rather than considering how the institutional pressures on them might be changed so as to make it easier to teach in culturally sensitive ways.

Similar considerations apply to the societal context of schooling. Schools function in the context of a societal division of labor and pattern of social relationships that need to be considered if we are to understand their basic purposes and politics. They must adapt not only to pupils, as Cazden advocates, but also to the larger community or society. Some of the phenomena Cazden considers could be clarified if considered in such a context, and such clarification could affect our sense of what teachers should do with their discourse in classrooms. For instance, understanding which differences make a difference or when ethnic borders become ethnic boundaries, could improve if viewed in the context of intergroup struggle and politics. How can a teacher organize a classroom in a way that minimizes occasions for the display of ethnic conflicts that dominate life in the wider community? Similarly, the particular ways in which Americans hunt for deficits, such as by looking for signs of who is intelligent or not, become more understandable when viewed against a broader societal (or even world) backdrop in which such individualistic rationalization has become a key to legitimacy.[29] Cazden's work may also be seen in this broader context as a contribution to the ideological debates in our society. For instance, in focusing on culture rather than social structure, she can be seen as implicitly emphasizing ethnic differences rather than differences in class.[30]

In the end, *Classroom Discourse* is exactly what it claims to be: an excellent report on what has been learned from sociolinguistic and ethnographic research on classroom talk and an application of that research to our understanding of what should be happening in the classroom. It helps to consolidate a scattered body of research, while presenting it in a way that makes it readily accessible to a wide range of readers, and it provides a way for teachers to begin to appreciate the beauty and artfulness of the verbal skills that each and every one of their students brings to school.

## Notes

1. Some of the personal experiences that have organized Cazden's focus are discussed in her "Four Comments," in *Children In and Out of School*, ed. Perry Gilmore and Allan Glatthorn (Washington, DC: Washington Center for Applied Linguistics, 1982), pp. 209–226.
2. Dell Hymes, *Foundations in Sociolinguistics: An Ethnographic Approach* (Philadelphia: University of Pennsylvania, 1974); see also Dell Hymes and John Gumperz, *Directions in Sociolinguistics: The Ethnography of Communication* (New York: Holt, Rinehart and Winston, 1972).
3. William Labov, *Language in the Inner City: Studies in the Black English Vernacular* (Philadelphia: University of Pennsylvania, 1972).
4. One of us (Ray McDermott) was a classroom teacher in an inner-city school in the late 1960s and found Cazden's early work very liberating. It gave a teacher the sense that even the most "difficult" children probably knew much more about what they were talking about than was immediately obvious.
5. Courtney Cazden, Vera John, and Dell Hymes, *Functions of Language in the Classroom* (New York: Teachers College Press, 1972).
6. Input-output studies of various types (for example, orthodox behaviorism in psychology, status-attainment research in sociology) have neglected inner processes and deeper explanations in the search for simple regularities relating inputs to outputs. R. P. McDermott and David R. Roth note in "The Social Organization of Behavior: Interactional Approaches" (*Annual Review of Anthropology*, 7 [1978]: 321–345) that "various biographical indices or facts about a person—gender, race, descent line, occupation, and the like—are assumed to gloss adequately the person's relations with others" but such methods "seldom allow for a careful description of the behavior of particular persons." More recently, Anthony S. Bryk, Valerie Lee, and Julia B. Smith suggest (in "High School Organization and its Effects on Teachers and Students: An Interpretive Summary of the Research," paper presented at the conference on "Choice and Control in American Education," University of Wisconsin-Madison, May 18, 1989) that "By typically using aggregate measures from individuals as proxies for organizational characteristics . . . school effects research has systematically underestimated organizational effects. Substantive conclusions from such research . . . are flawed by a misconception of *how* schools actually affect student learning." Noam Chomsky's critique of B. F. Skinner's approach to understanding verbal behavior in "Review of Verbal Behavior," *Language*, *35* ([1959]: 26–58) makes a related point, suggesting that the simple regularities between stimulus and response sought by Skinner are in principle inadequate to understand the complexities of linguistic behavior.
7. Clifford Geertz, *The Interpretation of Cultures* (New York: Basic Books, 1973).

8. Gregory Bateson suggested that in social interaction "longer cycles will always be enlarged repetitions or repeated reflections of pattern contained in the fine detail," "Communication," *The Natural History of an Interview*, unpublished ms.

9. Michael Cole, John Gay, Joseph Glick, and Donald Sharp, *Cultural Context of Learning and Thinking: An Exploration in Experimental Anthropology* (New York: Basic Books, 1971). This effort continues in Denis Newman, Peg Griffin, and Michael Cole, *The Construction Zone: Working for Cognitive Change in School* (New York: Cambridge University Press, 1989).

10. See, for example, Barbara Rogoff and Jean Lave, eds., *Everyday Cognition* (Cambridge: Harvard University Press, 1984); Jean Lave, *Cognition in Practice* (Cambridge: Cambridge University Press, 1988); Lucy A. Suchman, *Plans and Situated Actions* (Cambridge: Cambridge University Press, 1987); Donald Schön, *The Reflective Practitioner* (New York: Basic Books, 1983). Oddly enough, most of this work seems to be proceeding without mention of John Dewey's related efforts; for example, John Dewey, *How We Think* (Boston: D. C. Heath and Co., 1922).

11. Pierre Bourdieu's *Outline of a Theory of Practice* (New York: Cambridge University Press) seems to have been influential among anthropologists. For a discussion of critical theory and its relationship with other approaches in education, see Eric Bredo and Walter Feinberg, eds., *Knowledge and Values in Social and Educational Research* (Philadelphia: Temple University Press, 1982).

12. Paul Willis's 1977 account of a group of rebellious working class "lads" is an example (*Learning to Labor* [Lexington, MA: Lexington Books, 1977]). It depicts their rejection of conventional school roles and adoption of macho identities as resulting from a partial understanding of their positions in a class-stratified society.

13. In computational terms, the sequential structure emphasizes the "and" and the selectional structure the "or" branches of "and-or" trees.

14. Hugh Mehan, "Structuring School Structure," *Harvard Educational Review, 48* (1978): 32–64; Hugh Mehan, *Learning Lessons: The Social Organization of Classroom Behavior* (Cambridge: Harvard University Press, 1979); Courtney Cazden and Hugh Mehan, "Principles from Sociology and Anthropology: Context, Code, Classroom, and Culture," in Maynard Reynolds, *Knowledge Base for the Beginning Teacher* (New York: Pergamon Press, 1988), pp. 47–57.

15. The IRE sequence can be considered to be an instrumental one because it is virtually identical to the stimulus-response-reinforcement pattern found in instrumental conditioning in psychology. The pervasiveness of this pattern in U.S. classrooms is an interesting finding, since many other aspects of our culture also seem to follow an instrumental pattern. This pattern contrasts with that of rote learning, for example, in which one must only repeat a given answer rather than finding one's own, as well as with more passive operant conditioning, in which a new stimulus is a sign of valued or disvalued things to come that will occur whether one acts or not. For the use of different learning paradigms in analyzing cultures, see Gregory Bateson, "Social Planning and the Concept of Deutero Learning," in *Steps to an Ecology of Mind* (New York: Balantine, 1972, pp. 159–176).

16. John McHardy Sinclair and Richard Malcolm Coulthard, *Towards an Analysis of Discourse: The English Used by Teachers and Pupils* (London: Oxford University Press, 1975).

17. Susan Stodolsky, *The Subject Matters* (Chicago: University of Chicago Press, 1988).

18. Susan Philips, *The Invisible Culture: Communication in the Classroom and Community on the Warm Springs Indian Reservation* (White Plains, NY: Longman, 1983).

19. Shirley Brice Heath, *Ways with Words: Language, Life and Work in Communities and Classrooms* (Cambridge: Cambridge University Press, 1983).

20. Kathryn Au, "Participation Structures in a Reading Lesson with Hawaiian Children," *Anthropology and Education Quarterly, 11* (1980): 91–115.

21. R. P. McDermott and Kenneth Gospodinoff, "Social Contexts for Ethnic Borders and School Failure," in Aaron Wolfgang, ed., *Nonverbal Behavior* (New York: Academic Press, 1979); see also R. P. McDermott and Shelley Goldman, "Teaching in Multicultural Settings," in Lotty Van de Berg-Elderling, Ferry J. M. de Rijcke, and Louis V. Zuck, eds., *Multicultural Education* (Dordrecht, The Netherlands: Foris Publications, 1982), pp. 145–164.

22. There is considerable controversy between those who explain differences in minority school performance by cultural differences and those who explain them by socially structured differences in opportunity. Neither position confronts the more crucial issue of why these differences have to be explained at all. For a summary of the various positions, see *Anthropology and Education Quarterly, 18,* (1987): 312–367.

23. Lev Vygotsky, *Thought and Language* (Cambridge: Massachusetts Institute of Technology Press, 1986).

24. The contrast is analogous to that between sequential and selectional structures considered earlier.

25. Note the striking similarity between these concepts and Dewey's concepts of "continuity" and

"interaction," which he viewed as two aspects of fruitfully instructive experiences. John Dewey, *Experience and Education* (New York: Colliers, 1963).

26. Philip A. Cusick, *The Egalitarian Ideal and the American High School* (New York: Longman, 1983).

27. Fred Erickson and Jeffrey Schultz, *The Counselor as Gatekeeper: Social Interaction in Interviews* (New York: Academic Press, 1982), pp. 185–186.

28. Rebecca Barr and Robert Dreeben, *How Schools Work* (Chicago: University of Chicago Press, 1983); Larry Cuban, *How Teachers Taught: Constancy and Change in American Classrooms 1890–1980* (New York: Longman, 1984); see also Eric Bredo, "The Organizational Context of Teaching," unpublished ms.

29. See, for example, George M. Thomas, John W. Meyer, Francisco O. Ramirez, and John Boli, *Institutional Structure: Constituting State, Society, and the Individual* (Newbury Park, CA: Sage, 1987).

30. On the relations between culture and social structure and the fallacy of conflating them, see Margaret Archer, "The Sociology of Education," in Ulf Himmelstrand, ed., *The Social Reproduction of Organization and Culture* (Beverly Hills: Sage, 1986), pp. 59–87.

# Book Review

PATRICIA MARKS GREENFIELD
*University of California, Los Angeles*

THE PSYCHOLOGY OF LITERACY
by Sylvia Scribner and Michael Cole.
*Cambridge, MA: Harvard University Press, 1981. 335 pp.*

Sylvia Scribner and Michael Cole begin *The Psychology of Literacy* with the observation: "The notion that literacy introduces a great divide among human societies runs deep in contemporary social science" (p. 4). They further note claims going back to post-Homeric Greece concerning the psychological repercussions of literacy: "As literacy shapes culture, the argument goes, so it shapes human minds" (pp. 4–5). In its weak form, this argument refers to the progressive accumulation of knowledge from generation to generation made possible by the relative permanence of written texts.

Scribner and Cole are less interested, however, in the claim that literacy shapes the mind by allowing it to assimilate new information in written form than in the idea that mastery of a written language affects the very "processes of thinking—how we classify, reason, remember" (p. 5). This is the strong form of the argument. Essentially, their book is devoted to an exploration of this latter claim, using methods that join psychological with cultural analysis.

Theories concerning the cognitive impact of the written word can be found in the writings of the ancient Greeks. For example, Socrates argued, in Plato's *Phaedrus*, that writing might weaken memory by making the reader dependent on external memory aids while Plato, in *The Republic*, saw written communication as a way of promoting reason rather than emotion in human thought. However, neither possessed the empirical methods necessary to demonstrate scientifically the validity of his hypothesis. In modern times, Havelock (1963) provided evidence for Plato's views through a comparison of Homeric poems and Platonic dialogues, and Goody and Watt (1963) used historical analysis to posit a causal link between literacy and logic. Even in the latter study, the method of investigation is analysis of written texts, the products of literacy; the link between these products and individual cognitive processes required to produce or consume them must of necessity be assumed rather than tested. The empirical methods of psychology were required to supply this missing link.

*Harvard Educational Review* Vol. 53 No. 2 May 1983, 216–220

The first to attempt to provide this linkage was the Soviet psychologist Alexander Luria, who drew upon the theory of his compatriot Lev Vygotsky. Working in the 1920s and 1930s, Vygotsky attempted to provide a unified account of cultural and psychological change. His general thesis—presented in major English texts in 1962 and 1978—was that sociocultural changes form the basis for the development of higher memory and thinking processes. He had been strongly influenced by Marx's idea that there is no fixed human nature—that human beings continually make and remake themselves and their consciousness through productive activity: the use of tools transforms human nature. For Vygotsky, literacy was an important intellectual tool with the power of transforming the higher psychological processes. In the 1930s Luria tested Vygotsky's ideas by studying peasants in Central Asia who were undergoing a period of rapid change as a result of the Russian Revolution. Although his experiments were done before Havelock and Goody-Watt began their work, they were not published until 1976.

As Scribner and Cole relate, Luria "compared groups of traditional nonliterate farmers with other residents of the same villages who had gone through brief literacy courses or who had participated in short teacher-training programs" (p. 10). In a variety of experimental tasks dealing with perception, conceptualization, classification, and reasoning, he found consistent differences between the groups: the educational programs were associated with an abstract approach to problems and the ability to use techniques of formal logic. However, it was impossible to isolate the precise role of literacy in these group differences, for literacy was confounded with age and such cultural changes as collective management and agricultural planning.

Scribner and Cole see my work and that of David Olson as the next logical steps leading to their own. In my research in Senegal, carried out well after Luria's but published some ten years before, I had the opportunity to compare children from an oral culture with and without formal schooling (Greenfield, 1966; Greenfield, Reich & Olver, 1966; Greenfield & Bruner, 1969; Greenfield, 1972). Unlike Luria's groups, mine contained children who were the same in age and all other aspects of their background. However, despite the control of these background factors, one could not know to what extent the dramatic effects that resulted from schooling were caused by learning to read and write or by other aspects of formal education. David Olson's (1977) research was subject to yet another version of this problem. He drew his conclusions by comparing preschool children with school children of various ages and with educated adults. As a result, literacy effects could not be separated either from the effects of age or amount of schooling.

In Liberia, Scribner and Cole were able to isolate the effects of literacy because of the Vai, a people that invented and maintains its own writing system outside the context of formal education. The Vai made it possible, for the first time, to study the psychological effects of literacy independent of the effects of formal education. Further, the Vai provided a natural experiment, for within their single culture, three different literacies are to be found, each with its own particular set of learning conditions: Vai writing, mastered through informal means; Arabic, learned in the

Koranic school; and English writing, acquired in European-style schools. Thus, through the Vai people Scribner and Cole had the opportunity to assess the psychological consequences of different conditions of literacy learning.

Not even this set of conditions, however, would have sufficed to answer the fundamental question concerning the impact of literacy per se if the Vai had not also provided their own control group—a majority of the population who have not acquired any form of literacy. Unlike the situation in our society, illiteracy among the Vai carries no stigma, does not hamper everyday life or basic socialization, and, most important for the research, is not inextricably linked with any other social or psychological condition that would affect cognitive skills.

Scribner and Cole's genius was to find the Vai and to realize their potential for answering previously unanswerable questions about the psychological impact of literacy. But in order to realize this potential, Scribner and Cole had to muster an impressive array of psychological, linguistic, sociological, and anthropological tools; very few psychologists would have been equal to the task.

The authors began the experimental portion of their project by administering tasks designed to test the "great divide" theory of literacy. This theory presupposes, on the psychological side, the existence of highly generalized cognitive skills such as abstraction, classification, memory, and logic. Support for the theory would have been indicated by a pattern of results in which all literate groups did better than illiterate groups on tasks designed to assess one or more of these generalized skills. However, this was far from the pattern of results that actually emerged. In fact, there was not one measure designed to manifest a "great divide" between literates and illiterates on which all three types of literacy contributed to improved performance. If literacy in general did not create the "great divide," did any particular literacy have this effect? The answer was again negative: no single literacy made a positive across-the-board contribution to performance on this same set of tasks. The one effect that did emerge at this stage of the research was the positive impact of schooling on the general skill of verbal explanation. In the various experimental tasks, the topics to be explained were very diverse, ranging from reasoning about syllogisms to playing a board game. The authors conclude that it is not English literacy per se that fosters the generalized skill of verbal explanation, but rather other aspects of schooling. In particular, they ascribe importance to "teacher-pupil dialogue in the classroom. Teachers ask questions very much like those we asked: 'What made you give that answer? How do you know? Go to the board and explain what you did' " (p. 255).

Thus, the most generalized skill that emerged in the Vai research, the ability to construct verbal explanations, seemed to be a product not of literacy itself but of the verbal interaction that goes on in schools between teacher and pupil. Clearly such interaction is not limited to a particular medium of instruction. Indeed, it can form the social context for any medium. This fact has great educational significance, particularly as it relates to the role of electronic and other nonprint media in school instruction. The implication is that what is done in school—for example, the teacher's demand for explanations—is more crucial to learning than what medium is used to impart information. This hints that, in the educational process, print may not be a privileged medium of instruction. If there is a "great divide," it is created by schooling, not literacy.

In the face of their failure to find general literacy effects, the authors shifted strategy in the middle of their fieldwork. Instead of deriving hypotheses "from general abstract characterizations of literacy" (p. 158), they looked to "the functional uses of literacy among the Vai" (p. 159) as a source of hypotheses. This was an attempt to derive the cognitive consequences of literacy from knowledge of how literate Vai used reading and writing in everyday life. However, it often seems more accurate to characterize their new strategy as a switch from searching for instances of broad generalization of literacy skills to searching for instances of narrow generalization from the reading process itself. For example, the fact that Vai literacy, unlike Arabic or English, is based on a syllabary—symbols stand for syllables rather than sounds—was reflected in the finding that Vai literacy, but not Arabic or English, promotes the ability to integrate auditorily a series of separate syllables into a meaningful sentence. This effect is an instance of narrow generalization, because syllable integration is so closely related to the very process of reading Vai.

Another example of narrow generalization involved a cognitive process intrinsic to all three writing systems. This process was the auditory integration of separate words into a meaningful sentence. It must be carried out whether one reads Vai, English, or Arabic. Skill in auditory integration was measured by the comprehension of words spoken at an even pace and without intonation. On this task comprehension was positively affected by each of the three literacies.

In all these tasks, performance reflected a skill involved in the very acquisition or process of reading itself. Where that skill was part of only one literacy, task performance was promoted by that literacy alone. Where it was part of literacy in general, task performance was fostered by all three literacies.

There is, however, one skill area—communication—where Scribner and Cole go beyond the effects of reading-writing processes to explore the consequences of how a particular literacy functions in a particular society. In one of the communication tasks, the subject had to dictate a letter giving directions on how to play a new board game. The functional source for this task lay in the observation that the Vai syllabary is frequently used for letter writing. Indeed, Vai reading scores turned out to be a strong predictor of total information provided by subjects in their dictated letters. But the rub was that schooling was an even better predictor of these skills than Vai literacy. However, this finding may fit with the functional approach better than the authors realized. Although they had started with the hope that each of the three literacies would have a distinct set of functions, their background survey in fact indicated very similar functions for English and Vai. Specifically, English turned out to be used as much for letter writing by people literate in English as was Vai by people literate in Vai. Arabic, in contrast, was generally not used for letter writing. If letter-writing is functionally related to the communication task, as the authors hypothesize, then one would expect a positive contribution from both Vai literacy and English schooling, but not from Arabic literacy. This is precisely the pattern that emerged.

*The Psychology of Literacy* conveys more than important theoretical issues and substantive findings. Equally important are the methodological principles and techniques it presents. One notable feature is the use of ethnographically sensitive surveys to provide background information that is then used, through regression analysis, to assess the effects of many additional factors besides literacy status. Although regression analysis is a statistical technique from the discipline of psychology, the surveys, constituting Scribner and Cole's main tool of cultural analysis, integrate methods from sociology and anthropology. The experiments themselves involved techniques from both psychology—for example, the communication tasks—and linguistics—for example, phonological analysis. Such a combination of methods will be extremely useful for other researchers planning to investigate the impact of broad and complex sociocultural factors on individual cognitive or linguistic performance.

*The Psychology of Literacy* makes an important contribution on many levels. Theoretically, it develops the notion of socially organized practices as the mechanism by which a cultural skill affects cognitive processes. Here, Scribner and Cole provide a valuable addition to the Vygotskian theoretical framework for describing development. Empirically, the book contains a fascinating and rich set of findings. Methodologically, the research breaks new ground in combining the techniques of experimental psychology, linguistics, sociology, and anthropology. The result is a series of studies that are exact and yet sensitively adapted to their cultural context, both in procedure and interpretation. This book is also valuable methodologically because it shares with the reader the zig-zag road to knowledge and discovery that is so often covered up by a straight-line account in final publication.

Philosophically, *The Psychology of Literacy* should rid us once and for all of the ethnocentric and arrogant view that a single technology suffices to create in its users a distinct, let alone superior, set of cognitive processes. Educationally, we find that the development of cognitive skills demands more than the imparting of a particular technology, even if that technology is literacy; it depends crucially on how a particular technology is used and the web of practices and functions in which the technology is enmeshed.

## References

Goody, J., & Watt, I. The consequences of literacy. *Comparative Studies in Society and History,* 1963, 5, 27–68.
Greenfield, P.M. On culture and conservation. In J.S. Bruner, R.R. Olver, P.M. Greenfield, et al., *Studies in cognitive growth.* New York: Wiley, 1966.
Greenfield, P.M. Oral and written language: The consequences for cognitive development in Africa, the United States and England. *Language and Speech,* 1972, 15, 169–178.
Greenfield, P.M., & Bruner, J.S. Culture and cognitive growth. In D.A. Goslin (Ed.), *Handbook of socialization: Theory and research.* New York: Rand-McNally, 1969.
Greenfield, P.M., Reich, L.C., & Olver, R.R. On culture and equivalence: II. In J.S.

Bruner, R.R. Olver, P.M. Greenfield, et al., *Studies in cognitive growth*. New York: Wiley, 1966.

Havelock, E.A. *Preface to Plato*. Cambridge, Mass.: Harvard University Press, 1963.

Luria, A.R. *Cognitive development: Its cultural and social foundations*. Cambridge, Mass.: Harvard University Press, 1976.

Olson, D.R. From utterance to test: The bias of language in speech and writing. *Harvard Educational Review*, 1977, 47, 257–281.

Vygotsky, L.S. *Thought and language*. Cambridge, Mass.: MIT Press, 1962.

Vygotsky, L.S. *Mind in society: The development of higher psychological processes* (M. Cole, V. John-Steiner, S. Scribner, and E. Souberman, Eds.). Cambridge, Mass.: Harvard University Press, 1978.

# Book Review

JOSEPH C. GRANNIS, *Teachers College, Columbia University*

ALEXANDRA WHARTON GRANNIS, *St. Luke's Child Psychiatric Clinic, New York City*

CLASS, CODES AND CONTROL. VOLUME 1. THEORETICAL
STUDIES TOWARD A SOCIOLOGY OF LANGUAGE
by Basil Bernstein.
*London: Routledge & Kegan Paul, 1972. 238 pp.*

Language as a social institution is the powerful theme of Basil Bernsteins' work. A
precis of that work begins with his distinction between the *universal* "frames of consistency" represented in the syntax and morphology of a language, and the *distinctive*
linguistic forms or codes "which induce in their speakers *different* ways of relating
to objects and persons" (p. 123). Bernstein focuses particularly on a "restricted" and
an "elaborated" code which he associates with lower- or working-class and middle-
class speakers of English respectively. His argument is developed almost entirely in
the context of England, though it has been much used, and, in Bernstein's view,
abused, by Americans.

Most of the syntactical and morphological characteristics of the restricted and
elaborated codes, i.e., the regularities of their grammar and vocabulary, seem to
have been worked out by Bernstein in his early formulations of a "public" and a
"formal" language. The more recent work has added certain subtleties to these
characteristics, but has concentrated more on demonstrating their distribution among
different social strata and on defining more theoretically their social functions. Thus
in one of the earliest essays one finds the following contrasts.

*Public Language*

(1) Short, grammatically simple, often unfinished sentences, a poor syntactical
    construction with a verbal form stressing the active mode.
(2) Simple and repetitive use of conjunctions (so, then, and, because).
(3) Frequent use of short commands and questions.
(4) Rigid and limited use of adjectives and adverbs. (See pp. 42–43 for these and
    the additional features of public language.)

*Harvard Educational Review*   Vol. 43   No. 2   May 1973, 298–303

*Formal Language*

(1) Accurate grammatical order and syntax regulate what is said.

(2) Logical modifications and stress are mediated through a grammatically complex sentence construction, especially through the use of a range of conjunctions and relative clauses.

(3) Frequent use of prepositions which indicate logical relationships as well as prepositions which indicate temporal and spatial contiguity.

(4) Frequent use of impersonal pronouns (it, one).

(5) A discriminative selection from a range of adjectives and adverbs. (See p. 53 for these and additional features of formal language.)

Explication of individual meanings is the basic function of an elaborated code, whereas a restricted code assumes that the speakers share more of their meanings in common. Speakers of any social class make use of restricted code on certain occasions: in reference to experiences they have shared intimately and do not need to elaborate to each other, or in various ritualized situations, in church or, equally, in the opening gambits of a cocktail party. The basic reason Bernstein gives for middle-class speakers alone using elaborated code is that their stratum possesses "access to the major decision-making areas of the society." The elaborated code, existing at a psychological level between assumed deep linguistic structures and speech, orients a listener to the relative significance of different spoken signals, and regulates the listener's selection and organization of words, sequences, and extra-verbal signals for his reply. Middle-class parents socialize their children to the use of this code in anticipation of the decision-making the children will have access to. Working-class parents do not socialize their children for this decision-making, or do not reflect access to it in their own speech. Teachers not only use elaborated code in school, but they demand that children use it. The children respond as a function of their earlier socialization, middle-class children succeeding and working-class children failing to speak in elaborated code. Thus the relative positions of the social classes are maintained.

"For various reasons," Bernstein writes, "in particular the occupation of the mother before marriage and the role differentiation within the family, there will not be a one-to-one correlation between the use of a restricted code and the working class stratum, but the probability is certainly very high" (p. 91). The role differentiation referred to here is explicated elsewhere by Bernstein in terms of positional versus person-oriented families. This distinction is itself associated with the dynamics of restricted versus elaborated code, and a working-class family that happened to regard its members as more individuated persons might develop the open communications system of an elaborated code.

More often than not these days, one has to fight against the misconstruction of "significant" differences between social classes, or the extension of the terms of a difference to virtually every member of the classes compared. A finding that fourteen percent of middle-class parents, in comparison to "only" eleven percent of working-class parents, name creativity as something they value in their children's behavior, is liable to be translated as middle-class parents value creativity, working-class parents do not. Melvin Kohn finds that social class (or, more specifically, education and the condition of fathers' work) *consistently* predicts what parents value in their children, but at the same time he acknowledges that most of the variance is still not accounted for; yet Kohn then proceeds to associate middle-class parents with autonomy and working-class parents with conformity.[1] This is the sort of overgeneralization that one might expect to be involved in Bernstein's reasoning. But Bernstein's statistical confidence levels are high with relatively low *n's,* and one comes to appreciate how immediate and all-pervasive the association of a language code with class might be, and what potential this might have for socialization.

Bernstein makes empirical statements only about England, and, indeed, it makes sense that an English scholar would be the first to attend to class, codes, and control. Bernstein seems to have believed at one point that the language of the "negro subculture" in the U.S.A. is a form of restricted code. Today he would surely have no difficulty agreeing with the observation that Black English is a dialect that for many years has included both restricted and elaborated codes.

A more fundamental problem is Bernstein's definition of the function of restricted code. The very term "restricted," by comparison even with "public," has a deficit connotation. Bernstein's attempt to disown this, in fact to shift the deficit interpretation to others' misreading of his work, falls flat. The following passages are typical of his "Critique of the Concept of Compensatory Education."

> Now when we consider the children in school we can see that there is likely to be difficulty. For the school is necessarily concerned with the transmission and development of universalistic orders of meaning. The school is concerned with the making explicit and elaborating through language, principles and operations, as these apply to objects (science subjects) and persons (art subjects). One child, through his socialization, is already sensitive to the symbolic orders of the school, whereas the second child is much less sensitive to the universalistic orders of the school. The second child is oriented towards particularistic orders of meaning which are context bound, in which principles and operations are implicit, and towards a form of language-use through which such meanings are realized. The school is necessarily trying to develop in the child orders of relevance and relation as they apply to persons and objects, which are not initially the ones he spontaneously moves toward. (p. 196)
> Because a code is restricted it does not mean that a child is nonverbal, nor is he in the technical sense linguistically deprived, for he possesses the same tacit understanding of the linguistic rule system as any child. It simply means that there is a restriction on the *contexts* and on the *conditions* which will orient the child to universalistic orders of meaning, and to making those linguistic choices through which such meanings are realized and so made public (p. 197).

In the *applied* discourse of this and other of Bernstein's discussions of education, one seeks in vain for a more positive representation of the function of restricted code. Ironically, Bernstein himself defines the positive function of restricted codes in any number of *theoretical* passages. It is communality or unity.

> A restricted code is generated by a form of social relationship based upon a range of closely shared identifications self-consciously held by the members. An elaborated code is generated by a form of social relationship which does not necessarily presuppose such shared, self-consciously held identifications with the consequence that much less is taken for granted. (p. 108)
>
> So far as the child is concerned, in positional families he attains a strong sense of social identity at the cost of autonomy; in person-centered families, the child attains a strong sense of autonomy but his social identity may be weak. (p. 185)

Were we to speak of a "communal" code versus an "individuated" code, the ideological issue might be drawn more clearly.

What difference might it make if one asked how a communal code would function in school? We might see the necessity of it for expressions of solidarity, whether in spontaneous language or in the rites and ceremonies of the children's cultures of origin, so grossly neglected at the same time that "mainstream" rites and ceremonies are imposed upon children in school. We might understand better the function of a teacher's, or a parent's,[2] more abbreviated commands, in terms of their producing less social distance between the adult and the child than more elaborately justified requests, whatever the contribution of the latter might be to the children's cognitive facility. Again, we might connect a communal code to the sporadic finding that low-SES children have more positive self-concepts than middle-SES children (always a surprise, since we know how much better off the middle-class children are!).[3] Perhaps we could find that children from communal code families cooperated more than children from individuated code families, not in the sense of a highly role-differentiated form of cooperation, but in the sense of simple sharing of property, attention, jobs, and roles.

All this is highly speculative. It is meant to suggest a potential line of research growing out of Bernstein's theory, one that seems to have been neglected because of the ideological bias reflected in the terms "restricted" and "elaborated," especially as these terms have been applied to current emphases in educational practice. Bernstein's special theory, one might say, is couched in the general framework of *Gemeinschaft-Gesellschaft* that has been so productive for sociology, especially Durkheim's formulations of mechanical and organic solidarity.[4] It is because the *Gemeinschaft* concept has been fruitfully applied to other aspects of human activity that one expects it to yield in the study of language functions as well.

Two essays that are very provocative in this connection can be read in the book, *Functions of Language in the Classroom*, edited by Courtney Cazden, Vera John, and Dell Hymes.[5] Both essays, one by Stephen Boggs and the second by Susan Philips, contrast children's positive response to being addressed as members of a collective including themselves and adults, with their negative response to being addressed, by the teacher or the adult observer, as individuals. Both provide clues that the use of a communal or restricted language code is associated with the children's solidarity with each other and with adults. Only a few days after reading the Boggs and Philips essays, one of us happened to observe an elementary school celebration of Black

History Week, and was intrigued by the incongruity between the ritual mode of the different classes' presentations and the show and tell mode of the school principal as m.c. of the affair. Had the principal's language behavior been more oriented to the *communitas* of the occasion, it might not have detracted so from an otherwise profound event. For example, when the principal called upon one child to face the rest of the audience and "*explain* how we should behave," at which point the child "forgot" what he had thought he knew—quite like the children in analogous situations within their classrooms in the Boggs and Philips essays. Is there not as much to learn about creating community in a school as there is about individuating the children? The Cazden, John, and Hymes book testifies to the power of Bernstein's point of view, but at the same time it broadens the scope of the language functions considered.

A separate review could be written alone about the last chapter of *Class, Codes and Control*, "On the Classification and Framing of Educational Knowledge." Bernstein distinguishes between collected and integrated classifications of curricular contents, the first being characterized by strong boundaries insulating the curriculum contents, and the second characterized by weak boundaries reducing this insulation. He distinguishes also between strong and weak framing in the pedagogical relationship between teacher and pupil:

> Frame refers us to the range of options available to teacher and taught in the *control* of what is transmitted and received in the context of the pedagogical relationship. Strong framing entails reduced options; weak framing entails a range of options. Thus frame refers to the degree of control teacher and pupil possess over the selection, organization, and pacing of the knowledge transmitted and received in the pedagogical relationship. (pp. 205–206)

Bernstein treats classification and framing as the two formal variables of "knowledge codes." A collection code is characterized by strong content boundaries and a tendency to strong framing; an integrated code has weak content boundaries and a tendency to weak framing. The "tendency" wording is the reviewers', however. Bernstein writes explicitly about significant variations in the strength of the framing associated with one or the other knowledge code, and we have inferred the tendencies from the examples he discusses.

What is at stake here is the knowledge code itself that is transmitted to the learner— the form and the process of knowledge as it is given or constructed in the educational environment. Bernstein observes that there seems to be a long-run trend toward openness in English education, that is, toward more permeable content boundaries and looser or more flexible pedagogical framing. We might connect this with a parallel trend toward more individuated learning, stretching out the matter that is polarized in the contrast of restricted and elaborated codes, and note that there too Bernstein sees as the crucial issue the code that is made available to the learner. Just as we have argued with respect to language codes, therefore, we would urge that a sociology of knowledge should be alert to the positive functions of collected *and* integrated knowledge codes equally. Paradoxically, because the universality of the elaborated code and the integration of the integrated code are accomplished by *individuals* according to increasingly *internalized* standards, they *can* be associated with the disintegration of those external ties of the individual to the group that have constituted much of the meaning of specific language cultures and knowledge disciplines. A sociology of knowledge may be prone to the bias of favoring rational or rationalized systems over arbitrary or contextual ones. But the construction of the human creature is too complex to allow this. Durkheim saw the problem clearly. Bernstein is painting broad strokes and fine details alike on the canvas Durkheim stretched for us, but the picture that emerges must be full in its proportions.

## Notes

1. Melvin L. Kohn, *Class and Conformity: A Study in Values.* (Homewood, Ill.: The Dorsey Press, 1969).
2. Robert D. Hess and Virginia C. Shipman, "Early Experience and the Socialization of Cognitive Modes in Children," *Child Development,* 36 (Dec., 1965), pp. 869–886.
3. Norma Trowbridge, "Self Concept and Socio-Economic Status in Elementary School Children," *American Educational Research Journal,* 9 (Fall, 1972), 525–537.
4. Emile Durkheim, *The Division of Labour in Society* (Glencoe, Ill.: Free Press, 1933).
5. New York: Teachers College Press, 1972.

# Part III
*Multicultural/Bilingual Issues in Literacy*

# 11
# Literacy and Cultural Identity

BERNARDO M. FERDMAN
*State University of New York, Albany*

*Bernardo Ferdman discusses the implications of cultural diversity in a multiethnic society such as the United States for the process of becoming and being literate. Examining the relationships between literacy, culture, and cultural identity, the author argues that, in diverse societies, individuals who are becoming literate may hold different views of literacy that represent their culture-specific values, beliefs, and norms. Ferdman asserts that, as literacy is defined by culture, cultural identity mediates the process of becoming literate as well as the types of literacy activities engaged in. The author further argues that literacy education itself can also influence and shape the individual's cultural identity. Ferdman provides a theoretical framework that explains the mutual relationship between literacy and culture at the individual level and further elaborates and refines the concept of cultural identity. His work highlights the importance of developing a better understanding of the complex processes involved in literacy education.*

We are frequently reminded by public-service announcements on television and radio that being literate can change one's life: Life is better if one can read and write, the ads tell us. At first, there seems to be little that is controversial about this message. Nevertheless, although educators share the goal of developing more literate members of society—after all, this is a primary role of the schools—they disagree about what constitutes literacy and how best to achieve it. The television ads do not analyze the nature of the personal changes brought about by literacy, nor do they suggest how *becoming* and *being* literate are processes that can vary across individuals and groups and are shaped and given meaning by society.[1] Literacy, I believe, (and in this I concur with the ads) touches us at our core in that part of ourselves that connects with the social world around us. It provides an important medium through which

An earlier version of this paper was presented at the First Gutenberg Conference, *Towards A More Literate America: Perspectives on School and Society,* held at SUNY/Albany, February 27–28, 1988. I am grateful to Alan Purves and to the participants at the First Gutenberg Conference for their many helpful suggestions regarding this paper. I would also like to thank Niyi Akinnaso, Ana Mari Cauce, Débora Ferdman, and Janet Powell for carefully reading and thoughtfully commenting on prior drafts.

*Harvard Educational Review*   Vol. 60   No. 2   May 1990, 181–204

we interact with the human environment. For this reason, a consideration of the relationship of literacy and culture must be a fundamental component of any analysis of literacy and the individual.

While a number of writers (see, for example, Akinnaso, 1982, 1985; Goody, 1977, 1982; Goody & Watt, 1963; Ong, 1982; Said, 1983; Scribner & Cole, 1981) have debated and discussed the connections between literacy and culture and the human mind, few have directly addressed the implications of cultural diversity within a society for the processes of becoming and being literate. For example, Akinnaso (1981) and Goody (1982, 1986) discuss the cultural changes that accompany the introduction of literacy in oral societies. Similarly, Ong (1982) contrasts orality and literacy and the implication of their differences for understanding cultures based in one of the two modes. These analyses tend to use a societal frame of reference and therefore to assume a high degree of cultural homogeneity within societies. Other work (Goody, 1977) concentrates on the cognitive implications of the introduction of writing systems, thus emphasizing the individual level of analysis. Attention to intra-societal diversity, however, requires attending at once to issues on both societal and individual levels. In this paper, I discuss from a social psychological perspective the relationship between literacy and the individual in a multiethnic society such as the United States. More precisely, I explore how a person's identity as a member of an ethnocultural group is intertwined with the meaning and consequences of becoming and being literate. Each of us maintains an image of the behaviors, beliefs, values, and norms—in short, of the culture—appropriate to members of the ethnic group(s) to which we belong. This is what I call *cultural identity*. Cultural identity, I argue, both derives from and modulates the symbolic and practical significance of literacy for individuals as well as groups.

The goal of the paper is to provide a theoretical framework for thinking about the way literacy and culture influence each other at the level of the individual. After placing the issue in context, I elaborate and refine the construct of cultural identity and suggest how it can be useful in understanding the processes of literacy education.

Given great diversity in educational achievement among ethnic groups in the United States, the question of the relationship between literacy and cultural identity is driven by a desire to better understand the status of ethnic minorities and to find improved ways for schools to serve their members. At the same time, examination of this question can help to clarify literacy as a multifaceted and multilayered construct. A look at literacy education and acquisition in the context of an ethnically diverse society forces us to go beyond viewing these processes simply as the transmission and internalization of a set of cognitive functions or skills, and to consider both the symbolic aspects and the content of what is taught and learned. In doing so, we are also confronted with the need to clarify our underlying assumptions and values about the nature of such a society.

## The Role of Values

How ethnic differences in school performance should be addressed by educators has been a source of controversy and debate.[2] "Equal opportunity" is the ultimate goal; but there is disagreement on what this means and how to achieve it. Discussion of the relationship of literacy and culture takes place amid societal concern with issues of individual and collective rights: To what extent do individuals and groups in a multiethnic society have a right to define and maintain distinctive identities? And to what extent do these rights complement or conflict with each other? The United States proclaims the value of equal access to opportunity without barriers or advantages based on ethnicity, race, or gender. In one version of this value, individual merit and accomplishment are seen as the only legitimate sources of social and economic success. The educational system is promoted in this regard as "the great equalizer"—the institution that can and should provide citizens with the tools they need to be productive members of society. In this view, which emphasizes the similarities among people, fairness means measuring each individual by the same yardstick. It also means that all individuals must be treated similarly. To do otherwise would be to perpetuate inequities.[3] Another way to think about equal opportunity, however, is to emphasize the differences among people—in particular, those differences rooted in culture and therefore in group memberships. In this alternative view of equal opportunity, fairness involves choosing a yardstick appropriate to the person and group. To ignore group membership is to deny an important part of the individual. Indeed, treating everyone the same can result in the very inequities that are to be avoided (see, for example, Ferdman, 1988; Ferdman, 1989; Gordon, 1985; Thurow, 1987).

Divergent views on the proper nature of the relationship among culturally diverse ethnic groups in the society may be an underlying source of disagreement: Should each group pursue its own way and be free to maintain its own heritage, norms, and values, following a pluralist model? Or should one group's culture be emphasized and should assimilation be required? Or should some new "American" blend be developed, composed of something of each group, in line with the "melting pot" model? Debate over these alternatives has persisted throughout the U.S. history (see Feagin, 1989; Gleason, 1982; Hirschman, 1983) and is characteristic of plural societies (Babad, Birnbaum, & Benne, 1983; Berry, 1983, 1986). Ultimately, the choice is a value-laden one. An assimilation perspective emphasizes the dysfunctionality of differences and the maintenance of the dominant culture, and so demands that subordinate groups acculturate. The "melting pot" view, also referred to as "amalgamation," maintains that the ideal society takes something from each of its component ethnic groups to create a new culture ultimately shared by all. In contrast, the pluralist position prizes diversity and so holds that it is preferable for the various ethnic groups in a society to co-exist in a kind of "vegetable soup" (Babad et al., 1983), such that each group maintains its own culture to the extent and in the ways that its members wish to do so.

Depending on one's position in this debate, ethnic diversity in school achievement would be dealt with differently. Views that emphasize acculturation, or the "melting pot" ideal, would consider it more fair to use the same measure for all individuals, regardless of group membership. For example, students considered at risk of dropping out of school may be encouraged with magnet schools or other special programs.

Seen from strict assimilation or "melting pot" perspectives, the ethnic group to which any specific student belongs should matter little, so long as the opportunity to participate is available equally to all who are judged to need the program. It would also be unfair under these models of ethnic relations to institute special programs with different outcome goals or content for African-American, Italian-American, or Native-American students. Within these models, the fairest approach is to direct special programs to individuals, with needs defined in a global manner. Furthermore, success in the program should be defined similarly for all participants—for example, being able to read at or above a tenth-grade level.

If cultural pluralism is valued, however, individual merit needs to be defined in a culturally relativistic way that takes group membership into account. To the extent that the maintenance and development of distinctive ethnic cultures are valued, these cultures must be given consideration in the educational system. In formulating a drop-out prevention program, it would be not only practical, but also more fair, to explicitly link content and outcomes to the cultures of the participants. To the extent that groups differ, programs could be designed and implemented differently and selection criteria made group-specific. Success in this model would be conceived from a multitude of perspectives based on students' group membership and individual needs.

Literacy has become an important focus for this debate. Because schools are viewed as the institutions most responsible for literacy education in this society, these conflicting values affect the thinking and policy that shape the way children become literate.

### Perspectives on Individuals and Groups

Beyond requiring reflection on our values regarding intergroup relations, a look at literacy in a multiethnic context demands examination of the relationship of the individual to the group. If, in shaping individual development, the educational system and society at large are to pay attention to group-based diversity—whether the goal is to strengthen it or to reduce it—then we need a more focused understanding of the psychological concomitants of ethnic differences. Certainly, in spite of commonalities within ethnic groups, a good deal of within-group variance will also be present, especially in a heterogeneous society (Ferdman & Hakuta, 1985). That is, even valid group level characterizations are not automatically applicable to all or even most group members. Consequently, from a social psychological perspective, we need to better understand the interrelationships between collective and individual experience and behavior. We must conduct such an exploration at the intersection of the group and individual levels of analysis, at once considering both between-group and within-group diversity.

At least in part, the degree of within-group diversity, both real and perceived, may be a function of the predominant values regarding the type of ethnic relations desired in the society. Each model mentioned earlier—pluralism, assimilation, or "melting pot"—carries with it particular assumptions about the degree to which individual behavior and identity do or should follow from those of the group as a whole and thus may function as a filter for the interpretation of the links between the individual and the group levels. For example, a pluralist may consider it legitimate to interpret individual behavior in light of group patterns, while an assimilationist would prefer to focus on individual-level traits. In the illustration used earlier, the pluralist would be comfortable in considering a student's ethnicity in assessing the factors likely to lead to success in a drop-out prevention program, especially to the extent that specific connections could be made between cultural features of the group and the design of the program. Two students displaying the same behavior—say, speaking little in class—would be understood differently as a function of their different cultural backgrounds.[4] The assimilationist, in contrast, would prefer to stress individual characteristics—motivation, intelligence, or home environment, for example—without regard to ethnicity, and therefore with little or no thought to the differential meaning, expression, or incidence of these factors across groups. Alternatively, an assimilationist might recognize culturally based differences, but would prefer to eliminate rather than highlight them. For an advocate of assimilation, the meaning of individual behavior would either be self-evident or else construed from a mono-cultural perspective. So to understand a student who speaks little in class, his or her ethnic background would be seen as superfluous.

In turn, beliefs about the nature of the relationship of individuals and groups may affect which perspective is adopted on ethnic relations. For example, someone who sees groups simply as collections of similar individuals may be more likely to favor a "melting pot" approach, since this approach will not restrict individual freedom of choice. Such a vision of society allows plenty of room for individual differences— all the more so because such differences are not correlated with group membership. In contrast, those who view the group level as primary, as giving definition and meaning to the individual, would tend to prefer pluralism, because they will see individual freedom present only when the groups people belong to are allowed to flourish. From a pluralistic perspective, it is the denial and washing away of group boundaries that ultimately eliminates personal freedom.

## Literacy and Culture

Ethnic diversity, by its very nature, directs attention to the role of culture in the individual's transactions with the social world. Monica Heller (1987) provides a useful perspective on the type of culture that distinguishes an ethnic group:

> [For members of an ethnic group] shared experience forms the basis of a shared way of looking at the world; through interaction they jointly construct ways of making sense of experience. These ways of making sense of experience, these beliefs, assumptions, and expectations about the world and how it works underlie what we think of as culture. However culture is not only a set of beliefs and values that constitute our normal, everyday view of the world; it also includes our normal, everyday ways of behaving. (p. 184)

In this view, culture includes both specific behavioral characteristics typifying a group and the underlying views of social reality that guide those behaviors. This latter part is what Triandis (1972) termed "subjective culture . . . a group's characteristic way of perceiving its social environment" (p. viii). These definitions of culture suggest that a person's view of social reality is mediated by collective representations of that reality.

In a society tending toward homogeneity, it is easy to think of literacy simply in terms of specific skills and activities. Given broad cultural consensus on the definition of literacy, alternative constructions are either remote or invisible, and so literacy becomes a seemingly self-evident personal attribute that is either present or absent. In such an environment, literacy is experienced as a characteristic inherent in the individual. Once a person acquires the requisite skills, she also acquires the quality of mind known as literacy, together with the right to be labeled a literate person. Judgments about a person's degree of literacy are not dependent on the situation. Rather, because there is wide agreement on what constitutes a literate individual, a person carries the label regardless of whether or not she continues to demonstrate the behaviors that first earned her the designation. A person accepted as being literate is not considered to be any less literate when she is watching television or when she is sleeping than when she is writing a novel or reading the back of a cereal box.

In a multiethnic context, however, the cultural framing of literacy becomes more obvious. De Castell and Luke (1983) argue convincingly that "being 'literate' has always referred to having mastery over the processes by means of which culturally significant information is coded" (p. 373). In this view, literacy does not simply consist of a universally defined set of skills constant across time and place. Since cultures differ in what they consider to be their "texts" and in the values they attach to these, they will also differ in what they view as literate behavior.[5] An illiterate person is someone who cannot access (or produce) texts that are seen as significant within a given culture. That same person, in another cultural context, may be classified as being quite literate. When a number of cultures co-exist within the same society, it is more likely that we will encounter variant conceptions of what constitutes being literate.

Because culture exists as a product of social interaction and organization, de Castell and Luke ask us to view literacy as meaningful only in the social context of particular communities. Purves (1987) similarly points out the ways in which being literate involves mastering conventional wisdom and common knowledge and, in so doing, entering into a kind of "textual contract." What is important is that what is "common" and what is "conventional" are defined in reference to a group, to a particular community at a given point in time. This reference point constitutes culture and determines what will be construed as literacy. As Purves (1987) explains, "[b]eing literate . . . involves activities that bring various storehouses of knowledge into action when the situation calls for them" (p. 224). This knowledge base includes linguistic information, text models, and "socio-cultural norms of literacy acts" (p. 224) that all feed into defining behaviors and cognitive operations as literate. To become literate a person must master, in addition to a set of culturally defined skills, all the cultural information involved in decoding and producing texts, including the frames of reference for comprehending their contents.

In a culturally heterogenous society, literacy ceases to be a characteristic inherent solely in the individual. It becomes an interactive process that is constantly redefined and renegotiated, as the individual transacts with the socioculturally fluid surroundings. A new arrival to the United States from a small village in Malaysia, unable to read or write in English and unfamiliar with the Latin alphabet, would not immediately have all the skills required of a literate person in his new country and would in all likelihood be seen in the workplace as functionally illiterate. At home, however, he teaches his sons to read the Quran, maintains an elaborate accounting system for his lending society, and is revered as a teacher and wise person. As Scribner (1986) put it, "literacy is . . . a *social* achievement. . . . [It] is an outcome of cultural transmission. . . . Literacy has neither a static nor a universal essence" (pp. 8–9). Because culture is in flux, so are the definition and consequences of literacy (see, for example, Cook-Gumperz, 1986).

Literacy, then, in large part, involves facility in manipulating the symbols that codify and represent the values, beliefs, and norms of the culture—the same symbols that incorporate the culture's representations of reality. Because the processes referred to by de Castell and Luke are themselves part of the culture, to be defined as literate this manipulation must be done in a culturally appropriate manner. To be literate it is not enough, for example, to know how to sign one's name. One must also know when and where it is appropriate to do so.[6] Reading and writing behaviors must be done in the "right" way. "The enterprise of defining literacy," Scribner (1986) reminds us, " . . . becomes one of assessing what counts as literacy in some given social context" (p. 9). For example, the skills necessary to be considered literate in a society that employs pictographic writing can be quite different from those necessary in a society that uses an alphabetic system. Similarly, literacy for a supermarket shopper might be defined in terms of the ability to negotiate varieties of text printed on a number of different surfaces in a multitude of typefaces, with little emphasis on handling writing instruments or proper spelling. In contrast, literacy for a secretary/clerk might well include appropriate use of spelling and punctuation and the ability to decode many types of handwritten documents. In each of these situations, food-shopping and secretarial work, the particular distribution of skills may also vary from culture to culture. That is, cultures will have particularistic definitions of the behaviors and skills a person would need to demonstrate in order for him or her to be considered a literate foodshopper or literate secretary.

In addition to being skilled in the use of methods of representation such as the alphabet, writing implements, books, and so on, the literate person must be familiar with a particular configuration of meanings in context, to comprehend appropriately the content of what is encoded and decoded. *Becoming* literate means developing mastery not only over processes, but also over the symbolic media of the culture— the ways in which cultural values, beliefs, and norms are represented. *Being* literate implies actively maintaining contact with collective symbols and the processes by which they are represented. Thus, literacy goes beyond superficial transactions with a printed or written page and extends into the ability to comprehend and manipulate its symbols—the words and concepts—and to do so in a culturally prescribed manner.

The school is a particularly important institution for mediating the process by which the individual becomes literate and for reflecting societal views of what constitutes literacy. Roth (1984) put it this way:

> Social/cultural control is tied directly to the structure of knowledge and to the manner in which knowledge is presented in the schooling context. Schools, acting as agents for the culture, control the extent to which personal knowledge may enter into the public knowledge of school curriculum; they thus have a direct influence upon cultural continuity and change. In selecting what to teach and how it is to be taught and evaluated, schools reaffirm what the culture values as knowledge. . . .
>
> Because literacy provides a powerful means for individuals to make a personal tie to society in general, literacy acquisition, particularly reading instruction, holds implications for cultural transmission, that is, for how knowledge is transferred, reproduced, and transformed. The prime focus of 1st grade is to establish reading literacy so that the "knowledge" our culture sees as significant may be maintained. (p. 303)[7]

Roth's analysis certainly holds for a homogeneous society in which the schools are indeed "agents for the culture" of their constituents. To apply to a multicultural society, however, her view must be expanded to consider the relationship of the culture(s) represented by the school and those of its pupils.

In a multicultural environment, the individual who is becoming literate may be faced with an array of alternative methods and contents representing different views of literacy. The value placed on behaviors that are construed as literate in the context of one group will not be equivalent to the value given them by a different culture. For example, penmanship might be much more valued by the Chinese, who must spend long hours learning the appropriate brush-strokes for each pictogram, and who generally value the aesthetic qualities of text, than by North Americans, who might primarily emphasize the content. In a religious Christian community, it is likely that time spent reading the Bible is considered to be well spent; while among secular intellectuals, it may be considered more important to read the daily newspaper. Whereas those raised in upper-class New England may place a premium on being familiar with the classics of U.S. literature, midwestern farmers may be more concerned with their ability to read the latest commodity exchange tables and the manuals for their machinery. Educators in the United States tend to see creative writing by children as a valued activity, and this perspective is incorporated into school curricula. This may appear strange in other countries, however, where students are encouraged to learn and copy the work of great thinkers rather than to produce original work.

As part of their formal schooling, children encounter the preferences of the educational system, the school, and the teachers, regarding which behaviors to emphasize. These preferences have in turn been shaped by the sociocultural environment of the school and its agents (such as teachers, teacher assistants, principals, textbook writers, and editors). Other messages are conveyed through interactions with family and peers, the media, and even the various segments of the educational system. Whether these messages are congruent depends in part on the degree of cultural heterogeneity represented by the messengers. In educating their pupils toward literacy, schools vary in the degree to which they incorporate the cultural views of the ethnic groups to which their pupils belong. To the extent that schools tend to reflect the dominant culture, pupils from the dominant ethnic group are more likely than are ethnic minority students to find consistency between the various constructs of literacy. In either case, because literacy education tends to be left primarily to the school, children become literate in the cultural image represented by their school.

So it is that literacy education can constitute a profound form of socialization. A person who becomes literate does so in the context of a particular definition of literate behavior. She is, as Purves (1987) and others (Heath, 1986; Wallace, 1986) remind us, trained to internalize the behaviors appropriate to a functional member of a specific social community. In the case of a majority child attending majority schools, this is essentially transparent in that neither educator nor pupil need consciously attend to the ways in which they are engaged in a process of cultural transmission. In the case of minority group members, however, the process may be less smooth, depending on the extent to which their group's standards for cultural significance differ from the dominant group norms. For members of cultural minorities, the potential conflicts will be greater, as will the salience of group membership.

The meaning of the processes and symbols involved in literacy education will differ depending on what reference group the individual uses to interpret them. Thus, at the individual level, whether deliberately or not, the process of becoming and being literate involves becoming and being identified with a particular culture. The relationship of the individual to the group forms the basis for cultural identity. In the following sections, I elaborate on this point.

## Cultural Identity

From a social psychological perspective we are most concerned with the mutual influence of the individual and his social environment. Cultural identity is a concept that can help to conceptualize these links. In this section, I delineate the related but distinct constructs of group and individual cultural identity. By its very nature, culture is meaningful only with reference to the group, yet it is enacted by individuals. This is why culture is a central concept in understanding how the person and the collective are connected.[8] We must clarify what is meant by cultural identity to understand its interaction with literacy.

### The Group Level

An ethnic group's cultural identity involves a shared sense of the cultural features that help to define and to characterize the group. These group attributes are important not just for their functional value, but also as symbols. For example, for many Puerto Ricans in the United States, the Spanish language is not just a means of communication; it also represents their identification as Latinos and their difference from the majority culture. Even if Spanish reading and writing ability is absent, the desire to conserve some degree of Spanish speaking ability may reflect a desire to maintain distinctiveness from the surrounding society (see, for example Ball, Giles, & Hewstone, 1984; Hakuta, Ferdman, & Diaz, 1987). Group cultural identity has to do both with the particular features of the ethnic group and with the significance that is attached to these features in a societal context. A group's cultural identity will play an important role in the nature and outcome of the intergroup comparisons that it makes, and thus in the way the group comes to evaluate itself (see, for example, Ferdman, 1987; Montero, 1987; Tajfel & Turner, 1986). When a group perceives that its cultural features compare favorably with those of other groups, it should come to hold more positive images of itself. If, on the other hand, features central to the group's cultural identity are viewed negatively in the larger society, the group will probably incorporate a negative component into its self-evaluation.

Kochman (1987) makes a useful distinction between emblematic and nonemblematic ethnic indicators: "Emblematic indicators are those racial and cultural features that serve an identity function or otherwise mark and maintain social boundaries" (p. 220) between the in-group and the out-group. These are features that in-group and out-group members will tend to think of as "ethnic." Nonemblematic indicators are those cultural patterns that do not serve such functions, and of which in-group and out-group members may or may not be aware.[9] For example, anthropologists and other social scientists may identify characteristic features of the group's behavior that are not otherwise generally linked to the group.

As defined here, cultural identity at the group level involves those features of the group that are widely perceived as emblematic by the in-group. While outsiders may consider particular features as characteristic of most group members, thereby rendering them emblematic in Kochman's sense, these features would not necessarily form part of the group's collective cultural identity unless the in-group internalized this external point of view or had otherwise also incorporated these features into its self-image.

Smolicz (1981) uses the concept of core values similarly, although in a more restrictive sense than intended here. According to him, core values "generally represent the heartland of the ideological system and act as identifying values which are symbolic of the group and its membership" (p. 75). What is important in defining the centrality of a cultural feature is not the particular type of value or characteristic. Rather, "whenever people feel that there is a direct link between their identity as a group and what they regard as the most crucial and distinguishing element of their culture, the element concerned becomes a core value" (pp. 76–77). So, for example, while for some groups maintenance of the native language may function as a core value, for others, the centrality of the family or religious life may play this role. As elaborated here, then, an ethnic group's cultural identity is based on such core values, but also extends beyond them to include other features and values that the group generally perceives itself to possess and which help it to maintain its character as a group. This might nevertheless form part of the group's cultural identity, because it is a characteristic that is seen as identifying and distinguishing the group.

## The Individual Level

In conceptualizing cultural identity at the group level, I have assumed a certain degree of uniformity within the group. Nevertheless, although members of the same ethnic group will tend to demonstrate shared cultural features (this is in part what defines their common ethnicity), variation within groups will also be present. Individual members of ethnic groups will vary both in the extent of their identification with the group and in the degree to which their behavior is based on the group's cultural norms (see, for example, Boekestijn, 1988; Ferdman & Hakuta, 1985). In a multiethnic society in which members of different groups are in various degrees of contact with each other, a variety of options may be available to individuals regarding how to relate not only to other groups but also to their own. Ethnic group members will express their choices in part through the behaviors they demonstrate in different types of situations. Especially in the case of minority group members or immigrants, the extent to which an individual follows the group's typical cultural pattern may be an indication of the degree of that person's psychological assimilation or acculturation (Berry, 1986; Graves, 1967). Jones (1988) points out how such variation may also reflect minority group members' perceptions regarding the instrumentality[10] of particular behaviors in different contexts, such that an individual may behave in accordance with the group's cultural patterns in some situations but not in others. The distinction between the group and the individual level is important, in part because, as Berry (1986) puts it, "not every individual participates to the same extent in the general acculturation being experienced by his group" (p. 38; see also Berry, 1983) and conversely, because some individual group members may acculturate more rapidly than the group as a whole. Thus, over time, acculturation processes may affect both what the cultural features are at the group level (Taylor & McKirnan, 1984) and whether particular individuals demonstrate them (Berry, 1986). In addition, contextual factors may influence whether individuals are likely to behave in line with the group's cultural identity. Because of this intragroup variation, to render cultural identity useful as a psychological construct we must transpose it to the individual level. Beyond behavioral differences, we should expect within-group diversity in the degree to which particular features are seen as central to the group's identity.

At the individual level, cultural identity has to do with the person's sense of what constitutes membership in an ethnic group to which he or she belongs. Each person will have a particular image of the behaviors and values that characterize the group's culture. The term is distinguished here from the related and broader social psychological concept of *social identity*, as well as from *ethnic identity*. Tajfel and Turner (1986) define social identity as consisting "of those aspects of an individual's self-image that derive from the social categories to which he [*sic*] perceives himself as belonging" (p. 16). Their notion of social categories is quite broad, encompassing any type of group to which people perceive themselves as belonging.[11] Such categories of course include ethnicity, but can range from school sports teams to professional identifications, from social club memberships to gender or race classifications, and from nationality groups to psychological groups (for example, "jocks," "yuppies," "nerds"). Social identity incorporates both the person's knowledge of membership in particular social categories and the value and feelings attached to those memberships. Ethnic identity can be defined as the portion of an individual's social identity that is associated with membership in an ethnic group.[12] Cultural identity, while linked closely to both ethnic and social identity, is neither equivalent to them nor coterminous. While both ethnic and cultural identity help the individual to answer the question, "Who am I?", cultural identity is the component that associates particular cultural features with group membership. Social identity and ethnic identity deal with the symbolic aspects of social categorization—the boundary between the in-group and the out-group—and the associated affect. A particular individual, for example, may base her social identity primarily on gender, while her sister may focus more sharply on her Polish background. Thus, the first sister's ethnic identity as a Polish-American would be somewhat less strong than that of the second sister (see Babad, Birnbaum, & Benne, 1983).[13]

Cultural identity as defined here is a more specific construct. Cultural identity involves the perceived bases for a person's ethnic categorization—that which is inside the boundary—and the person's feelings about this content. The second sister's cultural identity includes the perception that being Polish generally implies being strongly Catholic and maintaining close family ties. It also incorporates her feelings about these features—she is somewhat ambivalent about the first, and she feels quite positive about the second. Cultural identity thus includes the individual's internalized view of the cultural features characterizing his or her group, together with the value and affect that the person attaches to those features.

Paralleling the distinction made here between cultural and ethnic identity, Keefe and Padilla (1987) discuss the difference between the processes of acculturation and ethnic identification. Acculturation involves changes in the cultural patterns shown by groups when they come into contact with one another. In ethnic identification, in contrast, "the particular assemblage of cultural traits becomes less important than the attitudes of members toward the people and culture of in-group versus out-group as well as members' self-identification" (p. 41). Thus, an individual may maintain a strong identification with a particular group while adopting new cultural traits. Similarly, Herman (1977), in studying the nature of Jewish identity, suggested that its analysis at the individual level must address both a) the nature of the individual's relationship to the Jewish group as a membership group; and b) the individual's perception of the attributes of the Jewish group, his or her feeling about them, and the extent to which its norms are adopted by him or her as a source of reference (p. 39). The first component involves aspects of the person's ethnic affiliation—in the present terms, both ethnic and social identity—while the second has to do with the ways in which that affiliation is represented—what I refer to as cultural identity.

Two people may perceive their identification as members in a particular group to be just as central to their ethnic identity, yet define its meaning quite differently. For example, for one Jew the primary features of being Jewish involve following the religious laws and becoming learned in the Bible and in the Talmud; while for another, religious observance is secondary or non-existent; more emphasis is placed on Jewish values and on supporting the State of Israel (Herman, 1977). Yet both claim an equally strong connection to the Jewish people. Similarly, Puerto Ricans living in New York and in Puerto Rico, while sharing an ethnic identification, will have divergent experiences and ways of looking at the world, with resulting differences in their cultural identities. For one, the experience of minority status and ethnic distinctiveness in an urban environment will play a relatively more central role; while for the other the Spanish language and living on the island will be relatively more important (Flores, 1985; Ginorio, 1987).

Thus, cultural identity involves those parts of the self—those behaviors, beliefs, values, and norms that a person considers to define himself or herself socially as a member of a particular ethnic group—and the value placed on those features in relation to those of other groups. Changes in those features would imply a shift in the person's way of thinking about him- or herself in a social context. Via his or her cultural identity, the individual answers the question, "What is the appropriate way for someone like me, for someone having my ethnicity, to interpret and to behave in the world?" While, at the group level, a collective set of emblematic cultural features that compose the group's cultural identity may exist, at the individual level, what is relevant is the person's particular perspective on the collective view. Individual members of an ethnic group will vary in the extent to which they perceive specific attributes as central to their cultural identity and in the value they give these attributes. In addition, they will vary in the degree to which they see themselves as representing these attributes.[14]

Status and power differentials between groups may play a role in the cultural identity individuals come to hold. In a multiethnic society, the minority group member[15] is typically identified in group terms, while members of the dominant group will be more likely to see themselves and to be seen by others in individual terms, "or at least as not belonging to any particular category" (Deschamps, 1982, p. 89; see also Tajfel, 1978). Guillaumin (1972) has suggested that minority groups tend to have complex views of the majority and not just of their own group; whereas, the majority tends to see the minority as a deindividuated mass. Thus, we might expect that members of minority groups will be more aware of their attributes as being associated with group membership and thus as forming part of their cultural identity. Members of the dominant group, in contrast, because they may be less accustomed to thinking of themselves in group terms, may be less conscious of the cultural sources for behavior. For them, identity may be construed primarily at the individual level and not be perceived as connected to the group's features. One implication of this is that minority group members are able to choose (and sometimes are forced) to adopt the dominant ("mainstream") perspective to interpret social reality.

## Cultural Identity and Literacy

Because literacy is a culturally defined construct, it follows that it should have close links to cultural identity. At the societal level, literacy education involves not just the imparting of particular skills, but also the transmission of values (de Castell & Luke, 1983). Kádár-Fülop (1988) points to the development of "language loyalty"—the encouragement of positive attitudes toward the language—as an important function for literacy education. De Castell and Luke (1983; 1987) forcefully show how literacy campaigns are carried out in the context of particular social agendas. In an ethnically diverse society, these values are not necessarily shared across groups. Indeed, de Castell and Luke (1987) write that:

> If literacy campaigns are seen primarily as attempts to forge or to impose a common cultural tradition, and only secondarily as attempts to disseminate competence at reading and writing, then we ought to reconsider the alleged current crises not as failures in the mass transmission of reading and writing but as failures of a far more fundamental kind: failures in the mass inculcation and perpetuation of a desired sociocultural tradition. (p. 428)

From a social psychological perspective, the question becomes one of describing the individual, interpersonal, and intergroup processes by which such failures (or successes) may come about.

The concept of cultural identity permits such an elaboration. The idea that cultural symbols have affective significance for the individual suggests that the process of becoming and being literate will tap into these feelings. When there is a mismatch between the definition and significance of literacy as they are represented in a person's cultural identity and in the learning situation, the individual is faced with making a choice that has implications for his or her acquisition of reading and writing skills, as well as for his or her relationship to particular texts and the symbols they contain. The student must either adopt the perspective of the school, at the risk of developing a negative component to his or her cultural identity, or else resist these externally imposed activities and meanings, at the risk of becoming alienated from the school; whereas, for majority children, the school's perspective is likely to parallel whatever cultural identity they have. This is less likely for members of ethnic minorities.

Henry Giroux (1987) points out how individuals' "stories, memories, narratives, and readings of the world are inextricably related to wider social and cultural formations and categories" (p. 177). In the context of literacy education, the issue has to do with what is experienced by the student as "owned" and what is experienced as "not owned" by his or her group. Which texts and which writing tasks does the student engage in as "ours" and which as "theirs"? When a child perceives a writing task or a text and its symbolic contents as belonging to and reaffirming his or her cultural identity, it is more likely that he or she will become engaged and individual meaning will be transmitted or derived. In contrast, those tasks and symbols that serve to deny or to devalue aspects of the individual's cultural identity, or even those that are neutral in relation to it, may be approached differently and with less personal involvement. For example, reading in a group setting and analyzing texts is an important component of Jewish religious practice. An Orthodox Jewish child who perceives these activities as important components of his cultural identity may become more involved in similar tasks at school because they are linked to his sense of who he is. A child who, for cultural reasons, is accustomed to reading aloud, with a group, may approach reading assignments at school differently from a classmate who thinks of reading as something that is done alone and silently. Another student, who believes that reading books assigned at school is not "something my people do," will probably be less likely to complete such assignments. This same child may be very adept, however, at reading other materials, such as comic books.

Two personal examples are in order here. As a child, I delighted in reading anything I could get my hands on. But one of my favorite types of stories as an eight- and nine-year-old was *midrashim*, myths and legends based on the Bible. If Norse legends were given to me, I was just as likely to read them; but, they did not have the same impact on me, and I did not see them in the same light. Because of my Jewish identity, my relationship to King David or to Abraham was a more personal and significant one than my connection with Thor. The Biblical stories, because they touched on my cultural identity, had practical and symbolic meanings that went beyond the story and extended into helping me learn more about myself and my group in a social context and gave me conceptual tools with which to interact with other group members. Similarly, when I want to read a Latin American author, I will do so in Spanish, my native tongue, rather than in an English translation. My choice is based not only on a desire to read the original, but also to reaffirm my connection with Latin American symbols and texts. In spite of ostensibly similar content, I experience the images and meanings differently in the two languages.

These examples highlight the ways personal meaning is derived from broader social meanings. However, the relationship of reading and cultural identity may not be a function of only the symbolic content of the text. The significance of the text itself and the context in which it is read may be at least as relevant, if nor more so. For example, therefore, if reading *The New York Times* contributes in an important way to my cultural identity, I will relate to that text differently from someone who approaches it as an outsider. Similarly, reading *The New York Times* every day will have a different meaning when I do it in New York than when I do it in Paris. While in both cases the activity may be similarly related to my cultural identity, in the latter case it may be seen as a more obvious statement of where I stand in relation to my social environment.

Relevant to this issue, Hakuta and I (Hakuta, Ferdman, & Diaz, 1987) conducted a study of Puerto Rican elementary school children and their parents in New Haven, Connecticut. We found some indication that reading Spanish newspapers reflected not only language proficiency but also degrees of identification with being Puerto Rican. At intermediate levels of English ability, twice as many of those respondents who planned to return to Puerto Rico, as compared with those planning to stay in

New Haven, reported that they regularly read *El Vocero,* a Spanish-language daily newspaper flown in from the island.[16]

Matute-Bianchi's (1986) research among Mexican-descent and Japanese-American high school students and Trueba's (1984) work in the Mexican-American barrio show that for ethnic minority group members, perceptions of themselves and others in a social context and of the value of their education in relation to those social perceptions contribute significantly shaping their attitudes toward school-related activities. In the California high school that she studied, Matute-Bianchi was able to distinguish five sub-groups among students of Mexican descent on the basis of how they identified themselves ethnically and which behavior patterns they perceived to go along with these labels. For some of the groups (the "Mexicans" and the "Mexican-Americans"), success in school was not viewed as incompatible with cultural identity. As they learned the dominant culture of the school, these students did not believe that they had to give up what they considered important about their identity as Mexicans. In contrast, for other groups (the "Chicanos"), maintaining their identity involved engaging in behaviors that ultimately reduce the chances for academic success:

> Chicanos and Cholos . . . appear to resist certain features of the school culture, especially the behavioral and normative patterns required for school achievement. These norms, assumptions, and codes of conduct are associated with being white or gringo or quaddie or rich honkie. To adopt these cultural features— that is, to participate in class discussions, to carry books from class to class, to ask the teacher for help in front of others, to expend effort to do well in school— are efforts that are viewed derivisively, condescendingly, and mockingly by other Chicanos. Hence, to adopt such features presents these students with a forced-choice dilemma. They must choose between doing well in school or being a Chicano. (Matute-Bianchi, 1986, pp. 253–254)

The Japanese-Americans who were interviewed by Matute-Bianchi were all successful students. They, in contrast to their peers of Mexican descent, did not see components of their ethnicity in conflict with their identities as students. Thus, they saw no need to behave differently in the school context from the ways of the dominant culture. This was the case even for students who outside of school participated in activities such as praying at a Buddhist temple, which is explicitly linked to their Japanese identity.

Trueba similarly found that the families he studied perceived a clear relationship between literacy in English and acculturation. As he put it:

> Posing as illiterate in some contexts was equivalent to keeping one's own identity as "cholo" i.e., as marginal in school and involved with peers in other activities. In the home, however, dedication to books and relative facility to deal with text signaled eagerness to make it in the Anglo world, and that had a price, because it required some adjustment in peer reference groups and in social activities. (Trueba, 1984, p. 33)

Thus, we may expect that those people who wish to become more acculturated will be more likely to engage in activities that will help them to acquire English literacy.

I have argued so far that cultural identity mediates the process of becoming literate as well as the types of literate behavior in which a person subsequently engages. At this point, it becomes possible to formulate more precise questions as a guide to future thinking and research about the ways cultural identity affects how and whether an individual becomes literate as a result of schooling:

1. How is literacy defined in the individual's group, and what is its significance? What behaviors are included in this definition?
2. What significance do particular texts have for the individual's cultural identity?
3. How do the particular pedagogical approach, the texts that are used, and the purpose of literacy as communicated by the school relate to the learner's motives and sense of identity (and more subtly, what messages does a reading and writing curriculum communicate about the value of the learner's culture)?
4. What relationship does the learner perceive between the tasks assigned in school and his or her cultural identity? Must the learner change the nature of his or her self-concept in order to do what is asked?

Attention to these questions by researchers and educators may help us to better understand how the meaning of literacy for individuals is influenced by their sense of themselves as cultural beings. In turn, such understanding should better serve members of a heterogeneous society as they acquire literacy.

Until now, the discussion has focused on the implications of cultural identity for literacy development. The relationship, however, is better seen as bi-directional. Not only will cultural identity mediate the acquisition and expression of literacy, but literacy education will also influence and mold the individual's cultural identity. Modifying the means by which the person interacts with others across time and space—that is, making the person "literate"—will eventually require the person to redefine (or reaffirm) his or her own view of the self in a social context. A clear example is that of the immigrant who seeks—or is forced—to acculturate not only by learning a new language but also by adopting a whole new set of symbols and meanings. I was struck, one recent November, by a picture in *The New York Times* showing newly arrived Vietnamese immigrant children in school dressed as Pilgrims and Indians in "celebration" of the Thanksgiving holiday. Clearly, they were being asked as a condition of citizenship to take as their own a new set of cultural icons and referents. The school was teaching the children not only to understand the images and associations evoked by Thanksgiving but to do so from the perspective of the dominant culture. In a more subtle but no less powerful way, the reading and writing activities that children are asked to engage in at school, to the extent that they are accepted, will ultimately affect not only the children's sense of who they are, but the ways in which they can figure out their cultural identity.

Literacy education, as de Castell and Luke (1987) so forcefully argue, can never be content-free. By providing the individual with the symbolic material with which to understand and transact with the social environment and by requiring him or her to do so in particular modalities, the range of possibilities for the person is channeled and narrowed. Certainly, this is a significant and indispensable part of socialization. The problem may arise for ethnic minority group members who as a result must dissociate from those aspects of themselves that would otherwise serve to provide them with a positive sense of identity in the social environment.

Linguists and psychologists (Erickson, 1984; Guiora, 1985; McEvedy, 1986) have pointed to the cognitive aspects of this channeling process as it occurs in learning a first or second language. Guiora and his colleagues (Guiora, 1985), for example, found that children who spoke languages with greater gender loadings (Hebrew) developed gender identity sooner than those speaking languages with little gender loading (English) or none (Finnish). McEvedy (1986) points out how the concept of *we* is very general in English, but much more fine-tuned among the Pitjantjatjarra of Australia, who employ different pronouns depending on exactly who is in the situation and how distant they are from the speaker. These arguments suggest that, for example, a French child who is educated in English and grows up without learning the French language will have a different experience of gender and of interpersonal relationships than a child educated in French, as a result of the use of different linguistic markers in the two languages.

The issue, however, extends beyond this, into the meanings that become attached to various symbolic representations as they relate to the person's sense of his or her integration into a cultural group and of the group's place in society, into what Erickson (1984) refers to as the "politics of social identity." Erickson summarizes Scollon and Scollon's (1981) work among Alaskan natives in this context:

> In their interpretation, Alaskan native teenagers come to see the acquisition of Western written literacy as a kind of metaphoric adoption of a new ethnic group identity. To become literate in school terms would be to disaffiliate symbolically from their parents and other members of the Alaskan native village, a few of whom are "literate" in traditional knowledge and skill, such as that involved in hunting, and many of whom are marginally literate in school-like practices of literacy. Caught in ambivalence between multiple cultural worlds, Alaskan native youth resist adopting the complete system of school-defined literacy, and then suffer the consequences of marginal acquisition. They do not belong fully to the old ways or to the new. (p. 539)

We might ask what happens to those Alaskan natives who do fully adopt "school-defined literacy." Their cultural identity, also, should be fundamentally altered. Indeed, in becoming and being literate in this way, the materials they now have access to, because they are mostly generated by other ethnic groups, will provide them with perspectives on their own ethnic group that are probably quite different from those originated by the Alaskans themselves.

It would appear, then, that the impact of literacy education as a socialization agent on individuals' cultural identity can be either destructive or constructive. When the person loses the capability to derive and create meaning in a culturally significant way, he or she becomes less, not more, literate. To the extent that successful learning, as defined from the school's point of view, forces the ethnic minority child to become disconnected from what is personally significant, his or her ability to construct a positive and coherent cultural identity will be weakened. I do not wish to argue, however, that children must learn only about the heritage and products of their own culture. Indeed, the opposite is true. James Banks (1977, 1981, 1987) presents a useful view of multi-ethnic education that aims towards inclusion rather than exclusion. He recommends providing all students with "cultural and ethnic alternatives" (1977, p. 8) so that they learn about both their own culture and those of others. One goal of this approach is to prevent minority group members from feeling that they must become alienated from their identity to do well. By explicitly incorporating into schooling a culture-sensitive approach, students can be allowed to discover how what they are learning relates to their ethnic identity. As they learn, they will then be able to better articulate their cultural identity. This process can occur not only as they discover what is their own; it is also facilitated through contrast, as they discover what belongs to others.

Literacy education, when it acknowledges the role of cultural identity, may serve to enhance self-esteem as it derives from a sense of self in a social context. If individuals can acquire the tools to better define their cultural identity—by, for example, comparing it with a range of possibilities—then learning about a range of cultural products[16] can be enriching. To do this, the individual who is becoming literate must be encouraged to consider the relationship of what is learned to the self and to the group, by calling attention to the ways in which alternative perspectives on the methods and contents of literacy are possible. When this is done, it may result in an environment that can more readily empower members of dominated groups (Cummins, 1986). Rather than aim for a curriculum that avoids discussions of ethnicity, the goal should be to facilitate the process by which students are permitted to discover and explore ethnic connections.

As pointed out earlier, the process by which literacy education shapes individuals' cultural identity takes place in an intergroup context. Because the definition of becoming and being literate at the societal level has to do in part with defining group boundaries and status, the debate over literacy in a multi-ethnic society reflects variant values regarding the proper place of the society's component groups. Implementing literacy education that authorizes and fosters variations in cultural identity implies realignments in groups' positions such that previously devalued groups— together with their cultures—become recognized and appreciated.[17]

The ongoing debate over cultural literacy (Hirsch, 1987) may be interpreted in this light: The controversy is about the issue of what should constitute cultural identity at the national level and what should be the nature of the relationship of minority and dominant groups in the society. In terms of the present discussion, the problem with Hirsch's recommendations is not the idea that Americans should be more familiar with a variety of terms and ideas. Rather, it is with the assumption that the meaning and significance of the terms are absolute. Hirsch's view of writing and reading skills as culture-bound makes good sense. The issue in regard to cultural identity, however, is that of the relevance of the content for the reader or writer. What does a particular concept symbolize in relation to the individual's sense of self as group member and in relation to the state of intergroup relations in the society?

In literacy education, attention must be given not only to teaching lists of important facts, but to develop individual skill in exploring the relationship of these facts to the self. Students must be encouraged to discover and decide for themselves—in the context of their cultural identity—what information and what values are conveyed. What makes a particular fact important and for whom? For example, the value attached to the concept *Crusades,* and even what is described by it, will probably be quite different for a Jewish, a Christian, and a Moslem individual. Thus, in the United States, the drive to educate all students about a set of "facts" in the name of literacy education can be seen by minorities as a thinly veiled guise for the imposition of a particular type of cultural identity. This way of pushing one version of knowledge may simply serve to allow the dominant group to maintain its position while still espousing democratic and meritocratic values.

How then can teachers and other educators better acknowledge their students' cultural identity and consider it in planning and providing more effective literacy education? I suggest that the first step in this process involves turning inward. Before helping others to do so, one must initially explore one's own values and attitudes about ethnic diversity, as well as one's degree of awareness of the role culture plays in one's own formation. A teacher should feel comfortable with his or her own background before attempting to delve into that of others. After doing this, I believe that educators will be more likely to adopt a strategy that recognizes cultural differences as important, but not the only source of individual variation. Teachers and other educators can become educated about other cultural forms that literacy can take and about the different cultural influences on their students. These can be incorporated into educational plans. In doing this, it is important not to automatically apply generalizations about a group to individual students. But avoiding stereotyping and over-generalization does not mean avoiding the reality of culture. Teachers can discover ways of encouraging students to explore the implications of their ethnicities and to engage in self-definition. Explicitly and positively linking classroom activities to the students' cultural identities could also be a way of motivating students; in the recent motion picture, *Stand and Deliver,* Jaime Escalante gained his students' interest through his high expectations and by connecting math to their Mayan forebears. By providing a range of literacy experiences and explicitly linking them to their cultural sources, teachers can give students more involvement and choice in their own formation.

## Conclusion

I have argued that cultural diversity plays an important role in influencing the relationship of literacy and the individual. People's perceptions of themselves in relationship to their ethnic group and the larger society, as reflected in what I have called cultural identity, can change, and in turn be changed, by the process of becoming and being literate. As the United States debates alternative visions of positive ethnic relations, those advocating the goal of extending literacy to all members of the society might well incorporate a view of all individuals as cultural beings. If this is done, perhaps more sensitive and articulated models of literacy acquisition can be developed that better take into account the social context in which literacy is defined and expressed. When everyone—minority and majority alike—is encouraged and supported in the development of a clear and strong cultural identity, we may well see a society, not of excessive uniformity and constraint at the individual level or undue divisiveness at the group level, as some might suggest, but rather, a society which would permit the full range of individual variation, choice, and flexibility, while at the same time recognizing the importance group identifications hold for individuals. In such an environment, perhaps literacy can indeed become a universal characteristic.

## Notes

1. *Becoming* and *being* are emphasized to stress the dynamic aspects of literacy. Rather than conceiving of literacy primarily as a passive characteristic of the individual and so considering someone to "be" literate regardless of what he or she does, in this article I focus on the active facets of literacy and on the ways in which literacy can be thought of as "a way of carrying out social transactions" (Carraher, 1988, p. 95). In this view, being literate means engaging in particular activities that so define persons as they transact with the social environment.
2. This debate itself forms part of the interethnic relations in the society. The lines dividing various points of view often follow ethnic boundaries. Moreover, the approach that is adopted has implications not just for pedagogy, but also for ethnic stratification. An example of this can be seen in the debates over bilingualism and bilingual education (for one account, see Hakuta, 1986), in which Hispanics are more likely to favor language transition programs that include a child's native Spanish over immersion programs using solely English (for example, Hakuta, 1984). We can expect that the type of program ultimately used in a particular school district will impact not only on how children learn, but also on the status and opportunities available to Hispanics in that district. It is in this sense that the struggle is over the relative power between groups and not simply an educational issue.
3. Note, for example, the proliferation of a mainstreaming policy for special populations that were previously segregated within the educational system.
4. For a useful discussion of an attributional perspective on intercultural education in multicultural societies, see Albert and Triandis (1985).
5. In their article de Castell and Luke (1983) show how the dominant definitions of literacy in American schools have shifted historically, from 19th century views that emphasized moral, religious, and civic aspects of literacy instruction, to more current views that emphasize functionality, basic skills, and measurability.
6. Reder (1987) gives the example of Hmong immigrants, who were able to produce a signature on documents, but did not comprehend what this implicated. When someone else would explain the legal implications, however, they would sometimes refuse to sign.
   Reder also points to a number of "collaborative literacy practices" in the communities he studied, in which two or more people work together to produce or decode texts. From an individualistic conception of literacy, we might view someone who requires or prefers help in reading or writing to be less literate than someone who works alone. In a different cultural context, however, it is the failure to collaborate that may be defined as less literate.
7. It must be noted that Roth's use of the term "culture" is somewhat imprecise and is more general than my usage of the term in this paper. She seems to use "culture" as a synonym for "dominant group" or "mainstream society." In either case, her use of the first person ("our" culture) is appropriate only for those groups adequately represented by the school. For those whose culture is different than that (or those) of the school, read "their" in place of "our."
8. The present analysis focuses on cultural identity as an aspect of ethnicity in a multi-ethnic society. This emphasis is not meant to suggest that other social categorizations—for example, gender, race, and class—do not play an important role in linking persons to groups and therefore in helping to form individuals' identities and world view. Indeed, it is probable that similar arguments to those presented here could be constructed linking literacy to these other components of people's social selves" (Babad et al., 1983). This paper, however, is restricted to exploring the relationship of literacy to cultural diversity as it derives from ethnic differences.

9. As Kochman (1987) puts it, "outgroup members are too far removed from the context in which such distinctive ingroup cultural patterns are displayed. Ingroup members, on the other hand, are often too close to their own culture to be able to see it" (p. 224).

10. By instrumentality, Jones (1988) refers to the utility of the behavior in obtaining desired outcomes.

11. Tajfel (1977) writes: "Any society which contains power, status, prestige and social group differentials (and they all do), places each of us in a number of *social* categories which become an important part of our *self*-definition (p. 654, author's emphases).

12. Because social identity may refer to any type of social group (see Tajfel, 1981; Ferdman, 1987) the concept is too broad if we are interested in focusing specifically on the individual's relationship with ethnic groups. The notion of ethnic identity, as it is defined here, is intended to serve this purpose.

13. Of course, every individual belongs to a number of social categories and so has many influences on his or her sense of self. Each of us constructs a social identity from these various components which include, in addition to ethnicity, categories such as gender, race, or socioeconomic status. The problem of how each person answers the question, "Who am I?" is complex and multifaceted. Ultimately, each individual derives a unique identity on the basis of his or her particular combination of experiences and group memberships (see Babad et al., 1983; Taylor & Dubé, 1986). Thus, although the focus here is on the ways in which ethnicity and culture influence a person's identity, this is not meant to suggest that these are mutually exclusive with other social categories. Indeed, there are interactions between group memberships such that being African American is incorporated differently by a middle-class woman than a working-class man.

14. Within-group variation in cultural identity need not be idiosyncratic. Differences in individuals' cultural identities could be systematically associated with other factors—socioeconomic status or place of residence, for example. We might expect that, in general, wealthy members of the English nobility will not have the same conception of what it means to be English as will poor laborers in Liverpool, in spite of a shared ethnic identification. A recent immigrant from Mexico living in a poor neighborhood of Los Angeles might have a different conception of Hispanic culture than a sixth-generation landowner in New Mexico, although both identify as Latinos.

   It should be noted that the construct of cultural identity is not meant to replace concepts such as social class. Although social class can interact with ethnicity in producing an individual's cultural identity, it can also operate independently to influence values, behavior, and experience. The concept of cultural identity, however, permits understanding some of the differences between members of the same social class who come from different ethnic backgrounds.

15. The term "minority group" is used here in the sociological sense to mean a group with less power than the dominant group and whose members are treated unequally and in an inferior manner in society (Feagin, 1984; Shaefer, 1988).

16. The question on the survey reads as follows: "If you had to move again, where would you like to move?" Respondents could mark one of five answers: 1) would stay in the same neighborhood, 2) would move to a different neighborhood, 3) would move to Puerto Rico, 4) would move to a different country (specify), or 5) would move to another city or state (specify).

16. I use the term *cultural products* to signify how all that is taught in schools is culturally produced.

17. In such a context, groups previously considered "minorities," groups whose members' cultural identity is largely disparaged within the society, could cease to be so designated. Groups could be understood in terms of their specific features and their uniqueness rather than in terms of their relative dominance and subordination.

# References

Akinnaso, F. N. (1981). The consequences of literacy in pragmatic and theoretical perspectives. *Anthropology and Education Quarterly, 12,* 163–200.

Akinnaso, F. N. (1982). On the differences between spoken and written language. *Language and Speech, 25,* 97–125.

Akinnaso, F. N. (1985). On the similarities between spoken and written language. *Language and Speech, 28,* 324–359.

Albert, R. D., & Triandis, H. C. (1985). Intercultural education for multicultural societies: Critical issues. *International Journal of Intercultural Relations, 9,* 319–337.

Babad, E. Y., Birnbaum, M., & Benne, K. D. (1983). *The social self: Group influences on personal identity.* Beverly Hills, CA: Sage.

Ball, P., Giles, H., & Hewstone, M. (1984). Second language acquisition: The intergroup theory with catastrophic dimensions. In H. Tajfel, C. Fraser, & J. Jaspars (Eds.), *The social dimension: European developments in social psychology* (Vol. 2). Cambridge: Cambridge University Press.

Banks, J. A. (1977). *Multiethnic education: Practices and promises.* Bloomington, IN: Phi Delta Kappa Educational Foundation.

Banks, J. A. (1981). *Multiethnic education: Theory and practice.* Boston: Allyn and Bacon.

Banks, J. A. (1987). *Teaching strategies for ethnic studies* (4th ed.). Boston: Allyn and Bacon.

Berry, J. W. (1983). Acculturation: A comparative analysis of alternative forms. In R. Samuda & S. Woods (Eds.), *Perspectives in immigrant and minority education.* New York: University Press of America.

Berry, J. W. (1986). Multiculturalism and psychology in plural societies. In L. H. Ekstrand (Ed.), *Ethnic minorities and immigrants in a cross-cultural perspective* (pp. 35–51). Berwyn, NY: Swets North America.

Boekestijn, C. (1988). Intercultural migration and the development of personal identity: The dilemma between identity maintenance and cultural adaptation. *International Journal of Intercultural Relations, 12,* 83–105.

Carraher, T. N. (1988). Illiteracy in a literate society: Understanding reading failure in Brazil. In D. A. Wagner (Ed.), *The future of literacy in a changing world* (pp. 95–110). Oxford: Pergamon Press.

Cook-Gumperz, J. (Ed.) (1986). *The social construction of literacy.* Cambridge: Cambridge University Press.

Cummins, J. (1986). Empowering minority students: A framework for intervention. *Harvard Educational Review, 56,* 18–36.

de Castell, S., & Luke, A. (1983). Defining 'literacy' in North American schools: Social and historical conditions and consequences. *Journal of Curriculum Studies, 15,* 373–389.

de Castell, S., & Luke, A. (1987). Literacy instruction: Technology and technique. *American Journal of Education, 95,* 413–440.

Deschamps, J. (1982). Social identity and relations of power between groups. In H. Tajfel (Ed.), *Social identity and intergroup relations* (pp. 85–98). Cambridge: Cambridge University Press.

Erickson, F. (1984). School literacy, reasoning, and civility: An anthropologist's perspective. *Review of Educational Research, 54,* 525–546.

Feagin, J. R. (1989). *Racial and Ethnic Relations* (3rd ed.). Englewood Cliffs, NJ: Prentice Hall.

Ferdman, B. M. (1987). *Person perception in interethnic situations.* Unpublished manuscript, Department of Psychology, Yale University, New Haven.

Ferdman, B. M. (1988, August). Values and fairness in the ethnically diverse workplace. In Faye Crosby (Chair), *Emancipation, justice and affirmative action.* Symposium conducted at the 2nd International Conference on Social Justice and Societal Problems, University of Leiden, Netherlands.

Ferdman, B. M. (1989). Affirmative action and the challenge of the color-blind perspective. In F. Blanchard & F. Crosby (Eds.), *Affirmative action in perspective* (pp. 169–176). New York: Springer-Verlag.

Ferdman, B. M., & Hakuta, K. (1985, August). Group and individual bilingualism in an ethnic minority. In K. Hakuta & B. M. Ferdman (Co-chairs), *Bilingualism: Social psychological reflections.* Symposium conducted at the meetings of the American Psychological Association, Los Angeles.

Flores, J. (1985). "Que assimilated, brother, yo soy asimilao": The structuring of Puerto Rican identity in the U.S. *Journal of Ethnic Studies, 13,* 1–16.

Ginorio, A. B. (1987). Puerto Rican ethnicity and conflict. In J. Boucher, D. Landis, & K. A. Clark (Eds.), *Ethnic conflict: International perspectives* (pp. 182–206). Newbury Park, CA: Sage.

Giroux, H. A. (1987). Critical literacy and student experience: Donald Graves' approach to literacy. *Language Arts, 64,* 175–181.

Gleason, P. (1982). American identity and Americanization. In W. Petersen, M. Novak, & P. Gleason, *Concepts of ethnicity* (pp. 57–143). Cambridge: Harvard University Press.

Goody, J. (1977). *The domestication of the savage mind.* Cambridge: Cambridge University Press.

Goody, J. (1982). Alternative paths to knowledge in oral and literate cultures. In D. Tannen (Ed.), *Spoken and written language: Exploring orality and literacy* (pp. 201–215). Norwood, NJ: Ablex.

Goody, J. (1986). *The logic of writing and the organization of society.* Cambridge: Cambridge University Press.

Goody, J., & Watt, I. (1963). The consequences of literacy. *Comparative studies in society and history, 5,* 304–345.

Gordon, M. (1985). Models of pluralism: The new American dilemma. In N. R. Yetman, *Majority and minority: The dynamics of race and ethnicity in American life,* 4th edition (pp. 523–530). Boston: Allyn and Bacon. Reprinted from M. Gordon (1981), Models of Pluralism: The new American dilemma. *The Annals of the American Academy of Political and Social Science, 454.*

Graves, T. D. (1967). Psychological acculturation in a tri-ethnic community. *Southwestern Journal of Anthropology, 23,* 337–350.

Guiora, A. Z. (1985, August). The psychodynamic aspects of bilingualism. In K. Hakuta & B. M. Ferdman (Co-chairs), *Bilingualism: Social psychological reflections.* Symposium conducted at the meetings of the American Psychological Association, Los Angeles.

Guillaumin, C. (1972). *L'idéologie raciste: Genèse et langage actuel.* Paris: Mouton.

Hakuta, K. (1984). Bilingual education in the public eye: A case study of New Haven, Connecticut. *NABE Journal, 9,* 53–76.

Hakuta, K. (1986). *Mirror of language: The debate on bilingualism.* New York: Basic Books.

Hakuta, K., Ferdman, B. M., & Diaz, R. M. (1987). Bilingualism and cognitive development: Three perspectives. In S. Rosenberg (ed.), *Advances in applied psycholinguistics, Volume 2: Reading, writing and language learning* (pp. 284–319). New York: Cambridge University Press.

Heath, S. B. (1986). The functions and uses of literacy. In S. de Castell, A. Luke, & K. Egan (Eds.), *Literacy, society, and schooling: A reader* (pp. 15–26). Cambridge: Cambridge University Press.

Heller, M. (1987). The role of language in the formation of ethnic identity. In J. S. Phinney & M. J. Rotheram (Eds.), *Children's ethnic socialization: Pluralism and development* (pp. 180–200). Newbury Park, CA: Sage.

Herman, S. N. (1977). *Jewish identity: A social psychological perspective.* Beverly Hills, CA: Sage.

Hirsch, E. D. (1987). *Cultural literacy: What every American needs to know.* Boston: Houghton Mifflin.

Jones, J. M. (1988). Racism in black and white: A bicultural model of reaction and evolution. In P. A. Katz & D. A. Taylor (Eds.), *Eliminating racism: Profiles in controversy* (pp. 117–135). New York: Plenum.

Kádár-Fülöp, J. (1988). Culture, writing and curriculum. In A. C. Purves (Ed.), *Writing across languages and cultures: Issues in contrastive rhetoric* (pp. 25–50). Newbury Park, CA: Sage.

Keefe, S. E., & Padilla, A. M. (1987). *Chicano ethnicity.* Albuquerque: University of New Mexico Press.

Kochman, T. (1987). The ethnic component in Black language and culture. In J. S. Phinney & M. J. Rotheram (Eds.), *Children's ethnic socialization: Pluralism and development* (pp. 219–238). Newbury Park, CA: Sage.

Matute-Bianchi, M. E. (1986). Ethnic identities and patterns of school success and failure among Mexican-descent and Japanese-American students in a California high school: An ethnographic analysis. *American Journal of Education, 95,* 233–255.

McEvedy, M. R. (1986). Some social, cultural and linguistic issues in teaching reading to children who speak English as a second language. *Australian Journal of Reading, 9,* 139–152.

Montero, M. (1987). A través del espejo: Una approximación teórica al estudio de la conciencia social en América Latina. In M. Montero (Ed.), *Psicología política latinoamericana* (pp. 163–202). Caracas: Editorial Panapo.

Ong, W. (1982). *Orality and literacy: The technologizing of the word.* London: Methuen.

Purves, A. C. (1987). Literacy, culture and community. In D. A. Wagner (Ed.), *The future of literacy in a changing world* (pp. 216–232). Oxford: Pergamon Press.

Reder, S. M. (1987). Comparative aspects of functional literacy development: Three ethnic American communities. In D. A. Wagner (Ed.), *The future of literacy in a changing world* (pp. 250–270). Oxford: Pergamon Press.

Roth, R. (1984). Schooling, literacy acquisition and cultural transmission. *Journal of Education, 166,* 291–308.

Said, E. W. (1983). *The world, the text, and the critic.* Cambridge: Harvard University Press.

Scollon, R., & Scollon, S. (1981). *Narrative, literacy and face in interethnic communication.* Norwood, NJ: Ablex.

Scribner, S. (1986). Literacy in three metaphors. In N. L. Stein (Ed.), *Literacy in American schools: Learning to read and write* (pp. 7–22). Chicago: University of Chicago Press.

Scribner, S., & Cole, M. (1981). *The psychology of literacy.* Cambridge: Harvard University Press.

Shaefer, R. T. (1984). *Racial and ethnic groups* (3rd ed.). Glenview, IL: Scott, Forsman.

Smolicz, J. (1981). Core values and cultural identity. *Ethnic and racial studies, 4,* 75–90.

Tajfel, H. (1978). *The social psychology of minorities.* London: Minority Rights Group.

Tajfel, H. (1981). *Human groups and social categories.* Cambridge: Cambridge University Press.

Tajfel, H., & Turner, J. C. (1986). The social identity theory of intergroup relations. In S. Worchel & W. Austin (Eds.), *Psychology of intergroup relations* (pp. 7–24). Chicago: Nelson-Hall.

Taylor, D. M., & Dubé, L. (1986). Two faces of identity: The "I" and the "we." *Journal of Social Issues, 42,* 89–98.

Taylor, D. M., & McKirnan, D. J. (1984). A five-stage model of intergroup relations. *British Journal of Social Psychology, 23,* 291–300.

Thurow, L. C. (1987). Affirmative action in a zero-sum society. In R. Takaki (Ed.), *From different shores: Perspectives on race and ethnicity in America* (pp. 225–230). New York: Oxford University Press. [Reprinted from Thurow, L. C. (1980). *The zero-sum society: Distribution and the possibilities for economic change.* New York: Basic Books.]

Triandis, H. C. (1972). *The analysis of subjective culture.* New York: Wiley.

Trueba, H. T. (1984). The forms, functions, and values of literacy: Reading for survival in a barrio as a student. *NABE Journal, 9,* 21–38.

Wallace, C. (1986). *Learning to read in a multicultural society: The social context of second language literacy.* Oxford: Pergamon Press.

# 12
# Empowering Minority Students: A Framework for Intervention

JIM CUMMINS
*Ontario Institute for Studies in Education*

*Jim Cummins examines the pattern of minority students' academic success and failure and presents a theoretical framework for predicting the effects of educational interventions. Cummins argues that attempts at educational reform, such as compensatory and bilingual education programs, have been relatively unsuccessful in the United States due to the relationships between educators and minorities. He points out that minority student groups, which demonstrate widespread failure in school, tend to be subordinate to the majority group. Cummins suggests that in order for programs to be accepted by minorities, and thus be successful, educators and policy makers need to empower minority students.*

During the past twenty years educators in the United States have implemented a series of costly reforms aimed at reversing the pattern of school failure among minority students. These have included compensatory programs at the preschool level, myriad forms of bilingual education programs, the hiring of additional aides and remedial personnel, and the institution of safeguards against discriminatory assessment procedures. Yet the dropout rate among Mexican-American and mainland Puerto Rican students remains between 40 and 50 percent compared to 14 percent for whites and 25 percent for blacks (Jusenius & Duarte, 1982). Similarly, almost a decade after the passage of the nondiscriminatory assessment provision of

Discussions at the Symposium on "Minority Languages in Academic Research and Educational Policy" held in Sandbjerg Slot, Denmark, April 1985, contributed to the ideas in the paper. I would like to express my appreciation to the participants at the Symposium and to Safder Alladina, Jan Curtis, David Dolson, Norm Gold, Monica Heller, Dennis Parker, Verity Saifullah Khan, and Tove Skutnabb-Kangas for comments on earlier drafts. I would also like to acknowledge the financial support of the Social Sciences and Humanities Research Council (Grant No. 431–79–0003) which made possible participation in the Sandbjerg Slot symposium.

*Harvard Educational Review*   Vol. 56   No. 1   February 1986, 18–36

PL94-142,[1] we find Hispanic students in Texas overrepresented by a factor of 300 percent in the "learning disabilities" category (Ortiz & Yates, 1983).

I have suggested that a major reason previous attempts at educational reform have been unsuccessful is that the relationships between teachers and students and between schools and communities have remained essentially unchanged. The required changes involve *personal redefinitions* of the way classroom teachers interact with the children and communities they serve. In other words, legislative and policy reforms may be necessary conditions for effective change, but they are not sufficient. Implementation of change is dependent upon the extent to which educators, both collectively and individually, redefine their roles with respect to minority students and communities.

The purpose of this paper is to propose a theoretical framework for examining the types of personal and institutional redefinitions that are required to reverse the pattern of minority student failure. The framework is based on a series of hypotheses regarding the nature of minority students' educational difficulties. These hypotheses, in turn, lead to predictions regarding the probable effectiveness, or ineffectiveness, of various interventions directed at reversing minority students' school failure.

The framework assigns a central role to three inclusive sets of interactions or power relations: (1) the classroom interactions between teachers and students, (2) relationships between schools and minority communities, and (3) the intergroup power relations within the society as a whole. It assumes that the social organization and bureaucratic constraints within the school reflect not only broader policy and societal factors but also the extent to which *individual educators* accept or challenge the social organization of the school in relation to minority students and communities. Thus, this analysis sketches directions for change for policymakers at all levels of the educational hierarchy and, in particular, for those working directly with minority students and communities.

## The Policy Context

Research data from the United States, Canada, and Europe vary on the extent to which minority students experience academic failure (for reviews, see Cummins, 1984; Ogbu, 1978). For example, in the United States, Hispanic (with the exception of some groups of Cuban students), Native American, and black students do poorly in school compared to most groups of Asian-American (and white) students. In Canada, Franco-Ontarian students in English language programs have tended to perform considerably less well academically than immigrant minority groups (Cummins, 1984), while the same pattern characterizes Finnish students in Sweden (Skutnabb-Kangas, 1984).

The major task of theory and policy is to explain the pattern of school success and failure among minority students. This task applies both to students whose home language and culture differ from those of the school and wider society (language minority students) and to students whose home language is a version of English but whose cultural background is significantly different from that of the school and wider society, such as many black and Hispanic students from English language backgrounds. With respect to language-minority students, recent policy changes in the United States have been based on the assumption that a major cause of students' educational difficulty is the switch between the language of the home and the language of the school. Thus, the apparently plausible assumption that students cannot learn in a language they do not understand gave rise in the late sixties and early seventies to bilingual education programs in which students' home language was used in addition to English as an initial medium of school instruction (Schneider, 1976).

Bilingual programs, however, have met with both strong support and vehement opposition. The debate regarding policy has revolved around two intuitively appealing assumptions. Those who favor bilingual education argue that children cannot learn in a language they do not understand, and, therefore, L1 (first language) instruction is necessary to counteract the negative effects of a home/school linguistic mismatch. The opposition contends that bilingual education is illogical in its implication that less English instruction will lead to more English achievement. It makes more sense, the opponents argue, to provide language-minority students with maximum exposure to English.

Despite the apparent plausibility of each assumption, these two conventional wisdoms (the "linguistic mismatch" and "insufficient exposure" hypotheses) are each patently inadequate. The argument that language minority students fail primarily as a result of a home/school language switch is refuted by the success of many minority students whose instruction has been totally through a second language. Similarly, research in Canada has documented the effectiveness of "French immersion programs" in which English background (majority language) students are instructed largely through French in the early grades as a means of developing fluent bilingualism. In spite of the home/school language switch, students' first language (English) skills develop as well as those of students whose instruction has been totally through English. The fact that the first language has high status and is strongly reinforced in the wider society is usually seen as an important factor in the success of these immersion programs.[2]

The opposing "insufficient exposure" hypothesis, however, fares no better with respect to the research evidence. In fact, the results of virtually every bilingual program that has been evaluated during the past fifty years show either no relationship or a negative relationship between amount of school exposure to the majority language and academic achievement in that language (Baker & de Kanter, 1981; Cummins, 1983a, 1984; Skutnabb-Kangas, 1984). Evaluations of immersion programs for majority students show that students perform as well in English academic skills as comparison groups despite considerably less exposure to English in school. Exactly the same result is obtained for minority students. Promotion of the minority language entails no loss in the development of English academic skills. In other words, language minority students instructed through the minority language (for example, Spanish) for all or part of the school day perform as well in English academic skills as comparable students instructed totally through English.

These results have been interpreted in terms of the "interdependence hypothesis," which proposes that to the extent that instruction through a minority language is effective in developing academic proficiency in the minority language, transfer of this proficiency to the majority language will occur given adequate exposure and motivation to learn the majority language (Cummins, 1979, 1983a, 1984). The interdependence hypothesis is supported by a large body of research from bilingual program evaluations, studies of language use in the home, immigrant student language learning, correlational students of L1–L2 (second language) relationships, and experimental studies of bilingual information processing (for reviews, see Cummins, 1984; McLaughlin, 1985).

It is not surprising that the two conventional wisdoms inadequately account for the research data, since each involves only a one-dimensional linguistic explanation. The variability of minority students' academic performance under different social and educational conditions indicates that many complex, interrelated factors are at work (Ogbu, 1978; Wong-Fillmore, 1983). In particular, sociological and anthropological research suggests that status and power relations between groups are an important part of any comprehensive account of minority students' school failure (Fishman, 1976; Ogbu, 1978; Paulston, 1980). In addition, a variety of factors related to educational quality and cultural mismatch also appear to be important in mediating minority students' academic progress (Wong-Fillmore, 1983). These factors have been integrated into the design of a theoretical framework that suggests the changes required to reverse minority student failure.

## A Theoretical Framework

The central tenet of the framework is that students from "dominated" societal groups are "empowered" or "disabled" as a direct result of their interactions with educators in the schools. These interactions are mediated by the implicit or explicit role definitions that educators assume in relation to four institutional characteristics of schools. These characteristics reflect the extent to which (1) minority students' language and culture are incorporated into the school program; (2) minority community participation is encouraged as an integral component of children's education; (3) the pedagogy promotes intrinsic motivation on the part of students to use language actively in order to generate their own knowledge; and (4) professionals involved in assessment become advocates for minority students rather than legitimizing the location of the "problem" in the students. For each of these dimensions of school organization the role definitions of educators can be described in terms of a continuum, with one end promoting the empowerment of students and the other contributing to the disabling of students.

The three sets of relationships analyzed in the present framework—majority/minority societal group relations, school/minority community relations, educator/minority student relations—are chosen on the basis of hypotheses regarding the relative ineffectiveness of previous educational reforms and the directions required to reverse minority group school failure. Each of these relationships will be discussed in detail.

## Intergroup Power Relations

When the patterns of minority student school failure are examined from an international perspective, it becomes evident that power and status relations between minority and majority groups exert a major influence on school performance. An example frequently given is the academic failure of Finnish students in Sweden, where they are a low-status group, compared to their success in Australia, where they are regarded as a high-status group (Troike, 1978). Similarly, Ogbu (1978) reports that the outcast Burakumin perform poorly in Japan but as well as other Japanese students in the United States.

Theorists have explained these findings using several constructs. Cummins (1984), for example, discusses the "bicultural ambivalence" (or lack of cultural identification) of students in relation to both the home and school cultures. Ogbu (1978) discusses the "caste" status of minorities that fail academically and ascribes their failure to economic and social discrimination combined with the internalization of the inferior status attributed to them by the dominant group. Feuerstein (1979) attributes academic failure to the disruption of intergenerational transmission processes caused by the alienation of a group from its own culture. In all three conceptions, widespread school failure does not occur in minority groups that are positively oriented towards both their own and the dominant culture, that do not perceive themselves as inferior to the dominant group, and that are not alienated from their own cultural values.

Within the present framework, the *dominant* group controls the institutions and reward systems within society; the *dominated* group (Mullard, 1985) is regarded as inherently inferior by the dominant group and denied access to high-status positions within the institutional structure of the society. As described by Ogbu (1978), the dominated status of a minority group exposes them to conditions that predispose children to school failure even before they come to school. These conditions include limited parental access to economic and educational resources, ambivalence toward cultural transmission and primary language use in the home, and interactional styles that may not prepare students for typical teacher/student interaction patterns in school (Heath, 1983; Wong-Fillmore, 1983). Bicultural ambivalence and less effective cultural transmission among dominated groups are frequently associated with a historical pattern of colonization and subordination by the dominant group. This pattern, for example, characterizes Franco-Ontarian students in Canada, Finns in Sweden, and Hispanic, Native, and black groups in the United States.

Different patterns among other societal groups can clearly be distinguished (Ogbu & Matute-Bianchi, in press). Detailed analysis of patterns of intergroup relations go beyond the scope of this paper. However, it is important to note that the minority groups characterized by widespread school failure tend overwhelmingly to be in a dominated relationship to the majority group.[3]

### Empowerment of Students

Students who are empowered by their school experiences develop the ability, confidence, and motivation to succeed academically. They participate competently in instruction as a result of having developed a confident cultural identity as well as appropriate school-based knowledge and interactional structures (Cummins, 1983b; Tikunoff, 1983). Students who are disempowered or "disabled" by their school experiences do not develop this type of cognitive/academic and social/emotional foundation. Thus, student empowerment is regarded as both a mediating construct influencing academic performance and as an outcome variable itself.[4]

Although conceptually the cognitive/academic and social/emotional (identity-related) factors are distinct, the data suggest that they are extremely difficult to separate in the case of minority students who are "at risk" academically. For example, data from both Sweden and the United States suggest that minority students who immigrate relatively late (about ten years of age) often appear to have better academic prospects than students of similar socioeconomic status born in the host country (Cummins, 1984; Skutnabb-Kangas, 1984). Is this because their L1 cognitive/academic skills on arrival provide a better foundation for L2 cognitive/academic skills acquisition, or alternatively, because they have not experienced devaluation of their identity in the societal institutions, namely schools of the host country, as has been the case of students born in that setting?

Similarly, the most successful bilingual programs appear to be those that emphasize and use the students' L1 (for reviews, see Cummins, 1983a, 1984). Is this success due to better promotion of L1 cognitive/academic skills or to the reinforcement of cultural identity provided by an intensive L1 program? By the same token, is the failure of many minority students in English-only immersion programs a function of cognitive/academic difficulties or of students' ambivalence about the value of their cultural identity (Cohen & Swain, 1976)?

These questions are clearly difficult to answer; the point to be made, however, is that for minority students who have traditionally experienced school failure, there is sufficient overlap in the impact of cognitive/academic and identity factors to justify incorporating these two dimensions within the notion of "student empowerment," while recognizing that under some conditions each dimension may be affected in different ways.

*Schools and Power*

Minority students are disabled or disempowered by schools in very much the same way that their communities are disempowered by interactions with societal institutions. Since equality of opportunity is believed to be a given, it is assumed that individuals are responsible for their own failure and are, therefore, made to feel that they have failed because of their own inferiority, despite the best efforts of dominant-group institutions and individuals to help them (Skutnabb-Kangas, 1984). This analysis implies that minority students will succeed educationally to the extent that the patterns of interaction in school reverse those that prevail in the society at large.

Four structural elements in the organization of schooling contribute to the extent to which minority students are empowered or disabled. As outlined in Figure 1,

FIGURE 1
*Empowerment of Minority Students: A Theoretical Framework*

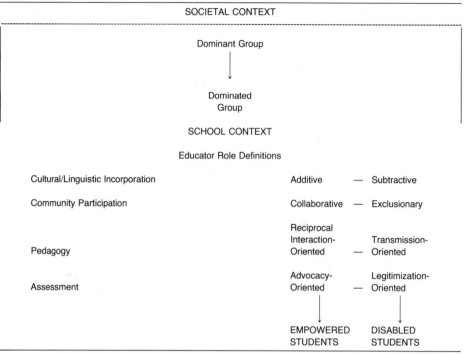

these elements include the incorporation of minority students' culture and language, inclusion of minority communities in the education of their children, pedagogical assumptions and practices operating in the classroom, and the assessment of minority students.

*Cultural/linguistic incorporation.* Considerable research data suggest that, for dominated minorities, the extent to which students' language and culture are incorporated into the school program constitutes a significant predictor of academic success (Campos & Keatinge, 1984; Cummins, 1983a; Rosier & Holm, 1980). As outlined earlier, students' school success appears to reflect both the more solid cognitive/academic foundation developed through intensive L1 instruction and the reinforcement of their cultural identity.

Included under incorporation of minority group cultural features is the adjustment of instructional patterns to take account of culturally conditioned learning styles. The Kamehameha Early Education Program in Hawaii provides strong evidence of the importance of this type of cultural incorporation. When reading instruction was changed to permit students to collaborate in discussing and interpreting texts, dramatic improvements were found in both reading and verbal intellectual abilities (Au & Jordan, 1981).

An important issue to consider at this point is why superficially plausible but patently inadequate assumptions, such as the "insufficient exposure" hypothesis, continue to dominate the policy debate when virtually all the evidence suggests that incorporation of minority students' language and culture into the school program will at least not impede academic progress. In other words, what social function do such arguments serve? Within the context of the present framework, it is suggested that a major reason for the vehement resistance to bilingual programs is that the incorporation of minority languages and cultures into the school program confers status and power (jobs, for example) on the minority group. Consequently, such programs contravene the established pattern of dominant/dominated group relations. Within democratic societies, however, contradictions between the rhetoric of equality and the reality of domination must be obscured. Thus, conventional wisdoms such as the insufficient exposure hypothesis become immune from critical scrutiny, and incompatible evidence is either ignored or dismissed.

Educators' role definitions in relation to the incorporation of minority students' language and culture can be characterized along an "additive-subtractive" dimension.[5] Educators who see their role as adding a second language and cultural affiliation to their students' repertoire are likely to empower students more than those who see their role as replacing or subtracting students' primary language and culture. In addition to the personal and future employment advantages of proficiency in two languages, there is considerable, though not conclusive, evidence that subtle educational advantages result from continued development of both languages among bilingual students. Enhanced metalinguistic development, for example, is frequently found in association with additive bilingualism (Hakuta & Diaz, 1985; McLaughlin, 1984).

It should be noted that an additive orientation does not require the actual teaching of the minority language. In many cases a minority language class may not be possible for reasons such as low concentration of particular groups of minority students. Educators, however, communicate to students and parents in a variety of ways the extent to which the minority language and culture are valued within the context of the school. Even within a monolingual school context, powerful messages can be communicated to students regarding the validity and advantages of language development.

*Community participation.* Students from dominated communities will be empowered in the school context to the extent that the communities themselves are empowered through their interactions with the school. When educators involve minority parents as partners in their children's education, parents appear to develop a sense of efficacy that communicates itself to children, with positive academic consequences.

Although lip service is paid to community involvement through Parent Advisory Committees (PAC)[6] in many education programs, these committees are frequently manipulated through misinformation and intimidation (Curtis, 1984). The result is that parents from dominated groups retain their powerless status, and their internalized inferiority is reinforced. Children's school failure can then be attributed to the combined effects of parental illiteracy and lack of interest in their children's education. In reality, most parents of minority students have high aspirations for their children and want to be involved in promoting their academic progress (Wong-Fillmore, 1983). However, they often do not know how to help their children academically, and they are excluded from participation by the school. In fact, even their interaction through L1 with their children in the home is frequently regarded by educators as contributing to academic difficulties (Cummins, 1984).

Dramatic changes in children's academic progress can be realized when educators take the initiative to change this exclusionary pattern to one of collaboration. The Haringey project in Britain illustrates just how powerful the effects of simple interventions can be (Tizard, Schofield, & Hewison, 1982). In order to assess the effects of parental involvement in the teaching of reading, the researchers established a project in the London borough of Haringey whereby all children in two primary level experimental classes in two different schools read to their parents at home on a regular basis. The reading progress of these children was compared with that of children in two classes in two different schools who were given extra reading instruction in small groups by an experienced and qualified teacher who worked four half-days at each school every week for the two years of the intervention. Both groups were also compared with a control group that received no treatment.

All the schools were in multiethnic areas, and there were many parents who did not read English or use it at home. It was found, nevertheless, to be both feasible and practicable to involve nearly all the parents in educational activities such as listening to their children read, even when the parents were nonliterate and largely non-English-speaking. It was also found that, almost without exception, parents welcomed the project, agreed to hear their children read, and completed a record card showing what had been read.

The researchers report that parental involvement had a pronounced effect on the students' success in school. Children who read to their parents made significantly greater progress in reading than those who did not engage in this type of literacy sharing. Small-group instruction in reading, given by a highly competent specialist, did not produce improvements comparable to those obtained from the collaboration with parents. In contrast to the home collaboration program, the benefits of extra reading instruction were least apparent for initially low-achieving children.

In addition, the collaboration between teachers and parents was effective for children of all initial levels of performance, including those who, at the beginning of the study, were failing in learning to read. Teachers reported that the children showed an increased interest in school learning and were better behaved. Those teachers involved in the home collaboration found the work with parents worthwhile, and they continued to involve parents with subsequent classes after the experiment was concluded. It is interesting to note that teachers of the control classes also adopted the home collaboration program after the two-year experimental period.

The Haringey project is one example of school/community relations; there are others. The essential point, however, is that the teacher's role in such relations can be characterized along a *collaborative-exclusionary* dimension. Teachers operating at

the collaborative end of the continuum actively encourage minority parents to participate in promoting their children's academic progress both in the home and through
involvement in classroom activities. A collaborative orientation may require a willingness on the part of the teacher to work closely with mother-tongue teachers or
aides in order to communicate effectively, in a noncondescending way, with minority
parents. Teachers with an exclusionary orientation, on the other hand, tend to regard
teaching as *their* job and are likely to view collaboration with minority parents as
either irrelevant or detrimental to children's progress.

*Pedagogy*. Several investigators have suggested that many "learning disabilities" are
pedagogically induced in that children designated "at risk" frequently receive intensive instruction which confines them to a passive role and induces a form of "learned
helplessness" (Beers & Beers, 1980; Coles, 1978; Cummins, 1984). This process is
illustrated in a microethnographic study of fourteen reading lessons given to West
Indian Creole-speakers of English in Toronto, Canada (Ramphal, 1983). It was found
that teachers' constant correction of students' miscues prevented students from focusing on the meaning of what they were reading. Moreover, the constant corrections
fostered dependent behavior because students knew that whenever they paused at
a word the teacher would automatically pronounce it for them. One student was
interrupted so often in one of the lessons that he was able to read only one sentence,
consisting of three words, uninterrupted. In contrast to a pattern of classroom interaction which promotes instructional dependence, teaching that empowers will aim
to liberate students from instruction by encouraging them to become active gener-
ators of their knowledge. As Graves (1983) has demonstrated, this type of active
knowledge generation can occur when, for example, children create and publish
their own books within the classroom.

Two major pedagogical orientations can be distinguished. These differ in the
extent to which the teacher retains exclusive control over classroom interaction as
opposed to sharing some of this control with students. The dominant instructional
model in North American schools has been termed a transmission model (Barnes,
1976; Wells, 1982). This model incorporates essentially the same assumptions about
teaching and learning that Freire (1970, 1973) has termed a "banking" model of
education. This transmission model will be contrasted with a "reciprocal interaction"
model of pedagogy.

The basic premise of the transmission model is that the teacher's task is to impart
knowledge or skills that she or he possesses to students who do not yet have these
skills. This implies that the teacher initiates and controls the interaction, constantly
orienting it towards the achievement of instructional objectives. For example, in first-
and second-language programs that stress pattern repetition, the teacher presents
the materials, models the language patterns, asks questions, and provides feedback
to students about the correctness of their response. The curriculum in these types
of programs focuses on the internal structure of the language or subject matter.
Consequently, it frequently focuses predominantly on surface features of language
or literacy such as handwriting, spelling, and decoding, and emphasizes correct recall

of content taught by means of highly structured drills and workbook exercises. It has been argued that a transmission model of teaching contravenes central principles of language and literacy acquisition and that a model allowing for reciprocal interaction among students and teachers represents a more appropriate alternative (Cummins, 1984; Wells, 1982).[7]

A central tenet of the reciprocal interaction model is that "talking and writing are means to learning" (Bullock Report, 1975, p. 50). The use of this model in teaching requires a genuine dialogue between student and teacher in both oral and written modalities, guidance and facilitation rather than control of student learning by the teacher, and the encouragement of student/student talk in a collaborative learning context. This model emphasizes the development of higher level cognitive skills rather than just factual recall, and meaningful language use by students rather than the correction of surface forms. Language use and development are consciously integrated with all curricular content rather than taught as isolated subjects, and tasks are presented to students in ways that generate intrinsic rather than extrinsic motivation. In short, pedagogical approaches that empower students encourage them to assume greater control over setting their own learning goals and to collaborate actively with each other in achieving these goals.

The development of a sense of efficacy and inner direction in the classroom is especially important for students from dominated groups whose experiences so often orient them in the opposite direction. Wong-Fillmore (1983) has reported that Hispanic students learned considerably more English in classrooms that provided opportunities for reciprocal interaction with teachers and peers. Ample opportunities for expressive writing appear to be particularly significant in promoting a sense of academic efficacy among minority students (Cummins, Aguilar, Bascunan, Fiorucci, Sanaoui, & Basman, in press). As expressed by Daiute (1985):

> Children who learn early that writing is not simply an exercise gain a sense of power that gives them confidence to write—and write a lot. . . . Beginning writers who are confident that they have something to say or that they can find out what they need to know can even overcome some limits of training or development. Writers who don't feel that what they say matters have an additional burden that no skills training can help them overcome. (pp. 5–6)

The implications for students from dominated groups are obvious. Too often the instruction they receive convinces them that what they have to say is irrelevant or wrong. The failure of this method of instruction is then taken as an indication that the minority student is of low ability, a verdict frequently confirmed by subsequent assessment procedures.

*Assessment.* Historically, assessment has played the role of legitimizing the disabling of minority students. In some cases assessment itself may play the primary role, but more often it has been used to locate the "problem" within the minority student, thereby screening from critical scrutiny the subtractive nature of the school program, the exclusionary orientation of teachers towards minority communities, and transmission models of teaching that inhibit students from active participation in learning.

This process is virtually inevitable when the conceptual base for assessment is purely psychoeducational. If the psychologist's task is to discover the causes of a minority student's academic difficulties and the only tools at his or her disposal are psychological tests (in either L1 or L2), then it is hardly surprising that the child's difficulties will be attributed to psychological dysfunctions. The myth of bilingual handicaps that still influences educational policy was generated in exactly this way during the 1920s and 1930s.

Recent studies suggest that despite the appearance of change brought about by PL 94-142, the underlying structure of assessment processes has remained essentially intact. Mehan, Hertweck, and Meihls (in press), for example, report that psychologists continued to test children until they "found" the disability that could be invoked to "explain" the student's apparent academic difficulties. Diagnosis and placement were influenced frequently by factors related to bureaucratic procedures and funding requirements rather than to students' academic performance in the classroom. Rueda and Mercer (1985) have also shown that designation of minority students as "learning disabled" as compared to "language impaired" was strongly influenced by whether a psychologist or a speech pathologist was on the placement committee. In other words, with respect to students' actual behavior, the label was essentially arbitrary. An analysis of more than four hundred psychological assessments of minority students revealed that although no diagnostic conclusions were logically possible in the majority of assessments, psychologists were most reluctant to admit this fact to teachers and parents (Cummins, 1984). In short, the data suggest that the structure within which psychological assessment takes place orients the psychologist to locate the cause of the academic problem within the minority student.

An alternative role definition for psychologists or special educators can be termed an "advocacy" or "delegitimization" role.[8] In this case, their task must be to delegitimize the traditional function of psychological assessment in the educational disabling of minority students by becoming advocates for the child in scrutinizing critically the societal and educational context within which the child has developed (Cazden, 1985). This involves locating the pathology within the societal power relations between dominant and dominated groups, in the reflection of these power relations between school and communities, and in the mental and cultural disabling of minority students that takes place in classrooms. These conditions are a more probable cause of the 300 percent overrepresentation of Texas Hispanic students in the learning disabled category than any intrinsic processing deficit unique to Hispanic children. The training of psychologists and special educators does not prepare them for this advocacy or delegitimization role. From the present perspective, however, it must be emphasized that discriminatory assessment is carried out by well-intentioned individuals who, rather than challenging a socioeducational system that tends to disable minority students, have accepted a role definition and an educational structure that makes discriminatory assessment virtually inevitable.[9]

## Empowering Minority Students: The Carpinteria Example

The Spanish-only preschool program of the Carpenteria School District, near Santa

Barbara, California, is one of the few programs in the United States that explicitly incorporates the major elements hypothesized in previous sections to empower minority students. Spanish is the exclusive language of instruction, there is a strong community involvement component, and the program is characterized by a coherent philosophy of promoting conceptual development through meaningful linguistic interaction.

The proposal to implement an intensive Spanish-only preschool program in this region was derived from district findings showing that a large majority of the Spanish-speaking students entering kindergarten each year lacked adequate skills to succeed in the kindergarten program. On the School Readiness Inventory, a districtwide screening measure administered to all income kindergarten students, Spanish-speaking students tended to average about eight points lower than English-speaking students (approximately 14.5 compared to 23.0, averaged over four years from 1979 to 1982) despite the fact that the test was administered in students' dominant language. A score of 20 or better was viewed by the district as predicting a successful kindergarten year for the child. Prior to the implementation of the experimental program, the Spanish-background children attended a bilingual preschool program—operated either by Head Start or the Community Day Care Center—in which both English and Spanish were used concurrently but with strong emphasis on the development of English skills. According to the district kindergarten teachers, children who had attended these programs often mixed English and Spanish into a "Spanglish."

The major goal of the experimental Spanish-only preschool program was to bring Spanish-dominant children entering kindergarten up to a level of readiness for school similar to that attained by English-speaking children in the community. The project also sought to make parents of the program participants aware of their role as the child's first teacher and to encourage them to provide specific types of experiences for their children in the home.

The preschool program itself involved the integration of language with a large variety of concrete and literacy-related experiences. As summarized in the evaluation report: "The development of language skills in Spanish was foremost in the planning and attention given to every facet of the pre-school day. Language was used constantly for conversing, learning new ideas, concepts and vocabulary, thinking creatively, and problem-solving to give the children the opportunity to develop their language skills in Spanish to as high a degree as possible within the structure of the pre-school day" (Campos & Keatinge, 1984, p. 17).

Participation in the program was on a voluntary basis and students were screened only for age and Spanish-language dominance. Family characteristics of students in the experimental program were typical of other Spanish-speaking families in the community; more than 90 percent were of low socioeconomic status, and the majority worked in agriculture and had an average educational level of about sixth grade.

The program proved to be highly successful in developing students' readiness skills, as evidenced by the average score of 21.6 obtained by the 1982–83 incoming kindergarten students who had been in the program, compared to the score of 23.2 obtained by English-speaking students. A score of 14.6 was obtained by Spanish-speaking students who experienced the regular bilingual preschool program. In 1983–84 the scores of these three groups were 23.3, 23.4, and 16.0, respectively. In other words, the gap between English-background and Spanish-background children in the Spanish-only preschool had disappeared; however, a considerable gap remained for Spanish-background students for whom English was the focus of pre-school instruction.

Of special interest is the performance of the experimental program students on the English and Spanish versions of the Bilingual Syntax Measure (BSM), a test of oral syntactic development (Hernandez-Chavez, Burt, & Dulay, 1976). Despite the fact that they experienced an exclusively Spanish preschool program, these students performed better than the other Spanish-speaking students in English (and Spanish) on entry to kindergarten in 1982 and at a similar level in 1983. On entrance to grade one in 1983, the gap had widened considerably, with almost five times as many of the experimental-program students performing at level 5 (fluent English) compared to the other Spanish-background students (47 percent vs. 10 percent) (Campos & Keatinge, 1984).

The evaluation report suggests that

> although project participants were exposed to less *total* English, they, because of their enhanced first language skill and concept knowledge were better able to comprehend the English they were exposed to. This seems to be borne out by comments made by kindergarten teachers in the District about project participants. They are making comments like, "Project participants appear more aware of what is happening around them in the classroom," "They are able to focus on the task at hand better" and "They demonstrate greater self-confidence in learning situations." All of these traits would tend to enhance the language acquisition process. (Campos & Keatinge, 1984, p. 41)

Campos and Keatinge (1984) also emphasize the consequences of the preschool program for parental participation in their children's education. They note that, according to the school officials, "the parents of project participants are much more aware of and involved in their child's school experience than non-participant parents of Spanish speakers. This is seen as having a positive impact on the future success of the project participants—the greater the involvement of parents, the greater the chances of success of the child" (p. 41).

The major relevance of these findings for educators and policymakers derives from their demonstration that educational programs *can* succeed in preventing the academic failure experienced by many minority students. The corollary is that failure to provide this type of program constitutes the disabling of minority students by the school system. For example, among the students who did not experience the experimental preschool program, the typical pattern of low levels of academic readiness and limited proficiency in both languages was observed. These are the students who are likely to be referred for psychological assessment early in their school careers.

This assessment will typically legitimize the inadequate educational provision by attributing students' difficulties to some vacuous category, such as learning disability. By contrast, students who experienced a preschool program in which (a) their cultural identity was reinforced, (b) there was active collaboration with parents, and (c) meaningful use of language was integrated into every aspect of daily activities were developing high levels of conceptual and linguistic skills in *both* languages.

## Conclusion

In this article I have proposed a theoretical framework for examining minority students' academic failure and for predicting the effects of educational interventions. Within this framework the educational failure of minority students is analyzed as a function of the extent to which schools reflect or counteract the power relations that exist within the broader society. Specifically, language-minority students' educational progress is strongly influenced by the extent to which individual educators become advocates for the promotion of students' linguistic talents, actively encourage community participation in developing students' academic and cultural resources, and implement pedagogical approaches that succeed in liberating students from instructional dependence.

The educator/student interactions characteristic of the disabling end of the proposed continua reflect the typical patterns of interaction that dominated societal groups have experienced in relation to dominant groups. The intrinsic value of the group is usually denied, and "objective" evidence is accumulated to demonstrate the group's "inferiority." This inferior status is then used as a justification for excluding the group from activities and occupations that entail societal rewards.

In a similar way, the disabling of students is frequently rationalized on the basis of students' "needs." For example, minority students need maximum exposure to English in both the school and home; thus, parents must be told not to interact with children in their mother tongue. Similarly, minority children need a highly structured drill-oriented program in order to maximize time spent on tasks to compensate for their deficient preschool experiences. Minority students also need a comprehensive diagnostic/prescriptive assessment in order to identify the nature of their "problem" and possible remedial interventions.

This analysis suggests a major reason for the relative lack of success of the various educational bandwagons that have characterized the North American crusade against underachievement during the past twenty years. The individual role definitions of educators and the institutional role definitions of schools have remained largely unchanged despite "new and improved" programs and policies. These programs and policies, despite their cost, have simply added a new veneer to the outward facade of the structure that disables minority students. The lip service paid to initial L1 instruction, community involvement, and nondiscriminatory assessment, together with the emphasis on improved teaching techniques, have succeeded primarily in deflecting attention from the attitudes and orientation of educators who interact on a daily basis with minority students. It is in these interactions that students are disabled. In the absence of individual and collective educator role redefinitions, schools will continue to reproduce, in these interactions, the power relations that characterize the wider society and make minority students' academic failure inevitable.

To educators genuinely concerned about alleviating the educational difficulties of minority students and responding to their needs, this conclusion may appear overly bleak. I believe, however, that it is realistic and optimistic, as directions for change are clearly indicated rather than obscured by the overlay of costly reforms that leave the underlying disabling structure essentially intact. Given the societal commitment to maintaining the dominant/dominated power relationships, we can predict that educational changes threatening this structure will be fiercely resisted. This is in fact the case for each of the four structural dimensions discussed earlier.[10]

In order to reverse the pattern of widespread minority group educational failure, educators and policymakers are faced with both a personal and a political challenge. Personally, they must redefine their roles within the classroom, the community, and the broader society so that these role definitions result in interactions that empower rather than disable students. Politically, they must attempt to persuade colleagues and decisionmakers—such as school boards and the public that elects them—of the importance of redefining institutional goals so that the schools transform society by empowering minority students rather than reflect society by disabling them.

## Notes

1. The Education of All Handicapped Children Act of 1975 (Public Law 94–142) guarantees to all handicapped children in the United States the right to a free public education, to an individualized education program (IEP), to due process, to education in the least segregated environment, and to assessment procedures that are multidimensional and nonculturally discriminatory.
2. For a discussion of the implications of Canadian French immersion programs for the education of minority students, see California State Department of Education (1984).
3. Ogbu (1978), for example, has distinguished between "caste," "immigrant," and "autonomous" minority groups. Caste groups are similar to what has been termed "dominated" groups in the present framework and are the only category of minority groups that tends to fail academically. Immigrant groups have usually come voluntarily to the host society for economic reasons and, unlike caste minorities, have not internalized negative attributions of the dominant group. Ogbu gives Chinese and Japanese groups as examples of "immigrant" minorities. The cultural resources that permit some minority groups to resist discrimination and internalization of negative attributions are still a matter of debate and speculation (for a recent treatment, see Ogbu & Bianchi, in press). The final category distinguished by Ogbu is that of "autonomous" groups who hold a distinct cultural identity but who are not subordinated economically or politically to the dominant group (for example, Jews and Mormons in the United States).

   Failure to take account of these differences among minority groups both in patterns of academic performance and sociohistorical relationships to the dominant group has contributed to the confused state of policymaking with respect to language minority students. The bilingual education policy, for example, has been based on the implicit assumption that the linguistic mismatch hypothesis was valid for all language minority students, and, consequently, the same types of intervention were necessary and appropriate for all students. Clearly, this assumption is open to question.
4. There is no contradiction in postulating student empowerment as both a mediating and an outcome variable. For example, cognitive abilities clearly have the same status in that they contribute to students' school success and can also be regarded as an outcome of schooling.
5. The terms "additive" and "subtractive" bilingualism were coined by Lambert (1975) to refer to the proficient bilingualism associated with positive cognitive outcomes on the one hand, and the limited bilingualism often associated with negative outcomes on the other.

6. PACs were established in some states to provide an institutional structure for minority parent involvement in educational decision making with respect to bilingual programs. In California, for example, a majority of PAC members for any state-funded program was required to be from the program target group. The school plan for use of program funds required signed PAC approval.

7. This "reciprocal interaction" model incorporates proposals about the relation between language and learning made by a variety of investigators, most notably in the Bullock Report (1975), and by Barnes (1976), Lindfors (1980), and Wells (1982). Its application with respect to the promotion of literacy conforms closely to psycholinguistic approaches to reading (Goodman & Goodman, 1977; Holdaway, 1979; Smith, 1978) and to the recent emphasis on encouraging expressive writing from the earliest grades (Chomsky, 1981; Giaccobe, 1982; Graves, 1983; Temple, Nathan, & Burris, 1982). Students' microcomputing networks such as the *Computer Chronicles Newswire* (Mehan, Miller-Souviney, & Riel, 1984) represent a particularly promising application of reciprocal interaction model of pedagogy.

8. See Mullard (1985) for a detailed discussion of delegitimization strategies in antiracist education.

9. Clearly, the presence of processing difficulties that are rooted in neurological causes is not being denied for either monolingual or bilingual children. However, in the case of children from dominated minorities, the proportion of disabilities that are neurological in origin is likely to represent only a small fraction of those that derive from educational and social conditions.

10. Although for pedagogy the resistance to sharing control with students goes beyond majority/minority group relations, the same elements are present. If the curriculum is not predetermined and presequenced, and the students are generating their own knowledge in a critical and creative way, then the reproduction of the societal structure cannot be guaranteed—hence the reluctance to liberate students from instructional dependence.

## References

Au, K. H., & Jordan, C. (1981). Teaching reading to Hawaiian children: Finding a culturally appropriate solution. In H. Trueba, G. P. Guthrie, & K. H. Au (Eds.) *Culture and the bilingual classroom: Studies in classroom ethnography* (pp. 139–152). Rowley, MA: Newbury House.

Baker, K. A., & de Kanter, A. A. (1981). *Effectiveness of bilingual education: A review of the literature.* Washington, DC: U.S. Department of Education, Office of Planning and Budget.

Barnes, D. (1976). *From communication to curriculum.* New York: Penguin.

Beers, C. S., & Beers, J. W. (1980). Early identification of learning disabilities: Facts and fallacies. Elementary School Journal, *81,* 67–76.

Bethell, T. (1979, February). Against bilingual education. *Harper's,* pp. 30–33.

Bullock Report. (1975). *A language for life.* [Report of the Committee of Inquiry appointed by the Secretary of State for Education and Science under the Chairmanship of Sir Alan Bullock]. London: HMSO.

California State Department of Education. (1984). *Studies on immersion education: A collection for United States educators.* Sacramento: Author.

Campos, J., & Keatinge, B. (1984). *The Carpinteria preschool program: Title VII second year evaluation report.* Washington, DC: Department of Education.

Cazden, C. B. (1985, April). *The ESL teacher as advocate.* Plenary presentation to the TESOL Conference, New York.

Chomsky, C. (1981). Write now, read later. In C. Cazden (Ed.), *Language in Early Childhood Education* (2nd ed., pp. 141–149). Washington, DC: National Association for the Education of Young Children.

Cohen, A. D., & Swain, M. (1976). Bilingual education: The immersion model in the North American context. In J. E. Alatis & K. Twaddell (Eds.), *English as a second language in bilingual education* (pp. 55–64). Washington, DC: TESOL.

Coles, G. S. (1978). The learning disabilities test battery: Empirical and social issues. *Harvard Educational Review, 48,* 313–340.

Cummins, J. (1979). Linguistic interdependence and the educational development of bilingual children. *Review of Educational Research 49,* 222–251.

Cummins, J. (1983a) *Heritage language education: A literature review.* Toronto: Ministry of Education.

Cummins, J. (1983b). Functional language proficiency in context: Classroom participation as an interactive process. In W. J. Tikunoff (Ed.), *Compatibility of the SBIS features with other research on instruction for LEP students* (pp. 109–131). San Francisco: Far West Laboratory.

Cummins, J. (1984). *Bilingualism and special education: Issues in assessment and pedagogy.* Clevedon, Eng.: Multilingual Matters, and San Diego: College Hill Press.

Cummins, J., Aguilar, M., Bascunan, L., Fiorucci, S., Sanaoui, R., & Basman, S. (in press). *Literacy development in heritage language programs.* Toronto: National Heritage Language Resource Unit.

Curtis, J. (1984). *Bilingual education in Calistoga: Not a happy ending.* Report submitted to the Instituto de Lengua y Cultura, Elmira, NY.

Daiute, C. (1985). *Writing and computers.* Reading, MA: Addison-Wesley.

Feuerstein, R. (1979). *The dynamic assessment of retarded performers: The learning potential assessment device, theory, instruments, and techniques.* Baltimore: University Park Press.

Fishman, J. (1976). *Bilingual education: An international sociological perspective.* Rowley, MA: Newbury House.

Freire, P. (1970). *Pedagogy of the oppressed.* New York: Seabury.

Freire, P. (1973). *Education for critical consciousness.* New York: Seabury.

Giacobbe, M. E. (1982). Who says children can't write the first week?, In R. D. Walshe (Ed.), *Donald Graves in Australia: "Children want to write"* (pp. 99–103). Exeter, NH: Heinemann Educational Books.

Goodman, K. S., & Goodman, Y. M. (1977). Learning about psycholinguistic processes by analyzing oral reading. *Harvard Educational Review, 47,* 317–333.

Graves. D. H. (1983). *Writing: Teachers and children at work.* Exeter, NH: Heinemann Educational Books.

Hakuta, K., & Diaz, R. M. (1985). The relationship between degree of bilingualism and cognitive ability: A critical discussion and some new longitudinal data. In K. E. Nelson (Ed.), *Children's language* (Vol. 5, pp. 319–345). Hillsdale, NJ: Erlbaum.

Heath, S. B. (1983). *Ways with words.* Cambridge: Cambridge University Press.

Hernandez-Chavez, E., Burt, M., & Dulay, H. (1976). *The bilingual syntax measure.* New York: The Psychological Corporation.

Holdaway, D. (1979). *The foundations of literacy.* Sydney, Australia: Ashton Scholastic.

Jusenius, C., & Duarte, V. L. (1982). *Hispanics and jobs: Barriers to progress.* Washington, DC: National Commission for Employment Policy.

Lambert, W. E. (1975). Culture and language as factors in learning and education. In A. Wolfgang (Ed.), *Education of immigrant students* (pp. 55–83). Toronto: O.I.S.E.

Lindfors, J. W. (1980). *Children's language and learning.* Englewood Cliffs, NJ: Prentice-Hall.

McLaughlin, B. (1984). Early bilingualism: Methodological and theoretical issues. In M. Paradis & Y. Lebrun (Eds.). *Early bilingualism and child development* (pp. 19–46). Lisse: Swets & Zeitlinger.

McLaughlin, B. (1985). *Second language acquisition in childhood: Vol. 2. School-age children.* Hillsdale, NJ: Erlbaum.

Mehan, H., Hertweck, A., & Meihls, J. L. (in press). *Handicapping the handicapped: Decision making in students' educational careers.* Palo Alto: Stanford University.

Mehan, H., Miller-Souviney, B., & Riel, M. M. (1984). Research currents: Knowledge of text editing and control of literacy skills. *Language Arts, 65,* 154–159.

Mullard, C. (1985, January). *The social dynamic of migrant groups: From progressive to transformative policy in education.* Paper presented at the OECD Conference on Educational Policies and the Minority Social Groups, Paris.

Ogbu, J. U. (1978). *Minority education and caste.* New York: Academic Press.

Ogbu, J. U., & Matute-Bianchi, M. E. (in press). Understanding sociocultural factors: Knowledge, identity and school adjustment. In California State Department of Education (Ed.), *Sociocultural factors and minority student achievement.* Sacramento: Author.

Ortiz, A. A., & Yates, J. R. (1983). Incidence of exceptionality among Hispanics: Implications for manpower planning. *NABE Journal, 7,* 41–54.

Paulston, C. B. (1980). *Bilingual education: Theories and issues.* Rowley, MA: Newbury House.

Ramphal, D. K. *An analysis of reading instruction of West Indian Creole-speaking students.* Unpublished doctoral dissertation, Ontario Institute for Studies in Education, 1983.

Rosier, P., & Holm, W. (1980). *The Rock Point experience: A longitudinal study of a Navajo school.* Washington, DC: Center for Applied Linguistics.

Rueda, R., Mercer, J. R. (1985, June). *Predictive analysis of decision making with language-minority handicapped children.* Paper presented at the BUENO Center 3rd Annual Symposium on Bilingual Education, Denver.

Schneider, S. G. (1976). *Revolution, reaction or reform: The 1974 Bilingual Education Act.* New York: Las Americas.

Skutnabb-Kangas, T. (1984). *Bilingualism or not: The education of minorities.* Clevedon, Eng.: Multilingual Matters.

Smith, F. (1978). *Understanding reading* (2nd ed.). New York: Holt, Rinehart & Winston.

Temple, C. A., Nathan, R. G. & Burris, N. A. (1982). *The beginnings of writing.* Boston: Allyn & Bacon.

Tikunoff, W. J. (1983). Five significant bilingual instructional features. In W. J. Tikunoff (Ed.), *Compatibility of the SBIS features with other research on instruction for LEP students* (pp. 5–18). San Francisco: Far West Laboratory.

Tizard, J., Schofield, W. N., & Hewison, J. (1982). Collaboration between teachers and parents in assisting children's reading. *British Journal of Educational Psychology, 52,* 1–15.

Troike, R. (1978). Research evidence for the effectiveness of bilingual education. *NABE Journal, 3,* 13–24.

Wells, G. (1982). Language, learning and the curriculum. In G. Wells, (Ed.), *Language, learning and education* (pp. 250–226). Bristol: Centre for the Study of Language and Communication, University of Bristol.

Wong-Fillmore, L. (1983). The language learner as an individual: Implications of research on individual differences for the ESL teacher. In M. A. Clarke & J. Handscombe (Eds.), *On TESOL '82: Pacific perspectives on language learning and teaching (pp. 157–171).* Washington, DC: TESOL.

# 13

# Toward a Social-Contextual Approach to Family Literacy

ELSA ROBERTS AUERBACH
*University of Massachusetts, Boston*

*Family literacy programs are designed to support low-income, minority, and immigrant families so that they can actively participate in their children's education. In this article Elsa Auerbach critically examines family literacy programs that accord with the "transmission of school practices" model, which promotes parents' efforts toward school-like literacy practices in the home. Drawing upon recent research findings, the author argues that the model is based on a number of false assumptions and warns that the programs function under a new version of the "deficit hypothesis," which assumes that the parents fall short of the skills necessary to promote their children's success at school. Auerbach proposes an alternative social-contextual model for family literacy that broadens the definition of family literacy.*

Why I didn't do the homework

Because the phone is ringing
the door is noking
the kid is yumping
the food is burning
time runs fast.

> *Rosa*

The work reported on this article was funded by Title VII Office of Bilingual Education and Minority Language Affairs, grant number G008635277, procurement number 003JH60021. The views, opinions and findings contained in this article are not to be construed as OBEMLA's position or policy, unless so designated.

The work reported on this article is the result of collaboration with UMass/Boston English Family Literacy project staff: Ann Cason, Rosario Gomez-Sanford, Loren McGrail, Andrea Nash, and Madeline Rhum. We owe a special debt of gratitude to the students whose work appears in the article and the many others who taught us about their ways of learning and teaching. We would also like to thank Candace Mitchell for her insightful critique of earlier drafts of this paper.

*Harvard Educational Review*   Vol. 59   No. 2   May 1989, 165–181

Rosa's writing is a window on her world. It reflects the tensions she faces as a young mother pursuing educational dreams in a new country. Given Rosa's strong motivation, her teacher was curious about why she hadn't done the homework. As Rosa explains, she is more than a student: she is also a parent, wife, cook, neighbor, member of an extended family and community, and someone who is trying to balance the demands of these many roles. Although she sees the importance of learning and has made the effort to enroll in English classes, she is asking her teacher to look at schoolwork in the context of her life and to understand the complex set of demands that sometimes takes priority over assignments.

Rosa's voice is both her own and the voice of many immigrant and refugee students. Her dilemma is their dilemma: how can parents with low proficiency in English and literacy find ways to integrate learning into their busy lives and, at the same time, provide a context for literacy development in their children's lives?

This dilemma is a challenge to educators: how should we view Rosa's situation, and what can we do to support her efforts? Rosa's class, part of the University of Massachusetts (UMass) at Boston English Family Literacy Program, is one of many set up around the country in recent years to provide English literacy instruction to parents of bilingual students so that they, in turn, can support the literacy development of their children.[1] In the UMass/Boston Program my colleagues and I have found that the way family literacy is defined has critical implications for addressing Rosa's dilemma. If it is defined narrowly to mean performing school-like literacy activities within the family setting, the social-contextual demands on family life become obstacles that must be overcome so that learning can take place. In this view, successful literacy and language acquisition are closely linked to the culture of schooling and to mainstream literacy practices; life demands are seen as taking parents away from literacy development and as conflicting with the demands of schooling (such as doing homework). This view implies that it is the teacher's job to make work on academic skills manageable and the parents' job to set aside time to work on these skills (see, for example, Simich-Dudgeon, 1987).

If, on the other hand, educators define family literacy more broadly to include a range of activities and practices that are integrated into the fabric of daily life, the social context becomes a rich resource that can inform rather than impede learning. In this more inclusive view, doing formal schoolwork and developing literacy are not necessarily synonymous. The acquisition of literacy skills is seen in relation to its context and uses (Heath, 1983; Street, 1984): literacy is meaningful to students to the extent that it relates to daily realities and helps them to act on them (Freire, 1970); divorced from such contexts and purposes, however, it can become one more burden. In this view, the teacher's role is to connect what happens inside the classroom to what happens outside so that literacy can become a meaningful tool for addressing the issues in students' lives.

The difference between these two perspectives on Rosa's dilemma is important because of its potential effect on policy and practice, as well as on students' learning. As the national focus on family contributions to literacy acquisition intensifies with, for example, the establishment of the Barbara Bush Foundation for Family Literacy and the passage of Even Start legislation (see Business Council for Effective Literacy [BCEL], 1989), it will become increasingly important to ground program development in a sound conceptual framework, informed by research, theory, and practice.

The UMass/Boston English Family Literacy Project staff has developed its own conceptual framework by examining not only current models for family literacy programs, but also the ethnographic literature on family contributions to literacy development as well as the evidence provided by the program's own students.[2] What we learned from students came not from formal "research" but from observing what they said, did, and showed in the course of day-to-day classroom interaction. The Project staff did not go into students' homes or communities to examine literacy uses and practices or to collect data; instead, we listened, read, and talked with students about literacy in their lives.

We found, as a result of this investigation, a gap between research and implementation: existing models for family literacy programs seemed not to be informed by ethnographic research or substantiated by what we learned from the students themselves. This article will discuss the results of this preliminary investigation and the assumptions behind current models for family literacy programs in light of recent research, both inside and outside the classroom; it will also suggest alternatives. While the perspective represented here focuses specifically on work with immigrant and refugee families, our sense is that the analysis and pedagogical implications may well be valid for other populations too (such as low literate native speakers of English), because it is informed by a broad base of research in a variety of cultural and economic contexts (Chall & Snow, 1982; Goldenberg, 1984; Heath, 1983; Taylor, 1983; Taylor & Dorsey-Gaines, 1988; Tizard, Schofield, & Hewison, 1982).

## The Context for the Family Literacy Trend

The attention now being paid to parental roles in literacy development must be seen in the context of the current alarmist concern about the "literacy crisis," the dropout rate, and declining academic achievement. This concern is often embedded in an analysis that links illiteracy and unemployment, claiming that inadequate literacy skills inhibit both personal and national economic advancement (see Shor, 1986, for an analysis of the context of this crisis). The makers of national educational policy argue that we must look beyond the school systems to the family in order to locate the cause of the problem. Former secretary of education Terrell Bell (1988) characterized this position with the comment: "Not even the best classroom can make up for failure in the family." The contention is that illiteracy breeds illiteracy: in an "intergenerational cycle of illiteracy," the "plague" passes from one generation to the next, creating a permanent, self-perpetuating "underclass" (see BCEL, 1989).

This analysis, in turn, is often justified by a series of studies on family literacy (although the authors of these studies may not agree with those who cite them); most of these focus on English-speaking families. One group of studies (Chall & Snow, 1982; Heath, 1983) examines a wide range of family literacy practices within and across social classes, showing that children whose home literacy practices most closely resemble those of the school are more successful in school. Other research (for example, Epstein, 1986; Topping & Wolfendale, 1985) indicates that parental involvement in children's schooling has a positive impact on school achievement. Taken together, these studies suggest that one explanation for the relative success in school of middle-class Anglo students is that their home environments provide them with the kinds of literacy skills and practices needed to do well in school. The fact that their parents use and transmit literacy in the specific ways that schools expect gives these children an advantage.

But what about those children from homes that do not promote middle-class "ways with words," whose parents are not involved with their children's schooling or do not speak English? Despite some of the researchers' intentions, these studies are often interpreted to mean that nonmainstream families may lack appropriate environments for fostering literacy development because of inadequate parental skills, practices, and materials (Bell, 1988).

Furthermore, research indicates that until recently little systematic institutional support existed to help parents develop specific skills or take an active role in education (Moles, 1982). Traditional forms of parent involvement—such as creating a home atmosphere conducive to learning, responding to school communications, helping at school, performing academic tasks with children, and working in parent advisory groups—have been limited in scope and often have not included low-income or language-minority families (Epstein, 1986). Many policymakers (Home and School Institute, for example, and The Academic Development Institute) and program designers use this body of research to recommend a systematic, school-based attempt to structure parental participation in children's education. According to this formulation, parents are responsible for helping teachers do their jobs, and schools are responsible for showing parents how to do so (Epstein, 1986).

## The "Transmission of School Practices" Model

The source of the problem is widely formulated as a lack of appropriate literacy practices in the home, and, further, in the case of bilingual families, lack of understanding of the language and culture of American schooling (see BCEL, 1989), compounded by a lack of institutional support for developing them. As a result, the solution is often formulated in terms of intervention programs that give parents specific guidelines, materials, and training to carry out school-like activities in the home. Simich-Dudgeon argues that parents with limited English proficiency must become their children's tutors, performing "structured academic activities that reinforce schoolwork" (1987, p. 3). Programs for these parents (see those described in *Issues of Parent Involvement and Literacy,* 1986) often focus on such practices as:

—Teaching parents about the American educational system and philosophy of schooling
—Providing parents with concrete methods and materials to use at home with children

—Assisting parents to promote "good reading habits"
—Training parents for home tutoring in basic skills (often extending a subskills approach to literacy with phonics, word-attack worksheets, and so on)
—Giving parents guidelines and techniques for helping with homework
—Training parents in how to read to children or listen to children read
—Training in "effective parenting"
—Giving parents a calendar or recipe book of ideas for shared literacy activities
—Teaching parents to make and play games to reinforce skills
—Teaching parents how to communicate with school authorities

While these programs take many forms (from competency-based behavior to behavior modification methods), what they have in common is their shared goal: to strengthen the ties between the home and the school by transmitting the culture of school literacy through the vehicle of the family. Parents are taught about mainstream ways of relating to print and about specific school literacy tasks that they can engage in with their children. The model starts with the needs, problems, and practices that educators identify, and then transfers skills or practices to parents in order to inform their interactions with children; its direction moves from the school/educator to the parents, and then to the children.

## Examining the Assumptions

As our Project staff reviewed the ethnographic literature on family literacy, as well as evidence from our own students, it became clear that a number of the assumptions implicit in this "transmission of school practices" model do not correspond to the realities of participants' lives. The first assumption is that language-minority students come from literacy-impoverished homes where education is not valued or supported. The second assumption is that family literacy involves a one-way transfer of skills *from* parents *to* children. Third, this model assumes that success is determined by the parents' ability to support and extend school-like activities in the home. The fourth assumption is that school practices are adequate and that it is home factors that will determine who succeeds. And fifth, the model assumes that parents' own problems get in the way of creating positive family literacy contexts.

Taken together, these assumptions contribute to a new version of the deficit hypothesis, placing the locus of responsibility for literacy problems with the family. The danger is that, left unexamined, these assumptions will justify a model that blames the victim by attributing literacy problems largely to family inadequacies.

### Assumption 1: Home Environments

The first assumption concerns the home literacy environments of language-minority students. The "transmission" model presents the homes of low-income and minority students and of students who speak English as a second language (ESL) as "literacy impoverished," with limited reading materials and with parents who neither read themselves nor read to their children, who do not provide models of literacy use and do not value or support literacy development (see, for example, BCEL, 1989).

A growing body of research, however, indicates that this does not reflect the reality of many low-income, minority, and immigrant families. Taylor and Dorsey-Gaines (1988) studied the literacy contexts of families living below the poverty level, in conditions where neither housing nor food could be taken for granted, where the parents often had not completed high school, and where families had been separated. They found that even in these homes where day-to-day survival was a struggle, "families use literacy for a wide variety of purposes (social, technical, and aesthetic purposes), for a wide variety of audiences, and in a wide variety of situations" (1988, p. 202). Homes were filled with print, and literacy was an integral part of daily life.

The Harvard Families and Literacy Study (Chall & Snow, 1982; Snow, 1987) investigated the home literacy practices of successful and unsuccessful low-income elementary school students in order to identify those factors and patterns of inter-action that contributed to the acquisition of literacy. This study also found a range of literacy practices and materials in the homes of working-class, minority, and ESL students:

> Perhaps the most surprising finding was the generally high level of literacy skill and literacy use among the parents of the children. For example, only twenty percent of the parents said they did not like to read and never read books. Thirty percent read factual books . . . and could name at least one favorite author. Fifty percent read a major newspaper on a regular basis and thirty percent could remember books from their childhoods. These low-income children also dem-onstrated considerable familiarity with literacy. The vast majority owned some books of their own and half owned more than 20 books. . . . *It seems then that explanations implicating the absence of literacy in low-income homes as the source of children's reading failure are simply wrong.* (Snow, 1987, p. 127, emphasis added)

In a study of the functions and meaning of literacy for Mexican immigrants, Delgado-Gaitan (1987) also found that each of the four families she investigated used a range of text types in a variety of ways that went beyond school-related reading. Despite the fact that parents had little prior schooling and did not perceive themselves as readers, they regularly used texts in English and Spanish (including letters from family members, newspapers, and their children's schoolbooks) as an integral part of daily life. Further, they wanted to develop their own English literacy as a way to support their children.

Study after study (for example, Chall & Snow, 1982; Delgado-Gaitan, 1987; Diaz, Moll, & Mehan, 1986; Goldenberg, 1984) has refuted the notion that poor, minority, and immigrant families don't value or support literacy development. In fact, often, quite the opposite seems to be the case for immigrants: those families most margin-alized frequently see literacy and schooling as the key to mobility, to changing their status and preventing their children from suffering as they did. For some, the desire to get a better education for their children may even be the central reason for coming to the United States (Delgado-Gaitan, 1987).

Beyond a general recognition of the importance of literacy, parents support it in specific ways. Each family in the Delgado-Gaitan study, for example, systematically rewarded children for work well done, completed homework, and good grades.

Moreover, these "illiterate" parents recognized that their support could extend beyond helping with skills:

> Some parents assisted their children in school work by sitting with them to do homework and working out the problem, showing them examples for solving their problems, encouraging them to do their homework before playing, reading to them, taking them to the community library and providing them with a space at the kitchen table to do their homework. (Delgado-Gaitan, 1987, p. 28)

Parents in each of these studies understood that supporting children academically went beyond helping with skills to include emotional and physical support. Our own students have repeatedly confirmed these findings. For example, one parent wrote:

> I help my kids by staying together with them, by talking to them. I help them by confronting them and telling them what's wrong or right just as they do me. I help them when they need a favor or money, just as they do me. It's just like you scratch my back, I scratch your back with my family.

*Assumption 2: Directionality of Literacy Interactions*

The phrase "you scratch my back, I scratch your back" points to a second false assumption of the predominant model—namely, that the "natural" direction of literacy learning is from parent to child, and, more narrowly, that the parent's role is to transmit literacy skills to the child. Interestingly, the example just cited was written through a collaborative mother-daughter writing process: the woman who wrote it was at a very beginning literacy level, and could only produce this text with the help of her daughter—it became a language-experience exercise for them.

This two-way support system characterizes the literacy interactions of many immigrant families. In fact, one study of parental involvement with very promising findings is based on a model of children reading to parents (Tizard, Schofield, & Hewison, 1982). This study found that children who read to their parents on a regular basis made significant gains, in fact greater gains than did children receiving an equivalent amount of extra reading instruction by reading specialists at school. Particularly significant was the fact that low parental English literacy skills did not detract from the results. This study suggests that the context provided by parents and their consistent support may be more important than any transfer of skills.

University of Massachusetts English Family Literacy Project work with immigrants and refugees indicates that the distribution and sharing of language and literacy practices in families is complex and by no means unidirectional from parents to children. Family members each contribute in the areas where they are strongest: instead of the parents assisting children with literacy tasks, the children help their parents with homework, act as interpreters for them, and deal with the outside world for them. Parents, in turn, often foster their children's first-language development and help in areas where they feel competent. One of the parents in our program wrote about how this works in her family:

> When I say some words wrong she corrects me. And sometimes I ask her how to say the word and she tells me. And I help her with her Spanish homework

because she takes a class in Spanish in her school. I feel very happy that she helps me, and that she knows good English. Sometimes she laughs at me and I laugh too.

This uneven distribution of language and literacy skills in immigrant families often leads to highly charged, emotionally loaded family dynamics. The fact that the children's English and literacy proficiency may be more developed than the parents' can lead to complicated role reversals in which parents feel that respect for them is undermined and children feel burdened by having to negotiate with the outside world for their parents. Diaz et al. found that since children often took responsibility for conducting transactions with important social institutions (banks, schools, and so forth), "they assumed control and power usually reserved for adults" (1986, p. 210).

A further example from one of our classes serves to illustrate the complexity of this parent-child role reversal. A teacher noticed that the handwriting in the dialogue journal of one of her students was not the student's own and, upon investigation, she learned that the student's daughter had written the journal for her mother. The teacher wrote back, inviting the daughter to keep a separate journal while letting the mother do her own work. The daughter responded with an entry about her own language use, ending with this:

> I'm glad my mother is going to school so she could speak English. It finally mean that I don't have to translate for her every time she watches a movie that she don't understand. I usually have to explain it to her. It must be hard for you to teach the students. You've also got to be patient. If one of your students don't understand what you mean then you have to explain it in a different way. I'll never be a good teacher because I'm not good at teaching.

Here the daughter is describing her own discomfort at being placed in the role of translator and teacher, a role she doesn't feel ready for. These comments suggest that in some families the power of the parents' learning may be that it reduces this parent-child literacy dependency, and frees the children to attend to their own development, including schoolwork.

What emerges from the composite of these studies and student writings is not at all a picture of deficit or literacy impoverishment, but instead a picture of mutual support—of family members working together to help each other in a variety of ways. Clearly a model that rests on the assumption of unilateral parent-to-child literacy assistance, with a neutral transfer of skills, misses important aspects of this dynamic and may in fact exacerbate already stressful family interactions.

*Assumption 3: Family Contexts of Successful Readers*

A third assumption concerns the nature of family contributions to literacy development. The recognition that certain ways of using literacy in the home may better prepare students for success in school is often accompanied by the assumption that children succeed because their families do specific school-like tasks with them—that home learning activities are the key to success for literate children and that literacy programs must provide support for this kind of interaction.

An examination, however, of the actual family contexts for the acquisition of literacy provides compelling counterevidence. Studies which examine the home literacy environments of successful readers (both lower and middle class) reveal a range of factors that contribute to literacy development. The Harvard study, for example, found no simple correlation between parents' literacy level, educational background, amount of time spent on literacy work with children, and overall achievement (Chall & Snow, 1982). Rather, the acquisition of literacy was found to be affected differentially by such factors. Indirect factors including frequency of children's outings with adults, number of maternal outings, emotional climate of the home, amount of time spent interacting with adults, level of financial stress, enrichment activities, and parental involvement with the schools had a stronger effect on many aspects of reading and writing than did direct literacy activities, such as help with homework.

Taylor's (1981, 1983) three-year study of six families of proficient readers provides further evidence that a wide range of home experiences and interaction patterns (rather than narrow, school-like reading and writing activities) characterizes homes of successful readers. Parents in this study often intentionally avoided "doing literacy" with their children in the ways they had been taught in school in order to avoid replicating what they remembered as negative experiences. The interactions around print varied from family to family and were, within each family, "situationally diffuse, occurring at the very margins of awareness . . ." (1981, p. 100). Specific types of interactions did not emerge as significant across families; rather, Taylor found that these interactions were *not* activities "which were added to the family agendas, but that they had evolved as part of everyday life" (1981, p. 100). She concludes:

> The approach that has been taken in recent years has been to develop parent education programmes which very often provide parents with a battery of specific activities which are designed to teach reading, and yet very little available information suggests that parents with children who read without difficulty actually undertake such "teaching" on any kind of regular basis. The present study suggests that there are great variations in approaches the parents have evolved in working with their children and that the thread that unites the families is the recognition that learning to read takes place on a daily basis as part of everyday life. (Taylor, 1981, p. 101)

A second study by Taylor and Dorsey-Gaines (1988) among poor urban families confirmed these findings, indicating that similar dynamics are at work across social classes. These studies indicate that successful readers' homes provide a variety of contexts for using literacy, and that literacy is integrated in a socially significant way into many segments of family life, and is not isolated as a separate, autonomous, add-on instructional activity. The more diverse the contexts for using literacy, the wider the range of literacy achievement factors affected.

*Assumption 4: School Contributions to the Acquisition of Literacy*

A further danger with the "transmission of school practices" model is that the focus may be shifted away from school roles and their interaction with home factors in literacy development. This view perceives what happens at home to be the key to school success, often assuming a direct correlation, even a cause-and-effect relationship, between home factors and school achievement. The flip side of this assumption is the claim that what happens at school is either less important or already adequate and need only be reinforced at home. Again, there is counter-evidence from a variety of sources.

For instance, Heath's (1983) ethnographic investigations of three rural communities in the Piedmont Carolinas found not a lack of literacy practices in the two poorer, working-class communities, but a difference in the ways that literacy was used and perceived. In each community, there was a wide and different range of uses of literacy at home. The relationship between home and school literacy practices was significant: the ways of using print in middle-class homes were similar to those of the school. Since authority is vested in those belonging to the mainstream culture, the literacy practices of the mainstream become the norm and have higher status in school contexts. Heath's analysis suggests that the problem is not one of deficit in the family environment, but one of differential usage and power.

In case studies that examined both home and school contexts, Urzua (1986) contends that it is *school* rather than *home* factors that shape differences in attitudes and abilities relating to literacy. She reports that two refugee children who had homes seemingly less conducive to literacy acquisition were more successful in school. Although their mothers were illiterate in their first language, did not speak or read English, and provided no reading materials in the home, these children progressed greatly in reading and writing. In contrast, another child whose home was filled with reading materials (books, maps, newspapers, dictionaries, and so forth), who had his own study space and school supplies, and whose parents overtly supported his literacy development, had enormous difficulties with reading and writing. Urzua asks, "What makes children like Vuong, loved and encouraged by parents who have offered many possibilities for literacy events in their home, face school with rigidity and approach literacy with fear?" (1986, p. 108).

She suggests that the answer to this question may be found in the classroom experiences. Both of the children who came from less literate home environments were in classes where the teacher valued writing. In these classes writing took place nearly every day, a variety of writing genres (such as autobiographies, fables, journals) was offered, and subskills work (spelling, phonics) was subordinated to the expression of meaning. In the class of the child who came from a home providing more support for literacy acquisition, however, students never wrote more than one sentence at a time, filled in the blanks in workbooks, copied dictionary definitions, and so forth. Urzua then asks, "How powerful are the influences of curriculum and instructional techniques. . . . which either teach children to find their own voices, or discourage them from doing so?" (1986, p. 108).

The Harvard study (Chall & Snow, 1982) offers further support for the view that school factors account as much as home factors for the acquisition of literacy. Classroom factors that affected literacy included the availability of a wide variety of reading materials, the amount and nature of writing, the use of the library, and the quality of instruction. The researchers found that in the early grades, "either literate, stimulating homes or demanding, enriching classrooms can make good readers" (Snow, 1987, p. 128). However, while strong parental factors could compensate for weak schooling up to grade three, even those children with positive home literacy environments fell back after this point if school practices were deficient. While positive home factors were sufficient to carry a child in the lower grades, both positive home and school factors were necessary for literacy development in the upper grades.

One particularly interesting finding of the Harvard study (Chall & Snow, 1982) is that even with such family-based factors as parental aspirations, the interaction with school factors is critical. When the researchers investigated the validity of the commonly held view that parents' hopes for their children affect their children's school success, they found that although these aspirations per se did not influence achievement, parental willingness to advocate for their children (talking to teachers about academics, and so on) did. The authors link this finding to teachers' expectations: parental involvement in an advocacy role is important because it shapes teachers' perceptions, which in turn influence student achievement. One of our students expressed this understanding succinctly:

> The parents should go to all of the meetings of the parent-teacher organization at the school one afternoon each month because you help your son's or daughter's progress in class. If you help the teacher, the teacher help your children.

The need to take on an advocacy role presents a particular challenge for low-income language-minority parents. They may, for cultural reasons, defer to the authority of the teacher and the school, assume that the teacher is always right, or feel unable to intervene on behalf of their children because of the power differential between themselves and school authorities. Further, the time pressures from working several jobs and dealing with the survival demands of poverty-level existence may impede advocacy. The studies suggest, however, that for less literate parents it is precisely this attitude of advocacy and critical examination of school practices that may be their most powerful tool in shaping their children's school achievement.

How can parents with limited language and literacy skills provide input into schooling? Some of our own students have suggested that this dilemma can be approached through "critical support"—that being an advocate can range from helping the teacher "so the teacher help the children," to monitoring children's progress and letting teachers know of parental concerns, to participating in parent advocacy groups. Taking this perspective, the family literacy class can become a context for critical and reflective thinking about education, as well as for modeling ways of shaping children's education.

*Assumption 5: The Social Context for Family Literacy*

A final problem with the "transmission of school practices" model rests with the focus on parents' inadequacies, which obscures scrutiny of the real conditions giving rise to literacy problems. The social context for parents' own needs and strengths is often ignored or seen as an inherently negative factor that ultimately undermines the possibilities for learning. This social context may include, as Rosa suggests, family obligations, as well as housing, health care, and employment needs. In one study, parents identify "family health problems, work schedules, having small children, receiving only 'bad news' from school, and fears for safety" (Moles, 1982, p. 46) as factors inhibiting participation. Taylor and Dorsey-Gaines (1988) argue that it is the lack of social, political, and economic support for parents in dealing with these contextual concerns that puts children at risk (as opposed to lack of support by parents for children's literacy development).

Cultural differences may also be perceived as impediments to participation. Some parents, for example, come from cultures that view education as the exclusive domain of schools (Oliva, 1986). The solution is then framed in terms of "overcoming" cultural differences and "molding" parents to conform to school-determined expectations: parents must reorder their priorities so that they can become involved in school-determined activities. In one case, for example, programs were advised to send home notes in the imperative, telling parents they *must* attend meetings (Tran, 1986). But in order to make parental involvement possible, programs must provide support services (such as child care and translators for meetings).

Certainly these are important ways to encourage involvement; nevertheless, the underlying formulation remains: social-contextual and cultural factors are considered external factors that need to be dealt with outside the classroom, through program structures. Inside the classroom, the assumptions, goals, processes, and content of parental involvement still follow a "from the school to the parent" model. The expectation that "obstacles" should (or can) be taken care of as a precondition to participation may result in reinforcing the advantage of students who come from the least complicated social contexts.

On the other hand, if we believe that the social context is not a negative external force and recognize that the conditions which shape family literacy are central to the learning dynamic itself, we can begin to make literacy work relevant for parents (Collier, 1986). Although being expected to conform to culturally unfamiliar school expectations and practices may intimidate parents and drive them away, being encouraged to explore their own concerns and to advocate for their own expectations may free parents to become more involved with their own and their children's literacy development. In this alternative formulation, housing, education, work, and health issues are acknowledged and explored in the classroom, with literacy becoming a tool for addressing these issues, and cultural differences are perceived as strengths and resources that can bridge the gap between home and school. As these issues become part of the curriculum content, literacy will become more socially significant for families, which, as Taylor and others so often remind us, is what characterizes the families of successful readers.

Again, this alternative perspective is supported by both researchers and parents. The study of Mexican families in San Diego (Diaz et al., 1986) confirms the importance of situating literacy in its social context. Rather than starting with mainstream ways of using literacy and transmitting them to families, researchers looked at community practices as the basis for informing and modifying school practices. Local residents were trained as ethnographers to collect data on community writing practices; they then worked with teachers to use this data in developing classroom instructional modules. The function of writing to address community issues proved to be important:

> Parents, students, and others all impressed us with their concern for social issues that permeate community life. Virtually every conversation that began as a discussion of writing eventually turned to the problems of youth gangs, unemployment, immigration, the need to learn English and the like. It became clear to us that writing, schooling and social issues are completely related phenomena in the community. (Diaz et al., 1986, p. 211)

Thus, by investigating community uses of writing, the researchers discovered essential social issues, which, when introduced into the classroom, became the vehicle for improving writing instruction. Student writing focused on the content of students' and families' interactions, life histories, conditions within the families, and parents' educational values. The underlying direction of curriculum development here is from the community to the classroom, rather than from the classroom to the community.

In Pajaro Valley, parents and children are involved in a project in which they read, discuss, and write children's stories together (Ada, 1988). Critical for this project is the positive value placed on the use of the home language both as a vehicle for communication within the family and as the foundation for children's academic success. Also important is the linking of readings to students' lives through a process of dialogue: readers share personal reactions and feelings, relate the story to their own experiences, critically analyze the events and ideas in the stories, and discuss real-life applications of this understanding. The process of sharing Spanish children's literature becomes the foundation for then asking children and parents to write their own stories about significant events in their lives. This kind of family literacy work draws on parents' cultural strengths and encourages critical thinking about key issues in family life.

Another project designed to build home and school links is the Chinle Navajo Parent-Child Reading Program (Viola, Gray, & Murphy, 1986). In this project, children bring books home and share them with their parents, either by reading or telling the stories. Children also write their own books based on Navajo stories they have heard from their parents and grandparents. In the process, the home culture is validated and promoted through literacy work; the parents' cultural knowledge contributes to rather than conflicts with school learning.

Work with parents in the UMass Project confirms the power of instruction centered around community and family issues. Through a process of co-investigation with students, our teachers have identified concerns about the new immigration law (the Immigration Reform and Control Act), housing, AIDS, language use at work, and bilingualism as relevant for their students. Students have developed their own language and literacy proficiency in the process of exploring these concerns through the use of collaboratively generated texts, thematic readings, language experience stories, Freirean problem-posing (Auerbach & Wallerstein, 1987; Wallerstein, 1983), dialogue journals, process writing, and photo stories. They have written letters to the editor about community problems, written and presented testimony for state funding hearings, and written about concerns for their children's schooling and their own language and literacy use in the community. One teacher reported that the quantity of her students' writings doubled when they wrote about immediate community issues such as day care. Not surprisingly, we have found that the quality of the work improves when the content is most closely linked with students' real concerns.

## Implications for Family Literacy Program Design

The analysis in this article points to a social-contextual model of family literacy that asks, How can we draw on parents' knowledge and experience to inform instruction? rather than, How can we transfer school practices into home contexts? The goal then is to increase the social significance of literacy in family life by incorporating community cultural forms and social issues into the content of literacy activities. This model is built on the particular conditions, concerns, and cultural expertise of specific communities, and, as such, does not involve a predetermined curriculum or set of practices or activities. Instead, the curriculum development process is participatory and is based on a collaborative investigation of critical issues in family or community life. As these issues emerge, they are explored and transformed into content-based literacy work, so that literacy can in turn become a tool for shaping this social context.[3]

This approach fosters a new formulation of what counts as family literacy. This broadened definition includes, but is not limited to, direct parent-child interactions around literacy tasks: reading with and/or listening to children; talking about and giving and receiving support for homework and school concerns; engaging in other activities with children that involve literacy (such as cooking, writing notes, and so on). Equally important, however, are the following, often neglected, aspects of family literacy work:

1. *Parents working independently on reading and writing.* On the most basic level, just by developing their own literacy parents contribute to family literacy; as parents become less dependent on children, the burden shifts and children are freer to develop in their own ways.
2. *Using literacy to address family and community problems.* Dealing with issues such as immigration, employment, or housing through literacy work makes it possible for literacy to become socially significant in parents' lives; by extension it models the use of literacy as an integral part of daily life for children.
3. *Parents addressing child-rearing concerns through family literacy class.* By providing mutual support and a safe forum for dialogue, parents can share and develop their own strategies for dealing with issues such as teenage sex, drugs, discipline, and children's attitudes toward language choice.

4. *Supporting the development of the home language and culture.* As parents contribute to the development of the home language and culture, they build the foundation for their children's academic achievement, positive self-concept, and appreciation for their multicultural heritage. By valuing and building on parents' strengths, the status of those strengths is enhanced.

5. *Interacting with the school system.* The classroom becomes a place where parents can bring school-related issues and develop the ability to understand and respond to them. They can explore their attitudes toward their own and their children's school experiences. They can assess what they see and determine their responses, rehearse interactions with school personnel, and develop support networks for individual and group advocacy.

The function of family literacy programs becomes the promotion of activities, events, and practices that correspond to this broadened definition. Our own attempts to implement this approach with bilingual parents include using reading and writing in a variety of ways:

1. To investigate home language use (for example, documenting who uses what language, to whom and when)

2. To explore family literacy practices (for example, evaluating critically a "how to help your children with homework" guide sent home by the school which includes questions like these: Which of these things do you already do? Which would you like to do? Which do you think are not possible? What do you do that's not already included here?)

3. To explore cultural issues (for example, writing about children's positive and negative attitudes toward the home language, participating in a community Spanish literacy day, writing about faith healing)

4. To model whole-language activities that parents might do with children (for example, telling stories, making books)

5. To validate culture-specific literacy forms (for example, reading, writing, and telling folktales and proverbs)

6. To explore parenting issues (for example, exchanging letters with American parents in an Adult Basic Education program, writing letters of advice to pregnant teenagers in a high school program)

7. To use literacy to explore issues of learning and teaching (for example, responding to pictures of different educational settings in terms of their own educational experiences and expectations for children's education)

8. To address community, workplace, and health care issues (for example, writing a class letter about police discrimination to a local newspaper, writing testimony for funding hearings on adult education and community services)

9. To practice advocacy in dealing with schools (for example, writing letters about concerns to children's teachers)

10. To explore political issues (for example, writing language-experience stories about the elections in Haiti)

We began this article by offering a window on Rosa's home context for literacy learning and by showing that schools need to take this context into account. This broader perspective on family literacy reflects our approach to addressing Rosa's challenge. We would like to end with another piece of Rosa's writing that illustrates how her writing has developed following this approach. It also illuminates the complexity of this challenge and her strengths in taking it on. Rosa paints here a picture of the richness of family interactions as she reflects on language and literacy use in her life:

At Home
I talk to my kids about school.
I ask . . . . ¿Como se portaron?
They say very good.
I continue to ask
about the food . . . and the homework.
They speak to me in english . . .
I say I am sorry . . .
Yo no entendi nada; por favor hablame
en Español. . . . The older boy says OK . . . OK
You study english you are supposed to
understand. They repeat again to me
slowly and more clearly. Yo les digo . . .
Muchas gracias. . . . I love you.

## Notes

1. Students in our classes reflect the diversity found in many immigrant and refugee communities: at any given time, there may be up to 25 language groups represented in the program. Students' first language (L1) and educational backgrounds range from no L1 literacy or ESL proficiency to strong L1 literacy and intermediate ESL proficiency—from students who sign their names with an X to students with teaching degrees in their homelands.
2. Our annotated bibliography of English family literacy (Nash, 1987) lists sources used in addressing the following questions: What are the ways that families contribute to literacy development? How do their contributions vary according to class and culture? What models are now being used to involve families in children's literacy development? What assumptions are these models based on? What are the particular issues that must be addressed in programs for non-English-speaking families and how is this being done? What alternatives are there to the predominant models?
3. Participants in the University of Massachusetts Family Literacy Project are documenting how this curriculum development process has been implemented in our classes. This curriculum development report (forthcoming, fall 1989), will include a discussion of how students' concerns are identified, a range of themes which have emerged in our classes, how language and literacy have been extended around these themes, and issues which have arisen in the process of putting this participatory, social-contextual approach into practice.

## References

Ada, A. F. (1988). The Pajaro Valley experience: Working with Spanish-speaking parents to develop children's reading and writing skills in the home through the use of children's literature. In T. Skutnabb-Kangas and J. Cummins (Eds.), *Minority education: From shame to struggle* (pp. 224–238). Philadelphia: Multilingual Matters.

Auerbach, E., & Wallerstein, N. (1987). *ESL for action: Problem-posing at work.* Reading, MA: Addison-Wesley.

Bell, T. M. (1988, October). Keynote address at *Adult Learners: Arizona's Future* conference. Phoenix, AZ.

Business Council for Effective Literacy. (1989, April). Newsletter.

Cazden, F. (1986). ESL teachers as language advocates for children. In P. Rigg & D. S. Enright (Eds.), *Children and ESL: Integrating perspectives* (pp. 9–21). Washington, DC: TESOL.

Chall, J. S., & Snow, C. (1982). *Families and literacy: The contributions of out of school experiences to children's acquisition of literacy*. A final report to the National Institute of Education.

Collier, V. P. (1986). Cross-cultural policy issues in minority and majority parent involvement. In *Issues of parent involvement and literacy. Proceedings of the symposium at Trinity College* (pp. 73–78). Washington, DC: Trinity College, Department of Education and Counseling.

Delgado-Gaitan, C. (1987). Mexican adult literacy: New directions for immigrants. In S. R. Goldman & K. Trueba (Eds.), *Becoming literate in English as a second language* (pp. 9–32). Norwood, NJ: Ablex.

Diaz, S., Moll, L., & Mehan, K. (1986). Socio-cultural resources in instruction: A context-specific approach. In *Beyond language: Social and cultural factors in schooling language minority children* (pp. 87–229). Los Angeles: California State Department of Education and California State University.

Epstein, J. (1986). Parent involvement: Implications for LEP parents. In *Issues of parent involvement in literacy. Proceedings of the symposium at Trinity College* (pp. 6–16). Washington, DC: Trinity College, Department of Education and Counseling.

Freire, P. (1970). *Pedagogy of the oppressed*. New York: Seabury Press.

Goldenberg, C. N. (1984, October 10–13). *Low-income parents' contributions to the reading achievement of their first-grade children*. Paper presented at the meeting of the Evaluation Network/Evaluation Research Society, San Francisco.

Heath, S. B. (1983). *Ways with words*. Cambridge, Eng.: Cambridge University Press. *Issues of parent involvement and literacy*. (1986). Proceedings of the symposium at Trinity College, June 6–7. Washington, DC: Trinity College, Department of Education and Counseling.

Moles, O. C. (1982, November). Synthesis of recent research on parent participation in children's education. *Educational Leadership, 40*, 44–47.

Nash, A. (1987). *English family literacy: An annotated bibliography*. Boston: University of Massachusetts/Boston, English Family Literacy Project.

Oliva, J. (1986). Why parent tutors? Cultural reasons. In *Issues of parent involvement and literacy. Proceedings of the symposium at Trinity College* (pp. 79–81). Washington, DC: Trinity College, Department of Education and Counseling.

Shor, I. (1986). *Culture wars: School and society in the conservative restoration, 1969–1984*. New York: Routledge & Kegan Paul/Methuen.

Simich-Dudgeon, C. (1987, March). Involving limited English proficient parents as tutors in their children's education. *ERIC/CLL News Bulletin, 10*(2).

Snow, C. (1987). Factors influencing vocabulary and reading achievement in low income children. In R. Apple (Ed.), *Toegepaste Taalwetenschap in Artikelen*, Special 2 (pp. 124–128). Amsterdam, ANELA.

Street, B. V. (1984). *Literacy in theory and practice*. Cambridge: Cambridge University Press.

Taylor, D. (1981). The family and the development of literacy skills and values. *Journal of Research in Reading, 4*(2), 92–103.

Taylor, D. (1983). *Family literacy: Young children learning to read and write*. Exeter, NH: Heinemann.

Taylor, D., & Dorsey-Gaines, C. (1988). *Growing up literate: Learning from inner city families*. Portsmouth, NH: Heinemann.

Tizard, J., Schofield, W. N., & Hewison, J. (1982). Symposium: Reading collaboration between teachers and parents in assisting children's reading. *British Journal of Educational Psychology, 52,* 1–15.

Topping, K., & Wolfendale, S. (Eds.). (1985). *Parental involvement in children's reading.* New York: Nichols.

Tran, B. T. (1986). Cultural issues in Indochinese parent involvement. In *Issues of parent involvement and literacy. Proceedings of the symposium at Trinity College* (pp. 65–66). Washington, DC: Trinity College, Department of Education and Counseling.

Urzua, C. (1986). A children's story. In P. Rigg & D. S. Enright (Eds.), *Children and ESL: Integrating perspectives* (pp. 93–112). Washington, DC: TESOL.

Viola, M., Gray, A., & Murphy, B. (1986, May). *Report on the Navajo Parent Child Reading Program at the Chinle Primary School.* Chinle School District, AZ.

Wallerstein, N. (1983). *Language and culture in conflict: Problem-posing in the ESL classroom.* Reading, MA: Addison-Wesley.

# 14
# Thinking about Bilingual Education: A Critical Appraisal

RICARDO OTHEGUY
*City College of New York and*
*City University of New York*

*There have been heated discussions for and against bilingual education. Here, Ricardo Otheguy presents the arguments put forth by critics of bilingual education programs as well as the opinions held by the general population. While not offering any definitive solutions to the debate, Otheguy uncovers the complexities of the issues surrounding bilingual education. By placing the issue within a historical perspective, he demonstrates that implicit in many of the critics' arguments are misguided notions of race and ethnicity. In addition, he highlights the confusion surrounding differences of opinion on the role of government in education and on the effect of policy on educational practice.*

Controversies surrounding innovations in education often extend beyond their natural limits, both in tone and duration, by exaggerated and oversimplified positions taken by the debaters. Such is the case with bilingual education in the United States. Disagreements emerged when it was new and small, controversy continued when it first received federal support, and it is still being debated at a time when many see it as having run its course.

A careful analysis of the complexities overlooked in the heat of argument appears as timely now as ever before. In communities that speak languages other than English, interest in bilingual programs does not seem to have waned.[1] Financial and moral backing for bilingual programs can still be found among some local politicians and school board members, in segments of large city school systems, in a few national

I would like to thank Wallis H. Reid, who provided many valuable comments on earlier versions of this manuscript, and Joan P. Levinson, whose many suggestions on style and substance were most useful, and whose encouragement and support were helpful during the writing of this article.

*Harvard Educational Review* Vol. 52 No. 3 August 1982, 301–314

foundations, as well as among some national politicians and members of several federal bureaucracies.[2] Yet poised against this support is notable opposition. The *New York Times,* for example, regularly rails against "expensive bilingual education programs" that never work, a fact its editors argue, that accords with "every known pedagogical theory and with common sense."[3] In addition, books such as Noel Epstein's *Language, Ethnicity and the Schools* have served as highly influential indictments of bilingual education, which is seen as part of a wave of "affirmative ethnicity" that has swept the country.[4]

In opposition also is the administration of President Reagan. The cancellation of federal regulations mandating specific services for bilingual pupils by school districts was announced in 1981.[5] Since the regulations had already been rejected by Congress during the previous administration, the announcement was an empty gesture, though it underscored the President's personally stated skepticism about bilingual education.[6] In addition, bilingual education is openly opposed by some teachers' unions and by many school administrators.[7]

Any examination of the oversimplifications that vitiate the arguments on both sides must start by questioning the almost universal acceptance of the term "bilingual education" as encompassing a unitary phenomenon—a single, coherent set of activities. In fact, however, the activities called bilingual education are quite diverse.

Yet in response to this misleading label, critics of bilingual education argue that it eliminates English as the common bond that eases the assimilation of immigrants; in promoting pluralism, these critics argue, bilingual education can lead to civil fragmentation and chaos. Supporters argue that non-English-speaking communities have as much right as English speakers to use schools to transmit their language to their children. They regard linguistic and cultural community between home and school as beneficial and necessary.

In centering the controversy on the label, debaters often fail to realize that bilingual education can employ practices that both retard and accelerate assimilation. In most bilingual programs, a part of the curriculum consists of teaching children English-as-a-second-language (ESL), presumably encouraging assimilation. Another consists of subject-matter instruction in the children's native language, presumably encouraging pluralism. The relative allocation of time and attention given to the student's first language and that to English varies enormously among states, school districts, and even among classes in the same school. Some bilingual teachers instruct primarily in the child's mother tongue. More teach primarily in English. Many programs stress literacy in the mother tongue; more emphasize English literacy. Some teachers maintain a clear separation between languages. Others switch back and forth, much as the children themselves do.[8] Practitioners obviously differ in their ideas on how best to run their bilingual classrooms, as well as in their ideas on assimilation, pluralism, language, and ethnicity.

These activities are simply too diverse to conduct a useful debate under a single rubric of assimilation versus pluralism. For this controversy to make any sense, the debaters need to base their arguments on observations of bilingual programs in operation. They may be surprised to learn, for instance, that federally funded bilingual programs have long been regarded as hastening the disappearance of the child's mother tongue rather than encouraging its survival.[9] At the present level of abstraction, the controversy centers on a phenomenon far clearer to critics and debaters than to participants and practitioners.

An image of bilingual education as a uniform phenomenon is created by many factors other than the single label. Many so-called bilingual programs were first funded from one source, Title VII of the Elementary and Secondary Education Act (1974). A decade of reports and evaluations led to a great tendency for schools to administer standardized tests to children in this program, tending to present bilingual education as a unitary set of practices with similar content. Another factor contributing to this image is related to who runs the programs. Most programs are implemented by Hispanic teachers and administrators, giving the impression of a united, ethnically identifiable enterprise. Moreover, these educators often identify themselves at conferences and professional meetings as advocates of a single cause. Hispanic community groups and elected officials, as well as Spanish-language magazines and newspapers, treat bilingual education as an important community issue, since the majority of children served by bilingual programs is Hispanic.[10] Any deviation from the regular school curriculum for students whose native language is not English is frequently labeled bilingual education, even if no element of the native language is involved.[11]

Just as it is not true that bilingual education is a unified movement whose practitioners share in a pluralist consensus, neither is it true that bilingual education is always federally supported and only responsive to Hispanic students. Though the impetus came originally from federal involvement, many bilingual programs are now supported by state and local funds.[12] The Supreme Court decision that gave bilingual education its strongest legal footing was based on a case brought by Chinese parents in San Francisco.[13] Bilingual programs serve children of many language backgrounds besides Spanish, including children from English monolingual homes. And, most important, the majority of Hispanic children in the United States do not attend bilingual classes at all.[14]

All references to the term "bilingual education," then, should be seen as denoting a complex set of educational activities characterized by several languages of instruction and by program diversity. The purpose here is not to evaluate or to argue for or against bilingual education, but rather first, to examine the assumptions of those who argue against using the home language of bilingual children in the schools, and second, to provide evidence that the appeal of these arguments rests on a reductionist oversimplification of the facts. While many of my observations will be applicable to non-English-speaking children with home languages other than Spanish, the discussion will focus on Hispanics, because of their proportionately large population in bilingual programs.[15] In addition, Hispanics comprise the largest political force advocating a language other than English as the medium of instruction and survival of the home language.

One aspect of the controversy about bilingual programs is the frequent comparison of the role of the government today in educating non-English-speaking children with its role during the turn of the century. The topic is a favorite of street-corner historians, who remember well that the government did nothing to help the immigrants adjust to their new surroundings. This theme surfaces frequently when bilingual programs are discussed—in private conversations, panels, lectures, meetings, articles, and most bitterly, in countless letters to the editor in newspapers throughout the United States. One such letter captures the tone and substance of this theme: "Perhaps what irritates Americans most is the insistence of many Hispanic-Americans that they not only have a natural right but also a constitutional right to be taught in Spanish at the taxpayers' expense, a claim put forward by no other group of any significance in our history."[16] The same theme also appears, for instance, in Noel Epstein's influential book attacking bilingual programs, where discussion of the immigrants then and now echoes widespread sentiment criticizing the government for interfering in "jobs long ago left to families, religious groups, ethnic organizations, private schools, ethnic publications, and others."[17]

Notwithstanding the obvious differences between European immigrants and Hispanics, and even more obvious changes in the federal government, the comparison is at the center of deeply felt emotions about bilingual education. Opponents of bilingualism always hark back to the wondrous results obtained through educational policies that encouraged immigrants to give up their languages. But proponents argue that this brilliant past was not really shaped by educational policies, nor was it as glorious as some remember it. They consider linguistic and cultural pluralism to be an asset that was squandered by previous groups and that should be preserved now.

We cannot join here the debate over how fast assimilation actually took place. Nor can we settle the question of whether the immigrants and their descendants "made it" or continue to live in a society stratified by national and linguistic origins.[18] But whatever truth is contained in the belief that they did succeed is related to other factors much more than to language. Economic advancement obtained by European immigrants is the product of the opportunities they found for economic and political involvement in the larger society, not of the sacrificial surrender of a native language. Many immigrants who achieved some modicum of economic success, then and now, did so operating businesses and shops with the benefit of very little skill in English. Moreover, English monolingualism has meant little in terms of economic advantages to most blacks and to the masses of poor descendants of poor European immigrants. Hispanics who now speak only English can often be found in as poor a state as when they first came. English monolingualism among immigrants tends to follow economic integration rather than cause it.[19]

This observation about language can also be made about education. The concern that bilingual education will keep Hispanics from "making it" is rooted in the belief that a monolingual education is what promoted other immigrant groups. Those other groups, however, did not receive much schooling, bilingual or otherwise. Rather, they prospered first, and only then were able to allow their descendants an opportunity for schooling.[20] The comparison fails because it is based on the myth of the public school's success in rapidly assimilating the immigrant child, when that child was, in fact, more often working in a shop than learning in a school.

The situation today is quite different. There is no doubt that bilingualism in the schools is the result of changing ideologies within and outside of education. It is also the result of simple changes in school demography. The proportion of children and adolescents who attend school now, as well as the number of years they spend in school, is much higher than in the turn-of-the-century decades of massive immigration. Since many children of the wealthy already attended schools then, the increase comes largely from children of the less affluent.[21]

Bilingual education is not new in the United States, but existed, under local auspices, from the early nineteenth century until well into the twentieth.[22] What is significant here, however, is not the similarities with the past but the differences. It seems pointless to focus on public schools that held classes in German in Baltimore and Cincinnati at the turn of the century. What must be taken into account, rather, is the unprecedented length of schooling today, and the massive attendance by rich and poor students of all ethnic backgrounds. At the heart of the problem is the belief today that the issues involved in educating large numbers of bilingual students in elementary and high schools can be compared to those issues of a former era when most children seldom completed grammar school.

In addition to demographic changes in school attendance there are also important changes in the general linguistic and ethnic demography of the two periods that render comparisons between them almost useless. During the period of European migration, the United States was home to large numbers of foreign-born people who spoke many different languages. In the first half of this century, however, no one group ever comprised more than 25 percent of all immigrants for any given year. And during the closing decades of the nineteenth century, the largest group was always primarily English-speaking. Today the country is much more widely English-speaking than ever before. English today is the usual language in 94 percent of U.S. households, up from 80 percent during the decades of massive immigration. The non-English-speaking population, on the other hand, is much less diverse. Spanish is spoken today six times more than the next most commonly spoken foreign language, Italian. In areas with high Hispanic concentrations—Florida, the New York metropolitan area, and the Southwest—Spanish speakers constitute 20 percent of all households and nearly 90 percent of all households with a language other than English.[23]

A final demographic factor is also relevant. A common observation in discussions contrasting the government's role in the two periods is that of permanence. Critics of bilingual education argue that Europeans migrated here to stay and thus became deserving of our support while Hispanics are here today and gone tomorrow, thus compromising their claim to our help. However, the common experience of Mexicans and Puerto Ricans today is shared by their earlier counterparts. With the exception of the Irish and the Jews, who largely remained in the United States, other Europeans traveled back and forth. They tried the United States, gave up, and went back to their native land, often took heart and tried again, and once more failed and went back. After the dust settled, a full 33 percent of those who immigrated to this country from 1908 to 1924 had returned to the old country for good.[24]

A proper comparison of European immigrants then and Hispanics now would require a look at the relationship of each group to the general population of their times. The experience of early generation European immigrants in the United States was a miserable one. Hispanics today not only get more schooling, but also have higher standards of living and have greater access to employment than did the southern and eastern Europeans at the turn of the century. But this comparison is true only if made across time. The proper comparison is not that of today's minorities with those who preceded them, but with those who share in today's society. Seen in these terms, the comparison of the two periods seems farfetched.

Although assessments made at different times and with different techniques are difficult to compare, a few things are clear. Immigrants then achieved levels of schooling similar to those of the native population. In the area of achievement as measured by the proportion of students held back a grade, immigrants were no worse than natives. The situation today is quite different. Hispanic enrollment is considerably less than that of majority children. The same holds true for employment. Immigrants in the early part of this century were often out of work in equal proportion to other citizens. Today, unemployment among Hispanics, particularly among the young, is spectacularly higher than among the white population.[25]

Comparison of the two groups usually overlooks another difference of great significance, namely, the role of the federal government in their respective histories. In order to place this role in its proper perspective, we need to examine the government's responsibility for creating the conditions that brought Europeans and Hispanics here. It would be inaccurate to portray the Europeans who sought this country as an escape from deprivation—and, in some cases, persecution—as entirely voluntary immigrants. It would be equally inaccurate to regard the United States government as a passive host to uninvited visitors. Immigrant labor was needed to work the factories and the mines and, in its familiar role as broker for capital and industry, the government wanted the immigration.[26] This was true then and remains true for the contemporary immigrant.

One important difference, however, is the limited role of the United States in creating the conditions of deprivation and persecution that prompted emigration from Europe. The federal government's contribution to world economic conditions then was small, and its role as a military power smaller yet. The presence of Hispanics in the United States, on the other hand, is to a much greater degree a consequence of U.S. government actions. Chicanos and Puerto Ricans are part of this country's population today because of the government's armed takeover of Mexican (1848) and Spanish (1898) territories. Unlike Europeans who traveled to the United States in the nineteenth and early twentieth centuries, Chicanos and Puerto Ricans were already living in territories annexed by the United States.

In the case of true immigrant Hispanics from Latin America, our government's role in creating the conditions they are leaving is larger than it was in the case of Europe. To be sure, socioeconomic conditions in Latin America are not entirely the making of "el imperialismo yanqui." The final, fateful step of immigration is an individual decision for which the immigrant bears ultimate responsibility. Still, the role of the U.S. government in sustaining a structure of privilege and a pattern of economic development that leads to emigration from Latin America is sadly familiar.[27] Thus Ecuadorians on Long Island, Hondurans in New Orleans, or Chicanos in Colorado can more readily attribute their presence here to the U.S. government than the Ukrainian, Sicilian, or Croatian immigrants of times past.

The greater premigration involvement of the U.S. government with Hispanics than with Europeans extends beyond territorial and economic colonialism to government activities that touch directly on education. The government had little involvement in the education or language policies of the countries from which the Europeans migrated. The opposite is true in the case of many Hispanics. For instance, after annexing Puerto Rico from Spain in 1898, the United States established English as the obligatory language for the children of people who knew nothing of the Anglophone world. Against bitter local opposition, the injunction against Spanish in schools was firmly enforced until 1952.[28]

There is little point in limiting discussion of U.S. government involvement in the life of Hispanics to the period since the advent of federally funded bilingual education. The involvement goes back a long way and includes, in the case of Puerto Rico, tax dollars spent to forcibly keep children from using their language in school. That the effort was only partially successful is a tribute to the tenacity and pride of Puerto Ricans.

These considerations should not be construed as promoting bilingual programs as compensation for past and present U.S. government actions. Rather, they argue for a more balanced view of history and government than is generally found in discussions of bilingual education. When we choose to look at current U.S. spending with a historian's view, we cannot help but notice government dollars being spent for purposes of developing children's native languages, promoting literacy, and encouraging cultural development—efforts that have become necessary in good measure to rectify past practices. In short, the familiar comparison between Europeans and Hispanics fails because it attempts to make a historical point while disregarding history.

An even more serious misunderstanding among critics of bilingual programs is their misconception of the government's role in education. No matter what people may think of diversity, assimilation, and cultural pluralism, strong objections to bilingual education are evoked when the question of cost is raised. Critics may argue that bilingual programs may be worthy of private support, but government, particularly

415

the federal government, should not support the teaching of languages other than English. Bilingualism, they argue, leads to little tangible educational improvement and increases the risk of de facto segregation and social tensions.[29] Given the current federal approach that has been characterized as "a significant cutting of educational expenditures for the poor and the handicapped and those minority groups that are bilingual,"[30] it is important to spell out the assumptions underlying this argument.

Instead of advocating a process through which current power arrangements evolve into new alignments, these critics appear to view politics and funding decisions as a procedure by which permanent arrangements are maintained. Such a perspective assigns an immutable role to government. This, in turn, makes possible an indictment of Hispanics and other minorities, not for wanting bilingual education, but for wanting the government to pay for it.[31]

The realization that funding decisions are the result of a political process and thus subject to constant revision and changes in power is a strong argument against this position. The objection to a policy on the grounds that it represents a change in one's conception of the role of the government runs counter to the democratic process. The heart of a democratic polity is precisely the articulation of change in the role of government and the adjudication of that change. In deciding whether federal expenditures for bilingual education are justified, it is simply not enough to rely on an inviolate conception of the government's role. We would be well served to remember that there is no absolute standard by which to judge the appropriateness of federal expenditure, or the magnitude of that expenditure. We have no strict criteria by which to assess whether bilingual programs should be funded by private sources only, or whether they are a public responsibility. If one believes that bilingual education belongs only in ethnic schools funded by the private resources of the community, then of course, bilingual programs that receive federal funds and operate in public schools are grossly overfunded. But if one believes that bilingual programs do belong in public schools and are legitimate recipients of public funds, then the programs are grossly underfunded, since they account for less than 2 percent of the federal education budget.[32] The process by which we address these questions is dependent on a changing political and cultural context, a context that has been subject to stereotyping and oversimplification.

The greatest oversimplification in this regard has been the assumption that private and public fundings of large American institutions are distinctly separate. In this view, private institutions such as business corporations derive the freedom to do as they please from their ability to pay their own way. Public institutions on the other hand must be supervised closely as they are supported by the tax monies of citizens. This notion reflects a naïve view. Just as large business corporations could not operate without government research and development funds, contracts, and investment, so would private education find it difficult to exist without government support. A recent Brookings Institution study estimated that public support of private colleges and universities amounts to approximately 45 percent of their direct and indirect educational and general operating costs.[33] Federal education funds aimed at providing remedial services in the United States flow to both public and private schools.[34] Criticism of educational programs supported by public financing must be examined in comparison to other uses of government funds or become subject to traditional American folk prejudices and to current political beliefs. Unless a case can be made for public support of the interests of so many private institutions while denying the interests of linguistic minorities, the argument is without force.

The history of education includes a long and controversial debate surrounding the issue of tax monies for education. After years of argument the issue is yet to be resolved, as illustrated by the recent debate about educational vouchers. People who speak foreign languages or practice different religions have traditionally used the political process to claim their share of tax money for the schooling of their children. There are remarkable parallels to the nineteenth-century argument that schools that excluded Catholic doctrine could not provide a real education to Irish children and were thus not truly public schools. The contemporary claim that schools excluding the Spanish language and Hispanic culture cannot provide a real education to Hispanic children is the modern version of the same argument. One can reject either or both of these claims, but one cannot do so by appealing to a historical consensus on uses of public funds for education as such a consensus has never existed.[35]

Much of the criticism of a government role in bilingual education trades on the unstated principle that English is the natural language of the country. Departure from this norm becomes the object of hard-nosed scrutiny. There is in fact no such federal or educational norm. The status of English in the United States is simply one of practical de facto reality, and is not supported by a federal mandate or constitutional amendment. Examples of government agencies spending public funds involving languages other than English are easy to find. For instance, on Hispanic radio stations in New York City the U.S. Army runs a recruitment campaign in Spanish paid for by federal dollars. Other federal dollars pay for thousands of signs in Spanish that encourage the use of food stamps in supermarkets throughout the land. The same allocations that pay for instruction in Spanish for Hispanic children in the United States paid for U.S. government led and sponsored instruction in Spanish in Fort Gulick, Panama, for "counter-insurgency" police agents in Latin America. This "School of the Americas" switched to Spanish as the medium of instruction in hopes of attracting more students, reasoning that it made little sense to instruct security agents in a language they did not understand.[36] Many of those who begrudge the cost of teaching children in Spanish here, knowingly or unknowingly seem willing to pay for instruction in Spanish for the henchmen of regimes that perpetuate the very social conditions that send these children's parents to the United States looking for a respite from poverty and oppression.

The suggestion that English is the "natural" language for government and education overlooks the long U.S. tradition of private ethnic schools. As of 1960, there were 2,000 such schools in this country, half of which used a language other than English as the medium of instruction. Their number is increasing, as is use of the mother tongue.[37] In addition, mention must be made of private colleges situated along the southern borders of the country that have recently attracted affluent Latin American students by offering technical and business courses in Spanish while the students learn English.[38] This is the same classic model of transitional bilingual education that is viewed with great skepticism when applied to these students' less fortunate compatriots who attend elementary and secondary public schools.

These manifestations of the American tradition in bilingual education are indispensable to an understanding of federally funded bilingual programs. When we see all levels of government use Spanish as a more practical medium to reach a large audience, use of the language in schools should not seem surprising. When we see that bilingual programs have been financed by the federal government when it suited military purposes, financing of programs for educational purposes does not seem so strange. When we see that English is not, nor has it ever been, the exclusive language of U.S. education, use of Spanish in public schools today does not seem so revolutionary. And when we see private institutions teaching courses in Spanish to attract fee-paying Hispanics, the English-only principle emerges as one applied only to institutions that cannot afford to have the principle waived.

The oversimplifications that surround discussions of bilingual education regarding historical, political, governmental, and linguistic issues are frequently compounded by a misguided approach to race and legal status. In the discussion thus far, juxtaposition of the Hispanic experience and that of European migrants was made to counter the strategy offered by critics of bilingual education programs and to provide a more careful analysis of the issue. Unlike the European immigrants, the majority of Hispanics residing in this country were born in the continental United States or in Puerto Rico.[39] They are, therefore, citizens by birth. In addition, Hispanics are mostly regarded by the larger society not simply as white members of a different ethnic group, as were the European immigrants, but as nonwhite members of a different race. Thus demands for use of Spanish in the schools must not be seen as demands made by foreigners but as coming from native-born Americans who dissent from generally held views on education. As such Hispanics are entitled to consideration of their political views within the American tradition of respect and encouragement of dissent.

To the extent that bilingual programs help to maintain communication in Spanish among Hispanic children, they may also curb the process of assimilation by identifying Hispanics as a distinct group. Conventional wisdom holds that as long as a group remains distinguished from the larger society, its members will remain poor. Because of their experience with racism in this country, many Hispanics have long ago given up the hope of disappearing as a distinct group.[40] The experience of blacks, who are the monolingual Americans with whom they are most in contact, is a lesson about melting into the larger society. Correlations between language and color among Hispanics lend credence to these speculations, as darker-skinned Hispanics tend to retain Spanish longer than those of lighter complexions.[41] The current demand for Spanish in the schools is an attempt to transform a problem into an asset. The problem is that people who had never regarded themselves as nonwhites now discover that they are not only members of an ethnic minority but of a racial minority too. Bilingual education affirms the distinctness of a different language and culture. The daily evidence of people of widely varying appearance identifying themselves as members of the same group tends to invest their language and their culture with a sense of nurturance and acceptance to withstand the dual pressure of immigration and racism.

Finally, the oversimplifications that characterize the bilingual education debate are most insidious with regard to the popular belief that the preservation of languages other than English in this nation plants the seed of social strife. Language alone is seldom the cause of unrest. History points to religious and economic differences as far more divisive than language. The worst strife of this multilingual country in the nineteenth century was the Civil War, fought along lines that had nothing to do with language. The Spanish Civil War was fought in a multilingual country by factions that did not correspond to language groups. The struggle between Catholics and Protestants in Ireland rages on despite their common language. Rivalries between Hindus and Moslems in India are only tangentially related to linguistic differences. And in Canada, French and English distinctions map onto social class differences that are as important as the language difference in explaining conflict between the groups.[42]

The variety of school activities subsumed under the term bilingual education in the United States makes it difficult to offer conclusive generalizations about bilingual education as a force for social cohesion or disintegration. Insofar as bilingual education has anything at all to do with this issue, its effects are likely to fall on the side of integration and social peace. Experience has shown that where no bilingual program exists Hispanic parents are less likely to approach the school and talk with teachers, that children are neglected by their teachers and tend to drop out, and that little effort is made to teach them English, preferring instead to classify them as slow learners or retarded. Indeed, these and other evils provided the impetus for bilingual education in the first place.[43]

Through instruction in Spanish and special efforts to teach English, bilingual programs have helped lower the dropout rates in many schools.[44] They have established an important link between the school and the home, as well as provided evidence to parents and students that their language is important. The emphasis given English in these programs is of particular interest, since it represents an explicit, concentrated, and large-scale effort to teach English literacy to foreign-speaking populations during the school day. The integrative effect is likely to far outweigh the fragmentation of these activities.

In any case, I do not suggest, as do some critics, that all the effort and resources should be devoted to the English component of these programs, ignoring the support that promotes the native tongue and culture. The political energy that produced bilingual education and the money to pay for it were generated for programs that, at least in principle, included the native language component. These energies would probably have dissipated if English were the only goal. Now that Hispanics and others have chosen a bilingual route for incorporation into the larger society, the odds of enticing support for English-only programs appear very small. Critics of bilingual education with a concern for civil order and social harmony should also concern themselves with issues of poverty, unemployment, and racial discrimination rather than concentrate on the use of Spanish in schools. In pledges of allegiance, it is liberty and justice—not English—for all that is to keep us indivisible.

There is great irony in the argument that bilingual education will keep Hispanics poor or discriminated against, for this is frequently the only argument rooted in a sense of the social good. This notion of what is good for society tends to preserve the status quo. For Hispanics who are poor, this offers little choice but to take their assigned places—with little command of English, with poorly developed Spanish, and with little sense of their common culture—within the present structure of powerlessness and poverty. That they should develop little enthusiasm for this position is not difficult to understand.

## Notes

1. See, for instance, survey data showing grassroots support for bilingual education among Puerto Ricans in New York in Language Policy Task Force, "Social Dimensions of Language Use in East Harlem," *Centro Working Papers*, No. 7 (1980). Centro de Estudios Puertorriqueños, City University of New York.

2. For examples of support from local boards, see statements from officials in the school boards in New York City, Dena Kleiman, "Views Vary on Approach to a Bilingual Education," *New York Times*, 3 Mar. 1979; and in San Diego, "San Diego Schools Reaffirm Support of Bilingual Education," *Forum*, 4, No. 7 (1981), 5; from national politicians, see Senator Edward Kennedy's speech to the 1981 Convention of the National Association for Bilingual Education reported in "Senator Kennedy Addresses NABE Convention," *NABE News*, 4, No. 5 (1981), p. 1; from foundations, see Alan Pifer, "Bilingual Education and the Hispanic Challenge," *Annual Report of the President of the Carnegie Corporation of New York* (New York: Carnegie Corporation, 1980).

3. See "In Plain English," Editorial, *New York Times*, 10 Oct. 1981; James Reston, "Reagan Against the Hispanics, *New York Times*, 4 Feb. 1981; "Bilingual Education and Federal Duty," Editorial, *New York Times*, 4 Feb. 1981; "Many Voices, But One Language," Editorial, *New York Times*, 12 Aug. 1979; and "Bilingual Goal, In Plain English," Editorial, *New York Times*, 26 Nov. 1976.

4. Noel Epstein, *Language, Ethnicity, and the Schools: Policy Alternatives for Bilingual-Bicultural Education* (Washington, D.C.: Institute for Educational Leadership, 1977); also, Richard Rodriguez, *Hunger of Memory: The Education of Richard Rodriguez* (Boston: Godine, 1981).

5. The HEW Memorandum, "Task Force Findings Specifying Remedies Available for Eliminating Past Educational Practices Ruled Unlawful under *Lau v. Nichols*," Office for Civil Rights, U.S. Dept. of Health, Education and Welfare, Summer 1975, known as the "Lau Remedies," contained regulations intended to help school districts comply with the Supreme Court decision of Lau v. Nichols, 414 US 563 (1974). These regulations were cancelled in 1981. For discussion of the regulations, see Shirley W. Hufstedler, "On Bilingual Education, Civil Rights, and Language Minority Regulations," *NABE Journal* 5 (1980), 63–71.

6. See "U.S. Education Chief Bars Bilingual Plan for Public Schools," *New York Times*, 3 Feb. 1981; and "Reagan Denounces Carter's Proposed Rules on Bilingual Education," *Washington Post*, 4 Mar. 1981.

7. The view of the American Federation of Teachers is best represented by the tone of articles and comments that appear in the *American Teacher*, such as "Bilingual Rules Draw Protest from Union," **65**, No. 2 (1980), 1. At a more local level, however, the UFT-sponsored column by Albert Shanker in the *New York Times* runs articles with titles such as "Bilingual Education Must be Expanded," 28 May 1978. The view of some administrators is reflected in articles in *The Executive Educator*, such as one by Louise Dyer, "Bilingual-Bicultural Education Is Ineffective and Ill-Considered," Jan. 1980, p. 44. For other bilingual opponents see, for example, Dick Dougherty, "The Kid Who Talked Funny," *The Courier News*, 2 Nov. 1979; and Mauricio Molina, "Less Spanish Please," *New York Times*, 12 Mar. 1980.

8. For discussion of varieties of classroom practices, see William Mackey, "A Typology of Bilingual

Education," in *Bilingual Schooling in the United States: A Source Book for Educational Personnel*, ed. Francesco Cordasco (New York: McGraw-Hill, 1976), pp. 72–90; for details of language use in bilingual programs, see Dorothy Legarreta, "Language Choice in the Bilingual Classroom," *TESOL Quarterly*, **11** (1977), 9–16; for varieties of approaches to bilingual education that have received federal sanction and federal funds, see discussion of the program in Fairfax County, Virginia in Fred Hechinger, "U.S. Ruling Fuels Controversy Over Bilingual Teaching," *New York Times*, 20 Jan. 1981.

9. For the claim that bilingual programs reduce rather than increase language maintenance when run according to federal regulations, see Joshua Fishman, "Minority Language Maintenance and the Ethnic Mother Tongue School," *Modern Language Journal*, **64** (1980), 167–173; but for some contradictory evidence, see Andrew Cohen, "Bilingual Schooling and Spanish Language Maintenance: An Experimental Analysis," *The Bilingual Review*, **2** (1975), 3–13; for discussion of the conceptual flaws of the attempt to "maintain" the child's home language, see Ricardo Otheguy and Ruth Otto, "The Myth of Static Maintenance in Bilingual Education," *Modern Language Journal*, **64** (1980), 350–357; for details on different views by practitioners, see survey by William Clarkson, "The Vernacular versus Standard Spanish in the Bilingual Classroom," *Hispania*, **60** (1971), 965–967; and the more informal sampling of views by Kleiman, "Views Vary on Approach to a Bilingual Education."

10. Abigail Thernstrom, "E Pluribus Plura: Congress and Bilingual Education," *The Public Interest*, No. 60 (1980), p. 21.

11. See Shirley W. Braun, "Bilingual Education, Old and New Style in a New York School District," *The Bilingual Review*, **2** (1975), 248–258; and William Mackey, "A Typology of Bilingual Education," in *Bilingual Schooling in the United States*, ed. Cordasco, p. 72.

12. The increase in support of bilingual programs from sources other than the federal government is seen, for instance, in the enactment since 1968 of 26 state laws mandating or permitting bilingual programs. See José E. Vega, "The Enactment of Bilingual Bicultural Education in Texas," in *Bilingual Education and Public Policy in the United States*, ed. Raymond V. Padilla (Ypsilanti: Eastern Michigan Univ. Dept. of Foreign Languages and Bilingual Studies, 1979), p. 109. This non-federal support can also be seen in the figures on numbers of bilingual teachers hired by large local school systems such as New York. In 1970 the Community School Districts of New York City employed 798 bilingual teachers, who constituted 1.4 percent of all teachers. By 1976 the number had more than doubled to 1,678 teachers who made up 3.6 percent of all teachers. See Lois Saxelby Steinberg, "The Bilingual Education Act and the Puerto Rican Community: The Politics of Implementing Federal Policy at the Local Level," in *Bilingual Education and Public Policy*, ed. Padilla, p. 170. By 1980 the number of bilingual teachers had risen to 2,000. See speech by Awilda Orta, Director, Office of Bilingual Education, New York City Board of Education, to the Bilingual Education Service Center, Hunter College, New York, 15 May 1981.

13. Lau v. Nichols.

14. The range and diversity of bilingual programs is reflected in nationwide allocations for basic grants under Title VII of the Elementary and Secondary Education Act. These allocations cover eleven different language groups. The highest allocation, as of 1979, had gone to Spanish (75.9 percent of all allocations) and the lowest to Arabic (0.23 percent). See National Clearinghouse for Bilingual Education, U.S. Office of Education, *Strengthening Bilingual Education: A Report from the Commissioner to the Congress and the President* (Rosslyn, Va.: Inter America Research Associates, June 1979), p. 5. The diversity found at the national level is also reflected in local figures. In the schools of New York City there are 85,000 children considered to be of limited English proficiency. Of them, 79 percent speak Spanish, 5 percent Chinese, 2.5 percent Haitian, 2.2 percent Italian, 2 percent Russian, 1.6 percent Greek, 1.4 percent Korean, and 1 percent Vietnamese, with 5.3 percent speaking other languages. See "Percent of Limited English Proficient Students by Ethnic/Language Groups Enrolled in New York City Public Schools, 1980–1981," in *Language Summary Information for Consent Decree-Lau Programs, Annual Statistics*, New York City Office of Bilingual Education, Center for Program Planning and Development. For figures on percentage of Hispanic children attending bilingual programs nationwide, see Susan G. Schneider, *Revolution, Reaction or Reform: The 1974 Bilingual Education Act* (New York: Las Americas Publishing, 1976), p. 6.

15. See National Clearinghouse for Bilingual Education, U.S. Office of Education, *Strengthening Bilingual Education*, p. 5.

16. Steven Teitelbaum, Letter, *New York Times*, 25 Feb. 1979.

17. Epstein, *Language, Ethnicity and the Schools*, p. 20.

18. Colin Greer, *The Great School Legend* (New York: Basic Books, 1972), p. 130; Irving Howe, *World*

*of Our Fathers* (New York: Harcourt Brace Jovanovich, 1976), p. 143; Diane Ravitch, *The Revisionists Revised* (New York: Basic Books, 1978), p. 73.

19. For the chronologies of monolingualism, level of education, and attainment of economic integration, see Joshua Fishman, *Bilingual Education: An International Sociological Perspective* (Rowley, Mass.: Newbury House, 1976), p. 15; and Thomas Sowell, *Race and Economics* (New York: David McKay, 1975), pp. 163; 207. See also Greer, *Great School Legend*, pp. 38; 83.

20. Fishman, *Bilingual Education: An International Sociological Perspective*, p. 15; and Sowell, *Race and Economics*, pp. 163; 207.

21. Even as late as 1910, 23.8 percent of people over the age of 25 had received less than five years of schooling, a figure which is down to 4.2 percent for 1970. As late as 1924, the dropout rate at grade eight was 25.9 percent of those who had finished fifth grade, a figure which was less than 1 percent by 1970. See National Center for Education Statistics, *Digest of Education Statistics* (Washington, D.C.: GPO, 1978), p. 14.

22. Joshua Fishman, *Language Loyalty in the United States* (The Hague: Mouton, 1966), p. 233.

23. U.S. Dept. of Commerce, *Statistical Abstract of the United States: 1977* (Washington, D.C.: GPO), pp. 34; 83; U.S. Census Bureau, *Historical Statistics of the U.S.: Colonial Times to 1970* (Washington, D.C.: GPO, 1975), p. 117; National Center for Education Statistics, *The Condition of Education* (Washington, D.C.: GPO, 1978), p. 37.

24. Howe, *World of Our Fathers*, p. 58.

25. For figures on the education of all children, see National Center for Education Statistics, *The Condition of Education*, table 2.22, p. 94; and U.S. Dept. of Commerce, *Statistical Abstract of the United States: 1977*, table 219, p. 137. For figures on the education of European immigrants, see Leonard Ayres, *Laggards in Our Schools* (New York: Survey Associates, 1913), p. 105; Raymond Callahan, *Education and the Cult of Efficiency* (Chicago: Univ. of Chicago Press, 1962), p. 42; and Francesco Cordasco, *Immigrant Children in American Schools* (Fairfield, N.J.: Kelley, 1976), p. 35. For figures on employment for Hispanics, see U.S. Dept. of Commerce, *Statistical Abstract of the United States: 1977*, table 639, p. 394; and table 642, p. 395. For figures on employment for European immigrants, see Isaac Hourwich, *Immigration and Labor* (New York: Putnam's, 1912; rpt. New York: Arno Press and *New York Times*, 1969), p. 127.

26. On efforts to recruit immigrants on the part of both federal and state governments, see Heinz Kloss, *The American Bilingual Tradition* (Rowley, Mass.: Newbury House, 1977), p. 84.

27. For the large part that the U.S. government and U.S. corporations have played in the economic underdevelopment of Latin America, see, for instance, Penny Lernoux, *Cry of the People* (New York: Penguin Books, 1980), esp. pp. 203–281. For a carefully argued case on U.S. responsibility for creating the conditions that led to immigration from Puerto Rico to the United States after World War II, see Manuel Maldonado-Denís, *Puerto Rico: Una Interpretación Histórico-Social* (México, D.F.: Siglo XXI Editores, 1969). For a similar argument about immigration from the Dominican Republic, see Lernoux, *Cry of the People*, pp. 236–247.

28. Manuel Maldonado-Denís, *Puerto Rico y Estados Unidos: Emigración y Colonialismo* (México, D.F.: Siglo XXI Editores, 1976), p. 123.

29. See for example, James Reston, "Reagan and the Hispanics," *New York Times*, 4 Feb. 1981; Philip W. Quigg, "Speaking the Same Language," *Newsweek*, 16 Oct. 1978; Jonathan Donald, Letter, *New York Times*, 20 Aug. 1979.

30. Martin Carnoy, "Proposed Education Budget Cuts by the Reagan Administration," in *A Balanced Budget for the People: Comments on the Reagan Budget* (Washington, D.C.: Institute for Policy Studies, 1981), p. 6.

31. For discussion of this "management" approach to government and its impact on bilingual education, see Christina Paulston, "Viewpoint: Research," in *Bilingual Education: Current Perspectives* (Washington, D.C.: Center for Applied Linguistics, 1977); and her *Bilingual Education Theories and Issues* (Rowley, Mass.: Newbury House, 1980), p. 39.

32. Josue Gonzalez, former director, Office of Bilingual Education, U.S. Department of Education. Information session at the Title VII Management Conference of 13 Jan. 1981, Washington, D.C.

33. Susan C. Nelson, "Financial Trends and Issues," in *Public Policy in Private Higher Education*, ed. David W. Breneman and Chester E. Finn, Jr. (Washington, D.C.: Brookings Institution, 1978), p. 105.

34. *New York Times*, 20 June 1979.

35. Diane Ravitch, *The Great School Wars* (New York: Basic Books, 1974), pp. 3–33; 46–47.

36. *New York Times*, 1 July 1978.

37. Joshua Fishman, "The Social Science Perspective," in *Bilingual Education: Current Perspectives*, p. 25.

38. Cecilia Beecher, "The New Mexico State University Spanish-Speaking Masters Program," *TESOL Quarterly,* **8** (1974), 79–81.
39. Dorothy Waggoner, "Non-English Language Background Persons: Three U.S. Surveys," *TESOL Quarterly,* **12** (1978), 247–263.
40. For an explicit equation of ethnic isolation among Hispanics with lack of economic advancement, see Alan Pifer, "Bilingual Education and the Hispanic Challenge," in *Annual Report of the President of the Carnegie Corporation of New York* (New York: Carnegie Corporation, 1980), p. 10. For a statement that mobility in other immigrants was derived at least in part from interacting with people outside their group, see Fishman, *Bilingual Education: An International Sociological Perspective,* p. 13; and Kloss, *American Bilingual Tradition,* p. 283.
41. Sowell, *Race and Economics,* p. 111.
42. See Alison d'Angeljan and Lisa M. Simand, "Bilingualism in Quebec: A Changing Perspective," in *Bilingual Education,* ed. Herman La Fontaine, Barry Persky and Leonard Golubchick (Wayne, N.J.: Avery Publishing Group, 1978), p. 122.
43. For the treatment of Hispanic children in schools without bilingual programs, and their frequent relegation to classes for slow learners, see U.S. Commission on Civil Rights, *Puerto Ricans in the United States: An Uncertain Future* (Washington, D.C.: GPO, 1976); and Jane Mercer, "A Policy Statement on Assessment Procedures and the Rights of Children," *Harvard Educational Review,* **44** (1974), 125–141. For the involvement of parents in bilingual programs, see *The Prospects for Bilingual Education in the Nation,* 5th Annual Report of the National Advisory Council for Bilingual Education, 1980–1981, pp. 49–52. For a critical appraisal of the effectiveness of parental participation in bilingual programs, see Rodolfo Rodriguez, "Citizen Participation in Selected Bilingual Education Advisory Committees," *NABE Journal,* **5** (1980–1981), 1–23; and Hermes T. Cervantes, Leonard Baca, and Daniel Torres, "Community Involvement in Bilingual Education: The Bilingual Educator as Parent Trainer," *NABE Journal,* **3** (1979), 73–83.
44. For the benefits of bilingual instruction in such areas as lower drop-out rate as well as in language development and academic achievement, see Christina Paulston, *Bilingual Education Theories and Issues,* p. 41; Rudolph Troike, "Research Evidence for the Effectiveness of Bilingual Education," *NABE Journal,* **3** (1978), 13–24; Paul Rossier and Wayne Holm, *The Rock Point Experience: A Longitudinal Study of a Navajo School Program* (Washington, D.C.: Center for Applied Linguistics, 1980), p. 41; *Prospects for Bilingual Education in the Nation,* pp. 5–14; Laraine T. Zappert and B. Roberto Cruz, *Bilingual Education: An Appraisal of Empirical Research* (Berkeley: Bay Area Bilingual Education League, 1977).

423

# 15

# Transitional Bilingual Education and the Socialization of Immigrants

DAVID SPENER
*University of Texas, Austin*

*David Spener focuses his argument on the role of transitional bilingual education (TBE) programs for immigrants with regard to U.S. governmental policies, the economy, and the employment situation. According to Spener, TBE programs provide only a limited period of native-language instruction and do not guarantee English mastery. Thus, these programs often prevent children from attaining fluency in either their native languages or in English. Spener argues that, as a result, immigrants are only prepared to fill the menial labor positions that are needed by society.*

Controversy abounds in this country regarding the education of immigrant children in the public schools. Specifically, this controversy has centered upon the language, or languages, to be used in the instruction of language-minority students. Both advocates and opponents of bilingual education make many claims about the relative merits of English-only instruction versus the use of the students' mother tongue (Cummins, 1984; Gersten & Woodward, 1985; Hakuta, 1986; Ovando & Collier, 1985). Some light can be shed on this debate by looking beyond the immediate issue of language use in the classroom to the role of immigrants to the United States in general. This article will first examine the economic and social situation of immigrants and other minorities in the United States, and then, with this context established, will examine the role of transitional bilingual education in the socialization of immigrants and ethnolinguistic minorities.

Those concerned about how public school students achieve their individual or familial goals in society cannot ignore the reverse side of educational policy: that is,

*Harvard Educational Review* Vol. 58 No. 2 May 1988, 133–153

how well the educational system prepares students to be able to perform tasks and occupy the social roles necessary to the social, political, and economic functioning of society. Educational policy at the macro level deserves scrutiny in conjunction with other aspects of governmental policy: By viewing the educational system as serving the needs of society instead of the individual student, we implicitly recognize that educational policy is not only related to, but is, in fact, largely determined by economic, social, and political factors.

Education is an integral part of the socialization process. It is future-oriented in that it prepares students to function productively in the niches of the social structures they will occupy as adults. As a part of the socialization process, education depends upon the features of the wider society—economic, technological, and political—for its direction. These features interact to form the *opportunity structure* of the society, that is, the array of social and economic positions open for a given individual to occupy on the basis of his or her particular socialization (Ogbu, 1978). How individuals confront society's opportunity structure may vary greatly, both in terms of starting position and degree of social mobility. How, then, immigrants to the United States confront its opportunity structure has important implications both for educational policy regarding immigrants and for their achievement levels in the educational system.

## The Role of Minorities in the U.S. Economy

The notion of the existence of an opportunity structure in U.S. society assumes that in order for available social and economic slots to be filled by appropriately "qualified" individuals, the nature of the structure itself must somehow be communicated to society members. It is the job of the family and the school to equip youth with the skills, knowledge, attitudes, and personal attributes for both high- and low-status social roles as adults, so that all slots are filled and all necessary societal functions are served. Moreover, the skills, knowledge, attitudes, and personal attributes that determine a low-status position in this society must be differentiated from those suitable for a high-status position. Given this, and assuming that all the slots are in some sense "necessary," it follows that some individuals must be socialized to occupy high-status positions, while others must be socialized or adapted to fill low-status positions. Under these differential socialization processes certain groups can be specially socialized to occupy certain positions in society. Indeed, historically, it has been the case that individuals from racial, ethnic, and linguistic minority groups have tended to occupy low-status positions in our society.

The perceptions of both immigrant and majority groups concerning opportunities in U.S. society for immigrant groups who are also members of racial and ethnolinguistic minorities matter in two ways. First, how both parents and children perceive the opportunities open to them in society and the combination of knowledge, skills, and behaviors that must be acquired in order to take advantage of them has an effect on how children are trained. Levine (1967) has posited two hypotheses about how children acquire the attributes for upward social mobility within the opportunity structure. In one, he suggests that parents of socially mobile children train them to adopt the attributes of a "successful" person in the society, thus helping their children to gain access to high-status positions. In the other, he proposes that children develop accurate perceptions of the possibilities for social advancement in response to differing "messages" received from society and adapt their behavior accordingly. Both of these hypotheses assume that social mobility depends on an individual's ability to adapt to the norm for mobility (Levine, 1967, cited in Ogbu, 1978).

Secondly, the perceptions of the majority group in society regarding minority group members are important, because in a society such as the United States the members of the majority White group control the opportunity structure. In his book *Minority Education and Caste: The American System in Cross-Cultural Perspective,* John U. Ogbu (1978) discusses discrimination against minority groups in terms of their socialization through public education. He describes situations in which groups controlling the opportunity structure ascribe to members of different minority groups only those attributes specific to low-status social and economic situations. If such ascription is intense, it creates an invisible but effective job ceiling above which it may be extremely difficult to rise. Ogbu goes on to contrast the different kinds of minority groups that may be present in a society and the ways in which their relation to the opportunity structure may vary according to their relative ascribed status and their perception of that status. Additionally, he distinguishes between caste-like minorities and immigrant minorities.

## Caste-like Minorities and Immigrant Minorities

According to Ogbu (1978), members of caste-like minorities are perceived by the majority group to be inherently inferior in all aspects of intelligence and ability to carry out the tasks associated with high-status jobs. They "enjoy" a pariah status which sharply circumscribes their economic, political, and cultural participation in society. Members of caste-like minorities do not compete freely with majority group members but, instead, are summarily excluded from certain jobs solely because of their caste status. Thus, they occupy the least desirable positions in society and face job ceilings which only a few may surmount. Children of caste-minority parents may be socialized for inferiority based on their parents' and their own perceptions of the adult statuses open to them. In addition, public schools may play subtle roles in educating and socializing caste-minority children for low-status positions as adults. Such "inferiorating" education can result from the following causes: negative teacher attitudes and expectations toward these children; teachers recruited from the majority group who are isolated from the minority community, thus inhibiting parent/teacher collaboration in the children's education; biased testing, misclassification of students as learning disabled, and ability group "tracking"; biased textbooks and curricula; use of clinical definitions of caste-minority children's academic problems which place the blame on the minority family for producing "inferior" children; and classroom dynamics that favor the more active participation of majority-group children (Cummins, 1984; McDermott, 1976; Ogbu, 1978). In addition to these factors

426

are the more commonly cited problems of overcrowding, decaying facilities, and drug abuse found in many schools with primarily minority children.

In Ogbu's classification scheme, immigrant minorities may be treated by the majority group in the host society much the same as caste-like minorities. That is, their political, economic, and social roles are circumscribed, and they face job ceilings similar to those for caste-minority members. Members of immigrant minorities, however, may react to the same opportunity structure in ways very different from caste-like minorities. Since a common reason members of immigrant minorities come to this country is to improve their condition relative to what they experienced in their homelands, they come into contact with the opportunity structure voluntarily. One of their personal measures of success, then, is not whether they have achieved parity in status with the majority group of the host society, but whether their situation has improved materially by immigrating—in which case, the member of an immigrant minority may actually accept discrimination as the price for personal advancement.

Furthermore, as strangers who may have established their own separate communities in the host country, immigrants are not as likely as native-born minorities to internalize the host society's caste ideology. Consequently, members of immigrant minorities may hold instrumental attitudes toward the host society, seeing it as a means to an end while holding on to either the hope of steady relative advance within it, or an improved economic position upon returning to the home country (Ogbu, 1978). Parents' instrumentalist attitudes toward the society in general may carry over to their children in school, who may see more immediate value in their education than caste-minority students whose families may not expect to advance.

There are several problems with Ogbu's caste-like versus immigrant minority dichotomy in describing the current situation for immigrants in the United States. First is the issue of race, which is noted but not fully developed in Ogbu's analysis. For Ogbu, the major caste-like minority in the United States is, of course, Black people, who constitute a pariah group whose main identifying characteristic is race. But Ogbu does not explicitly discuss the racial background of immigrant minorities in his classification scheme. This is an important omission, since historical experience in the United States has demonstrated that assignments of immigrant groups to low-status positions in the opportunity structure have often been made primarily upon the basis of race. During past waves of immigration to this country from Europe, the outward ethnolinguistic markers of immigrant minorities have disappeared after one or two generations. But for current immigrants from the Third World, race will not escape them even after linguistic and cultural barriers to their advancement have been overcome. The vast majority of those currently immigrating to the United States are non-White people from Latin America, the Caribbean, and Asia (Cockcroft, 1986; Dulles, 1966; Moyers, 1985; U.S. English, 1985).

Many current immigrants, especially Latin Americans, are racially and linguistically "lumped" by the White majority with Chicanos and Puerto Ricans, who, along with the Chinese in some areas, have become caste-like minorities by establishing themselves permanently in the United States over the course of several generations. For example, the experiences of Chicanos and Puerto Ricans show that, over time, immigrant minorities may become caste-like minorities who share a pariah status with Black people based principally on their race. The phenomenon of "lumping" new immigrants with ethnically similar caste minorities undermines Ogbu's contention that the children of immigrants may have a better chance at higher rates of success in school on the basis of their purported instrumentalist attitudes toward education. Failure to look at the racial background of immigrants also ignores the relatively ascribed statuses among different groups of recent immigrants. Numerous reports appear in the press comparing "successful" immigrant groups with those in the process of becoming caste-like minorities. Thus, "Korean-ness" may come to carry a positive racial stereotype, whereas "Mexican-ness" may come to be stigmatized (Matthews, 1985).

It is also important to consider other changes in the nature of immigration to this country. One difference is that a large number of new immigrants to the United States are coming not so much to better their economic situation as to escape war and physical repression in their native countries in Central America, Indochina, and the Caribbean. Because of their experiences of violence and physical and emotional trauma, they may have different aspirations and adapt themselves to the opportunity structure here in ways that are quite different from both established caste minorities and traditional immigrant groups. How these new refugees are received also differs. Some are welcomed with open arms by the U.S. government, while others live under constant threat of deportation by the Immigration and Naturalization Service (INS). Indochinese refugees, for example, are clearly being sent a different message about the array of opportunities open to them in this society than are Central American or Haitian refugees. Indochinese (who are not policed by the INS, need not fear deportation, and are eligible for public assistance) are recognized as victims of Communist aggression and are welcome in this country, while Central Americans and Haitians (who are policed by the INS, have reason to fear deportation, and are not eligible for any kind of public assistance) are perceived as taking away jobs from U.S. citizens (MacEoin & Riley, 1982).

The nature of economically motivated immigration itself has also changed since the first part of this century. Earlier groups of immigrants, from Southern and Eastern Europe, came to the United States at a time of rapid industrial expansion and were actively recruited to work in nearly all segments of a burgeoning industry. They came at a time of very real labor shortage, and although exploited, had a relatively large array of opportunities for placement and advancement, at least *within* the working class. This relative mobility was possible not only because of the labor shortage, but also because quite a large percentage of the working class was drawn from the ranks of first- and second-generation immigrants (Dulles, 1966).

Current immigrants, from Asia and Latin America, are entering a post-industrial United States which faces economic stagnation, high levels of unemployment—especially among members of the industrial working class—and a shift in the economy away from the production of goods toward the provision of services. As such, the opportunities for these new non-White immigrants tend toward low-level employment in the expanding service sector, seasonal farm labor, or membership in the strata of the chronically unemployed or underemployed (Harrington & Levinson, 1985). If these, in fact, are the roles open to most new immigrants to the United States, then we might well expect that government policies, including educational policy, will work in favor of socializing immigrants for such roles.

## The Role of "Illegal Aliens" in the U.S. Economy

Tove Skutnabb-Kangas of Denmark's Roskilde University has examined how the immigration and educational policies of several European countries relate to the roles played by immigrants in those countries. In her article "Guest Worker or Immigrant: Different Ways of Reproducing an Underclass" (1981), she analyzes post-World War II immigration to several Western European countries. Immediately following the war, these countries initiated guest worker programs to meet a severe labor shortage. Rapid post-war reconstruction and economic growth led the governments of these countries to recruit and hire, for a finite amount of time, unskilled and uneducated workers from Southern Europe and the Balkans to fill low-paying industrial and service jobs undesired by domestic workers.

Forty-plus years have passed since the end of World War II, and Europe has been rebuilt, but many guest workers have yet to return home, even though industrial production has slowed or been exported to the Third World, and high levels of unemployment have become chronic in the host countries. The continued residence of alien workers and their families in Western Europe with the tacit or official approval of the host countries has led Skutnabb-Kangas (1981) and others (Cockcroft, 1986; Dixon, Martinez, & McCaughan, 1982) to propose that immigrants have taken on a new function in modern, post-industrial nations. In the past, a host country would encourage immigration in order to meet labor shortages in an expanding economy. A primary role for immigrants in modern, post-industrial countries is to serve as a buffer between the domestic population, specifically the native-born working class, and the effects of periodic downturns in the economy. In essence, Skutnabb-Kangas sees immigrants as coming to constitute the modern caste minorities of Europe—the last hired, the first fired, the lowest status members of society. Nowhere does this view of the situation seem more real than in Great Britain today, where non-White immigrants compose the vast majority of the British underclass. If one accepts that the economies of the United States and Western European countries are similar, immigrants to the United States can be seen as additions to the ranks of caste-like minorities historically represented by Blacks, Chicanos, Chinese, Native Americans, and Puerto Ricans.

Although Skutnabb-Kangas's model for the new role of immigrants in post-industrial societies sheds some light on the situation in the United States, it does not directly address itself to one of the most provocative and controversial issues for U.S. immigration policy—the increasing presence of "illegal aliens" in the U.S. work force. Few public issues have generated as emotional a debate as the new wave of

Hispanic immigration across our southern border. The alarm with which this migration has been treated in the press has fostered widespread misunderstanding of its nature and has fueled nativist and racist sentiments among large segments of the country's population. Even normally restrained and cautious public officials, such as former CIA Director William Colby, have expressed fears of the development of "a Spanish-speaking Quebec in the U.S. Southwest," and have viewed illegal immigration from Mexico as "a greater threat to national security than the Soviet Union" (Cockcroft, 1986, p. 39). Television specials present images of "an army of aliens waiting to move forth across the border when night falls," and reporters interview White workers who feel that the United States is "being invaded as surely as [if] we had an enemy dropping bombs on us" (Moyers, 1985).

Nonetheless, by using the tools of analysis developed by Skutnabb-Kangas and by Ogbu, illegal immigration can be viewed quite differently. Some leaders in this country are less alarmed and more rational about immigration, as illustrated by William French Smith, the Reagan administration's first attorney general. Smith commented that the administration's goal was not to stem the flow of foreign workers into this country, but rather to "reduce and regulate" the flow and to channel foreigners "into jobs where they are needed" (Cockcroft, 1986, p. 220).

As noted above, Skutnabb-Kangas has suggested that immigrant workers serve as a buffer between native-born workers and the effects of economic downturn in developed nations. The historian and political economist James Cockcroft, in his book *Outlaws in the Promised Land* (1986), develops this analysis more completely in examining the role of undocumented Mexican workers in the U.S. economy. Cockcroft argues that thousands of "bad" jobs in the U.S. economy need filling, and employers face an acute shortage of laborers willing to fill those jobs. For Cockcroft, a "bad" job is one that does not pay a worker an adequate living wage, does not provide health and life insurance benefits, and exposes a worker to unsafe working conditions and unhealthy hours. Furthermore, Cockcroft points out that often the difference between a "good" job and a "bad" job is not intrinsic to the nature of the work or the level of skill required to perform it. The large difference in wages and benefits between an auto worker and an assembler of calculator parts in Silicon Valley, for example, cannot be accounted for by differences in skills, since neither job requires an extended period of special education or training; essentially the work performed in both jobs is similar. The auto worker has a better job because the work force in the auto industry is organized and has benefited for decades from union contracts with the major auto firms. In other words, workers have the ability to organize collectively under certain free-labor conditions to transform low-paying, undesirable jobs into better paying positions that are relatively attractive and difficult to obtain. In reality, Cockcroft maintains, there is no shortage of unskilled workers in the U.S. economy. Instead, he argues, there is a shortage of employers willing to pay a living wage and provide decent working conditions for their employees.

If, for example, seasonal farm labor paid better, there would be no seasonal labor shortage to be filled by undocumented Mexican workers in California's Central Valley. Farm labor jobs pay poorly because the work force in the agricultural sector of the economy is unorganized. Native-born or naturalized citizens, who enjoy the protection of federal and state labor codes won by decades of union organizing and who are eligible for social services, have no interest in taking these "bad" jobs. It is the role of illegal immigrants—the "outlaws" whose lack of protection by U.S. laws renders them unable to organize to raise wages or improve working conditions—to fill the "bad" jobs in the U.S. economy (Cockcroft, 1986). Cockcroft argues that illegal immigrants are recruited on the basis of their special "illegal" status to fill low-status slots in the U.S. opportunity structure outlined by Ogbu.

By extrapolating from the work of Skutnabb-Kangas (1980), it can be said that undocumented workers in the United States are not significantly different from the guest workers of post-war Western Europe, although they may not be officially recognized as such. Guest workers serve at the pleasure of the host country and can be ordered to return to their country of origin at any time. Their legal status is that of a policed labor force tightly constrained by the host government. They are denied the right to make demands for higher wages or for the provision of social services from business or government. They are like the immigrant minorities of Ogbu's model in that, even under the most draconian conditions in the host country, they may "enjoy" a higher standard of living than in their home countries. Guest workers are brought into the host country to do its most menial work for lower wages than the native-born work force would accept. The presence of guest workers in a country can also serve to elevate the status and pay of native-born or naturalized workers. This is because guest workers contribute substantially to expanding the gross national product and pay taxes to the host country while drawing substandard wages and receiving only token government expenditures for social services (Skutnabb-Kangas, 1981). While there has not been an official government guest worker program in the United States for over twenty years, the continued participation of "illegal aliens" in the U.S. work force suggests a tacit government guest worker policy, although the benefits to the naturalized work force may not be as directly correlated as in Great Britain's guest worker program.

The immigration reform legislation that was recently signed into law (Immigration Reform and Control Act, 1986) by President Reagan has received much attention. On the surface, it appears to take strong measures to halt the influx of undocumented workers, who many citizens believe threaten the livelihoods of "legal" workers. The efficacy of the measures mandated by the bill must be questioned, however. Although sanctions against knowingly hiring undocumented workers may discourage some employers, enforcement of this provision may or may not be vigorous. Consider the Bracero Guest Worker Program, for example, in which the U.S. government imported Mexican workers to work in agriculture to meet labor shortages. The workers stayed well after the return to a peacetime economy. Many believe that the Bracero program survived because it preserved a docile, cheap labor force for U.S. agribusiness. The historical record shows that many regulations governing the import and employment of workers in this program generally went unenforced, allowing employers to violate them with impunity (Cockcroft, 1986).

In spite of the fact that vast new expenditures have authorized the INS to strengthen and expand law enforcement and investigative capabilities, most knowledgeable observers agree that the agency lacks the capability to close the border and prevent the employment of "illegals" in this country (Brinkley, 1986; Matthews, 1986). Finally, the inclusion of a guest worker program for seasonal farm labor gives an additional indication that many of those individuals presently working illegally in the United States are, in fact, needed economically. Cockcroft (1986) notes that in the past, mass importation of Mexicans as "guest workers" has occurred simultaneously with their mass deportation as "illegals." The new immigration law seems less likely to eliminate illegal aliens from the work force than to police their presence in order to keep the "bad" jobs filled.

*The Effect of U.S. Economic Realities on Attitudes toward Minorities*

If immigrants, guest workers, and "illegal aliens" are performing services that are important to the U.S. economy by filling undesirable jobs, contributing to the growth of the GNP, and paying taxes, and if the existence of an underclass artificially raises the status of the White working class, why should the United States be witnessing an outpouring of anti-immigrant sentiment from the White working class at this time? One explanation lies in the nature of the changes in the U.S. economy and its export of "good" jobs (as defined by Cockcroft) to other countries where wages and corporate taxes are lower than those in the United States. The greatest loss of jobs in the economy has been in those heavy-manufacturing industries which, because of unionization and high profits during the period between the end of World War II and the end of the U.S. involvement in the Vietnam War, had paid high hourly wages, provided good benefit packages for their workers, and had been regulated by the government for standards of worker health and safety (Harrington & Levinson, 1985). The greatest growth in jobs, on the other hand, has been in the so-called service sector, where jobs were traditionally filled by members of the underclass, and in the high-tech field, where most firms are non-union (Bluestone, 1987). Huge cuts in government expenditures on welfare, combined with the loss of "good" jobs in the economy, have forced many members of the White, native-English-speaking working class to seek lower status jobs in the growth sectors of the economy (Harrington & Levinson, 1985). For the first time, many majority group members are competing with members of caste-like and immigrant minorities for suddenly scarce jobs (Bluestone, 1987). Traditionally, this competition has not existed, and it may be the perception of large numbers of White, native-born workers that such competition is unjust, especially when their chief competitors are not "Americans." Hostility toward foreigners from U.S. workers, however misplaced, should really come as no surprise under these conditions.

A second possible explanation concerns U.S. nationalism and its role in enhancing the self-perception of the domestic working class. The rise of the United States to the most powerful and economically successful nation in the world following World War II had the effect of raising the absolute status of all U.S. citizens in a world context, regardless of their relative status within the U.S. social hierarchy. Although mythical, this perceived status has had a powerful effect upon the psyche of U.S. workers. Another myth is that of the United States as a "melting pot," a nation of newcomers who have given up their old identities in order to assume the new, if somewhat vague, "American" identity. All newcomers then start at the bottom of the social ladder and climb in status as they progressively shed their foreign identities. As the economy is restructured, many assimilated Americans are experiencing a loss in relative status that forces them to work alongside and compete for jobs with foreign workers and other out-group members who, according to the myth, "belong" at the bottom of the social ladder because they are not Americanized. At this point, the fall in relative status is transformed into a fall in absolute status as the status of native-born within the United States falls to that of foreigners.

The perceived superior status of Americanized workers in the world might be preserved in several ways. One alternative, the deportation of foreigners so that the only workers remaining are culturally Americanized, is reflected in mounting pressures to stem the "tide" of illegal aliens entering the country and to deport those illegals already working. Another possibility is to drop the job ceiling for immigrant minorities even lower through intensified racial discrimination and violence. Consider the following recent events in Georgia, where the connection between anti-immigrant and non-English speakers has been used by lawmakers to prohibit the use of Spanish. In the small community of Cedartown, near the Alabama border, a meat-packing plant that was the town's largest source of jobs employed about one hundred Mexican workers alongside a large majority of White and Black employees. In 1985, many of the Anglo and Black workers walked off the job in a strike action organized by the Ku Klux Klan to protest the "discrimination" against U.S. workers by the company. The strike action followed the roadside slayings of two of the plant's Mexican employees in the previous three years by Klan members or associates ("Bill Pushes an Official State Prejudice," 1986). One of the Klan defendants was acquitted by an all-White jury ("Cedartown Strike," 1986). In 1986, the Georgia General Assembly passed a resolution declaring English to be the state's official language in order to reinforce "the cultural fabric of one language" within the state. The *Atlanta Constitution* stated in an editorial that it could not be seen as coincidence that the measure was introduced into the state legislature by the senator whose district includes Cedartown:

> It is such an obvious slap at dozens of Mexicans who came to Cummings' north-west Georgia district to work in a local meat-packing plant, only to find themselves targets of intense hatred and violence by local yahoos, that one wonders at the short span of some of the lawmakers' memories. ("Bill Pushes an Official State Prejudice," 1986, p. 22A)

The legislators' action in this light can be seen both as an effort to bestow official blessing upon state residents who speak English, and a repudiation of those residents who do not. The rapid growth in the number of Hispanic immigrants from diverse national and racial backgrounds to this country has contributed to the perception of the Spanish language as a racial characteristic, since Spanish is virtually the only feature common to all Hispanic immigrants (though not to all Hispanic residents), and because most new immigrants to the United States are coming from Latin America. If one accepts the notion that speaking Spanish functions as a racial characteristic of Hispanics in this country, can one ignore the racist implications of Georgia's English-speaking resolution?

In a related case in California, where there is a long history of violent crimes against Hispanic migrant workers and union organizers, and where it is traditional for the perpetrators of such crimes to go unpunished (Cockcroft, 1986), voters in 1986 overwhelmingly passed a ballot initiative declaring the primacy of the English language in public discourse ("An Official Language for California," 1986). The measure is intended to curtail the use of Spanish in the state government bureaucracy and in public schools.

A third alternative for preserving the status of Americanized workers, and the one that has the greatest implication for educational policy, is to insist that the immigrants who are allowed to remain in the United States become full-fledged, Anglicized Americans at the earliest possible date. Advocates of this path, among them the most strident critics of bilingual education, seem to fear that the price of cultural pluralism is the loss of a cultural basis for nationalism. All three of these remedies, however contradictory, are being applied simultaneously in the United States in the mid-1980s. At times, they are even cloaked in the rhetoric of the civil rights movement. A recent article written by a Black columnist in the *Washington Post,* for instance, questioned whether or not the United States could compete with a "homogeneous society like Japan" unless it, too, took steps towards homogenization by moving faster towards assimilating ethnic and racial minorities into the mainstream (Rowan, 1986).

## The Role of U.S. Educational Policy in Socializing Minorities for a Part in the Economy

Not surprisingly, current public demands to assimilate immigrant groups quickly, for their own good and for the good of the nation, have revolved around proficiency in the English language. English has become *the* public issue in the socialization of immigrant adults and children living in the United States. Increasingly, attempts are being made to ensure that mastery of the "standard" or "core" dialect of American English is represented as emblematic of an "American" identity. The public debate on the English language issue raised two concerns. First, it has always been true that millions of native-born U.S. citizens have never mastered standard English as defined by school textbooks, and that, since its founding, the United States has been multilingual (Hakuta, 1986; Shor, 1986). Second, it is necessary to question the extent to which mastery of English is necessary to carry out the functions of the roles open to adult immigrants in the U.S. opportunity structure. If, as a consequence of the imposition of a job ceiling on the upward social mobility of their members, immigrant minorities are restricted to "immigrant" jobs which do not require high English proficiency, it may be unrealistic to expect that immigrants will ever master "standard" English. A number of eminent linguists, most notable among them John Schumann, have hypothesized that individuals become proficient in a second language not so much due to the effects of formal instruction, but rather to the degree that second language proficiency serves their social and economic needs (Schumann, 1976, 1980). In this sense, proficiency in standard English is not a causal variable in an individual's social status, but rather, is reflective of the individual's opportunities to participate in social settings where standard English is the language of the participants (Schumann, 1980). The lack of proficiency in standard English on the part of many Black and White working-class Americans, in spite of years of public schooling, bears witness to the predictive value of Schumann's hypothesis.

Respect for the U.S. public education system has rested on the belief that public education is a great upward equalizer, giving children of low-status families the chance to surpass their parents' status through achievement in school (Shor, 1986). This belief parallels the melting pot myth which links social advancement to the process of "Americanization." Both notions presume that the opportunity structure of U.S. society will always have a surplus of higher status jobs to be filled by individuals who have adopted the language, values, and beliefs of the dominant White majority as they pass through the educational system. The presumption of a surplus of "good" jobs in the United States is dubious at best. Nonetheless, the "excellence in educaton" movement, spearheaded by the presidential commission's report on the nation's public schools (National Commission on Excellence in Education, 1983) rests on just such an assumption, and advocates the adoption of national curriculum standards aiming at the "Americanization" of students from groups outside the cultural mainstream. A focus on mastery of standard English is a major feature of the proposed new curriculum standards (Shor, 1986).

## The "Excellence in Education" Movement

Educational curriculum theorists, including Ira Shor of the City University of New York, have extensively analyzed the proposals for restoration of "excellence" in the nation's schools. Shor has commented in particular on the curriculum standards heralded by excellence movement leader Albert Shanker, president of the American Federation of Teachers. Shanker was disturbed by tendencies towards "permissiveness" and "cultural relativism" in the schools in the 1960s and 1970s, and began to argue for the re-establishment of standards of academic excellence in public schools. The "core curriculum" formulated by Shanker is described by Shor as follows:

> This theme of a universal course of study embodying a singular dominant culture took shape as a "core curriculum." That core of knowledge emanated from the center of authority outward to the periphery. It is based in Standard English, a

traditional reading list, and cleansed versions of history (the "American Heritage"). The "core curriculum" idea rejects the ideological diversity of the protest era. (Shor, 1986, p. 13)

Shor critizies the concept of the "core curriculum" in general because, he says, it "transmits an official value system disguised as universal knowledge" (Shor, 1986, p. 23). He also critizes the "core curriculum" for fostering a nationwide hysteria over an alleged "literacy" crisis in the United States based upon widespread lack of mastery of standard English, which has been a linguistic reality among Black people, immigrant groups, and lower class Whites in this country almost since its founding (Dulles, 1966; Hakuta, 1986; Johansen & Maestas, 1983; McDermott, 1976; Ovando & Collier, 1985; Rodriguez, 1981; Sennett & Cobb, 1972). Shor writes: "Curriculum and civilization were defined in the Literacy Crisis as resting on the authority of the elite language; that language was posed as a universal standard of culture rather than as a class-specific form of expression" (Shor, 1986, p. 65). Shor contrasts the English achievement standards of the core curriculum with more tolerant views regarding language usage:

> [in 1973] the largest organization of English teachers, the National Council of Teachers of English, had voted in its policy on "Students' Rights to Their Own Language." This egalitarian document described Standard English as a privileged dialect, and as one dialect among many in a diverse culture. It is no secret that most people speak a form of English different from the language of teachers, of literature, and of the elite. (Shor, 1986, p. 65)

The call for excellence in education, including the demand for assimilation of immigrant and caste-like minorities in the United States, is justified as necessary to raise the skills and productivity of the U.S. work force as the U.S. economy moves into new technological and trade frontiers in the twenty-first century. In spite of the fact that most evidence points to a *decrease* in the need for skilled laborers as the complexity of goods produced in the economy increases (Bluestone, 1987; Braverman, 1974), proponents of the excellence movement insist that the shortage of skilled, literate personnel in the labor market restricts U.S. ability to compete with the rest of the world. As evidence, they point to the declining productivity of workers and the falling academic test scores of students. The workers and students responsible for these declines are then seen as dragging down the rest of the society as it strives to enter a new age of high-tech prosperity. Members of immigrant and caste-like minorities, who often score lower on measures of academic achievement both because of cultural and dialectal differences and decades of discrimination, are easily targeted for this criticism. Minorities have, in fact, been scapegoated on numerous occasions, as shown in this excerpt from the conservative journal *Heritage Today:*

> The most damaging blows to science and mathematics education have come from Washington. For the past 20 years, federal mandates have favored "disadvantaged" pupils at the expense of those who have the highest potential to contribute positively to society. . . . By catering to the demands of special interest groups—racial minorities, the handicapped, women and non-English speaking students—America's public schools have successfully competed for

government funds, but they have done so at the expense of education as a whole. (Gardner, 1983, pp. 6–7)

The question of how the call for excellence in education is compatible with the decline in the number of "good" jobs available and skilled laborers needed in the U.S. economy is important if one accepts Shor's proposition that the educational system is "functional or dysfunctional to society at any instance to the degree it prepares student attitudes appropriate to the needs of an unequal social order" (Shor, 1986, p. 168). On the surface, it would seem that accepting the excellence program in the schools would lead to just the sort of dysfunction to which Shor alludes. Returning to Ogbu's job ceiling notion helps to reveal a way in which the imposition of new standards of excellence in the schools is highly functional.

In a sense, the United States is not experiencing a literacy crisis, but a crisis of an "overeducated" work force. Well-compensated, higher status jobs in the economy are in short supply relative to the number of workers "qualified" by their education and socialization to fill them (Bluestone, 1987; Cockcroft, 1986; Harrington & Levinson, 1985; Shor, 1986). As competition among workers for "good" jobs intensifies, employers can arbitrarily raise the qualifications a worker must have. The excellence movement in education is also expanding the grounds for exclusion from high-status jobs without regard to the real needs of the economy. Because the excellence movement seeks through its meritocracy to reward the "excellent" student who "excels" in the language and behaviors of the dominant elite, and to punish (through low grades and tracking) the "inferior" student who does not master the language and behaviors of the elite, the outcome of the movement will be to maintain a job ceiling for minorities. This serves to preserve the perceived superior status of the native-born White worker who is increasingly being called upon to accept employment in occupations formerly reserved for the underclass.

The United States offers immigrants an ambiguous social contract. It reads, more or less, as follows: "In order to participate in a non-marginal way in the U.S. economy, you must become an American by giving up your loyalty to your home country and language, and you must learn the language of the American elite. In order to become an American, you must meet certain standards. This country is in the process of raising its standards because, unfortunately, there are already too many Americans. If aren't allowed to become an American, there's still plenty of room for you in this country—at the bottom." Due to catastrophic economic conditions in much of the rest of the world, there are millions of people ready to sign on. A Mexican woman waiting to sneak across the U.S. border at Tiajuana put it this way: "We're sad about it, but what can we do? There is no opportunity in Mexico. Mexico is very poor, and the government doesn't help the people. . . . We are born to die. We know where we were born, but we don't know where we will end up" (Kelly, 1986).

*Assimilation as a Goal of Immigrant Educational Policies*

In spite of all the limitations on the social mobility of immigrants within the United States, the goal of almost any educational policy directed toward them will be assimilationist in some measure. The pace of the assimilation will vary as will the means of achieving it. The strategies that have been employed to implement immigrant educational policies in both the United States and Europe include so-called submersion, immersion, and transitional bilingual education programs. A question that must be raised at this point concerns the type of assimilation the United States aims to achieve through its educational policies. Is the goal to assimilate immigrant children into the dominant social group of the host society, or more to discourage their assimilation of the cultural and linguistic norms of their home country? In the United States, a long history of racism and the existence of a stratified opportunity structure combine to work against assimilation into the host society's higher status, dominant White group. What could be the rationale for assimilating immigrant children away from their own culture?

Ogbu's caste minority/immigrant minority model can provide some insight into this question. Ogbu (1978) noted that many immigrants hold instrumental attitudes toward the host society—by holding on to the hope of steady relative advancement within it or by an improved economic position upon returning to the home country. Viewing the host society instrumentally means concomitantly that immigrants view their stay as provisional, depending upon how they perceive their position in facing the opportunity structure. In Ogbu's view, it is the unassimilated status of immigrant minorities, best illustrated by the possibility of ultimately returning to the home country, that qualitatively distinguishes them from caste minorities. (A number of authors have studied the situation of immigrants standing at the crossroads between assimilation and return: See Ekstrand, Foster, Olkiewicz, & Stankovski, 1981.) That unassimilated status means that immigrants may hold onto attitudes, values, and behaviors that are incompatible with occupying a traditional caste-minority position within the U.S. opportunity structure.

The education of immigrant children enters the picture here in a most profound way. In order to prepare students for caste-minority status in the host society, whether in the United States or Europe, several things must be accomplished. First, children must let go their instrumentalist attitudes that view school and the host country as a means of personal advancement. Second, they must internalize the caste ideology of the host society. That is, they must not have a value system and a way of life independent of that of the society at large. Finally, they must be denied the possibility of returning to their home country should prospects for advance in the host country dim. How can schooling accomplish these aims? Official indoctrination might be one way. Another more politically acceptable way is to take away the immigrant child's language and culture and replace them with some form more suited to the social roles he or she can be expected to occupy as an adult in the host society. All three strategies mentioned earlier—submersion, immersion, and transitional bilingual education—can be effective means of achieving both assimilation and a progressive disengagement from the home language and culture. They may also play a role in educating immigrant children for low-status roles as adults.

The aim of educational approaches which prohibit mother-tongue instruction for immigrants is unquestionably and strongly assimilationist. The so-called submersion approach, which places limited-English-proficient children in English-only class-rooms in the hope that they will somehow learn the new language and adapt them-selves to the new culture, has been shown to have devastating consequences on the average immigrant child's cognitive development and academic achievement (California State Department of Education, 1982; Hakuta, 1986; Ovando & Collier, 1985). The immersion approach is also English-only, though the academic outcomes of immersion programs in the United States have only recently begun to be studied (Gersten & Woodward, 1985). The few programs in the United States that do use some degree of mother-tongue instruction and that have been implemented on a large scale are transitional bilingual education (TBE) programs. Since bilingual ed-ucation is currently embroiled in controversy, an examination of how it may function as an agent of socialization for immigrant children is worthwhile.

The goal of federally funded TBE programs in the United States has never been the "production" of bilingual, biliterate, bicultural adults capable of functioning competently in two languages and cultures. If this were the case, there would have to be numerous programs that promote the development of academic skills in im-migrant students' native languages in all school subjects through the end of high school. Virtually no such programs exist in this country. Since the 1974 reauthori-zation of Title VII of the Elementary and Secondary Education Act, the primary aim of such programs has been to raise the English proficiency of non-English-speaking children such that they may be able to participate "effectively" in classrooms where English is the sole medium of instruction (Ovando & Collier, 1985). Transi-tional bilingual education programs typically last only two to three years. The mother tongues of children in such transitional programs are used as necessary to introduce content material and to begin to develop the literacy competencies that will presum-ably help children learn to read and write in English. English instruction focuses on the development of students' oral command of the language as well as communicative competencies in English. After three years, or when students are deemed sufficiently proficient in English (whichever comes first), they are "mainstreamed" into regular English-only classrooms (Ovando & Collier, 1985). With formal instruction in the mother tongue completely terminated both as the medium of instruction and as a content subject very early on in students' education, they may be put on the road to *limited bilingualism.*

Limited bilingualism, that is, less than native-like proficiency in either the mother tongue or the second language, has been associated with impeded cognitive devel-opment and lowered academic achievement in a number of studies (California State Department of Education, 1982; Cummins, 1981; Hakuta, 1986). Research into bilingualism as a cognitive phenomenon has shown that second-language acquisition is most successful when there is a strong foundation in the mother tongue, and that conversational skills in a second language are learned earlier than the ability to use the language for academic learning (Hakuta, 1985). Research has also indicated that in order for bilingual children to match their monolingual peers' levels of cognitive and academic achievement, they must first attain a minimum linguistic threshold of near native proficiency in at least one of their two languages (Cummins, 1981, 1984; Skutnabb-Kangas, 1979). Cummins (1981) has gone further to suggest that it takes at least three to four years of formal schooling to attain such a threshold.

It is now widely accepted among researchers studying language acquisition that there are two dimensions of language proficiency (California State Department of Education, 1982; Hakuta, 1986; Ovando & Collier, 1985). The first dimension has to do with those skills associated with casual conversational use of the language, what Cummins has called BICS—basic interpersonal communicative skills. The second dimension concerns more formal intellectual understanding of the language and the ability to use it for intellectual or academic purposes. Cummins has called this dimension CALP—cognitive academic learning proficiency. Proficiency in one dimension, however, does not necessarily correlate positively with proficiency in the other. Moreover, it is generally believed that the BICS dimension is acquired before the CALP dimension (California State Department of Education, 1982; Cummins, 1984; Hakuta, 1986). The minimum linguistic threshold includes the development of CALP-level skills in a formal academic setting (Cummins, 1981, 1984).

## *Transitional Bilingual Education Programs*

Bilingualism research findings have important implications for transitional bilingual education programs. The overriding goal of TBE programs is to mainstream students into English-only classrooms. As a result, a major component of such programs is the development of English proficiency in the students. Unfortunately, most of the programs last only two to three years, not long enough for children to build up CALP level skills in either their mother tongue or English. Such children may be mainstreamed into English-only classes before they have attained the minimum linguistic threshold necessary to ensure their ability to carry out cognitively demanding academic tasks in English. Additionally, two to three years at the elementary level is regarded as insufficient time to allow for the development of CALP skills in the mother tongue. Students mainstreamed after only two to three years in bilingual classrooms will generally not be able to rely on a cross-language transfer of academic skills from their mother tongue to English to compensate for their CALP deficit in English. Consequently, language-minority students who are mainstreamed out of transitional bilingual programs may not be sufficiently prepared to participate and compete in English-only classrooms where English is the mother tongue of the majority of their peers.

The consequences of mainstreaming limited-English-proficient children into English-only classrooms extend beyond the cognitive and the personal. The social consequences include defining the terms of competition and social ranking in the public schools and influencing the perceptions that English mother-tongue students and teachers have of immigrant children in their classes. Immigrant children (as well as children of native-born linguistic minority parents) mainstreamed into regular classrooms from transitional bilingual programs may be presented before their teachers and classmates not as equal-but-different representatives of another language and culture, but rather as imperfect or inferior members of the domestic culture (Skut-nabb-Kangas, 1981). The differences most noted may be the immigrants' imperfect use and understanding of English, their poorer academic performance, and the color of their skin.

The process of mainstreaming limited bilingual students may potentially reinforce the racist stereotypes in U.S. society that limit the advancement of caste or caste-like minorities. The majority of recent immigrants to this country are non-White, and members of the White majority may consciously or subconsciously associate the cognitive deficits linked to poor educational policies with particular races and nationalities, particularly if transitional bilingual education programs are viewed in the same light as other forms of compensatory education. Intellectual inferiority would then be ascribed to immigrant groups on the basis of ascribed characteristics, since their school performance would still be perceived as deficient, even after they have received several years of special help in school. Blaming the victim, especially Black Americans, has been established as a given in the United States (Ogbu, 1978).

Research on bilingualism seems to indicate that early mainstreaming, the legal goal of short-term TBE programs, is flawed as a compensatory educational strategy for immigrant students (California State Department of Education, 1982; Cummins, 1981, 1984; Hakuta, 1985, 1986). It seems likely that many TBE programs are, in fact, turning out students whose CALP-dimension proficiency in both the mother tongue and English is inadequate for participation in English-only classrooms. On the surface, at least, it is on this issue that bilingual education is attacked. On another level, however, TBE may be an appropriate way for society to educate the children of immigrants.

If U.S. society needs to recruit and prepare new candidates for a growing number of low-status, poorly compensated slots in the opportunity structure, transitional bilingual education programs for non-English-speaking immigrants may be construed by the majority as part of a "reasonable" set of educational policies for the nation. If political and social considerations dictate that Black and other non-White and/or foreign-born people bear a greater share of the hardships, poverty, and unemployment in the U.S. economy, it is "reasonable" to expect the educational system to reflect such considerations. Black people and many new immigrants are already separated by means of race as they confront the opportunity structure. Educational policy can serve to reinforce caste distinctions in the society by providing, more or less intentionally, non-White people with an inferior education. In doing so, the educational system plays a role in creating a pool of adults who are "qualified" to be economically exploited, unemployed, or underemployed.

Reagan's Department of Education has vigorously attacked TBE programs because, it is claimed, they hinder non-English-speaking students' acquisition of English and keep them separated from mainstream students for too long. In fact, the criticism of TBE programs from within the government began under the Carter administration. Consider this statement by a former Secretary of Health, Education and Welfare, Joseph Califano: "[In bilingual programs] too little attention was paid to teaching

English, and far too many children were kept in bilingual classes long after they acquired the necessary proficiency to be taught in English" (Califano, 1981). Further, Ronald Reagan did not wait long after entering the White House to begin to speak out against bilingual school programs:

> It is absolutely wrong and against American concept to have a bilingual education program that is now openly, admittedly dedicated to preserving their native language and never getting them adequate in English so they can go out into the job market. (quoted in Hakuta, 1985, p. 207)

The attacks on transitional bilingual education are not consistent with the available research evidence on bilingualism, but they can be seen as consistent with trends toward the further lowering of the job ceiling for immigrants in the United States. New regulations governing the expenditure of funds for bilingual education promulgated by William Bennett, the Secretary of Education, seek to discourage the use of languages other than English in instruction and to encourage the early "mainstreaming" of students out of bilingual programs. Furthermore, the aim of native-language instruction under the new regulations is not to provide for children's overall academic success, but rather, to foster the acquisition of English. To this end, the Department of Education hopes to renegotiate many districts' compliance with the civil rights provisions of Title VII legislation (Orum, 1985). The National Council of La Raza, a national Hispanic-American civil rights organization, has commented that the Secretary of Education seems to believe that instruction in English-as-a-second-language alone is a sufficient educational remedy to meet the department's civil rights obligations as set by the *Lau v. Nichols* Supreme Court case of 1974 (Orum, 1985).

The provisions of the Department of Education's proposed new rules governing bilingual education programs receiving Title VII monies are as follows:

—DOE will provide for "maximum flexibility" on the part of local districts in designing programs to meet the needs of limited-English-proficient students. (In practice, this means that the native component of such programs may be eliminated.)

—Bilingual education programs will use native language instruction only to the extent necessary to achieve competence in English and to meet grade promotions and graduation requirements.

—No minimum amount of time or instruction is to be established to meet the standards of achieving English competence and meeting grade promotion and graduation requirements. (In other words, early mainstreaming of students is permissible.)

—The Secretary will fund proposals only if they can demonstrate the ability, financial or otherwise, to continue the project after Title VII monies are exhausted. Increased local responsibility for funding programs will be a priority. (U.S. Department of Education, 1985)

The last provision is of particular interest because of its implications for the many bilingual education programs located in poor districts. It appears that the Department of Education will fund only those projects in districts that can afford bilingual programs after federal start-up monies are spent. It is conceivable, then, that many districts will be denied federal bilingual education funds not because there is no demonstrable need for a bilingual program, but because the economically marginal status of the populations served cannot manage to foot the bill for the programs (Crawford, 1986). In relation to this point, Navarro (1985) notes that the rollback of bilingual education programs in the state of California is largely attributable to the real powerlessness of Hispanics there. In addition, he says that it is increasingly true that those who have a direct interest in public education policy are the disenfranchised, impoverished ethnic and racial minorities, while members of the dominant majority group in society are less and less willing to pay for such educational programs.

It is interesting to look at how the new DOE-proposed regulations define a "program of transitional bilingual education." According to the department, TBE refers to programs designed to meet the educational needs of limited English-proficient students and provide "structured English language instruction, and, to the extent necessary to allow a child to achieve competence in the English language, instruction in the child's native language . . ." (U.S. Department of Education, 1985). Clearly, the goal of such a program in this scheme—and the one criterion used to evaluate its success or failure (as well as the success or failure of the students participating in it)—is the acquisition of English as a badge of American identity. The insights gained from sociological and linguistic investigation seem to show that this goal serves the interest of society at the expense of the needs of language-minority students.

It remains to be seen whether or not TBE programs produce results in terms of student academic achievement. The research to date in bilingualism indicates, however, that in both the cognitive and affective domains, maintenance bilingual programs or two-way enrichment programs of longer duration (at least six years) would be far superior to transitional bilingual programs. Bilingual advocates need to consider whether or not they are preserving the essence of quality bilingual education when they seek to promote bilingual education through the defense of existing programs. If, in so doing, they defend compensatory programs whose graduates are consistently outperformed by their monolingual peers, they may inadvertently play a role in the negative stereotyping of the language and immigrant minorities whose cause they champion.

Finally, those who believe that compensatory educational programs for immigrants and language minorities play an important role in the advancement of minority civil rights need to be wary. The analysis presented in this article suggests that the existence of low-status social roles is necessary to U.S. society in some sense and that someone must fill those roles. Compensatory education assumes that low-status people suffer low status because of their lack of school success, and that if they were to become successful in school, their status would rise. In the United States, where race and ethnicity frequently form the basis of low status, such an assumption does not hold true. Educational advocates for immigrants and language minorities must look beyond strictly academic themes and examine the adult roles open to these students, in order to determine whether such programs do indeed facilitate both their advancement and mobility in our society.

## References

An official language for California. (1986, October 2). *New York Times*, p. A23.

Barreto, J., Jr. (1986, August 9). English isn't the only language we speak. *The Washington Post*, p. A19.

Bill pushes an official state prejudice [Editorial]. (1986, February 18). *The Atlanta Constitution*, p. 22A.

Bluestone, B. (1987). *The De-Industrialization of America*. New York: Basic Books.

Braverman, H. (1974). *Labor and monopoly capital*. New York: Monthly Review Press.

Brinkley, J. (1986, June 26). U.S. set to act on border drug flow. *New York Times*, p. 1.

Califano, J. (1981). *Governing America: An insider's report from the White House and the Cabinet*. New York: Simon & Schuster.

California State Department of Education, Office of Bilingual and Bicultural Education. (1982). *Basic principles for the education of language-minority students: An overview*. Sacramento: Author.

Cedartown Strike. (1986, February 15). *Mundo Hispanico*, Atlanta, p. 10A.

Cockcroft, J. D. (1986). *Outlaws in the promised land: Mexican immigrant workers and America's future*. New York: Grove Press.

Crawford, J. (1986, February 12). Bennett's plan for bilingual overhaul heats up debate. *Education Week*, p. 1.

Cummins, J. (1981). The role of primary language development in promoting educational success for language minority students. *Schooling and language minority students: A theoretical framework*. Evaluation, Dissemination, and Assessment Center, California State University at Los Angeles.

Cummins, J. (1984). *Bilingualism and special education: Issues in assessment and pedagogy*. San Diego: College Hill Press.

Cummins, J. (1986). Empowering minority students: A framework for intervention. *Harvard Educational Review*, *56*, 18–36.

Dixon, M., Martinez, E., & McCaughan, E. (1982, March). *Chicanas and Mexicanas within a transnational working class*. Paper presented at the Chicana History Project and Symposium, University of California at Los Angeles.

Dulles, F. R. (1966). *Labor in America: A history*. Arlington Heights, IL: AHM Publishing.

Ekstrand, L. H., Foster, S., Olkiewicz, E., & Stankovski, M. (1981). Interculture: Some concepts for describing the situation of immigrants. *Journal of Multilingual and Multicultural Development*, *2*, 269–295.

Gardner, E. (1983). What's wrong with math and science teaching in our schools. *Heritage Today*, *3* (May–June), 6–7.

Georgia General Assembly. (1985). *Georgia State House of Representatives Bill Number 717*.

Gersten, R., & Woodward, J. (1985). A case for structured immersion. *Educational Leadership*, *43*, 75–84.

Hakuta, K. (1985, September 27). Generalizations from research in second language acquisition and bilingualism. Testimony presented before the House Education and Labor Committee, Washington, DC.

Hakuta, K. (1986). *Mirror of language: The debate on bilingualism.* New York: Basic Books.
Harrington, M., & Levinson, M. (1985, September). The perils of a dual economy. *Dissent,* pp. 417–426.
Johansen, B., & Maestas, R. (1983). *El Pueblo: The Gallegos family's American journey, 1503 to 1980.* New York: Monthly Review Press.
Kelly, P. (1986, November 19). American bosses have jobs; Mexicans need work. *The Guardian,* New York, p. 11.
Levine, R. A. (1967). *Dreams and needs: Achievement and motivation in Nigeria.* Chicago: University of Chicago Press.
MacEoin, G., & Riley, N. (1982). *No promised land: American refugee policies and the rule of law.* Boston: Oxfam America.
Matthews, J. (1985, November 14). Asian-American students creating a new mainstream. *Washington Post,* p. A1.
Matthews, J. (1986, November 16). Few employers fear new immigration law: Threat of sanctions greeted with a shrug. *Washington Post,* p. A3.
McDermott, R. P. (1976). Achieving school failure: An anthropological approach to illiteracy and social stratification. In H. Singer & R. B. Russel (Eds.), *Theoretical models and processes of reading* (pp. 389–424). Newark, DE: International Reading Association.
Moyers, B. (1985, September). *Whose America is it?* Television documentary aired on CBS.
National Commission on Excellence in Education. (1983). *A nation at risk: The imperative for educational reform.* Washington, DC: U.S. Department of Education.
Navarro, R. (1985). The problems of language education and society: Who decides? In E. Garcia & R. V. Padilla (Eds.), *Advances in bilingual education research* (pp. 289–312). Tucson: University of Arizona Press.
Ogbu, J. U. (1978). *Minority education and caste: The American system in cross-cultural perspective.* New York: Academic Press.
Orum, L. S. (1985, October 31). Secretary Bennett's bilingual education initiative: Historical perspectives and implications. *Perspectivas Publicas,* a newsletter published by the National Council of La Raza, Washington, DC.
Ovando, C., & Collier, V. (1985). *Bilingual and ESL classrooms: Teaching in multicultural contexts.* New York: McGraw-Hill.
Rodriguez, R. (1981). *Hunger of memory: The education of Richard Rodriguez.* Boston: David R. Godine.
Rowan, C. T. (1986, October 7). The real issue Nakasone raised. *Washington Post,* p. A17.
Schumann, J. H. (1976). Second language acquisition: The Pidginization hypothesis. *Language Learning, 26,* 391–408.
Schumann, J. H. (1980). Affective factors and the problem of age in second language acquisition. In K. Croft (Ed.), *Readings on English as a second language,* 2nd ed. Cambridge, MA: Winthrop.
Sennett, R., & Cobb, J. (1972). *Hidden injuries of class.* New York: Random House.
Shor, I. (1986). *Culture wars: School and society in the conservative restoration, 1969–1984.* Boston: Routledge & Kegan Paul.
Skutnabb-Kangas, T. (1979). *Language in the process of cultural assimilation and structural incorporation of linguistic minorities.* Rosslyn, VA: National Clearinghouse for Bilingual Education.
Skutnabb-Kangas, T. (1981). Guest worker or immigrant: Different ways of reproducing an underclass. *Journal of Multilingual and Multicultural Development, 2,* 89–113.
U.S. Department of Education. (1985, November 22). Notice of proposed rule-making

for bilingual program implementation and general provisions. *The Federal Register,* *50* (226), 48352–48370.

U.S. English. (1985). *A kind of discordant harmony: Issues in assimilation.* Pamphlet, Washington, DC.

# 16
# Creative Education for Bilingual Teachers

ALMA FLOR ADA
*University of San Francisco*

*Research on bilingual education has suggested the need for the empowerment of language-minority students, their parents, and communities. In this article Alma Ada, focusing on the reflections of bilingual teachers in various areas in California, argues that bilingual teachers should not passively accept their unequal status with respect to other educators. Instead, she suggests that if bilingual teachers experience elements necessary for the empowerment of language-minority students, they will be in a better position to advocate for both themselves and their students. To accomplish this end, Ada proposes a "creative" approach to teacher training that helps bilingual teachers to better understand and examine the interpersonal, social, and political issues around them. She suggests that this approach serves not only to strengthen the image of bilingual teachers but to benefit language-minority students, their parents, and communities.*

Schools today, and teachers in particular, are under a great deal of criticism. Bilingual teachers, caught between the accepted practices they are required to follow and the sound theories and research that contradict those practices, are especially vulnerable to attack. Most bilingual teachers were not educated in bilingual programs, nor have they had the experience of teaching in bilingual schools that receive full societal support. In many instances they themselves have been victims of language oppression and racism; thus, in order to empower their students to overcome conditions of domination and oppression, they must first be empowered themselves. This paper,

Discussions at the First Working Conference on Critical Pedagogy held at the University of Massachusetts, Amherst, in February 1986, motivated me to write this paper. I would like to express my appreciation to the participants at this conference. I would also like to thank Paulo Freire, Tove Skutnabb-Kangas, Jim Cummins, Ellen Herda, and Dennis Parker, as well as my students in the Multicultural Program, University of San Francisco, for their enriching dialogue. This paper benefited from the insightful comments of my daughter Rosalma Zubizarreta and my editor and friend, Bernice Randall.

*Harvard Educational Review*   Vol. 56   No. 4   November 1986, 386–394

based on reflections of bilingual teachers in U.S. schools, will analyze the nature of the teacher training process and propose elements of an empowering process for training bilingual teachers.

All teachers must contend with the uncertainties arising from the lack of societal support for their profession, but the situation is doubly difficult for bilingual teachers.[1] Education in general is often criticized, but its critics talk of improvement, not of elimination. Bilingual education, on the other hand, faces opposition from a large proportion of the population, who would willingly do away with it.

Criticism of bilingual education comes from a variety of sources. Under the pervasive influence of the misused "melting pot" metaphor, some opponents fear that bilingual education will promote divisiveness among the general population. They see the maintenance of home languages as un-American. Other opponents, often members of language minority communities themselves, fear that participation in bilingual education will segregate and ostracize children and will jeopardize their future societal success.

## Subtractive versus Additive Bilingualism

The fear that home-language maintenance will hinder the acquisition of English is not borne out by research. Achieving high-language proficiency in English does not preclude maintaining proficiency in the mother tongue. Despite its widespread acceptance, the subtractive model of bilingualism, in which mastery of the second language is achieved at the expense of proficiency in the first, need not be the framework on which bilingual education rests. Additive bilingualism, in which a second language is acquired while maintaining and continuing to develop the first, is a healthy and viable alternative to subtractive bilingualism (Cummins, 1981, 1986; Dolson, 1985; Lambert & Tucker, 1972; Skutnabb-Kangas, 1984).

The benefits of additive bilingualism are many. Peal and Lambert's (1962) classic study suggested that having a dual repertoire to label and organize reality fosters students' cognitive flexibility. Since then, most research shows that bilingualism contributes positively to the cognitive, linguistic, and psychosocial development of children. Other, more subtle, advantages have been found; for example, enhanced metalinguistic development frequently correlates with bilingualism (for reviews, see Cummins, 1986; Dolson, 1985).

A major benefit, so obvious that it is frequently ignored, is the knowledge of two languages. There is a bitter irony in the fact that an English-speaking student may earn college credit for learning to speak another language, while a language minority child is encouraged not to use, and therefore lose, the same skill.

In addition to preserving a valuable skill, encouraging the maintenance and development of the home language can foster a bilingual student's identity and self-esteem, which tend to correlate with academic success. While it is difficult to determine whether the greater success of students in bilingual programs that emphasize the use of the first language is due to better promotion of cognitive/academic skills in the first language or to the reinforcement of cultural identity provided by the intensive use of the home language, Cummins (1986) states that "considerable re-search data suggest that, for dominated minorities, the extent to which students' language and culture are incorporated into the school program constitutes a significant predictor of academic success" (p. 25).

Finally, it should be noted that the maintenance of the home language strengthens family and community ties. Home language maintenance enhances communication between generations. When students are encouraged to forget the language of their families and communities, they may lose access to their heritage. Frequently heard comments along the lines of, "my parents made it without bilingual education," disregard the significant changes that have taken place in society, and fail to take into account the grief of immigrants whose sacrifices and efforts are rewarded by estrangement from their grandchildren, with whom communication is limited, at best.

## Beyond the Use of Two Languages

I believe the views of Freire (1982a, 1982b) and Aronowitz and Giroux (1985) are correct: schools do hold out the possibility of critical analysis and reconstruction of social reality through meaningful dialogue between teachers and students, by a process termed "transformative education." In this paper I refer to that transformative education process, which differs from the traditional reproductive education, as *creative education*.[2] Through creative education, students learn to understand and appreciate themselves, to use that understanding as a means of valuing the diversity of others, to reflect critically upon their experiences so that these can be a source of growth, and to respond creatively to the world around them. If bilingual students are to have an opportunity to validate their own language and culture—acknowledging both the difficulties faced by their ethnic groups and the possibilities open to them for effecting change and for making positive contributions to society—they must be participants in creative education. Only then will students and teachers be able to reclaim bilingualism as an asset for both individuals and society.[3]

Proponents of bilingual education suggest that the communicative and critical thinking skills that will empower students can best be developed, in the case of dominated minorities, through the utilization of the child's first language (Ada & de Olave, 1986; Cummins, 1986; Skutnabb-Kangas, 1984). These reasoning processes, once developed in the home language, are transferable to the second language, along with learning skills and academic content. Most important, the child's experience with success—a result of an additive approach that builds upon the child's existing knowledge—will create a positive attitude towards learning which will also be transferable to the second language.

However, if creative education is to be viable, teachers themselves must be empowered. Unfortunately, many teacher education programs seem designed to train teachers to accept social realities rather than to question them. Teachers are trained to conform to a mechanistic definition of their role rather than to recognize it as involving a relationship between human beings, with a possibility of growth for both

449

teachers and students. As a result, teachers frequently find themselves trapped in a series of ritualistic activities—taking attendance, maintaining order, creating and following lesson plans, testing and reporting test results—with little opportunity to step back from the reality in which they are immersed in order to analyze it critically and become true agents of transformation. In short, if a creative education is to be brought about, teachers must experience it themselves.

## Bilingual Teachers' Unheard Voices

Before something like creative education is introduced to teachers, it is important to know what those teachers' experiences have been. In order to listen to the voices of bilingual teachers, I engaged in dialogue with four groups of them and discussed the problems they face daily and the ways in which teacher education programs might better address those problems. In all, thirty-eight participants contributed to these reflections.[4]

All the participants welcomed the opportunity to discuss their teacher education. When first asked what their education had given or not given them, they were extremely enthusiastic about engaging in dialogue. Typical comments were quite broad: "We would need a year to discuss everything my teacher education failed to give me"; or "We could write a whole book about what my teacher education didn't provide." Yet, despite the promise of critical reflection that those initial statements held out, when the participants were asked to describe their education, they responded with a series of limited observations: "I wasn't given any preparation for class management"; "We were not told anything about all the bureaucratic requirements, all the forms we would have to fill out"; and "I needed to know how to handle A/V equipment."

As the dialogue came closer to tackling the issues and social realities they faced in their daily lives as teachers, the participants began to look at their experiences in a comprehensive way. As they realized the impact of having been led to look at their profession as a sequence of unrelated tasks, rather than as a vital life project that has impact on society, the teachers expressed recurrent themes of isolation, powerlessness, and insecurity. This realization emerged out of a broad criticism of their teacher-training programs and generated myriad questions that troubled these teachers: If children really benefit from learning in their mother tongue, why should we put a ceiling on how much first-language instruction they receive? What varieties of the home language are acceptable in the classroom? How much of their cultural heritage do children need in order to develop self-esteem? Should education be neutral, free from political implications? Will children not have a better chance of survival if they are taught to be "good Americans" rather than to question the ethics of the country they live in? How will children fare if they are exposed to creative education and helped to develop as critical thinkers for a brief period, and then later forced to return to a traditional style of education?

Although these questions were raised out of concern for the children, the questions by no means applied only to them. The questions had to do as well with the teachers' own identities, their ideologies and beliefs, their use of language, their culture, and the social realities that surrounded them. The concerns they expressed about the children reflected their own concerns about themselves as teachers in schools that often devalue their work because they are members of cultural groups that are often socially invisible.

## Isolation

The absence of support for bilingual education in the society at large reinforces the perception of many bilingual teachers that support is flagging within their own schools. Administrators and monolingual teachers, while applying pressure to have language minority students mainstreamed as soon as possible, often attack bilingual teachers for the lack of success of those very children who have been prematurely required to perform in a language whose mastery threshold they have not yet reached (Cummins, 1981).

The importance of peer support was mentioned in every group discussion. The mistaken perception of bilingual education as nonprestigious makes peer support networks among bilingual teachers a necessity. One, in suggesting that teacher-education programs should encourage future teachers to develop such support mechanisms, said that "especially in nonprestigious areas like bilingual education, it is imperative to receive affirmation from one's peers." The lack of peer support—and their being "locked" in classrooms with little interaction with the rest of the school, the district, and the community—results in a feeling of isolation among teachers in general, and bilingual teachers in particular.

All the groups agreed on the need for interaction with parents and community so as to involve them in the educational process. One teacher suggested that teacher education programs should include inservices from community leaders. Another pointed out that the need is twofold: to involve the community in the educational process and to get teachers involved in community action. A third teacher suggested that teacher education programs should include a form of internship in community projects so that teachers might gain a holistic view of the community and become involved in wider societal issues. In addition, all the groups saw education and teaching as political activities, and they considered it desirable for teachers to be politically aware.

## Sense of Inadequacy in Language Mastery

Since language performance plays a major role in the perception that others have of us and thus may affect our personal and professional success, feeling inadequate in the use of language is a painful experience. Bilingual teachers may feel inadequate in their language ability because of several factors. Those teachers whose mother tongue is English may not have had the opportunity to acquire full mastery of a second language—a sad reflection on our limited and deficient foreign language teaching. Members of language minorities who chose to become bilingual teachers may also have been victims of language oppression as children, when they were

451

scolded or punished in school for using their home language. Therefore it should not be surprising that many bilingual teachers lack confidence in their literacy skills. Yet if these individuals can acknowledge that the language inadequacy they experience stems from deeply rooted institutionalized oppression and is highlighted by the one-teacher model, they will be better able to understand what their students may be going through.[5] Instead of reproducing a negative outcome, these teachers' past experiences can serve as a positive, constructive example. However, in order to free teachers from feelings of inadequacy, we must examine the reasons for language limitations and then discuss ways to overcome them.

Future bilingual teachers would benefit from an opportunity to live, study, and, perhaps teach in a country where the language they will be teaching is spoken. Spending a few months in such an environment might be an ideal way to recapture, or to master, their language. This exposure might be beneficial in other ways as well. A successful bilingual teacher in one of the groups said the most valuable part of her teacher training had been the incentive it provided for her to visit and teach in Peru and Mexico. Observing different life styles, interacting with people in other countries, and having to teach under conditions very different from those she had always known gave her greater flexibility and creativity. She stated that she could better innovate because of her first-hand knowledge of diverse situations, and she derives strength from her experiences in unfamiliar places; she also feels the need to adopt a critical outlook because she has a new perception of the sociopolitical reality of the children who come to her classroom.

## Powerlessness

The lack of opportunity to explore conflicting issues in a psychologically-safe climate often leads to denial, defensiveness, and, most especially, powerlessness. Indeed, powerlessness was one of the recurring themes in all four discussion groups. Although the participants felt at first that their powerlessness stemmed from isolation and feelings of inadequacy, further examination revealed that the deeper causes were the interactive forces between the schools, the community, and the larger society.

The participants recognized that parents ought to be involved in the educational process because they are genuinely concerned about their children's education. For the most part, however, adequate mechanisms are not in place to facilitate real parent participation. Since parents are often perceived by the school authorities as uneducated and ineffective, they are given a limited role in decision making. In addition, parents sometimes withdraw their support of bilingual programs by choosing to take their children out of them or by discouraging the use of the home language. This lack of support increases the frustration felt by teachers. It is not widely understood by the teachers that parents withdraw support because they have internalized the negative view towards bilingual education that is widespread in society.

## Uncertainty Regarding Cultural Identity

To their feelings of powerlessness and language inadequacy many bilingual teachers add their own conflicts regarding their identity. In spite of the fact that the American society claims to respect the ideals of equality, diversity, and inclusion, the reality for language minority people has been inequality, the push for conformity to one standard, and exclusion. One of the greatest contradictions confronting minorities is that society urges them to become mainstream and thereby abandon their language and cultural traditions, but even after they assume the views and behavior of the majority culture in hope of increased acceptance, they often continue to be victimized by the same forces that compelled their conformity.

In the case of some Hispanics, the question of self-identity is doubly complicated. As one teacher explained: "One of the great puzzlements of my childhood was hearing my barrio cousins and friends say in school that they were Spaniards, not Mexicans. Because my father used to tell stories about how cruel and blood-thirsty the Spaniards had been and how they had destroyed the Indian civilizations, I could not believe that any of my classmates would want to call themselves Spaniards. To this day I am troubled by the fact that my home language is Spanish." This painful experience—of having a mixed heritage in which one represents the dominator and the other the dominated—is not uncommon among Hispanics. It is an unresolved issue felt throughout Latin America. Every one of us who has Spanish-speaking parents or grandparents in this hemisphere is a *mestizo,* either ethnically or culturally.

Guillén (1972) proposes a solution in a powerfully poetic image. By accepting his mixed heritage, he manages to unite the shadows of his two grandparents, the Spanish warrior and the African slave.[6] Such an acceptance would help us to keep in mind past inequities and the valuable lessons the knowledge of these past inequities provides. This knowledge would allow us to accept ourselves as a whole and give us the strength to struggle against present-day oppressors, who obviously are not the Spaniards of today.

In any case, these are issues that need to be addressed during the creative education process, since they strongly affect the Hispanic teacher's sense of identity and thus limit the ability to model self-worth for children.

## The Need to Integrate Theory and Experience

The participants saw the need for teacher education programs to integrate solid theory and ample experience in a mutually supportive manner. Many of them described their own educational experience as highly mechanistic. According to one teacher, "All we were told was how to set goals and objectives and how to write lesson plans. I wrote more than a hundred lesson plans, but I knew nothing about the classroom." Another teacher's complaint was that "all courses dealt with the ideal student, as if all students would be alike. We never heard anything about the students as real individuals." A third teacher said, "They gave us seminar syndrome. We never had the opportunity to experiment and explore. Now we do the same thing with our students. A lot of teaching goes on, but very little learning."

This brings us to the most crucial issue. Participants in all groups said that although they were very much concerned about the need to develop critical thinking in their students, they wanted to learn how to empower themselves first. The strongest criticism of teacher education was directed at the discrepancy between what the faculty in the schools of education taught and what they practiced. One participant expressed the shared complaint in this way: "They preached to us to teach creatively, but we were never allowed any creativity. They encouraged us to be good communicators, but the classes they taught were deadly. There was some lip service paid to the need for encouraging children to think, but we were expected to memorize and repeat."

Creative education recognizes that the process of learning is more than the accumulation of information. Some teachers came to this recognition on their own. One teacher said, "My teacher training wasn't great; the content was too remote. But I did get something—I learned myself. I learned how to learn, how to develop learning skills, how to organize my own learning style, and this has been the most useful thing for me." In discussing what a creative teacher education program should provide, another teacher commented, "It would offer the opportunity to look inside, to find their own biases, to learn not to be afraid of sharing intimacies and their own experiences. Students may not learn content, but they learn the teacher; they learn how to emulate the teacher. It is important to provide opportunities to validate the teacher's self-integrity."

## Summary

In order to provide creative education for language minority children, bilingual teachers themselves need to experience the liberating forces of this type of education. Teachers need to be validated as human beings, as conscientious, creative, intellectual human beings. They need the power that comes from communicating effectively, both orally and in writing, and the power that is built on solidarity. They need to understand the societal forces that have influenced their cultural and linguistic identity so that they can stop passively accepting their circumstances and become not only agents of their own transformation but also leaders in the world around them.

## Notes

1. Schools in the United States are currently perceived, as noted with considerable insight by Giroux (1986), as instruments of societal reproduction. As such, they are attacked by conservatives and radicals alike—by conservatives for failing to produce adequately trained workers for an increasingly complex technological economy; by radicals for legitimizing the prevailing societal value of the dominant corporate order and perpetuating the existing gender, racial, and class inequalities.
2. For an application of creative methodology to a language arts curriculum, see Ada and de Olave (1986).
3. The positive value of bilingualism increases as the country moves from an industrial society to a technological/informational one. It is indeed paradoxical that precisely when the country most needs communication skills in order to export its technology to the rest of the world, we should see the appearance of an "English-only initiative" aimed at discouraging the maintenance and development of such skills.
4. The first group comprised bilingual teachers working with migrant children in the Pajaro Valley School District, Watsonville, California; the second group were bilingual teachers in a number of communities between Santa Cruz and Salinas, California; the third group were bilingual teachers from the San Francisco Bay area; the fourth group included principals, counselors, and teacher educators, as well as teachers. Not all those in group four are engaged in bilingual

education, but they all work with minority populations in various areas in California. All members of groups two and three are pursuing a Masters of Education degree; those in group four are doctoral students. Although approximately 50 percent of them received their teacher education in California, the institutions they attended vary greatly (University of California at Davis, Berkeley, Santa Cruz, and Los Angeles; San Jose State University; Stanford University, University of Southern California). The others studied in Ohio, Michigan, New York, Massachusetts, Florida, and elsewhere.

5. The elite bilingual schools found in other countries, which include American schools abroad, use a two-teacher model of education. In a single classroom, each of two teachers provides instruction for half the day, speaking only in his or her native language and thus motivating the children to become proficient in that language. In that system, the children, not the teacher, are expected to become fully bilingual. In contrast, the one-teacher model, which is followed in most bilingual programs in the United States, requires a single teacher to teach all subjects in both languages. Yet, few teachers are equally proficient in both languages, precisely because there has not been a tradition of additive bilingual education in this country.

6. In the poem *Balada de los dos abuelos*, Guillén writes: "Sombras que solo yo veo,/ me escoltan mis dos abuelos./ . . ./Yo los junto./ . . . Los dos se abrazan./Los dos suspiran. Los dos/las fuertes cabezas alzan;/los dos del mismo tamaño,/bajo las estrellas altas;/los dos del mismo tamaño,/ ansia negra y ansia blanca;/los dos del mismo tamaño,/ gritan, sueñan, lloran, cantan./ Sueñan, lloran, cantan./ Lloran, cantan./ ¡Cantan!"

# References

Ada, A. F., & de Olave, M. de P. (1986). *Hagamos caminos*. Reading, MA: Addison Wesley.

Aronowitz, S., & Giroux, H. A. (1985). *Education under siege*. South Hadley, MA: Bergin & Garvey.

Cummins, J. (1981). The role of primary language development in promoting educational success for language minority students. In Office of Bilingual Education (Ed.), *Schooling and language minority students: A theoretical framework*. Los Angeles: California State University.

Cummins, J. (1986). Empowering minority students: A framework for intervention. *Harvard Educational Review, 56*, 18–36.

Dolson, D. (1985). The effects of Spanish home language use on the scholastic performance of Hispanic pupils. *Journal of Multilingual and Multicultural Development, 6*(2), 135–155.

Freire, P. (1982a). *Education for critical consciousness*. New York: Continuum.

Freire, P. (1982b). *Pedagogy of the oppressed*. New York: Continuum.

Giroux, H. A. (1986). *Radical pedagogy and the politics of student voice*. Unpublished manuscript.

Guillén, N. (1972). Balada de los dos abuelos. In *Abra Poética: 1920–1958*. Havanna: Institute Cubano del Libro, 137–139.

Lambert, W., & Tucker, R. (1972). *Bilingual education of children: The St. Lambert experiment*. Rowley, MA: Newbury House.

Peal, E., & Lambert, W. (1962). The relation of bilingualism to intelligence. *Psychological Monographs, 75*, 1–23.

Skutnabb-Kangas, T. (1984). *Bilingualism or not: The education of minorities*. Clevedon, Eng.: Multilingual Matters.

# 17

# Promoting the Success of Latino Language-Minority Students: An Exploratory Study of Six High Schools

TAMARA LUCAS, *ARC Associates, Oakland, California*
ROSEMARY HENZE, *ARC Associates, Oakland, California*
RUBEN DONATO, *University of Wisconsin, Madison*

*The failure of many high schools in the United States to meet the needs of diverse language-minority students is evidenced by high dropout rates and small numbers entering higher education. Not all schools, however, have failed to respond to the unique needs of these students. In this article Tamara Lucas, Rosemary Henze, and Rubén Donato discuss six high schools that have had positive success in educating Latino minority students. Through their analyses of these schools and their communities, the authors identify several factors that are related to successful schooling outcomes with these students, providing significant heuristics for future research.*

In "Effective Schools for the Urban Poor," Ron Edmonds states: "All children are eminently educable, and the behavior of the school is critical in determining the quality of the education. . . ." (1979, p. 20). This way of thinking diverges from

The authors wish to extend their thanks to all of the staff and students of the schools we visited. We greatly appreciated the hospitality and friendliness with which we were received and the unique perspectives which people took the time to describe to us in interviews. We also want to thank our colleagues Marie Mayen, Leticia Pérez, Huynh Dinh Te, William Tikunoff, Sau-Lim Tsang, Betty Ward, and Harriet Doss Willis for their work on various stages of this project and their support throughout. The information reported here was collected as part of a plan for providing technical assistance to Arizona secondary schools. The technical assistance project was conducted by the Southwest Center for Educational Equity, which is funded by the U.S. Department of Education, Office of Elementary and Secondary Education, under Title IV of the Civil Rights Act of 1964. The contents of this article do not necessarily reflect the views or policies of the Department of Education.

*Harvard Educational Review* Vol. 60 No. 3 August 1990, 315–340

often-cited "deficit" models of education, which account for student failure by reference to certain cultural, linguistic, and socioeconomic factors in students' backgrounds, thus making a liability out of difference. Language-minority (LM) students in particular have often been blamed for their underachievement in U.S. schools.[1] By considering them "difficult" or culturally and linguistically "deprived," schools have found it easy to absolve themselves of responsibility for the education of these students. Edmonds, on the other hand, places the responsibility for quality education squarely in the hands of the schools.

This assignment of responsibility for language-minority students has had a complex legal history. In 1973 the Supreme Court held, in the *Lau v. Nichols* decision, that public schools had to provide an education comprehensible to limited-English-proficient (LEP) students.[2] In an attempt to equalize educational opportunities for LEP students in U.S. schools, the Court stated: "Basic English is at the very core of what public schools teach. Imposition of a requirement that, before a child can effectively participate in the education program, he must already have acquired those basic skills is to make a mockery of public education" (*Lau v. Nichols*, 1973).

The *Lau* decision has had a powerful impact on the education of language-minority students. It marked the beginning of a national interest in educational equity for LM students and provoked policymakers throughout the country to respond to the special needs of this growing student population. After 1974, under pressure from the federal government, many states began to push school districts to develop programs for LM students. California, for example, passed a bill in 1976 mandating bilingual education in its public schools.[3] School districts in California with large numbers of LEP students were required by the state to demonstrate how they were going to serve those students. For the most part, however, school districts focused on LEP students in elementary schools and ignored the schooling of secondary LEP students.

However, secondary schools do enroll many students whose English proficiency is limited. For example, poor economic conditions in Mexico have caused large numbers of Mexican students to arrive in the Southwest, with or without their families. Political unrest and war have brought thousands of refugees to the United States from such countries as El Salvador, Nicaragua, Guatemala, Vietnam, Cambodia, Laos, and Afghanistan. Students of all ages often arrive with little or no knowledge of English. Because of wartime conditions in their countries, many students have had interrupted schooling and thus come unprepared not only in English, but also in content knowledge, basic study skills, and knowledge of school culture. Providing effective schooling for these students is particularly challenging at the secondary level, when students are expected to possess a wealth of implicit and explicit knowledge about how to be a student.

On the other hand, many immigrant students arrive in the United States with strong educational backgrounds; for example, those who have attended *"Secundaria"* in Mexico may have had higher levels of math than their U.S.-born peers. Secondary LM students, in other words, are extremely diverse, bringing with them educational, social, academic, and cultural experiences that may differ widely from those of members of the host culture. To assure academic success, schools must attend to this diversity through special programs and practices, and through increased sensitivity to students' needs. High drop-out rates, low standardized test scores, poor attendance records, and the small numbers of students going on to post-secondary education all attest to the failure of most high schools to meet the needs of this student population (See Arias, 1986; Brown & Haycock, 1984; Espinosa & Ochoa, 1986; Gingras & Careaga, 1989; Medina, 1988; Orfield, 1986; Orum, 1988; Rumberger, 1987; U.S. General Accounting Office, 1987).

Because we believe that schools are responsible for the quality of education students receive, and that given a good education, all students can achieve, we are interested in what makes some schools more successful than others. During the past fifteen years, some educational researchers have turned away from attempting to explain school and student failure and have focused instead on explaining success, producing a body of research known as the "effective schools" literature. This work, most of which comes from studies conducted in urban elementary schools, provides some insights into the attributes of successful schools, including strong leadership; high expectations of students; school-wide staff development; parent involvement and support; recognition of students' academic success; district support; collaborative planning; collegial relationships; and sense of community (Edmonds, 1979; Purkey & Smith, 1983).

The research on effective schools is not without its detractors, however. Critics have pointed to shortcomings in the literature, citing, for example, lack of generalizability to any but elementary schools; lack of attention to the variety of student populations and community contexts; an over-emphasis on attributes and lack of sufficient attention to complex processes and interrelationships; and a top-down strategy for school improvement growing out of the "implementation of attributes" approach (See Carter & Chatfield, 1986; Rosenholtz, 1985; Rowen, Bossert, & Dwyer, 1983; Stedman, 1987; Wilson & Corcoran, 1988).

One of the most frequent criticisms is that the effective schools literature has given little attention to what makes some schools more successful than others with language-minority students. Jennifer Bell (1989) has offered several reasons for this lack of attention. First, since most of the effective schools studies were conducted in schools which were predominantly Black and White in composition, LM students were not a major factor in overall student achievement. Second, with certain exceptions, most researchers did not consider language to be an important factor in student achievement. Third, the diversity of LM students was generally considered too difficult to account for in research design. Furthermore, since the public has been so sharply divided over bilingual instruction, research on LM students in the schools has focused primarily on the role of language in instruction rather than on the effectiveness of the whole school.

Recently, however, some studies have focused on effective schooling for language-minority students. Thomas Carter and Michael Chatfield (1986) reported on characteristics of three effective bilingual elementary schools, emphasizing processes over structures and attributes. The schools they described were characterized by such factors as: a well-functioning total system producing a school climate that promotes positive student outcomes; positive leadership, usually from the formal leaders; high staff expectations for students and instructional programs; strong demand for academic performance; denial of the cultural deprivation argument and stereotypes that support it; and high staff morale.

Bruce Wilson and Thomas Corcoran (1988) report on a number of middle and secondary schools that are successful with "at risk" students, which they define as students from poor and minority backgrounds (p. 130). Since some of the schools had sizable numbers of Latino and Asian students, we can assume that some of them were language-minority students, although the authors do not discuss the language backgrounds or English proficiency of students. The common elements of these successful schools include a positive attitude toward the students, a willingness to question conventional practices, a strong and competent leadership, a highly committed teaching staff, high expectations and standards, and an emphasis on high achievement in academics.

A number of studies have examined effective instructional practices for language-minority students in elementary bilingual programs (Ramírez, 1988; Tikunoff, 1985; Wong-Fillmore, McLaughlin, Ammon, & Ammon, 1985). However, there is little research of any kind at the secondary level, and little at either the elementary or secondary level that looks beyond effective classroom instruction to the broader issues involved in effective schooling for LM students. In a critique of the ways in which the "effective schools formula" has been applied, Stedman (1987) argues for a reconceptualization of the effective schools literature, focusing on "detailed descriptions of school organization and practice" (p. 217) and on providing "concrete guidance about what to do to make a school effective" (p. 218). Ways in which good schools foster cultural pluralism need to be documented, Stedman writes, and secondary schools need to be given more attention.

The exploratory study reported here intends to narrow these gaps in the existing research and to extend our knowledge about effective schooling. The study is based on information gathered at six secondary schools that have been recognized by local, state, or federal agencies for their success in providing a quality education for LM students, not only through effective classroom instruction but also through whole-school approaches. Because previous research, such as that described above, has primarily focused on successful instructional practices for LM students, our discussion will focus its attention on the whole school rather than on classroom practices per se.

It is improtant to point out that there is of course no formula or prescription for success; no single combination of variables will produce an effective school. Educators cannot simply adopt the features of these six schools and expect their institutions to become successful with LM students overnight. Schools can, however, begin to work toward such success by following the lead of these schools in ways that are appropriate and realistic for their particular school settings.

We believe that the most critical element in determining whether educators can work toward success for all students is the belief that all students can succeed. In

1979, Edmonds argued that the degree to which we effectively teach "the children of the poor" depends more on our political persuasions than on the information we gain from educational research. He asserted that we already know more than enough to successfully teach all students, and that the question is whether we *want* to teach all students. Recently, Shirley Jackson (1989) made a similar assertion. Yet many educators still appear uncertain as to whether schools can significantly influence the achievement and attainment of poor and minority youths, often claiming that parents do not support their children's educational efforts and implying that therefore schools cannot be blamed for failing to educate these children (Suro, 1990). In contrast, we hope that by presenting case studies of "living examples of success" (Carter & Chatfield, 1986, p. 229), we will not only encourage educators to believe that *all* students can succeed, but also provide them with concrete knowledge of what schools can do to help them.

## Background

In 1988, an initiative was undertaken by the Southwest Center for Educational Equity, at the request of and in collaboration with the Arizona Department of Education and representatives of six Arizona school districts, to develop strategies for Arizona high schools to serve language-minority students.[4] In surveying the literature on effective schooling, we realized that little was known about successful schooling for LM students at the secondary level. To gather information for the Arizona High School Initiative, we therefore conducted an exploratory study of schools promoting the achievement of this student population. We visited five high schools in California and one in Arizona that had large populations of Latino students and that had been recognized by local, state, and/or federal agencies for excellence.[5] Because the needs of different groups of LM students vary, and because we wanted to increase comparability of student populations across schools, we decided that schools working successfully with Latino LM students in particular would be the focus of this part of the initiative.[6]

## Methods

### Selection of Case Study Schools

The selection of case study schools was complicated by the lack of consensus about what constitutes an "effective" or "successful" school. After much deliberation over which criteria were the most relevant, we decided to take a two-pronged approach to site selection, using both qualitative and quantitative criteria. First, we sought nominations from a variety of people familiar with secondary schools with large numbers of language-minority students, consulting with educators at state, county, and district levels and asking them to recommend schools that they believed were successful with those students (Wilson & Corcoran, 1988). We then contacted the principals of the recommended schools to determine whether they had received any formal recognition from local, state, or federal agencies for their instructional programs for LM students and whether they could provide us with some quantitative evidence of their success—for example, average daily attendance rates, drop-out rates, numbers of Latino LM students going on to post-secondary education, and standardized test scores that compared favorably with other minority schools. While we recognize that "effectiveness is a construct, an abstraction" (Wilson & Corcoran, 1988, p. 26) and that this process did not capture the full range of possible indicators of success, we believe it enabled us to select six schools which are taking identifiable, positive steps to educate LM students.

## Data Collection

Data were collected at five school sites in California and one in Arizona.[7] Two to four project staff members visited each site for three days, thus providing multiple perspectives and allowing for intensive collection of information. The combined data from all six schools consisted of audiotapes and notes from structured interviews with 1 superintendent, 2 district-level bilingual program directors, 6 principals, 6 assistant principals, 5 school-level project and program directors, 15 counselors, 52 teachers and aides, and 135 students; 124 student questionnaires (35 from newcomers and 89 from non-newcomers); 54 classroom observations; schoolwide observations of the 6 schools; and various records and documents for each school, including policies regarding LM students, special program descriptions, transcripts for students who were interviewed, and other written information that interviewees gave us. Because we wanted above all to facilitate communication, we allowed students to use either English or Spanish for interviews and questionnaires, depending upon their preference. Students whose proficiency in English was very limited would not have been able to participate had they not been given the opportunity to use Spanish. Because the study sought to understand what contributes to the success of high school LM students, we were primarily interested in obtaining information from school staff who worked extensively and effectively with these students. Assistant principals, counselors, and teachers were selected to be interviewed if they 1) worked with large numbers of Latino LEP students, and 2) were recommended by others (administrators, counselors, teachers, students) as being especially effective with, and/or knowledgeable about, these students.

At each school, we asked a counselor, or in some cases a program director, to select students for us to interview. We requested six Latino students in each of four groups—high achievers, average achievers, students who had been doing poorly but had now improved, and students who had immigrated within the last two years. We also asked that students be non-native speakers of English. Though we succeeded in interviewing an average of 24 Latino LM students at each school, the distinctions among high achievers, average achievers, and "turnarounds" were not at all clear. For purposes of analysis, therefore, we grouped students only as newcomers or non-newcomers. Both groups included students from grades nine through twelve.

Sixty-one percent of the students interviewed were born in Mexico. The newcomers had arrived in the United States between the ages of fourteen and eighteen, while the non-newcomers were students born in the United States and students who had entered the United States in the early and middle grades. According to the student questionnaire, 72.5 percent of the students spoke Spanish at home, while 39 percent used Spanish at school. Ninety-eight percent of the students' fathers worked in labor- or service-related jobs, while 90 percent of the mothers worked as housewives or in service-related jobs.

In the aggregate, then, the Latino students we interviewed came from working-class backgrounds. However, they represented a tremendous range of educational and cultural experiences, from those whose entire education had been in the United States to those who had attended school in several different countries before coming here. Some students, according to the questionnaire, had had interruptions of several years in their schooling due to political unrest in their countries, while others had attended continuously. Factors such as these, combined with the different cultural identities of Mexicanos, Chicanos, Nicaragüenses, and other groups, made it clear that there is no such thing as a "typical" Latino student, and that a school successful with this population would have to be sensitive to differences in students' experiences and backgrounds.

## Data Analysis

Data analysis was a recursive process which began with the design of the study. The design, influenced by previous research on effective schooling, determined who would be interviewed and what other types of data would be collected. The questions used in interviews were formulated as new issues emerged from the data. Categories for analysis, inspired at first by the effective schools literature, were continually shaped as we interviewed, observed, and gathered documents at each site. Once information-gathering had ended, intensive analysis proceeded from within-site analyses to cross-site analyses:

1. Each person who visited a site wrote a report of the data that she or he collected from interviews, observations, and serendipitous encounters. These reports brought together all of the data collected by each researcher into one organized and accessible whole. Reports included information about the school context (community, school board, student body composition and ethnicity, language census), types of Latino LM students enrolled at the school, what seemed to be working based on what was reported and what we saw, and what improvements were suggested to better meet the needs of the students.

2. All individual reports about each school were then synthesized into one case study report per school to provide "a well-grounded sense of the local reality" in that setting (Miles & Huberman, 1984, p. 151).

3. The six case studies were then analyzed in order to compare perceived realities across these schools.

In this process, we developed both concrete descriptions of what we observed and categories or themes derived from the data and informed by other studies of effective schooling (see Merriam, 1988). This process resulted in highlighting eight features that existed across sites, as noted in the introduction. Although each school is unique, the eight features represent commonalities in the ways the schools were promoting success for language-minority students. Most of the study findings are derived from interviews with staff members and students—particularly when the same or similar features were mentioned by a large number of people in different schools—and from our informed observations. In many cases, the language of the findings reflects words or phrases we heard repeatedly. What we were told in interviews was also confirmed and concretized through classroom and school-wide observation and consultation of school records and documents.

## Findings

### School Profiles

Five of the six schools were relatively large, with 1,700 to 2,200 students. All had minority White populations, and in all but the smallest school, Latino students constituted the largest single group—more than one-third of the school population. The four schools with the larger proportions of non-White students (Nogales, Overfelt, Sweetwater, and Newcomer) also had larger proportions of non-White staff. In none of the schools, however, was the ethnicity of the staff comparable to the student population; in all of them, a much larger proportion of staff than students was White. The percentage of students participating in a school lunch program—a rough measure of their socioeconomic status—varied considerably among the six schools. At Anaheim and Artesia, fewer than 25 percent of the students received such aid, at Overfelt and Sweetwater, about 33 percent did so, and at Nogales and Newcomer 80 percent did so. Thus, socioeconomic status of students is not a feature shared by these schools overall, although as noted earlier, the Latino students whom we interviewed were largely working class.

### Key Features that Promote the Success of Language-Minority Students

Through the exploratory case studies and the analysis across cases, eight features emerged which we believe to be the most important in promoting the success of language-minority students at the six schools we visited. A more concise version of these eight features appears in Table 1.

### 1. Value is placed on the students' languages and cultures.

Rather than ignoring barriers to equality and perpetuating the disenfranchisement of minority students, the principals, administrators, counselors, teachers, and other support staff at the schools we visited celebrated diversity. They gave language-minority students the message that their languages and cultures were valued and respected, thus promoting the self-esteem necessary for student achievement. They communicated this sense of value and respect in a number of concrete ways, translating the ideal into an everyday reality.

TABLE 1

*Features of High Schools that Promote the Achievement of*
*Language-Minority Students*

1. *Value is placed on the students' languages and cultures* by:

   Treating students as individuals, not as members of a group
   Learning about students' cultures
   Learning students' languages
   Hiring bilingual staff with similar cultural backgrounds to the students
   Encouraging students to develop their primary language skills
   Allowing students to speak their primary languages except when English development is the
   focus of instruction or interactions
   Offering advanced as well as lower division content courses in the students' primary languages
   Instituting extracurricular activities that will attract LM students

2. *High expectations of language-minority students are made concrete* by:

   Hiring minority staff in leadership positions to act as role models
   Providing a special program to prepare LM students for college
   Offering advanced and honors bilingual/sheltered classes in content areas
   Making it possible for students to exit ESL programs quickly
   Challenging students in class and providing guidance to help them meet the challenge
   Providing counseling assistance (in the primary language if necessary) to help students apply to
   college and fill out scholarship and grant forms
   Bringing in representatives of colleges and minority graduates who are in college to talk to
   students
   Working with parents to gain their support for students going to college
   Recognizing students for doing well

3. *School leaders make the education of language-minority students a priority.* These leaders:

   Hold high expectations of LM students
   Are knowledgeable of instructional and curricular approaches to teaching LM students and
   communicate this knowledge to staff
   Take a strong leadership role in strengthening curriculum and instruction for all students,
   including LM students
   Are often bilingual minority-group members themselves
   Hire teachers who are bilingual and/or trained in methods for teaching LM students

4. *Staff development is explicitly designed to help teachers and other staff serve language-minority*
   *students more effectively.* Schools and school districts:

   Offer incentives and compensation so that school staff will take advantage of available staff
   development programs

   Provide staff development for teachers and other school staff in:
   –effective instructional approaches to teaching LM students, e.g., cooperative learning methods,
   sheltered English, and reading and writing in the content areas
   –principles of second-language acquisition
   –the cultural backgrounds and experiences of the students
   –the languages of the students
   –cross-cultural communication
   –cross-cultural counseling

5. *A variety of courses and programs for language-minority students is offered.* The programs:

   Include courses in ESL and primary language instruction (both literacy and advanced placement)
   and bilingual and sheltered courses in content areas
   Insure that the course offerings for LM students do not limit their choices or trap them in low-
   level classes by offering advanced as well as basic courses taught through bilingual and
   sheltered methods

*continued . . .*

TABLE 1
*Continued*

---

Keep class size small (20–25 students) in order to maximize interaction

Establish academic support programs that help LM students make the transition from ESL and bilingual classes to mainstream classes and prepare them to go to college

6. *A counseling program gives special attention to language-minority students* through counselors who:

Speak the students' languages and are of the same or similar cultural backgrounds

Are informed about post-secondary educational opportunities for LM students

Believe in, emphasize, and monitor the academic success of LM students

7. *Parents of language-minority students are encouraged to become involved in their children's education.* Schools can provide and encourage:

Staff who can speak the parents' languages

On-campus ESL classes for parents

Monthly parents' nights

Parent involvement with counselors in planning their children's course schedules

Neighborhood meetings with school staff

Early morning meetings with parents

Telephone contacts to check on absent students

8. *School staff members share a strong commitment to empower language-minority students through education.* This commitment is made concrete through staff who:

Give extra time to work with LM students

Take part in a political process that challenges the status quo

Request training of various sorts to help LM students become more effective

Reach out to students in ways that go beyond their job requirements, for example, by sponsoring extra-curricular activities

Participate in community activities in which they act as advocates for Latinos and other minorities

---

First, the ability to speak a language in addition to English was treated as an advantage rather than a liability. A number of White and Latino teachers and counselors who were not native speakers of Spanish had learned the language. Some spoke it well enough to understand some of what their students said; others had learned it well enough to teach bilingual content classes. Students commented in interviews that they appreciated efforts made by teachers to speak Spanish and were pleased to see that the teachers valued their language. One student noted that "when teachers are bilingual, it makes our learning easier. They treat us equally." Another described the school as *"una amiga bilingüe"* (a bilingual friend).

Although these high schools made English literacy a primary goal, they also encouraged students to enhance their native language skills in classes for those students who spoke Spanish. Four of the six high schools we visited offered Spanish courses for Spanish speakers. Of these, three of them offered both literacy skills instruction and advanced courses in Spanish. Advanced Placement (AP) Spanish classes at these schools gave native-Spanish-speaking students the opportunity to capitalize on their native language to obtain college credit. The principal at Nogales High School, where 89 percent of the students were Latino, had gone even further in demonstrating the value placed on Spanish. All students at this school were required to take five years of language instruction—four in English and one in Spanish. Students who passed a proficiency test in Spanish were free to take another language to fulfill the fifth year requirement; others had to take Spanish for Spanish speakers or Spanish as a second language, whichever was appropriate.

A less formal but no less effective way that educators showed respect for the students' language was to allow them to speak their native language when English language development was not the focus of instruction. Their philosophy was that nothing was gained from stifling a young person's desire to communicate in his or her primary language. Throughout the campuses of the high schools we visited, students were free to speak Spanish with each other and with school staff. The use of their native language was not restricted to informal settings. Five of the schools provided content courses in Spanish, thus giving students the opportunity to progress through the content areas while developing their English skills. They were not required to postpone taking advanced content courses until they were fluent in English.

Besides showing respect for students' native language, staff in these schools also celebrated the students' cultures. Perhaps the most transparent and readily accessible aspects of culture are customs, holidays, and overtly stated values. While many schools give lip service to these aspects of culture, for example, by celebrating *Cinco de Mayo* and serving tacos on that day, the schools we visited affirmed the customs, values, and holidays of the language-minority students' countries in deeper and more consistent ways throughout the year.

Teachers, for example, made it their business to know about their students' past experiences. Some had visited Mexican schools to better understand their students' previous educational experiences. A group of teachers from one school had observed mathematics teaching in a Mexican school. One of them said that understanding how Mexican students were taught math in Mexico made teaching them easier. He could say to students, "This is the way most of you were taught how to divide in Mexico. And that's OK. This is another way of doing it." Without denigrating what they had learned in Mexico, he would ask which way was easiest for them.

In addition, while faculty and staff were sensitive to the importance of students' language and cultures, they did not treat students simply as members of an undifferentiated ethnic group. They recognized students' individual strengths, interests, problems, and concerns rather than characterizing them by reference to stereotypes. The assistant principal at one school said, "Basically, Hispanic kids are no different from other kids; they want to learn. Those who fall by the wayside are those whose needs aren't being met. Who wants to fail everyday?"

Faculty and staff also knew that there is no such thing as a generic Latino LM student. Rather, people from Mexico, Nicaragua, El Salvador, Guatemala, Cuba, and other Spanish-speaking countries were known to have different histories and customs and to speak different varieties of Spanish. Mexican immigrants, Mexican Americans, and Chicanos were also recognized as different from one another, and variation among Mexican immigrants based upon socioeconomic background and educational attainment level was acknowledged. When asked to describe the Latino students at the school, one teacher responded with five categories: those who are "well off, well educated, not disenfranchised; the migrant kids who have little education; children born here of parents who have immigrated here; limited-English-proficient students who have been here ten to twelve years but have lived in insular communities and had no education in Spanish; and then Central Americans."

Respect for students' languages and cultures was communicated through support programs as well as academic programs. In some schools, special programs provided tutorial and counseling assistance. Teachers and Latino students were paired in mentoring and advocacy activities, thus increasing the sense among faculty of a personal connection with the students. Extracurricular programs involved activities that were relevant to Latino cultures. In one school, students could take a PE class called *Bailes,* in which they learned and performed dances from different regions of Mexico. In another, a student-run group published a monthly newspaper in Spanish called *El Mitotero.* Begun by a teacher, the paper was quickly "taken over" by the students themselves. They formed a committee and organized a formal club with officers and by-laws, which was then recognized by the school's student association. According to the teacher who started it, the paper is "very culturally-oriented—if you understand Spanish, you might understand the words, but if you are not familiar with the local Mexican culture, you will probably miss a lot of the 'double meanings' and cultural references." One issue of the newspaper was devoted to a debate about bilingual education. The newspaper staff interviewed students and teachers and then presented both pro and con sides of the debate, the former written in Spanish and the latter in English.

A final and important way in which these high schools showed respect for the students' cultures and languages was through their staffing. Faculty members who spoke the native languages of the language-minority students in the school and shared similar cultural backgrounds not only used this skill and knowledge to improve instruction for them, but also served as role models and advocates for these students. Comments of several faculty reflect their awareness of the roles they were playing. For example, the principal at Nogales High School said:

> When we hire teachers, we try to look for the best teachers, number one, but number two and most importantly, we try to get teachers that relate to our type of kids, and number three, if we can get teachers that are from this area, that are teachers that have graduated from this high school, teachers that have had to go through these problems, the growing-up problems, the educational problems from here, and have gone out and have become successful, then we have provided role models for our kids that are essential. I think probably that's one of the reasons I'm principal. We've had all kids of principals, but I think that the community itself has tried to hire administrators that, number one, relate to our community, and number two, have been here [for a long time]. The majority of the administration from this district is from here.

A teacher at another school said, "The students are very proud and the teachers support that. It's okay to speak Spanish, to be Mexican, not to know English." He believes that students at the school feel supported by the fact that teachers speak Spanish "in public." One student had come to him and reported with some incredulity, "Mr. W. [an Anglo] spoke Spanish to me in class!"

The head counselor at the same school said:

> Parents and students see us [Latinos] in leadership positions, not just in the cafeteria or as janitors. People in the school understand problems in the community and have lived it themselves. . . . For example, I understand if a student has to stay home all week to take care of kids. . . . Parents come in because I speak Spanish and can understand their problems. I'm not from a middle-class, elite, intellectual background.

A counselor at a third school said, "I have a sensitivity to these students that comes from my family background. I'm third generation here. I know what it is to leave your roots and live in a system different from that of your parents. Maybe that's why I have an urgency to push college." Students also referred to their teachers and others at the schools as role models. When asked to tell us about a faculty member who was particularly effective, one student commented, "Ms. V. has been a good role model. She speaks many languages and inspires me." Another student said, "Mr. A. encourages students to break stereotypes by being good in chemistry, physical science, and physics."

## 2. High expectations of language-minority students are made concrete.

Throughout the schools we visited, people recognized the importance of high expectations for Latino LM students. Such expectations form the foundation for the program features we describe. One principal put it this way: "I firmly believe that what you give to the best kids, you give to all," while taking into account special needs and equity issues. The professional staff members in the six schools we visited not only held high expectations of their students but had also taken concrete actions to demonstrate those expectations and to help students accomplish what was expected. Some of these actions already have been mentioned. For example, when students see people like themselves who have become teachers, counselors, and principals, they learn that professions like these are attainable.

Recognizing that language-minority students do not have information that mainstream students possess, school counselors who understood students' languages and cultures helped them plan their high school programs, find information about different colleges, apply to college, fill out financial aid forms, and apply for scholarships. Counselors also communicated with parents to gain their support for their children to apply for college, understanding that if going to college is a new idea to the student, it is probably completely unfamiliar, perhaps even threatening, to the parents. As one female student noted, "At first my parents weren't wanting me to go to college, but Mrs. C. [the counselor] convinced them that it was okay." College and university representatives were brought to the high school to talk with students. Former graduates of similar backgrounds who had gone to college were invited back

468

to the high school to share their experiences and to encourage others to follow in their path.

In classes, teachers challenged students with difficult questions and problems. Complex ideas and materials were made more accessible to LM students through visuals, board work, group work, reading aloud, and clear and explicit class expectations. Teachers did not talk down to limited-English-proficient students in "foreigner talk," but spoke clearly, with normal intonation, explaining difficult words and concepts as needed.

In all the schools we visited, student success was recognized publicly. In one high school, achievement in a particular class was recognized through a ritual in which the principal came to the class and congratulated the student. In another school, LM students who did well in particular areas (for example, most improved or perfect attendance) were recognized at a monthly "Student of the Month" luncheon during which teachers who had nominated the students presented certificates to them and spoke briefly about the students' accomplishments. Several high schools had special assemblies for students on the honor roll, where parents were invited and recognized while the students received certificates. "It makes you want to try harder when you get an award," noted one student. Latino LM students received these forms of recognition just as other students did.

*3. School leaders make the education of language-minority students a priority.*

Strong instructional leadership has been cited as a key ingredient of effective schools (Carter & Chatfield, 1986; Purkey & Smith, 1983). Effective school leaders, usually principals, are described as actively coordinating curriculum; monitoring students' academic progress; having a clear mission for the school which they communicate to staff, students, and parents; holding high expectations for student achievement and promoting the same among faculty and staff. In the high schools we visited, the principals were, in addition, sincerely committed to educating LM students and knowledgeable about effective teaching approaches for this population. All but one of the principals were bilingual minority-group members themselves. Although each had a unique leadership style, they all demonstrated a strong commitment to raising the achievement levels of minority students, including LM students. Sweetwater's principal, a Latino himself, said:

> One of our major roles in this community is to develop a sense of confidence that we can compete in all areas, not just athletics, that we can go out there and be just as good as anybody else. I guess if I had a wish, I would like for the kids in the school to absolutely believe and know in their hearts that they are as good as anybody on this planet.

Steps taken by this principal to support the success of language-minority students illustrate the types of leadership that we found in these schools. Sweetwater's principal was given the authority by the district to make virtually all decisions at the school, including hiring teachers of his choice. He had initiated several changes in the

469

education program for language-minority students. For example, all remedial classes were eliminated so that LM students would not receive "watered-down versions of content." When he came to the school, he discovered that bilingual classes were "remedial," that the school offered bilingual life science rather than biology and bilingual math rather than algebra. He quickly set out to "amend" the situation. Sections of physics, chemistry, and calculus were added along with summer sessions of geometry; the requirements for athletic participation were raised; the number of bilingual staff was increased from eight to thirty-three; the bilingual program was expanded to include advanced courses such as economics, biology II, and honors chemistry as well as lower division bilingual courses.

Although now credited with raising standardized test scores, tightening discipline, and raising the morale of students and teachers, the principal (and staff who supported his changes) encountered opposition from some staff members from the very beginning. When he eliminated the "remedial" classes in the school, for example, some teachers felt he was unrealistic; they argued that students were going to be lost in algebra. The principal recalled telling them that "students perform as well as they're expected . . . [and that] students in remedial classes in junior high school are still in remedial classes in the twelfth grade, often performing worse as time [goes] on." He believes students "will learn more in a classroom filled with students of mixed abilities than in a class composed solely of students with minimal math skills." He provided calculators for students, justifying their placement in basic algebra when others would think them more suited for remedial math: "If they're going to fail remedial math, why not have them fail basic algebra?"

We found that good leadership can and does come from program directors, department chairpersons, and teachers in high schools as well as from principals. In some schools, these individuals had taken on strong leadership roles vis-à-vis the education of LM students. At Artesia High School, for example, a separate ESL department had been formed, and it was the chair of this department who advocated most strongly for the education of LEP students. The principal at this school played a less active role in this area, though the previous principal, it should be noted, had been very active in making changes for the LM population. This example of a leader who is not a principal serves as a reminder that the strength for change does not necessarily have to come from the top. Though a strong principal who is deeply committed to the needs of LM students is certainly desirable, the principal is not the only person who can make a difference. Teachers, program coordinators, and department chairs can also take it upon themselves to be leaders in the education of LM students.

*4. Staff development is explicitly designed to help teachers and
other staff serve language-minority students more effectively.*

As Lisa Delpit writes, "It is impossible to create a model for the good teacher without taking issues of culture and community context into account" (1988, p. 291). Teachers who are expert in the instruction of mainstream students are not necessarily effective instructors of language-minority students. For this reason, professional development was a high priority for school administrators, teachers, and other professional staff at these schools. Teachers at Nogales High School in Arizona, for example, were encouraged to get an ESL or bilingual endorsement. Teachers received a salary bonus if they held such an endorsement and incorporated ESL or bilingual methods into their curriculum plans. In addition, staff at this school and others we visited received professional development through in-service workshops and conferences. Teachers received training in the principles of second language acquisition and effective instructional approaches for teaching language-minority students, such as sheltered content,[8] cooperative learning, and reading and writing in the content areas. Teachers and other staff learned about students' cultural backgrounds and experiences. Counselors became informed about cross-cultural counseling strategies. Professional staff worked to develop their ability in the native languages of their students, enabling them to communicate more effectively with LM students and their parents.

Most important, *all* teachers and other professional staff were encouraged to participate in professional development of the sort described here, not just those who taught specific classes for this special student population. It appeared that all school staff took responsibility for teaching these students. No one expressed the attitude that one group of teachers would "take care" of LM students and that the others therefore did not need to "worry" about them. In fact, one principal had set a policy prohibiting bilingual teachers from teaching bilingual classes the entire day. He believed that bilingual teachers should teach mainstream as well as bilingual classes so they would not forget what they were preparing LM students to do.

At Anaheim High School, a five-year plan developed to improve the achievement of Latino students included a strong emphasis on staff development and teacher empowerment. When the current principal first came to Anaheim High School in 1983, she convened the ten department heads, and together they examined the effective schools literature to establish a commonality of language and philosophy before instituting changes. These teachers developed a school plan. According to the principal, "[Empowering the teachers] was the best thing I could have done. I had ten advocates for change, and the plan was theirs, not mine. . . . You can force compliance, but you can't force commitment." Later, the principal and ten department heads shared the process they had gone through with all the teachers. One of the teachers who went through the process reflected, "There is an overall drive to help kids. That's one of the unique things about Anaheim High School. That mood was set by Mrs. C., and the turn-around is now being seen." At Anaheim, staff development was conceived of as teacher-motivated, rather than the traditional top-down process. A small cadre of teachers, with the support of the principal, made it their business to learn what could be done to improve the quality of education at their school and later served as models and teachers for the rest of the staff. A similar process occurred at Artesia High School, where a strong staff development program had been developed partly as a result of the school's participation in the state's School Improvement Program.

### 5. A variety of courses and programs for language-minority students is offered.

Too often LM students are placed and kept in a limited selection of low-level high school courses with the rationale that their English is not proficient enough to allow them to cope with more advanced classes. Often these classes are overfilled, leaving students with few opportunities to interact with the teacher adequately (Brown & Haycock, 1984). Yet LM students, like all students, do best when they have the opportunity to take a wide range of courses, including advanced courses that challenge them intellectually.

In these high schools, those who did not yet speak or write fluent English nonetheless were given the opportunity to progress in content courses appropriate to their academic level. Educators in these high schools did not assume that English proficiency matched content knowledge or cognitive skills. They recognized the fine but critical line between programs that failed to prepare LM students for college and those that facilitated their transition to an English language curriculum while providing continuing academic challenge through a variety of bilingual and sheltered courses. If, for instance, a student from Mexico had passed fundamental math and algebra in her country and had limited proficiency in English, she was able to take a geometry class taught in Spanish or one that used sheltered English methods. Advanced-Placement Spanish offered strong Spanish speakers the opportunity to receive college credit for studying Neruda and Cervantes, just as native-English-speaking students could receive advanced credit for studying Wordsworth and Hawthorne. Bilingual economics and bilingual honors chemistry allowed those who possessed the required content-area background to move beyond basics, doing advanced work in these areas while developing their English language competence. In addition to offering a wide range of courses to LM students, two of the schools also had special programs to facilitate their transition to mainstream classes, and another had a program to identify those who qualified for participation in the school's GATE (Gifted and Talented) program.

Special programs were also in place in all the high schools to promote LM students' academic and social growth. These programs have the net effect of extending learning time through before- and after-school activities, a feature which Wilson and Corcoran believe may be the "critical difference between a mediocre school and an excellent one" (1988, p. 58). In an advocate program, teachers were paired with students as tutors and advocates. BECA (Bilingual Excellence in Cognitive Achievement) provided tutoring, career planning, and multicultural awareness for both limited and fluent English-speaking Latino students at one high school. UCO (University and College Opportunity) encouraged and prepared underrepresented minority students in another high school to go to college. The Tanner Bill Program (or "SAT program," as it was known in one school) had a similar goal, though it targeted Latino students in particular. AVID (Advance Via Individual Determination) was a college-prep program for disadvantaged students in one high school that included one class specifically geared to LEP students. These are only a few of the special programs that either targeted or included LM students. A more complete listing appears in Table 2 along with names of the schools where the programs were offered.

*6. A counseling program gives special attention to language-minority students.*

In our interviews with students, one question asked them to identify the teacher or other staff member who had helped them the most. Many students referred to counselors as being key to their adjustment to the new environment and to their clarification of future goals. "At the beginning of the year," said one student, "I wasn't into school. Then I talked to Mrs. B [a counselor] and got into it. My mom said she was proud of me." In the schools we visited, there was at least one bilingual Latino counselor who was able to communicate effectively with newcomers as well as with longer term residents and understood the sociocultural backgrounds of the students. This person was also well informed about post-secondary educational opportunities for language-minority students—scholarships, fellowships, grants—and could guide the students in getting and filling out the appropriate forms. He or she could also communicate with parents about students' successes and problems in school and the value of a college or university education.

One case we heard of involved a twelfth-grade student who lived with her aunt and uncle because her parents were in Mexico. The parents were reluctant to let their daughter, who had been accepted at a reputable college, move away from the family. The counselor took it upon herself to call the parents and talk it over with them, eventually convincing them of the wisdom of letting their daughter take this opportunity. In a school with no bilingual counselor who cared as much as this one did, this student—and presumably others like her—would have missed her opportunity and become another statistic of the low college attendance of minority students.

Simply having one or more bilingual counselors on the staff who are sensitive to students' cultures does not necessarily mean that LM students have access to that counselor, however. In talking with counselors and students, we learned about the importance of having an effective method of assigning students to counselors. Schools used a variety of methods, including assignment by class level, alphabetical order, special needs, and various combinations of these. Those that were most effective made sure that language-minority students were assigned to a counselor who could communicate with them, was knowledgeable of post-secondary opportunities for language-minority students, and was sincerely committed to helping all students succeed in school and beyond.

In the better counseling program, case loads were relatively low, and bilingual Latino counselors were specifically designated for Latino LM students. At Sweet-

TABLE 2
*Courses, Programs, and Activities for Language-Minority Students at Six High Schools*

*Academic Courses and Programs*
–*ESL:* focus on English language development.
–*Transitional ESL/Booster courses:* for students who have completed the ESL sequence but need some extra help in order to succeed in mainstream English classes.
–*Sheltered English content classes:* content classes with English language development built in (includes advanced classes).
–*Spanish-language content courses:* content classes taught in Spanish (includes advanced classes).
–*Spanish for Spanish speakers:* basic literacy and advanced Spanish skills.
–*Math and reading labs (computer-assisted instruction):* work on basic skills at individual pace.

*Support Programs*
Some of these programs serve only Latino and/or LM students; most include but are not limited to Latino LM students. Some focus on helping students develop advanced skills; others focus on more basic skills.*
–*Advocate Program:* Teachers volunteer to be paired with students, act as advocates and tutors. (Nogales)
–*BECA (Bilingual Excellence in Cognitive Achievement):* tutoring, career planning, multicultural awareness for Latino LM students. (Overfelt)
–*UCO (University and College Opportunity Program):* to encourage and prepare underrepresented minorities to go to college. Students are assigned to a special counselor, go on field trips to colleges. (Overfelt)
–*AVID (Advance Via Individual Determination):* college-prep program for disadvantaged students of all ethnic backgrounds. Uses peer and college tutors. One class in the program is specifically geared to LM students. (Sweetwater)
–*SAT Program, funded by the Tanner Bill:* for Latino students who have potential for academic success. Teachers are specially trained, classes are small (25 students), teachers act as mentors for 10–12 students, parents are involved. (Anaheim)
–*MESA (Math, Engineering, Science Achievement):* college-prep program for disadvantaged students of all ethnic backgrounds with emphasis on science and math. (Overfelt)
–*PLATO (Programmed Logic for Automatic Teaching Operations):* This computer-based dropout program allows students to attend school part of the day and work part-time. They use computers for individualized instruction, get career and college counseling. Students can receive regular diploma. (Sweetwater)
–*High-Risk Program:* for students who have failed a class or two and/or have attendance problems. Students are assigned to work with mentor teachers who have had training to participate. All participate voluntarily.
–*Chapter I program:* for students in low socioeconomic brackets who have scored below the 36th percentile on the CTBS or equivalent. Focuses on basic math and language arts and the use of computers; 20 students per class. (Anaheim)

*Extracurricular Activities*
–*Bailes*—a group of students who learn and perform dances from different regions of Mexico. (Anaheim)
–*La Prensa Latina*—a student journalism group that produces a Spanish-language newspaper called *El Mitotero.* (Sweetwater)
–*International Club*—a student group that sponsors events to increase intercultural awareness. (Artesia)
–*Celebration of cultural events and holidays* such as *Cinco de Mayo* by the whole school.
–*MECHA (Movimiento Estudiantil Chicano de Atzlán)*—a group that represents the interests of Chicano, Mexican-American, and Mexican students on college and high school campuses. (Sweetwater)
–*Sports:* soccer and baseball are emphasized over football.

*Schools where these programs were operating are listed in parentheses.

water, in order to encourage counselors to guide all students toward post-secondary education, the procedures used to evaluate counselors took into account the test scores of the students with whom they worked, the number of students who applied to college, and the number of students who received college/university grants and scholarships. The head counselor said that four or five years before, they had realized that some people on the counseling staff were doing a much better job than others. They all sat down together and decided that helping students get money for college and go to college would be the priorities of the staff. The approach was later adopted for the whole district. It is a competitive approach, but "we work together. A counselor might say, 'What did you do that I didn't?' " At Artesia High School several Latino LM students indicated that their counselors worked with them on future plans, made sure they were doing well in classes, and advised them about the courses to take so they would have the option of going to a university. A College Aspiration Partnership Program (CAPP), developed by the counseling department at this high school, paired the school with several colleges and universities in the surrounding area. Language-minority students met with representatives of these institutions to learn the requirements for entry and procedures for applying for scholarships and other student support funds.

At Newcomer High, which unlike the other schools serves immigrant students for only a year before they make the transition to regular high schools, college counseling is not as large a component of the counselor's roles as helping students, many of them refugees, deal with the emotional and physical traumas they have experienced in leaving war-torn countries and coming to the United States. The counselors there, two of whom speak Spanish and one of whom speaks Chinese, see themselves as nurturers and facilitators of cultural adjustment. One of them described her roles: "I wear many hats; at times I'm a mother, a referral service to agencies, and I may have to be a comedian when needed." A student, commenting on her first day at the school, said, *"Para mi no fué tan extraño. La señora S. me presentó a los compañeros."* ("For me it wasn't so strange. Mrs. S. introduced me to friends.") It is the counselor's job, as well as that of teachers, to acquaint students with the expectations of the school system, particularly those areas that differ from one culture to another. Students learn, for instance, that in most U.S. classrooms student participation—including asking questions of the teacher—is expected and desired and that one shows respect to Anglo teachers by making eye contact while they are speaking. In addition to dealing with cross-cultural issues, counselors at Newcomer had to be experts at referring students to appropriate agencies for medical or psychological traumas which could not be handled at the school.

We realize that for schools which are only now beginning to see an increase in language-minority and LEP populations, it may be difficult to find qualified counselors who share the students' linguistic and cultural backgrounds. Until such counselors are found and hired, however, it is advisable to at least have a counselor who speaks the students' native language, who has been trained in cross-cultural counseling techniques, and who can bring to students' attention special funding and scholarship opportunities.

*7. Parents of language-minority students are encouraged to become
involved in their children's education.*

The parent participation feature was the least developed component of the high schools we visited. The principals, counselors, and teachers at all of the schools commented that more needed to be done to increase the schools' interaction with the parents of LM students. Yet they had taken steps to encourage parents to take an active part in their children's education. Several schools had Parent Advisory Committees that met monthly and included parents of LM students. These committees typically reached out to other parents for assistance with parent-sponsored multicultural activities. Some schools regularly sent newsletters to parents in their native languages.

Newcomer High School held a parent night once a month. Students and teachers in the school worked together to plan presentations about various aspects of the school's education program, including ways parents could help their children be better students. When we visited the high school, students were being prepared in their reading class to present to parents a play that dramatized some ways of "monitoring and motivating one's child," the topic for that month's meeting. The play was to be performed in Spanish, Chinese, Burmese, Vietnamese, Tagalog, and English. Afterwards, students would read several poems to parents—"Exile" by Pablo Neruda; "The Truth" by a student; and "The Road Not Taken" by Robert Frost. Finally, students would sing "The Impossible Dream."

The Tanner Bill program for Latino students at Anaheim High School required that the teachers and parents of participating students meet twice a month. In addition, the program coordinator held evening meetings several times a year in the neighborhoods of the students in the program. Representatives of colleges and universities in the area attended these meetings to inform parents of the college programs offered by their institutions, the entry requirements, and the scholarships and other support services available to language-minority students. Generally, the college and university representatives who attended spoke the parents' native language(s).

Nogales and Anaheim held early morning pancake breakfasts and invited parents to attend before they went to work; 800 people had attended Anaheim's most recent breakfast when we visited the school. Nogales also held monthly student-of-the-month breakfasts for parents and students in which a student in each department was honored, as well as an Honors Assembly each quarter in which parents were asked to stand up and be recognized with their children. More than 750 people attended the most recent Honors Assembly. Overfelt High School had a full-time community liaison who spoke Spanish and offered ESL classes for parents on the school campus. Parents of Overfelt students had also come out on weekends to paint the school. Several schools contacted parents by telephone to check on students who were absent or to inform parents when a student had become ill and was returning home. The person making the contact spoke the parents' native language.

Although we did not interview parents, comments from students indicated that many Latino parents were very supportive of their children's education. The language barrier, lack of familiarity with the U.S. educational system, and their own lack of educational experience made it difficult for some parents to help directly with homework; however, they encouraged their children in other ways to pursue the education they had not had the opportunity to receive. One student reported, "For my mom, the only thing is school. She said I could do anything; 'All I want is for you to finish school.' She pushes that I get educated. She herself dropped out and got married and regrets it. I dropped out too for awhile; it tore my mom and me apart." The theme of "becoming somebody" is a strong thread in the students' talk about their parents and their own goals for the future. "My dad is always telling me to work and study, to be somebody," said one. *"Quiero seguir estudiando para llegar a ser alguien en la vida"* ("I want to keep studying so that I can become somebody in life"), said another. These comments by students attest to the strong desire among these Latino parents to do whatever they are able to do to gain a good education for their children. The schools we visited were working hard to find ways of making the schools accessible to parents.

## 8. School staff members share a strong commitment to empower language-minority students through education.

The most fundamental feature of all, and the most difficult to describe in concrete terms, is the commitment we heard about from most if not all of the school staff and students we interviewed. This commitment goes beyond the value the staff places on students' languages and cultures and beyond the high expectations staff members hold for language-minority students. One can value the language and culture of a student and expect that student to be successful, yet still remain passive when it comes to promoting that student in the world. Commitment and empowerment of students involve staff members reaching out, giving extra time to further the goals of a few students, and taking part in a political process that challenges the status quo. In the words of Jim Cummins, "minority students can become empowered only through interactions with educators who have critically examined and, where necessary, challenged the educational (and social) structure within which they operate" (1989, p. 6).

Such commitment manifested itself in various ways at the schools we visited. Teachers and other staff at the schools were described as having students' best interests at heart and giving extra time and energy after school and during lunch or preparation time to counsel as well as teach them. For example, the Coordinator of Special Projects at Overfelt High School said that he had found the teachers there to be very eager to learn how to work effectively with language-minority students. He said that they considered it "a very serious endeavor" to be sensitive to the needs of such students, and that they frequently requested training of various sorts to help them become more effective. At all of the schools, students mentioned teachers who had given them special help and attention, often crediting them with providing personal counseling as well as academic support. Typical student comments included the following: "The teachers here don't just teach; they care about you" and "Teachers stay after school to explain what we didn't understand."

Activities at these schools promoted participation and empowerment of Latino

477

students outside the classroom as well. Through participation in MECHA[9] groups, Latino clubs, Spanish language newspapers, soccer teams, and other activities sponsored and advised by school staff, Latino students developed awareness and knowledge of their cultures and language as well as a sense of community and cooperation with other Latino and non-Latino students. School staff involved in these activities took their commitment beyond the classroom to help develop students as whole people. Through the *Ballet Folklorico* group at Anaheim, for example, students not only learned and performed various Mexican dances, but also learned about the different regions in Mexico where dances originated, and presented this information in performances as well. They thus deepened their own and others' knowledge and understanding of Mexican culture and history.

Besides their work in the school setting to promote the achievement and success of Latino and other language-minority students, staff at these schools also participated in various community activities, attended meetings, and held positions in their communities through which they acted as advocates for Latinos and other minorities. An assistant principal at Nogales High School, a Latino from the community, had been the mayor of Nogales. A teacher and MECHA advisor at Sweetwater High School, also a Latino, was elected to the City Council of National City in 1989. The principal at Anaheim High School described her work to develop an advocacy base in the community through her ongoing participation in a variety of community events and activities. She had gotten support from Anaheim graduates in the community, some business people, and many parents—both Latino and Anglo—by participating in community activities herself. Some of these people had spoken out at school board meetings advocating programs and services that were crucial to the success of the district's language-minority students. Sensitive to the fact that the way certain issues are discussed can trigger negative reactions and therefore interfere with the achievement of desired goals, she worked to communicate effectively with different audiences. Above all, she said, "I have not been naïve in thinking I can do it all by myself; I spent the first year getting a sense of who supported the equity issues that I'm concerned with."

It was evident at these schools that teachers, counselors, administrators, and other staff were highly committed to promoting the success of language-minority students in school and beyond. Besides promoting the achievement of such students, they acknowledged the educational and social structures that surround the students and challenged these structures in productive ways through concrete actions such as those described above. By taking their advocacy into the community, those who held elective offices and participated in community groups challenged negative attitudes and policies that may have been creating obstacles to the improvement of education for minority groups. Those who initiated and sponsored activities to expand LM students' knowledge and understanding of their own cultures and languages helped them develop a sense of identity and community that knowledge of their own backgrounds can provide. Those who were putting their extra energy into helping students with their academic work were fighting to raise the low achievement records of language-minority students. This commitment and accompanying action provided the framework within which the attributes and processes we have described above were developed and carried out.

## Conclusion

The eight features we have described appeared to be key to the success of language-minority students at the schools we visited. While the study was exploratory in nature, we believe it provides educators with a working model of effective education for language-minority students at the secondary level. These eight features can be thought of as a set of general recommendations, or perhaps as a checklist against which to compare other schools or programs.

Many of the key features we have described mirror features in the effective schools literature. The notions of high expectations, parent involvement, strong leadership, and staff development are common threads throughout the many studies that have been conducted. In addition, those studying schools with large numbers of minority and bilingual students found, as we did, that support services, a positive attitude toward students, and commitment to helping students achieve were crucial factors in the overall success of the schools. In these areas, our report offers further confirmation that, in order to be successful with language-minority students, high schools must place a high priority on services and attitudes that go beyond academic instruction.

But this study makes several additional contributions. The first of these is the focus on secondary schools with large numbers of LM students. Second, wherever possible, general features across schools have been operationalized through concrete examples of practices in particular schools. Much of the effective schools literature lists general attributes, but does not take the next step in describing ways of actually carrying out these broad manifestos. We have tried to provide not only food for thought but also suggestions for concrete action. Third, we have emphasized an integrated approach to secondary programs for language-minority students. The schools we visited provided strong academic preparation for these students in three areas—content knowledge and understanding, English language skills, and primary language skills. They also helped students develop their pride and identity as individuals, as members of ethnic groups, and as participants in a multicultural society by showing respect for students' languages and cultures, holding high expectations of students and acting upon them in concrete ways, guiding them in preparing for their futures, encouraging their parents to become involved in their schooling, and promoting student empowerment in school and in the larger community. This multifaceted approach manifested itself at all levels of the curriculum and throughout academic, support, and extracurricular programs at these schools.

Finally, this study strongly suggests that the diversity among students cannot simply be ignored. While the schools recognized the importance of integrating language-minority students with mainstream students and of providing equally challenging instruction for all students, they did not try to minimize differences among mainstream and Latino students or among Latino students themselves. Approaches to

479

schooling that value linguistic and cultural diversity and that promote cultural plu-ralism were welcomed and explored whenever possible (see Stedman, 1987). Stu-dents' languages and cultures were incorporated into school programs as part of the effort to create a context in which all students felt valuable and capable of academic success (see Cummins, 1989).

Though this study was exploratory in nature, we hope the findings will guide further research. Many more secondary schools with large numbers of language-minority students need to be visited for longer periods of time to determine whether the features which emerged in the six schools we studied apply to other similar schools. The features themselves need to be examined in greater depth so that educators can understand them more fully and apply them in appropriate contexts. For example, a study of parent involvement in language-minority student schooling should include extensive interviews with parents themselves as well as with students and school staff. Longitudinal studies of secondary schools with large numbers of language-minority students could increase our understanding of the processes schools go through in providing and maintaining effective schooling for such students. Schools with different populations of students also need to be examined—for example, students of different ethnic and language backgrounds, students who have lived in the United States for various lengths of time, students who are immigrants, refugees, and native-born citizens. Nevertheless, the study has extended our knowledge of what makes schooling work for a rapidly growing segment of the school population. We hope that this working model will also provide inspiration and a sense of pos-sibility to educators who are seeking an effective response to the needs of secondary language-minority students.

## Notes

1. We will use the phrase "language-minority (LM) students" to refer to those who come from families where a language other than English is spoken. Such students may or may not speak English fluently.
2. We will use the phrase "limited-English-proficient (LEP) students" to refer specifically to those language-minority students who are not yet fluent in English.
3. California State Department of Education, Assembly Bill 1329, 1976. In 1982, AB–1329 was revised as AB–507.
4. The Southwest Center for Educational Equity is funded by Title IV of the U.S. Department of Education to assist school districts in California, Arizona, and Nevada in their desegregation efforts in the areas of race, gender, and national origin.
5. Awards and recognition included a California Department of Education Distinguished School Award, a city Commendation Award, nomination as an exemplary school for the National Sec-ondary School Recognition Program, an award for the academic achievement of the school's graduates attending a university in the state, a U.S. Department of Education Excellence in Education Award, and selection as one of the "77 Schools of the Future" by *Omni* magazine.
6. The term *Latino* is used here because it is the term that the majority of people we interviewed used to describe their own ethnicity, when speaking on a broader level than their indivdual countries of origin.
7. Anaheim High School, Anaheim, CA; Artesia High School, Lakewood, CA; Newcomer High School, San Francisco, CA; Overfelt High School, San Jose, CA; Sweetwater High School, National City, CA; Nogales High School, Nogales, AZ.
8. The term *sheltered content* refers to an approach to teaching content classes for LEP students in English in which the development of English language skills is emphasized along with content area development. Teachers use whatever means they can to make the content comprehensible

and meaningful to the students: for example, simplified speech, vocabulary work, visuals, hands-on activities, and highly structured lessons (see Northcutt & Watson, 1986).
9. MECHA, or *Movimiento Esudiantil Chicano de Atzlán*, represents the interests of Chicano, Mexican-American, and Mexican students on college and high school campuses.

## References

Arias, B. (1986). The context of education for Hispanic students: An overview. *American Journal of Education, 95*, 26–57.

Bell, J. (1989, February). *Merging the research on effective instruction for LEP students with effective schools' research and practice.* Paper presented at the Annual Conference of the California Association for Bilingual Education, Anaheim, CA.

Brown, P. R., & Haycock, K. (1984). *Excellence for whom?* Oakland, CA: The Achievement Council.

Carter, T. P., & Chatfield, M. L. (1986). Effective bilingual schools: Implications for policy and practice. *American Journal of Education, 95*, 200–232.

Cummins, J. (1989). *Empowering minority students.* Sacramento: California Association of Bilingual Education.

Delpit, L. D. (1988). The silenced dialogue: Power and pedagogy in educating other people's children. *Harvard Educational Review, 58*, 280–298.

Edmonds, R. (1979, May 5). Effective schools for the urban poor. *Educational Leadership, 37*(1), 15–27.

Espinosa, R., & Ochoa, A. (1986). Concentration of California Hispanic students in schools with low achievement: A research note. *American Journal of Education, 95*, 77–95.

Gingras, R. C., & Careaga, R. C. (1989). *Limited-English-proficient students at risk: Issues and prevention strategies.* Silver Spring, MD: National Clearinghouse for Bilingual Education.

Jackson, S. (1989, May). Luncheon address, *Symposium on Excellence in Mathematics and Science Achievement: The Gateway to Learning in the 21st Century.* Sponsored by the Southwest Center for Educational Equity, San Francisco.

*Lau v. Nichols*, 414 U.S. 563, 566 (1973).

Levin, H. M. (1987). Accelerated schools for disadvantaged students. *Educational Leadership, 44*(6), 19–21.

Medina, M. (1988). Hispanic apartheid in American public education. *Educational Administration Quarterly, 24*, 336–349.

Merriam, S. B. (1988). *Case study research in education: A qualitative approach.* San Francisco: Jossey-Bass.

Miles, M. B., & Huberman, A. M. (1984). *Qualitative data analysis: A sourcebook of new methods.* Beverly Hills, CA: Sage.

Northcutt, L., & Watson, D. (1986). *SET: Sheltered English teaching handbook.* San Marcos, CA: AM Graphics and Printing.

Orfield, G. (1986). Hispanic education: Challenges, research, and policies. *American Journal of Education, 95*, 1–25.

Orum, L. S. (1988). *The education of Hispanics: Status and implications.* Washington, DC: National Council of La Raza.

Purkey, S. C., & Smith, M. S. (1983). Effective schools: A review. *The Elementary School Journal, 83*, 428–452.

Ramírez, D. (1988, April). *A comparison of structured English, immersion, and bilingual education programs: Results of a national study.* Paper presented at the Annual Meeting of the American Educational Research Association, New Orleans.

Rosenholtz, S. J. (1985). Effective schools: Interpreting the evidence. *American Journal of Education, 93*, 352–388.

Rowen, B., Bossert, S. T. , & Dwyer, D. C. (1983). Research on effective schools: A cautionary note. *Educational Researcher, 12*(4), 24–31.

Rumberger, R. W. (1987). High school dropouts: A review of issues and evidence. *Review of Educational Research, 57,* 101–121.

Stedman, L. C. (1987). It's time we changed the effective schools formula. *Phi Delta Kappan, 69,* 215–224.

Suro, R. (1990, April 11). Education secretary criticizes the values of Hispanic parents. *The New York Times,* pp. A1, B8.

Taylor, S. J., & Bogdan, R. (1984). *Introduction to qualitative research methods* (2nd ed.). New York: Wiley.

Tikunoff, W. (1985). *Applying significant bilingual instructional features in the classroom.* Rosslyn, VA: National Clearinghouse for Bilingual Education.

U.S. General Accounting Office. (1987). School dropouts: Survey of local programs (GAO/HRD-87-108). Washington, DC: GPO.

Wilson, B. L., & Corcoran, T. B. (1988). *Successful secondary schools.* New York: Falmer Press.

Wong-Fillmore, L., McLaughlin, B., Ammon, P., & Ammon, M. S. (1985). *Learning English through bilingual instruction. Final Report to the National Institute of Education.* Berkeley: The University of California.

# 18

# *The Silenced Dialogue: Power and Pedagogy in Educating Other People's Children*

LISA D. DELPIT
*Morgan State University*

*Lisa Delpit introduces and examines what she calls "the culture of power." In her discussion of the debate over skills-oriented versus process-oriented approaches to education, Delpit argues that Black and poor students often suffer from the good intentions of "progressive" educators whose educational reform programs do not necessarily provide students with knowledge of the rules needed to function in the culture of power. According to Delpit, social injustice is embedded in the social norms of communicative interaction of the group in power. Delpit argues that teachers must teach all students the explicit and implicit rules of power as a first step toward a more equitable education.*

A Black male graduate student who is also a special education teacher in a predominantly Black community is talking about his experiences in predominantly White university classes:

> There comes a moment in every class where we have to discuss "The Black Issue" and what's appropriate education for Black children. I tell you, I'm tired of arguing with those White people, because they won't listen. Well, I don't know if they really don't listen or if they just don't believe you. It seems like if you can't quote Vygotsky or something, then you don't have any validity to speak about your *own* kids. Anyway, I'm not bothering with it anymore, now I'm just in it for a grade.

I take full responsibility for all that appears herein; however, aside from those mentioned by name in this text, I would like to thank all of the educators and students around the country who have been so willing to contribute their perspectives to the formulation of these ideas, especially Susan Jones, Catherine Blunt, Dee Stickman, Sandra Gamble, Willard Taylor, Mickey Monteiro, Denise Burden, Evelyn Higbee, Joseph Delpit, Jr., Valerie Montoya, Richard Cohen, and Mary Denise Thompson.

*Harvard Educational Review*   Vol. 58   No. 3   August 1988, 280–298

A Black woman teacher in a multicultural urban elementary school is talking about her experiences in discussions with her predominantly White fellow teachers about how they should organize reading instruction to best serve students of color:

> When you're talking to White people they still want it to be their way. You can try to talk to them and give them examples, but they're so headstrong, they think they know what's best for *everybody*, for *everybody's* children. They won't listen, White folks are going to do what they want to do *anyway*.
>
> It's really hard. They just don't listen well. No, they listen, but they don't *hear*—you know how your mama used to say you listen to the radio, but you *hear* your mother? Well, they don't *hear* me.
>
> So I just try to shut them out so I can hold my temper. You can only beat your head against a brick wall for so long before you draw blood. If I try to stop arguing with them I can't help myself from getting angry. Then I end up walking around praying all day "Please Lord, remove the bile I feel for these people so I can sleep tonight." It's funny, but it can become a cancer, a sore.
>
> So, I shut them out. I go back to my own little cubby, my classroom, and I try to teach the way I know will work, no matter what those folk say. And when I get Black kids, I just try to undo the damage they did.
>
> I'm not going to let any man, woman, or child drive me crazy—White folks will try to do that to you if you let them. You just have to stop talking to them, that's what I do. I just keep smiling, but I won't talk to them.

A soft-spoken Native Alaskan woman in her forties is a student in the Education Department of the University of Alaska. One day she storms into a Black professor's office and very uncharacteristically slams the door. She plops down in a chair and, still fuming, says, "Please tell those people, just don't help us anymore! I give up. I won't talk to them again!"

And finally, a Black woman principal who is also a doctoral student at a well-known university on the West Coast is talking about her university experiences, particularly about when a professor lectures on issues concerning educating Black children:

> If you try to suggest that that's not quite the way it is, they get defensive, then you get defensive, then they'll start reciting research.
>
> I try to give them my experiences, to explain. They just look and nod. The more I try to explain, they just look and nod, just keep looking and nodding. They don't really hear me.
>
> Then, when it's time for class to be over, the professor tells me to come to his office to talk more. So I go. He asks for more examples of what I'm talking about, and he looks and nods while I give them. Then he says that that's just my experiences. It doesn't really apply to most Black people.
>
> It becomes futile because they think they know everything about everybody. What you have to say about your life, your children, doesn't mean anything. They don't really want to hear what you have to say. They wear blinders and earplugs. They only want to go on research they've read that other White people have written.
>
> It just doesn't make any sense to keep talking to them.

Thus was the first half of the title of this text born—"The Silenced Dialogue." One of the tragedies in the field of education is that scenarios such as these are enacted daily around the country. The saddest element is that the individuals that the Black and Native American educators speak of in these statements are seldom aware that the dialogue *has* been silenced. Most likely the White educators believe that their colleagues or color did, in the end, agree with their logic. After all, they stopped disagreeing, didn't they?

I have collected these statements since completing a recently published article (Delpit, 1986). In this somewhat autobiographical account, entitled "Skills and Other Dilemmas of a Progressive Black Educator," I discussed my perspective as a product of a skills-oriented approach to writing and as a teacher of process-oriented approaches. I described the estrangement that I and many teachers of color feel from the progressive movement when writing-process advocates dismiss us as too "skills oriented." I ended the article suggesting that it was incumbent upon writing-process advocates—or indeed, advocates of any progressive movement—to enter into dialogue with teachers of color, who may not share their enthusiasm about so-called new, liberal, or progressive ideas.

In response to this article, which presented no research data and did not even cite a reference, I received numerous calls and letters from teachers, professors, and even state school personnel from around the country, both Black and White. All of the White respondents, except one, have wished to talk more about the question of skills versus process approaches—to support or reject what they perceive to be my position. On the other hand, *all* of the non-White respondents have spoken passionately on being left out of the dialogue about how best to educate children of color.

How can such complete communication blocks exist when both parties truly believe they have the same aims? How can the bitterness and resentment expressed by the educators of color be drained so that the sores can heal? What can be done?

I believe the answer to these questions lies in ethnographic analysis, that is, in identifying and giving voice to alternative world views. Thus, I will attempt to address the concerns raised by White and Black respondents to my article "Skills and Other Dilemmas" (Delpit, 1986). My charge here is not to determine the best instructional methodology; I believe that the actual practice of good teachers of all colors typically incorporates a range of pedagogical orientations. Rather, I suggest that the differing perspectives on the debate over "skills" versus "process" approaches can lead to an understanding of the alienation and miscommunication, and thereby to an understanding of the "silenced dialogue."

In thinking through these issues, I have found what I believe to be a connecting and complex theme: what I have come to call "the culture of power." There are five aspects of power I would like to propose as given for this presentation:

1. Issues of power are enacted in classrooms.
2. There are codes or rules for participating in power; that is, there is a "culture of power."

3. The rules of the culture of power are a reflection of the rules of the culture of those who have power.
4. If you are not already a participant in the culture of power, being told explicitly the rules of that culture makes acquiring power easier.
5. Those with power are frequently least aware of—or least willing to acknowledge—its existence. Those with less power are often most aware of its existence.

The first three are by now basic tenets in the literature of the sociology of education, but the last two have seldom been addressed. The following discussion will explicate these aspects of power and their relevance to the schism between liberal educational movements and that of non-White, non-middle-class teachers and communities.[1]

*1. Issues of power are enacted in classrooms.*

These issues include: the power of the teacher over the students; the power of the publishers of textbooks and the developers of the curriculum to determine the view of the world presented; the power of the state in enforcing compulsory schooling; and the power of an individual or group to determine another's intelligence or "normalcy." Finally, if schooling prepares people for jobs, and the kind of job a person has determines her or his economic status and, therefore, power, then schooling is intimately related to that power.

*2. There are codes or rules for participating in power; that is,
there is a "culture of power."*

The codes or rules I'm speaking of relate to linguistic forms, communicative strategies, and presentation of self; that is, ways of talking, ways of writing, ways of dressing, and ways of interacting.

*3. The rules of the culture of power are a reflection of the rules of
the culture of those who have power.*

This means that success in institutions—schools, workplaces, and so on—is predicated upon acquisition of the culture of those who are in power. Children from middle-class homes tend to do better in school than those from non-middle-class homes because the culture of the school is based on the culture of the upper and middle classes—of those in power. The upper and middle classes send their children to school with all the accoutrements of the culture of power; children from other kinds of families operate within perfectly wonderful and viable cultures but not cultures that carry the codes or rules of power.

*4. If you are not already a participant in the culture of power,
being told explicitly the rules of that culture makes acquiring power
easier.*

In my work within and between diverse cultures, I have come to conclude that members of any culture transmit information implicitly to co-members. However, when implicit codes are attempted across cultures, communication frequently breaks down. Each cultural group is left saying, "Why don't those people say what they mean?" as well as, "What's wrong with them, why don't they understand?"

Anyone who has had to enter new cultures, especially to accomplish a specific task, will know of what I speak. When I lived in several Papua New Guinea villages for extended periods to collect data, and when I go to Alaskan villages for work with Alaskan Native communities, I have found it unquestionably easier—psychologically and pragmatically—when some kind soul has directly informed me about such matters as appropriate dress, interactional styles, embedded meanings, and taboo words or actions. I contend that it is much the same for anyone seeking to learn the rules of the culture of power. Unless one has the leisure of a lifetime of "immersion" to learn them, explicit presentation makes learning immeasurably easier.

And now, to the fifth and last premise:

*5. Those with power are frequently least aware of—or least willing to acknowledge—its existence. Those with less power are often most aware of its existence.*

For many who consider themselves members of liberal or radical camps, acknowledging personal power and admitting participation in the culture of power is distinctly uncomfortable. On the other hand, those who are less powerful in any situation are most likely to recognize the power variable most acutely. My guess is that the White colleagues and instructors of those previously quoted did not perceive themselves to have power over the non-White speakers. However, either by virtue of their position, their numbers, or their access to that particular code of power of calling upon research to validate one's position, the White educators had the authority to establish what was to be considered "truth" regardless of the opinions of the people of color, and the latter were well aware of that fact.

A related phenomenon is that liberals (and here I am using the term "liberal" to refer to those whose beliefs include striving for a society based upon maximum individual freedom and autonomy) seem to act under the assumption that to make any rules or expectations explicit is to act against liberal principles, to limit the freedom and autonomy of those subjected to the explicitness.

I thank Fred Erickson for a comment that led me to look again at a tape by John Gumperz[2] on cultural dissonance in cross-cultural interactions. One of the episodes showed an East Indian interviewing for a job with an all-White committee. The interview was a complete failure, even though several of the interviewers appeared to really want to help the applicant. As the interview rolled steadily downhill, these "helpers" became more and more indirect in their questioning, which exacerbated the problems the applicant had in performing appropriately. Operating from a different cultural perspective, he got fewer and fewer clear clues as to what was expected of him, which ultimately resulted in his failure to secure the position.

I contend that as the applicant showed less and less aptitude for handling the interview, the power differential became ever more evident to the interviewers. The

the applicant, became more and more uncomfortable. Their indirectness was an attempt to lessen the power differential and their discomfort by lessening the power-revealing explicitness of their questions and comments.

When acknowledging and expressing power, one tends towards explicitness (as in yelling to your 10-year-old, "Turn that radio down!"). When de-emphasizing power, there is a move toward indirect communication. Therefore, in the interview setting, those who sought to help, to express their egalitarianism with the East Indian applicant, became more and more indirect—and less and less helpful—in their questions and comments.

In literacy instruction, explicitness might be equated with direct instruction. Perhaps the ultimate expression of explicitness and direct instruction in the primary classroom is Distar. This reading program is based on a behaviorist model in which reading is taught through the direct instruction of phonics generalizations and blending. The teacher's role is to maintain the full attention of the group by continuous questioning, eye contact, finger snaps, hand claps, and other gestures, and by eliciting choral responses and initiating some sort of award system.

When the program was introduced, it arrived with a flurry of research data that "proved" that all children—even those who were "culturally deprived"—could learn to read using this method. Soon there was a strong response, first from academics and later from many classroom teachers, stating that the program was terrible. What I find particularly interesting, however, is that the primary issue of the conflict over Distar has not been over its instructional efficacy—usually the students did learn to read—but the expression of explicit power in the classroom. The liberal educators opposed the methods—the direct instruction, the explicit control exhibited by the teacher. As a matter of fact, it was not unusual (even now) to hear of the program spoken of as "fascist."

I am not an advocate of Distar, but I will return to some of the issues that the program—and direct instruction in general—raises in understanding the differences between progressive White educators and educators of color.

To explore those differences, I would like to present several statements typical of those made with the best of intentions by middle-class liberal educators. To the surprise of the speakers, it is not unusual for such content to be met by vocal opposition or stony silence from people of color. My attempt here is to examine the underlying assumptions of both camps.

*"I want the same thing for everyone else's children as I want for mine."*

To provide schooling for everyone's children that reflects liberal, middle-class values and aspirations is to ensure the maintenance of the status quo, to ensure that power, the culture of power, remains in the hands of those who already have it. Some children come to school with more accoutrements of the culture of power already in place—"cultural capital," as some critical theorists refer to it (for example, Apple, 1979)—some with less. Many liberal educators hold that the primary goal for education is for children to become autonomous, to develop fully who they are in the classroom setting without having arbitrary, outside standards forced upon them. This is a very reasonable goal for people whose children are already participants in the culture of power and who have already internalized its codes.

But parents who don't function within that culture often want something else. It's not that they disagree with the former aim, it's just that they want something more. They want to ensure that the school provides their children with discourse patterns, interactional styles, and spoken and written language codes that will allow them success in the larger society.

It was the lack of attention to this concern that created such a negative outcry in the Black community when well-intentioned White liberal educators introduced "dialect readers." These were seen as a plot to prevent the schools from teaching the linguistic aspects of the culture of power, thus dooming Black children to a permanent outsider caste. As one parent demanded, "My kids know how to be Black—you all teach them how to be successful in the White man's world."

Several Black teachers have said to me recently that as much as they'd like to believe otherwise, they cannot help but conclude that many of the "progressive" educational strategies imposed by liberals upon Black and poor children could only be based on a desire to ensure that the liberals' children get sole access to the dwindling pool of American jobs. Some have added that the liberal educators believe themselves to be operating with good intentions, but that these good intentions are only conscious delusions about their unconscious true motives. One of Black anthropologist John Gwaltney's (1980) informants reflects this perspective with her tongue-in-cheek observation that the biggest difference between Black folks and White folks is that Black folks *know* when they're lying!

Let me try to clarify how this might work in literacy instruction. A few years ago I worked on an analysis of two popular reading programs, Distar and a progressive program that focused on higher-level critical thinking skills. In one of the first lessons of the progressive program, the children are introduced to the names of the letter *m* and *e*. In the same lesson they are then taught the sound made by each of the letters, how to write each of the letters, and that when the two are blended together they produce the word *me*.

As an experienced first-grade teacher, I am convinced that a child needs to be familiar with a significant number of these concepts to be able to assimilate so much new knowledge in one sitting. By contrast, Distar presents the same information in about forty lessons.

I would not argue for the pace of the Distar lessons; such a slow pace would only bore most kids—but what happened in the other lesson is that it merely provided an opportunity for those who already knew the content to exhibit that they knew it, or at most perhaps to build one new concept onto what was already known. This meant that the child who did not come to school already primed with what was to be presented would be labeled as needing "remedial" instruction from day one; indeed, this determination would be made before he or she was ever taught. In fact,

Distar was "successful" because it actually *taught* new information to children who had not already acquired it at home. Although the more progressive system was ideal for some children, for others it was a disaster.

I do not advocate a simplistic "basic skills" approach for children outside of the culture of power. It would be (and has been) tragic to operate as if these children were incapable of critical and higher-order thinking and reasoning. Rather, I suggest that schools must provide these children the content that other families from a different cultural orientation provide at home. This does not mean separating children according to family background, but instead, ensuring that each classroom incorporate strategies appropriate for all the children in its confines.

And I do not advocate that it is the school's job to attempt to change the homes of poor and non-White children to match the homes of those in the culture of power. That may indeed be a form of cultural genocide. I have frequently heard schools call poor parents "uncaring" when parents respond to the school's urging, that they change their home life in order to facilitate their children's learning, by saying, "But that's the school's job." What the school personnel fail to understand is that if the parents were members of the culture of power and lived by its rules and codes, then they would transmit those codes to their children. In fact, they transmit another culture that children must learn at home in order to survive in their communities.

*"Child-centered, whole language, and process approaches are
needed in order to allow a democratic state of free, autonomous,
empowered adults, and because research has shown that children
learn best through these methods."*

People of color are, in general, skeptical of research as a determiner of our fates. Academic research has, after all, found us genetically inferior, culturally deprived, and verbally deficient. But beyond that general caveat, and despite my or others' personal preferences, there is little research data supporting the major tenets of process approaches over other forms of literacy instruction, and virtually no evidence that such approaches are more efficacious for children of color (Siddle, 1986).

Although the problem is not necessarily inherent in the method, in some instances adherents of process approaches to writing create situations in which students ultimately find themselves held accountable for knowing a set of rules about which no one has ever directly informed them. Teachers do students no service to suggest, even implicitly, that "product" is not important. In this country, students will be judged on their product regardless of the process they utilized to achieve it. And that product, based as it is on the specific codes of a particular culture, is more readily produced when the directives of how to produce it are made explicit.

If such explicitness is not provided to students, what it feels like to people who are old enough to judge is that there are secrets being kept, that time is being wasted, that the teacher is abdicating his or her duty to teach. A doctoral student in my acquaintance was assigned to a writing class to hone his writing skills. The student was placed in the section led by a White professor who utilized a process approach, consisting primarily of having the students write essays and then assemble into groups to edit each others' papers. That procedure infuriated this particular student. He had many angry encounters with the teacher about what she was doing. In his words:

> I didn't feel she was teaching us anything. She wanted us to correct each others' papers and we were there to learn from her. She didn't teach anything, absolutely nothing.
>
> Maybe they're trying to learn what Black folks knew all the time. We understand how to improvise, how to express ourselves creatively. When I'm in a classroom, I'm not looking for that, I'm looking for structure, the more formal language.
>
> Now my buddy was in [a] Black teacher's class. And that lady was very good. She went through and explained and defined each part of the structure. This [White] teacher didn't get along with that Black teacher. She said that she didn't agree with her methods. But *I* don't think that White teacher *had* any methods.

When I told this gentleman that what the teacher was doing was called a process method of teaching writing, his response was, "Well, at least now I know that she *thought* she was doing *something*. I thought she was just a fool who couldn't teach and didn't want to try."

This sense of being cheated can be so strong that the student may be completely turned off to the educational system. Amanda Branscombe, an accomplished White teacher, recently wrote a letter discussing her work with working-class Black and White students at a community college in Alabama. She had given these students my "Skills and Other Dilemmas" article (Delpit, 1986) to read and discuss, and wrote that her students really understood and identified with what I was saying. To quote her letter:

> One young man said that he had dropped out of high school because he failed the exit exam. He noted that he had then passed the GED without a problem after three weeks of prep. He said that his high school English teacher claimed to use a process approach, but what she really did was hide behind fancy words to give herself permission to do nothing in the classroom.

The students I have spoken of seem to be saying that the teacher has denied them access to herself as the source of knowledge necessary to learn the forms they need to succeed. Again, I tentatively attribute the problem to teachers' resistance to exhibiting power in the classroom. Somehow, to exhibit one's personal power as expert source is viewed as disempowering one's students.

Two qualifiers are necessary, however. The teacher cannot be the only expert in the classroom. To deny students their own expert knowledge *is* to disempower them. Amanda Branscombe, when she was working with Black high school students classified as "slow learners," had the students analyze RAP songs to discover their underlying patterns. The students became the experts in explaining to the teacher the rules for creating a new RAP song. The teacher then used the patterns the students identified as a base to begin an explanation of the structure of grammar, and then of Shakespeare's plays. Both student and teacher are expert at what they know best.

The second qualifier is that merely adopting direct instruction is not the answer. Actual writing for real audiences and real purposes is a vital element in helping students to understand that they have an important voice in their own learning processes. Siddle (1988) examines the results of various kinds of interventions in a primarily process-oriented writing class for Black students. Based on readers' blind assessments, she found that the intervention that produced the most positive changes in the students' writing was a "mini-lesson" consisting of direct instruction about some standard writing convention. But what produced the *second* highest number of positive changes was a subsequent student-centered conference with the teacher. (Peer conferencing in this group of Black students who were not members of the culture of power produced the least number of changes in students' writing. However, the classroom teacher maintained—and I concur—that such activities are necessary to introduce the elements of "real audience" into the task, along with more teacher-directed strategies.)

*"It's really a shame but she (that Black teacher upstairs) seems to
be so authoritarian, so focused on skills and so teacher directed.
Those poor kids never seem to be allowed to really express their
creativity. (And she even yells at them.)"*

This statement directly concerns the display of power and authority in the classroom. One way to understand the difference in perspective between Black teachers and their progressive colleagues on this issue is to explore culturally influenced oral interactions.

In *Ways With Words,* Shirley Brice Heath (1983) quotes the verbal directives given by the middle-class "townspeople" teachers (p. 280):

—"Is this where the scissors belong?"
—"You want to do your best work today."

By contrast, many Black teachers are more likely to say:

—"Put those scissors on that shelf."
—"Put your name on the papers and make sure to get the right answer for each question."

Is one oral style more authoritarian than another?

Other researchers have identified differences in middle-class and working-class speech to children. Snow et al. (1976), for example, report that working-class mothers use more directives to their children than do middle- and upper-class parents. Middle-class parents are likely to give the directive to a child to take his bath as, "Isn't it time for your bath?" Even though the utterance is couched as a question, both child and adult understand it as a directive. The child may respond with "Aw Mom, can't I wait until . . . ," but whether or not negotiation is attempted, both conversants understand the intent of the utterance.

By contrast, a Black mother, in whose house I was recently a guest, said to her eight-year-old son, "Boy, get your rusty behind in that bathtub." Now I happen to know that this woman loves her son as much as any mother, but she would never have posed the directive to her son to take a bath in the form of a question. Were she to ask, "Would you like to take your bath now?" she would not have been issuing a directive but offering a true alternative. Consequently, as Heath suggests, upon entering school the child from such a family may not understand the indirect statement of the teacher as a direct command. Both White and Black working-class children in the communities Heath studied "had difficulty interpreting these indirect requests for adherence to an unstated set of rules" (p. 280).

But those veiled commands are commands nonetheless, representing true power, and with true consequences for disobedience. If veiled commands are ignored, the child will be labeled a behavior problem and possibly officially classified as behavior disordered. In other words, the attempt by the teacher to reduce an exhibition of power by expressing herself in indirect terms may remove the very explicitness that the child needs to understand the rules of the new classroom culture.

A Black elementary school principal in Fairbanks, Alaska, reported to me that she has a lot of difficulty with Black children who are placed in some White teachers' classrooms. The teachers often send the children to the office for disobeying teacher directives. Their parents are frequently called in for conferences. The parents' response to the teacher is usually the same: "They do what I say; if you just *tell* them what to do, they'll do it. I tell them at home that they have to listen to what you say." And so, does not the power still exist? Its veiled nature only makes it more difficult for some children to respond appropriately, but that in no way mitigates its existence.

I don't mean to imply, however, that the only time the Black child disobeys the teacher is when he or she misunderstands the request for certain behavior. There are other factors that may produce such behavior. Black children expect an authority figure to act with authority. When the teacher instead acts as a "chum," the message sent is that this adult has no authority, and the children react accordingly. One reason this is so is that Black people often view issues of power and authority differently than people from mainstream middle-class backgrounds.[3] Many people of color expect authority to be earned by personal efforts and exhibited by personal characteristics. In other words, "the authoritative person gets to be a teacher because she is authoritative." Some members of middle-class cultures, by contrast, expect one to achieve authority by the acquisition of an authoritative role. That is, "the teacher is the authority because she is the teacher."

In the first instance, because authority is earned, the teacher must consistently prove the characteristics that give her authority. These characteristics may vary across cultures, but in the Black community they tend to cluster around several abilities. The authoritative teacher can control the class through exhibition of personal power; establishes meaningful interpersonal relationships that garner student respect; exhibits a strong belief that all students can learn; establishes a standard of achievement and "pushes" the students to achieve that standard; and holds the attention of the students by incorporating interactional features of Black communicative style in his or her teaching.

By contrast, the teacher whose authority is vested in the role has many more options of behavior at her disposal. For instance, she does not need to express any sense of personal power because her authority does not come from anything she herself does or says. Hence, the power she actually holds may be veiled in such questions/commands as "Would you like to sit down now?" If the children in her class understand authority as she does, it is mutually agreed upon that they are to obey her no matter how indirect, soft-spoken, or unassuming she may be. Her indirectness and soft-spokenness may indeed be, as I suggested earlier, an attempt to reduce the implication of overt power in order to establish a more egalitarian and non-authoritarian classroom atmosphere.

If the children operate under another notion of authority, however, then there is trouble. The Black child may perceive the middle-class teacher as weak, ineffectual, and incapable of taking on the role of being the teacher; therefore, there is no need to follow her directives. In her dissertation, Michelle Foster (1987) quotes one young Black man describing such a teacher:

> She is boring, bo::ing.* She could do something creative. Instead she just stands there. She can't control the class, doesn't know how to control the class. She asked me what she was doing wrong. I told her she just stands there like she's meditating. I told her she could be meditating for all I know. She says that we're supposed to know what to do. I told her I don't know nothin' unless she tells me. She just can't control the class. I hope we don't have her next semester. (pp. 67–68)

But of course the teacher may not view the problem as residing in herself but in the student, and the child may once again become the behavior-disordered Black boy in special education.

What characteristics do Black students attribute to the good teacher? Again, Foster's dissertation provides a quotation that supports my experience with Black students. A young Black man is discussing a former teacher with a group of friends:

> We had fu::n in her class, but she was mean. I can remember she used to say, "Tell me what's in the story, Wayne." She pushed, she used to get on me and push me to know. She made us learn. We had to get in the books. There was this tall guy and he tried to take her on, but she was in charge of that class and she didn't let anyone run her. I still have this book we used in her class. It's a bunch of stories in it. I just read one on Coca-Cola again the other day (p. 68).

To clarify, this student was *proud* of the teacher's "meanness," an attribute he seemed to describe as the ability to run the class and pushing and expecting students to learn. Now, does the liberal perspective of the negatively authoritarian Black

---

*Editor's note:* The colons [::] refer to elongated vowels.

teacher really hold up? I suggest that although all "explicit" Black teachers are not also good teachers, there are different attitudes in different cultural groups about which characteristics make for a good teacher. Thus, it is impossible to create a model for the good teacher without taking issues of culture and community context into account.

And now to the final comment I present for examination:

*"Children have the right to their own language, their own culture. We must fight cultural hegemony and fight the system by insisting that children be allowed to express themselves in their own language style. It is not they, the children, who must change, but the schools. To push children to do anything else is repressive and reactionary."*

A statement such as this originally inspired me to write the "Skills and Other Dilemmas" article. It was first written as a letter to a colleague in response to a situation that had developed in our department. I was teaching a senior-level teacher education course. Students were asked to prepare a written autobiographical document for the class that would also be shared with their placement school prior to their student teaching.

One student, a talented young Native American woman, submitted a paper in which the ideas were lost because of technical problems—from spelling to sentence structure to paragraph structure. Removing her name, I duplicated the paper for a discussion with some faculty members. I had hoped to initiate a discussion about what we could do to ensure that our students did not reach the senior level without getting assistance in technical writing skills when they needed them.

I was amazed at the response. Some faculty implied that the student should never have been allowed into the teacher education program. Others, some of the more progressive minded, suggested that I was attempting to function as gatekeeper by raising the issue and had internalized repressive and disempowering forces of the power elite to suggest that something was wrong with a Native American student just because she had another style of writing. With few exceptions, I found myself alone in arguing against both camps.

No, this student should not have been denied entry to the program. To deny her entry under the notion of upholding standards is to blame the victim for the crime. We cannot justifiably enlist exclusionary standards when the reason this student lacked the skills demanded was poor teaching at best and institutionalized racism at worst.

However, to bring this student into the program and pass her through without attending to obvious deficits in the codes needed for her to function effectively as a teacher is equally criminal—for though we may assuage our own consciences for not participating in victim blaming, she will surely be accused and convicted as soon as she leaves the university. As Native Alaskans were quick to tell me, and as I understood through my own experience in the Black community, not only would she not be hired as a teacher, but those who did not hire her would make the (false) assumption that the university was putting out only incompetent Natives and that they should stop looking seriously at any Native applicants. A White applicant who exhibits problems is an individual with problems. A person of color who exhibits problems immediately becomes a representative of her cultural group.

No, either stance is criminal. The answer is to *accept* students but also to take responsibility to *teach* them. I decided to talk to the student and found out she had recognized that she needed some assistance in the technical aspects of writing soon after she entered the university as a freshman. She had gone to various members of the education faculty and received the same two kinds of responses I met with four years later: faculty members told her either that she should not even attempt to be a teacher, or that it didn't matter and that she shouldn't worry about such trivial issues. In her desperation, she had found a helpful professor in the English Department, but he left the university when she was in her sophomore year.

We sat down together, worked out a plan for attending to specific areas of writing competence, and set up regular meetings. I stressed to her the need to use her own learning process as insight into how best to teach her future students those "skills" that her own schooling had failed to teach her. I gave her some explicit rules to follow in some areas; for others, we devised various kinds of journals that, along with readings about the structure of the language, allowed her to find her own insights into how the language worked. All that happened two years ago, and the young woman is now successfully teaching. What the experience led me to understand is that pretending that gatekeeping points don't exist is to ensure that many students will not pass through them.

Now you may have inferred that I believe that because there is a culture of power, everyone should learn the codes to participate in it, and that is how the world should be. Actually, nothing could be further from the truth. I believe in a diversity of style, and I believe the world will be diminished if cultural diversity is ever obliterated. Further, I believe strongly, as do my liberal colleagues, that each cultural group should have the right to maintain its own language style. When I speak, therefore, of the culture of power, I don't speak of how I wish things to be but of how they are.

I further believe that to act as if power does not exist is to ensure that the power status quo remains the same. To imply to children or adults (but of course the adults won't believe you anyway) that it doesn't matter how you talk or how you write is to ensure their ultimate failure. I prefer to be honest with my students. Tell them that their language and cultural style is unique and wonderful but that there is a political power game that is also being played, and if they want to be in on that game there are certain games that they too must play.

But don't think that I let the onus of change rest entirely with the students. I am also involved in political work both inside and outside of the educational system, and that political work demands that I place myself to influence as many gatekeeping points as possible. And it is there that I agitate for change—pushing gatekeepers to open their doors to a variety of styles and codes. What I'm saying, however, is that I do not believe that political change toward diversity can be effected from the bottom up, as do some of my colleagues. They seem to believe that if we accept and encourage diversity within classrooms of children, then diversity will automatically be accepted at gatekeeping points.

I believe that will never happen. What will happen is that the students who reach the gatekeeping points—like Amanda Branscombe's student who dropped out of high school because he failed his exit exam—will understand that they have been lied to and will react accordingly. No, I am certain that if we are truly to effect societal change, we cannot do so from the bottom up, but we must push and agitate from the top down. And in the meantime, we must take the responsibility to *teach*, to provide for students who do not already possess them, the additional codes of power.[4]

But I also do not believe that we should teach students to passively adopt an alternate code. They must be encouraged to understand the value of the code they already possess as well as to understand the power realities in this country. Otherwise they will be unable to work to change these realities. And how does one do that?

Martha Demientieff, a masterly Native Alaskan teacher of Athabaskan Indian students, tells me that her students, who live in a small, isolated, rural village of less than two hundred people, are not aware that there are different codes of English. She takes their writing and analyzes it for features of what has been referred to by Alaskan linguists as "Village English," and then covers half a bulletin board with words or phrases from the students' writing, which she labels "Our Heritage Language." On the other half of the bulletin board she puts the equivalent statements in "standard English," which she labels "Formal English."

She and the students spend a long time on the "Heritage English" section, savoring the words, discussing the nuances. She tells the students, "That's the way we say things. Doesn't it feel good? Isn't it the absolute best way of getting that idea across?" Then she turns to the other side of the board. She tells the students that there are people, not like those in their village, who judge others by the way they talk or write.

> We listen to the way people talk, not to judge them, but to tell what part of the river they come from. These other people are not like that. They think everybody needs to talk like them. Unlike us, they have a hard time hearing what people say if they don't talk exactly like them. Their way of talking and writing is called "Formal English."
>
> We have to feel a little sorry for them because they have only one way to talk. We're going to learn two ways to say things. Isn't that better? One way will be our Heritage way. The other will be Formal English. Then, when we go to get jobs, we'll be able to talk like those people who only know and can only really listen to one way. Maybe after we get the jobs we can help them to learn how it feels to have another language, like ours, that feels so good. We'll talk like them when we have to, but we'll always know our way is best.

Martha then does all sorts of activities with the notions of Formal and Heritage or informal English. She tells the students,

> In the village, everyone speaks informally most of the time unless there's a potlatch or something. You don't think about it, you don't worry about following any rules—it's sort of like how you eat food at a picnic—nobody pays attention to whether you use your fingers or a fork, and it feels *so* good. Now, Formal English is more like a formal dinner. There are rules to follow about where the knife and fork belong, about where people sit, about how you eat. That can be really nice, too, because it's nice to dress up sometimes.

The students then prepare a formal dinner in the class, for which they dress up and set a big table with fancy tablecloths, china, and silverware. They speak only Formal English at this meal. Then they prepare a picnic where only informal English is allowed.

She also contrasts the "wordy" academic way of saying things with the metaphoric style of Athabaskan. The students discuss how book language always uses more words, but in Heritage language, the shorter way of saying something is always better. Students then write papers in the academic way, discussing with Martha and with each other whether they believe they've said enough to sound like a book. Next, they take those papers and try to reduce the meaning to a few sentences. Finally, students further reduce the message to a "saying" brief enough to go on the front of a T-shirt, and the sayings are put on little paper T-shirts that the students cut out and hang throughout the room. Sometimes the students reduce other authors' wordy texts to their essential meanings as well.

The following transcript provides another example. It is from a conversation between a Black teacher and a Southern Black high school student named Joey, who is a speaker of Black English. The teacher believes it very important to discuss openly and honestly the issues of language diversity and power. She has begun the discussion by giving the student a children's book written in Black English to read.

| | |
|---|---|
| *Teacher:* | What do you think about that book? |
| *Joey:* | I think it's nice. |
| *Teacher:* | Why? |
| *Joey:* | I don't know. It just told about a Black family, that's all. |
| *Teacher:* | Was it difficult to read? |
| *Joey:* | No. |
| *Teacher:* | Was the text different from what you have seen in other books? |
| *Joey:* | Yeah. The writing was. |
| *Teacher:* | How? |
| *Joey:* | It use more of a southern-like accent in this book. |
| *Teacher:* | Uhm-hmm. Do you think that's good or bad? |
| *Joey:* | Well, uh, I don't think it's good for people down this a way, cause that's the way they grow up talking anyway. They ought to get the right way to talk. |
| *Teacher:* | Oh. So you think it's wrong to talk like that? |
| *Joey:* | Well . . . [*Laughs*] |
| *Teacher:* | Hard question, huh? |
| *Joey:* | Uhm-hmm, that's a hard question. But I think they shouldn't make books like that. |
| *Teacher:* | Why? |

| *Joey:* | Because they not using the right way to talk and in school they take off for that and li'l chirren grow up talking like that and reading like that so they might think that's right and all the time they getting bad grades in school, talking like that and writing like that. |
| --- | --- |
| *Teacher:* | Do you think they should be getting bad grades for talking like that? |
| *Joey:* | [*Pauses, answers very slowly*] No . . . No. |
| *Teacher:* | So you don't think that it matters whether you talk one way or another? |
| *Joey:* | No, not long as you understood. |
| *Teacher:* | Uhm-hmm. Well, that's a hard question for me to answer, too. It's ah, that's a question that's come up in a lot of schools now as to whether they should correct children who speak the way we speak all the time. Cause when we're talking to each other we talk like that even though we might not talk like that when we get into other situations, and who's to say whether it's— |
| *Joey:* | [*Interrupting*] Right or wrong. |
| *Teacher:* | Yeah. |
| *Joey:* | Maybe they ought to come up with another kind of . . . maybe Black English or something. A course in Black English. Maybe Black folks would be good in that cause people talk, I mean Black people talk like that, so . . . but I guess there's a right way and wrong way to talk, you know, not regarding what race. I don't know. |
| *Teacher:* | But who decided what's right or wrong? |
| *Joey:* | Well, that's true . . . I guess White people did. |

[*Laughter. End of tape.*]

Notice how throughout the conversation Joey's consciousness has been raised by thinking about codes of language. This teacher further advocates having students interview various personnel officers in actual workplaces about their attitudes toward divergent styles in oral and written language. Students begin to understand how arbitrary language standards are, but also how politically charged they are. They compare various pieces written in different styles, discuss the impact of different styles on the message by making translations and back translations across styles, and discuss the history, apparent purpose, and contextual appropriateness of each of the technical writing rules presented by their teacher. *And* they practice writing different forms to different audiences based on rules appropriate for each audience. Such a program not only "teaches" standard linguistic forms, but also explores aspects of power as exhibited through linguistic forms.

Tony Burgess, in a study of secondary writing in England by Britton, Burgess, Martin, McLeod, and Rosen (1975/1977), suggests that we should not teach "iron conventions . . . imposed without rationale or grounding in communicative intent," . . . but "critical and ultimately cultural awarenesses" (p. 54). Courtney Cazden (1987) calls for a two-pronged approach:

1. Continuous opportunities for writers to participate in some authentic bit of the unending conversation . . . thereby becoming part of a vital community of talkers and writers in a particular domain, and
2. Periodic, temporary focus on conventions of form, taught as cultural conventions expected in a particular community. (p. 20)

Just so that there is no confusion about what Cazden means by a focus on conventions of form, or about what I mean by "skills," let me stress that neither of us is speaking of page after page of "skill sheets" creating compound words or identifying nouns and adverbs, but rather about helping students gain a useful knowledge of the conventions of print while engaging in real and useful communicative activities. Kay Rowe Grubis, a junior high school teacher in a multicultural school, makes lists of certain technical rules for her eighth graders' review and then gives them papers from a third grade to "correct." The students not only have to correct other students' work, but also tell them why they have changed or questioned aspects of the writing.

A village teacher, Howard Cloud, teaches his high school students the conventions of formal letter writing and the formulation of careful questions in the context of issues surrounding the amendment of the Alaska Land Claims Settlement Act. Native Alaskan leaders hold differing views on this issue, critical to the future of local sovereignty and land rights. The students compose letters to leaders who reside in different areas of the state seeking their perspectives, set up audioconference calls for interview/debate sessions, and finally, develop a videotape to present the differing views.

To summarize, I suggest that students must be *taught* the codes needed to participate fully in the mainstream of American life, not by being forced to attend to hollow, inane, decontextualized subskills, but rather within the context of meaningful communicative endeavors; that they must be allowed the resource of the teacher's expert knowledge, while being helped to acknowledge their own "expertness" as well; and that even while students are assisted in learning the culture of power, they must also be helped to learn about the arbitrariness of those codes and about the power relationships they represent.

I am also suggesting that appropriate education for poor children and children of color can only be devised in consultation with adults who share their culture. Black parents, teachers of color, and members of poor communities must be allowed to participate fully in the discussion of what kind of instruction is in their children's best interest. Good liberal intentions are not enough. In an insightful study entitled "Racism without Racists: Institutional Racism in Urban Schools," Massey, Scott, and Dornbusch (1975) found that under the pressures of teaching, and with all intentions of "being nice," teachers had essentially stopped attempting to teach Black children. In their words: "We have shown that oppression can arise out of warmth, friendliness, and concern. Paternalism and a lack of challenging standards are creating a distorted system of evaluation in the schools" (p. 10). Educators must open themselves to, and allow themselves to be affected by, these alternative voices.

In conclusion, I am proposing a resolution for the skills/process debate. In short, the debate is fallacious; the dichotomy is false. The issue is really an illusion created initially not by teachers but by academics whose world view demands the creation of categorical divisions—not for the purpose of better teaching, but for the goal of easier analysis. As I have been reminded by many teachers since the publication of my article, those who are most skillful at educating Black and poor children do not allow themselves to be placed in "skills" or "process" boxes. They understand the need for both approaches, the need to help students to establish their own voices, but to coach those voices to produce notes that will be heard clearly in the larger society.

The dilemma is not really in the debate over instructional methodology, but rather in communicating across cultures and in addressing the more fundamental issue of power, of whose voice gets to be heard in determining what is best for poor children and children of color. Will Black teachers and parents continue to be silenced by the very forces that claim to "give voice" to our children? Such an outcome would be tragic, for both groups truly have something to say to one another. As a result of careful listening to alternative points of view, I have myself come to a viable synthesis of perspectives. But both sides do need to be able to listen, and I contend that it is those with the most power, those in the majority, who must take the greater responsibility for initiating the process.

To do so takes a very special kind of listening, listening that requires not only open eyes and ears, but open hearts and minds. We do not really see through our eyes or hear through our ears, but through our beliefs. To put our beliefs on hold is to cease to exist as ourselves for a moment—and that is not easy. It is painful as well, because it means turning yourself inside out, giving up your own sense of who you are, and being willing to see yourself in the unflattering light of another's angry gaze. It is not easy, but it is the only way to learn what it might feel like to be someone else and the only way to start the dialogue.

There are several guidelines. We must keep the perspective that people are experts on their own lives. There are certainly aspects of the outside world of which they may not be aware, but they can be the only authentic chroniclers of their own experience. We must not be too quick to deny their interpretations, or accuse them of "false consciousness." We must believe that people are rational beings, and therefore always act rationally. We may not understand their rationales, but that in no way militates against the existence of these rationales or reduces our responsibility to attempt to apprehend them. And finally, we must learn to be vulnerable enough to allow our world to turn upside down in order to allow the realities of others to edge themselves into our consciousness. In other words, we must become ethnographers in the true sense.

Teachers are in an ideal position to play this role, to attempt to get all of the issues on the table in order to initiate true dialogue. This can only be done, however, by seeking out those whose perspectives may differ most, by learning to give their words complete attention, by understanding one's own power, even if that power stems merely from being in the majority, by being unafraid to raise questions about discrimination and voicelessness with people of color, and to listen, no, to *hear* what they say. I suggest that the results of such interactions may be the most powerful and empowering coalescence yet seen in the educational realm—for *all* teachers and for *all* the students they teach.

## Notes

1. Such a discussion, limited as it is by space constraints, must treat the intersection of class and race somewhat simplistically. For the sake of clarity, however, let me define a few terms: "Black" is used herein to refer to those who share some or all aspects of "core black culture" (Gwaltney, 1980, p. xxiii), that is, the mainstream of Black America—neither those who have entered the ranks of the bourgeoisie nor those who are participants in the disenfranchised underworld. "Middle-class" is used broadly to refer to the predominantly White American "mainstream." There are, of course, non-White people who also fit into this category; at issue is their cultural identification, not necessarily the color of their skin. (I must add that there are other non-White people, as well as poor White people, who have indicated to me that their perspectives are similar to those attributed herein to Black people.)

2. *Multicultural Britain: "Crosstalk,"* National Centre of Industrial Language Training, Commission for Racial Equality, London, England, John Twitchin, Producer.

3. I would like to thank Michelle Foster, who is presently planning a more in-depth treatment of the subject, for her astute clarification of the idea.

4. Bernstein (1975) makes a similar point when he proposes that different educational frames cannot be successfully institutionalized in the lower levels of education until there are fundamental changes at the post-secondary levels.

## References

Apple, M. W. (1979). *Ideology and curriculum.* Boston: Routledge & Kegan Paul.

Bernstein, B. (1975). Class and pedagogies: Visible and invisible. In B. Bernstein, *Class, codes, and control* (Vol. 3). Boston: Routledge & Kegan Paul.

Britton, J., Burgess, T., Martin, N., McLeod, A., & Rosen, H. (1975/1977). *The development of writing abilities.* London: Macmillan Education for the Schools Council, and Urbana, IL: National Council of Teachers of English.

Cazden, C. (1987, January). *The myth of autonomous text.* Paper presented at the Third International Conference on Thinking, Hawaii.

Delpit, L. D. (1986). Skills and other dilemmas of a progressive Black educator. *Harvard Educational Review, 56,* (4), 379–385.

Foster, M. (1987). *"It's cookin' now": An ethnographic study of the teaching style of a successful Black teacher in an urban community college.* Unpublished doctoral dissertation, Harvard University.

Gwaltney, J. (1980). *Drylongso.* New York: Vintage Books.

Heath, S. B. (1983). *Ways with words.* Cambridge: Cambridge University Press.

Massey, G. C., Scott, M. V., & Dornbusch, S. M. (1975). Racism without racists: Institutional racism in urban schools. *The Black Scholar, 7*(3), 2–11.

Siddle, E. V. (1986). *A critical assessment of the natural process approach to teaching writing.* Unpublished qualifying paper, Harvard University.

Siddle, E. V. (1988). *The effect of intervention strategies on the revisions ninth graders make in a narrative essay.* Unpublished doctoral dissertation, Harvard University.

Snow, C. E., Arlman-Rup, A. Hassing, Y., Josbe, J., Joosten, J., & Vorster, J. (1976). Mother's speech in three social classes. *Journal of Psycholinguistic Research, 5,* 1–20.

# Essay Review

## Politics and Pedagogy: The Case of Bilingual Education

CARLOS J. OVANDO
*Indiana University*

BILINGUAL EDUCATION: HISTORY, POLITICS, THEORY,
AND PRACTICE
by James Crawford.
*Trenton, NJ: Crane Publishing, 1989. 204 pp.*

Why has bilingual education continued to be so controversial in the United States? What is the connection between the conflict over bilingual education and our path as a nation? Both the controversy and its impact on our nation's future are deeply grounded in the very nature of language itself. If language were nothing more than a set of words, a grammar, and sounds, there would probably be much less discord over our language education policies. However, language is so very much more than words, grammar, and sounds. It is, as folklorist Cratis Williams writes, "culture expressing itself in sound" (Quoted in Alvarez & Kolker, 1987). It gives individuals and groups their identity. As a lively and complex expression of culture, language enables members of society to transmit and exchange values, attitudes, skills, and aspirations as culture-bearers and culture-makers. I believe, therefore, that is it precisely because of this that language repeatedly emerges as a topic of national concern and interest.

Because of the power of language, bilingual education is more than just a useful pedagogical tool that addresses the learning needs of linguistic-minority students. It also involves complex issues of political power, cultural identity, and social status. These issues, on the surface, seem quite remote from the day-to-day realities of bilingual and English-as-a-second-language (ESL) classrooms across the United States. Yet these large sociopolitical and cultural issues are the bases, I believe, on which bilingual education is either so loved or so hated. In fact, I am convinced that the current debate on bilingual education is not just about pedagogical effectiveness—does it work or not—but about how language diversity fits within our prevailing national ideology.

In *Bilingual Education: History, Politics, Theory, and Practice*, James Crawford, the

*Harvard Educational Review* Vol. 60 No. 3 August 1990, 341–356

former Washington editor of *Education Week,* offers the reader an opportunity to understand thoroughly both the pedagogical issues and the powerful sociopolitical forces surrounding bilingual education. From a journalistic perspective, he offers four reasons language politics in the 1980s have emerged in such bold relief. Not surprisingly, these four reasons reflect both pedagogical and sociopolitical concerns.

1. The Bilingual Education Act of 1968 was enacted without the benefit of extensive public debate and with few precise guidelines. As a result, rather than providing an unambiguous framework for language policy, it has tended to exacerbate the issues.

2. As the number of immigrants from Asia and Latin America has increased, "language politics has become a convenient surrogate for racial politics" (p. 14). Many argue, for example, that the rhetoric of many English Only advocates shows evidence of thinly veiled racism.

3. Bilingual education has made life more difficult for those school administrators who dislike special programs in their districts. For administrators, bilingual education has meant a need to modify schedules, recruit teachers with new skills, and implement curricular changes.

4. Recent bilingual education research suggests a paradigm shift in the way we think languages are acquired and how they ought to be used in private and public life. Because of the growing understanding of the powerful connection between language and sociocultural identity, Americans have become increasingly opinionated about matters related to the functions of language in society.

With a paradigm shift under way—a shift that in some ways challenges the hegemony of English in the United States—it is not surprising that language minority education has lured a diverse assortment of curious participants and observers, including academicians, educators, politicians, religious leaders, parents, and journalists. Two journalists who have earlier written extensively on bilingual education are Fred Hechinger of *The New York Times* and Noel Epstein of *The Washington Post.* Interestingly, their interpretations differ markedly from Crawford's conclusions. Commenting on the role of the English language and the melting pot ideology in the creation of the American dream, Hechinger writes, for example, that "the facts of history are quite clear; they cannot be rewritten or revised. Those facts show clearly that the founding fathers viewed the United States as a country with a unified history, with unified traditions, and with a common language" (1978, p. 130). He argues that from its beginnings the United States was meant to be a nation ruled by English institutions, language, and cultural patterns. Consequently, the concept of the melting pot was a good one. The problem of integrating all Americans into this Anglo-Saxon cultural milieu came about, however, because of the highly discriminatory practices that did not allow all racial and cultural groups to "melt" (1978, p. 130). The source of the difficulty, as Hechinger sees it, is not the melting pot concept per se, but rather the reluctance of the dominant society to accept historically stigmatized racial and linguistic minorities who wanted to assimilate.

While Hechinger tends to deal more with broad national issues in a historical context, Epstein (1977) has written more specifically on federally sponsored bilingual education. (Such federal programs came about as a result of the Bilingual Education Act of 1968.) In his book, Epstein suggests that the United States is suffering from a "Columbus complex" and a "death wish" by officially affirming ethnolinguistic loyalties through native-language instruction in the public schools. He uses the metaphor of the Columbus complex to suggest that the federal government has undertaken an educational expedition without first having carefully charted the waters. By sponsoring bilingual programs it was blindly sailing into the unknown, hoping to stumble into islands here and there. He uses the death wish imagery to imply that the federal government has ventured into a dangerous and tortuous path that would encourage loyalties not only to other languages and cultures, but to other foreign countries as well. This policy, he argues, will stall the assimilation of indigenous minorities and newcomers into the American mainstream, and has the potential for tearing down the national fabric (Epstein, 1977).

I find Epstein's predictions exaggerated and off the mark. It is true that much of the initial impetus for bilingual education was guided by a great deal of intuition and by a lack of facts or scholarly guidance. However, after twenty years of federally sponsored as well as state-sponsored bilingual education, the national situation has not even come close to realizing Epstein's death wish metaphor. Ours is not a nation torn apart by clashing foreign loyalties. And the motives behind the bilingual legislation were positive in nature: a desire to correct the failed path of monolingual English instruction for students with limited English proficiency and a desire to carry out the principles of the civil rights movement. Such motives hardly constitute a death wish for the nation. It is within this framework that bilingual education has sought to nurture stronger citizenship among students with limited English proficiency by affirming their value as community members and by developing their literacy, their knowledge base, and their thinking skills.

Unlike Hechinger and Epstein, who focused primarily on the role of language as an instrument of national unity or separatism, Crawford takes a thoughtful and careful look at both the macro and micro issues associated with bilingual education in the U.S. experience. His book is a noteworthy addition to the literature on bilingual education as a political issue, but it also serves as an engaging and unusually well written primer for those not familiar with the overall history, rationale, development, implementation, and evaluation of federally sponsored bilingual education in the public schools. Crawford is the first journalist to date to conclude, after examining the field of bilingual education in a scholarly and thorough manner, that properly conceptualized bilingual instruction is not the misguided pedagogical process typically portrayed by the media. In fact, he argues the opposite—that for the past twenty years basic research in linguistics and cognitive psychology indicates that well-conceptualized bilingual education produces good cognitive and sociocultural results.

Beyond the field of journalism, there are of course many books and scholarly pieces on bilingualism written by linguists, sociologists, cognitive psychologists, legal experts, and educators. (For one overview, see Paulston, 1988, pp. 581–584). However, Crawford's book is one of the few comprehensive examinations of bilingual education written for the general public. Although other comprehensive works exist—such as *Bilingual and ESL Classrooms: Teaching in Multicultural Contexts* by Carlos Ovando and V. P. Collier (1985)—the intended audiences are quite different. In the process of surveying the field of bilingual education, Crawford sprinkles the discussion with rich storytelling detail that both engages the reader and sharpens his or her understanding of bilingual issues. Crawford has made extensive visits to a variety of bilingual classrooms across the country, and he takes advantage of his first-hand familiarity with bilingual programs to chronicle both the difficulties and the successes of these programs. In particular, he describes the shortcomings and the successes of various Native American bilingual programs and the positive results of the Eastman model in California. This type of detail is often missing from the academic literature. In addition to presenting the reader with a tour through actual bilingual classrooms, Crawford examines in great detail the anti-bilingual years of William Bennett's term as Secretary of Education and the English Only movement. This is "must" reading for anyone who wishes to understand the sociopolitical issues surrounding language politics in the 1980s.

By so carefully exploring virtually every aspect of bilingual education in the United States, Crawford enables the lay reader to gain a solid understanding of the field. He also enables the specialist to pause, look around, and reflect on where bilingual education has been in the past and where it may be headed. To date, most of the writing in bilingual education aimed at the general public has tended to be highly skeptical of the premise that instruction in the native language will benefit language-minority students. For example, in her book *Forked Tongue* (1990), Rosalie Porter provides examples of the dubious achievements of certain bilingual programs. Using her experiences with public school programs serving language-minority students in Newton, Massachusetts, she argues that alternative curricular and instructional approaches that do not use native-language instruction should be developed. But Porter's recommendation that students with limited proficiency in English spend the school day surrounded by English does not square at all with the persuasive evidence summarized by Crawford. Although he is as sympathetic to bilingual education as Porter is antagonistic, Crawford presents abundant data from all sides of the issues to let the reader make up his or her own mind.

It would be very difficult here to analyze every aspect of bilingual education that Crawford so ably explores. Because of the power of political issues over pedagogical realities, this discussion will focus on three areas that affect the current political status of bilingual education: the history of multilingual education in the United States, language loyalty issues, and the controversy over the effectiveness of bilingual programs.

## The Neglected History of Bilingual Education

In providing a context for discussing the current status of bilingual education, Crawford's historical analysis of the field offers the reader many surprises. Crawford points out that because the story has largely been untold and not carefully documented, the information vacuum has been filled by a variety of ethnic stereotypes, myths about U.S. history, and misconceptions about language. Unfortunately, such deceptive misinformation often serves the critics of bilingual education especially well.

Despite notions to the contrary, U.S. history is filled with examples of multilingual communities and regions. As early as 1664, for example, when Manhattan Island was obtained by the British, there were eighteen different European languages already spoken there. In addition, some five hundred Indian languages were present in North America at the time. In such multilingual contexts, some degree of bilingualism has always tended to develop because of the functional need for it. Given this background of long-standing multilingualism, Crawford remarks that it is quite ironic that the process of second-language acquisition has been only meagerly documented. The human story surrounding the process is little known, often misunderstood, and largely unappreciated. Bilingualism has taken root in ethnic enclaves both as a necessity for dealing with the larger English-speaking community and a way to provide support to an ethnic group in an alien environment; nevertheless, bilingual individuals generally have not received much affirmation in the United States. As Einar Haugen, a linguist who has done extensive research on Norwegian-English bilingualism in the United States, writes: "Bilingualism has been treated as a necessary evil, a rash on the body politic, which time might be expected to cure without the need of calling in the doctors" (1969, p. 2). For this and other reasons, the topic of bilingualism has not attracted the intellectual resources of the U.S. scholarly and scientific communities to the degree that one would expect for such an important topic.

One of several historical topics Crawford explores is the common presence of bilingual and non-English-language schooling in many communities in the United States before World War I. Crawford establishes that dual language instruction was pervasive during the nineteenth century, with many states passing laws that explicitly authorized bilingual education; a number of public schools provided instruction in such languages as German, French, Spanish, Norwegian, and Cherokee. So sophisticated were the bilingual processes among the Cherokees in Oklahoma in the 1850s that their literacy rate was higher than that of the White populations in Arkansas and Texas! In the year 1900, 600,000 children, or about 4 percent of the elementary school population, were receiving all or part of their instruction in the German language. However, this tolerant language policy was not fairly distributed across all language minorities. Crawford points out that our attitudes toward the language rights of oppressed racial minorities were (and continue to be) less generous than those toward users of northern European languages. In the past, for instance, unfair language policies have existed toward Spanish-speakers and speakers of Native American languages. Many adults with Spanish language backgrounds remember, as I do, being punished in school for speaking Spanish. One of the first words that some Native American children learned in the English-speaking school environment was *soap,* because having their mouths washed out with soap was one of the consequences of using their native language (pp. 25–26).

It was not until the first twenty years of the twentieth century (the "Americanization" period) that the ability to speak English was linked ideologically and politically to American loyalty and patriotism. Crawford suggests that by 1900 there were growing fears in the country about both the quantity and quality of new immigrants, especially those from southern and eastern Europe—Italians, Jews, and Slavs—who seemed unwilling or unable to assimilate to Anglo-American culture. The Dillingham Commission Report—a massive federal study on immigration—in fact claimed that these groups were not learning English and were not willing to assimilate as quickly as the Germans and Scandinavians. In yet another irony, Crawford reminds the reader that these same German and Scandinavian groups had themselves been criticized earlier for moving into the American mainstream too slowly.

This fear of nonassimilation, coupled with major industrialists' concerns over foreign labor agitators, led to the establishment of Americanization campaigns. Crawford argues that when the waves of immigration receded, the Americanization campaign of the early twentieth century might have fizzled had the United States not entered World War I. Because of the cultural and linguistic allegiances associated with their backgrounds, Americans of German ancestry became the target of much hostility. Speaking German was perceived as a subversive activity. In 1919 fifteen states passed laws mandating English as the language of instruction. Many states passed laws forbidding foreign language instruction below the ninth grade (p. 24).

The demise of the Americanization campaign occurred, according to Crawford, in 1924, when Congress established the most restrictive immigration program in U.S. history. The legislation was justified by its supporters as reducing the number of supposedly genetically inferior immigrants. This meant the virtual exclusion of newcomers from southern and eastern Europe, and for all practical purposes, from Asia as well. With the perceived threat from all these so-called undesirable immigrants gone, the coercive tactics used to Americanize new immigrants and to teach them English also disappeared. Although formal Americanization campaigns did not persist past the 1920s, Crawford blames state laws for destroying bilingual education in the United States for the next fifty years; it only reappeared in 1963 at Coral Way Elementary School in Dade County, Florida, (pp. 24–28).

Although Crawford does not offer any significant new insights into or interpretations of the history of bilingual education in the United States, he does an impressive job of providing the reader with an array of engaging primary sources documenting the nation's vivid and diverse multilingual history. This level of scholarship is often missing from journalistic writing and from books with a general appeal. Nevertheless, I think that with such a rich bibliography Crawford perhaps could have sharpened his interpretation further by pointing out more clearly a major paradox in our ethnolinguistic evolution. This paradox can be seen when one considers, for instance, the relationship between language and such important institutions as the visual and print media and churches. On the one hand, the U.S. government has been quite non-intrusive with regard to the establishment and operation of radio stations, TV networks, newspapers, the publishing industry, and churches—areas where the use of non-English languages has found ideal niches. On the other hand, the ugly reality of xenophobia has manifested itself throughout U.S. history, its opinions voiced by segments of society that question the wisdom of allowing so much linguistic and cultural freedom. This conflict between freedom of expression and the desire for monolingualism has changed over the years, but never disappeared.

## Language Loyalty and the English Only Movement: Common Sense, Myths, and Reality

The opposing assimilative and separatist potentials of language loyalty have played a part in heating up the debate over language politics. These are the basic issues at stake: Does bilingual loyalty ipso facto produce less patriotism? Conversely, does English monolingualism automatically ensure the unity of the country?

Despite sporadic antagonism toward specific ethnolinguistic minorities (for example, toward Spanish-speakers in the Southwest, toward Native Americans, and toward Germans during World War I and World War II), on the whole, Crawford argues, Americans have been tolerant of their rich and complex multilingual heritage. In fact, according to the prevailing view, it is a commitment to a shared set of democratic principles that has kept the country together—not English-language loyalty. And so, language choice has generally been accepted as a very personal right that should not be violated or modified by coercive governmental edicts. The standard assumption in the United States has been that citizens would come to accept of their own free will the function of English as the *lingua franca* of the republic. So successful has been this noncoercive process of the language shift to English in the United States that linguist Haugen was moved to make this observation: "America's profusion of tongues has made her a modern Babel, but a Babel in reverse" (1972, p. 1). In other words, it is surely the non-English languages in the United States that are truly vulnerable due to the aggressive pressure of the English language.

But if the English language is not in fact threatened by the linguistic diversity in U.S. society, then why is there a need to legislate its protection? The rationale for defending the hegemony of English derives in part from the perception that the traditionally rapid shift to English once made by immigrants has come to a screeching halt in the 1980s—that a new set of linguistic, and consequently patriotic, loyalties is being promoted by federally and state-sponsored bilingual education. Kathryn Bricker, executive director of U.S. English, expressed this fear in a television interview when she said that unless recent immigrants have as little access as possible to their home language, they will not learn English (1989). She implied that during the earlier waves of immigration, newcomers did not have much opportunity to use their native language and therefore learned English more quickly than today's immigrants. Similarly, Gerda Bikales, the former executive director of U.S. English, has expressed deep concern that a shared American culture established by earlier immigrants could slip away unless today's newcomers learn English quickly (cited in Crawford, p. 55). Allegedly, this threat to a national culture comes in part from the tide of immigrants from developing nations, especially from Asia and Latin America, who now are given native-language support in the schooling of their children.

But although the concerns may seem appealing on the surface, there is no doubt in my mind that the English Only movement runs counter to the basic principles of democratic pluralism. In fact, I believe that it is in the best national interest to encourage, nurture, and emphasize a multilingually competent citizenry. I agree with Crawford that bilingual education critics may have among them many wolves disguised in sheep's clothing. That is to say, within the ranks of the intellectually honest critics there may also be racist and xenophobic individuals masquerading as patriotic crusaders. Crawford shows that such racism is a factor in some of the U.S. English fan mail received by former secretary of education William Bennett. Here is part of one letter from a Florida critic:

> What hope is there of assimilating these foreigners into American life if we encourage and assist them in perpetuating their own language instead of learning to speak English? We not only have our taxes frittered away with supporting [illegal aliens] on relief . . . we must on top of that be taxed to educate their multitudinous offspring in their own language. (p. 13)

People with these sentiments cleverly use language as an intellectual and emotional magnet to attract ideological, financial, and political support from others who range across the political spectrum. For example, John Tanton, founder of both U.S. English and the Federation for American Immigration Reform (FAIR), was formerly an activist and leader in the Sierra Club and in Planned Parenthood, and was the national president of Zero Population Growth—all "mainstream" liberal organizations. At the same time, U.S. English has garnered support from such conservative organizations as the American Legion and from such well-known figures as Jacques Barzun, the late Bruno Bettleheim, Alistair Cooke, George Glider, Norman Podhoretz, Arnold Schwarzenegger, W. Clement Stone, and Rosalyn Yalow. Although they have since changed their stance, Walter Cronkite and Norman Cousins also supported U.S. English at one time. It is within this context that the 1980s, according to Crawford, have witnessed the emergence of language politics as an irresistibly engaging topic with great import for the kind of society that we wish to become: altruistic, tolerant, and pluralistic or coercive, restrictive, and isolationist.

Proponents of native-language restriction in the day-to-day affairs of the classroom, such as Porter (1990), Bricker (1989), and Herbert Walberg (1989), argue that the best way for children to learn English is to use it on a daily basis for social as well as academic purposes in the classroom and on the playground. Walberg states:

> For many immigrant children who are not proficient in English, the problems of second language and academic learning are more acute largely because they come from deprived socioeconomic backgrounds. More than others, these children need maximum exposure to English in school in order to learn it and because they may be deprived of such exposure at home and in their neigh-

borhoods. Because bilingual education deters the very factors that promote English mastery and other academic accomplishments, it can hardly be held out as their hope. (1989, p. 20)

The position of such proponents of native-language restriction is anchored in the intuitively appealing but misguided notion that for two hundred years immigrants have been successful in learning English and succeeding academically without native-language support. Accordingly, the reasoning goes, if our ancestors learned English without the crutch of native-language support, newcomers do not need it either.

The misguided motives of U.S. English assimilationists lead them to be concerned with how *quickly* schools can get these students to speak English rather than with what is the best way to provide them with a sound *education*. English Only proponents seem to forget that just speaking English, without a strong academic foundation, will not enable the large numbers of future minority workers to participate in a highly technological society, or, further, to contribute significant levels of social security payments in our rapidly aging society. Despite the sound arguments that an enlightened language policy is needed for the next century, a dangerous backlash against bilingual education has been growing as the English Only movement strengthens. This backlash can be seen in the restrictive language measures taken in sixteen states—most recently in Arizona, Colorado, and Florida—and in the expansion of federal Title VII funding for English-only approaches.[1] Individuals, racist or non-racist, may find the movement appealing because it can seem so logical that the best way to induct students into the American experience is to restrict the first language while giving a non-sugarcoated dose of 100 percent English on a sustained basis. As we will see shortly, however, there is ample evidence that this approach is usually unwise. Yet, as Crawford puts it, trying to convince a critic that bilingual education is the best route to full English proficiency is like trying to persuade someone that the best way to go West is to go East first. To gain access to English via the ancestral language may appear highly inefficient at first glance.

Many commonsense notions regarding language are incorrect, but they contribute to public doubts about bilingual education. As Crawford writes:

> Bilingual education still runs against powerful myths: That young children pick up new languages quickly and effortlessly. That prolonged reliance on the native tongue reduces students' incentives to learn English. That bilingualism confuses the mind and retards school achievement. In short, bilingual education defies common sense: If we instruct children in foreign tongues, how will we teach them to speak our language? (pp. 86–87)

## The Effectiveness Controversy

Just as he dispels myths about the history of language policy in the United States, Crawford provides a good synthesis of current and well-established research that, if accepted, can help clear the muddy waters of language policy. Crawford not only plays defense against the fallacies and dangers of the U.S. English movement, but he goes on the offensive and builds a solid case that bilingual education is tied both to the protection of civil rights and to good pedagogy. Citing the work of Kenji Hakuta and Catherine Snow (1986) among other researchers, he makes the following points:

1. Early childhood is not necessarily the optimum period in which to acquire a second language; older children and adults can actually be better learners. Thus the rush to immerse very young children in English may be inappropriate.
2. Language proficiency is a configuration of many different kinds of language abilities. Though children may quickly acquire simple, everyday social English, the English they need for academic success will take much longer to develop.
3. Skills learned in one language transfer to another. Children with a good academic foundation in their first language will do better in English in the long run.
4. Reading, especially for at-risk children, should first be taught in the native language. These skills will ultimately transfer into higher achievement in English.
5. Children are not handicapped cognitively by bilingualism, and some types of intelligence may actually be enhanced by the child's being bilingual (p. 89).

There is now a cumulative body of knowledge from linguistics and cognitive psychology that suggests that native language support in high-quality classroom environments produces good results. As he describes this research, Crawford notes that

> the past two decades have brought enormous advances in curricula, methodologies, materials, and teacher training. No longer stigmatized as slow learners, language-minority children are achieving at or near grade level by the time they leave well-designed bilingual programs, even in urban schools where failure was once the norm. (p. 12)

The Eastman School in the Los Angeles Unified School District is one particularly successful example that Crawford offers. A main component of the Eastman approach is the sustained validation of the students' first language during the entire schooling process. Students are encouraged to develop thinking and problem-solving skills in their first language, while they also receive sustained instruction in communication-based English as a second language (ESL). The results to date are so impressive that the Los Angeles School District has adopted the Eastman model for the many schools serving the district's 163,000 limited-English-proficient students (Gold, 1988, p. 4).[2]

Despite such successes as the Eastman School, the answers to questions about the effectiveness of bilingual education are not simple. The issues have become thoroughly entangled in current language politics, and political reality has more often than not had the upper hand over pedagogical outcomes and recommendations. However, an integrated and effective language policy goes beyond conventional wisdom to examine basic research and evaluation. And such research has indeed lured politicians, educators, parents, statisticians, linguists, and psychologists in search of evidence to argue for or against the merits of dual-language instruction. Both camps have found evidence to their liking, and both have tended to belittle each other's evidence. As we shall see, such research-based debates have become imbroglios over means, ends, and politics.

Politically influenced research seems to have started quite early in the evolution of federally sponsored bilingual education in the United States. Because there were no federally sponsored efforts prior to the passage of the Bilingual Education Act in 1968, it was important to build an experiential base. With this in mind, the Act funded demonstration projects that were required to submit an evaluation component at the end of their funding cycles. However, as Crawford points out, these evaluation results apparently were not of much interest to the U.S. Office of Education. According to Rudolph C. Troike, "It is a minor scandal that in 1975, all of the files of the evaluations accumulated since 1969 were discarded" (1986, p. 11). Why these early evaluation records were destroyed is a matter of conjecture. But it does illustrate the lack of seriousness of purpose related to data gathering for guiding public and educational policy. Moreover, according to Troike (1978), less than 0.5 percent of the $500 million appropriated for bilingual education during its first ten years went to research (p. 2). This minuscule amount certainly suggests that this component was not taken seriously.

It seems that both of the above—the absence of program evaluation data for the first few years of federal funding, and the lack of a sustained and well-funded research agenda—may have set the tone for the inconclusive and, by implication, negative results of the two well-publicized evaluation reports that Crawford examines. The first report was the American Institute for Research (AIR) study, a national evaluation of federally funded bilingual programs, published in 1977–78. This study involved more than seven thousand children, and is the largest single evaluation of Title VII programs ever done. Crawford notes that "after ten years of federal funding, AIR concluded, there had been 'no consistent significant impact' on the education of limited-English-proficient (LEP) children" (p. 87). This, of course, was wonderful ammunition for the anti-bilingual camp. The apparent conclusion was that bilingual schooling was no better than simple immersion schooling. Why then, the critics could argue, should the federal government mandate it or fund it?

The second evaluation, an extensive review of the bilingual research literature on program effectiveness, called the Baker-de Kanter Report, was published in 1981. This report was commissioned by the White House Regulatory Analysis and Review Group of the Education Department. The assignment went to Keith Baker, a sociologist, and Adriana de Kanter, a management intern, of the Office of Planning and Budget, the same division of the Education Department that had conducted the AIR study. Guided by legal-political concerns, Baker and de Kanter asked two questions:

1. Is there a sufficiently strong case for the effectiveness of TBE (transitional bilingual education) for learning English and nonlanguage subjects to justify a legal mandate for TBE?

2. Are there any effective alternatives to TBE? That is, should one particular method be exclusively required if other methods are also effective? (p. 92)

Baker and de Kanter initially examined more than three hundred bilingual studies. Of these, they found only twenty-eight to be valid and reliable according to their criteria; they considered the rest to be methodologically weak. Based on this analysis, which, as Crawford points out, left out some of the better-known bilingual success stories, they determined that, on the whole, the studies were inconclusive and that therefore the evidence of the value of bilingual education was apparently inconclusive. Baker and de Kanter recommended instead the use of structured immersion— a monolingual English approach in which content-area instruction is modified using ESL techniques.

According to Crawford, there are three flaws in the type of evaluation research represented by the AIR and the Baker and de Kanter reports:

> First, it tends to obscure the striking diversity of bilingual education program design and quality; availability of resources, materials, and trained staff; mix of English and native-language instruction; and students' social and linguistic backgrounds. Second, program evaluations face a series of technical obstacles—from tracking transient student populations to finding appropriate comparison groups—in judging bilingual education against its alternatives. Since the Supreme Court's 1974 decision in *Lau v. Nichols,* "no treatment" for LEP children has been legally forbidden as a violation of their civil rights. Finally, evaluations are subject to political pressures, for example, in crucial decisions about study design. Bilingual education practitioners clearly have a professional stake in defending their field. And the U.S Department of Education, the major source of research funding, has an ideological stake in vindicating the alternative methods that [former] Secretary William Bennett has called "promising." (p. 88)

The latest chapter in the effectiveness controversy deals with the research findings of a distinguished panel of ten educational researchers commissioned by the U.S. General Accounting Office (GAO) in 1987. In their conclusions, the majority of the panelists challenged the anti-bilingual position of the U.S. Education Department on five points:

1. The research showed positive effects of transitional bilingual education on students' achievement of English-language competence.
2. Evidence for students' learning in subjects other than English, although less abundant than data on second-language acquisition, also "supported [Title VII's] requirement for using native languages."
3. Research provided no reason to believe that English-only methods like structured immersion or stand-alone ESL offered promise for language-minority children in the United States.
4. There was no scientific basis for claiming that high Hispanic dropout rates reflected the failure of bilingual education, because no data had been gathered in this area.
5. The research was not so inconclusive, after all; there was enough evidence to indicate both the validity of native-language instruction and the groups of children most likely to benefit from it. (p. 79)

Considered by some to be the strongest pro-bilingual evidence to come out of the federal government, the report was, however, immediately challenged by officials from the U.S. Department of Education. Chester Finn, the abrasive secretary for educational research under Bennett, harshly criticized the GAO's methodology, saying that it was "biased and sloppy." Questioning the arbitrary composition of the panel, he concluded: "Our position on bilingual education is valid and unscathed by this inept report" (p. 79).

To me, these three studies—the AIR report, the Baker and de Kanter report, and the GAO report—illustrate only too clearly how research in bilingual education has become much too politicized for its own good. Politics instead of pedagogy has tended to drive bilingual educational policy and subsequent curricular and instructional outcomes. It appears that frequently educational and linguistic research and evaluation are either accepted or rejected according to the ideological framework of the policymakers. When the pedagogical outcomes are examined, they are often immediately associated with either the pro- or the anti-bilingual camp, and then the data become suspect. As a Californian colleague remarked a few years ago, "If only politicians could stay out of the field of bilingual education we could make progress in the classrooms" (F. Tempes, personal communication, February 20, 1983). He pointed out, for example, that just when teachers, parents, and school administrators at large were starting to accept the legitimate role of bilingual education in California's schools, suddenly politicians began to stir up political controversy about its validity. This type of controversy, of course, can wreak havoc on programs, because bilingual education is a complex pedagogical process that is insufficiently understood at best by many who currently influence its implementation or destruction.

Hakuta and Snow (1986) have taken the lead in criticizing the inappropriateness of evaluation research as a method for measuring the benefits of bilingual education. They suggest instead that policymakers and educators should be guided by basic research findings that focus on the linguistic and psychological development of the bilingual learner. However, I suspect that evaluation research—despite its crude "vote-counting" literature reviews—will continue to make waves. Recently, for example, Christine H. Rossell (1989), a political scientist, resurrected the Baker and de Kanter evaluation research controversy. Rossell was a key witness in the case of *Teresa P. et al. v. Berkeley Unified School District et al.* (1989). In this case, the plaintiffs charged that LEP students in the Berkeley School District were not succeeding in school for one of two reasons: either they were not receiving instruction in their native language by bilingually trained teachers, or the pull-out ESL tutoring for LEP students in regular classrooms was inadequate. Rossell argued successfully on behalf of the Berkeley School District that bilingual programs are not any better and are sometimes worse than English-only approaches. Dismissing virtually all basic research, she commented that "applied linguistics is a field of fads" (Crawford, 1989, p. 10). In a different context, Walberg, a panel member of the GAO commission, noted in a letter dissenting from the majority opinion "that the opinions of researchers and practitioners in bilingual education are 'suspect' because their jobs depend on such programs. Getting information from such sources is like asking your barber if you need a haircut" (U.S. General Accounting Office, 1987, p. 71).

These statements suggest to me once again the politicized nature of the debate among educators, social scientists, and policymakers. Although they have had more than twenty years in which to come to terms with bilingual education and the role of the federal government, pro- and anti-bilingual advocates, it appears to me, are not able to listen to each other objectively. In the meantime, the language curriculum, which could use the best research evidence available, suffers.

## Current Politics

The current stance of the Bush administration on bilingual education is somewhat ambiguous. On the negative side, Secretary of Education Lauro Cavazos has not supported funding developmental bilingual education programs, in which the native language is maintained. In January 1989 the secretary announced that the administration did not have any plans to fund such developmental programs (Crawford, 1989, p. 2). The Bush administration seems to prefer to continue the practice of flexible funding already in place under the Reagan administration. With flexible funding, English-only and structured-immersion applications are actively sought by Department of Education officials, rather than limiting the requests for proposals to programs that involve native-language instruction.

Nevertheless, there are also several positive notes and promising recent developments. The strident antibilingual rhetoric of the Bennett years is certainly gone. Throughout his career President Bush has demonstrated sympathetic tendencies toward Hispanic issues, and he has expressed some reservations in public about the English Only movement. Also, Rita Esquivel, the new director of the Office of Bilingual Education and Minority Language Affairs (OBEMLA), seems supportive of bilingual education, and has rekindled a warm relationship with the National Association for Bilingual Education (NABE). For example, she announced at the September 1989 meeting of state directors of Title VII bilingual programs that she had eliminated the Attachment Z letter from Title VII grants, which has put travel restrictions on attendance at the annual NABE conference. Also, she recently announced an OBEMLA competition for developmental bilingual programs in which English-proficient and limited-English-proficient students both receive instruction in another language ("OBEMLA Director," 1990, p. 5). In her speech at the April 1990 NABE conference, Esquivel spoke warmly and enthusiastically about the solid relationship that has been established between OBEMLA and NABE, and she received a standing ovation for her address. As part of her speech, she read a prepared message from Secretary Cavazos in which he stated that the Department of Education is strongly committed "to help children and adults with widely differing linguistic backgrounds learn English without neglecting their own language and cultural history."

However, as the English Only movement demonstrates, there are still many strong opponents of bilingual education, and without the luxury of the long-term view, bilingual educators will still have to be prepared for surprises. Whether or not we will indeed become a kinder and gentler nation for language minorities definitely remains to be seen. But a promising sign of the affirmation of bilingualism occurred in California in 1988, when the California State Board of Education officially adopted a new foreign language framework. With this framework, the value of nurturing bilingualism in *all* students was formally recognized by the California State Department of Education. According to this plan, by the mid-1990s all districts in California will have adopted a communication-based (as opposed to grammar-based) second-language plan for kindergarten through twelfth grade. ESL and the continued development of non-English home languages are integral parts of the framework (California State Department of Education, 1989). Such a move has long been overdue in the United States, and it will be interesting to see to what extent the plan is carried out, as well as to what extent other states follow suit.

At a time when technology is truly connecting everyone on the globe, the United States should take advantage of the rich linguistic resources that children from non-English-speaking backgrounds bring to its schools. Through the development of such linguistic and sociocultural resources, and not solely through foreign-language instruction, there is hope of creating a truly multilingual and multicultural society. Should the federal government and the states consider this idea seriously, it is conceivable that someday there could be legions of Americans able to communicate with persons around the world in their own languages—for humanitarian, spiritual, political, economic, cultural, educational, and commercial reasons.

At a time when I am often disheartened, Crawford's book reaffirms for me the urgent need to work toward a new public policy on language education. Sorting through the historical vagaries, the political furor, and the pedagogical realities, Crawford amply documents the success of high-quality bilingual programs, along with the strong pro-bilingual base of the past twenty years of research. Armed with the type of information and analysis that Crawford provides, our national language policy should be to affirm our many languages as national treasures. In contrast, our current implicit language policy is schizophrenic. On the one hand we encourage and promote the study of foreign languages for English monolinguals, at great cost and with great inefficiency. At the same time we destroy the linguistic gifts that children from non-English-language backgrounds bring to our schools.

Crawford does not specifically address the future of bilingual education, but he does provide the reader with a comprehensive mountain-top view of the past and the present—a valuable perspective for charting future directions. He appropriately concludes his book with a chapter on two-way bilingual education, a model in which speakers of English and speakers of a non-English language are placed together in a classroom to learn each other's languages and to work academically in both languages. Two-way bilingual education is an excellent way for language-majority and language-minority students to learn each other's languages and to establish successful cross-cultural communication skills. In such an egalitarian environment, the happenstance of one's mother tongue does not interfere with the fulfillment of dreams. Unlike Hechinger, who sees a nation dependent exclusively on English-language traditions and values, and unlike Epstein, who sees the United States as a country with a death wish, Crawford provides well-founded hope that—with reason and understanding—our society can move forward toward the twenty-first century to affirm the power, the beauty, and the functional need for language diversity.

It would of course be foolish to be so complacently optimistic about the future of linguistic pluralism in the United States. This vision of multilingual competency will not just self-convert into reality; realizing it will depend on educational and political activism. There are really two possible paths that we as a nation could take. One is the language-affirming path just described. The second alternative is to continue the predominant path of the 1980s by resisting the use of the home language for students with limited English proficiency. The basic research evidence indicates, though, that if we continue on this path, we are asking for trouble. Assimilation and language acquisition do not take place because we coerce people. Nor do they take place when children are deprived of their first language before they have mastered English. Rather, these processes occur when there is a culturally humane and pedagogically sound context that encourages minority students' cognitive and linguistic development. As a nation we need to be concerned primarily with providing a first-rate educational environment for limited-English-proficient persons, one that will enable them to participate meaningfully in a highly competitive, complex, and technological global society. We know that *both* sustained native language support and ESL are necessary in developing the limited-English-proficient student's full intellectual ability. The demography of the United States is changing as the increase in minority populations gallops ahead of the increase in the majority population. It is estimated that by the year 2000 Hispanic Americans, for example, may very well represent the largest minority in the country. In response to such demographic changes, we need sound educational planning and policies on how best to educate *all* children, not just native speakers of standard English. To continue to discount the value of the first language in the education of language-minority students is entirely and frighteningly imprudent.

## Notes

1. Not surprisingly, two years after the approval of the English-only measure in Arizona, Federal District Judge Paul G. Rosenblatt declared that the state's constitutional amendment was a violation of federally protected free speech (Barringer, 1990, p. 1).
2. For examples of other well-designed and successful bilingual programs, the reader may wish to consult Krashen and Biber's *On Course* (1988), in which seven programs and their achievement data are presented. Also of interest is Campos and Keatinge's (1988) description of the Carpintería preschool program. The Carpintería program has had striking success in preparing Spanish-dominant preschoolers for school through intensive development of the home language, using the native-language focus to foster cognitive development.

## References

Alvarez, L., & Kolker, A. (Producers & Directors). (1987). *American tongues: A documentary about the way people talk in the U.S.* [Videotape]. New York: The Center for New American Media.

Baker, K.A., & de Kanter, A.A. (1981). *Effectiveness of bilingual education: A review of the literature.* Washington, DC: Office of Planning, Budget and Evaluation, U.S. Department of Education.

Barringer, F. (1990, February 8). Judge nullifies law mandating use of English. *The New York Times*, p. A1.

Bricker, K. (1989, July 4). Interview on "American Agenda" (ABC News).

California State Department of Education. (1989). *Foreign language framework.* Sacramento, CA: Author.

Campos, S.J., & Keatinge, H.R. (1988). The Carpintería language minority student experience: From theory, to practice, to success. In T. Skutnabb-Kangas & J. Cummins (Eds.), *Minority education: From shame to struggle* (pp. 299–307). Clevedon, Eng.: Multilingual Matters.

Crawford, J. (1989, September 21). *Educating language minority children: Politics, research, and policy.* Paper presented at a conference of the American Speech-Language-Hearing Association: "Partnerships in Education: Toward a Literate America," Washington, DC.

Epstein, N. (1977). *Language, ethnicity, and the schools: Policy alternatives for bilingual-bicultural education.* Washington, DC: Institute for Educational Leadership, George Washington University.

Gold, D. (1988, May 18). Los Angeles plan focuses on native-language instruction. *Education Week*, p. 14.

Hakuta, K., & Snow, C. (1986). The role of research in policy decisions about bilingual education. In U.S. House of Representatives Committee on Education and Labor, *Compendium of papers on the topic of bilingual education* (pp. 28–40). Serial no. 99-R.

Haugen, E. (1969). *The Norwegian language in America: A study in bilingual behavior: Vol. 1. The bilingual community.* Bloomington: Indiana University Press.

Haugen, E. (1972). Language and immigration. In A.S. Dill (Ed.), *The ecology of language: Essays by Einar Haugen* (pp. 1–34). Stanford: Stanford University Press.

Hechinger, F. M. (1978). Political issues in education: Reflections and directions. In W. I. Israel (Ed.), *Political issues in education* (pp. 127–135). Washington, DC: Council of Chief State School Officers.

Krashen, S., & Biber, D. (1988). *On course: Bilingual education's success in California.* Sacramento: California Association for Bilingual Education.

OBEMLA director addresses TESOL members. (1990, March-April). *Forum, 13*(3), p. 5.

Ovando, C.J., & Collier, V.P. (1985). *Bilingual and ESL classrooms: Teaching in multicultural contexts.* New York: McGraw-Hill.

Paulston, C.B. (Ed.). (1988). *International handbook of bilingualism and bilingual education.* New York: Greenwood Press.

Porter, R. P. (1990). *Forked tongue: The politics of bilingual education.* New York: Basic Books.

Rossell, C.H. (1989, April 13). *The effectiveness of educational alternatives for limited English proficient children.* Paper presented at the Public Policy Conference on Bilingual Education, Washington, DC.

*Teresa, P. et al. v. Berkeley Unified School District et al.* (1989, February 14). U.S. District Court Case for the Northern District of California, Case No. C-37-2346DLJ.

Troike, R.C. (1978). *Research evidence for the effectiveness of bilingual education.* Rosslyn, VA: National Clearinghouse for Bilingual Education.

Troike, R.C. (1986). Improving conditions for success in bilingual education programs. In U.S. House of Representatives, Committee on Education and Labor, *Compendium of papers on the topic of bilingual education* (pp. 1–15). Serial No. 99-R.

U.S. General Accounting Office. (1987). *Bilingual education: A new look at the research evidence.* (GAO/PEMD-87-12BR). Washington, DC: U.S. Government Printing Office.

Walberg, H.J. (1989, April 13). *Promoting English literacy.* Paper presented at the Public Policy Conference on Bilingual Education, Washington, DC.

# Book Review

ROSEMARY C. SALOMONE
*St. John's University School of Law*

BILINGUAL EDUCATION: THEORIES AND ISSUES
by Christina Bratt Paulston.
*Rowley, MA: Newbury House, 1980. 90 pp.*

During the past fifteen years the proliferation of research on bilingual education in the United States has usually taken one of two forms: summative evaluations of bilingual projects funded under the Bilingual Education Act of 1968, or scholarly studies of language development and use conducted by linguists, psychologists, and sociologists. Findings from these reports have been inconclusive and, consequently, of minimal use to policymakers. The continuation of bilingual programs in the United States will require the articulation of a more solid theoretical base.

While economic growth during the early days of federal support could financially and politically tolerate, if not overtly promote, experimentation, the fiscal retrenchment of the 1980s has diminished this tolerance, pitting group against group in a struggle for limited resources. The concern for equality underlying congressional and judicial support in the 1960s and 1970s has now yielded to a demand for efficiency. If quality of education is defined only in terms of efficiency, that is, maximum output at minimum input in minimum time, with output measured only by achievement scores on standardized tests, then bilingual education may be doomed to extinction.

Bilingual educators are well aware that the process of developing dual language skills demands more time and resources that monolingual instruction, and that the output or success measures of bilingual education showing the most dramatic results have not been achievement scores. Rather, they have been psychological and social indicators, including improved self-image, decreased school absenteeism and drop-out rates, and increased parental involvement—all factors that ultimately promote social and economic success for the target population, both individually and as a group. It has therefore become critical for proponents of bilingual education to explore ways to reassess their methods of inquiry and to develop a methodology including these additional measures that can help justify bilingual education as educationally sound within the present political context.

*Harvard Educational Review*   Vol. 51   No. 4   November 1981, 605–608

*Bilingual Education: Theories and Issues* provides just such an exploration. Christina Bratt Paulston, a noted educator and applied linguist, analyzes the methodology used in past studies and proposes alternative methodological approaches within a sociological framework. In so doing, not only does she challenge the values underlying our educational system, but she also demonstrates how those values determine the type of research questions asked in measuring the success of an instructional approach. It is at this point that the book makes its most significant and well-developed statement. If educational researchers are to consider values other than efficiency, then their questions must move beyond a focus on achievement and lead to an exploration of alternative theoretical frameworks.

Paulston identifies seven variables by which bilingual programs must be examined:

1. the sequencing of the two languages for the development of literacy skills
2. the time allotted between the development of literacy skills in the two languages
3. the relative emphasis on the mother-tongue culture
4. the medium of instruction for specific subjects
5. teacher ethnicity and competencies
6. quality of programs, as measured by the competence of teachers and the adequacy of curricula and textbooks
7. the language of the surrounding school and community.

This last variable is particularly helpful in distinguishing the Canadian "immersion" programs, in which the children involved are from the dominant culture, from the "submersion" programs in the United States, where the children's native language is devalued in the larger society. Paulston's seven variables provide an operational framework with which researchers may describe programs and readers of such research may interpret findings and avoid inaccurate generalizations across programs. According to Paulston, what is needed is an empirically based feature analysis of models of bilingual education—that is, a study of those programmatic aspects that have proven most effective. What we find here is the worthwhile beginning of such an effort.

Drawing from the work of R.G. Paulston (1976), the author identifies two major paradigms, the equilibrium and the conflict paradigms, within which theoretical approaches to the study of bilingual education can be placed. She examines studies typical of each approach for their underlying assumptions, basic questions, and putative solutions.

According to Paulston, the evolutionary, structural/functionalist, and systems analysis theories fall within the equilibrium paradigm. "Basically, they are all concerned with maintaining society in an equilibrium through the harmonious relationship of the social components, and they emphasize smooth, cumulative change" (p. 16). By contrast, theoretical approaches within the conflict paradigm, such as group-conflict theory, cultural revitalization theory, and an anarchistic utopian approach, all emphasize the inherent instability of social systems and the concomitant conflicts over values, resources, and power.

The structural/functionalist (S/F) viewpoint has formed the dominant theory of social change in the United States in general and of bilingual education in particular. Based on the assumption that lack of social and economic success is due to unequal opportunity, those advancing this theory consider the objective of bilingual education to be the equalization of opportunity; that is, access to education through compensatory training in English. Researchers using this approach assume that increased instructional efficiency—as measured by scores on standardized achievement tests in English—will provide increased educational opportunity for the targeted population. The most common research design treats the bilingual program as the independent variable and achievement scores as the dependent variable. The author justifiably criticizes this model for its failure to produce findings that are generalizable across programs. As an example, she dicusses the problem of comparing findings from the Canadian immersion program studies, in which the target population is the middle-class, economically powerful Anglo majority, with those from Title VII programs in the United States, in which participants typically come from socially stigmatized ethnic minority groups. The S/F failure to acknowledge the intervening variable of social class renders the findings of these two types of studies incomparable. Paulston recognizes the value of psychometric evaluation research in providing descriptive evidence of program options useful in program modification. However, since such research fails to consider social, cultural, and political factors, she has serious reservations about the utility of such findings in determining national educational policy.

Group-conflict theory defines the problem not as one of unequal opportunity for schooling but rather as one of structured inequity in the general society. As distinguished from the S/F emphasis on instructional efficiency as a means to provide for the equalization of opportunity, conflict theory is based upon a more comprehensive concept of equity, specifically on the equitable distribution of goods, wealth, and services. Viewed from this perspective, bilingual education is not only a means toward efficient language teaching but also an attempt to cope with social injustice. Rather than limit the measure of program success to achievement levels, this approach would have the researcher look at changes in such social indicators as dropout rates, employment figures upon leaving school, and incidence of drug addiction, alcoholism, and suicide.

Although the author admits that presently there is no generally accepted framework of research on bilingual education from a group-conflict perspective, she suggests Schermerhorn's (1970) design as the most appropriate for research on ethnic relations. From this theoretical perspective, bilingual education is viewed as the direct result of ethnic groups in conflict and Schermerhorn's central question is, "What are the conditions that foster or prevent the integration of ethnic groups into their surrounding societies?" Language maintenance and language shift are considered as degrees of integration encompassing both assimilation and cultural pluralism as the dependent variable.

To clarify Schermerhorn's theoretical framework and to test its utility for bilingual education, Paulston considers several case studies, including the bilingual programs in St. Lambert, Canada (Lambert & Tucker, 1972), and Culver City, California (Campbell, 1972; Cohen, 1974). Focusing on the power relationships between the relevant groups in each situation, Paulston concludes that despite the similarity of programs and results, the major difference between the St. Lambert and Culver City programs is the trend toward integration in the former and the presence of conflict in the latter. In St. Lambert, the French immersion program was initiated by English-speaking parents from the economically dominant group who wished to gain political power as well. In Culver City, the educational system introduced Spanish as the language of instruction for English-speaking children. Parents in this case neither initiated the program nor perceived any strong sociopolitical benefits for their children. This difference in power relationships is a fundamental factor to be considered in comparing the instructional outcomes of these types of programs.

The most significant contribution of this book is that it forces us to question the values underlying the goals of bilingual education. The author's thesis, however, runs the risk of misinterpretation; she does not negate the value of evaluative research from the S/F perspective, but rather, sees this approach as a most useful "within program" technique for program refinement. What Paulston highlights is the inability of this approach to provide generalizable findings across programs, a limitation that must be underscored. Opponents of bilingual education have exaggerated unfavorable findings from recent studies of various bilingual programs as conclusive evidence of the failure of all bilingual instructional approaches.

For an "across program" comparison, however, the conflict paradigm offers a more valid approach. It offers information about important differences between programs despite deceptive similarities. The questions asked using this approach are quite different from those asked by the S/F theorists. The S/F researchers have sought answers as to "how" bilingual programs differ, mainly in terms of outcomes or achievement scores. As Paulston points out, however, their theory cannot answer such questions without considering the "why." Conflict theory, on the other hand, does seek to know "why" programs differ. Rather than view these two approaches as alternatives to each other, as does the author, they should be considered complementary. Conflict theory picks up where S/F theory leaves off, and together they can provide a more complete analysis of bilingual programs.

As a scholarly work, the book presents a novel approach to the examination of bilingual education and should therefore have considerable appeal to scholars. But it also has the potential to provide useful information to practitioners and policy-makers. For example, Paulston's seven variables beg for further elaboration and integration into the research framework established in the text. The author advocates a feature analysis of bilingual programs. Such an analysis may become critical as limited funds push the proponents of bilingual education to the bargaining table. Before we can bargain away any components of bilingual programs, we must first identify and prioritize those features that have proven to be the most successful.

This book suggests the theoretical foundation for such an analysis, thereby leading us one step closer to a clearer understanding of bilingual education.

## References

Campbell, R. Bilingual education for Mexican-American children in California. In P.T. Turner (Ed.), *Bilingualism in the Southwest*. Tucson: University of Arizona Press, 1972.

Cohen, A. The Culver City Spanish immersion program: The first two years. *Modern Language Journal*, 1974, 58, 95–103.

Lambert, W., & Tucker, R. *Bilingual education of children: The St. Lambert experiment*. Rowley, Mass.: Newbury House, 1972.

Paulston, R.G. *Conflicting theories of social and educational change: A typological review*. Pittsburgh: University Center for International Studies, 1976.

Schermerhorn, R.A. *Comparative ethnic relations: A framework for theory and research*. New York: Random House, 1970.

# Book Review

FRED GENESEE
*McGill University*

MIRROR OF LANGUAGE: THE DEBATE ON BILINGUALISM
by Kenji Hakuta.
*New York: Basic Books, 1986. 286 pp.*

Certain aspects of bilingualism have entered the public debate as a result of the historic and dramatic influx to the United States of non-English-speaking immigrants. Continued demographic changes have raised important issues concerning the nation's official language policy, the ethnolinguistic character of communities that have received particularly large numbers of such immigrants, the delivery of public education to linguistic-minority children, and the English-speaking majority's attitudes toward bilingualism and bilinguals. *Mirror of Language* is about bilingualism in its myriad aspects—educational, societal, cognitive, neuropsychological, developmental, and psycholinguistic. It is also about research on bilingualism: how researchers, past and present, conduct their research; how they interpret their results; and how research can influence, and be influenced by, social factors, including public policy. As suggested by his subtitle, Kenji Hakuta reviews a substantial amount of research on those aspects of bilingualism that have been the focus of attention and controversy for some time in the scientific community and, more recently, in the public arena.

The major issues, or debates, that Hakuta includes are: (1) the relationship between bilingualism and intelligence; (2) what it means to grow up bilingual; (3) cognitive aspects of learning and knowing two languages; (4) second-language learning in children and adults; (5) bilingualism in society; and (6) bilingual education. These issues are controversial at present in the United States because, aside from their relevance to changing demographic patterns, many English-speaking group members tend to view monolingualism as normal and bilingualism, therefore, as extraordinary, and indeed, possibly handicapping. *Mirror of Language* seeks to inform the public about bilingualism by using the knowledge base established by scientists to correct unfounded stereotypical impressions, and to encourage informed debate about bilingualism in the public arena. At the same time, the author reminds re-

*Harvard Educational Review* Vol. 57 No. 3 August 1987, 341–344

searchers of the multifaceted nature of bilingualism, and of the need to stimulate more interdisciplinary research.

Hakuta's delineation of each issue is a skillful integration of empiricism, social history, and scientific theory, drawn from different disciplines. The result is an in-depth picture of how social science and social scientists work. Early in the book, in the chapter "Bilingualism and Intelligence," Hakuta observes that social scientists and their work are products of their own times and are part of the fabric of social history. As history evolves, so too do the philosophies and methodologies of social scientists. He notes that in the United States, early research on the relationship between bilingualism and intelligence was shaped in part by the nature-versus-nurture debate, and by a concomitant interest in group differences in intellectual ability. Social scientists of the 1920s and 1930s favored the hereditarian perspective, which claimed that some sociocultural and racial groups were genetically inferior to others. Concerned with the rapid influx of immigrants from eastern and southern Europe after the first World War and armed with recently developed IQ tests, American scientists embarked upon a mammoth project to measure the intelligence of hundreds of immigrants as they arrived at Ellis Island. Not surprisingly, many scored very low, due both to invalid test instruments and absurd testing conditions. The poor test performance of these new Americans, who happened to be or were about to become bilingual, came to be associated with bilingualism in general. In sharp contrast, research on bilingualism and intelligence carried out in the 1960s at McGill University in Montreal was motivated by a growing interest in individual bilingualism within the province of Quebec and across Canada. Using different methodological techniques, research by Elizabeth Peal and Wallace Lambert refuted the earlier pessimistic view of bilingualism and instead showed bilinguals to be intellectually normal and in some ways superior to monolinguals.[1]

Hakuta, in the next chapter, discusses how research on bilingualism has been inspired and shaped in important ways by different scientific disciplines, especially psychology and linguistics. To illustrate this point, he describes in some detail the work of two early researchers on childhood bilingualism: Werner Leopold and Madorah Smith. Leopold, a linguist, observed and documented in meticulous detail his daughter's acquisition of German and English (pp. 45–58). In contrast, Smith, a psychologist, emphasized the measurement and evaluation of individual differences among a group of 1,000 Hawaiian children (pp. 59–65). Each of their approaches resulted in dramatically different pictures of early bilingualism in children. While Leopold's work has survived to become a classic of considerable contemporary merit and interest, Smith's work, which counted as "errors" those occasions when bilingual children chose to mix vocabulary from two languages, now appears dated and flawed. Hakuta goes beyond Leopold's personal legacy to show how changing philosophies in psychology and linguistics have altered the way scientists approach and investigate bilingualism in general. The reader will find Hakuta's personal insights and carefully integrated documentation in this and other chapters both informative and entertaining.

Discussion of scientific research belongs in the public forum precisely because that is where research findings and scientific knowledge can be applied to issues of general concern. Hakuta's contribution to the literature on bilingualism is commendable because he seeks to make research findings on various aspects of bilingualism part of the public debate and thereby to inform public opinion. This approach makes for interesting reading because Hakuta successfully imbues the sometimes esoteric and picayune findings of research with the excitement and relevance of public debate. His writing is erudite and engaging, yet not facile. The reader is eager to discover the next contentious issue to see what it is all about, in much the same way a well-written novel compels the reader to push ahead with the story.

A review of research—particularly that which is the focus of public debate—is especially useful when conducted by a researcher, because it brings to light relevant research results and their interpretations in ways acceptable to those who have generated them. This, in turn, can serve to expose the misrepresentations of non-scientists or of politicians who use research for their own ends. A case in point is the recent report by the United States General Accounting Office (GAO) that calls into question the Department of Education's use of research findings in ways that are compatible with federal policy on bilingual education but are inconsistent with the interpretations of expert researchers in the field.[2] Hakuta's analysis of the research on bilingual education and related issues supports the GAO's concerns with the ways in which government officials have used research results.

Reviewing research for public consumption in a book that is also intended for researchers is a challenging task. The author risks oversimplifying theoretical issues and empirical findings to accord with what are often simplistic public conceptualizations of complex issues. Moreover, issues of interest and concern for the researcher may be ignored because their importance may not be fully appreciated by the public and vice versa. Thus, the challenge in writing such a book is to present the scientific evidence within the parameters of the public debate while acknowledging the complexities that characterize the researcher's purposes and findings.

For the most part, Hakuta achieves this balance. Two of his chapters, for example, contain comprehensive and clear summaries of second-language acquisition in children and adults. Hakuta dispassionately and convincingly dispels the fears of many parents, educators, and some researchers (namely Madorah Smith) that second-language learning in childhood is arduous, handicapping, and fraught with problems. In the chapter on bilingual education, Hakuta carefully applies research findings to a number of issues in the current debate. He refutes claims that students' use of their native language detracts from their time to learn English; that since young children learn second languages more quickly than older learners do, minority-language students should be taught in English first; and that bilingual education is ineffective.

In this reader's opinion, however, there are instances where important complexities in the theoretical issues and empirical results have been lost. For example, in the chapter, "The Bilingual Mind," three rather complex and different theoretical issues are reduced to one. Studies on the neuropsychological aspects of bilingualism and second-language learning, information-processing in two languages, and learning through two languages are summarized in terms of the rather simplistic and now archaic distinction between independent versus interdependent representation of the bilingual speaker's two language systems. Research on neuropsychological aspects of bilingualism has sought, among other things, to examine the possibility that representation and processing of language, and possibly the neurological substrate for language learning in bilinguals, are influenced by the nature of the languages involved, the manner in which the languages are learned, and the stage of acquisition. This critical multidimensionality is lost in Hakuta's rendering.

Moreover, some issues have been left out altogether. Notwithstanding the cogent use of research findings to refute certain charges against bilingual education, Hakuta omits discussion of such topics as the nature of language proficiency and its relationship to academic achievement; the acquisition of literacy skills by children from backgrounds that provide limited experiences with literacy; and the role of sociocultural factors in the schooling of linguistic-minority children. These are issues of some importance in planning effective educational programs for linguistic-minority children and should, therefore, be examined more thoroughly in a book concerned with public policy.

In sum, *Mirror of Language* serves admirably to inform the public of diverse research findings pertinent to the ongoing public debate on bilingual education and bilingualism in the United States. As such, it is an effective counterpoint to the narrowness of much of the public discussion on these issues. The researcher-reader will be impressed and entertained by Hakuta's skillful integration of interdisciplinary research on bilingualism with social history. Researchers will undoubtedly find some gaps in Hakuta's coverage, but this is probably unavoidable in a book that seeks to reach a wide range of readers. In the final analysis, Hakuta draws a number of conclusions from both contemporary and past research that dispel a view of bilingualism and second-language learning as inherently problematic for the individual and society.

## Notes

1. Peal and Lambert, "The Relation of Bilingualism to Intelligence," *Psychological Monographs*, 76, No. 27 (1962), 1–23, Whole No. 546.
2. U.S. General Accounting Office, *Bilingual Education: A New Look at the Research Evidence* (Washington, DC: U.S. General Accounting Office).

# Book Review

JOHN BAUGH
*Stanford University*

TWICE AS LESS: BLACK ENGLISH AND THE PERFORMANCE OF
BLACK STUDENTS IN MATHEMATICS AND SCIENCE
by Eleanor Wilson Orr.
*New York: W.W. Norton & Company, 1987. 240 pp.*

In this book, Eleanor Wilson Orr concludes that Black English Vernacular (BEV) represents a barrier to success in science and mathematics. The data that she presents in support of this hypothesis were gathered over a nine-year period at the Hawthorne School in Washington, DC, an experimental high school that Orr founded with her husband, Douglas, in 1956. In 1972 Hawthorne opened its doors to approximately 320 inner-city students from the Washington, DC, public schools, tuition free. The selection process was random. Each public high school in the district would choose three students by lot, bringing forty-one students per year to Hawthorne. Ninety-eight percent of these students were Black, and, during the first two years of the cooperative program, 87 percent failed their mathematics and science courses.

*Twice as Less* attempts to account for this lack of success. Orr is quick to point out that these students were bright, hard working, and attended classes regularly. The traditional justifications for low achievement therefore did not apply in this instance. Although Orr and her staff had faced other educational problems with their middle- to upper-class students in the past, the new inner-city students presented novel challenges that these private school educators had not previously encountered. At the end of the second year of the cooperative program, the Hawthorne faculty concluded that excessive student failure centered on language; particularly "the usage by these students of such function words as prepositions, conjunctions, and relative pronouns and their usage in standard English" (p. 21). In cognitive terms Orr argues "that language may shape the way one perceives quantitative relations— specifically, that the way a BEV speaker may understand certain standard English expressions of quantitative relations can affect his or her understanding of those relations. That language may affect the way one *thinks* in mathematics and science is significant" (p. 11, my emphasis).

*Harvard Educational Review* Vol. 58 No. 3 August 1988, 395–403

To what extent, then, does *Twice as Less* confirm this hypothesized connection between the language, thought, and education of Black youth in science and mathematics? The book falls woefully short of this ambitious goal. Although Orr is to be commended for correctly pointing to sources of linguistic confusion that many BEV students confront in math and science, her conclusions regarding linguistic differences between BEV and standard English, as well as the cognitive assertions that grow out of her linguistic impressions, tend to be uninformed and somewhat naive.

Despite these limitations, this book has many virtues, including the obvious dedication Orr and her colleagues felt toward these students. Her unwillingness to accept their failure is laudable, as is her careful evaluation of students' work. In order to do justice to this book it is first necessary to survey the organization of the text, which, in turn, provides insight into some of the fundamental flaws in Orr's research.

At the outset she anticipates the potential controversy of this work. "Although it is clearly not my purpose to involve myself in the debate over the relationship between language and thought, I am very aware that what I document suggests that language may indeed play a part in shaping conceptual thinking" (p. 11). *Twice as Less* strives to confirm this hypothesis.

The introduction presents background information about the founding of Orr's school, the cooperative arrangement with the DC public schools, and a detailed discussion of the nature of the problem. Orr states that "students are required to translate each algebraic statement into a verbal statement; to identify what each expression in the algebraic statement represents; to state whether the given information requires the statement to be true, false, or indeterminate; and to write an explanation of their reasoning" (p. 38). This procedure is significant because it requires a high degree of linguistic sophistication and works best when students already have a solid educational foundation. Since many of the Black students who came to Hawthorne had weak literacy skills, Orr's requirement to provide written explanations of technical mathematical concepts tended to accentuate their existing educational deficiencies.

Ensuing chapters focus on specific types of mathematical problems, including problems of distance, motion, subtraction, and division. Each chapter contains detailed examples of students' work, their errors, and some preliminary discussion of the linguistic foundation for the misunderstandings that may have led students to wrong conclusions. Orr has provided sufficient detail to follow the essential steps associated with solving various problems and algorithms. Her presentation allows the reader to work out each problem and also to understand fully the linguistic sources of various misunderstandings. At times this exercise becomes somewhat tedious, because the essential linguistic points have already been made at the outset of each technical chapter. Nevertheless, readers should resist the temptation merely to accept these observations without careful, time-consuming evaluation, for they represent the center of Orr's thesis.

Chapter 6 introduces the linguistic evaluation of prepositions in BEV, including a historical survey and discussion of contemporary usage in BEV. With this linguistic evidence in hand, Orr attempts to demonstrate how various prepositions—such as *at, to, in, on, by, between*—function in standard English and in specific mathematical and scientific problems, with primary emphasis on evaluations of location and direction. Drawing heavily upon the Creole origin hypothesis (see Stewart, 1967, and Dillard, 1972), which emphasizes the African foundations of Black English, Orr correctly observes that "there can be little doubt that further investigation will show that the use of prepositions in BEV is not the same as in standard English" (p. 132). Moreover, this historical foundation leads her to posit "that the uses of prepositions that appear in [BEV students'] work do not appear in the work of White students who sit in the same classrooms and answer the same questions" (p. 132).

The next two chapters consider some essential linguistic facts in BEV, including introductions to composite sentences and comparisons. Both chapters consider vital syntactic and morphological issues, and, in the absence of formal linguistic analysis, would appear to be quite plausible to readers who are unaware of the grammatical intricacies of BEV. For example, Orr believes that "the grammar of standard English has been shaped by what is true mathematically" (p. 158). This is a dangerous assumption, to say nothing of the fact that Orr's investigation does not confirm this opinion. Again, there is no doubt that the inner-city students were confused by their assignments, but these errors do not imply that the linguistic evolution of standard English has been influenced by mathematical principles; this assertion is—quite frankly—wrong, and further, is inconsistent with historical linguistic facts for English or any other language.

Chapter 9 examines quantitative meanings, such as the derivation of the book's title, "Twice as Less." Problems pertaining to travel, speed, distance, age, and so on, are evaluated primarily on the basis of linguistic details that distinguish standard from nonstandard expressions. Orr examines the corresponding impact on mathematical failure, although it seems that her students' problems stem from linguistic as well as nonlinguistic sources. Some students, for example, do not understand the assignments—beyond the realm of mere linguistic difference or interpretation. Orr has chosen to concentrate on a narrow linguistic component, thereby veiling the overall complexity of student failure.

The final chapter summarizes major aspects of the hypothesis with some additional linguistic speculation: " . . . one should not assume that a student means by his or her nonstandard expression what is assumed a speaker of standard English means by the standard equivalent of the expression" (p. 73). Here, as elsewhere in the text, readers are asked to accept the notion that students' errors are the result of nonstandard mathematical perceptions, reflected by differences in language; no consideration is given to the possibility that their errors result from other sources. Orr therefore assumes that "if one's language restricts one to comparing quantities only by addition and subtraction, this perception could be automatic" (p. 184). Orr consequently concludes that BEV is a restricted code (see Bernstein, 1972), that prohibits speakers from conceiving of multiplication or division. This belief is reiterated in the final chapter. "To me, it is clear that the perceptions these students have of certain quantitative comparisons are shaped by the language they use. They come to school without an 'as . . . as' structure in the language they speak" (p. 185). This is a gross oversimplification of the actual state of linguistic affairs, and fails to consider the ramifications of alternative causes of confusion on the part of these students.

Educators will be most interested in suggested solutions to the problem Orr presents, and this assistance is reserved for a brief afterword. The final fifteen pages of the book provide a general discussion of the pressures on teachers to help high school students perform well on standardized tests, a practice she decries: ". . . nothing except an image is going to be changed by making the work easier so that fewer students fail. Furthermore, making the work easier is insulting; students know when they are being taught down to" (p. 205).

The first solution she offers advocates work with nonstandard irregular number systems. Such systems make "dependence on any numerical patterns impossible, one has no choice but to think on one's own, and to remain continuously conscious of what the numerical symbols represent" (p. 206). The second suggestion involves exercises that "develop the habit of visualizing when working with symbols" (p. 208). In this instance students draw pictures to aid them in solving problems, which typically deal with fractions; visual display allows the students to see the numerical relations. Such a procedure may indeed prove helpful to all students attempting to analyze fractions, not just those who speak BEV, because pictures may provide a clear basis upon which to illustrate partitive relationships; and these evaluative pictures may be worth thousands of words, regardless of the student's native language.

On balance, *Twice as Less* devotes nearly all of its attention to mathematics; very few examples from science are presented—which may well reflect another pedagogical policy. At Hawthorne "these students [did] not take any science until they had successfully completed algebra and geometry" (p. 211). This policy is then reflected in the scientific discussion, which is negligible. Logic offers a simple explanation; since the invited students failed their mathematics courses in such high numbers, readers are forced to conclude that because few of these students were able to pass the math requirements, even fewer took science courses. The scientific insights derived from Orr's thesis are therefore marginal to her hypothesis.

Anecdotal evidence from a single student, Mary, is presented in support of Orr's suggestions. It is most regrettable that more statistical evidence is not provided, because the collective success of typical Black students, as opposed to the proficiency of a single exceptional student, would constitute a more reliable endorsement of Orr's philosophy. In the absence of more data on the success or failure of most students in the cooperative program, one must accept Orr's views on faith rather than on rigorous scholarly grounds.

*Twice as Less* is written with two primary audiences in mind: educators and general readers. The limitations of the text could easily be missed by uninformed readers who lack thorough knowledge of BEV or, like Orr, believe that standard English has evolved under the influence of mathematical principles.

At this point I would like to consider other problems in Orr's book, including:

a. The atypical circumstances of the Hawthorne School,
b. The lack of familiarity among Hawthorne faculty with the language and educational difficulties of inner-city Black students,
c. Pedagogical contradictions, which forced students to tackle complex problems without adequate preparation,
d. Racial bias in Orr's hypothesis,
e. An impoverished research design,
f. Orr's lack of understanding of the complexity of BEV, including its historical foundations, and a misrepresentation of the language that students brought to school, as well as some other fundamental linguistic issues regarding basic principles of linguistic change,
g. The logical ramifications of this hypothesis in terms of multilingual comparisons,
h. Insensitivity to relevant cultural frames of reference,
i. The rejection of Orr's hypothesis by her primary linguistic consultant.

I will survey the problems individually, and then consider their collective consequences for the educational prospects of the Black student who is not tenacious enough to overcome misguided pedagogy.

## The atypical circumstances of the Hawthorne School

This observation is fairly straightforward. Hawthorne was an elite institution that, between 1956 and 1972, catered exclusively to the children of wealthy parents. Most privileged children with comparable backgrounds come from homes with highly educated parents who take strong personal interest in the educational welfare of their children. Indeed, it is for this very reason that private institutions survive; they represent a bastion of elite opportunity. Moreover, many students who attend private high schools have also attended private elementary schools with comparable privileges.

The cooperative agreement, then, placed poor inner-city Black students in a competitive relationship with wealthy White students. All students were required to produce the same work, although Orr's findings emphatically demonstrate that the inner-city students entered this competition on an unequal footing. To assume, then, that the atypical Hawthorne experience can be transferred to the public schools is questionable at best.

## The lack of familiarity with the language and educational difficulties of inner-city Black students

Hawthorne was not a typical elite private school, because it was receptive to the prospect of allowing public school children to attend classes. However, when this invitation was extended by the Board of Education of the DC schools, it would seem that neither party had fully considered the educational and social ramifications of such a cooperative arrangement.

Despite their considerable teaching experience, Orr notes, Hawthorne faculty were unsuccessful: ". . . for the first time, nothing we tried appeared to work, and we did not know why" (p. 19). Hawthorne's dedicated faculty were accustomed to success, and when they were confronted with high fates of failure they attempted to meet the challenge, albeit within the confines of their school.

With the advantage of hindsight it is clear that the Hawthorne faculty would have benefited greatly by some preparatory instruction and information regarding the educational difficulties of inner-city Black youth. As the program was organized, the Hawthorne faculty could not anticipate that they would be unprepared and ill equipped to serve the students from the cooperative program.

As with the Black English trial in Ann Arbor, Michigan (see Labov, 1982), the educational consequences of having an uninformed faculty were not exposed until after the students arrived at the school. These episodes have taught us how important it is to prepare and inform educators about Black English and the education of Black youth prior to the arrival of such students. Failing to do so merely perpetuates the high rates of failure that were experienced at Hawthorne and in Ann Arbor.

*Pedagogical contradictions*

"We were determined to trap them into situations where they would have no choice but to think" (p. 36). "The students were required to translate each algebraic statement into a verbal statement" (p. 38). "These difficulties are compounded by the lack of familiarity many of these students have with a variety of time prepositions. . . . they *think* in terms of the relations among distance, time, and speed indicated by one time preposition when the situation calls for another" (p. 98, my emphasis). Orr provides several examples of the alleged "lack of familiarity," but she fails to make the more accurate observation that students are unfamiliar with the "technical use" of various lexical items; some they know, others differ with semantic interpretation, and others are novel or unknown. Orr does not make such distinctions, and they are important if the student is to fully understand technical jargon.

Additional quotations would accentuate the circularity and contradictory nature of Orr's educational practices. By demanding that BEV students write their impressions of different problems, Orr has taxed their linguistic knowledge and literacy skills in order to illustrate their deficiencies. First, it is regrettable that students were "trapped" rather than "helped." Be that as it may, there is an inherent contradiction between her working hypothesis that BEV prevented students from thinking in terms of essential mathematical principles, and her insistence that these BEV speakers translate algebraic statements into verbal expressions.

If, for example, Orr assumes that BEV restricts conceptualization, then why would she force students to use BEV to translate mathematical or scientific algorithms? Such a practice is not only contradictory, but insures the confirmation of a self-fulfilling prophecy, since students have not yet learned the technical vocabulary of mathematics and science. As with every technical discipline, mathematics has specialized jargon that is simply not synonymous with standard English usage. If students are not provided with precise definitions of relevant concepts and the corresponding linguistic terms of reference, their failure is almost certain, regardless of linguistic background. The atypical circumstances at Hawthorne exacerbated the problem, as reflected by the excessive rates of failure among students in the cooperative program.

Public school educators who have been successful with inner-city students in mathematics and science have stressed the role of vocabulary enrichment (Beal, 1987). Surely students cannot be expected to invent the appropriate terminology on their own; yet, if educators do not fully appreciate BEV themselves, the definitions they give students may be even more confusing. This was the situation that Black students faced at Hawthorne: They were not adequately prepared to complete the same assignments as their privileged White peers, and yet this is what was demanded of them.

### Racial bias

The fact that a dedicated professional educator such as Orr, with the best interests of Black students at heart, is unaware of the racist implications in this study is alarming. As indicated, Hawthorne traditionally served a wealthy White clientele. When poor Black students arrived through the cooperative program, every effort was made to provide them with the same education as that of the wealthier White students. But the vast majority of the inner-city students failed. By concentrating exclusively on BEV, and ignoring many of the sociological, personal, economic, and other educational dimensions of the problem, Orr myopically concludes that Black language is the primary source of these students' difficulties.

If this were truly the case, a comparable study among poor White students would not yield similar rates of failure. Had Hawthorne entered into a cooperative arrangement with poor schools in Appalachia, for example, bringing 320 White students to her elite institution, Orr's hypothesis would lead us to assume that they would be more likely to succeed than the Black students because they do not speak BEV. However, even a casual survey of national statistics shows a strong correlation between social status and educational success, regardless of race (Conant, 1961; Labov, 1972; Williams, 1970). This crucial observation is not mentioned anywhere in *Twice as Less*. As a result, the racist implications of Orr's hypothesis are inescapable and inexcusable.

### Linguistic misunderstandings and inaccuracies

"That the students' nonstandard uses of the prepositions I have identified may be rooted in the grammar of Black English vernacular, or that they may be the product of the students' using two dialects that have lexicons that overlap, grammars that are in part distinct, and histories that are distinct, is of the utmost importance to educators" (p. 121). "They come to school without an *as . . . as* structure in the language they speak" (p. 185, emphasis in original).

The preceding statements are indicative of some false linguistic impressions that Orr has about BEV, and these fallacies are transferred to her hypothesis without qualification. In short, although Orr did conduct a survey of dated literature for BEV in support of her research, significant aspects of her historical conclusions and contemporary uses of BEV are emphatically wrong. For example, while the history of BEV is unique in America, it is by no means "distinct." Her historical survey of the subject is based exclusively on the Creole foundations of the dialect. The relevant sources of influence from standard English are simply not mentioned (see Traugott, 1972). This is a glaring oversimplification, and is detrimental to Orr's analysis and conclusions. The actual history of BEV is quite complex, and, while the Creole foundations of BEV are clear, they are by no means the exclusive source of influence.

This false historical impression leads Orr to other misconceptions regarding prepositions and comparatives in BEV and standard English, among other vital linguistic differences. As indicated above, Orr claims that in comparison to standard English, BEV uses single prepositions or the wrong preposition. Again, this over-simplifies the actual linguistic state of affairs. Consider the following example re-garding location, in which we shall add a preposition to the following sentence in order to indicate close proximity to the river's edge: "They were down _____the river." In standard English the preposition *by* is used for this purpose, but in BEV speakers can use several prepositions—not just one—to convey the same meaning. Thus, *by, at, to,* and occasionally, *on,* can be used to convey the same meaning. For readers who are unfamiliar with the actual linguistic facts, Orr's hypothesis seems highly plausible, and therein lies the danger.

Linguistic scholars have always known that the nonstandard languages of the world tend to exhibit greater variability than do their standard counterparts (Bloomfield, 1933). Many well-educated individuals, like Orr, do not fully comprehend the lin-guistic implications of this fact. For example, vulgar Latin exhibited more linguistic variability than did classical Latin. The historical evidence also shows that vulgar Latin, the language of the masses, was most responsible for the evolutionary changes in Latin, despite the fact that the educated elite attempted to preserve the classical form.

Similar principles can be found today, where standard dialects of well-educated individuals often absorb some aspects of nonstandard usage. Once these nonstandard features become integrated into the colloquial standard, they lose any prior stigma. As a result of this ongoing process, linguistic evolution is influenced by an intricate array of factors. Orr's thesis draws the following conclusion: standard English has evolved under the influence of the logical foundations of mathematics; there is, however, no evidence to support this misconception. Standard English is a prescrip-tive dialect; as such it tends to be more conservative—not more accurate—than corresponding nonstandard dialects.

Indeed, some nonstandard dialects, such as Black English, have unique gram-matical qualities that could provide useful linguistic distinctions for mathematics and science that cannot be conveyed through standard English. Within the auxiliary system, for example, BEV can distinguish between habitual events and momentary events depending on alternative lexical forms of the copula (See Baugh, 1983; Fasold, 1969; Labov et al., 1968). Standard English does not provide for this kind of semantic distinction in present-tense forms of the auxiliary. For example, "the train is traveling at 60 miles per hour" could be expressed differently in BEV: "the train ('s) traveling at 60 miles per hour" and "the train be traveling at 60 miles per hour" have differing meanings in BEV. The latter sentence indicates that the train would travel at a consistent speed, while the former example often refers to non-habitual, or momentary, states; a 60-mile-an-hour train which makes frequent stops would not (usually) be described using the "be" form of the nonstandard auxiliary verb. Thus, a speaker of Black English could use these alternative representations of the copula to distinguish between habitual states, such as fixed locations or constant motions, and transitional states, such as iterative motion or momentary events (see Baugh, 1983; Fasold, 1969; Labov et al., 1968).

I am not advocating that we attempt to adopt BEV in our mathematics classes, but it is obvious that Orr is simply unaware that aspects of Black English could be superior to standard English in the expression of specific mathematical relationships. This is clearly the case regarding Orr's belief that students do not bring the *as . . . as* construction with them to their classes; this assumption is wrong.

Based on my own research among high school students in Los Angeles in a community setting, it is quite clear that they do use such forms: "He big as Leroi," "Lola don't like Ricky as much as she like Leon." This list could go on. The essential point is that BEV speakers do have the *as . . . as* construction within their grammar. Orr has misunderstood the use of experimental repetition tasks in Labov et al. (1968); Labov and his colleagues were attempting to examine complex sentences that introduced several linguistic differences between BEV and standard English, including copula variability, negative concord, and comparatives. Labov observes specifically that "the major topic which is left untouched is the comparative. We will not attempt to survey, even briefly, the problems involved here, except to state that they are of such depth and complexity as to outweigh any other topic which we have treated" (p. 309). Speakers of standard English can easily appreciate the problem. In ordinary discourse few of us refer to comparisons as being "greater than" or "less than" something else. Imagine a parent saying, "My daughter is greater than my son, who is less than his cousin" versus "My daughter is older (bigger) than my son, who is younger (smaller) than his cousin." The technical mathematical uses of "greater than" and "less than" would be nothing less than an ambiguous insult if used in most colloquial conversation. When nonstandard speech patterns, such as those used in BEV, are added to the picture, the issues regarding the vast complexity of "comparatives" in standard English, BEV, and mathematical jargon become much clearer. Highly trained linguists have not yet solved these problems, and Orr's efforts oversimplify matters. She tends to treat her linguistic speculations as if they were empirical facts.

### An impoverished research design

The best scholarship, in all fields, reflects research that attempts to disprove—not confirm—the working hypothesis. Orr does not do this; rather, she seeks to confirm her hypothesis at every turn, ignoring relevant evidence beyond language, and restricting her study to the school that she owned.

This is a questionable research practice, and one that would not be tolerated by experienced scholars. Had Orr engaged in proactive research, including additional evidence from other Black students in the DC public schools, or data from poor White students in circumstances that would be comparable to the cooperative arrangement, then her conclusions would be more reliable. As the data now stand, other researchers interested in follow-up studies would have difficulty in thoroughly testing, replicating, or re-evaluating her results.

Shirley Brice Heath (1983) studied the language of poor Blacks in the Piedmont region of the Carolinas, and her research represents a superior model for this type of linguistic inquiry among disadvantaged American minorities. She did not merely look at the language usage in the schools, but went into the community, examining linguistic behavior as well as the ethnographic context that gave rise to language usage. Orr's research masquerades as rigorous scholarship, when, in reality, it is highly anecdotal and uncharacteristic of the educational circumstances that confront the vast majority of inner-city Black students.

## Logical ramifications for multilingual comparisons

"I believe that in the case of these three modes of expressing comparisons [that is, multiplicative, additive, and indefinite], the grammar of standard English has been shaped by what is true mathematically" (p. 159). Can we extend this assumption to the linguistically diverse standard languages of the world? Have standard German, Japanese, Russian, or Arabic similarly been shaped by mathematical truths? Such a suggestion is inconsistent with historical linguistic facts. Moreover, if we take Orr's hypothesis to its logical multilingual extremes, we would certainly expect to find statistical evidence to confirm that some of the world's languages are far better suited to mathematics and science than others. Orr has been influenced by research that advocates this type of linguistic determinism—that is, the belief that language controls thought—but these findings are both inconclusive and highly controversial (Bloom, 1981). In order to accept her hypothesis, one must believe, as Orr does, that BEV and standard English result in different modes of conceptual thinking. However, there are attractive alternatives to her opinion that consider historical and cultural data as well; moreover, these extralinguistic facts tend to complement linguistic observations that readily account for discrepancies in academic performance across class lines.

## Insensitivity to relevant cultural frames of reference

Many of the mathematical problems that are cited in *Twice as Less* suggest that students in the cooperative program were unfamiliar with essential extralinguistic facts. Some of the examples regarding evaluations of distances and locations reflect the fact that students from the cooperative program were simply unaware of geographical locations, whereas many of their wealthier White peers often knew exactly where different cities were located with respect to one another.

In these instances the personal lack of familiarity with the geographic dimensions of certain problems tended to reinforce the difficulties that Black students faced. Successful literacy programs with inner-city Black students have demonstrated that modification of educational material, by introducing culturally relevant and familiar concepts, results in greater educational achievement (Smitherman, 1981). Many of the students from DC, for example, would know where "Columbia Avenue" is located in relation to various national landmarks. If Orr and her colleagues had modified some of the assignments to capitalize on such familiar knowledge, their Black students would have had the benefit of additional personal familiarity with local points of reference. This type of information was often unavailable when problems referred to locations in Ohio, New York, or other areas unfamiliar to students in the cooperative program.

When problems with familiar reference points are introduced, the mathematical principles are not shrouded by inconsequential sources of confusion. Rather than adopt such a strategy, Orr calls for making the assignment "harder, so that it captures the students' minds—so that instead of arriving at answers easily, they have to puzzle through the possibilities" (p. 205). The introduction of familiar points of reference is not offered as a means of making the assignments "easier"; rather, such modification increases the likelihood that students will master the essential mathematical principles without unnecessary obfuscation.

*The rejection of Orr's hypothesis by the primary
linguistic consultant*

Dr. Walt Wolfram of the Center for Applied Linguistics in Washington, DC, was the primary linguistic consultant to Orr's project. He was most responsible for pointing out some of the linguistic distinctions that have been examined in *Twice as Less*. Wolfram's disassociation from Orr's research is perhaps the most damaging criticism of her study.

> Unfortunately, one comes away from Orr's work with the impression that her students could learn math if only the dialect difference could be taken care of. This is a gross simplification of a very complex problem. . . . At this stage, we thus have some preliminary hypotheses based on some anecdotal correlations; this, however, is very different from carefully controlled comparison and experimentation which establishes dialect differences as a causation of mathematical and scientific misinterpretation. . . . Math and science failure is a complex and serious problem, and the reduction of its cause to an interesting speculation about dialect differences serves neither the students who need help nor the educational system which has an obligation to serve the full range of student needs with respect to math and science. (Wolfram, 1987, pp. 1–2).

When viewed collectively, the limitations of *Twice as Less* far exceed its virtues. And, despite claims to the contrary, Orr's book merely serves to perpetuate racist myths about the relationship between language and thought. That she is unaware of the racist implications of her research is most disturbing. Although she did anticipate the potential controversy associated with this work, she said, "I can only hope that the problematic, sometimes volatile, issues that surround what I have to say in this book will not get in the way of what might otherwise be accomplished" (p. 12).

As with other educational theories that place the blame for low Black academic achievement exclusively at the feet of linguistic behavior (Farrell, 1983), *Twice as Less* emphasizes analysis of failure at the expense of examinations of success. The well-worn practice of analyzing such failures has contributed little to the long-term interests of Black students. They would be better served if researchers devoted as much attention to evaluations of programs in which Black students have experienced academic success.

## References

Baugh, J. (1983). *Black street speech: Its history, structure, and survival.* Austin: University of Texas Press.
Beal, B.B. (1987). *A study to identify items on the Iowa Test of Basic Skills which are associated with racial or ethnic group membership; to determine possible relationships between instructional needs and these items; and to develop recommendation strategies.* Denver: Denver Public Schools Department of Planning, Research, and Development.
Bernstein, B. (1972). Social class, language and socialization. In P. P. Giglioli (Ed.), *Language and social context* (pp. 157–178), London: Penguin Books.
Bloom, A. (1981). *The linguistic shaping of thought: A study in the impact of language on thinking in China and the West.* Hillsdale, NJ: Lawrence Erlbaum.
Bloomfield, L. (1933). *Language.* New York: Holt, Rinehart & Winston.
Conant, J.B. (1961). *Slums and suburbs.* New York: Signet Books.
Dillard, J.L. (1972). *Black English.* New York: Random House.
Farrell, T. (1983). IQ and standard English. *College Composition and Communication, 34,* 470–484.
Fasold, R.W. (1969). Tense and the form *be* in Black English. *Language, 45,* 763–776.
Heath, S.B. (1983). *Ways with words: Language, life, and work in communities and classrooms.* Cambridge: Cambridge University Press.
Labov, W. (1972). *Language in the inner city: Studies in the Black English Vernacular.* Philadelphia: University of Pennsylvania Press.
Labov, W. (1982). Objectivity and commitment in linguistic science. *Language in Society, 11,* 165–201.
Labov, W., et al. (1968). *A study of the non-standard English of Negro and Puerto Rican speakers in New York City.* Washington, DC: USOE Final Report, Research Project 3, p. 288.
Smitherman, G. (Ed.). (1981). *Black English and the education of Black children and youth: Proceedings of the National Invitational Symposium on the King Decision.* Detroit: Wayne State University, Department of Afro-American Studies.
Stewart, W. (1967). Sociolinguistic factors in the history of American Negro dialects. *Florida FL Reporter, 5*(11), pp. 22, 24, 26.
Traugott, E.C. (1972). *A history of English syntax.* New York: Holt, Rinehart & Winston.
Williams, F. (Ed.). (1970). *Language and poverty: Perspectives on a theme.* Chicago: Markham.
Wolfram, W. (1987). Black English and mathematics? The latest flap. *National Black Association for Speech, Language and Hearing Newsletter, 1*(3), 1–2.

# Notes on Books

MASAHIKO MINAMI

*The following books have been selected for review because of their interest to professionals in the field. These reviews originally appeared in various issues of the* Harvard Educational Review *in 1990 and 1991.*

## Sociolinguistics

UNFULFILLED EXPECTATIONS: HOME AND SCHOOL INFLUENCES ON
LITERACY
by Catherine E. Snow, Wendy S. Barnes, Jean Chandler,
Irene F. Goodman, and Lowry Hemphill.
*Cambridge: Harvard University Press, 1991. 251 pp.*

In *Unfulfilled Expectations*, Catherine Snow and her coauthors examine the salient factors in literacy development among low-income children in an industrial city of 100,000 located in the Northeast.

Other researchers have used the match-mismatch formulation to explain differences in discourse patterns as well as differences in behavioral expectations at home and at school when discussing academic success and failure across social class. While acknowledging the importance of such comparisons, the authors of *Unfulfilled Expectations* believe it is "also necessary to look elsewhere to understand the differences between the children who did well and those who did poorly" (p. 9). Thus, they emphasize the importance of the home and classroom environments and family-school relationships "within social class." Snow and her colleagues conducted an intensive two-year study of an ethnically diverse group of thirty-two children in grades two, four, and six, then they did a follow-up study five years later. The study sample was restricted to subjects of similar socioeconomic background.

The authors provide detailed ethnographic descriptions that present a multidimensional portrait of the children at home and at school. They discuss diverse environmental factors including family composition, parents' communication with the school, and the existence of rules about watching TV. The authors also portray differences in the classroom behavior of teachers across the grades, with a particular focus on curriculum and instruction. Thus, by vividly illustrating both the home and school environments, this study isolates some of the important factors that contribute to differences in performance among children of both above- and below-average academic achievement within the same socioeconomic status (SES).

The research team conducted a series of statistical analyses which suggest several models of behavioral interaction: the "Family as Educator" model (ch. 4) hypothesizes that families are most effective when they function directly as agents of education; the "Resilient Family" model (ch. 5) investigates the social, economic, and psychological stresses that adversely affect family behaviors; the "Parent-School Partnership" model (ch. 6) strongly supports the notion that parents who assist the school's efforts encourage their children's literacy achievement more successfully than parents who do not become "partners."

Two additional models are described: one proposes that home and school play complementary roles for the child's progress in literacy; the other assumes that deficits in either model are compensated by the other (ch. 7). Each of these hypotheses is important for different reasons. The assumption underlying each formulation is the significance of family support and the maintenance of close contacts between the family and school.

As presented in this book, combining ethnographic descriptions and statistical analyses does not create inconsistency between these two methodologies. On the contrary, when introducing a new hypothesis to account for the children's patterns of literacy achievements, the authors effectively integrate these two methodological approaches, thus strengthening the logical foundations of each. In fact, some of the proposed hypotheses might have been less convincing without the benefit of the other method of analysis.

At the end of the two years, the authors observed a positive correlation between maternal expectations and children's academic achievement, and thus were optimistic about the potential literacy achievement of low-income children. Unfortunately, the results of the follow-up study five years later showed that the authors' and parents' expectations were not fulfilled. In the original study, frequent parent-teacher contact was one of the most important factors contributing to children's academic growth. Five years later, the authors found that, because of increased parent-teacher miscommunications and misunderstandings, as well as teachers' biases against low-income families and their children, "parents were not as involved with teachers at the high school as they had been with teachers at the elementary school" (p. 191). Despite the fact that children's academic problems tend to become more serious in the higher grades, the frequency of parent-teacher contacts decreased, which, according to the authors, reflects the parents' sense of powerlessness and resignation. The authors report that parents felt either that "their continued involvement with their children's academic progress was not sought after," or that "they lacked the resources to be advocates for their children" (p. 192).

*Unfulfilled Expectations* examines the social, economic, and educational inequities that undermine high expectations for academic achievement by children from low-income families. This book powerfully portrays low-income families' commitment to and interest in their children's schooling in the face of overwhelming odds posed by the socioeconomic inequities of American society. As the authors state in their conclusion:

> We can only hope that society will not, in response to this discrepancy between early expectations and ultimate achievement, choose to lower its expectations for low-income American children. (p. 213)

SOCIAL LINGUISTICS AND LITERACIES: IDEOLOGY IN DISCOURSES
by James Paul Gee.
*New York: The Falmer Press, 1990. 224 pp.*

In *Social Linguistics and Literacies,* James Paul Gee defines the role of those who study linguistics and literacy as serving to eliminate racism, classism, and the social structure that supports such unfair systems. In seven chapters, Gee explores the concept of literacy, which has been construed as each individual's ability to read and write, and argues that this traditional view is too naive to capture the real picture of literacy. Instead, he emphasizes that languages are always social possessions and further claims that literacy has been used to consolidate the preestablished social hierarchy, especially in Western societies. The author thus proposes that literacy should be perceived from a more socioculturally situated standpoint.

In Chapter 2, Gee discusses issues surrounding literacy from a historical perspective—from Plato, one of the most influential figures in Western thought and literacy, to Paulo Freire, a contemporary Brazilian educator and advocate of critical literacy. Tracing this history, Gee describes how nonliterate people and people from under-represented groups have been oppressed in many respects. In Chapters 6 and 7, he further introduces the important notion of "Discourse" with a capital "D." According to his definition, Discourses, including more than sequential speech or writing, represent cultural models consisting of "words, acts, values, beliefs, attitudes, social identities, as well as gestures, glances, body positions and clothes" (p. 142). By naming such an aggregate Discourses, Gee rejects the traditional view of literacy, which has tended to perceive it as an autonomous, higher-level cognitive skill that is unrelated to a variety of social practices.

The concept of Discourses sheds light on socialization that reflects the relationship between the individual and society. Since the home serves as the primary agent of socialization, the individual's home-based Discourses reflect the values appreciated in his or her home culture. Once the individual has started to go to school, however, school-based Discourses, which tend to symbolize mainstream values, may seriously conflict with home-based Discourses that are based on nonmainstream cultures. In Chapters 4 and 6, Gee points out that the student's success at school largely depends on whether the two patterns of Discourses—the primary home-based Discourses and secondary school-based Discourses—parallel each other, and argues that in this regard, mainstream students are advantaged, whereas nonmainstream students are disadvantaged and are even at risk of being marginalized.

Gee's explanation may sound similar to a concept in discourse patterns in which school success or failure largely depends on whether school language use corresponds to home language use. However, Gee's position is innovative because he defines the entity of Discourses as a social aggregate that holds within itself a certain set of social values. Rather than simply using the linguistic match–mismatch conception, Gee goes one step beyond the ordinary framework of linguistics and succeeds in conceptualizing diverse sociocultural variables that are irrationally affecting students' school success and failure.

Throughout his discussions in *Social Linguistics and Literacies*, Gee criticizes mainstream school-based Discourses, which, by oppressing those who possess nonmainstream Discourses, have played an inhumane gatekeeping role in Western societies. He argues that historically, dominant Discourses (and present-day school-based Discourses in particular) have empowered those who have mastered these Discourses through the primary socialization at home, while facilitating unfair prejudices against those who have acquired different patterns of Discourses in their homes. In this book, Gee strongly encourages those who study linguistics and literacy to realize, understand, and further fight against such socially embedded unfairness.

LITERACY AS INVOLVEMENT: THE ACTS OF WRITERS, READERS, AND TEXTS
by Deborah Brandt.
*Carbondale, IL: Southern Illinois University Press, 1990. 159 pp.*

*Literacy as Involvement* offers educators and researchers a challenging view of reading, writing, and literacy skills. In five chapters, Deborah Brandt critically examines the prevailing "strong-text" view of literacy, in which one must be logical, literal, detached, and message-focused, like an expository text. She then reanalyzes literacy issues, presenting an alternate perspective of literacy in which metacommunicative skills are acquired through writer-reader involvement.

The literacy dichotomy has long been discussed in terms of an explicit, elaborated literate style versus an ambiguous, restricted oral style. This oral-literate dichotomy originated in the 1960s in British sociolinguist Basil Bernstein's theory of codes. According to his theory, students from middle-class families use an elaborated code, an explicit and decontextualized speech mode that generally matches school language use, while students from working-class families use a restricted code, an elliptical and context-dependent speech mode that generally does not correspond with school language. As Brandt puts it, "In match-mismatch formulations, students are deemed to be at risk in school literacy performance to the extent to which their home language is at odds with the so-called explicit, decontextualized language of the school" (p. 106). Although the oral-literate dichotomy has often been confused with social class and is thus controversial, Bernstein's theory has been incorporated into strong-text accounts of literacy and has influenced studies of literacy in the United States.

The main focus of *Literacy as Involvement* is to reassess strong-text characterizations of literacy and propose an alternate view. Brandt advocates that "literacy must be seen as a context-making rather than a context-breaking ability" because "skilled literates pull together and maintain *situated meaning*" (p. 38). Characteristics of literacy as contextualized and intersubjective run counter to the strong-text conceptions of literacy. With her analysis of expository texts from a cognitive-process perspective (ch. 2), the author further consolidates her position that the expert writer/reader has acquired a strategic, or in her terms metacommunicative, approach to written language, while the inexperienced writer/reader has not. Brandt, who claims that the strong-text notion of literacy merely answers the call of schooling for the masses, emphasizes the significance of establishing a sense of "we" between writer and reader (ch. 3).

In the concluding chapter, the author proposes that literacy in the United States should be understood and addressed in consideration of the diverse cultures represented in U.S. public schools. Brandt further critiques the social injustice embedded in the strong-text theories associated with the oral-literate dichotomy, in which children from middle-class communities are advantaged, while children from lower-class communities are disadvantaged. Brandt states, "It is not enough to say that everyone is welcome in the 'big tent' of literate culture without acknowledging that they will be bringing new materials with which to remake the tent" (p. 124). *Literacy as Involvement* is a thought-provoking book that demonstrates the need for educators from many societies to consider the significance of a plurality of literacies.

CONVERSATIONS ON THE WRITTEN WORD: ESSAYS ON LANGUAGE AND
LITERACY
by Jay L. Robinson.
*Portsmouth, NH: Heinemann, 1990. 335 pp.*

Jay Robinson and three of his colleagues invite the reader to join their *Conversations on the Written Word,* a book dedicated to teachers trying to help students become literate in secondary and collegiate classrooms. A collection of conversations among four different voices, the book is organized into four major parts with eleven chapters that focus on literacy from closely related but diverse perspectives. However, Carol Lea Winkelmann, one of the four contributing authors, points out that they all agree that the role of the teacher is that of an "experienced participant in the community rather than sole authority" (p. 117). She adds that learning should be defined as conversation that leads "students to feel more comfortable about being innovative and taking risks with their language" (p. 117).

The book also presents a collection of conversations between Robinson as a linguist in the present and the same Robinson trained as a medievalist in the past; thus, the book has autobiographical elements that describe a scholar who made a commitment to literacy education. Based on the conviction that literacy is the ability to participate fully in a set of social practices, the author connects two different disciplines of linguistics—namely, generative grammar, represented by Noam Chomsky, and sociolinguistics, represented by Dell Hymes and William Labov. Applying generative grammar theory, the author first discusses that, despite different surface features,

Standard English and other varieties of American English (e.g., Black English vernacular) share the same deep structure. He concludes that "Standard English is better because we assume it to be better" (p. 63). He then argues for other varieties of English, linking generative grammar with sociolinguist Labov's claim that nonstandard dialects are also highly structured systems. Thus, Robinson maintains that these two different disciplines of linguistics—generative grammar and sociolinguistics—form a continuum that simultaneously portrays the path the author followed as a linguist.

A majority of developmental psycholinguists describe literacy as depersonalized and decontextualized; Robinson and his colleagues disagree, warning that a depiction of language use as developing from context-bound orality to context-free literacy does not properly characterize literacy. The authors, whose perspectives are rather new in this field, present a convincing alternate picture that illustrates the development of literacy as a movement from one set of contexts (e.g., home language use) to another (e.g., classroom language use).

Throughout *Conversations on the Written Word*, Robinson and his colleagues propose that opportunities be equally provided to all students to practice and develop language competencies in response to concrete situations, especially in the classroom. The reader will thus come to understand the authors' firm belief that, without developing the competencies required in specific contexts, development of literacy is not feasible. To achieve this end, Robinson advocates functional literacy, defining it as the ability to create and act upon texts that are valued by oneself and others in a particular context. The authors, however, do not regard literacy as a set of basic or merely rudimentary skills; they hope, rather, that all students will be given equal opportunity to be engaged as active participants in a variety of forms of public discourse (p. 271). Readers of this book will realize that learning is always social, functional, and generative; that literacy is "the ability to participate fully in a set of social and intellectual practices" (p. 161); and, therefore, that nurturing students' literacy is crucial.

PORTRAITS OF WHOLE LANGUAGE CLASSROOMS
edited by Heidi Mills and Jean Anne Clyde.
*Portsmouth, NH: Heinemann, 1990. 307 pp.*

In *Portraits of Whole Language Classrooms*, Heidi Mills and Jean Anne Clyde are concerned about numerous misconceptions surrounding whole language, which abound despite its recent immense popularity. They have also realized that educators, especially teachers, need answers to many fundamental questions about the whole language approach such as: What is a typical day in a whole language classroom? and How do teachers put theory into practice with a variety of student populations? The editors try to answer such questions and demonstrate how whole language theory works in classroom practice.

*Portraits of Whole Language Classrooms* contains articles written by a diverse group of whole language teachers, all of whom highlight a typical day in their classrooms. Most of the sixteen chapters move from the beginning of a typical day into the teacher's personal reflection on a particular practice of the day. For example, in Chapter 4 Timothy O'Keefe, an elementary school teacher of long experience, describes a day with dinosaurs that progresses from children playing a dinosaur game to written conversations about dinosaurs accompanied by their drawings of dinosaurs, and later even includes dinosaur mathematics! This example illustrates the book's emphasis on the importance of incorporating mathematics and art into language learning.

The book begins by describing a daycare setting, then continues chronologically through preschool programs and elementary classrooms, to junior high and high schools. A whole language curriculum is established collaboratively through all grade levels, casting teachers as guides, participants, and learning in their own classrooms; thus, the teacher's roles are different than they would be in a traditional teacher-centered classroom. These roles are vividly illustrated in the book's descriptions of whole language classroom activities.

The editors also include other settings, such as a remedial education program and an ESL classroom. This information is important and timely: more than half a million immigrants from nearly one hundred different countries and cultures enter the United States each year, most speaking languages other than English. To master the new language, immigrant children who speak little or no English are placed in a variety of ESL programs. The description of one such program, in Chapter 11, demonstrates how whole language works with diverse student populations, as well as at different grade levels.

While *Portraits of Whole Language Classrooms* has a practical focus, particularly in relating whole language teachers' personal experiences in their classrooms, the examples presented are not intended as models for teachers to follow. They are, rather, meant to support the editors' belief that "language is inherently social" and, thus, "always occurs within a social context" (p. xxiv). The main theme running through the book is that encouraging children to use various phases of literacy "allows them the opportunity to expand their communication potential" and "to express their intended meanings more adequately" (p. xxiii). Thus, "a whole language curriculum . . . capitalizes on the social nature of learning" (p. xxv). In keeping with this ideal, whole language teachers who actively play a supportive role provide opportunities for children to learn from one another.

LEARNING TO BE LITERATE: THE DEVELOPMENT OF SPOKEN AND
WRITTEN LANGUAGE
by Alison Garton and Chris Pratt.
*New York: Basil Blackwell, 1989. 249 pp.*

In *Learning To Be Literate*, two Australian psychologists, Alison Garton and Chris Pratt, discuss language acquisition and later language skills development in children from birth to eight years of age. At the outset of their discussion, the authors define literacy as both spoken and written language. They admit that this is a much broader definition of literacy than is generally accepted, but they justify it by their belief that a strong connection exists between learning to talk and learning to read and write; in other words, early oral language development is directly related to the later development of written language. In Garton and Pratt's terms, literacy can be defined as "the mastery of spoken language *and* reading and writing" (p. 1). From this definition of literacy, therefore, it is clear that Garton and Pratt regard oral and written language as forming a continuum rather than a dichotomy, the more usual interpretation.

In the ten chapters of *Learning To Be Literate*, Garton and Pratt explain the relationship between young children's oral language acquisition and the later years of their language skills development in light of this literacy continuum. They do not necessarily follow children's chronological language development. In early chapters, for instance, they mainly explore young children's language developmental processes in light of diverse theoretical explanations such as Lev Vygotsky's and Jerome Bruner's social interaction theories (ch. 3). In later chapters, on the other hand, they focus more on the generally accepted notion of literacy, discussing such issues as the metalinguistic awareness necessary for a child to be literate (ch. 7).

In addition to advocating a continuity between oral and written language, Garton and Pratt also argue for the need for another continuum running between school language use and home language use. They aptly point out that, in spite of similarities in the nature of conversational interactions at home and at school, school language use may run counter to home language use (p. 111). Among the pictures used in this book to familiarize readers with the issues discussed, a photograph titled "language in the classroom" (p. 110) especially emphasizes the teacher's need to understand children whose habitual uses of language are different from those valued at school, because of their ethnic or cultural background. To illustrate these differences (and, likewise, individual differences), the authors cite, along with research findings in the United States, research findings and school practices in Australia; such cross-cultural material is unique, and is clearly one of the charms of this book. The concluding chapters (8, 9, and 10) discuss practical issues around improving children's learning to read and write at school. Throughout the book, the authors try to avoid introducing difficult technical terms, so that anyone interested in this field can understand their discussion. When it is necessary to introduce technical terms, however, they take pains to explain the subtle differences of similar terms, such as "motherese," "baby talk," and "child-directed speech" (pp. 24–29).

In *Learning To Be Literate*, Garton and Pratt discuss and describe young children's language acquisition and later language skills development both at home and at school. The authors emphasize the significance of social contexts and interactions for children in learning to be literate. Garton and Pratt make it clear that the two types of continua are not separated from each other but are, in reality, closely related to and interwoven with each other.

FIRST LANGUAGE ACQUISITION
by David Ingram.
*New York: Cambridge University Press, 1989. 572 pp.*

"How do children learn to talk?" This is the question posed by this book. Simply exposed to a language, children seem to master almost all of its linguistic features. Sometime during the second year of life (anywhere from twelve to eighteen months), children begin to utter their first words; during the following four to five years, language acquisition and development occur quite rapidly. By the time children enter school, they have mastered the major structural features of their language.

The purpose of this book is to respond to these mysterious developmental features and processes of language acquisition. First, the author presents a historical overview of the field. Then, he discusses recent developments in our understanding of how children learn to talk, in particular the roles of innate, cognitive, and social factors in language development, as well as individual differences. This book thus deepens the overall understanding of language acquisition.

## Narrative

DEVELOPING NARRATIVE STRUCTURE
edited by Allyssa McCabe and Carole Peterson.
*Hillsdale, NJ: Lawrence Erlbaum Associates, 1991. 367 pp.*

Allyssa McCabe and Carole Peterson have been interested in ways to analyze children's narrative structure. Their new book, *Developing Narrative Structure*, consists of eight chapters written by scholars who, in diverse ways, identify and analyze mechanisms of children's narratives. The underlying theme throughout is the editors' and the contributors' wish that the book might serve to facilitate people's better understanding of children from diverse ethnic backgrounds.

The main theme of the book is particularly relevant to the school setting. David Dickinson (ch. 7), for example, discusses how children are socialized in culturally specific ways during the preschool and early school years. He specifically studies (1) how teacher-child interaction varies during activity time, depending on whether the teacher is stationary or moving about the classroom, and (2) how teacher-child talk varies between lunch time and activity time. Along similar lines, McCabe and Peterson (ch. 6) discuss how adults from different cultures evaluate children's narrative differently. Emphasizing the role of social interaction, they examine the influence of environment on children's narratives through interaction with their parents. This focus is based on the authors' belief that a child's early narrative style in the home influences or even determines the narrative style that he or she will later carry over to the classroom.

In order to encourage and stimulate children from different cultures, it is important to know those cultures' specific communicative styles. Using "sharing time" (an oral language activity in early elementary classrooms) data, Sarah Michaels (ch. 8) shows that teachers accustomed to a discourse with a clearly identifiable topic tend to misunderstand children whose culture allows them to use a discourse consisting of a series of implicitly associated personal anecdotes. Pointing out that children's habitual ways of communicating at home may not necessarily work in the school setting, Michaels appeals to educators to better understand children from different cultures.

The editors of *Developing Narrative Structure* include articles that deal with issues reflecting children's age and topic genre, as well as structural differences as a function of culture. Judith Hudson and Lauren Shapiro (ch. 3), for instance, provide the reader with a deep insight into children's narratives, which, according to these authors, reveal how children "translate their knowledge into narratives" (p. 89). Comparing different types of narratives, they closely examine how the selection of the topic affects children's narrative production and investigate how components of the narrative differ among children of different ages.

Age differences, however, work under the influence of a specific culture. As Deborah Hicks (ch. 2) discusses, studies of children's narrative structure reveal similarities for children of a given age in each cultural setting. The notion of cultural influence on narrative is also supported by Elizabeth Sulzby and Liliana Zecker (ch. 5), who study emergent literacy, young children's "everyday encounters with the print in their environments" (p. 175). As McCabe, one of the editors, puts it in the preface, "People should be encouraged to engage in a little more structural analysis before coming to a conclusion about the quality of some narratives" (p. xiv). The collection of studies included in *Developing Narrative Structure* thus provides educators, researchers, and others interested in narrative development with useful information about children from diverse cultural backgrounds.


ACTS OF MEANING
by Jerome Bruner.
*Cambridge: Harvard University Press, 1990. 179 pp.*

In his most recent book, *Acts of Meaning*, cognitive psychologist Jerome Bruner once again foreshadows the direction that the field of developmental psychology will take in the ensuing years. Although Bruner is one of the founders of information processing, in this book he highlights its shortcomings and calls for a "new look" at human development.

For Bruner, this "new book" emphasizes the meaning-making that emerges through social interactions mediated by culturally constructed narratives. In the first chapter, "The Proper Study of Man," he discusses his frustration with developmental theorists' overreliance on information processing models of human development and outlines his concept of narrative as the central psychological process involved in meaning-making.

According to Bruner, narratives serve as the mediating factor between mind and culture, through which canonical or normative patterns of behavior develop. Narratives also act as the framework within which deviations from canonical forms are assessed, understood, and explained. Thus, Bruner defines meaning-making as the construction of an individual's logic through interaction with others.

In subsequent chapters, Bruner discusses this concept in more detail. In Chapter 2, he discusses the importance of folk psychologies, which can be seen in indigenous theories of "mind" and "motivation"; in Chapter 3, he discusses how children acquire narrative skills. The concluding chapter calls for a shift from an overemphasis on empirical research, such as that of the information processing programs, to a study of the emergence of the "self" within the context of a specific culture. *Acts of Meaning,* written by one of the most distinguished thinkers in human development, is an insightful summary of the past trends in the field, and is, perhaps, a prophetic glimpse into the future. Bruner's breadth of knowledge makes for thought-provoking and enjoyable reading for anyone interested in human culture.


NARRATIVES FROM THE CRIB
edited by Katherine Nelson.
*Cambridge: Harvard University Press, 1989. 350 pp.*

Studies of language development and discourse analysis are focused increasingly on the communicative social interactions in the beginning stages of children's speech patterns. *Narratives from the Crib* is an analysis of the sequentially organized narratives of a toddler, Emily, between the ages of 21 and 36 months, as well as her interactions with her parents. Each of the nine chapters approaches Emily's cognitive capacity and communicative skills from a different perspective. In Part One, the authors examine Emily's construction of her worldview; in Part Two, they emphasize her language and discourse development; in Part Three they analyze her construction of self. While each contributor has a different focus, they all agree that social interactions have a significant impact on young children's narrative acquisition and development.

The underlying theme of this book is how the young child views the world and situates herself within it through monologic and dialogic discourse. Lev Vygotsky, the noted Russian psychologist, suggests that children's cognitive skills develop through interactions with more mature members of society and are then internalized after long practice. In chapter two, Jerome Bruner maintains that for learning to take place, children must have opportunities for appropriate cooperative interactions. Katherine Nelson, editor of *Narratives from the Crib* and author of chapters one and eight, also supports these ideas. Nelson describes Emily's monologic narrative organization as a developmental process moving in the direction of adult models. Each of these theorists provides evidence that strongly supports the social-interactionist paradigm.

The view that parental talk provides a verbal framework for children's representations of past events implies that early social interactions shape young children's narratives into culturally preferred patterns. Two-year-old Emily is, thus, in the process of acquiring canonical sequence-of-event-description. Many chapters of this book remark on the striking similarity between Emily's speech and her parent's prebedtime routines. Bruner and Joan Lucariello explain such canonicality as "the appropriate folk description of human action" (p. 76). The evidence in this case suggests that parents, either implicitly or explicitly, provide their children with culturally and socially appropriate narrative forms and routines.

As described above, when social-interaction theories are applied to the study of young children's narratives, parents are considered to be the primary agents providing the framework within which their children learn a particular narrative style. Interestingly, all of the contributors to *Narratives from the Crib* point out the sharp contrast between Emily's pre-sleep monologic narratives—which are richly textured—and her conversational activities—which are short, sparse contributions to dialogue with her parents. This distinction may imply that, because of a certain set of constraints embedded in the dialogic framework, parents' utterances tend to be projected forward, while children's are likely to be projected backward (ch. 3).

This phenomenon, described by Bruner as "scaffolding," encompasses a variety of parental supports for language development in the young child. In dialogic speech, the parent tends to be dominant; thus, his or her utterances are more likely to be projected forward. This circumstance does not deny, however, the validity of the social-interaction approach. As Nelson points out, "the result of the integration of parental input and child representation in verbal form is the monologic organization" (p. 63). Looking at Emily's narratives from these perspectives clearly delineates the important differences between monologues and dialogues.

*Narratives from the Crib* goes beyond a simple description of language development. It provides the reader with diverse but integrated examinations of Emily's cognitive, linguistic, and social development. Furthermore, this book supports the social-interaction theory by presenting detailed analyses of the young child's developing mind in terms of language, narrative, and thought.

Narrative Thought and Narrative Language
edited by Bruce K. Britton and Anthony D. Pellegrini.
*Hillsdale, NJ: Lawrence Erlbaum Associates, 1990. 278 pp.*

In one way or another, researchers in linguistics, anthropology, and psychology have tried to address the relationship between the mind and narrative forms. The articles in *Narrative Thought and Narrative Language* originate from the conference of the same name held at the University of Georgia in 1987. Its ten chapters explore a variety of issues, from "scaffolding" to psychoanalysis, that illustrate how narrative processes reflect the nature of the mind. The underlying theme throughout this volume is that "the narrative is the window of the mind," and distinguished scholars such as Jerome Bruner, Wallace Chafe, and David Olson discuss narrative in diverse ways.

For example, chapter four examines the joint construction of stories by preschool children and adults based on Bruner's notion of "scaffolding"; that is, the context in which adults provide guidance and support to children in the process of narrative production and comprehension. Chapter ten discusses psychoanalysis from the perspective of how narrative theory has created a paradigm shift in current understandings of psychoanalytic processes.

Although the focus of this volume differs from chapter to chapter, the diverse treatment of the subject suggests that the relationship of narrative thought and language to cognition is an important medium of research, from both a developmental and a psychoanalytic viewpoint.

The contributors to this volume examine several important concepts in narrative discourse analysis. In chapters one, five, and six, for instance, the authors discuss the framework of what Jerome Bruner has termed "the dual landscape of narrative." In this framework, the landscape of action is a canvas on which the narrator paints the world of action in the story. The landscape of consciousness, on the other hand, describes "how the world is perceived or felt by various members of the cast of characters, each from their own perspective" (p. 2). Developmentally, the child's acquisition of these two vehicles for thought and language production is crucial to understanding his or her progress in narrative production. To understand and appreciate the story, Janet Astington (ch. 6) emphasizes the importance of the simultaneous comprehension of these two landscapes by the young child. Astington argues that "this is what the four-year-old, but not the two-year-old, can achieve" (p. 153). This interesting interpretation of the dual landscape of narrative will surely contribute much to studies of cognitive development and other related disciplines.

The concept of the dual landscape of narrative suggests that the nature of the mind is simultaneously constrained by a specific culture and society. Wallace Chafe, a longtime advocate of the notion of "idea units," highlights these constraints of culture and society differently from proponents of "the dual landscape narrative." According to Chafe, the idea unit restricts the narrator to verbalizing only one new concept at a time. For the production of successive idea units, Chafe argues that the individual mind is guided by the schema—prepackaged expectations or interpretations that naturally follow unique culture-specific perspectives (ch. 2). The discussion of narrative under such restrictions is further supported by David Olson's argument that, instead of a simple reflection of past events, narratives are laid out over events, and thus are comprehensible and memorable (ch. 3). That the mind and narrative do not stand alone without the influence of a specific culture and society is another important idea articulated in this book.

*Narrative Thought and Narrative Language* provides an interesting approach to understanding the relationship between the human mind and narrative forms. Through the discussions of narrative production, comprehension, and interpretation, this book, as Chafe's title indicates (ch. 2), gives the reader the time to reflect on "some things that tell us about the mind."

# About the Contributors

ALMA FLOR ADA is Professor and Director of Doctoral Studies in International Multicultural Education in the School of Education at the University of San Francisco. An advocate of bilingual education and of the rights of all children and their parents to quality education, her interests also include critical pedagogy, education as an instrument for social change, adult literacy, and cross-cultural understanding. She is author of numerous children's books, including *The Gold Coin*. Her other publications include *A Magical Encounter: The Use of Spanish Children's Literature in the Classroom* and *Home School Interaction: Parents and Children as Protagonists and Authors*.

ELSA ROBERTS AUERBACH is Assistant Professor of Bilingual/ESL Graduate Studies and Coordinator of the Bilingual Community Literacy Training Project at the University of Massachusetts, Boston. Her work focuses primarily on adult ESL and literacy, with particular emphasis on participatory approaches to curriculum development and workplace ESL. She is involved in both university and community-based adult ESL teacher education. She is coauthor of *ESL for Action: Problem-Posing at Work* (with N. Wallerstein, 1987), and author of *Making Meaning, Making Change: A Guide to Participatory Curriculum Development for Adult ESL and Family Literacy* (forthcoming). She is also author of numerous articles on the ideology of adult ESL texts and approaches to curriculum development.

JOHN BAUGH is Professor of Education, Linguistics, and Anthropology at Stanford University School of Education, where his current professional focus is educational applications of sociolinguistics. Other research interests include ethnography of speaking and communication, linguistics and the law, and linguistic variation in U.S. vernaculars. His publications include *Black Street Speech: Its History, Structure, and Survival* (1983), "Language and Race: Some Implications for Linguistic Sciences" in F. Newmeyer (Ed.), *Linguistics: The Cambridge Survey* (1988), and "The Politicization of Changing Terms of Self-Reference among American Slave Descendants" in *American Speech* (1991).

URSULA BELLUGI is a Professor and Director of the Laboratory for Cognitive Neuroscience at The Salk Institute for Biological Studies, and Adjunct Professor at the University of San Diego. She is a co-recipient of the 1991 Neuronal Plasticity Prize awarded by the Foundation IPSEN of Paris. Her major professional interests are the biological foundations of language and cognitive neuroscience. She is the author of numerous publications, including *What the Hands Reveal about the Brain* (with H. Poizner and E. S. Klima, 1987) and "Once More with Feeling: Affect and Language in Atypical Populations" in *Development and Psychopathology* (with J. Reilly and E. S. Klima, 1991).

ERIC BREDO is Associate Professor in the Department of Educational Studies at the University of Virginia, Charlottesville. Currently on sabbatical, he is a visiting scholar at Stanford University and a visiting scientist at the Institute for Research on Learning in Palo Alto, California. His professional interests include social contexts of teaching and learning, and education and social theory. He is author of "After Positivism, What?" in *Educational Theory* (1989), "Is the Answer in the Text?" in *Educational Foundations* (1990), and *Grace in Teaching* (1991).

ROGER BROWN is John Lindsley Professor of Psychology at Harvard University, where his professional interests include sociolinguistics and politeness theory. He is a recipient of the Fyssen International Prize in Cognitive Sciences. His publications include *Words and Things* (1958), *Social Psychology* (1965), *Psycholinguistics: Selected Papers* (1970), *A First Language* (1973), and *Social Psychology: The Second Edition* (1987).

HERLINDA CANCINO is Professor of Education at San Francisco State University. Her professional interests focus on second-language acquisition and the influence of language on cognition and self-concept. Her publications include *Grammatical Morphemes in Second Language Acquisition: Marta* (1976) and *First Language Transfer in the Acquisition of English Locative Prepositions and Genitives by Four Spanish Speakers* (1980).

JOHN B. CARROLL is Professor of Psychology Emeritus at the University of North Carolina at Chapel Hill. His research interests include the psychology of language performance abilities and individual differences in human cognitive abilities. He was formerly the Roy E. Larsen Professor of Educational Psychology at Harvard University. His publications include *The Study of Language* (1953), *Modern Language Aptitude Test* (1959), *and Perspectives on School Learning: Selected Writings* (1985).

CAROL CHOMSKY, Lecturer on Education at the Harvard Graduate School of Education, is interested in child language development and reading. She works on applications of technology in the classroom, and develops educational software in the areas of language and reading. She is author of *The Acquisition of Syntax in Children from 5 to 10* (1969), and of "Reading, Writing, and Phonology" (1970) in the *Harvard Educational Review*.

MICHAEL COLE is Professor of Communication and Psychology at the University of California at San Diego. His current research focuses on cultural theories of mind and human development. He is the editor of *Soviet Psychology,* and coauthor of *The*

*Cultural Context of Learning and Thinking* (with J. Gay et al., 1971), *Culture and Thought* (with S. Scribner, 1974), *Psychology of Literacy* (with S. Scribner, 1981), and *The Development of Children* (with S. Cole, 1989).

JIM CUMMINS, Professor in the Curriculum Department at the Ontario Institute for Studies in Education, is interested in bilingual education, critical pedagogy, and language education. His publications include *Bilingualism and Special Education: Issues in Assessment and Pedagogy* (1984) and *Empowering Minority Students* (1989).

LISA D. DELPIT, on leave from her position as Associate Professor of Education at Michigan State University, is presently a Senior Research Associate at Morgan State University's Institute for Urban Research in Baltimore. Her research concerns include literacy development, teacher education, and teaching and learning in multicultural settings, with particular emphasis on ensuring that poor communities and communities of color have a voice in determining educational policy. She is a recent recipient of a MacArthur Prize Fellowship, and is currently researching a volume on issues of diversity in teacher education.

RUBEN DONATO, Assistant Professor in the Department of Educational Policy Studies at the University of Wisconsin at Madison, is interested in Mexican Americans in schools, historical and contemporary issues, and educational equity and policy studies for Latino students in public schools. His publications include *Multicultural Teacher Education: Research in the 1990s* (with V. Florez, 1990), "Segregation, Desegregation, and Integration of Chicano Students: Problems and Prospects" (with M. Menchaca and R. Valencia) in R. Valencia (Ed.), *Chicano School Failure and Success: Research and Policy Agendas for the 1990s* (1991), and "Segregation in Desegregated Schools: A Question of Equity" in *Equity and Excellence* (with H. Garcia, in press).

KIERAN EGAN is Professor of Education at Simon Fraser University in British Columbia, where his major professional interest is in curriculum. He is author of *Teaching as Story Telling* (1986), *Primary Understanding: Education in Early Childhood* (1988), *Romantic Understanding: The Development of Rationality and Imagination, Ages 8–15* (1990), and *Imagination in Teaching and Learning* (1991).

BERNARDO M. FERDMAN is Assistant Professor in the departments of Psychology and of Latin American and Caribbean Studies at the State University of New York at Albany. His professional focus is on ethnic identity. He is coauthor of "Bilingualism and Cognitive Development: Three Perspectives" in S. Rosenbert (Ed.), *Advances in Applied Psycholinguistics, Vol. II: Reading, Writing and Language Learning* (with K. Hakuta and R. M. Diaz, 1987). His forthcoming publications include "The Dynamics of Ethnic Diversity in Organizations: Toward Integrative Models" in K. Kelley (Ed.), *Issues, Theory and Research in Industrial/Organizational Psychology,* and an edited volume, *Literacy across Languages and Cultures* (with R.-M. Weber and A. Ramirez).

PAULO FREIRE, former Secretary of Education for São Paulo, Brazil, is now an advisor to that city's government. He has also served as Special Advisor in Education to the World Council of Churches in Geneva, Switzerland, and was Professor of Philosophy of Education at the Catholic University of São Paulo and the State University of Campinas, Brazil. His publications include "Cultural Action and Conscientization" in the *Harvard Educational Review* (1970), *Pedagogy of the Oppressed* (1971), and *Literacy: Reading the Word and the World* (with D. Macedo, 1987).

JAMES PAUL GEE is Professor of Linguistics in the Department of Linguistics at the University of Southern California, and a member of the executive board of the Literacies Institute in Newton, Massachusetts. Currently a Visiting Professor in the Education Program and the Psychology Department at Clark University in Worcester, Massachusetts, his research interests include discourse, sociolinguistics, and socio-cultural approaches to literacies. His recent publications include *Social Linguistics and Literacies: Ideology in Discourses* (1990), "A Linguistic Approach to Narrative" in the *Journal of Narrative and Life History* (1991), and *The Social Mind: Language, Ideology, and Social Practice* (in press).

FRED GENESEE, Professor of Psychology at McGill University, is interested in the simultaneous acquisition of two languages in children, the metalinguistic development of bilingual children, and learning to read a second language. His research activities have also focused on individual differences in second-language learning, the neuropsychological correlates of bilingualism, and the effectiveness of alternative approaches to bilingual education. He is author of *Learning through Two Languages: Studies of Immersion and Bilingual Education* (1987).

ALEXANDRA WHARTON GRANNIS is a Supervisor and Language and Learning Abilities Specialist at St. Luke's Child Psychiatric Clinic in New York City. She has a particular interest in early language development.

JOSEPH C. GRANNIS is Professor of Education and a Senior Research Associate in the Institute for Urban and Minority Education at Teachers College, Columbia University. His major professional interests are educational environments and urban schools. Among his publications on these topics is "Task Engagement and the Distribution of Pedagogical Controls: An Ecological Study of Differently Structured Classroom Settings" in *Curriculum Inquiry* (1978).

PATRICIA MARKS GREENFIELD is Professor of Psychology at the University of California, Los Angeles. Her professional interests include research into the effects of media on children, the application of child language research to chimpanzee language, and cultural influences on cognitive socialization and development in Senegal and Mexico. She is coauthor of *Studies in Cognitive Growth* (with J. S. Bruner et al., 1966), *The Structure of Communication in Early Language Development* (with J. H. Smith,

1972), and *Infant Curriculum: The Bromley-Heath Health Guide to the Care of Infants in Groups* (with E. Tronick, 1973).

KENJI HAKUTA is Professor of Education at Stanford University and Chair of the Board of Trustees at the Center for Applied Linguistics in Washington, DC. He is interested in bilingualism and bilingual education, language acquisition, and language maintenance and loss. His publications include "Grammatical Description versus Configurational Arrangement in Language Acquisition: The Case of Relative Clauses in Japanese" in *Cognition* (1981), and *Mirror of Language: The Debate on Bilingualism* (1986).

MARY HENRY is Assistant Professor of the Social Foundations of Education at Washington State University, where her major professional interest is the ethnography of schooling. She is author of several articles, including "Voices of Academic Women on Feminine Gender Scripts" in the *British Journal of Sociology of Education* (1990), "Expectations of Students and Teachers: A Gifted Classroom Observed" in *Gifted Education International* (1991), and "School Rituals as Educational Contests" in the *International Journal of Qualitative Studies in Education* (forthcoming).

ROSEMARY HENZE, an Education Specialist at ARC Associates in Oakland, California, recently completed a study of bilingual education in a Southwestern Alaska school district. She is currently working with teachers in Northern California to develop more culturally responsive pedagogy. Her publications include "Literacy in Rural Greece: From Family to Individual" in F. Dubin and N. Kuhlman (Eds.), *Cross Cultural Literacy*, and *Informal Teaching and Learning: A Study of Everyday Cognition in a Greek Community*, both of which will appear in 1992.

ROBERT W. KOPFSTEIN, Reading Instructor at Saddleback College in Mission Viejo, California, is also an Instructor at the Institute for Reading and a member of the Reading Advisory Council at California State University, Fullerton. His major professional interest is reading and education. His publications include "After the Basics, Then What?" in *Institute for Reading Forum* (1979), *Study Skills Evaluation: Why Does Who Do What and How?* (1980), and "Bromeliads Televised" in the *Journal of the Bromeliad Society* (1984).

TAMARA LUCAS is a Research Associate at ARC Associates in Oakland, California, where her primary interest is in the education of language-minority students in the United States. Among her publications are "Personal Journal Writing as a Classroom Genre" in J. K. Peyton (Ed.), *Perspectives on Journal Writing* (1990), "Meaning Construction in School Literacy Tasks: A Study of Bilingual Students" in *American Educational Research Journal* (with J. A. Langer, L. Bartolome, and O. Vasquez, 1990), and "Diversity among Individuals: Eight Students Making Sense of Classroom Journal Writing" in D. Murray (Ed.), *Diversity as Resource: Redefining Cultural Literacy* (forthcoming).

R. P. McDermott is Professor of Education at Stanford University. His research is in cultural anthropology, with a focus on writing systems and their use in various cultures and on the organization of behavior in educational settings. His publications include "Inarticulateness" in D. Tanner (Ed.), *Linguistics in Contexts* (1989).

Peter L. McLaren is Renowned Scholar-in-Residence, Associate Professor of Educational Leadership, and Associate Director of the Center for Education and Cultural Studies at Miami University of Ohio School of Education and Allied Professions. His professional interests are critical pedagogy, critical ethnography, and cultural studies. He is co-editor (with H. Giroux) of the publication series "Teacher Empowerment and School Reform." His recent publications include *Life in the Schools* (1989), *Postmodernism, Post-Colonialism and Pedagogy* (1991), and *Radical Pedagogy: Post-Colonial Politics in a Postmodern World* (forthcoming). Two co-edited books are in press: *Paulo Freire: A Critical Encounter* (with P. Leonard) and *Postmodernism, Politics, and Praxis* (with C. Lankshear).

David R. Olson is Professor of Applied Psychology at the Centre for Applied Cognitive Science at the Ontario Institute for Studies in Education, where his major research interests are cognition and literacy. He is co-editor of *Literacy, Language and Learning* (with N. Torrance and A. Hildyard, 1985), *Literacy and Orality* (with N. Torrance, 1991), and *Developing Theories of Mind* (with J. Astington and P. Harris, 1989). He is also author of *The World on Paper* (forthcoming).

Ricardo Otheguy is Professor of Linguistics and Bilingual Education at City College of New York, and Professor of Linguistics at the Graduate School of the City University of New York. His professional interests include bilingual education, language contact, and grammatical analysis. His publications include "Transferring, Switching, and Modeling in West New York Spanish: An Intergenerational Study" in the *International Journal of the Sociology of Language* (1989). He is also co-editor of *English across Cultures: Cultures across English: A Reader in Cross-Cultural Communication* (with O. Garcia, 1989).

Carlos J. Ovando is Professor of Education at Indiana University School of Education. He is interested in second-language acquisition, cross-cultural communication, issues in the education of language-minority students, and curriculum theory and practice. His publications include "Bilingual-Bicultural Education: Its Legacy and Its Future" in the *Phi Delta Kappan* (1983), *Bilingual and ESL Classrooms* (with V. Collier, 1985), "Language Diversity and Education" in J. Banks and C. Banks (Eds.), *Multicultural Education: Issues and Perspectives* (1989), and "Intermediate and Secondary School Curricula: A Multicultural and Multilingual Framework" in *The Clearing House* (1990).

CHARLES READ is Professor of Linguistics and Associate Dean of the Graduate School, Department of Linguistics, at the University of Wisconsin, Madison. His major professional interests are linguistics and education, in particular phonetics and phonology in the foundations of reading and writing. He is author of *Children's Categorization of Speech Sounds in English* (1975) and *Children's Creative Spelling* (1986), and has written numerous articles on the linguistic bases of reading and spelling.

DANIEL P. RESNICK, Professor of History at Carnegie Mellon University, is interested in literacy studies, history of education, and assessment. He edited and contributed to *Literacy in Historical Perspectives* (1981), and is coauthor of "Varieties of Literacy" in A. E. Barnes and P. N. Stearns (Eds.), *Social History and Issues in Human Consciousness: Some Interdisciplinary Connections* (with L. B. Resnick, 1989), and "Assessing the Thinking Curriculum" in B. R. Gifford and M. C. O'Connor (Eds.), *Future Assessments: Changing Views of Aptitude, Achievement and Instruction* (with L. B. Resnick, 1991).

LAUREN B. RESNICK is Director of the Learning Research and Development Center and Professor in the Department of Psychology at the University of Pittsburgh. Her research focuses on assessment, the nature and development of thinking abilities, and the relationship between school learning and everyday competence. She is author of *Education and Learning to Think* (1987) and "Literacy in School and Out" in *Daedalus* (1990), and co-editor of *Perspectives on Socially Shared Cognition* (with J. Levine and S. D. Teasley, 1991).

HAROLD ROSEN is Emeritus Professor of Education at the University of London Institute of Education. His professional interests include narrative theory and its educational significance, and, more broadly, language in education. He is coauthor of *The Language of Primary School Children* (with C. Rosen, 1972) and *The Languages and Dialects of London Schoolchildren* (with T. Burgess, 1979). He has recently written a number of articles and papers on narrative.

ROSEMARY C. SALOMONE, Professor of Law at St. John's University School of Law in Jamaica, New York, is interested in legal and policy issues related to educational equity. She is currently working on a book that focuses on First Amendment rights of students to freedom of conscience and speech. She is also author of *Equal Education under Law* (1986), and her articles on law and education have been published in the *Journal of Law and Education, Hastings Constitutional Law Quarterly,* and *Urban Education*.

SYLVIA SCRIBNER, who died in July 1991, was Professor of Psychology in the Developmental Psychology Program of the Graduate Center of the City University of New York, as well as Director of the Laboratory for Cognitive Studies of Work. Her publications include *Culture and Thought* (with M. Cole, 1974) and *Psychology of Literacy* (with M. Cole, 1981).

CATHERINE E. SNOW is Professor of Education and Academic Dean at the Harvard Graduate School of Education. She has published extensively in the fields of first- and second-language acquisition, literacy development, and parent-child interaction. Among her recent books are *Children's Language: Volume 7* (co-edited with G. Conti-Ramsden, 1990) and *Unfulfilled Expectations: Home and School Influences on Literacy* (with W. S. Barnes et al., 1991).

DAVID SPENER, an ESL specialist, has been a Program Associate with the National Clearinghouse on Literacy Education at the Center for Applied Linguistics in Washington, DC. Currently pursuing doctoral studies in sociology at the University of Texas, Austin, he is interested in the sociology of immigration, and in race and ethnic relations. He has taught ESL at the University of the District of Columbia, in a program for Asian refugees in Maryland, and at the Centro Colombo-Americano in Medellín, Colombia. He is editor of *Adult Biliteracy in the United States* (forthcoming).

# Author Index

Ada, A. F., 403, 449
Adams, M., 85, 89
Aguilar, M., 382
Akinnaso, F. N., 348
Alatis, J., 76
Althusser, L., 256
Alvarez, L., 513
Ames, L. B., 118
Ammon, M. S., 459
Ammon, P., 459
Anastasiow, N., 207
Anderson, R. C., 154, 167
Antinucci, F., 91
Apple, M. W., 281, 282, 488–489
Applebee, A. N., 197
Arias, B., 458
Aristotle, 178
Arlman-Rup, A., 492
Arnove, R., 266
Aronowitz, S., 449
Ashton, P. T., 196
Au, K. H., 325, 378
Auerbach, E., 404
Austin, J. L., 172
Ayres, L., 145

Babad, E. Y., 349, 358
Bailey, N., 86, 87
Bailyn, B., 137
Baker, C. L., 102, 115
Baker, K. A., 374, 513, 514
Bakhtin, M. M., 270
Baldwin, J., 298
Ball, P., 356
Banks, J. A., 365
Bannatyne, A. D., 209
Barclay, J. R., 154, 167
Barnes, W. S., xv, 542
Bartlett, F., 188
Barzun, J., 510
Bascunan, L., 382
Basman, S., 382
Bates, E., 91
Baugh, J., 537, 538
Beers, C. S., 381
Beers, J. W., 381

Bell, J., 458
Bell, T. M., 393, 394
Bellugi, U., 77, 79, 83, 84, 85
Benne, K. D., 349, 358
Bennett, W. J., 288, 289, 294, 302, 510
Berg, I., 275
Berko, J., 42
Bernstein, B., xi, xiv, 532; Class, Codes and
    Control. Volume 1. Theoretical Studies toward a
    Sociology of Language, 339–344
Berry, J. W., 357
Berthoff, A., 292
Bettelheim, B., 197
Bettleheim, B., 510
Bever, T. G., 105, 154
Biemiller, A., 119
Birnbaum, M., 349, 358
Bloom, A., 288, 289, 295, 298, 539
Bloom, L., 85, 86, 89, 155
Bloome, D., 209, 229
Bloomfield, L., 160, 536
Bluck, R. S., 162
Bluemnberg, H., 179
Bluestone, B., 432, 436, 437
Boas, F., 194
Bobcock, R., 277
Boekestijn, C., 357
Boggs, S., 342
Bonvillian, J., 92
Bossert, S. T., 458
Botkin, P., 240
Bourdieu, P., 267
Bowen, J., 76
Bowles, S., 267
Braine, M. D. S., 14
Brandt, D., xi, xiv, xvii; Literacy as Involve-
    ment: The Acts of Writers, Readers, and Texts,
    545–546
Branscombe, A., 491
Bransford, J. D., 154, 167
Braverman, H., 436
Bresnan, J. W., 105
Bricker, K., 509, 510
Brinkley, J., 432
Britton, B. K., Narrative Thought and Narrative
    Language, 553–555

Britton, J., 499
Brown, P. R., 458
Brown, R., ix, 77, 79, 81, 83, 86, 87, 88, 90, 98, 111, 112, 156
Bruner, J. S., xii, xiv, 152, 156, 161, 212, 217, 220, 236, 282, 334; *Acts of Meaning*, 551–552
Buck-Morss, S., 196
Buhler, K., 155
Bullock Report, 384
Bunzel, R., 240
Burger, R., 268
Burgess, M. A., 144
Burgess, T., 499
Burke, P., 183
Burt, M. K., 77, 78, 79, 87, 385
Business Council for Effective Literacy, 393, 394, 395
Butterworth, G., 85, 89

Cabral, M., 292
Califano, J., 441–442
California State Department of Education, 439, 440, 441, 517
Campbell, F., 207
Campbell, R., 524
Campos, J., 378, 384, 385
Cancino, H., 80, 81, 86
Careaga, R. C., 458
Carnoy, M., 208
Carpenter, P., 170
Carroll, J. B., 156
Carroll, L., 201
Carter, T. P., 458, 459, 460, 469
Cassirer, E., 188, 189
Cavazos, L., 516
Cazden, C., xiii, 81, 84, 86, 87, 89, 208, 267, 281, 282, 342, 383, 499; *Classroom Discourse: The Language of Teaching and Learning*, 320–330
Cedartown Strike, 433
Cellerier, G., 124
Center for the Study of Reading, 245
Chafe, W., 153, 166
Chall, J. S., x, 146–147, 156, 208, 393, 396, 399, 400, 401; *Stages of Reading Development*, 117–121
Chandler, J., xv, 542
Changeux, P., 124
Chapman, R., 217
Chase, S., 153
Chatfield, M. L., 458, 459, 460, 469
Childs, C., 240
Chomsky, C., ix, x
Chomsky, N., ix, 26, 28, 76, 89, 99, 102, 105–106, 114, 123–126, 153, 155, 165, 169

Clanchy, M., 267
Clark, E., 169, 170
Clark, H. H., 154
Clark, M., 210
Clark, R., 270
Clyde, J. A., 547
Cobb, J., 436
Cockcroft, J. D., 427, 429, 430, 431, 432, 434, 437
Cohen, A. D., 79, 377, 524
Colby, W., 430
Cole, M., 152, 168, 228, 238, 239, 240, 321–322, 348; *The Psychology of Literacy*, 333–337
Coleman, J., 207
Coles, G. S., 381
Collier, V. P., 402, 424, 436, 439, 440, 506
Comrie, B., 114
Cooke, A., 510
Cook-Gumperz, J., 228, 267, 268, 281, 282, 353
Cooper, D. E., 189, 199
Copperman, P., 121
Corder, S. P., x, 77, 78, 79, 80
Corvoran, T. B., 458, 459, 461, 472
Coulthard, R., 324
Cousins, N., 510
Cox, B., 229
Crawford, J., 443, 508, 510, 511, 515, 516; *Bilingual Education: History, Politics, Theory, and Practice*, 503–518
Cremin, L., 137
Cronkite, W., 510
Cropsey, J., 270
Cross, T., 216
Culicover, P., 98, 106
Cummins, J., 373, 374, 375, 376, 377, 378, 380, 381, 382, 383, 424, 426, 439, 440, 441, 448, 449, 451, 477, 480
Curtis, J., 379
Cusick, P., 329

Daiute, C., 382
Dale, E., 208
D'Arcy, P., 245
Darlington, R., 208
Davis, F. B., 208
deBlauw, A., 219
deCastell, S., 281, 352, 360, 363
DeJong, J., 228
de Kanter, A., 513, 514
de Kanter, A. A., 374
de Laguna, G., 155, 156
Delgado-Gaitan, C., 396
Delpit, L. D., 470, 485, 490
Demientieff, M., 497–498

de Olave, M. de P., 449
DePaulo, B., 92
Derrida, J., 268
Deschamps, J., 359
DeStefano, 208
de Villiers, J., 86, 87, 90
de Villiers, P., 86, 87, 90
De Vries, G. J., 268
Diaz, R. M., 356, 361, 379
Diaz, S., 396, 398, 402, 403
Dillard, J. L., 532
Dittmar, N., 207
Dixon, M., 429
Dodds, E. R., 178
Dolson, D., 448
Donaldson, M., 169
Dornbusch, S. M., 500
Dorsey-Gaines, C., 393, 396, 399, 402
Duarte, V. L., 372
Dubber, C., 219
Dulay, H. C., 77, 78, 79, 87, 385
Dulles, F. R., 427, 428, 436
Dumas, G., 79
Durkheim, E., 188
Durkin, D., 210, 225
Duskova, L., 79
Dwyer, D. C., 458
Dylan, B., 158

Eagleton, T., 267, 282
Edmonds, R., 457, 458, 460
Edwards, A. E., 207
Egan, K., 187, 188, 198, 199, 200, 202, 281
Eisenberg, A., 228
Ekstrand, L. H., 438
Eliade, M., 192, 193
Ellison, R., 298
Ellul, J., 163
Epstein, J., 394
Epstein, N., 410, 412, 505
Erikson, E., 487
Erikson, F., 364
Ervin, S., 14
Ervin-Tripp, S., 89
Escalante, J., 366
Espinosa, R., 458
Esquivel, R., 516
Evans-Pritchard, E. E., 178

Farnham, G., 144
Farr, M., 208
Farrell, T., 235
Fasold, R. W., 537, 538
Feagin, J. R., 349, 356
Feldman, S., 154
Ferdman, B. M., 350, 356, 357, 361

Ferguson, C. A., 92
Ferreira, M. E., 261
Feuerstein, R., 376
Filby, N., 170, 237
Finnegan, R., 189
Fiorucci, S., 382
Flavell, J., 240
Flood, J., 208
Flores, J., 359
Fodor, J. A., 105, 124, 125, 154
Ford, W. G., 168
Foster, M., 494
Foster, S., 438
Fox, L., 245
Frankfort, H. A., 190, 193
Franks, J. J., 154, 167
Fraser, E., 91
Frauenfelder, U., 82, 89
Frazxer, J. G., 178
Freire, P., 44, 267, 279–280, 381, 392, 449;
    *Literacy: Reading the Word and the World*,
    286–304
Fries, C., 75
Frost, R., 476
Fry, C., 240
Fry, G. W., 275
Frye, N., 157, 172

Gadamer, H. G., 153
Gardner, H., 197
Gardner, R. C., 91, 93
Garrett, M. F., 105, 154
Garton, A., *Learning To Be Literate: The Devel-
    opment of Spoken and Written Language*, 548–
    549
Garvey, C., 90
Gates, A. I., 117, 118
Gay, J., 152, 168
Gedike, F., 143
Gee, J. P., viii, xiii, xiv, 267, 282; *Social Lin-
    guistics and Literacies: Ideology in Discourses*,
    544–545
Geertz, C., 321
Geisel, T., 218, 220
Gelb, I. J., 159
Gersten, R., 424, 439
Giacobbe, M. E., 227
Gibson, E. J., 145
Giles, H., 356
Gillis, M., 85, 86, 88
Gingras, R. C., 458
Ginorio, A. B., 359
Gintis, H., 267
Giroux, H. A., 267, 289, 292, 360, 449
Givon, T., 102
Gleason, J. B., 227

Gleason, P., 349
Gleitman, H., 226
Gleitman, L., 117, 118, 226
Glider, G., 510
Gold, D., 512
Goldenberg, C. N., 393, 396
Goldfield, B., 219, 220
Gombrich, E., 159
Goodman, I. F., xv, 542
Goodman, K. S., 156, 289
Goodman, N., 164
Goodman, Y., 289
Goodnow, J., 152
Goody, J., xi, 152, 157, 159, 161, 162, 179,
    186, 187, 191, 192, 194, 195, 239, 267,
    270, 333, 348
Gordon, M., 349
Gough, J., 92
Gould, S., 180
Graff, H. G., 289; *The Legacies of Literature:
    Continuities and Contradictions in Western Cul-
    ture and Society*, 266–283
Graves, D. H., 381
Graves, T. D., 357
Gray, A., 403
Gray, M., 158
Gray, W. S., 117, 118
Greenfield, P., 152, 165, 236, 237–238, 240,
    334
Greif, E., 227
Grice, H. P., 154
Griffin, J., 183
Grimshaw, J., 109, 110
Griswold, C. L., 268, 271
Guillaumin, C., 359
Guillén, N., 453
Guiora, A. Z., 364
Guizot, F., 141
Gumperz, J., 487
Gwaltney, J., 489

Hakuta, K., xiv, xv–xvi, xvii, 85, 88, 89, 90,
    91, 350, 356, 357, 361, 379, 424, 434, 436,
    439, 440, 441, 442, 512, 515, 871, 876;
    *Mirror of Language: The Debate on Bilingual-
    ism*, 526–529
Halle, M., 26, 28
Halliday, M. A. K., 172
Hamburger, H., 106
Hanes, M. L., 207
Harman, G., 165
Harrington, M., 429, 432, 437
Hassing, Y., 492
Hatch, E., 88, 91, 92
Haugen, E., 507, 509
Hauke, R., 245

Havelock, E. A., 152, 157, 159, 160, 161,
    184, 185, 193, 235, 266, 267, 269, 270,
    271, 333
Hayakawa, S. I., 153, 287
Haycock, K., 458
Hayek, F. A., 187
Heath, S. B., xiii, 209–210, 228, 267, 281,
    282, 288, 325, 355, 376, 392, 393, 400,
    492, 493, 539; *Ways with Words*, 310–319
Hechinger, F. M., 504
Heller, M., 351
Hemphill, L., xiv, xv, 542
Henle, M., 155, 168
Herman, S. N., 358, 359
Hernandez-Chavez, E., 87, 385
Hertweck, A., 383
Hewison, J., 380, 393, 397
Hewstone, M., 356
Hildyard, A., 167, 170
Hirsch, E. D., 267, 288, 289, 295, 296–297,
    365
Hobson, C., 207
Hoefnagel-Höhle, 209
Hollis, M., 178, 179
Holm, W., 378
Holquist, M., 270
Homer, 182, 184, 269
Hornsby, J., 236
Horton, R., 179, 195
Huang, J., 89, 90, 91
Huberfman, A. M., 463
Huddy, L., xvi
Hymes, D., xiii, xiv, 267, 313, 321, 342

Ilg, F. I., 118
Illich, I., 288
Ingram, D., *First Language Acquisition*, 550
Inhelder, B., 164, 198
Innis, H., 152

Jackson, S., 460
Jacob, F., 124
Jacobsen, T., 190
Jain, M., 80
James, C., 80
Jarvis, P., 240
Jenkyns, R., 178
Johansen, B., 436
Johansson, E., 137, 273
John, V., 321, 342
Johnson, M. K., 154, 167
Johnson-Laird, P. N., 168
Jones, J. M., 357
Joosten, J., 492
Jordan, C., 378
Josbe, J., 492

Jowett, B., 191
Jungeblut, A., 268
Jusenius, C., 372
Just, M., 170

Kádár-Fülop, J., 360
Keatinge, B., 378, 384, 385
Keefe, S. E., 358
Keenan, E., 90
Keller-Cohen, D., 91
Kelly, P., 437
Kemey, H., 236
Kennedy, M., 208
Kermode, F., 271
Kindleberger, C., 139
Kirk, G. S., 183
Kirsch, I., 268
Kleinmann, H., 82
Klima, E., 83, 84, 85
Knapp, H., 196, 197
Knapp, M., 196, 197
Kneale, M., 160
Kneale, W., 160
Kochman, T., 356
Kohn, M., 341
Kolker, A., 513
Korzybski, A., 153
Kozol, J., 267
Krashen, S., 86, 87

Labov, W., 277, 321, 535, 536, 537, 538
Lado, R., 78
Lakoff, G., 165
Lambert, W., 93, 448, 524, 527
Larsen-Freeman, D., 86, 87, 88
*Lau v. Nichols*, 457
Leach, E., 186
Lemke, J. L., 267
Leopold, W., 527
Lévi-Bruhl, L., 186, 187, 188, 193, 195
Levin, H., 145, 276
Levine, R. A., 425, 426
Levinson, M., 429, 432, 437
Lévi-Strauss, C., 179, 180, 181, 185, 188,
    189, 190, 192, 194, 202, 272
Lloyd, P., 169
Loban, W., 208
Locke, J., 163
Lockridge, K., 137
Lofti, A., 220
Lonergan, B. J. F., 171
Lord, A. B., 158, 183, 188
Lord, C., 85, 86
Luckmann, T., 171
Luke, A., 281, 352, 360, 363
Lukes, S., 187

Luria, A. R., 191, 334
Luther, M., 153, 157, 166
Lyons, J., 160

McCabe, A., viii; *Developing Narrative Struc-
    ture*, 550–551
McCarthy, J. J., 102
McCaughan, E., 429
Maccoby, M., 236
McDermott, R. P., 426, 436
Macedo, D., 279; *Literacy: Reading the Word
    and the World*, 286–304
MacEoin, G., 428
McEvedy, M. R., 364
McKirnan, D. J., 357
McLaughlin, B., 75, 375, 379, 459
McLeod, A., 499
McLuhan, M., 152, 157, 162
Macnamara, J., 109, 110, 156, 169
McNeill, D., 155
McPartland, J., 207
Madden, C., 86, 87
Maestas, R., 436
Maimonides, M., 158
Malécot, A., 35
Malinowski, B., 179, 192, 193, 195, 310
Martin, J., 76
Martin, N., 245, 499
Martinez, E., 429
Marx, K., 249, 334
Mason, J., 218
Massey, G. C., 500
Matthews, J., 428, 432
Matute-Bianchi, M. E., 361, 362, 376
Medina, M., 458
Mehan, H., 320, 324, 383
Mehan, K., 396
Meihls, J. L., 383
Menyuk, P., 208
Mercer, J. R., 383
Merriam, S. B., 463
Michaels, S., xi, 228, 267
Miles, M. B., 463
Miller, P., 207, 228
Miller, W., 14
Mills, H., *Portraits of Whole Language Class-
    rooms*, 547–548
Milon, J., 84, 85
Milroy, J., 277, 278
Milroy, L., 277, 278
Modiano, M., 236
Moles, O. C., 394, 402
Moll, L., 396
Montero, M., 356
Mood, A., 207
Morson, G. S., 270

Mosher, F., 236
Moyers, B., 427, 430
Mulford, R., 86
Mullard, C., 376
Murphy, B., 403
Musgrove, F., 274

Nadander, D., 199
National Commission on Excellence in Education, 435
Navarro, R., 443
Neimark, E. D., 154
Nelson, K., 156, 169, 217; *Narratives from the Crib*, 552–553
Nemoianu, A., 228
Nemser, W., 77
Neruda, P., 476
Newton, B., 245
Nickel, G., 76
Nickerson, N., 167, 170
Nietzsche, F., 269
Ninio, A., 217, 220

Oakes, J., 276
Ochoa, A., 458
Ogbu, J. U., 373, 375, 376, 425, 426, 427, 438, 441
Ohmann, R., 267
Oliva, J., 402
Olkiewicz, E., 438
Oller, J., 76, 77
Olson, D. R., xi, 161, 167, 170, 172, 180, 208, 236–237, 238, 267, 334
Olver, R. R., 236, 334
O'Malley, J. M., xv
Ong, W. J., xi, 162, 164, 171, 180, 181, 186, 190, 191, 197, 200, 266, 267, 269, 270, 348
Opie, I., 196
Opie, P., 196
Orfield, G., 458
Orr, D., 530
Orr, E. W., xvii; *Twice as less: Black English and the Performance of Black Students in Mathematics and Science*, 530–541
Ortiz, A. A., 373
Ortony, A., 154, 167
Orum, L. S., 442, 458
Ovando, C. J., 424, 436, 439, 440, 506

Padilla, A. M., 358
Paley, V. G., 197
Papert, S., 124
Paris, S. G., 154
Parisi, D., 91
Parker, R., 245
Parry, M., 152, 157, 183

Passeron, J. F., 267
Pattison, R., 266
Paulston, C. B., 375, 506; *Bilingual Education: Theories and Issues*, 521–525
Peabody, B., 182, 183, 190
Peal, E., 448, 527
Pellegrini, A. D., 553
Perlmann, R., 227
Peters, A., 219
Peterson, C., viii, 550
Philips, S., 325, 342
Piaget, J., 123–126, 154, 164, 168–169, 198, 227, 237, 238
Piattelli-Palmarini, M., 105
Pike, R., 167
Pinker, S.; *Language Learnability and Language Development*, 98–114
Pitcher, E. G., 197
Plato, 162, 177, 178, 184, 185, 190, 234, 235, 258, 267, 279, 333; attack on writing, 268–272
Podhoretz, N., 510
Politzer, R., 79
Porter, R. P., 506, 510
Potter, M., 236
Pratt, C., 548
Prelinger, E., 197
Premack, D., 125
Purkey, S. C., 458, 469
Purves, A. C., 352, 355
Putnam, H., 125, 178

Ramirez, A., 79
Ramírez, D., 459
Ramphal, D. K., 381
Ravitch, D., 188
Reagan, R., 442
Reich, L. C., 334
Reid, J. F., 171
Reisch, L., 236
Richards, I. A., 171
Richards, J., x, 76, 77, 80
Ricoeur, P., 164, 170
Riley, N., 428
Rivers, W., 76
Rivlin, A., 208
Robinson, J. L., xvii; *Conversations on the Written Word: Essays on Language and Literacy*, 546–547
Rodriguez, R., 436
Rosansky, E., 81, 86, 87
Rosenholtz, S. J., 458
Rosier, P., 378
Ross, J. R., 103
Rossell, C. H., 515
Roth, R., 354

Rowan, C. T., 434
Rowe, C. J., 268
Rowen, B., 458
Rozin, P., 117, 118
Rueda, R., 383
Rumberger, R. W., 458
Russell, B., 164, 172
Russell, D. H., 117, 118

Said, E. W., 348
Salas, D., 262
Salus, M., 208
Sanaoui, R., 382
Sanderson, M., 137
Sartre, J. P., 250
Scarry, R., 219
Schachter, J., 81
Schermerhorn, R. A., 523
Schieffelin, B., 228
Schneider, S. G., 374
Schofield, W. N., 380, 393, 397
Schumann, J., 76, 77, 81, 93, 435
Schutz, A., 171
Schwarzenegger, A., 510
Scollon, R., xiii, xvi, xvii, 208, 217, 228, 267, 268, 364
Scollon, S., xiii, xvi, xvii, 208, 217, 228, 364
Scollon, S. B. K., 267, 268
Scott, M. V., 500
Scribner, S., 152, 226, 228, 238, 239, 240, 267, 274, 275, 282, 348, 353; *The Psychology of Literacy*, 333–337
Sears, D. O., xvi
Selinker, L., 77, 79, 82
Sennett, R., 282, 436
Seuss, Dr. (T. Geisel), 218, 220
Shanker, A., 435
Shapira, R., 92
Sharp, D., 152, 168
Shor, I., 393, 434, 435, 436, 437
Shuy, R. W., 208
Siddle, E. V., 490, 492
Simich-Dudgeon, C., 392, 394
Simons, H. D., 208
Sinclair, J., 324
Skinner, B. F., x
Skutnabb-Kangas, T., 373, 374, 377, 429, 430, 431, 440, 441, 448, 449
Slotnick, N. S., 154
Smith, F., 156
Smith, M., 527, 528
Smith, M. S., 458, 469
Smith, W. F., 430
Smitherman, G., 540
Smolicz, J., 356

Snow, C. E., xv, xvi, 92, 209, 217, 219, 220, 227, 393, 396, 399, 400, 401, 492, 512, 515
Socrates, 162, 190–191, 268, 270, 271, 333; *Unfulfilled Expectations: Home and School Influences on Literacy*, 542–544
Söderbergh, R., 210
Solomon, 158
Sonstroem, A., 236
Spearitt, D., 208
Sprat, T., 163
Stankovski, M., 438
Staudenmayer, H., 155
Stearns, M. S., 208
Stedman, L. C., 458, 459
Stenson, N., 76, 77
Stewart, G., 239
Stewart, W., 532
Sticht, T., 245
Stockwell, R., 76
Stone, L., 137
Stone, W. C., 510
Strauss, L., 270
Street, B., 267, 282, 392
Stubbs, M., 208
Sulzby, E., 229
Suppes, P., 154
Suro, R., 460
Sutton-Smith, B., 196
Svartvik, J., 77, 83
Swain, M., 80, 82, 377

Tajfel, H., 356, 357, 359
Tannen, D., 208, 209, 228
Tanton, J., 510
Taplin, J. E., 155
Tarone, E., 82
Taylor, B., 80
Taylor, C., 177
Taylor, D., 393, 396, 399, 402
Taylor, D. M., 357
Tempse, F., 515
Thabalt, R., 142–143
*Theresa P. et al. v. Berkeley Unified School District et al.*, 515
Thorndike, E. L., 120, 131, 244
Thorndike, R., 208
Thurow, L. C., 349
Tikunoff, W. J., 377, 459
Timpane, P. M., 208
Tizard, J., 380, 393, 397
Todorov, T., 197, 270
Topping, K., 394
Torrance, N., xi
Tran, B. T., 402
Traugott, E. C., 537

Triandis, H. C., 351
Troike, R. C., 381, 382, 515
Trueba, H. T., 282, 362
Tucker, R., 448, 524
Turner, F. J., 178
Turner, J. C., 356, 357
Tyler, R., 201

UNESCO, 235
U.S. English, 427
U.S. General Accounting Office, xv, 458,
    514–515, 516
Urzua, C., 400

Vernant, J. P., 189, 190
Vico, G., 183, 198, 199
Viola, M., 403
Virgil, 182
Vygotsky, L. S., x, 282, 327, 334; *Thought and
    Language*, 127–133

Wagner, D., 220
Wagner-Gough, J., 88, 91
Walberg, H. J., 510–511
Walker, A., 298
Wallace, C., 355
Wallerstein, N., 404
Wardhaugh, R., 76
Wason, P. C., 168
Watt, I., 152, 186, 191, 192, 333, 348
Watt, I. P., 267

Weber, E., 143
Weber, R., 85
Weinfeld, F., 207
Wells, G., xi, 216
Wexler, K., 98, 106
Whorf, B. L., xvii
Williams, C., 503
Williams, F., 536
Williams, R., 282–283
Willis, P., 267, 315
Wilson, B. L., 458, 459, 461, 472
Wilson, B. R., 178
Wilson, J. A., 190
Wolf, F. A., 183
Wolfendale, S., 0
Wolfram, W., 540
Wong-Fillmore, L., 85, 90, 92, 375, 376, 380,
    382, 459
Wood, M., 182
Woodward, J., 424, 439
Woodworth, R., 244
Wright, J., 240
Wright, R., 298

Yalow, R., 510
Yap, K. O., 208
Yates, J. R., 373
Yerkes, R., 144
York, R., 207

Zapf, D., 245
Zinn, H., 281

# Subject Index

Academic failure, among minority students, 373–375

*Acts of Meaning* (Bruner), 551

Additive bilingualism, subtractive bilingualism versus, 448–449

Aesthetic value, of myths, 188

Affrication, preschool children's knowledge of phonology and, 29–32

Age, spontaneous spelling and, 39. *See also* Children

Alaskans, cultural identity of, 364

Alphabet, 160–162; Greek, 161; phonemic, 159–160

Alternations, preschool children's knowledge of phonology and, 38–42

*Although* construction, 58–60, 61, 62. *See also* Linguistic research

American Indians, family literacy among, 403

Arabs, literacy among, 274

Articulatory overlap, nasals and, 35–36

*Ask* construction, 54–58, 64. *See also* Linguistic research

Assessment, empowerment of minority groups and, 382–383

Assimilation, as goal of immigrant educational policies, 437–440

Assimilation model, of multiethnic society, 349, 351

Audiolingual method, second-language acquisition and, 76

Authoritarianism, in schools, 492–495

"Bicultural ambivalence," 376

Bilingual education, 374, 409–420, 503–518; *Bilingual Education: History, Politics, Theory, and Practice* and, 503–518; *Bilingual Education: Theories and Issues* and, 521–525; creative education for teachers in, 447–454; diversity of, 410–411; effectiveness of, 511–516; English Only movement and, 509–511; funding for, 416; government role in, 412–414, 415–418; group-conflict theory of, 523; history of, 506–509; immigrant groups and, 412–414; isolation of teachers in, 451; *Mirror of Language: The Debate on Bilingualism* and, 526–529; poli-

tics of, 516–518; private schools and, 417–418; sense of inadequacy in language mastery and, 451–452; structural/functionalist viewpoint of, 523, 524; transitional, *see* Transitional bilingual education

*Bilingual Education: History, Politics, Theory, and Practice* (Crawford), 503–518

*Bilingual Education: Theories and Issues* (Paulston), 521–525

Bilingual Education Act of 1968, 504

Bilingualism, limited, 439; subtractive versus additive, 448–449. *See also* Bilingual education; Second-language acquisition

Bilingual Syntax Measure (BSM), 78, 87, 385

Black(s). *Twice as Less: Black English and the performance of Black Students in Mathematics and Science* and, 530–541. *See also* Ethnic groups

Black English Vernacular (BEV), 297, 530–541. *See also* Hawthorne School

Bootstrapping, 110, 111

Bracero Guest Worker Program, 431–432

Brazil, literacy in, 258–259

Carpinteria, empowerment and, 383–386

Catholicism, literacy and, 274

Chicanos. *See* Ethnic groups; Hispanics

Children, knowledge of phonology, 20–46. *See also* First-language acquisition

Chile, literacy in, 258, 261–262

Civic-national schooling, literacy criteria and, 139–143

*Class, Codes and Control. Volume 1. Theoretical Studies toward a Sociology of Language* (Bernstein), 339–344

Classification, in oral cultures, 194–195

*Classroom Discourse: The Language of Teaching and Learning* (Cazden), 320–330

Codification, in literacy process, 255

Cognitive academic learning proficiency, 440

Communication, in classrooms, 320–330; language versus literacy and, 209–217. *See also* Literacy; Reading

Composition, without writing, 182–185

Comprehension, literacy and, 166–167; psycholinguistic models of, 154

Concept, 129

Conscientization, 300

Contentives, imitation of, in first-language acquisition, 7–9

Content Question Rule, 103–104

Continuity assumption, first language acquisition and, 108

Contrastive analysis, of second-language acquisition, 75–76

Conventionality, language versus literacy and, 226–227

*Conversations on the Written Word: Essays on Language and Literacy* (Robinson), 546–547

Critical literacy, 287, 289–304; canon of prescribed works and, 295–301; Freire's perspective on, 291–295

Cultural deficit view, 322

Cultural differences, in classroom, 325–328

Cultural difference view, 322

Cultural dominance view, 322–323

Cultural identity, 355–359, 357, 358; at group level, 355–356; at individual level, 357–259; literacy and, 347–367; power and, 495–501; uncertainty regarding bilingualism and, 452–453

Cultural literacy, 287, 288–289

Cultural politics, 292

Culture, oral: of power, 483, 484; value placed on, success of language-minority students and, 464–468. *See also* Orality

Curriculum, to stimulate development of orality, 199–201

Dative Alternation, 99, 106–107, 112

Dative Transformation, 100–101

Decoding, reading and, 170–171

Decontextualization, language versus literacy and, 217–219

Deductive empirical science, development of, 163–164

Deep structure, surface structure and, 155–156

*Developing Narrative Structure* (McCabe and Peterson), 550–551

Dialects, 297

Differentiation, in first language acquisition, 15–17

Discourse analysis, of second-language acquisition, 90–92

Eastman School, 512

*Easy to see* construction, acquisition of, 51–52. *See also* Linguistic research

Economy, immigrants and, 428–429

Education, communication in classroom and, 320–330; creative, for bilingual teachers,

447–454; cultural deficit view and, 322; cultural differences and, 322, 325–328; cultural dominance view and, 322–323; differential treatment in, 325–328; empowering minority students and, 372–387; excellence in, 435–437; functional approach to literacy and, 238–246; illiteracy and, 302; of immigrants, assimilation as goal of, 437–440; implications of orality for, 195–203; language codes and, 341–343; of language-minority students, 456–480; literacy, 355, 362–363, 365–366; literacy and, 234–246; occupation related to, 275–276; power in, 483–501; preschool children's knowledge of phonetics and, 44–46; purposes of, 276; structure of classroom lessons and, 323–325; theoretical stance required by, 248–253; *Ways with Words* and, 310–319. *See also* Schools; Bilingual education; Transitional bilingual education

Elaborated code, social class and, 340

Elementary and Secondary Education Act (1974), 411, 439

Elite-technical schools, literacy criteria and, 138–139

Empowerment, 372–387; Carpinteria example of, 383–386; of language-minority students, 477–479

Endocentric constructions, in first-language acquisition, 13

English language, Black English vernacular and, 297, 530–541; dialects of, 297

English Only movement, 509–511, 516–517

Error(s), interference, in second-language acquisition, 77–79; intralingual, in second-language acquisition, 77, 78–79; longitudinal study of, 80–81; overgeneralization, in first-language acquisition, 13; overgeneralization, in second-language acquisition, 80; oversimplification, in language acquisition, 79; systematic, in second-language acquisition, 75–76; unique to second-language acquisition, 80

Error analysis, of second-language acquisition, 77–83

*Essay Concerning Human Understanding, An* (Locke), 163

Essayist technique, 162–165

Ethnic groups, caste-like versus minority, 426–429; caste status of, 376; communication in classroom and, 321; cultural identity of, 358–359, 361–362; economic effects on attitudes toward, 432–434; education and, 310–319; empowering students of, 372–387; intergroup power relations and, 376–383; literacy and cultural identity and, 349–350; literacy as tool for oppression of, 281; power and education of, 483–501; psychological concomitants of ethnic differences and, 350; role of educational policy in socializing for economic participation, 434–444; role in U.S. economy, 425–429. *See also* Language-minority students; *specific groups*

Expansions, imitation with, first-language acquisition and, 9–12

Expectations, of language-minority students, making concrete, 468–469

Failure, language versus literacy and, 225–226

Family literacy, 391–406; context for current emphasis on, 393–394; design of programs for, 404–406; directionality of literacy interactions and, 397–398; family contexts of successful readers and, 398–399; home environments and, 395–397; school contributions to, 399–401; school practices model for transmission of, 394–404; social context for, 401–404

First-language acquisition, 3–19; Chomsky's contribution to, 99–107; imitation and reduction in, 6–9; imitation with expansion in, 9–12; induction of latent structure in, 12–19; *Language Learnability and Language Learning* and (Pinker), 98–114; locus of meaning and, 155; negation in, 83–84; order of acquisition of grammatical structures and, 48–64; Pinker's contribution to, 107–114; reading background and activity and, 64–67; second-language acquisition research and, 77; universal aspects in, 83

*First Language Acquisition* (Ingram), 550

Flaps, preschool children's knowledge of phonology and, 32–33

Formal language, 340

France, literacy in, 138–143

Functional literacy, 146, 286, 287

*Functions of Language in the Classroom* (Cazden, John, and Hymes), 321–322

Functors, imitation in first-language acquisition, 8–9

Funding, for bilingual education, 416

Government, role in education of non-English-speaking people, 412–414, 415–418

Government and Binding (GB) theory, 106

Grammar(s), defined, 50; developmental sequence in acquisition of, 48–72; first-language acquisition and, 77; nontransfor-

mational, 105–106; transformational, 75–76, 99–107

Grammatical structures, order of acquisition of, 48–72; morphemes in second-language acquisition and, 87–89

Greek(s), cognitive impact of written word and, 333; rational thinking and, 177–178

Greek alphabet, 161

Hawthorne School, 530–541; atypical circumstances of, 534; lack of familiarity with language and educational difficulties of inner-city Black students, 534–535; linguistic misunderstandings and inaccuracies and, 536–538; pedagogical considerations and, 535–536; racial bias at, 536

Hispanics, bilingual education and, 411–412, 414–415; cultural identity of, 358–359, 361–362; family literacy among, 402–403; group cultural identity and, 355–356; promoting school success of, 456–480. *See also* Ethnic groups; Bilingual education

Holophrases, 3–4

Home, literacy in, 228–229

Ideographic writing systems, 159

Illegal aliens, role in U.S. economy, 429–434

Illiteracy, 302. *See also* Literacy; Reading

Illiterate people, as marginal, 251–252

Imitation, expansion and, in first-language acquisition, 9–12; reduction and, in first-language acquisition, 6–9

Immigrants, illegal, 429–434. *See also* Bilingual education; Ethnic groups; Transitional bilingual education; *specific groups*

Immigration reform and Control Act (1986), 431

Incorporation, in second-language acquisition, 91

"Insufficient exposure" hypothesis, 374

Intelligence testing, development of, 144. *See also* IQ scores

"Interdependence hypothesis," 375

Interlanguage, 77

IQ scores, linguistic stages correlated with, 65–67, 68; socioeconomic status correlated with, 67

Jews, cultural identity of, 358–359

Knowledge, concept of, 250

Language, dissimilarities in development of literacy and, 225–228; effect of literacy on, 165–172; formal, 340; literacy compared with, 208–229; perceived as cause of social unrest, 419; Piaget/Chomsky debate about learning and, 123–126; public, 339; reality and, 164; sense of inadequacy in mastery of, bilingualism and, 451–452; as social institution, 339–344; thought and, 127–133; value placed on, success of language-minority students and, 464–468. *See also* Orality; Speech

Language acquisition, literacy and, 169–170. *See also* First-language acquisition; Second-language acquisition

Language development, stages in, 48–72

*Language Learnability and Language Learning* (Pinker), 98–114

Language-minority (LM) students, counseling program for, 473–475; courses and programs for, 472–473; empowerment of, 477–479; parent involvement and, 475–477; promoting school success of, 456–480

Language of thought, 109

Latent structure, induction of, in first-language acquisition, 12–19

Latinos. *See* Ethnic groups; Hispanics

Learnability theory, 98

Learned helplessness, empowerment of minority students and, 381

Learning, language versus literacy and, 225; Piaget/Chomsky debate about language and, 123–126; structure-dependent, 110

*Learning To Be Literate: The Development of Spoken and Written Language* (Garton and Pratt), 548–549

*Legacies of Literacy: Continuities and Contradictions in Western Culture and Society, The* (Graff), 266–283

Letters, children's reversals of, 41–42

Lexical causatives, 112

Lexical Functional Grammar (LFG), 105–106, 107–108

Lexical redundancy rule, 101–102

Liberation, literacy as tool for, 282–283

Limited bilingualism, 439

Limited-English-proficient (LEP) students, promoting school success of, 457

"Linguistic mismatch" hypothesis, 374

Linguistic research, on linguistic stages, 48–72; on reading background and activity, linguistic stages and, 64–68; on second-language acquisition, 74–93

Linguistic stages, 48–72; differentiation of, 67–68; IQ scores correlated with, 67, 68; reading background and activity and, 65–67, 68; socioeconomic status correlated with, 67

Linguistic theory, literacy and, 165–166

Listening, metaphorical, 189. *See also* Reading aloud, by others

Literacy, cognitive impact of, 333–337; comprehension and, 166–167; critical, 287, 289–304; cultural, 287, 288–289; as cultural action for freedom, 248–263; cultural identity and, 347–367; as development, 236–238; dissimilarities in development of language and, 225–228; education for, 365–366; effects on linguistic theory, 165–166; effects on reasoning, 167–169; functional, 146, 286, 287; functional approach to schooling and, 238–246; function within society, 336–337; "great divide" theory of, 335–336; history of, 266–283; in home, 228–229; language compared with, 208–229; mainstream approaches to, 294–295; orality versus, 229–230, 235, 348; process of, as act of knowing, 253–263; schooling and, 234–246; social class differences in reading achievement and, 207–230; solidification of social hierarchy and, 277–279; as tool for liberation, 282–283; as tool for oppression of nondominant groups, 281. *See also* Family literacy; Reading

*Literacy: Reading the Word and the World* (Freire and Macedo), 286–304

*Literacy as Involvement: The Acts of Writers, Readers, and Texts* (Brandt), 545–546

Literacy criteria, 135–148; changing, 145–147; civic-national schooling and, 139–143; elite-technical schools and, 138–139; policy implications of, 147–148; Protestant religious education and, 137–138; teaching methods and, 143–145

Literary canon, critical literacy and, 295–301

Logical reasoning, locus of meaning and, 154–155

Mathematics, eighteenth-century focus on, 139

Maturation, language versus literacy and, 209

Meaning, locus of, 152–156; in oral language tradition, 157–158; writing and, 158–160

"Melting pot" model, of multiethnic society, 349, 351

Memory, orality and, 187–190

Metaphor, orality and, 196–197, 199

Metaphorical listening, 189

Minority groups. *See* Ethnic groups; *specific groups*

*Mirror of Language: The Debate on Bilingualism* (Hakuta), 526–529

Morpheme(s), grammatical, in second-language acquisition, 87–89

Myths, 199; aesthetic and utilitarian value of, 188

*Narrative Thought and Narrative Language* (Britton and Pellegrini), 553–555

*Narratives from the Crib* (Nelson), 552–553
Nasals, preschool children's knowledge of phonology and, 33–36
National Association for Bilingual Education (NABE), 516
National Council of La Raza, 442
Negation, in second-language acquisition, 83–86
Noun phrases, in first-language acquisition, 17–18

Occupation, education related to, 275–276
Office of Bilingual Education and Minority Language Affairs (OBEMLA), 516
Opportunity structure, 425
Orality, 177–203; classification and explanation and, 194–195; foundations of science and, 200–201; impact of writing on, 158; implications for early childhood education, 195–203; literacy versus, 229–230, 235, 348; meaning in, 157–158; memory and, 187–190; participation and conservation and, 190–194; path to literacy from, 179–180; rediscovery of, 182–195; thought modes and, 179; variations in, 186–187
Overgeneralization, children's spontaneous spelling and, 42; of lexical causatives, 112

Palatalization, preschool children's knowledge of phonology and, 31
Parents, focus on inadequacies of, family literacy and, 401–404; involvement in education of language-minority students, 475–477; participation in schools, 379–381
Past, orality and, 192
Pedagogy, empowerment of minority students and, 381–382
Performance analysis, of second-language acquisition, 83–90; grammatical morphemes and, 87–89; negation and, 83–86; routine formulas and prefabricated utterances and, 89–90
Phonetization, 159
Phonology, preschool children's knowledge of, 20–46
Phrase structure rules, 99
Phrase structure tree, 99–100
Pluralist model, of multiethnic society, 349, 350–351
Plurals, spontaneous spelling and, 41–42
Poetry, orality and, 182–185
Policy, empowering minority students and, 373–375; literacy criteria and, 147–148
*Portraits of Whole Language Classrooms* (Mills and Clyde), 547–548
Power, in education, 483–501
Powerlessness, bilingualism and, 452

Power relations, intergroup, 376–383
Practice, language versus literacy and, 226
Prefabricated utterances, 83; in second-language acquisition, 89–90, 91
*Promise* construction, acquisition of, 52–54, 64. *See also* Linguistic research
Protestantism, literacy and, 274
Protestant religious education, literacy standards and, 137–138
Psycholinguistics, comprehension and, 154; ethnographic approach to, 321–322; research in, *see* Linguistic research; transformational grammars and, 105
*Psychology of Literacy* (Scribner and Cole), 333–337
Public language, 339

Race, education and, 310–319. *See also* Black(s); Ethnic groups
Reading, exposure to, in curriculum, 72; locus of meaning and, 156; social class differences in achievement in, 207–230; stages of development of, 117–121; utterances and, 170–171. *See also* Literacy
Reading aloud, by others, language acquisition and, 64–68
Reading background, linguistic stages and, 64–68; socioeconomic status correlated with, 67, 68
Reading comprehension, socioeconomic status correlated with, 67
Reading vocabulary, socioeconomic status correlated with, 67
Reality, language and, 164
Reasoning, 177–178; literacy and, 167–169; locus of meaning and, 154–155
Rebirth, orality and, 192–183
Reciprocal interaction model, of pedagogy, 381, 382
Recontextualization, in classroom, 327–328
Reduction, imitation with, first-language acquisition and, 6–9
Redundancy, nasals and, 35–36
Repetition, in second-language acquisition, 91
Restricted code, social class and, 340–342
Reversals, of letters, made by children, 41–42
Rhyme, orality and, 189, 196–197
Routines, language versus literacy and, 219–220
Royal Society of London, 163

Scaffolding, 212; in classroom, 327, 328
School(s), assessment in, 382–383; attendance at, changing patterns of, 145; civic-national schooling and, literacy and, 139–143; collaborative-exclusionary dimension of, 380–381; community participation in, 379–

381; cultural/linguistic incorporation in, 378–379; elite-technical, literacy criteria and, 138–139; empowerment of students and, 377–386; excellence in, 435–437; mediation of process of becoming literate by, 353–355; pedagogy in, 381–382. *See also* Bilingual education; Education

Schooling. *See* Bilingual education; Education; School(s); Teachers; Teaching; Transitional bilingual education

Second-language acquisition, 74–93; avoidance of structures and, 81; contrastive analysis of, 75–76; cross-sectional studies of, 87; discourse analysis of, 75, 90–92; error analysis of, 75, 77–83; future research directions for, 92–93; gradual nature of, 81–83; grammatical morphemes and, 87–89; input to learner in, 92; longitudinal studies of, 87–89; negation and, 83–86; performance analysis of, 75, 83–90; routine formulas and prefabricated utterances and, 89–90; sociolinguistic analysis of, 92

Self-esteem, literacy education and, 365

Semantic bootstrapping, 110, 111

Semantic contingency, 210

Sentences, meaning of, 153–156

Social identity, 357–358

Socialization, literacy education as, 355, 362–363, 365; of minority groups, for part in economy, 434–444

*Social Linguistics and Literacies: Ideology in Discourses* (Gee), 544–545

Social unrest, language perceived as cause of, 419

Socioeconomic status, elaborated versus restricted code and, 340–344; literacy and, 277–279

Socioeconomic status (SES), IQ correlated with, 67; linguistic stages correlated with, 67; reading background correlated with, 67, 68; reading vocabulary and comprehension correlated with, 67

Sociolinguistic analysis, of second-language acquisition, 92

Speech, competence versus performance and, 50; displaced, 5; telegraphic, 8. *See also* Language; Orality; *headings beginning with term* Language

Spelling, standard, 45–46; spontaneous, 22–46

*Stages of Reading Development* (Chall), 117–121

Stress, imitation in first-language acquisition and, 8–9

Structural linguistics, second-language acquisition and, 75–76

Structure-dependent distributional learning, 110

Subject, missing, acquisition of ability to assign, 53–58, 62–63

Subtractive bilingualism, additive bilingualism versus, 448–449

Success, language versus literacy and, 225–226

Surface structure, deep structure and, 155–156

Sweden, literacy in, 138, 272–274

Syllabaries, 160; development of, 159

Syllabic segments, preschool children's knowledge of phonology and, 36–38

Syntax, acquisition of, 3–19, 50; adjustment of rules in language development, 61; in second-language acquisition, 92

*Taking Inventory of Children's Literary Background*, 65, 66–67

Teachers, bilingual, creative education for, 447–454; of language-minority students, staff development for, 470–472. *See also* Education; School(s); Teaching

Teaching, implications of orality for, 201–202; language versus literacy and, 225. *See also* Education; School(s); Teachers

Telegraphic speech, 8

Text, utterance and, 156–165

Third World, "salvation" of, 259

Thought, impact of literacy on, 333–337; language of, 109

*Thought and Language* (Vygotsky), 127–133

Time, in oral cultures, 191

Transformational grammar, 75–76, 99–107

Transitional bilingual education (TBE), 424–444; program for, 440–444

Transmission model, of pedagogy, 381

*Twice as Less: Black English and the Performance of Black Students in Mathematics and Science* (Orr), 530–541

*Unfulfilled Expectations: Home and School Influences on Literacy* (Snow), 542–544

Unique entry principle, 113

Utterance, text and, 156–165

Vai, literacy among, 274–275, 334–337; schooling among, 334–337; writing system of, 239–243

Values, literacy and cultural identity and, 348–350

Verb, missing, acquisition of ability to identify, 53–58, 62–63

Vocabulary, reading, socioeconomic status correlated with, 67

Vowel(s), nasalization of, 35–36; preschool children's knowledge of phonology and, 24–26